HELL'S GATE

THE BATTLE OF THE
CHERKASSY POCKET
JANUARY - FEBRUARY 1944

Douglas E. Nash

HELL'S GATE

by
Douglas E. Nash

First Published March 2002

RZM Imports, Inc.
One Pomperaug Office Park, Suite 102
Southbury, CT 06488 USA
Tel. 203-264-0774 Fax. 203-264-4967
e-mail: rzm@rzm.com
www.rzm.com

Book Production Team
Layout and Design by Todd Rose
Text edited by Jeffery Hufnagel
Map Design by Fletch Brendan Good
Additional Photographic Research by Remy Spezzano
Jacket Design by Todd Rose

Photograph Credits:
U.S. National Archives, Bundesarchiv, Battle of Korsun-Shevchenkovsky Museum,
72.Inf.Div.Veteran's Association, 88.Inf.Div.Veteran's Association, Wiking Division
Veteran's Association, Freiherr von Dörnberg, Eberhard Heder, Willy Hein,
Günther Jahnke, Fernand Kaisergruber, Walter Schaefer-Kehnert, Bernd Lerch,
Hans-Kurt Menedetter, Gerhard Meyer, Douglas Nash, Hans Queitzsch,
Horst Scheibert, Karl Schierholz, Andreas Schwarz, Rolf Stoves, Munin Verlag.

ISBN 0-9657584-3-5

Printed and Bound in Canada
by FREISENS Corporation

John 3:16

To my wife Jill and Doug Jr., Drew and Deanna,
without your love and support this book would not have been possible,
and Thomas McGuirl.

TABLE OF CONTENTS

BOOK I: SETTING THE STAGE

BOOK II: THE RUSSIAN STEAMROLLER

BOOK III: VON MANSTEIN TO THE RESCUE

BOOK IV: DAYS OF DESPERATION

BOOK V: NOW OR NEVER

TABLE OF CONTENTS

BOOK VI: THE BREAKOUT

BOOK VII: CONGRATULATIONS AND RECRIMINATIONS

LIST OF MAPS

TITLE	PAGE

"The flood tide devoured itself, not us!" So proclaimed the title of a map study on the Battle of the Cherkassy Pocket published a few years ago by veterans of the Wiking Division.

On 17 to 18 February 1944, the men of the SS-Panzer Division "Wiking," along with the attached SS-Volunteer Brigade "Wallonie" and the Estonian Volunteer Battalion, stood side by side with their comrades from divisions of the Army as more than 30,000 German soldiers, supported by combat units outside the pocket, bravely and steadfastly were able to fight their way free.

Douglas E. Nash, a staff officer in the U.S. Army, has with this book success-fully undertaken for military history readers of all countries the mission of making understandable the tragedy experienced by the German soldiers trapped in the pocket. Nash depicts the operational events on both the German and Soviet sides of the front, without any sense of bias.

The author has dedicated an incredible amount of time and care towards this endeavor. His source material stems both from American and Russian archives, as well as from other sources. Most significantly, he has interwoven verbal and written accounts by eyewitnesses into a carefully researched document.

Nash has been to the area; accompanied by a Cherkassy survivor from the Walloon Brigade and a Ukrainian friend, he was able to locate and identify many key areas of the battlefield, where on account of the nature of the terrain the fighting was heaviest.

It gives me great satisfaction that men from the circle of my comrades and I were able to make files and recollections of personal experiences available to the American officer and author of this book. Douglas Nash and I have been on friendly terms since 1995.

May this book promote understanding among its readers and above all, to soldiers of all ages.

I dedicate my concluding thoughts to all those who died or are still missing in action, whose sacrifices during the encirclement battle came to a tragic end.

***SS-Obersturmführer*
Willy Hein**

Willy Hein
Former captain and tank company commander,
5.SS-Panzer Division "Wiking"
September 1998

PREFACE

The Gniloy Tikich (pronounced neeloy teekitsch) is a small stream typical of those found in the Ukraine west of the mighty Dnieper River. From its headwaters in the swamps north of Zhashkov, it meanders southeasterly through nearly one hundred kilometers of rolling Ukrainian farmland before it empties into the much larger Gniloy Taschlik at Mydanovka, which itself merges with the Shpolka River. During the summer, it meanders along its bed. It is usually no more than three or four feet deep and is fordable in many places. During the winter, it is often covered with a thick sheet of ice and can support the weight of a truck. Its course is lined with shrubs or trees.

The only thing which makes this stream noteworthy is the steepness of its banks, mute testimony to the power the Gniloy Tikich possesses when the Spring thaw melts the accumulated blanket of snow, common to Ukrainian winters. Then, the snow seems to melt all at once, sending millions of gallons of water into the stream, causing it to overflow its banks and flood surrounding lowlands. Crossing it is out of the question, except for the few bridges which dot the landscape. The only thing, however, unusual about the winter of 1944 was that the Spring thaw came two months early.

It was along the banks of this stream where the final acts of a wartime tragedy took place, where nearly 50,000 men of the once-mighty German Wehrmacht faced their personal Calvary. Well over six feet deep, twenty yards wide, and flowing with the power provided by millions of cubic feet of melting snow, the Gniloy Tikich proved to be the last and most formidable obstacle faced by the encircled troops of Gruppe Stemmerman, the survivors of the breakout from the pocket west of a town named Cherkassy. Many would find their watery graves here. Many others would cross it and find salvation. All those who experienced the battle and the narrow escape would be marked by it for the rest of their lives, regardless of what happened to them the remainder of the war.

Virtually unknown in the English-speaking world, the Battle of Cherkassy (also known as the Korsun Pocket) still stirs controversy in both the former Soviet Union and in Germany, the protagonists during this epic struggle. Although small in scale when compared to the gigantic battles of Moscow, Stalingrad, and Kursk, the Battle of the Cherkassy Pocket occupies a prominent place in the Russo-German War. It was at Cherkassy where the last German offensive strength in the Ukraine was drained away, creating the conditions for the victorious Soviet advance into Poland, Rumania, and the Balkans during the summer and autumn of 1944. Eclipsed by a war of such gigantic proportions that saw battles of over one million men or more as commonplace, the events which occurred along the banks of the Gniloy Tickich have faded into obscurity. However, to the 60,000 German soldiers who were encircled there at the end of January 1944, this was perhaps one of the most brutal, physically exhausting, and morally demanding battles they had ever experienced. Fully thirty-four percent of them would not escape.

Yet all of this was in the future. When German troops withdrew behind the Dnieper River during September and October of the previous year, they thought they had finally found safety and a respite from months of withdrawals and delaying actions fought against the victorious Red Army that followed on the heels of their defeat at the Battle of Kursk the previous July. Many looked toward the time when they would be able to occupy comfortable bunkers and fighting positions constructed by the laborers of Organization Todt, the German paramilitary construction corps. Many others looked towards a pause in the fighting, with the possibility of receiving leaves or passes to visit their loved ones in Germany or in other countries of Europe.

Few imagined that their previous experiences would only serve as a harbinger of worse times to come. Even fewer could have imagined having to swim a roaring stream in the middle of a Ukrainian winter. If any of them had ever heard of the towns of Cherkassy, Korsun, or Zvenigorodka at all, it was from the early stages of the German advance in Russia, when Hitler's troops had passed through them on their way to the Dnieper River crossings in August and September 1941. By the Fall of 1943, of course, few of these original Ostkämpfer were still in the ranks and all that anyone knew was that these towns were safely in "the rear."

To the Soviets, this battle marked a point in the Russo-German War when their own military capability and strength surpassed that of their hated opponent. After this battle, the men of the Red Army's First and Second Ukrainian Fronts proved that they could face their enemy confident in their ability to conduct mobile warfare on an equal, if not superior, footing. Cherkassy, like the Battle of Kursk six months before, marked a moment when the elite panzer divisions were again bled white with negligible gains; only this time eight of Hitler's panzer divisions reached a point from which they would never recover and two entire infantry corps were virtually destroyed as effective fighting formations.

The Battle of Cherkassy was not just about the progress that Joseph Stalin's Red Army of Workers and Peasants had made since its near defeat in July and August of 1941; it was also an intensely personal battle for soldiers of both sides as well. From the infantryman in his water-filled foxhole, who had to withstand days and weeks of constant combat with little or no rest, to the tank crewmen who engaged in dozens of one-on-one battles with enemy tanks, to the harried and overworked staffs of both sides who struggled to make some sense of the situation, and to the generals and field marshals who matched wits with one another, the Battle of Cherkassy stands out as one of the most bitterly fought, desperate battles which characterize a war singular in its brutality, destructiveness, and inhumanity. Like the equally ferocious fighting that characterized the Battles of Demyansk, Velikiye Luki, Rschev, and Cholm, Cherkassy pitted outnumbered and poorly positioned German soldiers fighting heroically against overwhelming masses of Soviet troops, artillery, and tanks. But this time, with a difference.

While all of these other battles found German soldiers fighting outnumbered against poorly directed suicidal human wave attacks and clumsily employed armor, the Red Army encountered during the Battle of Cherkassy by the Germans was a highly maneuverable, flexible force. The ordinary

German Landser was to witness a degree of cooperation between all Soviet combat branches that he found unnerving. In the past, he knew, as long as he kept his cool he could outfight his opponent, even though outnumbered. Now, it did not seem to matter much anymore, because no matter how skillfully he fought or how many Soviet soldiers he killed, sooner or later he would be overwhelmed.

This period of the war also bore witness to an increasingly common occurrence experienced by German soldiers on the Eastern Front: encirclement. As the German losses mounted and tactical flexibility was increasingly constrained by Hitler's headquarters thousands of kilometers away, the Red Army's increasing numerical superiority would eventually overwhelm thinly-spread German defenses. Stand-fast orders would insure that German units would remain pinned to their defensive positions, while Soviet mechanized troops sought out their enemy's command and logistics installations.

The disaster of Stalingrad was merely the first and most famous of these encirclement battles; many were to follow in its wake. The loss of Field Marshal Paulus's 6.Armee at Stalingrad, with the capture of over 100,000 men, had a profound effect on German Army morale in Russia as well as Germany's overall strategic situation. Stalingrad also had an impact on the Soviet Supreme Command, or STAVKA, in that Stalin's marshals would persistently try to stage another larger, strategically decisive encirclement. Cherkassy was supposed to have been such a victory.

The reason that the Battle of Cherkassy did not become a Stalingrad on the Dnieper is due to a variety of factors, not the least being the incredible heroism displayed by soldiers of both sides. By all calculations, the Red Army should have repeated their success at Stalingrad here along the wind-swept fields of Ukraine, but did not. Although the encircled German divisions lost or abandoned nearly all of their equipment, most of the troops managed to escape, making this battle akin to a German Dunkirk, with all of the implications of a moral victory.

Despite the evidence that their Korsun-Shevchenkovsky Operation was still an impressive Soviet military victory, Marshals Zhukov's and Koniev's triumph was tarnished by the fact that they had lied to Stalin in order to conceal the escape of so many Germans, exaggerating German casualties to make the victory seem more grand, more impressive. In fact, the controversy continues to this day, obscuring the significance of what occurred here and reducing this accomplishment into a mere argument over the German body count.

Although the Battle of Cherkassy has received mention in many post-war accounts, few books have been written about it, except for several official Soviet versions which clash with actual reports written immediately after the battle. German accounts of the battle have been limited to articles in veteran's association magazines, or individual chapters in books dealing with the Russian Front in general. When dealt with in official publications, Cherkassy is most often used as an example of what not to do during an encirclement operation or as a exhibit to illustrate the folly of Adolf Hitler's demand that his troops yield not one foot of ground.

There has yet to be an account written from the individual soldier's perspective, that describes his experiences of being encircled, fighting and marching for days on end, and of his escape from the pocket. I hope that this book will shed some light on these experiences, while highlighting the simple devotion to duty, heroism, and self-sacrifice of the average Landser or Ivan. As memories fade and surviving veterans dwindle in number, may this book serve as a reminder of what can be accomplished by well-led soldiers facing overwhelming odds, how resilience can overcome diversity, and how the human spirit can triumph even in defeat.

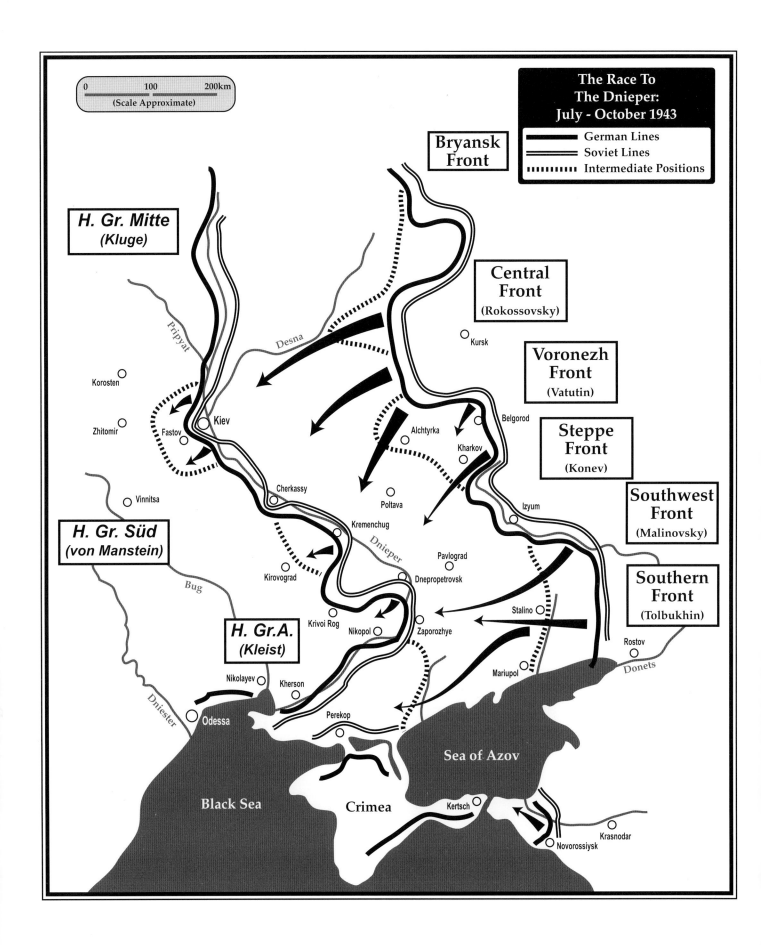

The Race To
The Dnieper:
July - October 1943

— German Lines
= Soviet Lines
···· Intermediate Positions

Bryansk
Front

Central
Front
(Rokossovsky)

Voronezh
Front
(Vatutin)

Steppe
Front
(Konev)

Southwest
Front
(Malinovsky)

Southern
Front
(Tolbukhin)

H. Gr. Mitte
(Kluge)

H. Gr. Süd
(von Manstein)

H. Gr.A.
(Kleist)

Pripyat

Desna

Korosten

Zhitomir

Kiev

Fastov

Kursk

Alchtyrka

Kharkov

Belgorod

Vinnitsa

Cherkassy

Poltava

Izyum

Kremenchug

Dnieper

Pavlograd

Kirovograd

Krivoi Rog

Nikopol

Dnepropetrovsk

Zaporozhye

Stalino

Mariupol

Rostov

Donets

Bug

Nikolayev

Kherson

Dniester

Odessa

Perekop

Sea of Azov

Black Sea

Crimea

Kertsch

Krasnodar

Novorossiysk

0   100   200km
(Scale Approximate)

I

SETTING THE STAGE

Chapter One
THE SAGA OF ARMY GROUP SOUTH

"The time for grand-style operations in the East is now past."
— *Adolf Hitler to Erich von Manstein, in Barbarossa*[1]

When *Hauptmann* (*Hptm.*, or captain) Ernst Schenk returned to the Ukraine to retake command of his battalion in late December 1943 after several months of convalescence, what he found was not encouraging. When he had been evacuated to Germany with severe wounds shortly after the Battle of Kursk, his regiment, *Grenadier Regiment* (*Gren.Rgt.*) 110, had consisted of three nearly full-strength battalions.

Schenk, an experienced 30-year old professional soldier from the town of Dinkelsbühl in Franconia, had been with his regiment since 1939. He knew his regiment had been in constant action during his absence, but expected to find it still intact upon his return. To his surprise and dismay, it was no longer a regiment at all; in fact, due to heavy fighting during the retreat of the previous autumn, each of the regiment's battalions had suffered such losses that they had to be combined into one battalion-sized unit, now renamed *Regimentsgruppe* (*Rgt.Gr.*) 110.[2]

The situation was exacerbated by the fact that no replacements had been made available to his unit or his division, *112. Infanterie-Division* (*Inf.Div.*). In fact, casualties had been so high and the manpower situation so critical that even his decimated division had been renamed a *Divisionsgruppe* (*Div.Gr.*), and that it, in turn, had been assigned to *Korps Abteilung* (*K.Abt.*) B, which consisted of three *Div.Gr.112, 255,* and *332* - all of which had suffered considerably during the summer battles in the Ukraine and the retreat to the Dnieper River defensive line that autumn.

What had happened to Schenk's regiment and division had become a common occurrence in Germany's *Heeresgruppe Süd* (Army Group South), since the retreat to the Dnieper and bitter defensive fighting had burnt many divisions out, necessitating extreme measures, such as combining shattered units in the hopes of getting further use out of them. The replacements that Army Group South desperately needed were being funneled to the west, where they were being used to build up divisions slated to repulse the expected Allied amphibious landing along the channel coast. Until that battle had been won, according to Hitler, the *Ostheer* (the German Army in Russia) would have to make do with what it had until forces could be switched back to the East.

In his *Führer* Directive 51, issued on 3 November 1943, Hitler stated that although the Soviet danger to Germany was still extant, a greater threat had arisen in the West - the long-awaited Anglo-American invasion. Hitler directed that "I can no longer take the responsibility for allowing the Western Front to be weakened for the benefit of other theaters of war."[3]

Hauptmann Ernst Schenk, *Commander, Rgt.Gr.110, Korpsabteilung B. (Photo courtesy of Ernst Schenk)*

After all, if worse came to worse in the east, Hitler felt that his armies could possibly trade space for time. The Soviet Union, as the reasoning went, was, after all, a vast land whose borders were still safely hundreds of miles away from the *Reich*. Whether Hitler would be willing to yield large amounts for territory in exchange for the advantage gained was an open question - previously, he had displayed a tremendous reluctance to give up ground that his armies had conquered.

So, Ernst Schenk found an amalgamated battalion with too many new faces and a great deal of old ones missing, such as *Oberleutnant* (*Oblt.*) Kaiser and *Hptm.* Grimm, men with whom he had faced many critical situations and had become close friends. Both had been killed in action during the retreat to the Dnieper, when his division had been forced to fight a series

Hauptmann Schenk, *(second from right) at his battalion command post on the outskirts of Bobritsa, early January 1944. (Photo courtesy of Ernst Schenk)*

of rearguard actions. Now he missed them greatly. His battalion-sized *Regimentsgruppe* consisted of about 400-500 infantrymen and 100 or so supporting troops, holding a front about four kilometers in length near the town of Kanev. The battalion's heavy weapons by now consisted of several medium mortars and a dozen machine guns, scarcely enough to provide supporting fire to the infantry.

His sector of the front was already thinly occupied and became even more so when his battalion had to take over their neighboring battalion's sector on its left in early January 1944, adding another eight kilometers to his already thinly-manned line, with a troop density of less than 40 men per kilometer. To visit his men in their widely spaced, snow-covered bunkers, Schenk would travel alone on skis with his submachine gun slung around his neck, since the Soviets frequently infiltrated his lines in attempt to kill messengers or seize prisoners.[4] However, he believed that these visits were important to boost his troops' morale to ascertain true conditions at the forward outposts, where most of the fighting actually took place.

At his command post in Bobritsa located at the right flank of *Div.Gr.112* (and rightmost flank of its higher headquarters, *XXXXII.Armeekorps* (*A.K.* or corps), Schenk could look to the east, where the mighty Dnieper slept under its thick coat of ice; to his south lay the city of Kanev, which the Soviets had failed to seize the previous October during their daring airborne operation which had ended in disaster. Kanev itself was now occupied by troops from the reconnaissance battalion of *5.SS-Pz.Div. Wiking*, covering the left flank of the neighboring *XI. A.K.*

From Schenk's vantage point, it seemed as if the war had simply fallen asleep; there had not been any significant Soviet offensive activity in *K.Abt.B*'s sector since his return from convalescent leave, though *88.Inf.Div.* on the *Korpsabteilung's* left flank had been in motion for weeks. However, the constant threat of local small-scale Soviet attacks or patrols, always a factor to be reckoned with on the Eastern Front, kept Schenk's men in a constant state of alertness, contributing greatly to their already strained physical condition and morale.

One soldier who experienced these conditions was *Gefreiter* Hans Queitzsch from the town of Halle. Trained as a medic, he was sent to the Eastern Front on 27 September 1943, where he was soon assigned to *6.Kompanie* (*Kp.*), *Gren.Rgt. 258 of 112.Inf.Div.* as an infantryman. Eighteen years old at the time, Queitzsch still believed in Hitler and in final victory, but this prepared him little for the reality he faced when he went into the trenches. His company, reduced in strength to about 65 men, occupied defensive positions along the Dnieper adjacent to *Schenk's Rgt.Gr.110.* From here, he got to experience the everyday life of a *Landser* first-hand.

The hygiene conditions in our positions were catastrophic. In Nov./Dec.'43 we were occupying positions near Bobritsa, where it was relatively quiet. In a nearby village, someone had erected a washing facility. We filled an old washbasin with hot water and five of us at a time would jump in. In another hut nearby, someone would wash and try to iron our uniforms. Unfortunately, it did no damage to the lice. Later on in the fighting, such washing became impossible. We soon became filthy and infested with lice. The only chance we had to wash then was to find a bucket and clean oneself the best one could. Sometimes we even had to use snow mixed with soap, so we could at least wash our hands and faces. Cutting our hair soon became a problem. The last haircut I received was before I left for the front in September 1943. The next one I got was after being wounded and flown out of the pocket on 9 February 1944.

Our spare set of underwear was kept in our Tornister (back packs), which were stored in the company baggage train. Only once, on 9 December, were we allowed to get them and change our underwear and socks. To store our personal effects, we had only our breadbag and uniform pockets. The uniforms themselves we wore day and night and were unable to exchange them for clean ones. Whenever a thawing spell happened, we were soon covered from top to bottom in mud from our foxholes. Fortunately, our uniform pockets had flaps which at least kept them from filling up with dirt. Our breadbag and canteen became lumps of mud.

Whenever the temperature fell below freezing, we suffered. Sometimes the tea or coffee in our canteens was full of ice. Every squad had a small bunker stove, but we were not always able to keep it going, if we had to occupy positions in an open field where there was no wood. If the stove produced too much smoke, it immediately drew mortar or machinegun fire. The more frequently we changed positions, the less we were able to keep clean or to build warm bunkers.

Besides the cold, we were often tortured by lice. Whenever one stood guard duty out in the open, they rarely bothered a man. However, whenever one returned to his foxhole and warmed up a bit, the lice would be so bad you couldn't stand it. Of the one or two hours between guard, one could only get an hour or so sleep because of them. During the day, we rarely had the opportunity to

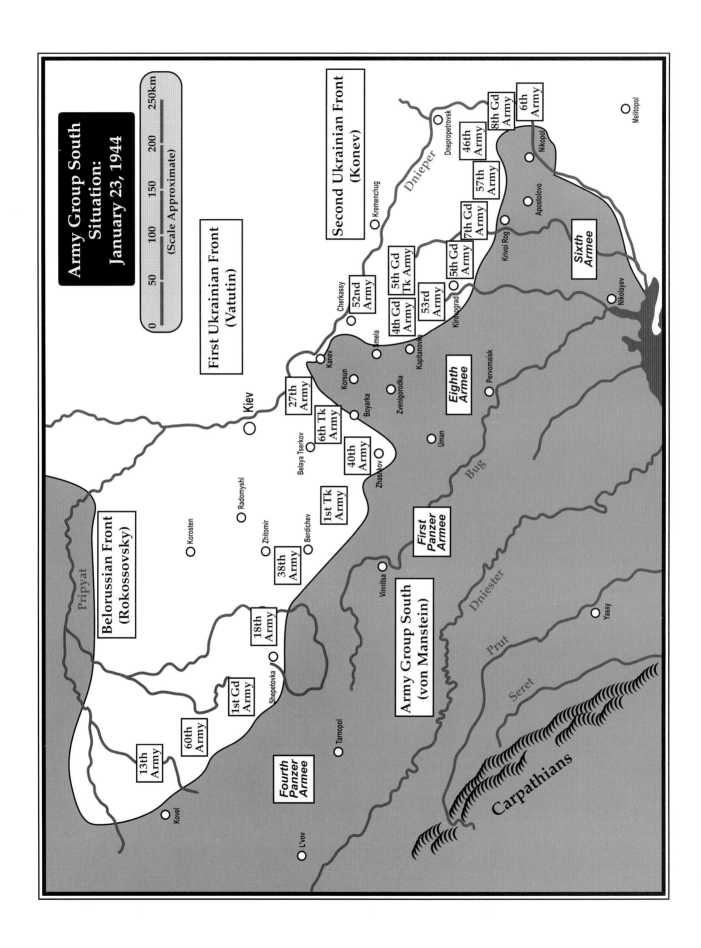

Army Group South Situation: January 23, 1944

(Scale Approximate)
0 50 100 150 200 250km

First Ukrainian Front (Vatutin)

Second Ukrainian Front (Konev)

Belorussian Front (Rokossovsky)

Army Group South (von Manstein)

8th Gd Army
6th Army
46th Army
57th Army
17th Gd Army
5th Gd Tk Army
52nd Army
4th Gd Army
5th Gd Army
53rd Army
Sixth Armee
27th Army
6th Tk Army
40th Army
1st Tk Army
Eighth Armee
First Panzer Armee
38th Army
18th Army
1st Gd Army
60th Army
13th Army
Fourth Panzer Armee

Melitopol
Dnepropetrovsk
Nikopol
Apostolovo
Krivoi Rog
Nikolayev
Kremenchug
Cherkassy
Kirograd
Kapitanovka
Smela
Kaniv
Korsun
Boyarka
Zvenigorodka
Pervomaisk
Kiev
Belaya Tserkov
Zhashkov
Uman
Radomyshl
Zhitomir
Berdichev
Korosten
Vinnitsa
Shepetovka
Tarnopol
Kovel
L'vov
Yassy

Pripyat
Dnieper
Bug
Dniester
Prut
Seret
Carpathians

sleep, because there was always something to do. Foxholes and guard posts had to be kept in order, water had to be fetched if a spring was nearby, wood had to be gathered, weapons and equipment had to be maintained, messages had to be brought back and forth to the company headquarters and so on . . . [5]

Neither Schenk nor Queitzsch, nor any other German soldiers for that matter occupying positions in the *Dneprknie* ("Dnieper-knee" because the bend in the Dnieper River near Kanev) had any idea of the magnitude of the storm about to be unleashed at them. Glad to have finally stopped retreating, keeping alive and warm were the most pressing priorities of the men in Schenk's battalion and the rest of the German soldiers occupying defensive positions in the Ukraine in the third winter of the war in the East. None of them knew that they would soon be fighting for their lives in circumstances far worse that any of them would imagine.

The road to the Battle of the Cherkassy Pocket began at Kursk six months before with the failure of Hitler's Operation *Zitadelle*. It was here during the first two weeks of July 1943 that the Third Reich's last attempt to regain the strategic initiative in the East with carefully hoarded armored reserves stalled in the face of successive Red Army defensive belts and massive armored counterattacks. When Hitler was forced to call off the offensive due to the Allied landing in Sicily that same month, Stalin was able to seize this opportunity to launch his own counteroffensive.

By 20 July 1943, six *Fronts* of the Red Army (a Front was the equivalent of a German Army Group) had joined in the attack, forcing the German Army to slowly fall back, especially in the Ukraine. The Soviet goal was to beat the Germans to the Dnieper River, deny them the bridges leading to safety on its western bank, and carve up their armies, corps and divisions piecemeal. They very nearly succeeding in carrying out this plan (Map 1). The Germans won the race to the Dnieper River, though just barely. Skillful handling of the remaining German reserves by *Generalfeldmarschal* (Field Marshal) Erich von Manstein, the commander of Army Group South, and his subordinate commanders avoided catastrophe repeatedly. Practicing a form of mobile warfare rarely equaled by the pursuing Soviets, von Manstein used his divisions, particularly his panzer divisions, to deftly parry the blows of the Red Army, which repeatedly attempted to encircle the steadily withdrawing Germans, though without success. Kharkov, though it fell to the Soviets for the third and final time of the war in August 1943, saw the corps and divisions of *Armeeabteilung Kempf* (Army Detachment Kempf, later to become *8.Armee*) deal a series of bloody counterattacks against the pursuing armies of General Vatutin's Voronezh Front.

On 19 August, General Pavel Rotmistrov's 5th Guards Tank Army, which had triumphed over *II.SS-Pz.Korps* at Kursk, lost 184 of its own tanks to the guns of *III.Pz.Korps'* armored divisions - *3.Pz., 2.SS-Pz.Gren.Div. Das Reich*, and *Wiking*.[6]

The Soviet attack was stopped in its tracks. However, Stalin was adamant - he wanted Kharkov liberated at all costs. Several hundred additional Soviet tanks were thrown at the German defenders, slowy forcing them back from the outskirts of the city, though at enormous cost to the attackers. When the city was about to be surrounded, von Manstein, defying Hitler's desire to hold the city, ordered the defending *XI.A.K.* of General Stemmermann to withdraw on 22 August, thus allowing its troops to escape the fate of Stalingrad, for the time being.

So fluid was the situation during this withdrawal that not even Hitler could react in time to tie up von Manstein's hands. Even so, von Manstein was forced to fly for personal conversations with Hitler no less than seven times during the course of the retreat.[7] For his part, von Manstein was trying to save as many divisions, tanks, and soldiers as possible because he knew that everything would be needed to hold the Dnieper defensive line.[8] Skillfully executed German delaying tactics such as those displayed at Kharkov continued to inflict painful losses on the Red infantrymen and armored units, forcing the pursuit by the Red Army to slow to a crawl just when victory was in their grasp.

While the German rearguard held the Soviets at bay, the rest of Army Group South converged on seven Dnieper Crossings - from north to south, Kiev, Kanev, Kremenchug, Dnepropetrovsk, Zaparozhye, Bereslav, and Kherson - and streamed across to safety. By 30 September, nearly all German troops had been successfully evacuated across the Dnieper.[9] Despite overwhelming superiority in tanks, men, guns, and aircraft, the Fronts of Marshals Popov, Rokossovsky, Vatutin, Konev, and Malinovsky could not bring the Germans to bay. Although the Germans had won the race to the river, the battle to hold the line had only begun.

To hold this extensive defensive postion, which stretched over 400 miles from Kiev to the Black Sea near Kherson by early September 1943, Army Group South had only 37 divisions, none of which were at full strength. This total equated to approximately 80 men per mile of front, a laughably inadequate number for so challenging a task.[10] Once again, the *Ostheer* had been tasked to do too much with too little. The overextended front of Army Group South would soon be pierced at many locations, with its ultimate collapse only a matter of time. Even had positions been prepared for von Manstein's divisions, they would only have delayed the Soviet advance.

The safety of the long hoped-for German defensive positions at the so-called "Wotan Line" and "Panther" positions along the Dnieper proved illusory. These defensive positions were supposed to have been fully prepared with field fortifications, troop shelters, communication wire and trenches. They were supposed to have been stocked with ample amounts of ammunition and other supplies to enable weary German forces to recover their strength and to easily ward off the expected Soviet offensive. However, the local German civil administration and Nazi Party officials had completely failed to carry out this task, so bad was the level of cooperation between the party and the Army. Additionally, the order, Führer Directive 10 issued on 12 August 1943 that authorized Army Group South to prepare the Dnieper fortifications, had come too late for those officials responsible for the task to do much anyway.[11]

The withdrawing troops of Army Group South subsequently found that these positions were completed in only a few locations, such as at Kiev. A few, at best, had been surveyed by construction crews of Organization Todt (Germany's paramilitary construction corps). Most positions had not been prepared at all. In many places along the river, large stands of trees and bushes grew up to its edge, making observation and fire difficult, should the Soviets attempt a crossing. Many other places along the river were suitable for fording by the Soviets, but these locations went unreported to the newly arriving defenders, who in many cases would have precious little time to reconnoiter these positions themselves.

The men of Army Group South were thus bitterly disappointed by what they saw when they finally arrived at what they had thought would be veritable rest areas. *Oberst* (colonel) Hans Schmid, an officer from the *57.Inf.Div.*, which took up its new positions along the Dnieper south of Kanev on 23 September, had this to say:

> They [the troops] had hoped to find prepared positions behind the Dnieper where they could have a rest from fighting. But they found there neither prepared positions nor a reception party, other than the Russians. The result was to dash their spirits to the ground.[12]

Many officers and men such as he were thoroughly shocked by what they found after escaping across the Dnieper. Having believed their nation's own propaganda broadcasts, the German troops simply could not believe that so little had been done to prepare defensive positions for them. However, lack of prepared defensive positions was not the only problem faced by the men of von Manstein's *1.* and *4.Pz.Armee* and *8. Armee*, to which the bulk of the German soldiers fighting in the Ukraine were assigned. Their enemy had not granted them permission to enjoy their respite, either.

By the first week of October 1943, the Red Army had established bridgeheads at several points along the river. Although the Germans had succeeded in destroying every bridge along the Dnieper after their last units had crossed to safety, Soviet soldiers had carried out numerous small - scale crossings using whatever material was available, such as rafts made from planks lashed together, fishermen's rowboats, and rope ferries. Soviet commanders and troops displayed tremendous personal initiative during this period, contrary to German assertions that their opponent lacked such, much to their surprise.

Several of these tiny bridgeheads, established hastily by a few hundred men at the most, were quickly transformed into major staging areas in a remarkably short time, large enough to hold regiments, divisions, or even corps. The Germans recognized the danger posed by these positions popping up along their flanks and rear, but in many cases could not spare the manpower to completely wipe them out. Not all Soviet attempts to force the Dnieper succeeded, however.

One particularly ill-fated Soviet enterprise was an attempt to seize the river crossing at Kanev through the employment of airborne troops from 24 to 25 September. This attempt, spearheaded by the 1st, 3rd and 4th Guards Parachute Brigades, was intended to seize the bridge at Kanev and hold it long enough to deny it to the withdrawing *XXIV. Pz.Korps* and for Vatutin's mechanized forces to disrupt German defenses long enough to form a deeply entrenched bridgehead. A supporting attack was to be made further south at Moshny by the 1st, 2nd and 4th Parachute Brigades.

However, the plan was badly flawed, poorly planned, and ended in disaster when the Germans quickly moved mechanized units such as *Wiking* and *19.Pz.Div.* into the threatened area and killed or captured 80 percent of the parachutists. One airborne drop landed in the assembly area of one company of *Gren.Regt. 258* from *112.Inf.Div.* near the town of Grigorovka. Awestruck, the German defenders could not believe their eyes, since none of them had ever seen a sight such as this before, as hundreds of parachutes filled the sky above them in broad daylight.

It only took a couple of moments before the Germans regained their composure and began a fearsome slaughter which accounted for several hundred men of the 5th Guards Parachute Brigade, whose aircraft had strayed off course.[13] The few surviving Soviet parachutists who escaped capture melted into the forest, particularly in the Irdyn Swamp west of the town of Cherkassy, joining forces with the partisans already active there.[14]

Other Soviet bridgeheads, such as the ones at Lyutezh, Zaporosche, and Melitopol, were a harder nut to crack. Despite desperate German counterattacks in October and November 1943, these bridgeheads could not be eliminated and became springboards for future offensives to liberate the entire Ukraine. Massive offensives, involving hundreds of thousands of Soviet troops, tanks, and guns from the Lyutezh bridgehead northwest of Kiev in the north, from Zaporozhye in the center, and from Melitopol in the south exploded in mid-October 1943. By the end of November, the German defensive positions along the Dnieper were in shambles and the future survival of Army Group South was in jeopardy.

Army Group South's first major counteroffensive, carried out by *General der Panzertruppe* (*Gen.d.Pz.Tr.* or General of Armored Troops) Raus's *4.Pz.Armee*, was launched from mid-November to early December 1943, retaking the important transportation hub of Zhitomir, but ultimately succeeded only in slowing the Red Army's rate of advance. Despite temporary local gains and impressive numbers of tanks destroyed by Raus's panzers, the Soviets, spearheaded by General Vatutin's newly-renamed First Ukrainian Front, had smashed through *1.* and *4.Pz.Armee* in late December 1943. Hundreds of square miles of territory were liberated; some Soviet advance elements had even penetrated deep into the Pripyat marshes, which divided Army Group South from Army Group Center, creating the famous *Wehrmachtsloch* (Hole in the *Wehrmacht*) separating the two army groups which remained open until withdrawing German forces sealed it off in late April 1944.[15]

Following further Soviet gains in early January 1944 during the Zhitomir-Berdichev and Kirovograd operations, the only portion of the Dnieper positions still held by the Germans, with the exception of the tiny Nikopol bridgehead to the south, was a stretch that ran from Kanev in the north to a few kilometers northwest of Cherkassy, a total of roughly 80 kilometers. This left Army Group South with an overly extended frontage nearly 800 kilometers long in mid-January 1944 that ran from Rovno, in the north, southeast to Zhitomir, Kanev, Korsun, Shpola, Kirovograd, and to Nikopol, where the frontline angled southwest towards Kherson on the Black Sea (Map 2).

It offered a situation unique in the annals of the Eastern Front, in that some of the German divisions actually occupied positions facing west, instead of east, as they had been accustomed to since, June 22 1941, the day they invaded the Soviet Union. Many German defenders, as attested to by letters during the fighting and after the war, found this prospect quite unnerving, because if they were ordered to retreat, they would have to march to the east first![16]

The bulge in the German frontline near Kanev, which jutted out conspicuously towards the Dnieper, was not the result of any far-reaching plan by the German High Command, but was instead a by-product of constant battles along the length of the Dnieper from October 1943 to January 1944. This bulge, dubbed the "Kanev Salient" by the Soviets, existed because the Soviets had simply stopped attacking west and southwest, if only temporarily. What was more remarkable is that instead of withdrawing from the developing trap which anyone, even the simplest infantryman, could see, the Germans were ordered by their highest military authority, Hitler himself, to remained in their positions and prepare for a renewed offensive towards the east. This vexed von Manstein and his staff, since they knew that the Kanev Salient was an open invitation towards encirclement by the Soviets.

Unfortunately, von Manstein's forces were now prevented from withdrawing from this vulnerable position because of a "stand-fast" directive, issued by Hitler, which only he could countermand.[17] Although Hitler considered himself a brilliant strategist and tactician, the evidence suggests that he possessed middling talent as a strategist at best and that his tactical concepts dated back to World War One.[18] In fact, his "stand-fast" directive, which had been an ad hoc measure that was credited with preventing the rout and destruction of the German armies before Moscow during the winter of 1941-42, was fast becoming doctrine by the third winter of the war in the East.

Essentially, the stand-fast order, formalized 8 September 1942 as a "*Führer* Defense Order," recognized the growing numerical superiority of the Red Army and sought to defend and retain as much terrain as possible by emphasizing reliance on static defensive positions. Units were not to abandon positions until they had exhausted all ammunition, in effect dooming them to fighting to the last man or to certain encirclement, long after any chance for success had passed. According to one noted authority on the subject "What Hitler really wanted . . . was a return to the rigid, terrain-holding linear defense that the Germans had practiced before the adoption of the 'Elastic Defense' during the winter of 1916-17."[19] Hitler's increasing interference in operational and tactical decisions meant that German commanders could ignore the order at their own peril.

Despite the disaster at Stalingrad, where an entire army had been lost because its commander, Field Marshal Paulus, adhered to Hitler's stand-fast policy rather than yield to his conscience, Hitler continued to believe in his military infallibility.

Characteristically, Hitler, in his role as head of the *Oberkommando des Heeres* (German Army High Command or *OKH*), which was responsible for the conduct of the war in the East, saw this salient as an opportunity, rather than an enormous risk. Poised as it was along the Dnieper, Hitler believed that the salient would serve as an ideal springboard for a renewed offensive aimed at retaking Kiev from the rear and throwing the Red Army back across the river, soon to be followed by a renewed offensive aimed at Moscow.[20] The head of state of the Third Reich and the *OKH* could harbor such grandiose plans because he sincerely believed that the Red Army had exhausted itself during the winter battles in the Ukraine, creating an opportunity for the *Wehrmacht* to strike against an unprepared opponent. His imagination, unfettered by knowledge of true conditions and the state of his units which could only be gained by actually visiting front-line positions and seeing how his troops actually lived, left Hitler free to fantasize.*

However, the commander and leaders of Army Group South did not possess such sanguine views of the situation and knew that their formations did it possess the combat power required to accomplish so grand a task. *Generaloberst* Karl Zeitzler, then serving as *OKH* Chief of the General Staff, also attempted to persuade Hitler to allow a withdrawal, but without success. Unfortunately, by this stage of the war, the vaunted General Staff of the *OKH* had been relegated to little more than a conduit for the issuance of orders from Hitler to his field commanders in the East, and exercised precious few of the powers that it has previously enjoyed prior to and during the First World War. Even von Manstein's strenuous objections to holding the salient and retaking Kiev had no effect. Hitler believed that superior willpower alone was sufficient to achieve his ends. The Kanev salient therefore would remain - there was to be no withdrawal and the troops presently occupying positions there would dig in, while Army Group South would begin preparations to concentrate its armored and mechanized divisions for the grand counteroffensive.

Occupying this salient were two corps of *Army Group South, XI.* and *XXXXII.A.K.*, with a total effective strength of six divisions and one independent brigade. Both of these hard-pressed corps had been involved in combat operations for weeks without pause and were exhausted. Neither had any standing forces in reserve worth mentioning, since all units of both corps were spread rather thinly in order to cover the huge frontage. Complicating matters was the fact that each belonged to a different army - *XXXXII.A.K.* in the western half of the salient was under the control of *1.Pz.Armee*, while *XI.A.K.* in the east came under the control of *8.Armee*.

---

* Hitler assumed the mantle of Commander-in-Chief of the Army on 19 December, 1941 after relieving Field Marshal von Brauchitsch for disagreeing with the former's decision to stand fast before Moscow in the face of the Soviet counteroffensive. This, according to one noted source, diminished the Army's operational and tactical authority in comparison to the Navy and Air Force, which remained under their own commanders. (Source: Albert Seaton, The Russo-German War, 1941-45, p. 212.)

Above: *Five Ukrainian peasant children pose for an SS photographer somewhere in Wiking's defensive sector, February 1944. All appear to be adequately dressed and fed, though all appear to be shy before the camera. The boy with the balalaika appears to be wearing a cast-off Soviet winter cap and boots. German soldiers often brought food from their field kitchens for the local population and like all soldiers everywhere, gave children treats such as bonbons or candy. (U.S. National Archives)*

Above: *An SS-Kriegsberichter NCO Candidate from Wiking samples some roast grains, probably sunflower seeds, offered by a local somewhere in Wiking's defensive sector. After living close together for months, German soldiers and the local inhabitants often developed a wary trust between one another. (U.S. National Archives)*

Above: *An SS-Kriegsberichter engaged in friendly conversation with an elderly local man. In many instances, German troops were quartered in the homes of local civilians and were expected by their commanders to treat the people as justly and as courteously as the tactical situation permitted. (U.S. National Archives)*

Above: *In this scene inside a typical Ukrainian private dwelling, the host of the house, here wearing a beard reminiscent of the Tsarist period, holds forth at the dinner table. German soldiers often shared meals with the families they were quartered with, often using their own rations to supplement the family's meals. (U.S. National Archives)*

Left: *A Ukrainian woman baking bread in her home. Despite Soviet accusations of widespread German looting, this home seems remarkably intact. Taken late January/early February 1944. (U.S. National Archives)*

Above: *A typical Ukrainian tie stove with a bed made atop for sleeping, in this case occupied by members of the Wiking's Kriegsberichter unit. Their clothing and equipment hang nearby. (U.S. National Archives)*

Right: *A typical Ukrainian windmill, which dotted the landscape and were used as landmarks by both sides. Made almost entirely of wood, windmills like this one were used to mill wheat or to drive sawmills.*
(U.S. National Archives)

Left: *A friendly-looking Ukrainian girl drawing water from a village well. Although not stylishly dressed, her clothes appear to be in good repair. (U.S. National Archives)*

Each reported back to and drew their logistical support from their respective higher headquarters, which would immensely complicate command, control, and resupply of their forces during the initial stages of an encirclement. Why both corps were not put under the command of a single army headquarters, with the danger of encirclement so evident, remains a mystery. Perhaps von Manstein did not want one or the other subordinate army commanders to have too few or two many corps under his immediate span of control.

Of all of Adolf Hitler's field marshals, Erich von Manstein was arguably one of his best. An acknowledged master of large-scale mechanized operations, he was perhaps the only one of Germany's military leaders who had the skill and ingenuity that the situation demanded. Indeed, he had thwarted the Red Army many times in the past, especially in the epic fighting withdrawal to the Dnieper River defensive line. In addition to his proven military abilities, he also possessed the moral courage to stand up to Hitler and tell him when he was wrong, even when he knew that it was extremely risky to do so.

Probably the only other generals who possessed this same sense of conviction were Heinz Guderian and Walter Model, who also clearly spoke their mind to their Führer. This was a quality in rare supply by January 1944, since by this stage of the war, Hitler had sacked most of his best field commanders, such as von Rundstedt (whom he reappointed to command in the West), von Bock, and von Leeb. Truly, von Manstein was in a small class of that rare breed - the true Prussian officer in the mold of von Schlieffen, von Moltke, and Ludendorff.

Born 24 November 1887 as Erich von Lewinski, he was adopted by his mother's sister, who was childless. Raised in a military family (his adoptive father was General von Manstein), Erich attended the Cadet Corps in Berlin at Gross Lichterfelde. During World War One, he served in *2.Reserve-Regiment* of the Guards on both the Eastern and Western Fronts, until being severely wounded in November 1914. For the remainder of the war, he served on progressively higher level staffs, taking part in the Battles of Verdun, the Somme, and the final German offensive in the West, where he was serving when the war ended. Between the wars, he continued to serve in a variety of staffs, proving his mettle as a resourceful and contemplative general staff officer. In 1935, he became Chief of Operations Branch of the German Army, an extremely powerful and influential position.

When his chief Freiherr von Fritsch, Commander in Chief of the German Army was sacked by Hitler in February 1938, von Manstein was sent to command *18.Inf.Div.*, gaining valuable practical experience in the command of a large organization. Later that year, he had been appointed to serve as the chief of staff of an army. Chosen by Generaloberst von Runstedt to serve as his army's chief of staff during the invasion of Poland, von Manstein soon became embroiled in the controversy regarding which plan of action to follow for the upcoming invasion of France. His plan, which envisioned an end run around the Maginot Line by attacking through the Ardennes Forest with armored forces, was eventually adopted by Hitler, though by that time von Manstein had been placed in command of *XXXVIII.A.K.*, which saw extensive service under his leadership during the Battle of France.

Generalfeldmarschal Erich von Manstein, *Commander, Army Group South. (U.S. National Archives)*

In March 1941 he was chosen to command *LVI. Pz.Korps*, which he led as part of Army Group North during the initial stages of Operation Barbarossa, dashing from East Prussia to Lake Ilmen, nearly reaching the gates of Leningrad. Then, he was unexpectedly transferred to Army Group South, where he assumed command of *11.Armee*. While leading his army into the Crimea, his troops conquered the fortress of Sevastopol in July 1942. In recognition of this accomplishment, he was promoted to field marshal by a grateful Hitler. Transferred with his headquarters staff to the Leningrad Front in August 1942, he was charged with the responsibility of taking that city. Although his army did ward off a Soviet counteroffensive and destroyed one of the attacking armies, the renewed attack on Leningrad had to be broken off on account of the situation far to the south.

Von Manstein was placed in charge of Army Group Don in December 1942 and given an even greater task - rescuing the encircled Sixth Army in Stalingrad. Despite winter weather, enormous supply problems and unrelenting attacks from the Red Army, troops of his improvised army group nearly succeeded in reaching the beleaguered forces, approaching so close to the pocket that they could see flashes of gunfire across the steppe. When Paulus refused to break out on his own responsibility, the encircled troops in Stalingrad were doomed and von Manstein was forced to watch helplessly as his relief column was finally forced back.

Deeply affected by this ordeal, von Manstein was able to restore some measure of good fortune to German arms when

Marshall of the Soviet Union Georgi K. Zhukov,
STAVKA Represetative for the Korsun-Shevchenkovsky Operation, later Acting Commander, First Ukrainian Front. (Photo courtesy of the Battle of Korsun-Shevchenkovsky Museum, Korsun, Ukraine)

his army group, soon to be renamed Army Group South, dealt a crushing blow to the Soviets when his forces encircled Vatutin's Voronezh Front and retook Kharkov in March 1943, saving the right wing of the German Army in Russia. This feat, which is still regarded by military historians as being one of the most brilliantly executed campaigns of World War Two, earned him the Oak Leaves to his Knight's Cross.[21]

In the summer of 1943, he led his army group during the abortive Kursk offensive, where his forces achieved far greater penetrations into the Soviet defensive positions than did Field Marshal von Kluge's forces of Army Group Center. Afterwards, von Manstein conducted his brilliant withdrawal to the Dnieper River, of which, by January 1944, there was only one small stretch still in German hands. The Battle of the Cherkassy Pocket would perhaps be the greatest challenge of his military career.

His opponent during the late winter Kharkov counteroffensive and the Battle of Kursk was another of the war's great field commanders, Deputy Supreme Commander-in-Chief and First Deputy Defence Commissar of the Soviet Union, Georgy Konstantinovich Zhukov. They would be pitted against each other once again, this time over the fate of the Kanev Salient.

Georgy Zhukov, born 2 December 1896 in the village of Strelkovka in the Kaluga Province, was the son of poor peasants. He served in the First World War as an NCO in the cavalry, specializing in patrols behind the enemy lines, for which he was awarded two St. George's Crosses, one of Imperial Russia's highest military awards. Dissatisfied with the Czar and the political and economic situation then obtaining in Russia, he joined the Red Guards in January 1918. He was promoted to captain and led a cavalry squadron during the Russian Civil War. For his leadership during the Battle of Tsaritsyn in 1919, he was awarded the Soviet Union's Order of the Red Banner. By 1923, he was commanding a cavalry division at 27.

During the nineteen-twenties and thirties, Zhukov combined field and staff service, all the while continuing his military studies at night. He was far more interested in his profession than many of his contemporaries, who were amazed that he spent his free time in his quarters studying maps. In one efficiency report, his commander, future Marshal of the Soviet Union Konstantin Rokossovsky, characterized Zhukov as "strong-willed and decisive . . . has a broad range of initiative and knows how to apply it in practice."[22] However, the Soviet Union nearly lost this promising young leader who would later play so large a role in his country's victory, before the war even began.

When the great purge of Red Army leadership was ordered by Stalin in 1937, Zhukov was at that time commanding the 3rd Cavalry Corps. When notified by a Plenum of the Communist Party Central Committee led by Molotov that his signature was on several incriminating documents linking him to so-called reactionary elements, Zhukov confronted Molotov with an emphatic denial which, if not believed by Molotov, was accepted by the Plenum. Nevertheless, Zhukov was transferred to assume Deputy Command of the Bialystok Military District, considered a demotion at the time.

Summoned to a meeting at the Kremlin on orders of Defense Commissar K. Voroshilov on 1 June 1939, Zhukov feared the worst, since such a request usually led to the person's arrest and subsequent trial. Zhukov was surprised when he was ordered to Khalkin-Gol in Mongolia to command the military district there, then threatened at the time by Japanese expansion in neighboring Manchuria. In the subsequent battle and decisive defeat of the Japanese Army, Zhukov proved beyond a doubt his capability as a talented and hard-driving leader of large mechanized forces.

When the German invasion of the Soviet Union began, Zhukov had been serving as the Chief of the Red Army's General Staff since January 1941. In the ensuing disasters which led from one to another between June and July 1941, Zhukov was chosen to coordinate the actions of several of the *Fronts* involved in the fighting, though he chafed at being a staff officer instead of leading troops into battle. He got his wish on 30 July 1941, when Stalin took command of the Reserve *Front*, then being hastily assembled to defend the approaches to Moscow. From this point until the end of the war, Zhukov was constantly in motion, serving as a Stalin's one-man fire brigade, being moved to take command of one crisis spot after another. In September he was charged with defending Leningrad at the head of the *Front* charged with that city's defense. Leningrad, under his energetic and ruthless leadership, held.

When the Western and Reserve Fronts were in danger of collapse near Vyazma in October, Zhukov was sent there by Stalin to assess the situation and to take charge if necessary. This he did, but by November 1941, Moscow was being directly threatened by the German's Operation Typhoon, their final all-out effort to take the Soviet capital. Recalled to coordinate the actions of the various Fronts charged with Moscow's defense, Zhukov again was characteristically energetic, alternatingly exhorting and chiding Front commanders. The German failure to take Moscow and their subsequent defeat at the gates of the city are well-known, but Zhukov was one of the key players behind the scenes who made sure that the great victory was achieved.

From August 1942, when he was named Deputy Supreme Commander-in-Chief and First Deputy Commissar, to July 1943, he served in practically all of the key battles as the Front Coordinator for Soviet Supreme Command or *STAVKA*, including Stalingrad, Kharkov, and Kursk. As a *STAVKA* "Coordinator," his duties required him to direct strategic and campaign planning of all big *Front* operations, both in their preparation and execution.[23] During this time, he was rarely in Moscow. Rather that sit at a desk, he preferred to be at the front lines, assisting the commanders in developing and putting their battle plans into action.

He also helped coordinate the actions of several *Fronts*, if a large-scale operation required that they work together to achieve an objective. For the upcoming offensive to eliminate the Kanev Salient, Zhukov was ordered by Stalin to the Ukraine to coordinate the activities of the First and Second Ukrainian *Fronts*. Although he knew his position was an important one, Zhukov would have preferred to command these large formations instead of serving as a glorified staff officer. He would soon get his chance.

For by 12 January 1944, the Kanev Salient, which comprised an area 125 kilometers wide and 90 kilometers deep, had also attracted the notice of Stalin. Both Zhukov and his leader saw the German forces still arrayed along the Dnieper as both a threat poised to the overextended inner flanks of the two Soviet *Fronts* concerned (the First and Second Ukrainian), as well as an opportunity. If the Red Army acted decisively, its forces could encircle and destroy the Germans occupying the salient, applying the recipe proven so successful at Stalingrad the year before and thereby weaken the entire German defense in the Ukraine.[24] Perhaps, if they acted quickly, these German corps and divisions could be destroyed during a rapidly executed encirclement operation, before they had the opportunity to escape the noose clearly being drawn about them.

With any luck, it could be done without a great deal of costly fighting, like the famous German blitzkrieg operations proven so effective during the early days of the war. Unlike Hitler's grandiose plan to retake Kiev and continue the victorious advance to Moscow, the Soviet plan had an air of practicality around it - at least Stalin had the forces available to execute his plan, should he decide to do so. And he had the initiative, something which Germany had irrevocably lost the previous summer, not just on the Eastern Front, but in all its

theaters of war. The Third Reich was now on the strategic defensive everywhere.

Both Hitler's and Stalin's decisions and von Manstein's and Zhukov's leadership would soon significantly affect the conduct of operations of the entire southern front of the war in the East and the fate of thousands of men. The situation in the wake of the Soviet offensive in the Ukraine and the race to the Dnieper in the late summer and fall of 1943 had provided Stalin and his generals an excellent opportunity to carry out another operation on the scale of Stalingrad. They vowed not to let this opportunity slip through their grasps, as it had repeatedly since Kursk. Hitler's obstinate desire to retain every inch of territory, combined with his reckless disregard of the advice of his experts, would only serve to make the task of the Soviets that much easier, or so it seemed to them at the time.

That the Battle of Cherkassy would not become another Stalingrad on the Dnieper was due to a number of factors, none of which had anything to do with *der Führer's* supposed skills as a *Feldherr* (a great captain). Instead, many other factors would combine to influence the outcome, not the least of which was the plan drafted by the Soviets themselves. The true outcome would also be greatly influenced by the soldiers and their leaders on both sides, who had been fighting each other since 22 June 1941.

End Notes

[1] Alan Clark, *Barbarossa: The Russian-German Conflict, 1941-45.* (New York: Quill Books, 1985), p. 380.

[2] Letter from Ernst Schenk, Dinkelsbühl, Germany to author, dated 26 July 1996. Original in author's possession.

[3] Earl F. Ziemke, *From Stalingrad to Berlin: The German Defeat in the East.* (Washington, D.C.: The United States Army Center of Military History, 1966), pp. 216-217.

[4] Schenk letter.

[5] Letter from Hans Queitzsch, Halle/Salle Germany, to author, dated 22 January 1998, pp. 1-4.

[6] Peter Strassner, *European Volunteers: The 5th SS-Panzer Division Viking.* (Winnepeg, Canada: J.J. Fedorowicz Publishing, 1988), p.124-125.

[7] Clark, p. 372.

[8] Paul Carell, *Scorched Earth.* (New York: Ballantine Books, 1971), pp. 354-355.

[9] Erich von Mastein, *Lost Victories.* (Novato, CA: Presidio Press, 1982), p. 475.

[10] Ziemke, p. 174.

[11] Albert Seaton, *The Russo-German War 1941-45.* (Novato, CA: Presidio Press, 1971), p. 378.

[12] Strassner, p. 129.

[13] Carell, pp. 403-405.

[14] Hellmuth Reinhardt, MS # P-116, *Russian Airborne Operations.* (Washington, D.C.: Department of the Army, Office of the Chief of Military History,1952), pp. 59-60.

[15] Ziemke, p 233.

[16] Mayer, Gerhard. *Im Kessel Tscherkassy bei Regimentsstab Artillerie-Regiment 188, 88.Infanterie-Division,* (Heilbronn, Germany: Unpublished private manuscript, 1987), p. 127.

[17] Ibid, p. 226.

[18] Ronald Lewin, *Hitler's Mistakes.* (New York: William and Morrow, Inc., 1984), pp. 125-126.

[19] Timothy Wray, *Standing Fast: German Defensive Doctrine on the Russian Front during WWII.* (Fort Leavenworth, KS: Combat Studies Institute,1986), p. 120.

[20] Alex Buchner, *Ostfront 1944: The German Defensive Battles on the Russian Front, 1944.* (West Chester, PA: Schiffer Military History, 1991), pp. 20-21.

[21] Correlli Barnett, ed. *Hitler's Generals.* (New York: Quill Books, 1989), p. 221.

[22] Harold Shukman, ed. *Stalin's Generals.* (New York: Grove Press, 1993), p. 344.

[23] Ibid, p. 353.

[24] *Sbornik materialov po izucheniiu optya voiny* (Collection of Materials on the study of war experience). No. 14 (Moscow: Voennoe Izdatel'stvo Narodnogo Komissariata Oborony, 1945). Translated into English and republished as "The Korsun-Shevchenkovsky Operation, January-February 1944," in *The Journal of Slavic Military Studies.* (London: Frank Cass and Company, June 1994), p. 299-300. Henceforth referred to as *Sbornik.*

Chapter Two
OPPOSING FORCES

"Our mobility, which had always given us an advantage over the vast but slow Soviet formations, was now only a memory."

— *Guy Sajer, The Forgotten Soldier* [1]

The German forces occupying the Kanev salient had been marching and retreating since the failure of Operation *Zitadelle* the previous July. For six long months, von Manstein's men had known no other existence except fighting by day and marching by night, often with the threat of encirclement hovering nearby. Instead of finding prepared defensive positions behind the safety of the Dnieper, the troops of Army Group South often found no prepared positions at all and may even have found a Soviet reception committee in their designated sectors, which they would have to drive out or destroy before they could construct a front line.

Weary and gaunt, German infantrymen in ragged uniforms successfully kept the Soviet armies at bay and fought to hold most portions of the Dnieper Line, although by December 1943 there was not much left to hold - except for the bridgehead at Nikopol and the Kanev salient, virtually all of the west bank of the Dnieper had been given up in the face of unrelenting Soviet pressure.

Despite the strain of constant fighting, the units of von Manstein's army group still retained a measure of their fighting capability. Although outnumbered and outgunned, the Germans were still superior to the Soviet armies in tactical flexibility, staff work, and initiative of commanders at the divisional level and below. Under von Manstein's leadership, the men of Army Group South had been able to withstand most of the Red Army's attacks, though he himself could see that the end was in sight, if drastic measures were not taken soon.

Von Manstein felt that if Hitler continued to deny him the freedom of action and the reinforcements that he felt he needed, at a certain point in the near future he would no longer be able to successfully keep the Soviets at bay. There were no longer enough troops, tanks, guns and aircraft to hold his thinly spread front, much less to launch any kind of attack designed to regain the initiative in the Ukraine, as Hitler was constantly badgering him to do.

For in fact, many of von Manstein's divisions were at the end of their rope. Oberst Schmid of *57.Inf.Div.* captured their condition succinctly when he described conditions in his own division:

> The division's fighting strength has been weakened by the months-long battle against an enemy superior in men and material. The infantry battalions are at only 20 to 40 percent strength. Fighting morale has sunk. Within the unit is an apathetic indifference. The troops have been living under conditions in which the most primitive essentials of life have been lacking . . . harsh words of embitterment and lack of faith in the High Command are voiced by the troops.[2]

Although not all of the divisions in Army Group South were in such bad shape, by no means was this division out of the ordinary. All of von Manstein's divisions had suffered to a greater or lesser extent. The German soldier of World War Two is even today still legendary for his resilience and faith in his commanders, but even the *Landser* had a breaking point. Whether their morale would bear up to the stress and strain posed by weeks of encirclement remained to be seen.

Generaloberst Hans Valentin Hube, *Commander, First Panzer Army. (Bundesarchive 84/19/17)*

Von Manstein's Army Group South in mid-January 1944 consisted of three field armies - Fourth Panzer Army in the north, First Panzer Army in the center, and *8.Armee* in the south, adjoining General Hollidt's *6.Armee* in the Dnieper Bend, part of Field Marshal von Kleist's Army Group A. Two of von Manstein's armies each had a corps in the Kanev salient - *1.Pz.* and *8.Armee*, commanded by *Generaloberst (Gen.O.)* Hans Hube and *General der Infanterie (Gen.d.Inf.)* Otto Wöhler, respectively. Both were experienced commanders and had led their troops well during the grueling withdrawals to the Dnieper the previous autumn.

The *1.Pz.Armee's Gen.O* Hans Valentin Hube assumed command 29 October 1943, at the height of the Dnieper battles, relieving Eberhard von Mackensen, who had lost the Führer's confidence. Hube was to prove a steadfast, competent commander, whose aggressive leadership style had earned him the name *Der Mensch* (the man) for his affection for front-line soldiers and willingness to share dangers with them. Born 29 October 1890 in Naumburg, he had served in World War One, where he lost an arm while serving on the Western Front. During the interwar period he wrote the definitive textbook on the infantry tactics, *Der Infanterist*, and served as the commander of the *Infanterie-Lehr Regiment*, the Army's premier infantry formation. He commanded troops in Poland in 1939 and earned the *Ritterkreuz* (Knight's Cross) 1 August 1941 while leading *16.Pz.Div.* during Operation Barbarossa. Ordered out of the Stalingrad pocket immediately prior to the surrender, Hube was transferred to the Italian front, where he commanded the German effort to delay the Allied invasion force on Sicily.

Although the collapse of the Italian forces enormously complicated his mission of delaying the Allied advance on the island, the evacuation of Axis forces safely to the Italian mainland was a minor military miracle and caused Hube to be seen as the type of leader in short supply by Hitler, who was casting about for loyal commanders who would stand and fight, a quality which Hitler, unfairly, had thought was lacking among his senior officers on the Russian Front. Hube's performance during the fall and winter Dnieper Line battles had justified Hitler's confidence in his choice, as Hube skillfully handled his corps and divisions, particularly his armored and mechanized units, which repeatedly blunted the blows of General of the Army Rodion I. Malinovskiy's Third Ukrainian *Front*, though losing the Dnepropetrovsk bridgehead and much of the lower Dnieper in the process.

On 3 January 1944, Hube's army was pulled out of the line and transferred to the northwest, where it was inserted between Raus's crumbling *4.Pz.Armee* and *8.Armee*, a move which stabilized the situation for the time being. That von Manstein could order such a movement showed that he had confidence in Hube and knew him as a fearless commander, though he thought him to be unjustifiably optimistic and too prone to Hitler's influence.[3] *1.Pz.Armee* was the more powerful of the two armies having elements in the Kanev salient, with two panzer corps and two infantry corps under its command.

8.Armee was composed of one panzer corps, two infantry corps, and the *Pz.Gren.Div. Grossdeutschland* occupying a corps-sized sector. The army commander, *Gen.d.Inf.*

Generalobrst Otto Wöhler, *Commander, Eighth Army. (Bundesarchiv)*

Otto Wöhler, had been with *8.Armee* since 15 August 1943, when it had previously been known as Armee-Abteilung (army detachment) *Kempf*, after its then-commander, *Gen.d.Pz.Tr.* Werner Kempf, had been relieved by von Manstein. Wöhler, born 12 July 1894 at Grossburgwedel, also fought in World War One and served in the post-war *Reichsheer*. A seasoned general staff officer, he had caught the attention of von Manstein, who made him his chief of staff when the latter was given command of *11.Armee*.

Wöhler served with von Manstein until April 1942, when he was assigned as the chief of staff for Army Group Center under Field Marshal von Kluge. His first combat command was *I. A.K.*, which he led from April to August 1943, before being given command of *8.Armee*. Von Manstein was particularly pleased to have Wöhler assigned once again to his command, stating that "Wöhler's cautiousness and sang-froid, which have stood up to such severe tests in the Crimea, would be of particular value in the present situation."[4] Indeed, Wöhler had fought with distinction and skill during the summer and fall of 1943. His cool-headedness would be crucial asset in the days to come.

In the area which would bear the immediate brunt of the upcoming Soviet attack, *1.Pz.Armee* and *8.Armee* had a total of 130,000 men deployed in four corps with approximately 100 combat-ready tanks and assault guns.[5] The German forces in the Kanev salient itself were the aforementioned *XI.* and *XXXXII. A.K.*, with a combined total of 65,000 men. Each answered to a higher headquarters, a factor which would initially complicate

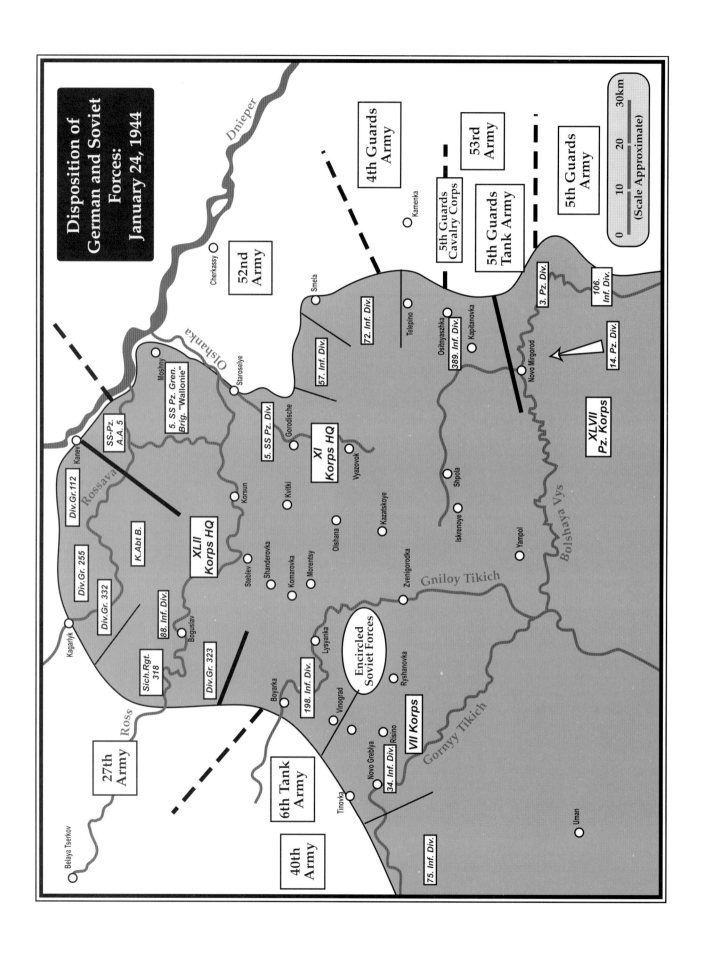

Disposition of German and Soviet Forces: January 24, 1944

30km
20
10
0
(Scale Approximate)

Dnieper

4th Guards Army

5th Guards Cavalry Corps

53rd Army

5th Guards Tank Army

5th Guards Army

Kamenka

52nd Army

Cherkassy

Smela

3. Pz. Div.

106. Inf. Div.

Telepino

72. Inf. Div.

Osltnyaszhka

389. Inf. Div.

Kapitanovka

Novo Mirgorod

14. Pz. Div.

Olshanka

Moshny

5. SS Pz. Gren. Brig. "Wallonie"

Staroselye

57. Inf. Div.

Gorodische

5. SS Pz. Div.

XI Korps HQ

Vyazovok

XLVII Pz. Korps

SS-Pz. A.A. 5

Kanev

Div.Gr.112

Korsun

Kvitki

Shpola

Rossava

Div.Gr. 255

K.Abt B.

XLII Korps HQ

Steblev

Shanderovka

Komarovka

Morentsy

Olshana

Kazatskoye

Iskrenoye

Yampol

Bolshaya Vys

Div.Gr. 332

Div.Gr. 323

88. Inf. Div.

Boguslav

Zvenigorodka

Gniloy Tikich

Kagarlyk

Sich.Rgt. 318

Encircled Soviet Forces

Lysyanka

Ryshanovka

Gornyy Tikich

Boyarka

198. Inf. Div.

Vinograd

VII Korps

27th Army

Ross

6th Tank Army

Novo Greblya

Risino

34. Inf. Div.

Tinovka

Uman

40th Army

Belaya Tserkov

75. Inf. Div.

the mission of defending the pocket. *XI.A.K.*, commanded by *General der Artillerie* Wilhelm Stemmermann, was the leftmost corps of Wöhler's Army. Its rightmost boundary lay to the south, in the vicinity of the village of Krasnossilka, where it linked up with *Generalleutnant* (*Gen.Lt.*) Nikolaus von Vormann's *XXXXVII.Pz.Korps*. Its sector stretched over 100 kilometers to the northwest along the Dnieper, where its left flank linked up with *XXXXII.A.K.* on the outskirts of Kanev (refer to appendix 11, Correlation of Force).

Stemmermann, who would soon bear the burden of responsibility for all of the encircled troops, was born 23 October 1888 in Rastatt and served in World War One as an artillery officer. When the war began in 1939, he was serving as chief of staff of *XIII.A.K.* In January 1941, Stemmermann was given command of *296.Inf.Div.* and led it through the first year of the Russian campaign until he was severely wounded on 1 March 1942. A quiet, reserved, and unassuming man, he was promoted to command *XI.A.K.* on 5 December 1943, only a few weeks prior to the encirclement.[6]

Stemmermann's western neighbor was *XXXXII.A.K.* This formation was the easternmost corps of Hube's army, sharing its right boundary with Stemmermann's left flank at Kanev. *XXXXII.A.K.'s* own left flank was tied in with *Gen.d.Inf.* Ernst-Eberhard Hell's *VII.A.K.'s* right flank near the village of Medvin. The corps commander, *Gen.d.Inf.* Franz Mattenklott, was on detached service. Consequently, acting command had been entrusted to his senior division commander, *Gen.Lt* Theobald Lieb. Lieb, born 25 November 1889 in Freundenstadt, was also a World War One veteran, as were nearly all of his contemporaries. He commanded *Inf.Rgt.27* during the invasion of Poland and was promoted to the rank of *Generalmajor* on 1 June 1941 and given acting command of *290.Inf.Div.* in time for the invasion of the Soviet Union.

Posted to Germany in April 1942, he was briefly given command of *306.Inf.Div.* in the East from February to March 1943. Promoted to *Generalleutnant* on 1 June 1943, he was given command of his third division, *112.Inf.Div.*, on 3 September 1943, leading it during the grueling withdrawal to the Dnieper Line, where it performed steadfastly. On 2 November, he took command of *K.Abt.B*, leading it until called to temporarily assume command of *XXXXII.A.K.*[7] A vain and imperious man, Lieb had little sympathy for National Socialism and possessed an independent streak which made him a difficult subordinate. These latter qualities would stand Lieb in good stead during the trials to come.

Both corps had taken up defensive positions in the Kanev salient during the first two weeks of January, in the wake of the Soviet's successful Zhitomir-Berdichev and Kirovograd offensives. As mentioned previously, the corps of Lieb and Stemmermann shared the only part of the Dnieper River still in German hands, where an 80-kilometer stretch had been held since early October 1943 (Map 3). Both corps were seriously understrength, by an average factor of 50 percent. *XI.A.K.* consisted of four divisions - *57.*, *72.*, and *389.Inf.Div.*, and *5.SS-Panzer Division Wiking*, itself reinforced by the *SS-Freiwilligen Sturmbrigade Wallonien* (Walloon Volunteer Assault Brigade), consisting of French-speaking Belgians.

General der Artillerie Wilhelm Stemmermann, *Commander, XI.Armeekorps (shown here as an Oberst)* *(U.S. National Archives)*

The aforementioned *57.Inf.Div.* originated in southern Bavaria, where it had been created from reservists in 1939. A veteran division, it had fought in Poland in 1939, France in 1940, and throughout the Russian Campaign. Despite low morale at the time of the Dnieper crossing, it still had a deservedly good reputation and retained some degree of defensive capability. Its two main combat elements were *Gren.Rgt.199* * and *217*. Its third regiment, *Gren.Rgt.179*, had been disbanded several months before due to heavy losses. This regiment was temporarily replaced by *Rgt.Gr.676*, on loan from *Div.Gr.332* of *K.Abt.B*. At the time of the encirclement, it still fielded 50 artillery pieces of various caliber and eight antitank guns.[8]

The division's commander was *Generalmajor* (*Gen.Maj.*) Adolf Trowitz, an artilleryman from Dessau. Born in 1893, he was an experienced commander who had previously commanded *122.* and *332.Inf.Div.* before assuming command of *57.Inf.Div.* on 19 September 1943.[9] Trowitz's division occupied a sector on the eastern half of the salient several kilometers west of the town of Smela. Sandwiched between *72.Inf.Div.* on its right and *Wiking* on its left, its front faced north, where the partisan-infested Irdyn Swamp lay. After inspecting his new sector in January 1944, Trowitz stated "Short of men, digging all day, a huge sector of the front to defend and no sleep at night; no man can do that."[10]

---

* Otherwise known as Infanterie Regiment "List"

Generalleutnant Theo Helmut Lieb, *Acting Commander, XXXXII.Armeekorps. (Bundesarchiv 87/135/11)*

its officers and NCOs. Its commander, *Oberst* Dr. Hermann Hohn, who was born in Renchen in 1897, had climbed the ladder of command within the division, having commanded an infantry battalion and two of its infantry regiments before being named as division commander on 23 November 1943, a high tribute indeed for a relatively junior officer.[12] A bold and energetic commander, Hohn fostered a sense of esprit within the division that would manifest itself repeatedly during the encirclement.

The third division in Stemmermann's corps was the Hessian *389.Inf.Div.*, formed in France in the summer of 1943. A relative newcomer to the Eastern Front, this division, nicknamed the "Rheingold Division," had been rebuilt from another division of the same number which had been destroyed at Stalingrad the previous winter. It had been transferred from occupation duty along the French Coast in October 1943 and was immediately thrown into the battles for the Dnieper Line, where its performance had been less than stellar. Its own grenadier regiments - *Gren.Rgt.544, 545,* and *546*, had suffered heavy losses among its infantry companies during the retreat from Cherkassy in late December 1943 to early January 1944.

To augments its weakened ranks, a battalion each from *Gren.Rgt.331* and *339* from *167.Inf.Div.* had been attached. Despite this welcome addition to the division's strength, it still had fewer than one man for every 15 meters of frontage. Its commander, *Gen.Maj.* Kurt Kruse, born 1895 in Neustrelitz, was also an a World War One veteran and an artilleryman like his corps commander. Prior to assuming command of the division on 1 June 1943, he had commanded *Art.Rgt.186*.[13] Situated on the far right flank of the corps, he shared boundaries with the neighboring *3.Pz.Div.* of XXXXVII.Pz.Korps on the right and with Hermann Hohn's *72.Inf.Div.* to its left.

Kruse's division had the dubious distinction of being located at the point of main effort of the planned Soviet attack and would soon have 14 enemy divisions hurled against its defenses. Hard hit during the previous month's fighting, it still fielded 26 artillery pieces and 12 antitank guns and would soon need every one of them. Despite its previously displayed shortcomings, *389.Inf.Div.* was to give a good account of itself during the upcoming battle and had developed field fortifications in its sector to a high degree, a fact noted in the Soviet after action report.

Oberst Hermann Hohn, *Commander, 72.Inf.Div., XI. Armeekorps (shown here as a Generalmajor). (Photo courtesy of 72nd Infantry Division Veteran's Association)*

Its neighbor to the right, *72.Inf.Div.*, was another veteran unit. Created in September 1939 by combining two regular army regiments from the Mosell region, *Gren.Rgt.105* and *124*, with a reserve regiment, *Gren.Rgt.266*, it had given an especially good account of itself in the West in 1940, in Greece in 1941, and on the Eastern Front, where it had been in action continuously since 22 June 1941. It had earned special accolades for its part in the siege of Sevastopol, where it took the Sapun Heights and Fort Maxim Gorky.

Transferred to Army Group Center in 1943, it fought at Kursk before being transferred back to Army Group South in the Fall. Briefly encircled in the town of Cherkassy itself during December 1943, it was mentioned twice in the *Wehrmachtbericht* (Armed Forces Daily Communiqué) for its conduct. After breaking out and withdrawing with its neighboring units to the hills southwest of Cherkassy, its front in the Kanev Salient faced to the east and was anchored along the south to north-flowing Sukhoi Tashlyk River. Its left flank linked up with *57.Inf.Div.* in the town of Smela. Still fairly well equipped with heavy weapons by early 1944 standards, *72.Inf.Div.* possessed at the time of encirclement 45 artillery pieces of various caliber and 14 antitank guns.[11]

Unlike the neighboring *57.Inf.Div.*, *72.Inf.Div.* still possessed excellent morale, a tribute to the energy and dedication of

Generalmajor Fritz Trowitz, *Commander, 57.Inf.Div., XI Armeekorps. (Bundesarchiv 155/2110/10A)*

The fourth division of *XI.A.K.* was *Wiking*. Established on 1 December 1940 originally as a motorized division of the *Waffen-SS* (Hitler's elite guard), by combined several existing SS infantry regiments, it was famous for being the first division of the *Waffen-SS* that incorporated large numbers of Europeans of "nordic" descent, such as Scandinavians, Dutch, and Belgians, as well as a few minorities from other countries, such as Switzerland and Finland. Its first commander, *General der Waffen-SS* Felix Steiner, had inculcated the men of the division with his own fighting spirit and formed into a formidable combat force that quickly earned a reputation in the Eastern campaign as being a highly reliable, hard-hitting unit.

Although it was not engaged during Kursk, it has performed well during the retreat to the Dnieper, winning recognition for its spectacular defense of Kharkov on 20 August 1943 from its army commander, General Wöhler, when it destroyed 84 Soviet tanks in a single day.[14] Reorganized in November 1942 as a *Panzergrenadier* (mechanized infantry) Division, it added a tank battalion to its structure and was lavishly equipped with a complement of heavy weapons which added substantially to its offensive punch, though it was forced to give up one of its three infantry regiments. The two remaining *Panzergrenadier* regiments, named *Germania* and *Westland*, each had three battalions, one more than a comparable army *Pz.Gren.Rgt.* In October 1943, it had again been redesignated, this time as a panzer division, though the tank regiment's headquarters and its

new second battalion were still being raised and equipped in Germany and would not join the division until April 1944, well after the battle.

Its commander since November 1942 was *SS-Brigadeführer und Generalmajor der Waffen-SS* Herbert O. Gille. Gille, born on 8 March 1897 in Bad Gandersheim in the Harz Mountains, had served as an artillery officer from 1914-1918. Joining the *SS-Verfügungstruppe* (the forerunner of the *Waffen-SS*) in 1934, he was commanding *Wiking's* artillery regiment by 1940, leading it through the first two years of the Russian campaign. He was widely respected and admired within the division and was like a father to his men. Decorated for bravery numerous times, he had already been awarded the Knight's Cross with Oak Leaves by November 1943. Optimistic and self-confident by nature, no task seemed too hopeless or impossible to him.[15]

Although Gille was considered by his fellow SS and Army generals to be a dedicated and professional soldier who could be ruthless as the situation required, he was no Nazi. In fact, according to one authority on the subject, Heinz Höhne, Gille was "an entirely non-political officer who would have nothing to do with ideology." One particular incident which occurred earlier during the war highlights his attitude towards the National Socialist Party and the SS hierarchy. When he was paid a visit by *Obersturmbannführer* (*Ostubaf.*) Jakob Fick, *Wiking's* "ideological observer," while fighting in Russia during January 1942, Gille, who was then serving as the division's artillery commander, made it plain that Fick was not welcome.

Generalleutnant Kurt Kruse, *Commander, 389.Inf.Div.,XI.Armeekorps. (Bundesarchiv 78/77/19)*

During their conversation in front of several other witnesses, Gille growled to him that "Wearing the brown shirt is not permitted in this aristocratic artillery regiment. I'll put a clean-out squad into your room."[16] Fick reported Gille's attitude in a letter to his superior at Himmler's headquarters, *Obergruppenführer* Karl Wolff, but nothing came of it, probably due to General Steiner's intervention on behalf of his subordinate, an example of the intense loyalty that he felt towards the men in his division while he served as its commander.

Gille's resolve, not to mention the impressive combat power of his division, would add a great deal of stiffening to the German defensive effort during the upcoming battle. On the eve of the encirclement, his division still fielded 36 artillery pieces, including 16 self-propelled guns. With nearly 14,000 men in the field, *Wiking* was the strongest division in the Kanev salient. Although two of its *Pz.Gren.* battalions were absent (one was in Yugoslavia while the other was being re-equipped in Germany with new armored personnel carriers), it had been augmented by the attached *SS-Freiwilligen Batl. Narwa*, composed of Estonian volunteers. The Walloon Volunteer Brigade was also attached, though it functioned somewhat independently.

Gille's division also possessed a tank battalion with 25 Pz. IV L48 tanks, a dozen or so Pz. III's in its training company, plus an additional six assault guns, thus making it the only division in Stemmermann's corps with any offensive punch.[17] However, *Wiking* was initially arrayed along the Dnieper River defensive line from Kanev to Orlovets, well away from the Red Army's point of main effort.

Also present under *XI A.K.'s* order of battle was the Walloon Brigade, officially known as *5.SS-Freiwilligen Sturmbrigade Wallonien*. Originally attached to the Army, which it joined on the Eastern Front during the summer of 1942, it had fought on the Don Front and in the Caucasus Mountains, earning the respect of their German comrades-in-arms for their daring-do and enthusiasm, if not for their military skill. Transferred to the *Waffen-SS* on 1 June 1943, it was organized as an independent motorized brigade with its own artillery, engineers, antitank and antiaircraft elements.

Temporarily attached was a *Sturmgeschützabteilung* (*StuG.Abt.*, or assault gun battalion) with ten self-propelled 7.5 cm guns, on loan from *4.SS-Pz.Gren.Div. Polizei*, then undergoing refit in the Balkans. Intended as a showpiece of German-European cooperation, its members hoped that their membership in the SS would serve as a basis for a new all-European army that would be united in the battle against Communism. Whether Heinrich Himmler, in his capacity as *Reichsführer-SS*, actually intended to grant them that desire was an open question.[18]

The brigade's commander was *SS-Obersturmbannführer* (lieutenant colonel) Lucien Lippert, a 29-year old former Belgian Army general staff officer. Lippert had graduated at the head of the class at the military academy in Brussels and was known for his competent, calm leadership. His second-in-command was *Hauptsturmführer* (*Hstuf.*, or captain) Leon Degrelle, leader of the Belgian Rexist movement and a pre-war Belgian politician of some renown who hoped that his brigade's service in the East would help earn a separate homeland for his fellow Walloons in the Belgian province of Burgundy.

With 2,000 men, the brigade was under the operational control of *Wiking* and occupied a 12-kilometer long sector stretching from Moshny near the Dnieper to the town of Staroselye. It had been engaged in defensive and offensive operations against the Red Army, including partisans, since it had arrived in the area on 11 November 1943.[19] Described by one Soviet source as composed of nothing less than "underworld thugs and adventurers of the worst kind," the Walloons saw themselves as the embodiment of the finest traditions of Belgian and European civilization. The brigade had yet to conduct maneuvers with all of its units, hence Gille's decision to assign a German operations officer and liaison officer.

In addition to its infantry divisions, *XI.A.K.* also had under its establishment three independent artillery batteries with a total of 15 pieces ranging in caliber from 10.5 cm howitzers to 17 cm cannons. The corps also had four engineer *Abteilungen*, ranging in size from a company to a battalion. Another corps troops unit was *StuG.Brig. 239*, with its 17 assault guns provid-

Members of Walloon Brigade at headquarters in Staroselye, late January 1944 (note Walloon Brigade tactical marking on truck's left fender). (Photo: Kaisergruber)

Oberscharführer Gustav Schreiber, *of SS Pz.Gren.Rgt. Germania, looking across the frozen Dnieper from one of his company's defensive positions, late January 1944. (Jarolin-Bundesarchiv)*

ing the only other armored force besides that of the SS. The corps also had the usual amount of signal, ordnance, supply, transport and repair units so necessary to the function of modern armies.

In all, *XI.A.K.* had approximately 35,000 men assigned as of 24 January 1944, not counting several thousand auxiliaries and *Hiwis* (Russian POWs-turned German volunteer helpers).[20] Stemmerman had no reserves, except what could be put together from *Wiking*. His only advantage was that his opponent opposite his thinly-spread units did not know exactly where the German main line of resistance lay, forcing them to conduct a reconnaissance in force the day prior to the attack.

The German force occupying the northern and western portion of the salient was *XXXXII.A.K.*, consisting of two battered divisions. It had only 30,000 men and no tanks or assault guns. In the northern portion of the salient, from Kanev on the Dnieper, where it tied in with *XI.A.K.*, to the town of Boguslav was *K.Abt.B*. As previously described, this force was composed of the remnants of three shattered infantry divisions - *Div.Gr.112, 255,* and *332.* Each of these regimental-sized units consisted of two amalgamated infantry battalions, such as Ernst Schenk's, and a regimental infantry gun and antitank companies. Grouped under a corps standard on 2 November 1943 with the division staff and support units provided by the now-disbanded *112.Inf.Div., K.Abt.B* was employed tactically as a division.

Despite the losses which had necessitated its creation, General Lieb is quoted as having said that it had "the strength of a good division." [21] As Lieb had moved up to temporarily com-

SS-Sturmbannführer Lucien Lippert, *SS-Freiwilligen Sturmbrigade Wallonien. (Photo: Andreas Schwarz and 88.Inf.Div. Veterans Association)*

mand the corps in General Mattenklott's absence, *Oberst* Hans-Joachim Fouquet was named to serve as the acting commander. Born 1895 in Braunschweig, Fouquet had served as a junior lieutenant in World War One in the artillery. After interwar service in the *Reichsheer*, he had served as the commander of *Art.Rgt.223* of *223.Inf.Div.* during Operation Barbarossa. Fouquet's command had 43 artillery pieces and nine antitank guns, including one powerful *Panzerabwehrkanone* or *PAK 43*, the new 8.8 cm antitank guns then being introduced. Most of the *Korpsabteilung's* sector consisted of wide-open steppe, ideally suited for attack by tanks at this time of year. However, it would only be lightly attacked, a factor which made it the first source for reserves to shore up other crumbling portions of the salient when the attack came.

XXXXII.Armee Korps' other infantry division, *88.Inf.Div.*, was located to the left of *K.Abt.B*, facing to the west, where it tied in with *Gen.Lt.* Hans-Joachim von Horn's *198.Inf.Div.* of neighboring *VII.A.K.* in the vicinity of Medvin.[22] The division

SS-Brigadeführer Herbert Otto Gille, *Commander, 5th SS-Panzer Division "Wiking," XI Army Corps. (Bundesarchiv 73/128/43)*

was formed 1 December 1939 mainly out of Bavarian reservists from the Nuremberg and Bayreuth areas, as well as many Austrians. It participated in the Battle of France, where it had remained on occupation duty along the French Biscay Coast.

Transferred to Russia in December 1941 at the height of Army Group Center's crisis, it gave a good account of itself in the desperate winter fighting that followed, especially since the unit was deployed into combat without winter clothing or equipment. It took part in the Battle of Kursk in July 1943 and the withdrawal battles to the Dnieper, joining Army Group South on 11 September 1943, when it was nearly encircled during the Battle of Kiev.[23] On the eve of the Soviet offensive, *88.Inf.Div.* had a polyglot of different units under its control, though only 5,400 of its troops actually belonged to the division.[24]

In addition to its own *Gren.Rgt.245* and *248* (its third regiment, *Gren.Rgt.246*, had been disbanded), it also had the attached *Div.Gr.323* with its two battalions, as well as *Gren.Rgt.417* from *168.Inf.Div.*, which was fighting elsewhere. Rounding out the division were elements from *Sicherung-Regimenter* (*Sich.Rgt.*, or security regiments) *318* and *177* of *213.Sich.Div.* With these disparate units, *88.Inf.Div.* covered a wide frontage. Forced out of the town of Biala Zerkov at the end of December 1943, the division was exhausted and nearly worn out but did not consider itself defeated.[25]

Its commander, *Gen.Lt. Graf* von Rittberg, was born 1898 in Strasbourg, Alsace of German parents. Also a veteran of the artillery from World War One, he served with the *Reichsheer* between the wars. His command experience included leadership of *Art.Rgt.31* and *131* in both the Battle of France and on the Eastern Front from 1940 to 1943. He assumed command of *88.Inf.Div.* on 12 November 1943, while it was engaged in defensive battles near Zhitomir. It fielded 22 artillery pieces of various makes as well as seven antitank guns, but no assault guns or tanks. Its chief asset was its artillery regiment, which, though small, was very experienced. This ability would prove to be of great value when the division would face the brunt of Vatutin's impending attack.

Unlike Stemmermann's corps, which had a modicum of corps-level artillery support, Lieb's corps had only one artillery battery in general support of his divisions. He also had only one engineer battalion, as well as other supporting corps troops - supply units, ammunition and supply depots, and so forth. Also present in the salient were one *Landesschutz* (home guard) battalion of middle-aged reservists and *Armenisches Inf.Btl.810*, composed of Armenian volunteers of dubious loyalty. Except for two companies of railroad construction engineers, that was the sum total of German forces in the salient - in all, slightly over 65,000 men, 50 tanks and assault guns, 218 artillery pieces and infantry guns, and 51 antitank guns.[26] When the amount of front to be defended was factored in, this seemingly impressive amount of firepower was rather thinly spread indeed - in practical terms, it amounted to slightly less than two pieces of artillery per kilometer, hardly sufficient for a peacetime firepower demonstration, much less for a battle against the Red Army.

Oberst Fouquet, *Acting Commander, Korpsabteilung B, XXXXII.Armeekorps. (Photo courtesy of Andreas Schwarz and 88.Inf.Div. Veterans Association)*

However, to make up for their inferiority in numbers, the units of both corps had worked feverishly to prepare their defensive positions against the Red Army offensive they knew would come. The Soviet after-action report described German defenses as being extremely well constructed, with many dugouts, bunkers, artillery firing positions and communications trenches. Key terrain was used effectively, as well as the many small rivers and streams which reinforced the power of the defense.[27] The men of *XI.* and *XXXXII.A.K.* had been forced to rely on field fortifications as a substitute for manpower. In addition to the well-constructed defensive positions, the Soviets also thought that another strength of their enemy was the large number of troops he appeared to have in the salient. This assumption, though false, would greatly influence the Soviet plan of operations.

The melange of different German units described previously presented a bounty of information to the Red Army's military intelligence specialists whose job was to construct the German order of battle in the salient. In addition to the five named divisions in the salient, there were numerous elements from other divisions attached to the two corps in various capacities. As mentioned, these included battalions or regiments from three other divisions, as well as various army troops, such as artillery, engineers, assault gun units, and railway units. Due to a number of means - prisoners, radio intercept, aerial reconnaissance, etc. - the Red Army was able to paint, to its way of thinking, a fairly complete picture of what lay in the objective area. Its intelligence officers were even able to obtain a German map detailing *XXXXII.A.K.* defensive positions.[28]

The Soviet intelligence specialists interpreted this data and determined that there were ten German divisions in the salient, as well as the Walloon brigade, instead of only six. They labeled each division as being present and in full strength, a common technique which attests to the Red Army's extreme caution when calculating necessary force ratios to launch an operation. Due to this conservative method, the Red Army estimated that the Germans fielded in the salient over 130,000 men, 1,000 artillery pieces, and 100 tanks, an amount that was twice again as much as what the Germans actually had (in regards to artillery, the Germans had only a quarter of that amount).[29]

Paradoxically, though the Soviets had overestimated the number of Germans in the salient, they had underestimated their ability to hold out during an encirclement as well as German capability to quickly launch a relief effort. This was a clear-cut case of Soviet military intelligence forming an erroneous estimate of the German situation. Nevertheless, to the Soviets, this appeared to be a dense and powerful grouping, which had the capacity to threaten Kiev or Kirovograd and must therefore be eliminated. The truth, as has been shown, was quite different.

Despite Hitler's desire to retake Kiev, the German forces arrayed in the salient were barely enough to defend it, much less conduct an offensive. Forced to defend a frontage of over 200 kilometers, the two corps were hard-pressed to man a continuous screenline. Gaps between adjacent units were covered by foot patrols during the day. Local reserves of company or battalion size were used to counterattack breakthroughs and restore the front.[30] Compounding these difficulties were the already mentioned shortage of manpower, plus the added shortages of heavy weapons, (especially tanks and self-propelled guns), motor vehicles, fuel, ammunition, and signals equipment. Ukrainian partisans roamed the steppes, attacking both German and Soviet alike.

The only bright spot in this otherwise gloomy litany was the fact that the German occupation authorities only two weeks before had stockpiled tons of food at the airfield in the town of Korsun-Shevchenkovsky. This had been done on the order of *1. Pz.Armee*, which wanted the supplies moved in anticipation of a withdrawal of *XXXXII.A.K.* to the Ross River defensive line two weeks before.[31] Although Hitler had turned down this request, the food and other supplies had already been moved and there they remained. At least if the Germans had to die, they could do so now with a full stomach.

Another problem was the German defenses lack of depth, a fact which nearly everyone from Army Group headquarters down to the most junior company commander recognized. Once the Red Army had broken through the German defenses, there would be nothing to keep them from driving to the Bug River, the Black Sea, or even the Rumanian frontier. The Black Sea port of Odessa, lifeline to the marooned *17.Armee* in the Crimea, was only 200 kilometers from the Second Ukrainian Front's headquarters at Kirovograd. Army Group South, like both *XI.* and *XXXXII.A.K.*, possessed few reserves; all available armored or mechanized formations were committed to ongoing defensive operations.[32]

In fact, the Red Army's failure to drive to the Black Sea would later baffle von Manstein, since he believed that was what he would have done had he been in the Red Army's place. In the event of a major deep attack by the Red Army, there would be little he could do to stop them.[33] The Red Army's concentration on the annihilation of the troops soon to be trapped in the salient at the expense of far greater gains would be a source of relief and puzzlement to the hard-pressed Germans. For, in fact, the once-mighty *Wehrmacht* was now a shadow of the force which entered Russia two and a half years before.

Generalleutnant Graf von Rittberg, *Commander, 88.Inf.Div., X XXXII.Armeekorps. (Photo courtesy of Hans-Kurt Menedetter)*

By the winter of 1943-44, the German Army was no longer able to make good its losses of men and materiel. One symptom of this situation was the necessity of resorting to the creation of corps detachments, as previously mentioned. These organizations, created by the combination of two or three burnt-out divisions of regimental strength, was an attempt to provide corps commanders a unit that at least could carry out division level operations. The existence of *K.Abt.B* would soon confound the Red Army's order of battle calculations for the Germans, counting three divisions when in fact there was really only one.

In addition, every German division in the salient was charged with defending wide frontages. For example, *Wiking* had to defend a frontage along the Dnieper that was over 80 kilometers long.[34] Hitler's decision to defend every inch of ground in effect dispersed combat power at a time when it was most badly needed. Worse, units were forced to occupy ground poorly suited for defense when a short withdrawal would have allowed them to make the best use of key terrain. The situation was further complicated by Hitler's refusal to allow von Manstein to evacuate the Kanev salient, despite numerous requests by von Manstein, Hube, and Wöhler to *OKH,* i.e., Hitler, in early January to do so.

Thus, by mid-January 1944, Hitler's *1.Pz.* and *8.Armee* were overextended and exhausted. Von Manstein had no reserves available to counter any Soviet thrust, unless he decided to take units from other armies within his army group, which in any case were already engaged with ongoing operations. He had been forced to resort repeatedly to this tactic for the past four months, robbing Peter to pay Paul, but von Manstein could not conduct a static defense indefinitely. Thus, Army Group South was extremely vulnerable to the mobile operation which Stalin and his generals were contemplating.

Another factor which was beginning to affect the performance of the Germans was that their morale was no longer as high as it had been. Reverses of the previous Summer and Fall had led to a sense of fatalism in the ranks, except for elite units of the *Panzertruppen* or *Waffen-SS*. Belief in final victory was no longer certain. The so-called *Untermenschen* (subhumans) of the Soviet Union had turned out to be formidable opponents after all. The individual German soldier had come to fear the Red Army and had developed a great deal of respect for *Ivan*, their term for the individual Soviet soldier. The trend towards increasing competence of the Red Army in mechanized warfare was another foreboding development.

What many German soldiers feared most was becoming encircled and abandoned to their fate, as Paulus' *6.Armee* had been at Stalingrad. This crisis in confidence would manifest itself on several occasions during the battle.[35] That the Red Army was becoming increasingly proficient at mechanized warfare and, in fact, was becoming nearly equal in ability to the Germans was recognized by 1942-43, but seldom mentioned publicly. Even a hard-bitten *Waffen-SS* General, Max Simon, wrote admiringly of the Red Army's skill and tenacity, stressing that German toughness and self-sacrifice were no longer enough to guarantee eventual German victory.[36]

The quality of Germany's soldiers was also no longer what it had been on 22 June 1941, when the *Wehrmacht* had been the world's finest army. Within its ranks were now men who previously had been considered medically unfit to serve, too old, or two young. The standards of training at their home-based *Ersatz und Ausbildung* (Replacement and Training) battalions had fallen off and training had been shortened as well. Noticeably, National-Socialist fervor appeared to be lacking. Many personnel from the *Luftwaffe* and *Kriegsmarine* (German Navy) had also been involuntarily transferred to ground combat units, where they complained bitterly about conditions in the front lines. One frequently quoted account which describes this situation was related by *SS-Sturmbannführer* (Major) Karl Kreuz, who was commanding an artillery battalion of *2.SS-Pz.Div. Das Reich* at the time:

> Towards the end of the month we at last got some replacements . . . They were mostly young chaps from the training barracks with a few officers and non-commissioned officers who had served in Italy. In no time they were complaining about the cold. They kept fires going during the day as well as the night, and were breaking up a lot of wooden outhouses for fuel which would have been valuable later. I had occasion to speak sharply to them about this and one of them answered that on that day the thermometer had fallen to ten below, and was this not abnormal? I told him that he would soon

Above: *Panzer III of Wiking's tank training company, January 1944. (Jarolin Bundesarchiv 95/58/14)*

Above: *Panther grinding its way through the Ukrainian mud. (Bundesarchiv 72/69/39)*

count himself lucky when the thermometer was not ten but twenty-five below, and that in January it would fall to forty below. At this the poor fellow broke down and sobbed . . . [37]

The reality was that the German Army, after the first year of the war in Russia, when it suffered 800,000 casualties alone, could no longer make good its enormous losses in manpower. Even the *Waffen-SS*, Hitler's elite guard, was forced to accept ethnic Germans from Eastern Europe as well as non-Germans to solve the manpower crisis. *Wiking* even had Finns, Estonians, and Latvians in its ranks, though these men usually performed very satisfactorily and were welcomed as comrades-in-arms by their German brethren.

As German losses mounted, as replacements arrived increasingly unprepared for war in the East, and as morale continued to suffer, the overall efficiency of combat elements began to show clear signs of decline. While combing rear echelon establishments for further replacement manpower was a short-term solution, this in turn led to an increasingly strained logistical situation which also affected combat efficiency. Clearly, no army on earth could withstand such a trend indefinitely. However, while it, too, had suffered enormous casualties (by December 1943, the Soviets had suffered nearly 19 million casualties of all types), the Red Army was going in the exact opposite direction - the longer the war in the East lasted, the better it became.[38] The forces which were chosen to pinch off and destroy the troops in the Kanev Salient clearly had benefited from this trend. Their power would clearly overshadow that of the German's during this battle.

For the execution of the Red Army's Korsun-Shevchenkovsky Operation which was to lead to the what became known in the West as the Battle of the Cherkassy or Korsun Pocket, *STAVKA*, through Marshal Zhukov, directed on 12 January 1944 that the First and Second Ukrainian *Fronts* immediately conclude offensive operations in their respective sectors and begin planning for a double envelopment to trap the German forces in the salient.[39] Each *Front* therefore did not begin the operation at full strength, since both had been continuously engaged against German forces in the Ukraine since mid-November 1943 and would have little time to prepare for this new operation. Vatutin's Front was especially arrayed over a very wide sector along an east-west axis running from the Dnieper river in the east to the town of Shepetovka in the west, where elements of his force were still engaged in battle against General Raus's *4.Pz.Armee*. To carry out his part of the operation, Vatutin would be able to commit only three of his armies - the 27th , the 40th, and the newly-created 6th Tank Army. The first two of these armies had been in position since the cessation of the advance during the second week of January, and were already familiar with their sectors as well as the German units opposite them.

Colonel-General Nikolai Fedorovich Vatutin, commander of the First Ukrainian *Front*, had become one of Stalin's youngest and most trusted *Front* commanders. Born of Russian peasant stock in 1900, little is known of his personal life. His military service began in World War One, when he served in a Czarist cavalry regiment. Joining the Bolsheviks in 1917, he rose from the ranks to command of a cavalry division during the Russian Civil War of 1919 to 1921, an indication of his dynamic leadership ability and tactical acumen, as well as his communist fervor. A graduate of the Frunze Academy, he was untouched by the purge which claimed the lives of so many of his contemporaries. Most likely, he kept his personal views to himself, a rule of survival which many officers senior in rank to him had violated, with fatal results.

His career had been meteoric since the outbreak of the war, when he was then serving as the Deputy Chief of the Soviet General Staff. When the German invasion of the Soviet Union was launched in June 1941, Vatutin was sent to command an army in the Ukraine under Marshal Timoshenko, where he experienced defeat at the hands of von Runstedt's Army Group South. Often characterized as a rash, excitable leader, his boldness and daring attracted the favorable attention of Stalin, when Zhukov pointed out to him that these were qualities which made him ideally suited for a commander of mobile forces.[40] Vatutin's first Front command had been that of the Northwest Front, which he was charged with on 29 March 1942, in order to destroy the German encircled forces in the Demyansk Pocket.

Although the Germans eventually slipped through his grasp, Vatutin had proved himself an able and energetic commander who could be relied upon by *STAVKA* to get results.[41] He had fought against the best armies the Germans had to offer, and, though not always successful, had learned his craft well. Described by one account as "massive, square-faced, and pugnacious looking," Vatutin's broad head was set so close to his shoulders that his troops called him "the man without a neck," who was a hard driver, but one who shared the hardships of the field with them.[42] Vatutin had been the commander of the First Ukrainian Front, formerly known as the Voronezh *Front*, and before that the South-west Front, since October 1942. The three armies that Vatutin would soon hurl against the Germans defending the salient were also seasoned formations and had gained in competence as well.

The 27th Army, under Lt.Gen. Sergei Georgievich Trofimenko, with three rifle divisions and the 54th and 159th Ukreplenii Rayon (Fortified Regions), was First Ukrainian Front's left-most army, with its eastern flank abutting the Dnieper River near Kanev. The 206th Rifle Division abutted the Dnieper and faced *K.Abt.B*. The two fortified regions faced part of this force, as well as most of the sector occupied by *88.Inf.Div.* Its 337th and 180th Rifle Divisions, both designated as breakthrough elements, were arrayed against the inner flanks where *88.* and *198.Inf.Div.* shared tactical boundaries. In addition to these forces, Trofimenko also had three heavy mortar regiments, three artillery regiments, and one heavy anti-tank regiment, as well as the usual number of engineers, supply, and transport personnel, providing Trofimenko with a total personnel strength of 28,348 men, barely a corps-sized unit by German standards. As a reminder of its primarily static role, 27th Army had no tanks assigned.

General of the Army Mikhail F. Vatutin, *Commander, First Ukrainian Front, shown here with his political officer.*
(Photo courtesy of the Battle of Korsun-Shevchenkovsky Museum, Korsun, Ukraine)

The most peculiar units in Trofimenko's order of battle were the aforementioned 54th and 159th Fortified Regions. These bizarre (to a Western way of thinking) organizations were organized around a division headquarters staff designed purely for static employment and relied upon a large number of automatic weapons, mortars, and artillery instead of masses of troops to serve as a reinforced security force designed to hold areas of the front line in order for the Soviet High Command to mass troops elsewhere. It's main elements were the 404th, 496th, 512th, and 513th Artillery Machine Gun Battalions. Although ill-suited for attack, these so-called fortified regions could tie down a disproportionate amount of German troops, whose commanders often believed that they faced a much stronger opponent. This forced the Germans to keep more men in the line than the situation actually warranted, which would tie them down while the main attack took place elsewhere.

The 40th Army under Lt.Gen. Filipp Fedoseevich Zhmachenko, to the right of Trofimenko, consisted of three rifle corps (50th, 51st, and the 104th) fielding a total of nine rifle divisions and one airborne division, the 4th Guards. Located opposite *VII.A.K.*, Zhmachenko's army was reinforced for its mission of helping to create the breakthrough conditions for the follow-on armored assault. At 33,726 men, 40th Army was still well under established strength, but it had been bolstered with up to seven artillery regiments, several mortar regiments, and three heavy antitank regiments. Since the bulk of these forces would be thrown against one German infantry

division, *198.Inf.Div.*, success seemed virtually assured.

The newly-established 6th Tank Army under General Andrei Grigorevich Kravchenko would deliver the offensive punch. It consisted of two corps - 5th Guards Tank and 5th Mechanized - both of which had distinguished themselves during the heavy fighting around Kiev during the previous December. The Guards Tank Corps consisted of three guards tank regiments - 20th, 21st, and 22nd, equipped for the most part with T-34 tanks. The tanks corps also had 6th Guards Motorized Rifle Brigade in support. 5th Mechanized Corps consisted of three mechanized brigades - 2nd, 9th, and 45th, as well as 233rd Tank Brigade, partially equipped with U.S. M4 Sherman tanks.[43] Both corps had three or four self-propelled (SP) artillery regiments, an SP antitank regiment, and supporting elements.

To make up for the new tank army's shortage of infantry, Vatutin had attached to it 47th Rifle Corps, originally part of Trofimenko's Army, with its three rifle divisions - 136th, 167th, and 359th. In 6th Tank Army, Vatutin had an organization that he hoped would make up for its lack of numbers by the experience of its men and daring of its commanders, such as General Volkov, commander of 5th Mechanized Corps. However, Kravchenko would have to make do without a proper army staff - there had not been time to raise and train one. Nor would he be provided with the required signal apparatus to communicate both with his subordinate corps and with Vatutin's staff. In order to obtain the minimum level of staffing needed to plan and control his part of the Operation, Kravchenko would use the staff

Lieutenant General Sergei G. Trofimenko, *Commander, 27th Army, First Ukrainian Front. (Photo courtesy of the Battle of Korsun-Shevchenkovsky Museum, Korsun, Ukraine)*

Lieutenant General of Tank Troops Andrei G. Kravchenko, *Commander, 6th Tank Army, First Ukrainian Front. (Photo courtesy of the Battle of Korsun-Shevchenkovsky Museum, Korsun, Ukraine)*

and communications means of the 5th Guards Tank Corps.

Born in the Ukraine in 1899, Kravchenko joined the revolution in 1917 as an 18-year old factory worker. Shortly thereafter, he joined an infantry battalion of the Red Army and took part in the Russian Civil War, rising to command 1st Regiment, 44th Rifle Division by 1921. While assigned as a student to the Poltava Infantry School to receive professional military training, he befriended an older student, Nikolai Vatutin, who would become Kravchenko's commander twenty years later. Heavy-set for his average height, he had what was described as a "simple Russian face," which hardly made him stand out in an army of workers and peasants.

A complex and quiet man, he moved and thought with a quick agility that belied his stolid appearance. Between the wars, Kravchenko served in the normal variety of command and staff positions. In the mid-1920s, he was posted to the Leningrad Armored Tank Course. One of his instructors who greatly influenced his thoughts on tank warfare, then an infant science, was Marshal Mikhail Tukhachevskiy, the father of the Soviet armored force. Tukhachevskiy found Kravchenko an attentive student. In his evaluation of the junior officer, the Marshal, who was to be murdered on Stalin's orders after a show trail in 1937, remarked that Kravchenko was a "good student of military affairs, erudite, good soul, with uncompromising character . . . " [44]

The year 1939 saw Kravchenko serving as the Chief of Staff for 61st Rifle Division, an important posting. When the Russo-Finnish War began in 1939, Kravchenko was ordered to

help form 173rd Motorized Rifle Division and accompany it to the Karelian isthmus to take part in the Red Army's enormously costly winter offensive. Despite the poor showing of Soviet forces, he performed his duties well and was awarded the Order of the Red Banner for his personal bravery. From 1940 to 1941, he served as the Chief of Staff of 18th Mechanized Corps when the German invasion began. His experiences from 1941 to 1944 were typical of those of many of his contemporaries. Despite his own bravery and leadership, his corps was shattered and was forced to retreat. He commanded successively 31st Tank Brigade, then as Chief of Staff of 1st Tank Corps, then command of 2nd Tank Corps in the summer of 1942. He learned his trade the hard way, by fighting, and often, losing.

Promoted to Major General, he assumed command of 4th Tank Corps just in time for the Stalingrad counteroffensive in November 1942, where his corps had helped closed the ring around *6.Armee* when it linked up with 4th Mechanized Corps on 23 November 1942 near Kamyshi. It was during this battle that Kravchenko earned his reputation as a superb leader of armor. Taking over 5th Guards Tank Corps in February 1943, he led it during the Battle of Kursk, where he fought the vaunted *Grossdeutschland* Division to a standstill, and the pursuit of the retreating Germans to the Dnieper. He particularly distinguished himself during the November 1943 drive to liberate Kiev, when his corps helped spearhead the attack from the Lyutezh bridgehead and seized the northern portion of the city. In recognition of his and his corps' deeds, Kravchenko

Colonel General Philip F. Zhmachenko, *Commander, 40th Army, First Ukrainian Front. (Photo courtesy of the Battle of Korsun-Shevchenkovsky Museum, Korsun, Ukraine)*

Marshall of the Soviet Union Ivan S. Konev, *Commander, Second Ukrainian Front. (Photo courtesy of the Battle of Korsun-Shevchenkovsky Museum, Korsun, Ukraine)*

was awarded the star of the Hero of the Soviet Union. He had clearly demonstrated the ability for further promotion and showed great promise as a leader, factors which contributed to his old friend Vatutin's choosing him as the man to command the new Sixth Tank Army.

The command was new, but its subordinate elements were very experienced, though battle-scarred. Since all of Kravchenko's tank and mechanized units had been involved in heavy fighting only the week before against *Gen.Lt.* Balck's *XXXXVIII.Pz.Korps* near Vinnitsa, his army had considerably fewer tanks and assault guns, with a total of 190, as opposed to the authorized strength of 375.[45] The role of his two infantry armies would be to keep the Germans penned up along the northern and northwestern part of the salient, where little German offensive action was expected, as well as helping to form a defensive belt against any German relief attempt.

Their relative lack of mobility would serve as a drag on Kravchenko's forces, since once the tank army achieved a penetration, the infantry would not be able to keep up, leaving the tanks vulnerable to infantry and antitank weapons. Besides the combat elements mentioned above, Vatutin's *Front* also possessed 8 additional artillery and mortar brigades or battalions, plus an SP antitank regiment, equipped with SU-76 assault guns. In all, Vatutin initially would commit nearly 90,000 men, 210 tanks or assault guns, and hundreds of tubes of artillery and heavy mortars from his *Front*.

To the east, deployed in the vicinity of Kirovograd, was General Konev's Second Ukrainian Front. The Second

Ukrainian Front had occupied positions from Cherkassy in the northwest, where its right flank rested on the Dnieper River, to Kirovograd in the southeast since the first two weeks of January, when it had tried, without success, to trap *XXXXVII.Pz.Korps* of *8.Armee*. Despite the considerable losses suffered during this offensive, Konev's Front would still be able to initially commit over 165,000 men and 323 tanks and assault guns for this operation. His *Front's* mission would be to attack the German salient from the east to the west and link up with the First Ukrainian Front in the vicinity of Zvenigorodka, thereby completing the encirclement of the forces in the Kanev salient.

Konev had become one of Stalin's most effective Front commanders, who, like most of his contemporaries in the Red Army of 1944, had learned his trade the hard way. Ivan Stepanovich Konev, born 28 December 1897 into a peasant family in the village of Lodeino in Northern Dvina, served as a sergeant in the Czar's Army during the First World War. Throwing in his lot with the Bolsheviks, he served as a political commissar from 1918 to 1921, when he was elevated to an even higher position in the Communist Party as a delegate to the Party Congress. During the Russian Civil War, he served in a variety of party and military positions, proving himself to be a resourceful and ruthless leader.

During the interwar period, Konev commanded a rifle division, then a corps, and graduated from the prestigious Frunze Academy, the USSR's general staff school. His communist credentials were never in doubt, since he was one of the few Soviet general officers not liquidated during the brutal purge of the officer corps conducted by Stalin in 1937. In May 1941, one month before the outbreak of the Russo-German War, Konev was posted to the Belaya Zerkov-Cherkassy District, where he was to command 19th Army. Thus, he became very well acquainted with the area where he would be leading his much larger Front two and one half years later.

In the summer of 1941, he led his army in the defense against von Runstedt, where it was mangled in the subsequent retreat to the Dnieper. Despite his initially unpromising performance as an army commander, Konev was appointed commander of an army group, Western Front, on 21 September 1941, since Red Army commanders of any ability were in such short supply. Konev's luck continue to worsen, as five armies under his command were encircled and forced to surrender to the Germans near Vyazma a month later. Threatened with a military tribunal and possible execution by Stalin for his alleged mishandling of his command (actually, most of the fault lay with Stalin), Konev was rescued by Marshal Zhukov who vouched for him and requested that Stalin place him on his own staff of the Kalinin Front as Deputy.

Here, Konev was entrusted with increasing leadership duties and took over the command itself 17 October 1941 when Zhukov was recalled to Moscow, somewhat of a vindication of Konev, who less than a month before had been threatened with a firing squad. Konev's command played a key role in the defense of Moscow, winning the coveted Order of Kutuzov for leadership of his command. In August 1942, he was given command again of Western Front and in quick succession commanded the Northwestern and Steppe Fronts, leading the latter during the decisive battle of Kursk. This command, later to be renamed Second Ukrainian Front, had played a key role in the pursuit of the Germans to the Dnieper.

Konev was known among Soviet circles as an ambitious, brutal leader who ruthlessly pushed his subordinates to their utmost. Nevertheless, he got results, which, in Stalin's eyes, made any personal shortcomings forgivable. He was also extremely brave and took what many nowadays would call needless risks, frequently visiting front-line positions while the fighting raged to see the situation for himself. Another characteristic of Konev was that he preferred meticulous preparation for operations and methodical execution, with particular emphasis on using deception and overwhelming amounts of artillery preparatory fires, in contrast to Vatutin, who was much more of a gambler.[46]

By far the larger and more powerful of the two *Fronts*, Konev's force contained some of the most famous and battle-experienced units in the Red Army. In addition to 52nd and 53rd Armies, Konev's *Front* would commit 4th Guards Army and 5th Guards Tank Army. Arrayed to the north, on the eastern face of the salient, lay Lt.Gen. Konstantin Apollonovich Koroteyev's 52nd Army, composed of 73rd Rifle Corps with two rifle divisions, the 254th and 294th. With its right flank resting on the Dnieper, it faced the bulk of *Wiking* and the Walloon Brigade. To its left, was situated 78th Rifle Corps, with 373rd Rifle Division and one regiment of the 254th, whose remainder was assigned to 73rd Corps. 78th Rifle Corps faced the bulk of *57. and 72.Inf.Div.*

In addition to the forces already listed, Koroteyev's army had a separate artillery regiment, two heavy mortar regiments, and several antitank regiments, as well as an antiaircraft division. While this sounded impressive on paper, 52nd Army was extremely understrength, with a total of 15,886 personnel assigned and no armored forces. Because of these realities, Koroteyev's troops would play a supporting role throughout the battle, primarily serving to harass, pin down, or pursue the retreating German forces.

To 52nd Army's left was positioned 4th Guards Army, which would play a key role in the upcoming battle. To carry out its mission of serving as the initial breakthrough force, Maj.Gen. Aleksandr Ivanovich Ryshov's 4th Guards Army had been considerably reinforced. As a rule, Guards armies were allocated more manpower, more artillery and tanks, and possessed better morale, having proven themselves as fighting organizations during previous campaigns. For this operation, Ryshov had been reinforced to a total of 45,653 men, with ample supporting artillery. To the north bounding with 52nd Army lay 20th Guards Rifle Corps, with 5th and 7th Guards Airborne Divisions, 62nd Guards, and 31st Rifle Division. This corps was located opposite part of the German *72.Inf.Div.* and the northern flank of *389.Inf.Div.*

South of this corps lay 21st Guards Rifle Corps, occupying a very narrow sector opposite the bulk of *389.Inf.Div.* With four divisions - 69th and 94th Guards Rifle and the 252nd and 375th Rifle Divisions, the corps had concentrated a considerable amount of combat power opposite its thinly-spread opponent. Ryshov's Army had been considerably strengthened with artillery in order to blast the German lines. In addition to the batteries possessed by the rifle divisions themselves, the army fielded three artillery brigades, two artillery regiments, and one heavy mortar regiment, as well as an antiaircraft division. Ryshov also had been assigned one tank regiment with 27 tanks to help with the breakthrough. With such a force arrayed against them, who could withstand an assault from such a force?

To 4th Guards Army's south lay the other breakthrough formation, 53rd Army under Lt.Gen. Ivan Vasil'evich Galanin. Like its neighbor to the north, Galanin's force had also been reinforced to a strength of 51,043 men, making it the largest Soviet force scheduled to take part in the battle. It boasted three corps and an entire artillery division. To the north, where it joined 4th Guards Army was 26th Rifle Corps, with three divisions, 1st Guards Airborne Division, 25th Guards Rifle Division, and 6th Rifle Division, all of which were opposite the south flank of the hapless *389.Inf.Div.*

To the corps' south, opposite the sector held by *3.Pz.Div.* and *106.Inf.Div.* of *XXXXVII.Pz.Korps*, lay 75th Rifle Corps, with three assigned rifle divisions - 138th, 213th,and 233rd, crammed together into a narrow ten kilometer-wide assembly area. To its left lay the neighboring 48th Rifle Corps, which also had three divisions assigned - 14th, 66th, and 89th Guards Rifle Divisions, all of which were opposite the bulk of *320.Inf.Div.* and the weakened *11.Pz.Div.* Additionally, 53rd Army had been assigned two additional rifle divisions, 78th Guards Rifle and 214th Rifle Divisions, as well as 16th Artillery Division, with four artillery brigades and one heavy mortar brigade.

To add to the already overwhelming number of artillery batteries arrayed against the Germans, Galanin's army had been given two more artillery regiments, an artillery brigade, an anti-aircraft division, and a heavy mortar regiment. 53rd Army also had one tank regiment, the 189th, assigned with its 21 tanks. It, too, was expected to quickly liquidate any Germans who may have been fortunate enough to survive the initial artillery barrage. To the south of Galanin's force was positioned 5th Guards Army, which would play only a supporting role in the operation, primarily tasked with tying down any German reinforcements which might be thrown into the coming battle.

Konev's striking force for the operation would be Fifth Guards Tank Army commanded by General of Tank Troops Pavel Rotmistrov, an eccentric veteran of the Bolshevik Revolution who wore round horn-rimmed glasses and sported an old-fashioned walrus mustache, quite a incongruent sight among the other clean-shaven Soviet generals. However, despite his scholarly appearance, Rotmistrov was a natural-born cavalryman and had forged an extremely well-led, capable organization. Born in 1902, his career was remarkably similar to that of Kravchenko, his fellow tank army commander. His first experience with tanks occurred in 1935, when he was assigned to the Far East Army near the Manchurian border as its chief of armored forces.

His first combat experience as a commander took place in Finland in December 1939. When he arrived at the front, he was immediately placed in command of a tank battalion in 35th Light Tank Brigade, when its previous commander had been killed.[47] The inept handling of armor by the Red Army during this winter war made a deep impression on Rotmistrov, who felt that Soviet tank forces needed to be handled with more imagination. He felt that their being relegated to infantry support made them vulnerable to enemy antitank tactics. During this campaign, he learned a great deal about how one fights in bitter winter conditions with armor, lessons that would stand in good stead later in the war against Germany.

When war broke out in June 1941, the chief of all Soviet armored troops, Lt.Gen. Yakov Fedorenko, tried to obtain Rotmistrov as his chief of staff. Rotmistrov would not hear of it and insisted that his place was with the troops in the field, not sitting in some headquarters safe in the rear. Fedorenko insisted, but he was undeterred. Grasping at straws, Rotmistrov wrote a letter to Joseph Stalin, explaining his desire for front line service. Surprisingly, Stalin approved his request, though Fedorenko was unhappy about his subordinates circumventing the normal chain of command.

In September 1941 he assumed command of 8th Tank Brigade on the Leningrad Front, where it was able to retard the forward advance of the Germans and buy time for the defenders of Leningrad to complete the city's defenses. Shortly thereafter, his brigade was switched to the front of Moscow, where it threw itself in the path of the German drive and was cut to bits in the process. Hastily reformed, it took part in Zhukov's winter counteroffensive which threw the enemy back from the gates of Moscow, earning him the Order of Lenin and his brigade being renamed 3rd Guards Tank Brigade in recognition of their dedication and bravery.

Lieutenant General Konstantin A. Koroteyev, *Commander, 52nd Army, Second Ukrainian Front. (Photo courtesy of the Battle of Korsun-Shevchenkovsky Museum, Korsun, Ukraine)*

Colonel General of Tank Troops Pavel O. Rotmistrov, *Commander, 5th Guards Tank army, Second Ukrainian Front. (Photo courtesy of the Battle of Korsun-Shevchenkovsky Museum, Korsun, Ukraine)*

Lieutenant General Ivan V. Galanin, *Commander, 53rd Army, Second Ukrainian Front. (Photo courtesy of the Battle of Korsun-Shevchenkovsky Museum, Korsun, Ukraine)*

Guards Lieutenant General Oleksandr I. Ryzhov, *Commander, 4th Guards Army, Second Ukrainian Front. (Photo courtesy of the Battle of Korsun-Shevchenkovsky Museum, Korsun, Ukraine)*

In the Spring of 1942, Rotmistrov was ordered to form 7th Tank Corps, leading it throughout the summer battles against the German drive on Stalingrad. Although his new tank corps was shot up and reduced to 35 tanks, it could not prevent the German assault on Stalingrad. While his corps was licking its wounds, he was summoned to Moscow in early November 1942 and was asked by Stalin himself how would he, Rotmistrov, destroy the Germans then fighting in the city. Rotmistrov told him that the Red Army should conduct a deep encirclement and trap them, while continuing the attack against their rear areas.

Whether his plan was the one finally accepted or not, it does show to a certain extent how much respect Rotmistrov had within the Red Army. During von Manstein's effort to relieve Stalingrad in mid-December 1942, it was Rotmistrov's tank corps, fighting under the command of the Second Guards Army, that helped bring the German relief attempt to a halt at Kotelnikovo, only 25 miles short of their goal. For his leadership, Rotmistrov was awarded the newly instituted Order of Suvorov. Active in the effort to reduce the Stalingrad Pocket, Rotmistrov's corps again was committed to heavy fighting.

In late January 1943, Rotmistrov was ordered to form 5th Guard Tank Army near the town of Millerovo, 400 miles southeast of Kursk. During the spring and early summer of 1943, he trained his new command thoroughly in the art of mobile warfare, of which he had come to be recognized as the Red Army's expert. His new tank army proved itself at Kursk during the great tank battle at Prokhorovka 11-13 July 1943, when it stopped *II.SS-Pz.Korps* in the largest tank battle of the war,

forcing the Germans to withdraw just when it seemed as if they were finally gaining the upper hand. In the pursuit of Army Group South to the Dnieper and the bloody battle for Kirovograd, his troops had distinguished themselves, earning him the trust of Konev, his *Front* Commander. Rotmistrov's drive, dedication, and skill, as well as his penchant for daring and initiative, were the qualities that would be required for this upcoming operation.

Rotmistrov's tank army consisted of 18th Tank Corps under Major General V.I. Polozkov, 20th Tanks Corps of Lieutenant General I.G. Lazarev, and 29th Tank Corps under Major General I.F. Kirichenko. Each tank corps had three tank brigades and one motorized infantry brigade assigned, as well as up to four artillery regiments in direct support. Rotmistrov's army also had 25th Tank Brigade in reserve. When tallied, Rotmistrov fielded 22,301 men and 197 tanks and assault guns. This force and Kravchenko's tank army would be chosen to effect the initial encirclement of the German forces in the Kaniev Salient, as detailed in the following chapter.

The last, but certainly not the least, formation in Konev's order of battle was 5th Guards Cossack Cavalry Corps commanded by Major General A.G. Selivanov. This formation, composed of 11th and 12th Guards Cavalry Divisions and 63rd Cavalry Division, offered an all-terrain striking capability due to the fact that its troops were primarily on horseback. Used for the purpose of exploiting breakthroughs over difficult ground, this corps had been in *STAVKA* reserve and had been allocated to Konev for the coming attack. Due to the poor road network in the area, its cross-country mobility made it a powerful addition to Konev's force. Manned by Cossacks from the Don River basin, known for their ferocity, these formations preferred to close with and destroy their enemy with drawn sabers, but were well-equipped with modern weapons which gave them added flexibility their ancestors had lacked during the time of the Czar. Each Cossack division had three cavalry regiments, as well as mortars and antitank units.

In addition, the corps itself had two light tank regiments, which by this stage of the war were usually composed of SU-76 assault guns or U.S. lend-lease M4 Shermans, as well as a mortar regiment, antitank regiment, and a SU-85 tank destroyer regiment.[48] Since these formations were small and light, their logistical requirements were not nearly as great as that of comparable tank or infantry formations, while having the added advantage of being able to keep pace with fully mechanized units. Their addition to the order of battle would immensely complicate the German's defensive effort. For this operation, Selivanov corps, with 20,258 men and 76 tanks and assault guns, would be positioned behind Rotmistrov's tank army and await the signal to exploit the breakthrough.

As well as these forces already mentioned, both Vatutin and Konev would be able to count on other assets from *STAVKA* reserve being apportioned to them, such an multiple rocket-launcher regiments, independent tank brigades, self-propelled antitank regiments, engineer units, and antiaircraft formations, bringing the total number who would be involved in the attack to over 336,000 men.[49] Besides these, an added bonus was the many and varied partisan units operating in the German rear areas, which kept them in a constant state of armed unrest. Some of these partisan forces, such as those operating in the Irdyn Marshes and the Cherkassy Forest, were firmly under the control of their commissars and obeyed orders unquestioningly, if not always enthusiastically. Other units, such as those composed primarily of Ukrainian nationalists, attacked both sides indiscriminately, but at least their presence forced the hard-pressed German rear services to maintain a high state of alert.

Despite the impressive numbers of troops, tanks, and guns soon to be arrayed against the so-called "Hitlerites," the various elements of the First and Second Ukrainian *Fronts*, though flush with victory, had suffered considerably during the past several months. They had thrown the Germans across the Dnieper, carried out many river crossing operations and had liberated Kiev. Because of this, most of Vatutin's and Konev's armies, corps, and divisions were less than full strength. For example, when it was committed later to the battle, one tank corps of 1st Tank Army, which entered the battle after operations had already commenced, had only 30 tanks remaining out of 189 authorized.[50] However, shortage of equipment was a minor problem when compared to a far more serious situation which had begun to arise during the pursuit to the Dnieper.

By January 1944, the Red Army was extremely short of good replacements, a legacy of the tremendous losses suffered during the summer and fall of 1941, when it had lost over three million men killed, captured, or wounded.[51] The shortage of manpower was particularly felt in the infantry, where many divisions were operating at less than half of their authorized

strength. By that point of the war, the manpower shortage had grown so acute than advancing Red Army units would encircle newly-liberated villages, round up the able-bodied men (ranging in age from thirteen to sixty) and immediately impress them into their ranks.[52]

These so-called "booty" Ukrainians swelled depleted Soviet ranks and restored them to some level of their authorized strength. A disadvantage to this method of gaining recruits, of course, was that these individuals were untrained and untested in battle. Many of these men were sent into battle still wearing their civilian clothes. Many units of the First and Second Ukrainian *Fronts* were replenished with these men whose lack of experience and training undoubtedly contributed to the decline of fighting efficiency of the average Soviet infantry formation. However, this deficiency was made up elsewhere by the vast improvement in their mechanized forces and the improvement of headquarters staffs from the corps to *Front* level.

Even with its shortages of infantry, the Red Army had calculated that it would enjoy at least a two-to-one superiority in men, a five-to-one superiority in tanks , and, most importantly to the Soviet way of thinking, a seven-to-one superiority in artillery in the area of the Kanev salient. In Konev's area, he alone would employ over 1,700 pieces of artillery against the Germans, an enormous quantity in comparison to what the Germans could offer.[53] Actually, the odds were even more in their favor, since Konev had overestimated the number of pieces of artillery they had facing him. The odds for the encircled German divisions

Lieutenant General Alexei G. Selivanov, *Commander, 5th Guards Don Cossack Cavalry Corps, Second Ukrainian Front. (Photo courtesy of the Battle of Korsun-Shevchenkovsky Museum, Korsun, Ukraine)*

General der Fliegertruppe Seidemann, *Commander VIII. Flieger-Korps. (Bundesarchiv 649/5355/14)*

would worsen as the battle developed. However, the advantage possessed by the Soviets was not brought about by sheer numbers alone, but also by the introduction of weapons that were equal to or better than those of the Germans. Not only that, but the men of the Red Army were becoming adept in their use both tactically and operationally.

By 1944, both sides had developed combined arms formations which used some of the most modern weapons systems available. Both had lethal, effective main battle tanks such as the Russian T-34/85 mounting an 8.5 cm gun and the German Pz. V *Panther*, mounting a high velocity 7.5 cm gun. Both were widely recognized at the time as being the best fighting vehicles in the world. But by early 1944, the only advantages German armored formations had in battles with Red Armor was the superior training of their crews, quality of unit leadership at the regimental level and below, and the fact that every German tank had a radio, facilitating command and control at the platoon, company, and battalion level, while those of the Red Army, except for its command tanks, had none.

However, the Germans had to rely on an equal number of older, less modern tanks such as the Pz. IV, which first saw combat service during the invasion of Poland. Although well-liked by its crews, the Pz. IV had less armor and poorer maneuverability in comparison to the T-34 and Panther, although its 7.5 cm L48 main gun could still hold its own. The Red Army also fielded a variety of other tanks, ranging from the newly-introduced Joseph Stalin II (JS2) with a 12.2 cm gun (which saw its debut in this battle) to the M4 Sherman. The only truly decisive factor, however, when considering armor in the Battle of the

Cherkassy Pocket was that the Red Army employed at the outset nearly five times as many tanks as the Germans did. Even the mighty German Pz. VI *Tiger* tank, with its deadly 8.8 cm high-velocity gun and thick armor, could not redress the balance.

The story was the same with artillery. Although the German's self-propelled artillery systems were far superior in quality and responsiveness to anything the Red Army had, the Soviets had seven to twelve times as many guns. This is due in part to the Red Army's tendency to use artillery in mass as a substitute for the infantry which it had employed previously in the assault role and which it no longer had in abundance. The Soviets also fielded many guns and howitzers which out-ranged those of the Germans, making those of the former much less vulnerable to counter-battery fire, the bane of artillerymen. The preferred Red Army tactic by this phase of the war was to fire at preplanned targets and use rolling barrages very similar to methods introduced in World War I.[54] Gun densities of hundred of barrels per kilometer were not uncommon.

Although this method was inefficient, it proved devastating against hasty field fortifications. It was also a simple system to use, requiring no detailed training. During the opening stages of the coming attack, artillery support was more than adequate, but the high rates of fire required to sustain the offensive could not be supported once the attacking echelons had advanced into the German's operational depth due to the condition of the main supply routes. Consequently, the accustomed level of fire support was not as high as it had been in previous operations, which would affect the course of their operation.[55]

German armored divisions did possess certain numbers of half-tracked armored vehicles, known as *Schutzenpanzerwagen*, or SPW (predominately of the *Sd.Kfz.251 HANOMAG*-type) for mechanized infantry, but these had become relatively scarce. By January 1944, most *Panzergrenadiers* (mechanized infantry) rode in trucks, many of which were of foreign design and lacked all-wheel drive capability. To make up for their near-total lack of half tracks, the Red Army relied on the expedient of placing their mechanized infantry on the back decks of their tanks. Although these *Tankodesantniki* suffered grievous losses during combat owing to their vulnerability to small arms and artillery fire, it did allow the infantry to ride with the tanks into battle. For the most part, however, the infantrymen of both armies went into battle the old-fashioned way - on foot, although both sides did maintain some horse cavalry organizations.

In regards to overall mobility, the Red Army had an advantage over the *Wehrmacht*. In 1944, there were few paved roads in European Russia. Most *Rollbahnen* (main supply routes) were dirt roads improved with a layer of gravel or log corduroy. During the summer, they were veritable dust bowls; during the spring thaw, they often became an endless morass. Both sides used thousands of impressed civilian laborers, prisoners of war, and penal battalions to improve and maintain these roads.[56] These lines of communication were always a significant planning factor whenever either side was preparing for an operation, but the fact that the winter thaw came two months early would immensely complicate planning by the supply and transportation staffs

Lieutenant General Stepan A. Krasovsky, *Commander, 2nd Air Army. (Photo courtesy of the Battle of Korsun-Shevchenkovsky Museum, Korsun, Ukraine)*

Colonel General Sergei K. Goryunov, *Commander, 5th Air Army. (Photo courtesy of the Battle of Korsun-Shevchenkovsky Museum, Korsun, Ukraine)*

and units of both the *Wehrmacht* and Red Army.

Not only did the Red Army's wide-tracked tanks have better trafficability in the mud than most German armored vehicles, the Red Army had the additional advantage of possessing thousands of four-wheel drive American-made Studebaker and Ford 2 $^{1}/_{2}$ ton trucks, courtesy of the U.S. lend-lease program. These trucks, compared to the German Ford and Mercedez two-wheel drive commercial vehicles, were far more rugged and durable, allowing Soviet combat service and support units to keep up with mechanized forces even when terrain was unfavorable.[57] When faced with totally impassible road conditions, both sides would also be forced to resort to aerial resupply, with the accompanying need to control the air over the battlefield.

Air power, though employed heavily by the Soviets, would not prove to be decisive for their coming operation. Soviet air support for the upcoming offensive was provided by Second Air Army, under Lt.Gen. of Aviation Stepan Akimovich Krasovsky, responsible for supporting the First Ukrainian *Front*, and Fifth Air Army, under Lt.Gen. of Aviation Sergei Kondrat'evich Goryunov, responsible for supporting Second Ukrainian *Front*. Each air army had several air corps assigned, with component bomber, fighter, and ground attack divisions. The aircraft of the Red Air Force had been vastly improved from the obsolescent models destroyed mostly on the ground during the first months of the war. Its airmen now flew the latest models, such as the Yak-9 fighter, Pe-2 light bomber, and the dreaded Ilyushin IL-2 *Stormovik*, perhaps the most successful ground-attack aircraft of the war.

Although the Red Air Force had made great strides since it was nearly destroyed in June 1941, its employment was still poorly integrated into the overall concept of operations and did not support the scheme of maneuver for the two *Fronts*, a sign that the Red Air Force had yet to develop proficiency in air-to-ground cooperation. Command and control of Red Air Force elements were also weak. However, the Red Air Force would enjoy air superiority for much of the battle and attacks by Ilyushin IL-2 *Stormoviks* would make life miserable for the Germans in the salient. In all, the Red Air Force would have 768 aircraft available for the operation, outnumbering the Germans in the air by at least three to one.

German air support was provided by General Hans Seidemann's *VIII.Flieger-Korps*, which included both tactical and airlift assets, such as *Jagdgeschwader* (Fighter Wing) 52, *Stukageschwader* (Dive Bombing Wing) 2, and *Transportgeschwader* (Transport Wing) 3. These units were overextended because they were required to provide air support to all of Army Group South. By the third year of war in the Soviet Union, the *Luftwaffe* could no longer provide air superiority since it, too, had suffered irrecoverable losses in air battles fought in the skies over Kursk.

This, coupled with the requirement to send additional fighter squadrons to Western Europe to take part in the air defense of the Reich against the Anglo-Allied air offensive, left the German Air Force on the Eastern Front chronically weak. It could control the skies for limited periods over specific objectives and could inflict punishment upon packs of Soviet tanks, but was becoming increasingly irrelevant and was in danger of being engulfed by resurgent Soviet air power. Even the bravery of men such as *Oberstlt.* Hans-Ulrich Rudel, the legendary *Stuka* tank-buster, and *Oblt.* Erich Hartmann, called the "Black Devil of the Ukraine" by Soviet fliers for his incredible skill as a Messerschmidt Me-109 pilot, could no longer stem the onrushing tide of Red air power.

Due to a number a factors, primarily weather and shortage of improved airfields, effective use of close air support would be limited for both antagonists. While *Stormoviks* and Yak-9s seemed to fill the skies during the battle, it was only on rare occasions where their employment was orchestrated with operations of ground troops. When they were, the effect was deadly. The Germans would make extensive use of airlift assets in support of the soon-to-be encircled corps. German fighter aircraft focused primarily on protecting these transports, while Rudel and his *Stuka* wing would inflict punishing blows to Soviet armor whenever they could fight their way through swarms of fighter aircraft.

The Red Air Force also began to carry out numerous orchestrated night attacks during the final stages of the battle, which were widely noted in both wartime and postwar Soviet literature. The effect of these attacks were chiefly psychological, though the threat to the German aerial resupply operation was a constant danger, forcing the Germans at times to cancel air drops.[58] Lack of these critical supplies would have an adverse impact on both sides' armored formations, testifying to the immense importance of logistics in modern mechanized warfare.

The Germans made matters worse by overburdening their already strained logistics system. One of the *Wehrmacht's* weaknesses was its reliance on what the Red Army would call "creature comforts." As did most Western armies of the day, the German Army devoted a great deal of their logistical infrastructure to mail, depots, field kitchens, repair shops, clothing, and baggage trains. The requirement to haul these items placed an additional demand on the available transport and tended to clog the already poor road network with hundreds of superfluous vehicles. This could have potentially disastrous consequences during the conduct of a retreat or when mobile forces were trying to shift rapidly from one threatened sector of the front to another.[59]

The Red Army, which was accustomed to doing without a lot of such frills, focused its logistical effort instead on providing fuel and ammunition to its combat units. Their soldiers could and did live on the land for extended periods and were exhorted to use captured German food supplies as frequently as possible. Their ability to subsist on a bare minimum of rations amazed the Germans, who often tied the degree of combat worthiness to the amount of bread their soldiers received in their daily ration.[60]

Another expedient used by both sides to overcome transportation difficulties was the utilization of native horse and wagon (or sled) combinations. The so-called *panjewagen*, pulled by ponies, was used extensively to haul food, fuel, ammunition, wounded and nearly everything else, through roads that would hopelessly mire a truck or even a half-track. By the winter of

1943-44, both sides were using thousands of these small carts pulled by the shaggy little ponies.[61] Both sides also used rail, another time-tested means of transportation, as much as possible, to carry supplies as well as a means to shift forces from one part of the front to another. The advantages of rail transport, however, were limited. As in World War One, once a train arrived at the front, it had to be unloaded by hand. Mechanized units would have to conduct the remainder of their movement on muddy roads. Supplies proceeded to the units in the field from the railhead in trucks or *panje* wagons.

One notable characteristic of the Russian campaign was the use by both sides of armored trains as a tactical expedient. Such a train was used during the Battle of Cherkassy by Wöhler's *8.Armee* to make up for his lack of sufficient mobile field artillery. It was not unusual for this *Panzerzug* to approach to within eight-to-ten kilometers of the front lines and provide badly needed fire support to the beleaguered German *XXXXVII.Pz.Korps* fighting to the southeast of the encircled forces.[62] Even so, its impressive firepower - it carried several 10.5 cm howitzers as well as heavy antitank guns - would not redress the balance in favor of the Germans. Besides, the Red Army's plan would not rely merely on firepower - mobility and flexibility of its forces and the initiative of its commanders would play an even greater role.

Thus, all of these planning factors - condition of troops, weapons, logistics and organizational structure would all contribute to the course of the upcoming battle. For the Soviet plan to work, it would have to take into account all of these factors in order to guarantee a quick and relatively cheap victory. The Germans, in turn, would have to marshal their remaining strength and frustrate Vatutin's and Konev's plan, while not yielding one inch. To overcome the anticipated German resistance, the Soviet plan would have to capitalize on the Red Army's greatest strengths at this stage of the war - its fledgling tank armies, artillery, air force, as well as superior numbers.

To tie down German reserves, especially armor, the plan would also have to incorporate deception, psychological warfare, and diversionary attacks. To further confuse the Germans, the operation would have to be launched quickly, since the Germans were accustomed to lengthy Soviet delays between major operations. However, the Red Army had never been tasked with carrying out an offensive quite like this one before. With this sense of urgency in mind, on 10 January 1944, shortly after the conclusion of Konev's successful Kirovograd Operation, Stalin ordered Marshal Zhukov, as the designated *STAVKA* representative for this operation, to draw up a plan to eliminate the Kanev Salient in the shortest possible time. The Germans must not be allowed to escape.

End Notes

1 Guy Sajer, *The Forgotten Soldier*. (New York: Ballentine Books, 1971), p. 308.

2 Strassner, p. 129.

3 John R. Angolia, *On the Field of Honor: A History of the Knight's Cross Bearers*. (San Jose, CA: R. James Bender Publishing, 1980), pp. 80-81 and Erich von Manstein, Lost Victories (Novato, CA: Presidio Press, 1982), pp. 352-53.

4 von Manstein, p. 456.

5 LTC David Glantz, "From the Dnieper to the Vistula: Soviet Offensive Operations - November 1943 - August 1944," 1985 *Art of War Symposium,* (Carlisle Barracks, PA: U.S. Army War College, 1985), p. 128.

6 Angolia, pp. 331-332.

7 Ibid, pp. 332-333 and Kurt Mehner, *Die Deutsche Wehrmacht 1939-1945: Führung und Truppe.* (Norderstedt, Germany: Militair Verlag Klaus D. Patzwall, 1993), pp. 51, 86.

8 *Geschütz-Bestand der Gruppe Stemmermann,* 17 February 1944, *An der Gruppe Mattenklott, Panzerarmeeoberkommando 1,* Microfilm Group T-313, Roll 69.

9 Guenther Jahnke and Bernd Lerch, *Der Kessel von Tscherkassy 1944.* (Donauwoerth, Germany: Merkle Druck Service, 1996), p. 23.

10 Strassner, p. 129.

11 *Geschütz-Bestand der Gruppe Stemmermann.*

12 Angolia, pp. 217-218.

13 Jahnke and Lerch, p. 31.

14 Gordon William, *Loyalty is My Honor: Personal Accounts from the Waffen-SS.* (London: Motorbooks International, 1995), p. 181.

15 Jahnke and Lerch, p. 15.

16 Höhne, Heinz. *The Order of the Death's Head.* (New York: Ballantine Books, 1983), p. 544.

17 Ewald Klapdor, *Mit dem Panzerregiment 5 im Osten.* (Siek, Germany: Privately published, 1981), pp. 186-187.

18 Richard Landwehr, Jean-Louis Roba and Ray Merriam, *The Wallonien: The History of the 5th SS-Sturmbrigade and 28th Volunteer Panzergrenadier Division.* (Glendale, Oregon: Weapons and Warfare Publications, 1984), pp. 5-6.

19 Ibid, p. 10.

20 Glanz,p. 128.

21 U.S. Department of the Army Pamphlet 20-234, Operations of Encircled Forces: *German Experiences in Russia.* (Washington, D.C. U.S. Government Printing Office, 1952), pp. 19-20.

22 Buchner, p. 23.

23 Hans-Kurt Menedetter, *Chronik der Artillerie Regiment 188.* (Fürth, Germany: Traditionsverband der ehemaligen 88.Infantrie-Division, 1960), p. 4-7 and Samuel W. Mitcham, Jr., Hitler's Legion's: *The German Army Order of Battle, World War II.* (New York: Stein and Day, 1985), p. 104.

24 Interview with Hans Kurt Menedetter, Vienna, Austria, 2 July 1996.

25 Menedetter, pp. 66-67.

26 *Kriegsgliederung Gruppe Stemmermann, 30 January 1944, Armeeoberkommando 8,* Chefsachen January-June 1944, Microfilm Grouping T-312, Roll 65. (National Archives, Washington, D.C.).

27 *Sbornik,* pp. 326-327.

28 Ibid, pp. 324-325.

29 Glanz, p. 304.

30 Nilolaus von Vormann, *Tscherkassy.* (Heidelberg, Kurt Vowinckel Verlag, 1954), p.61.

31 Department of the Army Pamphlet 20-234, *Operations of Encircled Forces: German Experiences in Russia.* (Washington, D.C.: Department of the Army, 1952), p.15.

32 Ziemke, *Stalingrad to Berlin*, p. 227.

33 Paul Carell, *Scorched Earth.* (New York: Ballantine Book, 1973), p. 467.

34 Leon Degrelle, Campaign in Russia. (Torrance, CA: Institute for Historical Review,1985), p. 161.

35 Ziemke, pp. 214-216.

36 James Lucas, *War on the Eastern Front.* (New York: Stein and Day, 1979), pp. 53-54.

37 Alan Clark, *Barbarossa: The Russo-German Conflict, 1941-45.* (New York: Quill Books, 1965), pp. 369-70. Incidentally, Clark misattributes this quote to a Major Gustav Kreuz of the Army's 182.Inf.Div. In actuality, it was Karl Kreuz, who went on to co mand *Das Reich's* artillery regiment by the war's end, who made this statement.

38 David M. Glantz and Jonathan M. House, *When Titans Clashed: How the Red ArmyStopped Hitler.* (Lawrence, KS: University Press of Kansas, 1995), p. 292.

39 "Documents on Korsun-Shevchenkovsky Given," *Voyenno istoricheskiy zhurnal, No. 2* (February 1984). (Moscow:*Voyenno istoricheskiy zhurnal,* 1984), p. 35.

40 Georgi Zhukov, *Reminiscences and Reflections.* (Moscow: Progress Publishers, 1985), p. 249.

[41] Earl F. Ziemke, *Moscow to Stalingrad: Decision in the East.* (Washington, D.C.:U.S. Army Center of Military History, 1987), p. 194.

[42] Anna Rothe, Ed., *Current Biography: Who's News and Why, 1944.* (New York: The H.W. Wilson Company, 1944), pp. 703-704.

[43] Dmitriy Loza, "How Soviets Fought in U.S. Shermans." *Armor Magazine,* (July-August 1996), (Fort Knox, KY: Armor Magazine, 1996), p. 21.

[44] Richard Armstrong, *Red Army Tank Commanders: The Armored Guards.* (Atglen, PA: Schiffer Publishing Company, 1994), p. 385.

[45] Ziemke, *Stalingrad to Berlin*, p. 506.

[46] Harold Shukman, ed., *Stalin's Generals.* (New York: Grove Press, 1993), pp. 100-101.

[47] Armstrong, pp. 305-306.

[48] Trevor Dupuy, James Dunnigan, and David Isby, eds. *War in the East: The Russo-German Conflict 1941-45,* (New York: Simulations Publications, Inc. 1977), p.124.

[49] Glanz and House, p. 298.

[50] Glanz, "From the Dnieper to the Vistula," p. 128.

[51] R. Ernest Dupuy and Trevor N. Dupuy, *The Encyclopedia of Military History.* (New York: Harper and Row, 1970), p. 1080.

[52] Ziemke, *Stalingrad to Berlin,* pp. 279, 281.

[53] *Sbornik*, p. 302.

[54] Viktor A. Matsulenko, *Operatsii i boi na Okruzheniye* (Encirclement Operations and Combat), (Moscow: Voyenizdat, 1983), p.55.

[55] Zhukov, p. 242.

[56] Glantz, "From the Dnieper to the Vistula," pp. 134-135.

[57] Clark, pp. 371-372.

[58] Claude R. Sasso, "Soviet Night Operations in World War II," *Leavenworth Papers, No. 6.* (Fort Leavenworth, KS: U.S. Government Printing Office, 1982), pp. 15-16.

[59] Degrelle, p. 208.

[60] *XXXXII.A.K.* report 9 February 1944 to Headquarters, *1.Pz.Armee.*

[61] Lucas, pp. 105-106.

[62] *8.Armee Kriegstagebuch*, 12 February 1944.

Chapter Three
THE SOVIET PLAN FOR A SECOND STALINGRAD

"It was about this time that we began to hear a new name: Georgi Zhukov. Whenever things were going badly for us, whenever we felt the presence of a powerful and flexible opponent, our commanders gave a knowing smile: Zhukov."
— *Erich Kern in Dance of Death* [1]

The Red Army's plan to eliminate the Kanev Salient, dubbed the Korsun-Schevchenkovsky Operation, would incorporate elements of Soviet operational design which had been tried in various forms in previous operations, but which had not been synchronized to such a degree as this operation would demand. The operational plan would rely for its success on a combination of operational deception, diversionary attacks, and deeps attacks by *STAVKA's* operational reserve - the tank armies of the First and Second Ukrainian *Fronts*. The Soviet operation would also incorporate the use of massive artillery concentrations on narrow sectors to totally disrupt the German tactical defenses, close air support, echelonment of attacking elements, and military intelligence to determine German capabilities and intentions. The incorporation of all of these elements would require an unprecedented degree of command and control by *Front* and army commanders, as well as initiative at lower levels of command where the fighting would actually take place. Whether the Red Army possessed the capability to carry out such a complex operation remained to be seen.

The origin of the Soviet tactical plan can be traced to recommendations made to *STAVKA* by Marshal Zhukov during the second week of January 1944, immediately following the completion of the Zhitomir-Berdichev and Kirovograd operations.[2] Zhukov and the commanders of the First and Second Ukrainian, *Fronts*, Vatutin and Konev, whose operations had created the Kanev Salient, saw the German grouping in the bulge that angled towards the Dnieper as a potential threat to their flanks, especially Vatutin's, which extended 250 kilometers west from the river.[3] The salient additionally threatened the Red Army's freedom of action, in that its size and depth prevented close cooperation between the two *Fronts*.

Of more concern to *STAVKA* was the possibility that the salient could be used to conduct deep attacks into the rear of Vatutin's *Front* or into the flank of Konev's *Front*, with the goal of retaking Kiev and Kirovograd, respectively, which was exactly what Hitler was proposing to do.[4] The fact that von Manstein's army group did not have the strength to conduct such a large scale operation, despite Hitler's grand designs, seems to have eluded the Soviets. *STAVKA's* thoughts on the issue were probably influenced by the powerful counterattacks that von Manstein had launched during his Korosten-Zhitomir counterattack in December, where the Germans had inflicted considerable destruction on Vatutin's strung-out armored formations. Perhaps von Manstein could repeat this performance; at any rate, *STAVKA* was not going to take any chances. Zhukov, on orders

from Stalin, flew to the Ukraine, where he briefed Vatutin and Konev on the concept of the plan and gained their approval and agreement. Zhukov passed their recommendations to *STAVKA*, where the chief of the General Staff, Marshal Vasilevsky, quickly gained Stalin's approval.[5]

The Soviet field commanders were in agreement. Zhukov quickly concurred with Vatutin's and Konev's assessment of the threat posed to their flanks by the German salient at Kanev. Furthermore, Konev saw what he believed to be far more than an opportunity to straighten out the front line. Based on Soviet intelligence reports, Konev believed that the bulk of *8.Armee* was in the trap that was about to be sprung. Rather than bag a few divisions, the Soviet marshal believed that he could achieve another victory on the scale of Stalingrad and decisively tip the balance in the Ukraine in the USSR's favor.[6]

Konev's beliefs were based on information which indicated, from a variety of sources (including POWs, radio intercepts, etc.), that ten German divisions and a motorized brigade lay within the Kanev salient (these units included *57., 72., 82., 88., 112., 167., 168.,* and *332.Inf.Div., 213.Sich.Div., 5.SS-Pz.Div. Wiking* and the *Walloon Brigade*). Since Soviet military intelligence habitually estimated German units at their full authorized strengths, Konev, as well as Vatutin and Zhukov, believed that there were at least 100,000 Germans within the area encompassed by the Kanev salient.[7]

To Soviet military intelligence specialists, this represented the bulk of the combat power of *8.Armee*, which occupied a considerable portion of the area in question. According to one source, Colonel Kvach, a staff officer at *STAVKA*:

> The German 8.Armee under General Wöhler is in the salient near Kanev. It comprises no fewer than nine of the best motorized divisions of the Wehrmacht as well as a division of the Waffen-SS and the "Wallonia" motorized brigade. Another Stalingrad is in the making.[8]

It was therefore not surprising that the Red Army would soon dedicate so much effort towards this operation. If it were successful, the German defensive effort in the Ukraine would likely collapse, bringing the Red Army to the Rumanian border.

Why did not the Soviet commanders plan anything beyond the immediate encirclement and annihilation of the German units in the Kanev salient? To this day, there is no evidence to suggest that Zhukov and the Front commanders considered striking deeper into the German defenses. The Korsun-Shevchenkovsky Operation's plan envisioned only shallow penetrations aimed at cutting the salient off at its base. This is puzzling, since Red Army doctrine since 1936 stressed deep battle concepts with particular emphasis on large-scale envelopment operations. Even the 1944 Red Army Field Regulations emphasized striking into the operational depth of the enemy. Yet in this case the Red Army's leaders, with the *STAVKA's* approval, chose not to.

To have been true to established doctrine, the operation should have been targeting towards the linkup of the two Fronts at Uman or Perwomajsk. Both towns were 75 and 100 kilometers further south, respectively, of Zvenigorodka. Both were major rail and supply centers for Army Group South and Army Group A. Either would have been a suitable operational objective for a deep attack by the two Fronts. Their seizure would have jeopardized Manstein's entire right flank and would have encircled or at least threatened the rear of both the German *8.* and *6. Armee.* Subsequent operations launched from Uman or Perwomajsk could have been directed at the port city of Odessa, where supplies for the beleaguered *17.Armee* in Crimea were shipped. Certainly upon first inspection, this appears to have been a logical and obtainable goal. However, the Red Army's experience with deep operations in the previous two years had been overwhelmingly negative.

Two unsuccessful deep operations serve as excellent examples. The first was the Spring 1942 counteroffensive near Kharkov. In this operation, the Red Army's Southwest Front, using three armies, attempted to strike deep in order to encircle *6.Armee* near Kharkov. Due to a variety of reasons, most predominantly the poor planning by inexperienced staffs, poor supervision by Marshal Timoshenko, and stiff German resistance, the offensive failed. A determined German counterattack by Army Group Kleist sealed off the Soviet penetration. By 28 May 1942, the Red Army had lost over 240,000 men and 1,200 tanks. Such a massive defeat one month prior to the German 1942 summer offensive contributed substantially to the subsequent Soviet defeats that followed in its wake. The loss of the carefully built up Soviet armor reserve (two tank corps were annihilated) would not be made good until four months later.[9]

Another example of a Red Army deep attack gone awry was the counteroffensive in the wake of the encirclement of *6.Armee* at Stalingrad. Believing that German defenses in the Donets Basin were finished, *STAVKA* urged Southwest Front under Marshal Vatutin and Voronezh Front under Marshal Golikov, to drive to the Dnieper on 30 January 1943, a distance of over 200 kilometers. Having just rescued Army Group Don from the lower Don and Caucasus, its commander, von Manstein, was faced with a crisis. Instead of holding ground, von Manstein conducted a classic mobile defense. Drawing the Red Army formations deeper into the German operational depths, he counterattacked 19 February 1943 with hastily assembled reserves. In four weeks of heavy fighting, he not only threw back the Red Army offensive, but cut off and destroyed the army-sized "Popov" Group.[10] This was reason to instill caution in even a bold commander as Vatutin. After this disaster, few Red Army commanders wanted to risk another similar deep operation.

Another factor which influenced the thinking of the Soviet commanders, besides an aversion to risking another deep attack, was the belief that they would need all available forces to encircle and annihilate the large German grouping trapped in the salient. Any forces diverted to push the Germans further back would not be available to fight the main battle. As the operation was to prove, this would be an accurate assumption. Although committing more reserves from the *STAVKA* pool could have influenced the outcome of the battle, evidence suggests that these assets were being withheld for subsequent operations. In sum, there is no evidence to suggest that Zhukov even considered penetrating further and cutting off the entire southern wing of Army Group South by pushing to the Black Sea at Odessa, a mere 200 kilometers from Zvenigorodka.[11]

On 12 January 1944, *STAVKA,* through Zhukov, sent the order to the First and Second Ukrainian Fronts which assigned the tasks of encircling and destroying the German forces in the Kanev salient in the shortest possible time.[12] This order, signed by Stalin himself, stated that in order to accomplish this task, the two Fronts would link up somewhere in the vicinity of the Ukrainian towns of Shpola and Zvenigorodka. It was envisioned by *STAVKA* that the destruction of the German forces in the salient would improve the operational position of the Front's boundaries, as well as shorten the overall frontage, making more troops available for subsequent operations. It would also remove the threat to Kiev and Kirovograd. Following the completion of this operation, Soviet forces would then have the opportunity to develop an assault force for breaking out of the Ukraine and reaching the southern Bug River.[13]

The plan itself was quite straightforward. The operation would begin with an attack in the east on 24 January by Konev's Second Ukrainian *Front.* Using the 5th Guards Tank Army as his spearhead, Konev planned to pass them through the attacking infantry armies whose mission was to tie down and destroy the German positions in the vicinity of Kapitanovka. Once clear of the German front line tactical defenses, this army would drive to the base of the salient and seize the towns of Shpola and Zvenigorodka, cutting the German lines of communication to the salient. The 5th Guards Tank Army would then link up with the 6th Tank Army from Vatutin's *Front* attacking from the west near Tinovka.[14] The plan made no mention of striking into the operational depths of the enemy. In this respect, it lacked the subsequent deep operations which characterized the Stalingrad Operation of the previous year.

Zhukov passed on *STAVKA's* insistence that the operation should begin by the time specified, which gave Vatutin and Konev a mere two weeks to prepare their front to resume the offensive. This was quite an unusual departure from the normal standard operating procedure, since heretofore the Red Army normally required a great deal of planning and preparation time (usually one to two months) before launching an operation of this magnitude. This preparation time normally allowed the commanders involved to train and position units, stockpile ammunition, and conduct detailed rehearsals.

Vatutin and Konev would not have this luxury. In essence, the Korsun-Shevchenkovsky Operation would not have sufficient time for commanders to make thorough preparations.

According to one source, in many respects this operation fell into the category of an "operational-level hasty attack."[15] The fact that this operation took place on the heels of the just-completed Zhitomir - Berdichev and Kirovograd operations meant that the forces that were to be engaged were considerably understrength, as mentioned in the previous chapter. Troops were exhausted, losses in infantry and armor had been high, and tanks as well as other systems were in need of maintenance.[16] The Soviets apparently believed that despite these shortcomings, the operation would be concluded quickly.

The operation would unfold in three distinct phases. The first phase involved the penetration of enemy defenses in the tactical zone on the first day. The second phase consisted of the encirclement of the enemy in the course of the next three to four days, followed by the third phase, which involved the liquidation, or *unichtozhenie* of the surrounded enemy.[17] The belief that this operation would be accomplished so quickly was probably due to the overpowering amount of combat power - artillery, tanks, and tactical aviation - which would be brought to bear at the points of penetration and to carry out the encirclement itself. The plan also assumed that the Germans would not be able to react quickly enough to influence events should they assemble a relief force.

Zhukov expected the encirclement phase to take two or three days to complete. The destruction of the encircled forces was expected to take an additional three or four days as specified by the doctrine laid out in the 1944 Field Service Regulations. In the first instance, Zhukov was to prove correct. The second assumption was to prove wildly optimistic, evidence that the Soviets had greatly underestimated German capabilities. In any case, Zhukov, Vatutin, and Konev wanted to act quickly to take advantage of the German's exposed condition before they realized the danger and withdrew from the salient.[18]

As previously mentioned, one possible explanation for the optimism that this was going to be a short and decisive operation was Zhukov's and the *Front* commanders' confidence that they possessed sufficient forces to quickly complete the operation.[19] Another reason was that they expected the deception plan and planned diversionary attacks to tie down German mobile reserves to such an extent, that if they were able to free themselves and move to relieve the encircled units, it would be too late.[20]

As it developed, the attack could not be launched on the date indicated and was postponed to 25 January. The reason for this last-minute change was due to the inability of Second Ukrainian *Front's* 4th Guards Army to pinpoint the German main line of resistance at the points of penetration occupied by *389.Inf.Div*. Konev asked for and received permission to use 24 January to conduct a reconnaissance in force to locate the outpost line and identify the German main line of defense. This was successfully completed by the evening. The attack would begin as scheduled the following Tuesday morning, 25 January.[21]

In general, the operation would consist of "shattering, simultaneous concentric attacks" by the First Ukrainian *Front* attacking from the west and the Second Ukrainian *Front* attacking from the east. Strong shock groups of infantry, reinforced with independent tank brigades and artillery, would attack from

the two adjacent Front's internal flanks and deliver powerful blows to the weakest sector of the German front. The link up point of the encircling forces would be in the vicinity of the town of Zvenigorodka, which would sever the German main supply route to Uman.[22] Following the completion of this phase, the Fronts would then create an external ring of encirclement to ward off any relief attacks and an internal ring of encirclement to destroy the encircled German forces and prevent them from breaking out.

Konev, attacking first, would use Ryshov's 4th Guards Army and Galanin's 53rd Army to penetrate the German defenses in the Verbovka - Vasilevka region, a width of 19 kilometers. These adjacent armies would use a total force of 14 infantry divisions to create conditions favorable (i.e., punch a hole) for the commitment of the *Front's* operational reserve, Rotmistrov's 5th Guards Tank Army, from the vicinity east of Krasnossilka. After penetrating the German defenses, the tank army was to drive rapidly via Kapitanovka and Shpola in the general direction of Zvenigorodka, where it would link up with the advancing units of the First Ukrainian *Front*.[23]

To achieve the breakthrough, Konev would rely on massive amounts of artillery preparation to flatten the German fighting positions, assembly areas, and wire entanglements located in the breakthrough sectors. From *STAVKA* reserves, Konev received ten artillery brigades and eleven mortar regiments, including several regiments of 12 cm multiple rocket launchers, the dreaded *Katyusha*, giving the Soviet commander over 1,000 tubes to pulverize the German defenses.[24] Known by the Germans as *Stalinorgel* (Stalin's organ), these weapon systems could launch 36 rockets in less than ten seconds. Their impressive firepower, plus that of the tube artillery, gave the attacking armies a density of over 100 barrels per kilometer, or an artillery force ratio of 14 to 1.[25]

The 5th Guards Tank Army, scheduled to conduct the deep attack after the breakthrough had been achieved, consisted of three tank corps - the 18th, 20th, and 29th. Each corps consisted of two or three tank and mechanized infantry brigades, giving the army a total strength of 197 tanks.[26] Although at only 50 percent strength, the tank army still possessed considerable offensive striking capability. Its tank corps were equipped primarily with T-34/85 medium tanks, though the Soviets possessed a number of assault guns as well, such as the SU-85 and SU-76 models. In addition, a few of the new Joseph Stalin II super-heavy tanks, armed with the 12.2 cm main gun, would also make their battlefield debut.

Once the tank army had reached Zvenigorodka, it would then face south, where it would block anticipated German relief attempts from the Novy-Mirgorod area. The 4th Guards Army and Koroteyev's 52nd Army would follow the tank army and build the inner encirclement ring. They would be aided by Selivanov's 5th Cavalry Corps, which would exploit its speed and maneuverability to break up and splinter the German pocket piecemeal, hastening its destruction. 53rd Army in the south would protect the left flank of the tank army as it advanced and reinforced the outer ring.[27] All of the armies scheduled to conduct the operation received attachments of troops, tanks, and artillery from other armies of the Second

Ukrainian *Front* to increase their combat power.[28]

The First Ukrainian *Front*, attacking one day after Konev's on 26 January, would attack using Zhmachenko's 40th and Trofimenko's 27th Armies from the area of Tinovka. Unlike Konev's *Front*, which used infantry armies to achieve the penetration, Vatutin would place his operational reserve, Kravchenko's 6th Tank Army, in the front lines, intermingled with units of his infantry armies. Vatutin was forced to do this because his overall combat power was low, due in part to the losses his *Front* had suffered during the previous two weeks.[29] Even as the Soviet offensive was taking place, other elements of First Ukrainian *Front*, such as 38th Army and 2nd Tank Army would be heavily engaged in the Vinnitsa region, forcing Vatutin from time to time to direct his attention to his far right flank.[30]

Despite this distraction, Vatutin would still be able to amass sufficient combat power to achieve favorable force ratios in the breakthrough sector, but not nearly as much as Konev had in his. Once the German defenses had been breached in the Tinovka area, the 6th Tank Army would drive to Zvenigorodka. The tank army's right flank would be guarded by the 40th Army. Both armies would form the outer encircling ring oriented towards the southwest, where a relief attempt would be expected from the Uman area. 27th Army, on the left, would form the internal ring, seeking to push the defenders out of Boguslav and away from the Ross River.[31] Much would hinge on the ability of 6th Tank Army to maintain the outer ring of encirclement.

Kravchenko's 6th Tank Army, though impressive on paper, had only been in existence for five days. Organized on 21 January 1944, the army consisted of only two corps - 5th Guards Tank Corps and 5th Mechanized Corps - one corps short of what was authorized. It was not even provided a headquarters staff or support organizations. General Kravchenko, who had been the commander of the tank corps, was named army commander, and thus was "dual hatted," since he still had to control his old 5th Guards Tank Corps. The shortage of infantry was partially made up by the attachment of 27th Army's 47th Rifle Corps, as well as by the forcible impressment of untrained "booty Ukrainians."[32] Still, Vatutin retained a marked advantage over the German defenders.[33]

Upon first inspection, the area chosen for this large-scale operation did not appear to be conducive for tank operations. The terrain of the Kanev-Zvenigorodka-Cherkassy area on the right or west bank of the Dnieper river was hilly, with considerable swampy and forested areas. The terrain was strongly cut with *balki* (gorges) and streams which aided the defense. These topographical features created numerous commanding heights, which provided excellent observation and fields of fire for five to ten kilometers when weather permitted.[34] The rather broken terrain and lack of improved roads posed numerous challenges for the attackers, who would rely on armored and mechanized units to create the encirclement.

In addition to the hilly terrain, numerous small rivers flowed within the region, most of which flowed from the west to the east, to empty into the Dnieper. The most significant of these were the Ross River, in the northern part of the salient, the Olshanka River, at the east of the salient, and the Gniloy Tikich,

which flowed from north to south, before it angled back towards the Dnieper, at the southern boundary of what was to become the German pocket. During the winter, all of these rivers would be sixty to one hundred meters wide, 0.6 to 2 meters deep, and swiftly flowing.[35] If defended, these rivers would prove major obstacles to offensive action. These rivers would prove to be a double-edged sword. Not only could they slow a Red Army attack if bridges were not seized intact, but could also be used as obstacles to block the anticipated German relief attempt.

The entire area was predominately farmland, dominated by collective farms with wide-open fields where wheat and sunflowers were grown during the summer. Most streams and rivers were bordered by dense shrubbery. The few forest were normally located on hilltops. Most roads were mere farm tracks which disappeared during the winter when they were covered by snow. The only roadway which could be considered "all weather" were the two rail lines which crisscrossed the area.[36] The region was also densely populated, presenting a rich bounty of potential recruits to fill the gaps in the ranks of the advancing Red Army. Numerous villages were scattered throughout the entire area, and their inhabitants were constantly utilized to clear or repair roadways by both sides.

The roadways deteriorated rapidly in winter due to the weather conditions at this time of year in the Ukraine. It was not uncommon for the region to receive several feet of snow each winter, followed by a rapid thaw which turned the roads into an endless morass, known as the *rasputitsa*. Temperatures could hover below freezing for months; overnight, a thaw could set in and reduce a frozen yet passable road into a quagmire, severely restricting movement by armor. Only the *panje* wagon with its sturdy little horses or tracked vehicles could get through. What made winter in the Ukraine during the beginning of 1944 so unusual was that the spring thaw would begin nearly two months early, catching both Germans and Soviets by surprise. Still, when Zhukov, Konev, and Vatutin drafted their plan, weather and trafficability was not considered to pose a serious problem for the upcoming operation. Weather forecasts predicted that the weather would be clear and temperatures below freezing, with periodic snow storms during late January and early February.[37] With both numbers and terrain seemingly in their favor, the Soviets wanted to obtain added insurance by crafting an intricate and tightly orchestrated deception plan which would fool the Germans into thinking that the attack would come elsewhere.

In order for the operation to succeed, the Soviets felt that Army Group South had to be deceived about the time and place of the attack. Von Manstein could not be allowed to have the time or the opportunity to switch his powerful mobile units from his flanks to relieve his encircled units in the pocket. This was absolutely vital to the Soviet plan, since the Red Army did not have an appreciable number of armored units in *STAVKA* reserve during this period of the war, so great had the loss in tanks during the operations to clear the right bank of the Dnieper from October 1943 to January 1944.[38] If von Manstein was able to quickly move one or more panzer corps to the threatened area, he would be able to inflict wholesale punishment upon Vatutin's and Konev's forces. Despite the heavy fighting that had raged throughout the Ukraine, Army Group South still mustered 18 of the 25 panzer or mechanized divisions then operating on the entire Soviet-German front, an impressive force to be reckoned with, even though most of these divisions could muster barely 50 tanks each.[39]

To achieve this aim, Konev implemented a massive deception plan for his *Front* designed to prevent German armor from relieving their soon-to-be encircled comrades. It consisted of two components. The first involved the use of diversionary attacks in the area south of Kirovograd. The other would use classic *maskirovka* procedures to make German military intelligence analysts believe that the Second Ukrainian *Front's* main effort would be elsewhere.

Maskirovka, or operational deception, involves the use of a variety of measures designed to conceal the true location of the Red Army's forces, as well as means to simulate the presence of forces elsewhere, thus misleading the enemy as to the actual location and size of the attacking forces. Ideally, *maskirovka* would also lead to gaining complete surprise over the enemy, thus dealing him an important psychological blow.[40] To achieve this, Konev's Front created dummy radio nets, false troop concentrations using mannequins and loudspeakers, dummy tanks and artillery firing positions and field fortification. The bulk of these were located to the southwest of Kirovograd, immediately in front of the *8.Armee's XXXXVII.Pz.Korps*.[41] To the uninitiated observer, it appeared as if Konev's operational reserve, 5th Guards Tank Army, was preparing a major attack from Kirovograd towards Uman in the west.

Meanwhile, the real 5th Guards Tank Army was shifted 19-23 January from the Kirovograd area nearly 100 kilometers north to its assembly area for the upcoming attack in the Krasnossilka area.[42] Movement was conducted at night under stringent radio silence. Units moved into camouflaged assembly areas and remained hidden until the start of the operation.[43] To prevent German aerial reconnaissance from detecting the move, the Red Air Force carried out aggressive counter-reconnaissance missions throughout Konev's sector.

To further tie down Wöhler's mobile forces, Konev ordered his 7th Guards and 5th Guards Armies (both infantry formations) to carry out feints against German defenses in the Kirovograd region on the 23 January.[44] Konev's intent was that Wöhler would commit his available armor, as well as any other units von Manstein might bring up, to this attack, tying them down and denying them the flexibility to react when the real offensive began farther to the north. This, combined with surprise, was judged by Konev to be sufficient to carry out his part of the operation.[45] But what about Vatutin's deception plan?

Vatutin's *Front*, from the sources available, does not seem to have used *maskirovka* in the design of its operational plan at all. Apparently, Vatutin did not have as great a need to mount a deception plan, since his forces were still conducting operations near Vinnitsa, in contrast to Konev, whose forces had halted 15 January after liberating Kirovograd and were in static positions. Vatutin had two armies - 2nd and 3rd Tank - that were engaged in bitter fighting with *1.Pz.Armee's III.* and *XXXXVI.Pz.Korps*, over 150 kilometers to the west from where he would initiate his part of the Korsun-Shevchenkovsky Operation. The evidence

indicates that Vatutin hoped that Hube's eyes would be looking to the west, rather to the east where the main blow would fall against Lieb's and Stemmerman's corps.[46]

Another facet of Vatutin's plan was that his creation of a new tank army, the 6th, in an area not expected by the Germans, had the same effect as a deception plan, even though it was not intended. The appearance of this army would surprise the Germans, since they believed that all available Soviet tank armies of Vatutin's Front were committed far to the west, as well as the bulk of *1.Pz.Armee's* armor. Vatutin knew that Lieb's corps had no armor to speak of and would be relatively helpless to stop him. Besides, Vatutin's and Konev's *Fronts* would not be the only ones involved in the deception plan.

To further confound the Germans, *STAVKA* ordered General of the Army Rodion Malinovskiy's Third Ukrainian Front to launch a limited offensive in the vicinity of Krivoi Rog. This operation, scheduled to begin 31 January, would hit the boundary of the German 8. and 6.Armee. The regroupment of forces necessary to launch the operation would contribute further to the confusion of German military intelligence.[47] Thus, the intent of the overall deception plan would be to make the Germans look to the far south and western portions of their Ukrainian defenses, instead of the center where the encirclement operation would actually take place. But was the deception plan, the use of operational *maskirovka*, successful?

The deception plan, for all the effort that went into it, did not work. Ironically, German military intelligence analysts saw the coming attack from the direction where *maskirovka* had been most heavily employed in Konev's sector and had begun to shift reserves before the blow fell. Vatutin's attack on the other hand, using his 6th Tank Army in the first echelon of the breakthrough formations, was to prove an almost total surprise, though he used hardly any deception measures to speak of. Despite this initial success, Vatutin's units were to suffer the most from the failure of the planned diversionary attacks. What accounted for this less than successful outcome?

Although Army Group South did not know the time and place of the impending Soviet attack, its intelligence analysts had deduced that a large operation against their exposed forces in the Kanev salient would probably take place sooner rather than later. Indeed, von Manstein and his subordinate commanders had requested repeatedly to *OKH* (and by extension, Hitler) that their forces be withdrawn immediately, but to no avail.[48] They knew from bitter experience that the salient was a lucrative target that the Red Army would not pass up. The question was when would they attack.

This belief was buttressed by a general assessment prepared by *Fremde Heere Ost*, the German intelligence agency for the Eastern Front. On 15 January 1944, it stated that the Red Army's main effort for the remainder of the season would be Army Group South. The Red Army's goal would be pushing towards the Black Sea and the Rumanian border, encircling and destroying German units isolated farther to the east.[49] On the heels of this assessment was another one carried out by 8. Armee on 21 January, four days prior to the beginning of the Soviet offensive.

This assessment stated that *8.Armee* should expect a fresh Russian offensive designed to envelop and encircle the troops deployed in the Kanev Salient. It went on to predict that the attack would probably be directed in the Zvenigorodka-Uman area, remarkably similar to the actual Soviet intentions. German sources state that although this estimate was correct in general terms, it was not as specific as the commanders required.[50] A shortage of signal intelligence capabilities, aerial reconnaissance aircraft, and human intelligence would continue to deny Army Group South the specific details regarding Red Army capabilities and intentions at the operational level. However, at the tactical level, units were making preparations to defend against the coming attack

At 1930 hours, 20 January 1944, *8.Armee* signal intelligence discovered the presence of a tank army in the Krasnossilka area. The following day, it was confirmed that this was 5th Guards Tank Army, which had indeed moved north from the Kirovograd area. Due to inadequately supervised radio silence, the movement of Rotmistrov's Army had been detected.[51] Radio reconnaissance had also detected signs indicating the installation of dummy tank concentrations west of Kirovograd. The intelligence estimate for *8.Armee* that day concluded:

> In the Kirovograd region we noticed today a shifting of the main attack north to the area east of Novo-Mirgorod. Therefore, in a resumption of offensive operations here we would expect first of all to see an introduction into operations of strong units for a penetration to Novo-Mirgorod . . . the staff of 5th Guards Tank Army and sapper units are displacing northward . . . mine removal is occurring in the central sector of XXXXVII.Pz.Korps and on the internal flanks of the panzer corps and XI.A.K.[52]

Hube's *1.Pz.Armee* intelligence section was also busy. On 23 January 1944, it had detected Soviet offensive preparations on the internal flanks of *XXXXII.* and *VII.A.K.* near Tinovka. These took the form of local Red Army attacks to seize favorable jumping-off positions for a large scale attack. Patrols had detected movement of additional elements of the First Ukrainian *Front* into assembly areas close to the front lines.[53] *1. Pz.Armee's VII.A.K.* also had its hands full eliminating a division-sized Soviet force encircled two weeks previously in its rear area. Whether this buildup was designed to rescue these units or was part of a much larger plan could not be determined. However, deserters from the 5th Guard Tank Corps and 5th Mechanized Corps were picked up the same day. The significance of their presence was apparently missed. Kravchenko's 6th Tank Army remained undetected.

From 21-24 January, both German armies detected increasing Red Army activity indicating further offensive preparations. Tanks were seen moving up in greater numbers, along with the first sightings of multiple rocket launchers, a sure sign of offensive preparations. *8.Armee* issued warning orders to its *11.* and *14.Pz.Div.* to prepare to displace north to counter any Soviet move to break through from the Kapitanovka area.[54] *1. Pz.Armee*, concerned with its two-corps counterattack east

of Vinnitsa, sent only a tank destruction detachment (infantry with hand-held weapons) to *VII.A.K.* opposite Tinovka.[55] *XXXXVII.Pz.Korps'* commander, General von Vormann, did not await the upcoming attack passively. On 24 January, the same day Konev launched his reconnaissance in force a few kilometers to the north, he had General Fritz Bayerlein's *3.Pz.Div.* carry out a spoiling attack in combination with *Luftwaffe* reconnaissance aircraft. Bayerlein's tanks during the evening destroyed a large enemy assembly area of troops and vehicles west of Krasnossilka.[56] Without a doubt, the Germans had solid evidence that Konev was preparing to conduct an attack within the next two or three days. Von Vormann ordered his corps on full alert.

To Konev's surprise, when he launched his reconnaissance in force on 24 January, he found the German defenders fully prepared and awaiting the attack. Stemmerman had already begun moving an armored *Kampfgruppe* (battle group) from *Wiking* to reinforce *389.Inf.Div.*, where the main blow would fall. The two panzer divisions previously placed on alert by General Wöhler were already displacing north. A third was pulled out of line west of Kirovograd with orders to move north as soon as possible.[57] Wöhler's Army was reacting quickly to meet the offensive they knew was coming with what seemed adequate countermeasures. The only thing the men of *XI.A.K.* and *XXXXVII.Pz.Korps* did not know was how powerful the impeding Soviet attack would be.

Despite the already described massing of forces, the successful outcome of the Soviet's Korsun-Shevchenkovsky Operation hinged to a large degree on a deception plan which employed both *maskirovka* and diversionary attacks. Neither achieved results to the degree intended. Konev's offensive preparations, despite his elaborate deception plan, were detected by the Germans five days prior to his Front's attack. General Wöhler had begun to move two armored divisions and parts of two others to the threatened area so that they would be present when the operation commenced. Their arrival would have a significant effect on the Second Ukrainian *Front's* timetable.

Vatutin's *Front*, which relied on ongoing operations to the west to divert the *1.Pz.Armee's* attention, used little, if any, *maskirovka* in its operational plan. Due to the employment of the newly-raised 6th Tank Army, Vatutin's *Front* would surprise the defenders, who had expected small-scale attacks. Both Fronts would soon surprise the Germans with the scale of their assaults, because they had thought the Red Army incapable of launching such a large-scale operation so soon after the Zhitomir-Berdichev and Kirovograd Operations.

The diversionary attacks lacked the offensive punch necessary to tie down German armored reserves and confuse the Germans as to the true location of the main attack, especially in the *1.Pz.Armee's* area. The evidence suggests that Army Group South was not overly concerned by these diversionary attacks, thus enabling von Manstein to rapidly shift units to come to the aid of the encircled forces. Third Ukrainian *Front's* attacks at Krivoi Rog and Nikopol, though serious, did not prove to be anything that would keep *6.Armee* under General Hollidt from sending one panzer division to von Manstein's aid. The chief result of the deception plan's failure on the Red Army's Korsun-

Generalmajor Fritz Bayerlein, *Commander, 3.Pz.Div. at beginning of battle, seen here in Afrikakorps uniform.* *(Bundesarchiv 75/25/25)*

Shevchenkovsky Operation was that the operation would last three times longer than its planners had anticipated and would require far more hard fighting than desired to achieve the goal of encircling and cutting the Germans off from their supplies and annihilating them.

Logistics, too, would play an important role in the upcoming operation. The short preparation period gave Vatutin's and Konev's staffs little time to devote their attention to this most important aspect of Red Army offensive operations. Mother nature also hampered preparations. Konev, in his report of the operation, described the weather and terrain as being "exceptionally unfavorable" for conducting preparations.[58] In his words, sudden thaws and muddy roads "made it difficult to move troops and supply them with fuel and ammunition." Zhukov, as STAVKA representative for the operation, stated that the Fronts were unable to fully build up material reserves (troop strength, combat vehicles, fuel, ammunition, and food) needed to conduct the operation in the manner they were accustomed. However, due to the perceived nature of the German threat, he believed that the operation could not be delayed any further.[59]

According to the Soviet after-action study of the operation, all troop movements and logistical preparations were carried out on time, despite the pressure to adhere to the timetable.[60] This feat deserves recognition, in that Konev's and Vatutin's *Fronts* were able to carry out this tremendous task in

less than half the time than usual. This contributed to the German surprise when the operation commenced. Although the Germans had expected the operation and had predicted its location, they could not believe that the Red Army could recover so quickly from the two operations mentioned previously.

Great effort was expended in making the forces ready. Both Konev and Zhukov mentioned that preparations continued night and day under conditions of great secrecy. Regrouping of assault units continued up to the day the operation commenced. Reconnaissance of German positions was conducted continuously, with the aim of identifying which units lay on the opposite side of the battle front. Patrols penetrated the German lines to gather intelligence and take prisoners, which further helped flesh out the enemy order of battle. This technique, of course, partially explains how the Soviets believed so many German divisions were in the salient. As mentioned previously, some of these reconnaissance efforts were poorly conducted. In the Second Ukrainian *Front* sector, Konev had to postpone his assault by one day, so he could launch a reconnaissance in force along his front to determine exactly where the German defenses were. This, in fact, did occur and succeeded. Although the Germans were forewarned, Konev had sufficient time to shift forces to reflect the new information.[61]

Red Army engineers and sappers were also busy in the days and weeks leading up to the operation. In terrible winter conditions, Red Army troops laid 135 kilometers of lateral roads in the Second Ukrainian Front area alone. Mine clearing efforts continued apace up to the point the assault units began their attack. The after-operations study states than 20,000 mines were cleared in front of the 4th Guards and 53rd Armies.[62] Engineers were also busy erecting dummy frontline positions, part of the *maskirovka* plan. In addition, they repaired 475 kilometers of roads, repaired or reinforced 24 bridges and cleared 180 passages in German wire obstacles, usually under fire.[63]

Thus, in record time, the Red Army units slated to prepare for the upcoming operation had conducted a thorough, if hurried preparation phase. As the war progressed, it was able to match this record of preparation time repeatedly, much to the consternation of the Germans, who had taken slow and deliberate Soviet preparations as a matter of course. The speed with which this task was accomplished impressed and amazed them.

Due to a number of factors, the Soviet's planned Korsun-Shevchenkovsky Operation had every chance of achieving success. The relatively simple concept of operations, utilizing tank armies to conduct deep attacks to achieve the encirclement, allowed the *Front* commanders to concentrate enormous combat power at two selected points to ensure that the encirclement could be achieved quickly and the entrapped Germans wiped out. It included an intricate deception plan that utilized both *maskirovka* and diversionary attacks. Preparations, though hastily executed, were adequate.

The Red Army possessed other advantages for this operation as well. It enjoyed an overall superiority in numbers of tanks, guns and troops. Knowledge of German order of battle and terrain were complete (in fact, in the case of the number of defenders, they had greatly overestimated German strength). The Red Army also held the initiative and could dictate both the time and the place of the attack. The Germans, tied down to an overextended front line, could only await the overpowering attack that they knew would come sooner or later. The Germans were extremely vulnerable in the Kanev salient due to Hitler's stand-fast decree which prevented a timely withdrawal, an exposed salient inviting a double envelopment, thinly held flanks, and overall exhaustion and weakened condition of German units. *XXXXII.A.K.* had no tanks or assault guns at all. Von Manstein's armored forces were busy elsewhere. The eyes of Hitler and his high command were so directed towards the Anzio beachhead in Italy and the fighting around Leningrad that little attention was paid to what was about to occur along the Dnieper.

The Germans, however, did possess some advantages that would threaten the successful completion of the Soviet operation. These were Manstein's willingness to disobey Hitler, still-superior German tactical ability (especially at the division level and below), and their ability to rapidly switch units from one part of the front to another. Soviet underestimation of still-powerful German capabilities would markedly affect the operation as it developed, much to the Red Army's surprise. The German's detection of the actual movement of Konev's 5th Guards Tank Army and *8.Armee's* discovery of the deception plan five days prior to the offensive gained enough time to begin moving the few armored formations out of the line elsewhere to ward off the upcoming attack. Certainly, the Red Army would not find this operation to be an easy one.

The Red Army, in the lead-up to this operation, made several mistakes that would be to their disadvantage later. Their ambitious deception plan, though doctrinally sound, was hastily implemented. Troops were poorly trained or disciplined to practice proper radio listening silence, thus tipping off the Germans as to the location of the attack. The Red Army, perhaps due to Stalin's urgings, was eagerly seeking a repeat of their victory at Stalingrad by totally annihilating a large grouping of German forces. They lacked sufficient infantry and armor to simultaneously reduce the pocket and ward off relief attacks. Their reliance on artillery would receive a blow when insufficient ammunition could be brought forward due to the mud. The Red Air Force would prove that it was not yet capable of close cooperation with ground forces. The Soviet command structure left no one in overall command at the scene of the operation. Zhukov, though serving as the *STAVKA* coordinator, could allocate reinforcements and advise the *Front* commanders, but could not direct their actions.

One puzzling aspect of the operational plan was that it directed no action beyond the immediate annihilation or *unichtozhenie* of the encircled forces. The initial deep attacks that would encircle the German salient would not be followed up by subsequent deep attacks to continue pushing the German front line further back. This concentration on total destruction of the enemy, at the expense of greater gains, was a persistent feature of Bolshevist-influenced Red Army doctrine. It not only demanded destruction of the German forces in the pocket, but the death or captivity of every one of its defenders; *do kontsa* (to the very end).[64] Their single-minded dedication to this goal may have caused the Red Army commanders to overlook the

greater gains that were possible had they sent their armored spearheads deeper where there were no defenses. All that lay beyond Zvenigorodka were postal and supply units and 200 kilometers of empty space stretching to the Black Sea.

Thus, the stage was set not for a neat, clean, and decisive operation concluded in a week's time, but rather one that was drawn out and costly to both sides. The plan drafted by Zhukov and the *STAVKA* and the *Front* commanders utilized several operational concepts which, although impressive on paper, would reveal weaknesses that would materialize when put to the test of battle. The use of the tank armies to conduct deep strikes was well planned, but 6th Tank Army was a new, untested headquarters. The deception plan and use of diversionary attacks would prove to be beyond the capability of the Red Army to execute at this stage. Artillery, which was becoming increasingly critical for smashing German tactical defenses in lieu of infantry, would not be able to keep up with the advancing tank spearheads. Soviet military intelligence would prove to be far too conservative in its analysis of the German order of battle and too limited in its assessment of German capabilities.

All of these elements of the Soviet operation would show the need for greater synchronization during the planning stages and better command and control during the conduct of operations. This plan, which required rapid and violent maneuver, combined with an effective deception operation, evolved into a slugfest where both sides fought to exhaustion with neither totally achieving their stated objectives, as the following chapter will describe.

End Notes

[1] Erich Kern, *Dance of Death* (New York: Collins, 1951), p. 111.

[2] Glantz, "From the Dnieper to the Vistula," p. 133.

[3] *Sbornik*, p. 299.

[4] Ibid., p. 300.

[5] Ibid.

[6] Zhukov, p. 238.

[7] von Vormann, p. 66.

[8] Ibid.

[9] Earl F. Ziemke and Magna E. Bauer, *Moscow to Stalingrad: Decision in the East* (Washington, D.C.: U.S. Army Center of Military History, 1987) p. 282.

[10] Ziemke, *Stalingrad to Berlin*, pp. 94-97.

[11] Ibid., pp. 65-66.

[12] "Documents on Korsun-Shevchenkovsky Given," Voyenno Istoricheskiy Zhurnal, No.2 (February 1984), (Moscow: Voyenno-Istorichesky Zhurnal, 1984), pp. 35.

[13] Ibid., p. 36.

[14] Ibid.

[15] Glantz, "From the Dnieper to the Vistula," p. 124.

[16] Ibid., pp. 127-128.

[17] Ibid., p. 140.

[18] Ibid., p. 136.

[19] Zhukov, p. 239.

[20] Sergei Sokolov, *Battles Hitler Lost* (New York: Jove Books, 1988), p. 114.

[21] *Sbornik*, p. 307.

[22] Ibid., pp. 302-303

[23] Ibid., p. 303.

[24] Ibid., p. 303.

[25] Ibid., p. 303.

[26] Glantz, "From the Dnieper to the Vistula," p. 128.

[27] *Sbornik*, pp. 303-304.

[28] Ibid., pp. 306-307.

[29] Glantz, "From the Dnieper to the Vistula," pp. 134-135.

[30] David Glantz, *Soviet Military Deception in the Second World War* (London: Frank Cass and Company, LTD, 1989), pp. 311-312.

[31] *Sbornik*, pp. 304-305.

[32] Ibid., p. 305.

[33] Glantz, *Soviet Military Deception*, p. 314.

[34] *Sbornik*, p. 301.

[35] Ibid.

[36] Ibid., p. 302.

[37] Ibid.

[38] Glantz, "From the Dnieper to the Vistula," pp. 124-125.

[39] Sokolov, p. 112.

[40] Glantz, *Soviet Military Deception*, p. 315.

[41] *Sbornik*, p. 308.

[42] Ibid., p. 306.

[43] Ibid., p. 307.

[44] Glantz, *Soviet Military Deception*, p. 315.

[45] Sokolov, p. 114.

[46] Glantz, *Soviet Military Deception*, pp. 311-312.

[47] Ibid., p. 311.

[48] von Vormann, p. 56.

[49] Glantz, "From the Dnieper to the Vistula," p. 179.

[50] Ibid., pp. 179-180.

[51] *8.Armee Kriegstagebuch* (KTB) entries from 20-21 January 1944.

[52] Glantz, *Soviet Military Deception*, pp. 319-322.

[53] *1.Pz.Armee* KTB, entry dated 23 January 1944, p. 2.

[54] *8.Armee* KTB, entry dated 23 January 1944.

[55] *1.Pz.Armee* KTB, entry dated 23 January 1944.

[56] von Vormann, p. 58.

[57] *8.Armee* KTB, entry dated 24 January 1944.

[58] Sokolov, p. 113.

[59] Zhukov, p. 239.

[60] *Sbornik*, p. 305.

[61] Ibid., p. 307.

[62] Ibid., pp. 309-310.

[63] Ibid., p. 310.

[64] Raymond Garthoff, *Soviet Military Doctrine* (Glencoe, IL: The RAND Corporation, 1953), 150, 155.

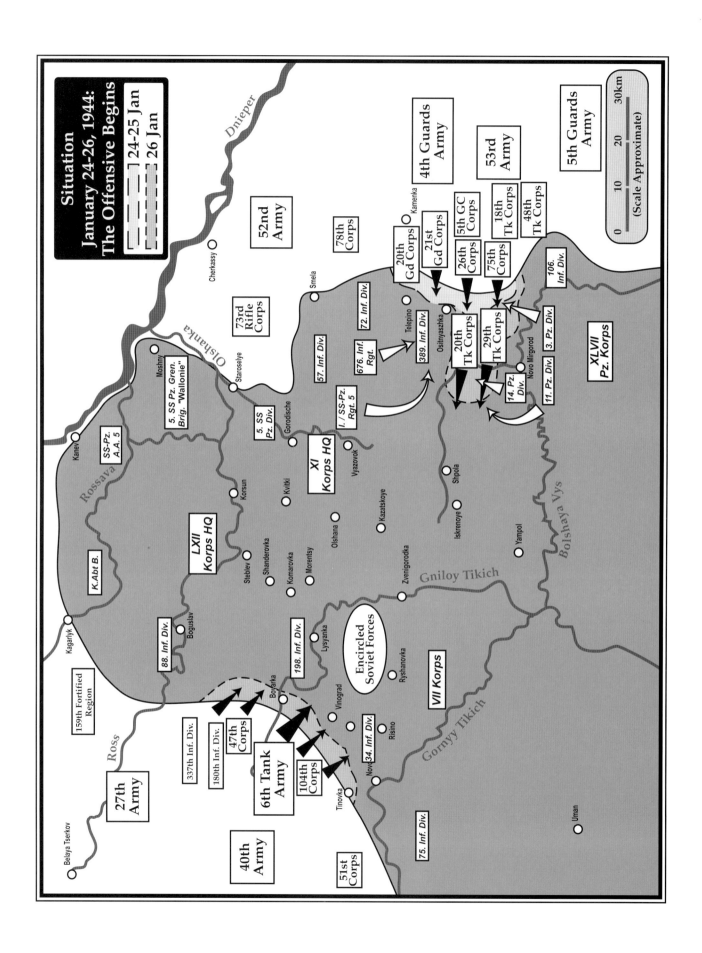

THE RUSSIAN STEAMROLLER

Chapter Four

THE HAMMER FALLS - KONEV ATTACKS

"If the end should come one day…it should really be the field marshals and generals who stand by the flags to the last."
— *Adolf Hitler, quoted by Erich von Manstein.* [1]

As described in the previous chapter, Zhukov and the commanders of the First and Second Ukrainian *Fronts* planned to conduct their Korsun-Shevchenkovksy Operation in three distinct phases. The first phase, the creation of the breakthrough, was to begin on 25 January 1944, when Konev's *Front* attacked in the east. The following day, Vatutin's *Front* would begin its attack in the west. The second phase was the actual encirclement operation itself, which was accomplished by the deep attacks launched by the two tank armies on 28 January 1944, though an unbroken line of encirclement would not be formed until 4 February. The third phase, the destruction or *unichtozhenie* of the encircled German forces, would take until 20 February.

The failure of operational *maskirovka* and the diversionary attacks would complicate the execution of the operation. As will be seen, although the initial phases would go according to plan, the German's refusal to conform to Soviet expectations would force the Red Army to redeem the operation by combat. In addition, as the operation unfolded, key combat support elements, such as artillery and close air support, would not keep pace with the movements of the tank armies. Without their accustomed numerical advantage and fire support, the Soviet commanders would be forced to confront the Germans on nearly even terms, where German tactical superiority was still telling. The coordination between the infantry, artillery, and armored forces would further contribute to Soviet difficulties, though in the end the situation would be for the most part redeemed by the versatility and flexibility of the *STAVKA* coordinator and the *Front* commanders.

As each phase of the battle unfolded, the Soviet commanders would be confronted by numerous efforts by the trapped Germans to break out of the encirclement or efforts to effect their relief from the outside. These efforts to relieve the German forces in fact constituted a separate and distinct phase which the Soviet commanders had to contend with, occurring simultaneously with the phase dedicated to the destruction of the encircled forces. At times, the Germans came within a hair's breadth of not only escaping with all their forces intact, but accomplishing the encirclement and destruction of the Red Army forces carrying out the operation. Thus, despite Zhukov's, Konev's and Vatutin's belief that the battle would result in a quick, easy victory, the outcome was neither.

Throughout the days leading up to the start of the battle, troops, tanks, guns, and horse cavalry of the Red Army continued to pour into their assembly areas. Rifles and machine-guns were cleaned and oiled, tanks were given one last going-over by anxious crews, and gunners checked their pre-arranged targets

Leader of Gruppe Stemmermann's sole tank force, **SS-Sturmbannführer Hans Köller***, (first from left). Commander, 1Abt., SS-Pz.Rgt.5 "Wiking" during award ceremony near Kharkov, August 1943. (Jarolin-Bundesarchiv 81/16/17A)*

once more. Commanders carried out last-minutes inspections of their attack sectors. Soviet reconnaissance patrols set out each day in hopes of locating German defensive positions for destruction or of capturing a German for interrogation. All the while, aggressive Red Air Force patrols scoured the air, doing their best to keep German reconnaissance aircraft from discovering true Soviet intentions. However, what seemed to the Germans to be a prelude to the attack took place on 24 January, effectively confirming General Wöhler's expectations.

Since the attack date for Konev's *Front* was postponed from 24 January to the following day due to the poor reconnaissance of the forward edge of the German defenses, his troops received another day of breathing space to prepare; that is, everyone except the units detailed to go back again and find out where the German front line actually was. They also had to find out where the German covering force was - that is, the thin screen line posted well forward of the main line of defense in order to provide early warning of a Soviet attack and to delay it until the main defensive positions could be alerted. This lack of solid information on the actual whereabouts of the Germans, particularly the positions of *389.Inf.Div.*, led to major fighting when the commanders of 4th Guards and 53rd Armies were ordered by their *Front* headquarters to go back again and do it right.[2]

Monday, 24 January began with cold, clear skies. The reinforced Soviet infantry battalions chosen to perform the reconnaissance task moved out at in the early morning hours to see whether what was out in front of them were genuine forward defensive positions for *Winterfritz* (Russian slang for the stereotyped poorly clothed and freezing German soldier) or the covering force. These battalions, reinforced with one horse-drawn 7.62 cm cannon, two or three tanks, and other supporting forces such as engineers, moved forward as silently as possible and surprised the German outposts. Quickly taking advantage of the opportunity, as many as 16 of these battalions pressed forward and penetrated the forward edge of the enemy's defenses between the villages of Verbovka and Vasilivka, forcing units of General Kruse's *389.Inf.Div.* to withdraw to their intermediate positions. By the close of the day, several Soviet battalions had managed to penetrate the German front line from four to six kilometers and capture Verbovka, causing a great deal of consternation at *8.Armee*.[3]

Wöhler's army headquarters began to suspect something was afoot when it received radio reports from *XI.A.K.* at 0730 hours that same day describing limited Soviet attacks and a penetration of unknown size near the villages of Burtki and Balandino. An hour later, the situation had clarified sufficiently to cause Stemmermann at *XI.A.K.* headquarters concern, especially the attack near Burtki, which was directed along the seam of his boundary with von Vormann's neighboring *XXXXVII.Pz.Korps*. Although Stemmermann thought that this minor Soviet gain was not the actual awaited main attack, he did believe that it was launched by the Soviets with the intention of clarifying the situation and seizing more advantageous jump-off positions for the subsequent attack. Not taking any chances, the *XI.A.K.* commander ordered *SS-Stubaf.* Hans Köller's armored *Kampfgruppe* of the *Wiking*, composed of the tank battalion, a *Panzergrenadier* battalion, and the self-propelled artillery battalion, to be move to the threatened sector and prepare to counterattack to retake Burtki, if need be.[4] Fortunately, Stemmermann had ordered the armored battlegroup two days previously to expect such a mission, so it was able to move out quickly.

To the south, Vormann's corps reported to *8.Armee* that there was enemy reconnaissance activity along his entire front, with small attacks being launched along his right flank against *3.SS-Pz.Div. Totenkopf*, which were easily repulsed. In addition, his corps was being subjected to harassment and interdiction fire from Soviet artillery, though nothing that caused him any great concern. To break up apparent Soviet assembly areas forming in front of the boundary between his and Stemmerman's corps, von Vormann ordered his artillery to conduct *Feuerüberfälle* (ambushes by fire), with good results. Later that morning, a *Stuka* attack was successfully launched against Soviet forces assembling near Balandino, which had been seized by troops of 21st Guards Rifle Corps. By 1100 hours, Army Group South's Chief of Staff, *Gen.Lt.* Theodor Busse, radioed Wöhler and asked what was going on. Wöhler informed him that the Soviets were probably trying to clear minefields and wire obstacles, as well as gain favorable attack positions, in order to launch the main assault the following day. Wöhler was to be proven correct.[5] In addition, Wöhler told Army Group South that he predicted that the main effort would come from the Krassnossilka area, along the boundary of the two corps in question.

I./Gren.Rgt.545, the sole reserve force possessed by *389.Inf.Div.*, was committed by General Kruse at 1430 hours, along with several assault guns from *StuG.Abt.228*, to retake some trenchlines on the hilltop near the village of Kochanivka, which an estimated 300 Soviet troops had occupied after killing or driving off the German outposts. By 1650 hours, the armored *Kampfgruppe* from *Wiking* had arrived and quickly retook Burtki from the north. Most disturbing to Stemmermann was the report that the German tanks had bagged seven Soviet tanks, where none had previously been reported, and had received scattered fire from multiple rocket launchers, somewhere to the east. If this was a Soviet reconnaissance in force, what would the real attack be like? And if the dreaded *Katyushas* were being employed, were they in the path of the main attacking force? Worst of all was the realization by Stemmermann that at this early juncture, he had already committed all of his available reserves - and the main attack had not even come yet.[6] Additionally, the situation south of Burtki was unclear. *XI.A.K.*'s Chief of Staff, *Oberst* Heinz Gädke, suspected that several battalions of Soviet troops had occupied positions on the wooded hilltops south of the village.

Oberst i.G. Gädke, *Chief of Staff, XI.Armeekorps (shown here as a Generalmajor). (Photo courtesy of Andreas Schwarz and 88.Inf.Div. Veterans Association)*

The Soviet probing attacks continued for the rest of the day and into the night. Despite the troops' best efforts, the battalions of the Hessian *389.Inf.Div.* were being slowly overwhelmed or ejected from their forward positions. Early that evening, Stemmermann radioed *8.Armee* that his intelligence section had identified elements of three Soviet divisions in the contested area - 6th Rifle and 31st and 69th Guards Rifle Divisions. It got worse as the night went on. Stemmermann reported that the situation was now "a pure question of numerical strength" and that the *Grabenstärke* (foxhole strength) of the units involved were rapidly eroding. As a precaution, Stemmermann ordered the one battalion of *Gren.Rgt.676*, attached to *57.Inf.Div.* near Smela nearly 50 kilometers to the north, to be pulled out of the line, loaded on trucks and moved to the town of Pastorskoya. There, ten kilometers to the northwest of Burtki, they could be used to reinforce the hard-pressed *389.Inf.Div.* However, they would not arrive in time to prevent Kruse's division from being slowly ground to bits.

The Division's *Füs.Btl.389* (organized as an infantry-heavy reconnaissance unit) was holding steady along the corps boundary which it shared with the neighboring *3.Pz.Div.,* but *Gren.Rgt.546* to its immediate north, though it had fought well, had several of its infantry companies wiped out to the last man in heavy defensive fighting. As the night wore on, more Soviet infantry battalions supported by tanks moved forward to take advantage of the ground gained that day. Stemmermann, appearing frantic, kept contacting *8.Armee* and asking when he could count on the arrival of *14.Pz.Div.* to bolster his sagging right flank. He radioed *8.Armee* at 1900 hours and notified Wöhler that continuation of the enemy attack was to be expected the following day and went on to report that he was lacking infantry, reporting that "I only have 1,500 men to cover 21 kilometers of front!"

After Köller's armored *Kampfgruppe* had retaken Burtki, it moved out to deal with another crisis at the seam of *XI.* and *XXXXVII.Pz.Korps*, where *Füs.Bt.389* had reported that it was in danger of being overwhelmed. After the battlegroup departed, the Soviets counterattacked and threw the meager force from *389.Inf.Div.* out of Burtki and brought up 25 to 30 of its own tanks from 4th Guards Army reserve. Soviet aircraft from 5th Air Army had also appeared by this time. Despite the oncoming darkness, they made matters worse throughout *XI.A.K.*'s sector by attacking ground targets and preventing German reconnaissance aircraft from entering the skies over the battlefield. By that evening, Burtki and the neighboring village of Kochanivka were finally lost for good. The division headquarters of *389.Inf.Div.* had lost contact with *Füs.Btl.389* and the division's front line was only sporadically held by isolated strong points, but at least there had been no deep penetrations.[7]

Stemmerman also requested that *8.Armee* detach *14.Pz.Div.* from von Vormann's corps and place it under his corps' operational control.[8] *8.Armee* duly complied, notifying Stemmermann that the division, under the command of *Gen.Maj.* Martin Unrein, would be attached to his corps at 0300 hours on the 25th, but it would be in transit most of the day. To get to the threatened area of Stemmermann's right flank, General Unrein and his men would have to move out of an assembly area on *XXXXVII.Pz.Korps'* far right flank and move to an attack position near Novo-Mirgorod, requiring a road march of four to five hours.

In comparison to Stemmermann's almost panicky response to the day's developments, *8.Armee* headquarters, and Army Group South as well, appear to have only been mildly concerned. Although a Soviet attack was expected the following day, the commanders and staffs of both army and army group believed that a counterattack by Unrein's *14.Pz.Div.* in concert with other units of *XI.A.K.* could restore the front line within the next several days. After all, there had been no other serious enemy attacks along the corps' front that day, and Stemmermann could still move other units from within his corps if he had to, as he had already begun to do with the regiment from *57.Inf.Div.* Just to be sure, Wöhler directed that *I./Art.Rgt.108*, an independent army artillery battalion, then supporting *Pz.Gren.Div. Grossdeutschland* at the boundary of von Vormann's corps, as well as *11.Pz.Div.*, be moved immediately to come to the aid of Stemmermann's command. With any luck, that ought to do it, at least the staff of *8.Armee* must have thought as they went to bed that evening.

Had they known what was in store the following day, they would not have slept at all. At 0600 hours on Tuesday, 25 January, 4th Guards and 53rd Armies swung into the attack, their infantry divisions having taken full advantage of the forward jump-off positions seized the day before. The Soviet

preparatory artillery barrage ranged along a 40-kilometer sector of *XI.A.K.* which not only engulfed the hasty defensive positions of *389.Inf.Div.*, but also pummeled the positions of its neighboring division to the north, Hermann Hohn's *72.Inf.Div.* Forward German positions reported enemy advance elements approaching the Raygorod-Smela sector, a sure sign of an impending major attack.

To the south, von Vormann's corps reported massive drumfire artillery barrages upon *3.Pz.Div.* positions near Yamki which lasted over half an hour and caused it to lose contact with the right flank of *389.Inf.Div.* At 0800 hours, General von Vormann ordered *3.Pz.Div.*, now temporarily under the command of *Oberst* Lang (General Bayerlein had been ordered back to Germany to form a new division), to attack north to throw back an enemy unit of unknown strength that was advancing towards the west and to restore contact with *389.Inf.Div.* However, the planned attack got off to a slow start when the division had to first protect its own left flank against an enemy attack.[9] Soon, Lang had to worry about becoming encircled himself.

Matters in Kruse's sector had taken a turn for the worse when an early morning Soviet attack from the direction of Burtki scattered the hastily entrenched elements of *Gren.Rgt.546*, creating the first serious gap in the German's defenses. The ground had been too frozen for the men of the *Rheingold* Division to dig foxholes the night before, so they had to do the best they could, which was not enough to protect them from the murderous fire from the Soviet artillery barrage. The

Red Army's 25th and 66th Guards Rifle Divisions and 1st Guards Airborne Divisions surged through the German defenses, though not without loss. Although the German infantry had been overwhelmed in places, their supporting artillery still functioned, and upon the wide-open fields west of Burtki and Balandino, the effect of the shelling on the massed infantry formations was terrible to behold, so dense had the attack formations of the Soviet forces been.

Generalmajor Martin Unrein, *Commander, 14.Pz.Div. (From Bender and Odegard, Uniforms, Organization, and History of the Panzertruppe)*

Before being shot or bayoneted in their fighting positions, the desperate grenadiers of *389.Inf.Div.* also claimed a terrible toll in dead and wounded with their MG-42 machine-guns, mortars, and machine pistols. One Soviet source afterwards stated that this particular division's defenses had been especially hard to overcome; for a Soviet source to mention this must mean that they suffered high losses indeed.[10] Still, the Soviet troops took their losses and kept coming, threatening the remaining German defensive positions centered around the village of Ossitnyashka with 15 tanks and scores of *tankodesantniki*. This village would soon become a focal point of the action in this sector, since it constituted the northern shoulder of the first major Soviet penetration.

Köller's armored battlegroup from *Wiking*, which had pulled back during the evening of 24/25 January to rearm and refuel, was recommitted by *XI.A.K.* shortly after 0800 hours to attack north towards Ossitnyashka, south of which lay nothing but a "gaping hole in the front."[11] To Stemmermann, this was clearly a major crisis which required that his only armored reserve be re-committed to battle immediately. Two hours later, *Wiking's* tanks collided with a Soviet tank formation of between 25-30 tanks, probably the same group that had helped take Burtki the night before. In an engagement at nearly point-blank range, Köller's battalion destroyed 13 T-34s without loss. Six other Soviet tanks, in their haste to disengage, ran afoul of anti-tank mines placed at the southern edge of Ossitnyashka and were also destroyed. Sensing the seriousness of the situation there, Stemmermann ordered Köller to remain in the village to buttress the German defense in that sector. His force was soon to be joined by one battalion from *57.Inf.Div.'s* attached *Gren.Rgt.676* which had arrived by truck the evening before. For the time being, the attacking Soviet guards infantry began to work their way further south, where their attack seemed to be going much more favorably.

With Köller and his tanks elsewhere, the attack along the boundary of the two German corps began to gather steam. At the same time the SS tank crews were shooting up one Soviet armored unit, 15 kilometers further south another unit with 30 T-34s had penetrated as far as the northwest corner of the town of Raymentarovka, directly along a road which constituted the corps' boundary. Although only a control feature on a map, such boundaries often are lucrative objectives for an attack and are sought after, since coordination between neighboring units which report to different higher headquarters can often be poorly or haphazardly carried out. This can make units placed along such boundaries vulnerable to attack, since a neighboring unit may be unsure of how to act or whether it has permission to engage.

This situation was no different. When troops of *3.Pz.Div.* observed the Soviet tanks beginning to move past out of range to the north, it merely reported its observation to corps headquarters; it did not yet have permission to leave its fighting positions and conduct an attack. Besides, weren't *Wiking's* tanks there to take care of such things? To be fair, *3.Pz.Div.* itself was under attack from the east and north, and was pinned down by heavy artillery fire and Soviet ground-attack aircraft. It had enough problems of its own to worry about, such as whether the Soviets were planning to get around its open left flank and attack it from behind as well.

Gen.d.Pz.Tr. Nikolaus von Vormann was also busily engaged. An experienced panzer officer, he was born in Neumark, West Prussia in 1895. An infantryman in 1915, von Vormann had served as a *Leutnant* in *Inf.Rgt.26* during World War One. During service with the *Reichsheer*, he lost his right eye in a training accident involving hand grenades. By 1938, he was serving as the first general staff officer (*1a*) with *X. A.K.* and was appointed the following year to serve as a liaison officer for the *OKH* in the *Führerhauptquartier*. Promoted to *Generalleutnant* on 1 July 1943 while commanding

General der Panzertruppe Nikolaus von Vormann, *Commander, XXXXVII.Pz.Korps, Eighth Army. (Bundesarchiv 84/116/16)*

23.Pz.Div. on the Eastern Front, he had only recently taken command of his panzer corps on 26 December 1943.[12] A military historian by profession, he was a competent and methodical tactician who has left us with one of the finest accounts of the battle from the perspective of *XXXXVII.Pz.Korps.*

But now von Vormann had his hands full. Not only did he have to contend with attacks along his entire front, he had to determine which one was the main effort and which ones were merely supporting attacks or deceptions. Furthermore, Soviet artillery barrages were being reported along the length of his entire front. Although the situation in *3.Pz.Div.* sector worried him, he was more concerned with getting *14.Pz.Div.* from Novo-Mirgorod to the blocking position that he and Stemmermann had picked out west of the town of Kapitanovka. This position offered several advantages, in that the Red armor would have to pass through this town, which clearly lay astride the path of the main Soviet route of advance. It also would be on high ground that was bounded to the east by wide-open fields that would turn this area into a killing ground for Soviet tanks. To von Vormann's way of thinking, and to that of Wöhler, his superior, a blocking force of two panzer divisions (*11.Pz.Div.* was also en route), coupled with a successful holding action at the shoulders of the Soviet penetration, would be sufficient.

While von Vormann was trying to get *14.Pz.Div.* moved into position, Stemmermann was viewing the continued collapse

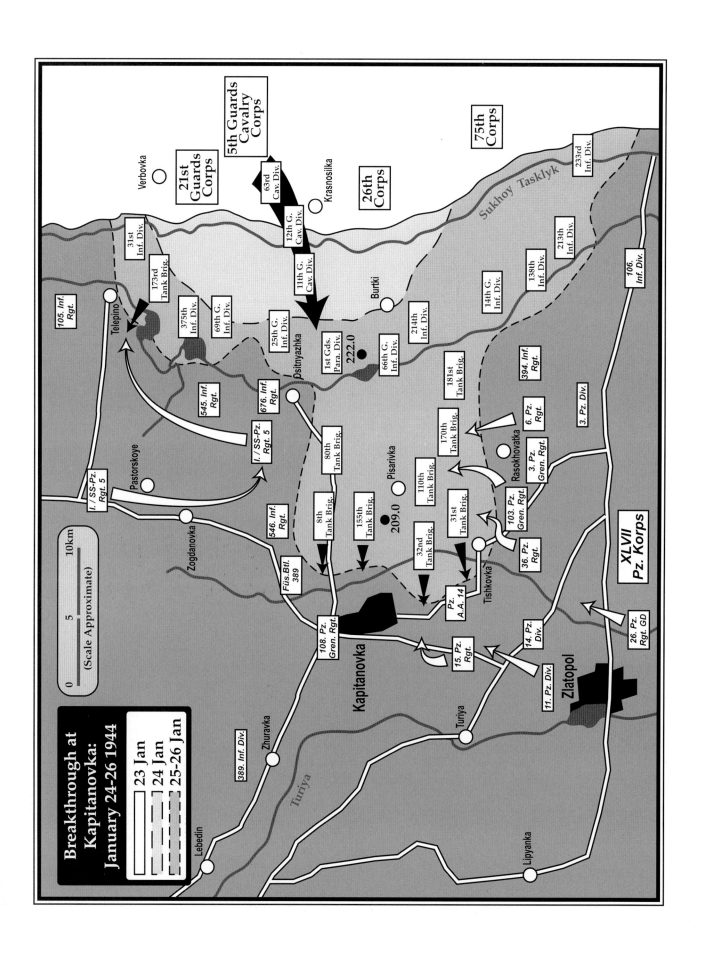

Breakthrough at
Kapitanovka:
January 24-26 1944

23 Jan
24 Jan
25-26 Jan

of *389.Inf.Div.* with alarm; at the rate it was eroding, there would soon be nothing left between the right flank of *72.Inf.Div.* and the left flank of *3.Pz.Div.*, save the *Wiking* battlegroup and the battalion from *Gren.Rgt.676* holding Ossitnyashka. This 21-kilometer gap had to be closed as soon as possible. To carry out this task, Stemmermann requested permission to move the entire *57.Inf.Div.* out of its sector west of Smela and insert it between *72.Inf.Div.* and *389.Inf.Div.* which still held a coherent ten-kilometer sector of front between Ossitnyashka and Telepino. The request to move this unit had to be passed all the way up the chain of command to Army Group Headquarters, where *Gen.Lt.* Busse would have to approve the move.

Busse was well aware of the risk this movement would entail, since it would partially denude Stemmermann's front of infantry, but approved the movement anyway, since there was little other choice. To cover the gap created by the move of *57.Inf.Div.*, *Wiking*, minus its armored battlegroup, would shift its boundary to the right, while *72.Inf.Div.* would shift its to the left. Both divisions were now seriously overextended. Should they be hit in the next wave of the Soviet offensive, they would be hard pressed indeed. The second battalion from *Gren.Rgt.676* duly began moving out at 1115 hours, the advance guard for the main body of Trowitz's Bavarians. About the same time, the advance elements of *14.Pz.Div.* finally arrived in their assembly areas near the town of Kapitanovka. The division was immediately subordinated to *XI.A.K.* control and given the mission of preventing a Soviet breakthrough towards Novo-Mirgorod, which lay astride the major route of advance to the city of Pervomaisk, the shortest route to the Black Sea.

At this point of the Soviet offensive, both Army Group South and *8.Armee* still believed that Zhukov was going after bigger game - the entire southern wing of Hitler's armies in the Ukraine. If the Red Army broke through, there would be nothing to stop them. General Konev had other ideas. Instead of heading south, he was heading west, and his forces' line of march clearly showed that they were heading in that direction. Instead of punching a hole and turning to the left, they were continuing through in a straight line. This began to become evident when von Vormann reported to Wöhler at noon that Soviet elements were heading west towards the towns of Rossoshovatka and Pissarevka. *3.Pz.Div.* was still pinned in its forward positions by a large Soviet force and could do little to affect the situation. Was this then the clear breakthrough the Soviets had wanted? (Map 4)

Gille, *Wiking's* commander, was one of those who were not at first inclined to believe the first reports that the Soviets had broken through. After all, a similar event had occurred several weeks before, when a handful of T-34s had broken through on 7 January and had penetrated all the way to Zvenigorodka. To deal with the situation, Gille had dispatched two Pz. IVs under the command of *Uscha.* Hans Fischer from Köller's *1.Kompanie*. After a game of cat and mouse that lasted long into the evening, Fischer's and the other tank, with the help of two 8.8 cm anti-aircraft guns and a platoon of infantry, were able to corner the Soviet tanks and destroy them one by one, though not after some tense moments when his own tank was cornered by a T-34 near a bridge. After

returning to his battalion, Fischer and the others were congratulated by their battalion commander. None of them knew at the time that the real Soviet attack was only two weeks away and shrugged the incident off.[13]

The Germans forces in the western portion of the salient had not remained undisturbed either. The ordinary front line soldiers of *XXXXII.A.K.* knew something was up - Soviet patrols and small assault parties were becoming more numerous, as were pre-registration of artillery fires. Since sounds carry further in bitter cold, the Germans could also hear the rattling and creaking of tank treads which sounded quite near. In fact, they were - much closer than they would imagine. The Germans also stepped up patrol activity, for they, too, needed to know Soviet intentions and to gather prisoners. On several occasions, opposing patrols would stumble into each other during the night, and the ensuing sounds of rifle fire and grenades would awaken the entire section of the front. The commander of *K.Abt.B's Rgt.Gr.110*, Ernst Schenk, knew something out of the ordinary was developing when a sentry shot and killed a Soviet general on 25 January in no-man's land. The previous evening, its members repulsed a determined Red Army reconnaissance in force which penetrated the *Regimentsgruppe's* forward positions in the vicinity of Troshtshin. After several hours of hand-to-hand combat, the front line was finally restored, leaving the men of Schenk's unit wondering what was next in store for them.[14]

While Schenk's grenadiers were fighting near Troshtshin, events 100 kilometers to the southeast were rapidly coming to a head. Konev, dissatisfied with the rate of progress of the infantry assault being carried out by Ryshov's and Galanin's armies, began to get impatient. According to the plan's timetable and painstaking calculations of force ratios, the German tactical defenses should have been completely smashed by late morning, enabling him to commit Rosmistrov's 5th Guards Tank Army.[15] *389.Inf.Div.* was still holding things up, so unexpectedly tough had been its resistance. The gap in the German defenses between Ossitnyashka and Yamki was still too narrow for Rotmistrov to commit his armor, yet Konev had to act quickly.

Soviet intelligence had reported the movement of *11.* and *14.Pz.Divs.*, as well as other German formations, towards

Panzer IV from Wiking, early February.
(Jarolin-Bundesarchiv 81/16/17A)

Kapitanovka. If the decisive breakthrough was to be achieved, and if he was to beat his rival Vatutin to Zvenigorodka, Konev would have to alter his plan and commit his armor without delay. If the Germans were allowed to establish a firm defensive line, his Front's entire operation could be jeopardized. To reestablish momentum, he shifted 20th and 29th Tank Corps from Rotmistrov's tank army positioned near Krassnossilka to the first echelon of the attacking infantry armies to the vicinity of Kochanivka. They were to create their own penetration, without waiting on the infantry to do it for them as planned.

While Rotmistrov was repositioning Lazarev's and Kirichenko's tank corps, the fighting raged on. Soviet infantry which had moved into the gap between *XI.A.K.* and *XXXXVII.Pz.Korps* were being engaged with artillery from both German corps. General Hohn's *72.Inf.Div.* reported that his right flank unit was under attack by infantry. By 1700 hours, Hohn's troops had lost contact with the left flank of *389.Inf.Div.* when the village of Yekaterinovka fell to troops from the Soviet 31st Rifle Division. Ossitnyashka came under attack again that afternoon, and by evening its defenders reported that Soviet troops had seized the northeastern part of town, after several hours of close-in fighting. During the battle for this modest little village, 15 more Soviet tanks were destroyed by troops of *Gren.Rgt.676* and Köller's *Kampfgruppe*, but they were slowly being pushed back. The troops were radioed by corps that they would have to hold at all costs, since their position would be used to "anchor" the northern shoulder of the penetration for the planning counterattack by *11.* and *14.Pz.Divs.*, whose formations were finally beginning to close on their new sectors.

Although the advance elements of Unrein's *14.Pz.Div.* had begun arriving near Kapitanovka by late morning, its main body did not arrive until mid-afternoon. While it awaited the arrival of *11.Pz.Div.*, Unrein organized his division into three *Kampfgruppen* - one in the south (or right), formed around *Oberstlt.* Mummert's *Pz.Gren.Rgt.103*, would focus on the defense of the town of Rossoschovatka; the one in the north (or left), formed around *Pz.Gren.Rgt.108* under the command of *Major* Heinz von Brese, would defend the town of Kapitanovka. Each of these two *Kampfgruppen* were composed of a *Pz.Gren.Rgt.* augmented by an artillery battalion and antitank guns. The division's third *Kampfgruppe* consisted of *Pz.Rgt.36* commanded by *Oberst* Willy Langkeit, though by this time it was a regiment in name only, since it only had 11 serviceable tanks and assault guns left, which had been formed into one battalion. The regiment's second battalion was in France being equipped with new *Panther* tanks, and would not make it back to the East until the summer of 1944.[16] To the rear, the division's reconnaissance battalion, *Pz.Aufkl.Abt.14*, had been positioned along a creek to prevent any Soviet armor from crossing and to act as a general reserve.

Near Kapitanovka, von Brese had established contact with elements of *389.Inf.Div.* which had been pushed out of their defensive positions that morning. Before the *Panzergrenadiers* of *K.Gr.* von Brese could get settled in, they were struck at 1545 hours by Soviet tanks and infantry attacking out of the fog which had settled in around this area of the

battlefield. After the Germans quickly knocked out several Soviet tanks at nearly point-blank range, the pack of T-34s turned to the south in an attempt to work their way around von Brese's right flank, whereupon they ran into *K.Gr.* Mummert, holding Rossoshovatka. After a brief fight, the Germans were thrown out of the village by the Soviet assault, but were able to counterattack and retake it later that evening. Things were not going well to the east of *14.Pz.Div.*, where troops from 1st Guards Airborne Division seized the eastern part of Ossitnyashka after severe fighting, often hand-to-hand. Stemmermann reported at 1900 hours that *389.Inf.Div.'s* infantry battalions were down to an average strength of 40-50 men each and that several artillery batteries had been lost, so rapid had been the Soviet advance in some areas of the front.

Despite the seriousness of the situation, General Wöhler told Stemmermann that he still believed that the arrival of *11.Pz.Div.* the next morning would enable him to restore the front line. Wöhler also told von Vormann to have any of his remaining armor prepared to pull out of their positions and move north, just in case.[17] By 2000 hours, the point became moot when it was reported that a force of 70 to 80 Soviet tanks, most probably part of 29th Tank Corps of 5th Guards Tank Army, was reported to be attacking in the direction of Kapitanovka. Rotmistrov's guardsmen had finally made their appearance.

Despite this development, *8.Armee* and its subordinate corps continued their plan for restoring the front line to begin the following day. The last entry for 25 January in the Army *Kriegstagebuch* (war diary) read:

> Intentions for 26 January . . . close the gap on the inner flanks of the XXXXVII.Pz.Korps and XI.A.K. through offensive action of 14.Pz.Div. Retake the south flank of 72.Inf.Div. and close the gap northwest of Yekaterinovka. Continue the regrouping of XI.A.K. in order to free up 57.Inf.Div. . . . .

Today this assessment carries an air of unreality about it, since the storm that was about to be unleashed upon the German forces would soon make the realization of these goals impossible and even their further survival would be in doubt.

The storm broke the next day, 26 January, when one tank brigade of Kirichenko's 29th Tank Corps threw *K.Gr.* Mummert out of Rossoshovatka in an early morning assault. To the north, another one of Kirichenko's brigades became embroiled in fighting in and around Kapitanovka with von Brese's troops, though the Germans managed to hold onto the village. An attack by 5th Guards Airborne Division threw out the battalion from the *72.Inf.Div.* defending Yekaterinovka, forcing the Germans to take their right flank back several kilometers southeast of the town of Losanovka. Stemmermann notified Wöhler at 0825 hours that the situation "had developed most unfavorably."

In fact, Stemmermann's hopes that *14.Pz.Div.* would be able to attack and reestablish contact with von Vormann's corps were dashed when that division soon found itself fighting for its very survival. Wöhler's staff still had not grasped the seriousness of the situation, when *8.Armee* ordered Stemmermann during the same radio conversation to attack south with *14.Pz.Div.*, reestablish contact with von Vormann, and throw the Soviets back.[18] Stemmermann's thoughts are not recorded, but he must have felt a great deal of frustration. To make matters worse, Wöhler told him to explain why had he split up *14.Pz.Div.* into two main groups. Stemmermann replied that the Unrein had done so on his own accord, based on the tactical situation.

For its part, *14.Pz.Div.* was not having an easy time of it. After being thrown out of Rossoschovatka, the men of *K.Gr.* Mummert retreated to the low hills a kilometer west of the town, where the pursuing Soviets of 29th Tank Corps were unable to dislodge them. Another wave of T-34s caused Mummert and his troops to lose contact with von Brese's force, leaving the latter unit isolated near Kapitanovka. German outposts in Ossitnyashka, eight kilometers to the east, reported that dozens of tanks with infantry aboard were bypassing their positions heading towards von Brese's positions, most likely 31st Tank Brigade of Kirichenko's corps. By this point, both von Brese's unit and Mummert's to the south had been reduced to a combat strength of between 250 to 300 men, far below their authorized level. Langkeit's armored group, which had fought back and forth all day, had only four tanks still operational. Though Unrein's panzer division had warded off or slowed the advance of Kirichenko's troops and tanks, eventually the superior numbers of their enemy would tell. Soviet tanks were also reported heading west near the bridge at Tishkovka, between von Brese's and Mummert's forces. The only force standing in the path of Kirichenko's tanks was *Pz.Aufkl.Abt.14*, reinforced with the division's combat engineer battalion, under the command of *Major* Rehm. Rehm had no tanks of its own, only some light antitank guns.

To the east of Kapitanovka, the early-morning attempt by *Wiking's* armored *Kampfgruppe* to attack from Ossitnyashka southwest towards Pissarevka and link up with *14.Pz.Div.* failed when it ran into strong defensive fire from enemy tanks and anti-tank guns. When a battalion-sized Soviet force made a penetration to the north near Telepino and was reported heading in the direction of Yekaterinovka, Köller's battlegroup was ordered to execute an about-face and roll as quickly as possible to come to the aid of *72.Inf.Div.*, whose right flank regiment, *Gren.Rgt.105,* was now in immediate danger of being enveloped. That left *II./Gren.Rgt.676* isolated in Ossitnyashka, though it still had tenuous contact with a regiment from *389.Inf.Div.* to its right, which at any rate had its own problems to worry about. To hold the key town of Ossitnyashka, which controlled the main road leading to Kapitanovka, the men of *II.Batallion* were ordered to remain and either await a link up with *14.Pz.Div.*, which was supposed to attack in its direction from Kapitanovka, or the return of Köller's tanks.

Events were developing rapidly (Map 5). It was about this point that the first major crisis in command for the German forces took place. While Konev and his commanders had to contend with the slow pace of the attack thus far, the Germans had far more serious matters to deal with. It was becoming evident

Generalleutnant Wend von Wietersheim. *Commander, 11.Pz.Div. (Photo courtesy of Walter Schaefer-Kehnert)*

by mid-morning that *14.Pz.Div.* was not going to succeed and that *11.Pz.Div.* would not arrive in time to launch a coordinated attack. Indeed, *11.Pz.Div.,* commanded by *Gen.Lt.* Wend von Wietersheim, would soon be ordered to relieve the enemy pressure on Unrein's *14.Pz.Div.* and then attempt to reestablish contact with the forces holding Ossitnyashka, thus reestablishing a coherent defense line. An additional cause of concern was the delay in the movement of Trowitz's *57.Inf.Div.* from its old positions in the north to the south, where it was now intended to be used to plug the gap yawning from Yekaterinovka to Ossitnyashka.

His men were still in the process of handing over their positions to *Wiking* and would not be able to move until nightfall, too late for them to influence the fighting that day. A more serious matter was that it was beginning to appear that the entire eastern front held by *XI.A.K.* would have to be taken back further west to an intermediate defensive line, in order to prevent its front from being pierced in several locations and outflanked to the south. This intermediate defensive line, code named *Hamsterstellung* (the Hamster position) lay several kilometers to the west and had already been surveyed to a limited extent. *Oberst* Gädcke, at *XI.A.K.* headquarters, was in favor of moving to this line as soon as possible, before things got out of control.

However, movement to this line would require a general withdrawal from Smela, to the north, to Ossitnyashka in the south. Neither *XI.A.K.* nor *8.Armee* had the authority to order such a move. Only Army Group South, in the person of Field Marshal von Manstein himself, with Hitler's permission, could do so. Unfortunately, the army group commander was not at his headquarters in Vinnitsa. He had been called that day by Hitler and ordered to attend a meeting of all army group and army commanders on the Eastern Front at the *Wolfschanze* (Hitler's "field headquarters" of the *OKW*) near Rastenburg in East Prussia on Thursday, 27 January.

The purpose of the meeting was to allow Hitler to give an address on the need for National Socialist education within the Army, a ludicrous event staged to secure a pledge of loyalty from his senior officers, which von Manstein found highly insulting. His rejoinder to Hitler's statement that "even Field Marshals and generals should stand by the flags to the last" brought the meeting to an end when Hitler stormed out of the room, perplexed at von Manstein's effrontery (von Manstein had called out "and so they shall, *mein Führer!*").[19] Until von Manstein returned to Vinnitsa, no actions could be taken, with the exception of those that had already been authorized. Meanwhile, while the decision was delayed, hundreds of men continued to fight and die around the hills and fields of Kapitanovka and Ossitnyashka.

While Stemmermann's and Wöhler's staffs were deliberating, the Red Army continued to probe to the west. At 0930 hours 26 January, it was reported that ten Soviet tanks had broken through near Kapitanovka, slipped past *Maj.* Rehm's reconnaissance battalion, and had been spotted moving southwest towards the town of Zlatopol, while others were reported firing upon German supply troops in Zhurovka, which lay to the northwest. The Russians had broken through! *8.Armee* acted quickly. Believing that it had a better appreciation of events than either von Vormann or Stemmermann, Wöhler's headquarters placed *11.Pz.Div.* directly under its control and directed it to attack as soon as possible from Pissarevka in the south to Kapitanovka in the north, destroy any Soviet forces it encountered, and establish contact with *14.Pz.Div.* As soon as this occurred, von Weitersheim's division was to prepare to attack in concert with Unrein's division the following day to close the gap through which troops of 4th Guards and 53rd Armies were pouring. With two panzer divisions attacking together, *8.Armee's* Operations Officer, *Oberst* Fritz Estor, evidently believed that the situation would be made right.[20] Had both divisions been at full strength, they probably could have done so. As it was, *14.Pz.Div.* had been whittled down to about 50 percent of its authorized strength and was in the process of being broken apart by the 29th Guards Tank Corps.

Shortly after announcing the decision to assume tactical control of *11.Pz.Div.*, General Wöhler radioed Stemmermann directly at 0945 hours and informed him that, in addition to the seven Soviet airborne and infantry divisions already identified opposite the battered *389.Inf.Div.*, army intelligence had also definitely detected the approach of Lazarev's 20th Guards Tank Corps. It was evidently heading in the direction of Kapitanovka and probably indicated that the Soviet main effort was being directed against *XI.A.K.*, since Konev's infantry had been unable to push back *3.Pz.Div.*, holding firm on von

Vormann's corps left flank. Although he could not permit *72.Inf.Div.* or what remained of the *389.Inf.Div.* to pull back to the *Hamsterstellung*, Wöhler did agree with Stemmermann's order to move the right flank of *72.Inf.Div.* several kilometers to the west in order to maintain contact with its struggling neighbor to the south. Wöhler stated that he naturally wanted his corps commander to exercise as much freedom of action as was in his authority to grant. This could not have been much consolation for Stemmermann, who still had yet to feel the brunt of the Soviet attack.

The official Soviet records do not have much to say regarding events of 26 January in the area of the Second Ukrainian *Front*. Despite the seizure of a 21-kilometer wide strip up to ten kilometers deep, the shattering of one German infantry division, and the commitment of one of its tank corps near Kapitanovka, the expected breakthrough had not yet occurred. True, a tank company had slipped past the German force holding that town, but that did not create the conditions required to commit all of Rotmistrov's armor. The German resistance had been far tougher than expected, and *8.Armee* had reacted far more quickly than anyone in Konev's staff had anticipated. *14.Pz.Div.* seemed to have materialized out of thin air. When another panzer division, von Wietersheim's *11.Pz.Div.*, had been encountered by mid-afternoon, Konev and Rotmistrov were faced with a dilemma - do we stop and destroy them, or keep on going? By mid-afternoon, it seemed as if they would not be able to carry out either course of action.

Except for the ten kilometer gap between these two divisions, and the other slightly larger one between Ossitnyashka and Raymentorovka near the positions of *3.Pz.Div.*, things appeared to be looking up. Plus, Trowitz's *57.Inf.Div.* was on the way and would arrive by nightfall in an assembly area near Tashlyk, between *389.* and *72.Inf.Div.* True, things still appeared very serious, but the Soviet offensive seemed to be losing steam. Even their artillery fire seemed to be slackening. *8.Armee* apparently believed that *11.Pz.Div.* would be able to restore the line on Stemmermann's right flank, who could then take care of the other hole in his front on his own. Army Group had already been told about the need to withdraw to the *Hamsterstellung*, and as soon as Field Marshal von Manstein returned, he would surely grant a speedy approval, or so the German staff officers must have thought.

This sense of satisfaction was shattered at 1130 hours when a radio report from neighboring *1.Pz.Armee* was received. To their shock and disbelief, the staff officers, after decoding the message, read that the enemy had launched an attack in the west against the inner flanks of *1.Pz.Armee's XXXXII.* and *VII.A.K.* In the message, *1.Pz.Armee's* 1a, *Oberstlt.* Martin von Graevenitz, stated that it appeared that the Soviet goal was to attack in the direction of Shpola and link up with forces of the Second Ukrainian Front, attacking from the east.[21] Two hours later, this report was followed by another which stated that attacking Soviet forces had broken through *XXXXII.A.K.* with 30 tanks and were last seen heading towards the town of Medvin. *8.Armee* passed the news to Stemmermann shortly thereafter, and notified him that in case *XXXXII.A.K.* was permitted to withdraw, he would have to be ready to pull his own left flank back, too. Stemmermann replied that he was only too glad to do so, the sooner the better.

Meanwhile, the attack by *11.Pz.Div.* was making good progress. By early afternoon, its leading *Panzergrenadier* regiment had advanced as far as Kamenovatka, twelve kilometers south of Kapitanovka, while its *Pz.Rgt.8*, detouring through Zlatapol, saw no signs of the reported Soviet tank company that had broken through earlier. The division encountered and destroyed several T-34s en route east of the Kapitanovka-Zlatapol road, and observed a strong enemy force of tanks holding the northern part of the village of Tishkovka, only five kilometers south of their objective. Reports from von Brese, whose group had been thrown out of their positions earlier that day, indicated that there were 30 or so Soviet tanks with infantry occupying Kapitanovka, so seizing it would not be easy.

At 1540 hours, the lead element of *11.Pz.Div.* reported that it had observed about 40 enemy tanks approaching from the east, which had suddenly appeared from the direction of Rossoshovatka. *8.Armee*, exercising direct control of the division, ordered it to both continue its advance towards Tishkovka and to stop the tanks coming from Rossoshovatka, while its *Pz.Rgt.8* with its dozen or so tanks hooked around to the left and linked up with the remaining elements of *14.Pz.Div.* west of Kapitanovka. At this stage, the Soviet formations seemed to have momentarily lost their offensive drive, and were content with holding a few key villages while their reinforcing echelons closed up. In fact, German observers on the outskirts of Ossitnyashka reported that motorized columns of troops, trucks, tanks and guns were passing through the area heading west.

Although evening was rapidly approaching, *11.Pz.Div.* pushed on, seizing part of the town of Pissarevka several kilometers east of Tishkovka by 1900 hours against only minor resistance. It had also ambushed a Soviet column heading west near the town, inflicting considerable losses, including the destruction of three tanks. The division radioed *8.Armee* that it planned to continue its attack in the morning, seize the remainder of Pissarevka, and close the gap between it and XI.A.K. In response, *8.Armee* notified the division commander, von Wietersheim, that an assault gun battalion, *StuG.Abt.905*, would be attached to him the following day to augment his weak tank regiment, which only had one battalion, the other one having been sent to France to be equipped with Panthers, the same as the *14.Pz.Div.'s* had.

As the day drew to an end, the boundary between *389.* and *72.Inf.Div.* saw more heavy fighting. One regiment from *389.Inf.Div.*, *Gren.Rgt.545* (reduced in strength to only a weak battalion), reported that it had just driven off a large enemy force that was trying to approach between the villages of Pastorskoya and Bogdanovka. German artillery and infantry coordinated their efforts, with good effect. One eyewitness to the event, Fw. Anton Meiser, a artillery forward observer from *IV./Art.Rgt.389*, later reported:

Along a broad front, especially on the right, all hell had broken loose. As a preventive measure, I ordered the batteries to fire another round of our [artillery] blocking concentration to check its accuracy… it was dead on. Then

suddenly, all was quiet. Shortly thereafter, from the opposite side of the slope, we heard the roar [of the Soviet battle cry] Urrah! Thousands of Russians [seemed to] leap from their foxholes and charged directly towards us. It appeared that our lads would be overwhelmed by the [enemy's] masses. Then, however, the fire from our machine guns swept across the front and scythed through the enemy ranks . . .

Cries of pain soon mixed with the roar of their battle cry. I then ordered our artillery to begin shooting its blocking fire concentration, with terrible effect. The oncoming Russian tide hesitated. But there was no cover to be had. The MG-42s started rattling again. The Russians fell in heaps. Now, the first ones began to run back; that is, they tried to. Many remained lying there for eternity. The machine gun fire finally slackened, but rifle shots continued to ring out as our men shot at the hastily withdrawing Ivans. The attack had been driven off, as far as I could see. The first "work" had been done . . . [22]

The bodies of over 500 Soviet troops were counted later that day. To the left of *389.Inf.Div.*, *72.Inf.Div.'s Gren.Rgt.105*, commanded by *Major* Robert Kästner, warded off a determined Soviet attack at 1700 hours against Yekaterinovka.

This assault, led by 20 tanks in support of 20th Guards Rifle Corps, was driven off after 10 of the tanks were knocked out. Kästner's neighbor to the north, *Maj.* Rudolf Siegel's *Gren.Rgt.266*, reported strong enemy reconnaissance activity all along his sector, but they, too, were driven off.[23] As far as Stemmermann was concerned, his troops could not withdraw to the *Hamsterstellung* soon enough. Still, Army Group South refused to grant permission until it had been allowed to do so.

Despite the carnage the day had seen, Stemmermann felt that, with the exception of the breakthrough at the boundary between his and von Vormann's corps, his troops for the most part had been able to hold their positions. During the day, *389.Inf.Div.* had destroyed 22 Soviet tanks, while *14.Pz.Div.* had destroyed five. *Wiking's* armored battlegroup had destroyed another dozen or so. Stemmermann calculated that of the 120 tanks that had pierced his front lines in the past three days, as many as 90 of these had been destroyed. True, the old front line positions of *389.* and part of those of *72.Inf.Div.* had been given up, but at least the current front appeared to be holding together, as shaky as it was. This, despite the fact that his corps had been attacked that day by nine identified infantry and airborne divisions, as well as elements of two tank corps. On balance, his troops had fought very well indeed.

That evening, Wöhler radioed Stemmermann and informed him that he had been attacked that day by 12 to 14 divisions, not nine, and that he should expect the same the following day. The missing Soviet tank company that had last been seen near Zlatapol had turned up near the outskirts of the town of Lebedin, over 30 kilometers to the west, where they had been temporarily halted by an ad-hoc *Kampfgruppe* formed from supply and service troops of *389.Inf.Div.* Nevertheless, Wöhler

Generalleutnant Hans Speidel, *Chief of Staff, Eighth Army.*
(Bundesarchiv 72/32/6)

informed his corps commander that he should plan to continue his attack to seal off the enemy penetration and reestablish the front line between his corps and von Vormann's. Although he was still forbidden to withdraw to the *Hamsterstellung*, Wöhler permitted him to take back the right flank of *72.Inf.Div.* further back to the rail line that ran northwest of Yekaterinovka southwest to Bobrinskaya, as a sort of an intermediate position, quickly named the *Sehnenstellung* (bow-string position) that would enable Hohn's troops to remain in contact with Kruse's battered *389.Inf.Div*. This, at least, was better than nothing.

In addition to dealing with the battle within his own part of the front, Wöhler also had to keep abreast of the confused situation further to the west, where the troops of Vatutin's First Ukrainian Front had reportedly broken through and were heading east. In a radio conversation between the two army commanders, Hube of *1.Pz.Armee* suggested that it was senseless for the both of them to keep holding on to the sector that bulged east towards the Dnieper. He went on to say that it was too difficult to keep supplied anyway, and had ordered that everyone except a thin security force be left behind, so he could honestly tell von Manstein and Hitler that "he was still holding the Dnieper Front."

Wöhler agreed, stating that he had also passed on similar orders to his own troops along the river. Shortly thereafter, at 2200 hours, Gen.Lt. Hans Speidel, the Chief of Staff of *8. Armee*, received a telephone call from General Busse at Army

Group South. Speidel updated von Manstein's chief of staff on the tactical situation and told him about the attack planning for the following day. Then Busse gave Speidel the bad news - permission to pull back to the Hamsterstellung had been refused. Both *1.Pz.* and *8.Armee* were to reestablish their old front line positions as soon as possible.

Speidel said that doing so was unrealistic and would lead to an untenable situation, especially if the army's main supply routes were severed. Busse replied that he did not have the authority to countermand the order from Hitler's headquarters, "even if it led to the front being blown away."[24] With Field Marshal von Manstein away in East Prussia, his hands were tied. Later than same day, both Wöhler and Hube would have to depart for the same conference as well, leaving both armies short of their key decision-makers just at the moment when they were most badly needed.

Thus the curtain fell on what had been a very eventful day, though it was only a prelude to what was to happen next. *1. Pz.Armee*, for its part, was also experiencing the same type of events which had already occurred to their eastern neighbor - now, its soldiers, too, would face the same fate that was threatening the men of *8.Armee* - encirclement! Had they known what Pavel Rotmistrov had in store for them the following day, they would have real reason to fear. For once, the Soviets would do something totally unexpected. Instead of stopping to deal with the two German panzer divisions, as the Germans expected him to do, Rotmistrov had ordered his two forward guards tank corps - 20th and 29th - to forget about their flanks or what was behind them and to press ahead. In fact, the phantom tank company that *XI.A.K.* thought had slipped through was not a company of tanks at all, but a powerful force of nearly one hundred tanks, infantry, and artillery. And they were driving for Shpola, deep in the German rear.

End Notes

1   von Manstein, p. 511.
2   *Sbornik*, p. 307.
3   Ibid., p. 311.
4   Eighth Army *Kriegstagebuch* (KTB), entry dated 24 January, p. 1.
5   Ibid., p. 2.
6   Ibid., p. 3.
7   Ibid., p. 5.
8   Ibid., p. 4.
9   Eighth Army KTB entry dated 25 January, p. 1.
10 Glantz, "From the Dnieper to the Vistula," p. 141.
11 Eighth Army KTB entry dated 25 January, p. 1.
12 Jahnke and Lerch, p. 60.
13 Fischer, Hans. *Erlebnisbericht Einsatz Januar 1944.* (Versmold,Germany: Unpublished private manuscript in possession of the author, January 1998).
14 Ernst Schenk, *Das Badische Infanterie-Regiment 110.* (Heidelberg, Germany: Privately Published 1957), p. 55.
15 Glantz, p. 139.
16 Rolf Grams, *Die 14.Panzer Division, 1940-1945.* (Friedberg,Germany: Podzun-Pallas Verlag, GmbH, 1986), p. 164.
17 Eighth Army KTB entry dated 25 January 1944, p. 6.
18 Ibid, p. 8.
19 von Manstein, p. 513.
20 Eighth Army KTB entry dated 26 January 1944, p. 3.
21 Ibid, p. 4.
22 Anton Meiser, *Die Hölle von Tcherkassy: Ein Kriegstagebuch 1943-1944.* (Schnellbach,Germany: *Verlag Siegfried Bublies*, 1998), p. 181.
23 Rudolf Siegel, *Bericht über die Kämpfe im Kessel von Tscherkassy und des grossens Kessels von Korsun in der Zeit vom 11.1943 bis 17.2.1944*, (Stuttgart, Germany: Unpublished Report, 1944), p. 26.
24 *Eighth Army* KTB entry dated 26 January 1944, p. 9.

Chapter Five

VATUTIN STRIKES

"Today, the weather is our friend."
— *Junior Lieutenant Mikhail Prikhod'koi.* [1]

hat Field Marshal von Manstein had feared most occurred at dawn on Wednesday, 26 January, when the other component of the Soviet offensive, the First Ukrainian *Front*, began its attack. While the attention of Army Group South was diverted by the attack in *8.Armee*'s sector, and while *1.Pz.Armee* was tying up loose ends resulting from the partially successful counterattack it conducted northwest of Uman during the second week of January, three armies of General Vatutin's *Front* burst forth from their positions between the towns of Tarashcha and Zhazhkov along a frontage of 70 kilometers.

Like the offensive preparations being made at the same time in the east, Vatutin's had been detected by German intelligence as early as 23 January, three days before his attack actually began. The tip-off was an assault launched that morning by an overwhelming force of at least two regiments against the village of Koshavatoye, then held by a battalion from *88.Inf.Div*. The defenders were thrown out of the village after several hours of severe fighting, after which the victorious Soviet soldiers were observed busily digging in. A German counterattack later that day by a battalion from *K.Abt.B* failed to drive the Soviet forces out, compelling *Gen.Lt.* Lieb, acting commander of *XXXXII.AK.*, to pull his shattered lines back to the east several kilometers.[2]

Why such a full-scale attack was launched against such a seemingly minor objective only became clear after analysis showed that Koshavatoye furnished excellent jump-off positions for a subsequent attack. In his *Kriegstagebuch* (*KTB*) entry for 23 January 1944, the chief of staff of *1.Pz.Armee*, *Gen.Maj.* Walter Wenck, offered General Lieb little comfort by noting that "The army has made it completely clear, that conducting combat operations with the limited means in this sector is especially difficult...despite this fact, the corps must stand fast in this crisis..."[3] In fact, the crisis for Lieb's corps had only just begun.

The following day, 24 January, radio intercepts and interrogation of prisoners confirmed that both 5th Guards Tank Corps and 5th Mechanized Corps, with approximately 70 tanks, had been identified in the area west of the town of Tinovka, where the Red Army was most likely building its point of main effort for the impending attack.[4] When Lieb requested to be reinforced with additional antitank forces, all *1.Pz.Armee* had to provide him was one tank-hunting battalion equipped with *Panzerfäuste*, hardly a force able to stand up to a determined tank attack on open ground. Nevertheless, it was all that the army could spare.

An early casualty of the fighting, this SS-Unterscharführer of one of Wiking's Panzergrenadier Regiments has been bandaged and is awaiting evacuation, forest north of Staroselye, late January 1944. Note the whitewashed helmet, a common practice if white helmet covers were unavailable.
(U.S. National Archives)

Since the existence of Kravchenko's newly-formed 6th Tank Army had not yet been detected, the Germans did not expect a major effort along this portion of the front. *1.Pz.Armee's* conclusion was that the armored forces assembling near Tinovka were there for the purpose of launching a relief attack towards the town of Tichonovka, where a Soviet corps had been encircled the week before. Here, during the course of the German's early January counterattack against the forces of the Soviet 38th and 40th Armies that were threatening Uman, part of these forces, including 13th Guards and 167th Rifle Divisions, as well as 6th Motorized Rifle Brigade, had been cut off. Since then, they had been resisting efforts by *82.Inf.Div.* to eliminate them. Therefore, Hube and his staff assumed that any future attack would be of limited scope and duration, certainly not a major offensive. Of course, to the German and Soviet infantrymen who were engaged in these costly struggles, it made little difference whether one died in a small battle or a large one. All that mattered for them was to live one day longer and not to let down one's comrades.

On the day prior to the onset of the Soviet operation against the western portion of the Kanev Salient, *1.Pz.Armee* was far more concerned about operations 100 kilometers to the west, where *III.Pz.Korps* was still attempting to wipe out the remnants of some of Vatutin's other units that had been trapped during the previous two weeks of fighting. Tank battles were still raging to the west when the enemy situation opposite Lieb's corps was summarized as being "local attacks aimed at tying down and diverting German attention," while only a relief attack was expected from the direction of Tinovka towards the encircled Soviet troops in Tichonovka, 30 kilometers away.[5] Although the report mentioned that three T-34s had been spotted as well as the movement of another enemy division into the area, *1.Pz.Armee*

Generalleutnant Hans Joachim von Horn, *Commander, 198.Inf.Div. (Photo: Andres Schwarz and 88.Inf.Div. Veterans Association)*

seemed little concerned. Apparently, Hube and his staff believed that they could deal with any situation on the army's right flank after the situation on its left flank was resolved. The army would simply switch the entire *III.Pz.Korps* to the affected area after its other mission had been completed.

After a shattering half-hour barrage from several hundred guns, Vatutin's spearhead, General Kravchenko's newly-created 6th Tank Army, attacked in the first echelon. His two corps were immediately bogged down in frontal battles with the German *VII.A.K.'s 34.* and *198. Inf.Div.* Soviet records speak of the enemy fighting stubbornly all along the front, causing the Red Army's offensive in the west to "develop more slowly than anticipated."[6]

Vatutin's decision to commit the bulk of his attacking forces in a frontal attack had been a mistake. The supporting Soviet infantrymen were mowed down by the determined German defenders. Even Kravchenko's armor made little headway.

Within the *VII.A.K.* sector, the German defenders claimed to have destroyed 82 Soviet tanks during the first three days of the offensive alone.[7] General von Horn's divisional artillery, consisting of *Art.Rgt.235*, even destroyed enemy tanks using direct fire. An attempt by 5th Mechanized Corps, commanded by Lieutenant General M.V. Volkov, and 58th Rifle Division to seize the town of Repki ended in failure when the German defenders of *Gren.Rgt.308* of *198.Inf.Div.* held firm against repeated tank-supported infantry assaults. The *Baden-Württembergers* of *Gen.Lt.* Hans-Joachim von Horn's *198.Inf.Div.* could not, however, prevent the neighboring town of Pavlovka, along the boundary shared with the neighboring *34.Inf.Div.*, from falling

after several hours of house-to-house fighting, but were able to keep the attackers from 359th Rifle Division from penetrating any further than that. The story was the same along the entire portion of the front held by *VII.A.K.*

While the Red Army made limited gains of two to three kilometers in most places, it had yet to make a clean breakthrough in that corps' sector. The Soviet's 47th Rifle Corps from 40th Army had made gains of up to seven or eight kilometers opposite von Horn's *198.Inf.Div.*, but could not break through the secondary lines of defense. The German infantrymen had been too well entrenched and had fought stubbornly. The thick morning fog, while it had helped conceal approaching Soviet units, also made it more difficult for their commanders to control their units. By the end of the day, the Soviet main effort against *VII.A.K.* had ground to a halt, forcing Vatutin to cast about for a more favorable path of advance.

The only bright spot in this otherwise gloomy day for Vatutin was in the area of Trofimenko's 40th Army, where an attack against the left flank of *Gen.Lt. Graf* von Rittberg's *88.Inf.Div.* gained considerable ground. Here, 180th and 337th Rifle Divisions, supported by 30 tanks, tore an 18 kilometer-wide hole in the defenses between the villages of Luka and Dibnizy, held by the attached *Gren.Rgt.417*, and headed northeast towards the large town of Boguslav. They were brought to a temporary halt on the town's southern outskirts by a hastily assembled scratch force from *88.Inf.Div.*, after creating a sense of panicked uncertainty in the area. Another advance, probably by elements of 180th Rifle Division, drove to the southeast along the main supply route towards Medvin, separating the left flank of *Graf* Rittberg's division from the right flank of von Horn's *198.Inf.Div.* One account, by Oberst Keiser, commander of *Gren.Rgt.326*, arrayed on the division's right flank, described the events which occurred:

The night of 25/26 January passed without anything worth reporting. We had already become accustomed to tank noises during the past few days and they no longer made an impression on us. But then around 0540 hours, an artillery drumfire barrage broke out upon our forward positions, especially against those that closed up with 88.Inf.Div. on the right. The earth shook all along our 30 kilometer-wide front. This means the main attack! Shortly after 6 a.m., the shellfire ceased. We raised our heads. Outside [our positions] there was heavy fog, that limited our observation to 100 meters or less . . . I decided to carry out a personal reconnaissance with my adjutant…now and then we halted and listened in all directions, but all was still. Were the Russians just bluffing? Suddenly, five Sherman tanks appeared out of the fog in front of us, the enemy must have broken through! . . . It was now high time to get back to my command post . . . Around noon the fog cleared…we observed a strong enemy force heading towards Medvin . . . of our right neighbor . . . there was no sign . . . We had been separated from them by the enemy breakthrough.[8]

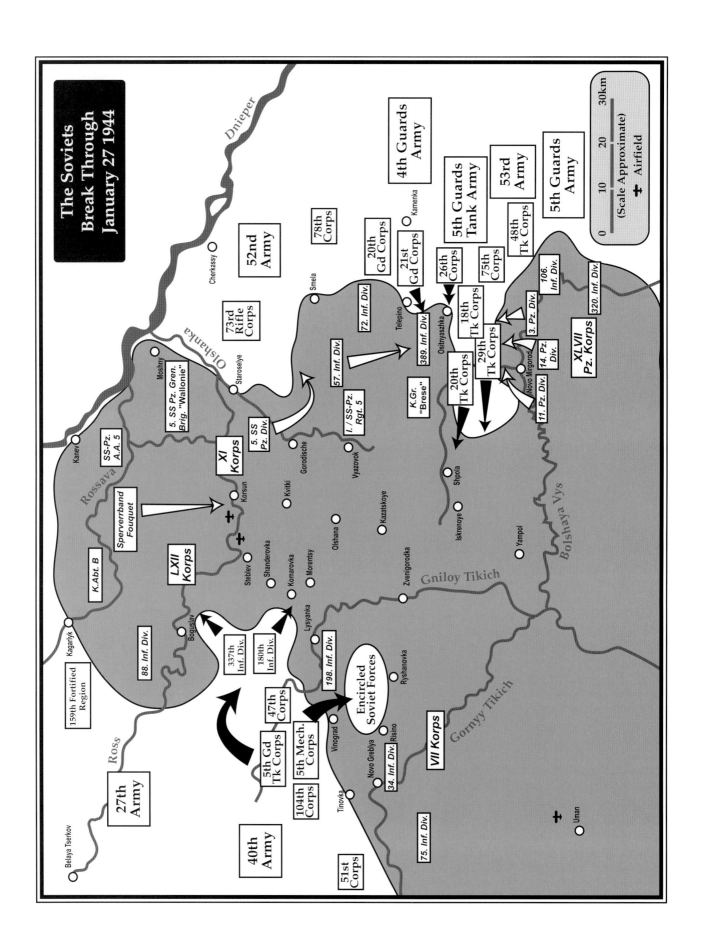

Because the left flank of *88.Inf.Div.* had begun to give way, von Horn was forced to extend his own division's right flank to keep in contact with his northerly neighbor. Several companies were switched from other regiments in the division to the right flank, weakening the positions elsewhere and creating favorable conditions for a breakthrough which the First Ukrainian *Front* would undoubtedly exploit the following day. Indeed, *1.Pz.Armee* fully recognized the danger. Wenck wrote in the army's war diary later that evening that:

> At the widely-spread, thinly occupied front along the army's right sector, the continuation of the enemy attack is anticipated with concern . . . the danger that the [two] corps will experience strong [enemy] pressure along their inner flanks, despite ruthless weakening of other front sectors . . . and the fact that they cannot hold for long, is completely recognized by the Army.[9]

1.Pz.Armee's intelligence section made an important discovery on this day - the identification of Kravchenko's 6th Tank Army. A *KTB* entry stated that this discovery "raises the possibility that the opponent is pursuing (with these attacks) more than locally limited objectives," an accurate, though understated, assessment.[10] Wenck also foresaw that the situation in *VII.* and *XXXXII.A.K.* sectors could grow more serious, so he recommended that the army begin drafting plans for ending ongoing operations on the army's far left flank by *III.Pz.Korps* and prepare to quickly switch mobile units to the east to restore the situation there. In this, he was prophetic.

Indeed, the troops of Trofimenko's neighboring 27th Army had advanced over 12 kilometers by the end of the first day, overshadowing the efforts of 6th Tank and 40th Armies. This penetration, located though it was along a secondary route of attack, offered Vatutin and his commanders the opportunity they were looking for. To take advantage of this promising development, Kravchenko, with Vatutin's permission, moved his army's 5th Tank Corps, under the command of Lieutenant General V.M. Alekseyev, during the early morning hours of 27 January near Tinovka, where it was having little success, to the north, where 47th Rifle Corps was attacking. For closer cooperation, 47th Rifle Corps was subordinated to 6th Tank Army commander. After a night march of over 50 kilometers along badly rutted roads, the tank corps, in conjunction with the infantrymen of 47th Rifle Corps, was able to launch its attack that afternoon and quickly penetrated the German defenses north of Boyarka.

Vatutin's ploy paid off (Map 6). The Germans had been caught completely off guard by this maneuver, since they did not believe that the Red Army was capable of such a quick reaction - in the past, after all, their enemy had always moved slowly and most predictably. *1.Pz.Armee* expected that the main attack would continue from the Tinovka area, where the tank army had been identified, towards Uman or Zvenigorodka. While Vatutin's forces had been stymied elsewhere, 5th Tank Corps rapidly drove through Medvin and Lysyanka that Thursday afternoon, 27 January. This force easily brushed aside

SS-Untersturmführer Hans-Georg Jessen, *the leader of 4./SS-Pz.Abt.5, observes the fighting from the commander's cupola of his StuG III, near Staroselye, late-January 1944. (U.S. National Archives)*

weak German roadblocks thrown up to impede its advance, slicing down the seam that separated the German's *VII.A.K.* from *XXXXII.A.K.*

As Kravchenko's tanks continued their penetration and exploitation of the German defenses, the units of Zhmachenko's 40th Army, as well as 5th Mechanized Corps, continued their attacks against *Gen.d.Inf.* Hell's *VII.A.K.* Although the Red Army scored gains of several kilometers, it failed to punch a whole wide enough through which to push the bulk of the mechanized corps, since the Germans stubbornly held on at the shoulders of the penetration that formed near the village of Pavlovka, northwest of the key town of Vinograd.

In day-long battles with the German defenders, both sides suffered serious losses in men and materiel. General Hell's Corps claimed to have destroyed 34 Soviet tanks that day alone.[11] Vinograd, astride a main German supply route, changed hands several times, falling into the hands of Soviet 104th Rifle Corps late that evening. *34.Inf.Div.* reported an enemy attack in division strength, supported by 40 tanks, along the boundary it shared with the neighboring *198.Inf.Div.* This tank unit, most likely the independent 233rd Tank Brigade attached to 5th Mechanized Corps, pushed southeast of Vinograd, then turned to the north, where it relieved the Red Army units which had been encircled around Tichonovka two weeks before.

Above: *A StuG III from 4th Kompanie, SS-Pz.Abt.5 Wiking, during the course of a counterattack north of the town of Staroselye, has hit an antitank mine. Here, the crew is busily engaged in reattaching the track while under enemy fire, late January 1944. (U.S. National Archives)*

Above: *Another StuG III from the same unit advances to provide some needed assistance to the crew of the mine-damaged vehicle. (U.S. National Archives)*

Above: *SS Grenadiers from Wiking using probes to search the packed snow for antitank mines in advance of their supporting StuG IIIs from 4./SS-Pz.Abt.5, on the road from Staroselye to Baybuzy. (U.S. National Archives)*

Above: *SS Grenadiers from Wiking clear snow away from a mine they have just detected on the road. (U.S. National Archives)*

Above: *A Wiking StuG III with supporting infantry riding on top prepares to continue the counterattack near Staroselye. (U.S. National Archives)*

Above: *Their first objective taken, these SS Grenadiers have attached a captured Soviet 4.5 cm antitank gun to the tow pintle of their supporting StuG III. (U.S. National Archives)*

Above: *SS Grenadiers occupy a shallow depression during their counterattack north of Staroselye. (U.S. National Archives)*

Above: *A StuG III from 4./SS-Pz.Abt.5 continues the counterattack in the forest north of Staroselye. Note the snow capes being worn over the gray SS winter Anorak. (U.S. National Archives)*

These forces joined 233rd Tank Brigade's spearhead, lending it some of the infantry strength it sorely lacked. By the late evening however, the Soviet attack nearly everywhere else had finally been brought to a halt and contact between the two German divisions of *VII.A.K.* restored, though not without hard fighting, as described in *198.Inf.Div.'s* account:

> Like a stormflood the enemy poured through the breaks [in our line] that his artillery had created. Individual battalions and companies of the division clung to their strongpoints in fortified villages and defended them the entire morning . . . despite [these efforts], enemy tanks at the onset were able to plunge through the thin front between these strongpoints, with the aid of the fog and soon penetrated the artillery positions . . . Against the division today the enemy had thrown three fully-rested and tank-reinforced infantry divisions. In spite of this overwhelming commitment of men and materiel, and the bitter losses to the defenders, the enemy was unable to bring about a breakthrough in our division's sector.[12]

The situation was much worse on the corps' far right flank, where contact with neighboring *XXXXII.A.K.* had been lost the previous evening. Horn's *198.Inf.Div.* had reported the movement during the day of 20 Soviet tanks and 30 trucks loaded with infantry (probably the vanguard of 5th Guards Tank Corps) racing in a southerly direction from Medvin in *88.Inf.Div.'s* sector, but was unable to do anything to stop them. The *Luftwaffe*, which could have helped slow the enemy's advance, was nowhere in sight. General Hell believed that his right flank was being rapidly turned and successfully begged *1.Pz.Armee* for permission to pull his right flank back along the main supply route running from Medvin to Lysyanka, which allowed him to temporarily block this avenue of approach and keep the Soviet armor from penetrating to the town.

This town was critical for several reasons - not only was it *198.* and *88.Inf.Div.s'* main supply base, but the main supply route for *XXXXII.A.K.* ran through it as well. The road that ran east towards the town of Zvenigorodka also ran through Lysyanka. It was defended solely by supply troops of the two infantry divisions as well as "line of communication units" of *1. Pz.* and *8.Armee* - postmen, judge advocates, farriers, and troops of the *Feldkommandantur* (the regional area administrative command). They were poorly suited to withstand a concerted tank attack with infantry support. *1.Pz.Armee* rightly noted that an advance towards Zvenigorodka, combined with Soviet approach from the direction of Konev's Second Ukrainian Front from the east, would spell encirclement for both corps in the salient. In the words of Walter Wenck, "The time to make a decision [to pull out of the salient] has come to the final hour."[13]

As noted above, the most threatening Soviet activity against *1.Pz.Armee* on 27 January was taking place in *XXXXII.A.K.* sector. There, Kravchenko's armored spearheads had sliced through the gap between *88.* and *198.Inf.Divs.* and were moving south, east, and northeast, where they encountered

Generalmajor Walter Wenck, *Chief of Staff, First Panzer Army. (Photo: The Decline and Fall of Nazi Germany and Imperial Japan: A Pictorial History of the Final Days of World War II by Hans Dollinger)*

little resistance. *K.Abt.B* also came under attack that day, when the positions held by *Div.Gr.332* near Yanovka came under attack. This was most likely launched by troops of the Soviet 159th Fortified Region, timed to divert German attention and tie down units which could have been used to shore up the tottering left flank of *Graf* Rittberg's division. A unit from *Div.Gr.323*, *Kompanie* Knauss, was moved to Luka and counterattacked Soviet forces from 337th Rifle Division holding the town of Dibnizy, in an attempt ordered by *Graf* Rittberg to reestablish contact with *VII.A.K.*[14] The attempt failed in the face of strong Soviet resistance.

Faced with this situation, Lieb, *XXXXII.A.K.'s* commander, contacted *1.Pz.Armee* headquarters that day with a request to withdraw his corps' left flank back to the Ross River line running from Boguslav in the east to the town of Steblev in the southeast. Only this way, he believed, could he hold his front together in the face of continued Soviet attacks.[15] Better yet would be obtaining permission to withdraw his entire corps south of the Ross River - at least in this manner, he would be able to free enough battalions to seal off the breach. Although *1. Pz.Armee* informed Lieb that it would think about the proposal, it could not issue the order until Army Group South granted the permission to do so.

Once again, Hitler's order that prevented the yielding of territory without his express permission would significantly delay tactical operations when quick decisions were most urgently needed. The absence of Field Marshal von Manstein and his decision-making ability was affecting *1.Pz.Armee*, just as it was *8.Armee* fighting to the east. Both armies would have to do they best they could within the parameters set by Army Group South until its commander returned from the *Führer's* conference in Rastenburg the next day, 28 January. Rather than await a decision, Lieb ordered his units to prepare to withdraw anyway.

While Lieb was busily engaged in the effort to pull his left flank back to the safety of the Ross River, the forward detachment of 6th Tank Army, 233rd Tank Brigade, had reached the southwestern outskirts of Lysyanka along the main supply route, easily brushing aside efforts to block the route. While this brigade was moving to the northeast, the bulk of 5th Guards Tank Corps was beginning to attack towards the southeast from the direction of Medvin, which had fallen to the Red Army earlier that day. The weather was cold and road conditions were favorable, though a light rain set in that afternoon.

At midday, 233rd Brigade's 1st Tank Battalion, commanded by Captain Nikolai Masyukov, reached the outskirts of the town with his accompanying *tankodesantniki* aboard. Described in a contemporary account as a small regional town then used as a German supply base, Lysyanka stretched out along a broad valley, through which ran a shallow creek, the Gniloy Tikich. Its houses could only be seen from a relatively close range. Two key roads intersected in the town - the route running north-south from Zvenigorodka to Korsun-Shevchenkovsky and the east-west route running from Talnoye to Taratsha. It was along this latter route that the tanks of 1st Tank Battalion were racing to the east.

Maslyukov's battalion, equipped with M4 Shermans or *Emchas*, quickly overran the scratch German battalion-sized force organized to defend the town. Using terrain to good advantage, the Soviet tankers were able to envelop the town from both the north and south. The Germans were caught totally off guard by the speed and shock of the tank attack and their defense quickly collapsed. One German security outpost at the western edge of town, which was alerted by the sound of advancing tanks, was silenced when the lead Sherman ran over its position and performed a pivot steer, burying its occupants alive. The town was in Soviet hands by early evening, with its thousands of tons of German food, ammunition, and clothing. Noteworthy was the tank battalion's choice of conducting a "psychological attack" with both headlights and sirens blazing. In an account written after the war by one of the *Emchisti* crewmembers:

> The piercing light of the headlamps pulled the road out of the darkness, along with the adjacent fields, houses, and trees. It blinded the enemy infantry . . . the powerful howl of the sirens ripped into the night. It assaulted the eardrums and placed a heavy load on the brain. The enemy fire, initially somewhat dense, began to weaken. The "psychological attack" bore fruit . . . [16]

With no antitank weapons to speak of, the Germans were helpless. To evade capture, the defenders either withdrew to the north, where they would soon be encircled with the rest of the forces in the Kanev Salient, or to the south, where they would soon be incorporated into makeshift *Alarmeinheiten* (emergency units), culled from a variety of different elements caught up by the Soviet offensive. This latter category included over 1,800 men from the *88.Inf.Div.'s Trossteile* (rear services).[17] Their absence would severely complicate the logistical support of their division, soon to be trapped in the pocket without them. After capturing Lysyanka, 233rd Tank Brigade left some infantry and a few tanks behind to hold the town and pressed on towards Zvenigorodka, where they hoped to link up with the advance elements of Rotmistrov's 5th Guards Tank Army.

The seizure of Lysyanka made *198.Inf.Div's* position untenable. With at least a Soviet tank corps somewhere behind his right flank, General von Horn was forced to pull back his rightmost regiment and realign his division so that its front now faced to the north, not to the west as it had two days before. Its right flank was now anchored at the town of Chessnovka, its left at the outskirts of Vinograd, which von Horn's troops had retaken once again by nightfall, reestablishing contact with *34.Inf.Div*.[18] To the right of his division lay absolutely nothing but nearly 100 kilometers of empty space, an open invitation to further Soviet attack. As bad as von Horn's situation was, that of *Graf* Rittberg's *88.Inf.Div.* was even worse. One account by *Oblt.* Hans Menedetter, describes the action as experienced by the division's *Art.Rgt.188*, which was heavily engaged that day in support of the division's beleaguered infantry between Olshanitza and Savarka:

> It was a time in which every soldier - from the lowliest gunner to the regimental commander - performed his duty to the utmost and which placed the highest demands upon our [draft horses] and equipment as well. The batteries fired - without [the benefit of] prepared positions - against the constantly increasing numbers of the enemy until the barrels grew white hot, in order to help bring to a halt the massed assaults of two enemy armies.[19]

Not only had contact been lost with *Graf* Rittberg's neighbor to the south, but elements of the Soviet 337th Rifle Division were reported to be attempting to get in behind his left flank and were even rumored to be in Boguslav, the linchpin of his Ross River defensive line, still in the process of being occupied by German troops on the evening of 27 January.

At least things had quieted down in *K.Abt.B's* sector, where little had happened since the Soviet attack against Yanovka had been driven off earlier that day. In a radio conversation that evening between Lieb at *XXXXII.A.K.* and the 1a of *1.Pz.Armee*, Lieb was told to "ruthlessly weaken" his northern front held by Oberst Fouquet's *K.Abt.B* and send them to reinforce his left flank. By nightfall, Lieb already had troops from this command in motion, since they had been prepared to do just that since the day before. In fact, the evidence suggests that Lieb

During the course of the Wiking counterattack, several Soviet prisoners, including one wounded Ivan, are marched out of the forest under the watchful eyes of two Wiking Grenadiers. (U.S. National Archives)

Wiking StuG III with several Panzergrenadiers on board continues the counterattack, north of Staroselye, late January 1944. (U.S. National Archives)

had already begun pulling his troops back even before he received the order, a prudent move under the circumstances, though in direct contravention to his *Führer's* orders.

The day ended on a mixed note. While General Hell's *VII.A.K.* had held firm, it had lost ground on the right, where *198.Inf.Div.* had been forced to swing its right wing back in order to prevent being outflanked. General Lieb's *XXXXII.A.K.* was in the process of being cut off from its neighboring corps and its supplies would now have to be routed through the town of Korsun, rather than Lysyanka. *Graf* Rittberg's *88.Inf.Div.*, though weakened, was in the process of withdrawing to the Ross River line in an orderly manner. Far more uncertain was the situation to the east, where Wöhler's *8.Armee* was battling Konev's Second Ukrainian *Front*. *1.Pz.Armee* had already received disturbing reports of Soviet tanks being reported near the town of Lebedin, only 60 kilometers from Zvenigorodka, and 100 kilometers from the spearheads of the 6th Tank Army, which was reported to be in Lysyanka.

To *1.Pz.Armee*, the enemy's intentions were becoming quite clear. All of his movements seemed to indicate that he was aiming for Zvenigorodka and the encirclement of the forces in the Kanev Salient. After the Red Army had carried out this task, what would be next? It seemed likely that he would continue moving south, attempting a deep penetrations into the operational depths of Army Group South, but there was no way of knowing for sure. Closer to home, Hube and his staff foresaw the need to assemble a relief force to reestablish contact with the soon-to-be-encircled corps in what would become known to the world as the *Kessel von Tscherkassy* (the Cherkassy Cauldron), although technically it should have been named after the town of Korsun, since Cherkassy had been given up nearly a month earlier, when a smaller encirclement battle involving *Oberst* Hohn's *72.Inf.Div.* had taken place.

1.Pz.Armee had already asked Army Group for permission to begin assembling such a relief force, to be built around *III.Pz.Korps*, but was refused by Busse at Army Group Headquarters "in the sharpest of terms."[20] To get around this obstacle, Wenck, as Army Chief of Staff, informed the

commanders of the corps concerned - *III.Pz.Korps, VII.* and *XXXXII.A.K.* - that they would be issued oral instructions by him personally to begin preparing for such a relief effort. He was forced to do so in order to prevent Army Group South from discovering his intentions either through written messages, through the telephone, or through radio traffic, which could then be countermanded by Busse.[21] How low had the level of trust sunk between higher-level staffs since the outbreak of the war!

The Red Army no longer had such problems. Since the outbreak of the war, the pernicious influence of Communist Party commissars upon the efficiency of military staffs had been curtailed considerably, resulting in more trust between staff officers at higher levels of command, not less. As these staff officers gained confidence and experience, the level of trust increased. While Hitler was placing increasingly restrictive controls on his army group, army, corps, and division commanders, Stalin was becoming more content with the delegation of authority to leaders such as Marshals Vasilevsky and Zhukov.

While Army Group South's decision-making authority was paralyzed by the absence of its commander, Vatutin's and Konev's forces had made great gains in the space of only three days. At a point when the German commanders needed freedom of action to fight the battle as they saw fit, they were forced to watch helplessly as two Soviet tank armies sliced their way deep into the rear areas of *1.Pz.* and *8.Armee*, bringing the encirclement of the forces in the Kanev Salient closer to realization. Even the best efforts of the hard-fighting German infantry, artillerymen, panzer crews and combat engineers would amount to nothing unless they were intelligently led. An indication of what they could do was shown the following day, when the battle against the Soviet breakthrough in the east would reach its climax.

End Notes

[1] Loza in Armor, p. 22.

[2] *1.Pz.Armee* KTB entry dated 23 January 1944, p. 1.

[3] Ibid., p. 1.

[4] *1.Pz.Armee* KTB entry dated 24 January 1944, p. 1.

[5] *1.Pz.Armee* KTB entry dated 25 January 1944, p. 1.

[6] *Sbornik*, p. 314.

[7] *1.Pz.Armee* KTB entry dated 26 January 1944, p. 3.

[8] Gerhard Graser, *Zwischen Kattegat und Kaukasus: Weg und Kämpfe der 198.Infanterie-Division, 1939-1945*. (Tübingen, Germany: Kameradhilfswerk und Traditionverband der ehemaligen 198.Infanterie-Division, 1961), p. 284.

[9] *1.Pz.Armee* KTB entry dated 26 January 1944, p. 1.

[10] Ibid.

[11] *1.Pz.Armee* KTB entry 27 January 1944, p. 2.

[12] Graser, p. 285.

[13] Ibid, p. 1.

[14] Dr. Andreas Schwarz, *Datentafel 323.Infanterie-Division*. (Fürth, Germany: Traditionsverband der 88.Infantrie-Division, e.V., 1966), p. 41.

[15] *1.Pz.Armee* KTB entry dated 27 January 1944, p. 1.

[16] Loza, pp. 22-23. Incidentally, this account mentions that the Germans had placed five Tiger tanks in the town of Lysyanka. This is patently false, since neither *VII.* nor *XXXXII.A.K.* had such tanks, which in fact did not appear in this area until the *3.Pz.Div.*, with Heavy Tank Regiment *Bäke* arrived on the scene nearly a week later. This account undoubtedly is an example of how many Soviet veterans felt the need after the war to embroider their own exploits as a means of showcasing the superiority of the Communist system.

[17] Chief of Staff Files, *Abteilung 1a, Nicht in Kampfraum XI. und XXXXII.Armee Korps befindliche Teile*, Headquarters, *8. Armee*, 18 February 1944, p. 3.

[18] Graser, p. 285.

[19] Menedetter, *Chronik der Artillerie-Regiment 188*, pp. 66-67.

[20] *1.Pz.Armee* KTB entry dated 27 January 1944, p. 1.

[21] Ibid, p. 2.

Chapter Six

THE DAM BREAKS

"In Russia, he who defends, loses."
— *Nikolaus von Vormann in Tscherkassy*[1]

While the Soviet tanks formations had made impressive gains against *8.Armee* on 26 January and *1.Pz.Armee* on 27 January , the Germans were by no means encircled yet. By itself, armor can do little more than block the main routes into and out of the salient. It would take the slow-moving infantry of the Red Army to build up the inner and outer encircling rings, and this would take days to carry out. However, the infantry armies - 4th Guards, 52nd, 53rd, 27th, and 40th Armies - were still hung up in both the east and west on the German's first-line tactical defenses by the hard-fighting troops of *34., 72., 88., 198.,* and *389.Inf.Div.*

Additionally, Rotmistrov's and Kravchenko's forces were extremely vulnerable themselves to being cut off from their logistical tail - the area they had broken through in both east and west were very narrow corridors, subject to intense German artillery bombardment. Without additional quantities of fuel and ammunition, the Soviet armor would become immobilized and vulnerable to a German counterattack. To make matters worse for the Soviet tank and mechanized units, on the morning of 27 January, *XXXXVII.Pz.Korps* finally began its counterattack to seal the penetration for good, or so it was hoped.

It was high time, too - the morning report from *XI.A.K.* to *8.Armee* stated that enemy tanks had been reported at the outskirts of Shpola.[2] In fact, this was confirmed when *Wiking's* radio interception platoon monitored a Soviet radio transmission later that day. The message, apparently from an officer from a Soviet tank unit to his higher headquarters, proceeded thusly: "I am in Shpola and there are no Germans to be seen anywhere. What should I do?," followed by an exasperated reply from his superior, "Keep going, keep going, you asshole!"[3]

The attack, as laid out by General von Vormann, was to begin on the morning of Tuesday, 27 January with three panzer divisions. *3.Pz.Div.,* in the south along the shoulder of the Soviet penetration, would attack in a northerly direction from its current position near Vasilivka and retake the town of Raymentorovka, thereby severing the major highway heading west towards Zlatapol. Both *11.* and *14.Pz.Div.,* ten kilometers northwest of *3.Pz.Div.,* would attack side by side, *11.Pz.Div.* on the left, *14.Pz.Div.* on the right, and continue their drive north. There, they would seize Kapitanovka, form a front facing east and destroy any following Soviet units that tried to break through. Any Soviet tanks that had already broke through would be left to "wither on the vine." *Maj.* von Brese's *Pz.Gren.Rgt.108*, still occupying defensive positions north of Kapitanovka, would attack south and reestablish contact with its parent division, General Unrein's *14.Pz.Div.*

Köller's armored *Kampfgruppe* from *Wiking* with its 25 remaining *Pz.IVs* would launch an attack to the south towards Pisarevka from its current positions west of Ossitnyashka, as long as the situation on the right flank of *72.Inf.Div.* did not grow worse. The hard-pressed *389.Inf.Div.* would continue to hold its positions and would cooperate with General Trowitz's *57.Inf.Div.* in its counterattack designed to restore the front between Yekaterinovka and Pastorskoye. Trowitz's Bavarians, after a night march from their old positions along the Irdyn front, had finally moved into its assembly areas near Tashlyk the evening before. The day started out looking quite promising for the beleaguered defenders - this plan offered the best chance yet to put things right again.

Another good sign was the attachment of an additional tank battalion to provide more offensive capability to *11.Pz.Div.* This battalion, *I./Pz.Rgt.26*, had been borrowed from *Pz.Gren.Div. Grossdeutschland*, then situated nearly 100 kilometers further south, where it defended a sector southwest of Kirovograd. Equipped with 61 brand-new *Panthers*, the battalion had only recently been transferred to the Russian Front from the West, where it had just completed its training. Originally destined for *26.Pz.Div.*, then fighting in Italy, it was diverted earlier that month to *Grossdeutschland* as a temporary substitute for that division's own *Panther* battalion, also being formed in France at the same time.[4]

Commanded by *Maj.* Glaesgen, this battalion never made it to *26.Pz.Div.,* but fought with various *Grossdeutschland* units until the end of the war. Wöhler had been trying to wrest permission for its employment in his counterattack from Army Group South for several days; by the evening of 26 January, he was finally granted permission to begin its movement to the north, which began the following morning. Along with its tanks, the battalion was augmented by several elements of *Grossdeutschland's* own panzer regimental headquarters, such as repair and recovery teams, as well as an antiaircraft platoon.

However, it would not arrive to bolster *11.Pz.Div.* until late in the evening of 27 January, and would not be able to take part in operations that day at all. Even then, the battalion's employment would be strictly limited by Army Group. Since it was *8.Armee's* only substantial tank unit, Busse, Army Group South's chief of staff, wanted it pulled out after Wöhler's counterattack was finished, so it could be quickly made available for use elsewhere, should the need arise.[5]

The German counterattack began at 0530 hours, when *11.Pz.Div.* crossed its line of departure. Three hours later, its infantry battlegroup had entered the village of Pissarevka, situ-

German infantrymen moving up to take part in the relief operation. (Bundesarchiv 690/209/33)

ated at the division's right flank, driving the Soviet defenders out. At the same time, the division's armored battlegroup, composed of *Pz.Rgt.15, a Panzergrenadier* battalion mounted in half tracks, and *II./Pz.Art.Rgt.119*, was attacking on the left towards Tishkovka. An hour later, von Wietersheim, the division commander, reported to Speidel, *8.Armee's* chief of staff, that the attack was going well so far.

Not only had his division penetrated north as far as Kapitanovka, it had also established contact with *K.Gr.* von *Brese's* from *14.Pz.Div.*, cut off the previous day. When von Wietersheim's forces entered the town, the Soviet units holding it withdrew to the northwest without offering a fight, which seemed odd. The seizure of Kapitanovka cut off the bulk of 20th Tank Corps, leaving its commander, Lazarev, separated from two of his three brigades. Soviet convoys passing through the area, unaware of the German counterattack, were shot up and destroyed by German tanks patrolling up and down the supply routes.[6]

Von Brese was given the order by *8.Armee* to stand fast where he was and have his unit act as a roadblock, as long as there was no strong enemy pressure. Von Wietersheim's *11.Pz.Div.* was to orient to the east in order to block the road from Ossitnyashka to Kapitnovka, clear out the rest of the latter town, and tie in with the flank of the neighboring *14.Pz.Div.* near Pissarevka, still held by the enemy, in order to seal off the enemy penetration.[7] The latter division was to consolidate its position near Rossoshovatka and link up with *3.Pz.Div.* southeast of Raymentorovka, a mere 12 kilometers. Then the front would be stitched back together again, if all went as planned.

However, Rotmistrov, Konev's tank army commander, did something doctrinally uncharacteristic of Soviet leadership, at

least until this occasion. Instead of stopping to deal with the German counterattack and reestablishing contact with the following main body of the Second Ukrainian *Front*, he ordered his lead unit, Lazarev's 20th Guard Tank Corps, to continue attacking towards west towards Shpola and southwest towards Zlatapol. He ordered Lazarev to disregard his flanks and not stop until his corps had linked up with the spearheads of Kravchenko's 6th Tank Army at Zvenigorodka. Kirichenko's 29th Corps would follow as soon as it could disengage from the enemy. 4th Guards and 53rd Armies would deal with the Germans and widen the breach. If Rotmistrov's forces ran out of fuel and ammunition, they would be resupplied by air. This had not been an easy decision for Rotmistrov.

On 26 January, he believed that his forces risked being bogged down in the Kapitanovka area and he had already received reports that additional German tank forces were en route that evening. Kirichenko, whose tank-heavy force had sustained heavy losses near Rossoshovatka, requested permission to go over to the defense. Lazarev's 20th Tank Corps in the north, whose spearhead that night had reached as far as Lebedin, was ordered to continue the attack the following day. Kirichenko would defend until Rotmistrov's reserve, 18th Tank Corps, commanded by Major General of Tank Troops V.I. Polozkov, had closed up by the morning of 27 January. Then, both corps would attack, bust through the Germans, and keep moving west, with Kirichenko's corps to protect Lazarev's left flank.[8]

The German's first realization on 27 January that something was amiss came at 0935 hours when *XI.A.K.* reported that four to five enemy tanks were in reported to be in Shpola. They had been spotted earlier that morning when the *Schienenbus* (powered railcar), operated by *Wiking* as a sort of supply and taxi service, moved south towards the town and noticed groups of Soviet tanks approaching from the east. In order to determine which forces were in the corps' rear area, *Wiking* sent a military police patrol (no other combat forces were available) to the town to conduct a reconnaissance. They confirmed the railcar's report and added that more tanks were passing through the town heading west towards Zvenigorodka.[9] A steady stream of trucks and tanks were also reported on the road between Shirovka and Lebedin and between Lebedin and Shpola.

At nearly the same time, *Oberst* Lang's *3.Pz.Div.* reported that his left flank had come under renewed heavy attack by Soviet tanks and infantry, necessitating the commitment of his division's armored battlegroup to restore the situation. Soviet tanks that had got in around the division's left flank were reported to be attacking the unit's rear service and support units.[10] Although *3.Pz.Div.'s* few remaining tanks knocked out seven T-34s, the Soviet tanks forced the delay of the planned attack to link up with *14.Pz.Div.* at Rossochovatka.

At 1050 hours, *14.Pz.Div.* reported further enemy forces assembling east of Rossoshovatka, where it had knocked out ten Soviet tanks since 0600 hours. A patrol from *11.Pz.Div.* reported that it had encountered strong enemy forces assembling in the woods two kilometers west of Kapitanovka. The Soviets appeared to be massing everywhere. Despite these disturbing developments, General Speidel at *8.Armee* Headquarters declared to Army Group South headquarters that "the enemy east-west connection is cut off at the present time," which indeed was technically correct.[11] The Soviet spearhead was cut off, but could the new German front hold?

Over the next several hours, the situation deteriorated rapidly. At 1430 hours, Rossoshovatka was lost after changing hands several times, despite the renewed efforts of *3.* and *14.Pz.Div.* to hold them, by now panzer divisions in name only. Ten Soviet tanks charged into Tishkovka and broke through to the west. Forces from *11.Pz.Div.* holding Kapitanovka were driven out by a strong enemy force. General von Wietersheim reported that his troops were fighting for their lives against renewed enemy tank attacks. A second wave of 22 T-34s thundered through the armored battlegroup holding Tishkovka and headed west towards Lebendin. These tanks were most likely from 80th Tank Brigade, the second echelon unit of Lazarev's 20th Guards Tank Corps.

Another Soviet tank attack, reinforced by infantry, crashed into Tishkovka two hours later. There simply were not enough German infantry or tanks to help hold the gains of that morning, and artillery was a poor substitute when combating mobile forces. *8.Armee* had ordered *320.Inf.Div.* to hand over its sector to the neighboring *10.Pz.Gren.Div.* near Panchevo, march 50 kilometers, and take over *3.Pz.Div.'s* position, a maneuver which would require several days before that panzer division could be freed up. Until then, *11.* and *14.Pz.Div.* would have to do the best they could.

One eyewitness to the attack on Tishkovka was *Hptm.* Walter Schaefer-Kehnert, commander of *II./Pz.Art.Rgt.119* of *11.Pz.Div.* Schaefer-Kehnert, a 26 year-old reservist from the town of Kehnert on the Elbe, had been serving with his division

He watched the Soviet tide roll through Kapitanovka.
Hauptmann Walter Schaefer-Kehnert, *Commander, 2.Btl., Pz.Art.Rgt.119, 11.Pz.Div.*
(Photo courtesy of Walter Schaefer-Kehnert)

since its inception in late 1940. A veteran of the Battle of France, the invasion of Yugoslavia, and the Eastern Front, he had been commissioned in 1940 as a signals officer. Wounded during the Battle for Moscow in January 1942, he was wounded again in the hip during von Manstein's abortive offensive to relieve Stalingrad in December 1942, recovering in time to take part in the Battle of Kursk and the retreat to the Dnieper. He had earned the *Deutsche Kreuz in Gold* (German Cross in Gold) for his repeated bravery in action, an award he referred to jokingly as the "Party Badge for the Nearsighted," because of the large swastika it bore in its center.* Nevertheless, its wearers were highly respected.[12]

He was present in Tishkovka when it was attacked that afternoon. His account, preserved in a letter he wrote home shortly after the battle was over, gives a glimpse of what the fighting was like:

---

* The *Deutsche Kreuz* in Gold was also known as *das Sturmabzeichen für Ritterkreuzträger*, or "the assault badge for Knight's Cross Holders."

Tanks and infantry attacked us in the flank again [that afternoon] and succeeded in occupying the center of the town. Two of our [battle group's] battalions were cut off in the northern part of town, including two of my battery commanders, Reissland and Kamieth, who were manning their observation posts, while we sat in the south with the guns. The situation had gotten completely out of control. Our tanks outside of the town had formed a hedgehog for self-defense . . . On the map, red (for Soviet) and blue (for German) [tactical symbols], were all mixed together. That night, my two battery commanders were able to sneak back through the enemy-occupied town. They were quite a sight to see, and we embraced each other [in joy], when we met up . . . [13]

14.Pz.Div.'s armored battlegroup, *K.Gr. Langkeit*, again retook Rossoshovatka, for the second time in as many days, but it was no use. Soviet tanks and infantry from 29th Guards Tank Corps and the newly-committed 18th Guards Tanks Corps began pouring through the ever-widening gap between Kapitanovka and Rossoshovatka, despite the desperate efforts of the Germans to stop them. Dozens of tanks were knocked out, but the flood was unaffected. The divisional history of *14.Pz.Div.* provides a gripping account of the battle that followed:

In the middle of the fire from all our [division's] weapons the enemy pushed inexorably to the west. What did it matter to him, whether his riflemen were mowed down in rows, if tank upon tank were left behind in flames? More and more armored vehicles festooned with masses of infantry pushed forward in endless columns, closely followed by galloping cavalry formations, flowed around the remaining islands of resistance and continued onward.[14]

To the amazement of the Germans, over 100 T-34s thundered past their defensive positions. Although *3.*, *11.*, and *14.Pz.Divs.* attempted to stem the flood, waves of T-34s kept heading west, losing dozens of tanks to German fire. *XXXXVII.Pz.Korps'* plan to restore the front line came too late. With fewer than 50 tanks of its own, the corps was simply overrun.

Rotmistrov's daring plan had succeeded and the bulk of his tank army had broken through to the west. Another account of the battle is provided by Nikolaus von Vormann, *XXXXVII.Pz.Korps'* commander:

Without regard to losses - in the truest sense of the term, the Red masses flooded to the west during the afternoon past the tanks of 3., 11., and 14.Panzer Divisions, who were firing with every barrel, as well as past our heavy artillery fire. An amazing, shatteringly dramatic picture! No other true comparison could fit [this amazing scene]: the dam had broken, and the massive unending flood plunged over the flat landscape,

where [our] tanks, surrounded by our few remaining infantry, stood out like cliffs in a firestorm. Our amazement rose further still, when in the late afternoon through the middle of our Sperrfeuer (blocking fire), tightly-packed cavalry formations [of the enemy] galloped towards the west. It was an unforgettable, incredibly shattering scene.[15]

General Konev, who was present in Rotmistrov's command post while the breakthrough was occurring, was impressed with Rotmistrov's control of this maneuver. Konev praised his tank commander's self-control and tactical acumen, commenting that Rotmistrov "clearly led the actions of his subordinate corps and brigades, sensibly assessing the situation and taking well-grounded decisions."[16]

How much Rotmistrov's decision was influenced by Konev's desire to get to Zvenigorodka first is not known. Had Rotmistrov's breakthrough at Kapitanovka failed, his commander would not had been so generous in his praise, to put it mildly. Konev was well known for his penchant for relieving commanders who had failed him; two days before, he had relieved the first commander of the 4th Guards Army, General Ryshov, and replaced him with General Smirnov, for failing to conduct an adequate reconnaissance of the German positions opposite his sector, leading, perhaps in Konev's opinion, to the slow development of the initial attack.

To protect the breakthrough corridor, Konev ordered that several antitank brigades be dispatched to the Kapitanovka area immediately, as well as a rifle division from 4th Guards Army. The horsemen who had broken through were from Selivanov's 5th Cavalry Corps, whose mission was to begin the exploitation phase of the breakthrough, as well as to bolster the strength of Rotmistrov's infantry-starved formations. It was these cavalrymen whom the German eyewitnesses had marveled at. One Soviet account of the decisive breakthrough that day credits Rotmistrov's boldness for saving the Second Ukrainian *Front's* operation.[17] In addition, Rotmistrov ordered 29th Tank Corps to take up the defense of the Vodyanoye-Lipyanka line with its front facing toward the south, directly perpendicular to the direction of attack of the German panzer divisions.[18]

By ordering his formations to keep pressing forward, without waiting for the infantry armies to catch up, Rotmistrov was able to throw the German defenses off balance and create the conditions for a large-scale encirclement. Despite this unfavorable development, some officers in the German chain of command were slow to believe its import. Even Army Group South's operations and intelligence officers, despite reports to the contrary, still believed that the Red Army did not have the strength to conduct such a grand operation and felt that the situation would soon be "balanced out."[19] Hampering the German conduct of the battle that day was the fact that Stemmermann controlled one Panzer division, von Vormann another, and *8. Armee* directly controlled a third.

Even in the best of situations, this would have been an awkward command arrangement. Besides, Stemmermann had been more involved in events which were occurring farther to the north, where things had gone badly and could not devote his full attention to what was taking place near Kapitanovka. Consequently, *8.Armee* issued an order at 1800 hours 27 January designed to simplify the previous command and control arrangement, and make the new one more streamlined. Von Vormann's corps quickly incorporated *14.Pz.Div.*, which had been temporarily under command of *XI.A.K.*, and *11.Pz.Div.*, which had been under the direct control of *8.Armee.* Furthermore, von Vormann's *XXXXVII.Pz.Korps* took over responsibility for the entire sector encompassing the breakthrough.[20] Von Vormann welcomed the switch, since this would make his already difficult assignment somewhat easier, at least on paper.

For the following day, 28 January, General von Vormann was issued another set of instructions. They would prove to be just as difficult to carry out as his orders had been that day. His corps was to reestablish the connection between his corps and *XI.A.K.*, from *3.Pz.Div's* left flank to the *XI.A.K's* southern flank near Pastorskoye, cut the Soviet supply arteries (again), and destroy all of the Soviet tanks that were still occupying ground in the area encompassing Pissarevka, Kapitanovka, and Turiya. Meanwhile, the fighting continued.

Another wave of Soviet tanks roared through Tinovka, scattering another attempt by von Wietersheim's *11.Pz.Div.* to reestablish contact with his troops in the northern part of the ten kilometer-long village. Contact with *K.Gr. von Brese* was lost again. The second attempt by Martin Unrein's *14.Pz.Div.* that day to retake Rossoshovatka was bloodily repulsed that evening. Although his division was able to knock out 14 T-34s, the division had suffered 310 casualties in the past 36 hours and had only six tanks and assault guns left in operating condition.[21] Fortunately for von Vormann, the vanguard of *I./Pz.Rgt.26* had arrived in its assembly area and would be available for the attack the following day.

It had arrived on the battlefield in the nick of time. Both *11.* and *14.Pz.Divs.* would regroup that evening for another attempt at cutting off Rotmistrov's tank army the next day. Little did any of them realize that Rotmistrov cared little whether he was cut off or not; in fact, the bulk of his army had already passed to the west of Kapitanovka and it was now the job of the infantry armies following in his wake to clear his supply routes, for the Soviet tank general was after far bigger game than three shot-up panzer divisions. He intended to bag the 100,000 Germans believed to be in the Kanev Salient. His leading tank units were only a few kilometers away from their goal of Zvenigorodka; in a few more hours, the town would be theirs, for the Germans seemed to have little in the way of tactical reserves to stop them, even had they tried. A great victory was clearly within Pavel Rotmistrov's grasp.

While the drama to the south was unfolding, the situation to the north in the middle of *XI.A.K's* sector was deteriorating alarmingly. The day began promisingly enough when *72.Inf.Div.* began withdrawing to the "Bowstring" position in good order. This move would allow it to maintain a coherent front while keeping in contact with the battlegroup of *389.Inf.Div.* on its right near Yekaterinovka. However, by 0820 hours, a renewed attack from the south and southwest by units of 21st Guards

Rifle Corps (31st and 375th Rifle Divisions and 69th Guards Rifle Division) had pushed back the center of 389th Division to Pastorskoye. To prevent a breakthrough, *57.Inf.Div.*, which was preparing to move from its assembly area south of Tashlyk to take over the right flank of *389.Inf.Div.,* dispatched a combat-ready detachment towards Pastorskoye via Makeyevka.

At the same time, *72.Inf.Div.* reported a number of resolutely-led Soviet attacks against the right flank of its newly-occupied position. Although the defense of Pastorskoye was shored up by the counterattack of *57.Inf.Div.,* the situation took a dramatic turn for the worse when an enemy battalion broke through *72.Inf.Div's* right flank held by Richard Kästner's *Gren.Rgt.105* near the railway station at Serdjukovka and headed towards Tashlyk. Another enemy battalion accompanied by four tanks, most likely from 7th Guards Airborne Division, broke through three kilometers to the northeast at the village of Krasny Chutor, and headed towards Yekaterinovka.

Kästner's regiment would get hit from behind if it did not react quickly enough. A counterattack was immediately carried out by his northerly neighbor, *Gren.Rgt.266,* led by *Hptm.* Strathof, using a 2 cm self-propelled antiaircraft gun and a PaK 40 7.5 cm antitank gun. After a short but sharp battle, the enemy was driven back.[22] The enemy attack towards Tashlyk inexplicably stopped when it came to the rail line. The other battalion-sized enemy force near Pastorskoye was thrown back and surrounded in a large wood north of the village in a counterattack launched by *57.Inf.Div.*

It was a scene reminiscent of the famous Dutch boy trying to plug the crumbling dike with his fingers and toes. As soon as one Soviet breakthrough was ironed-out, another one occurred a few kilometers to the north or south. The three German infantry divisions in the area simply did not have enough men to be everywhere at once. Another battalion-sized force broke through at Krasny Chutor at 1430 hours that afternoon, but was thrown out in another counterattack launched by *57.Inf.Div.* By 1700 hours, three major attacks against *72.Inf.Div.* had been reported, and its front had been pierced again between the railway station at Serdjukovka and Krasny Chutor. A gap nearly six kilometers wide had been ripped wide open.

A previously unidentified Soviet unit, 254th Rifle Division, had been detected in the area. The time had come when *72.*, *57.*, and *389.Inf.Div.* had to be moved back to the *Hamsterstellung*, before it was too late. At 1740 hours, Stemmermann called Speidel and begged him to grant permission for his troops to fall back immediately. Speidel demurred, stating that he had already requested permission from Army Group South to do so, and was awaiting a reply.[23]

Speidel had in fact done so. An hour after his conversation with the commander of *XI.A.K.*, Speidel contacted Busse again, brought him up to date on the tactical situation, and told him that he felt compelled to order the withdrawal to the *Hamsterstellung*. Busse stated that he understood the seriousness of the situation, but could not authorize the withdrawal. He was acting on Field Marshal von Manstein's instructions, now nearly two days old, to hold firm and wait until a panzer corps could be freed from the *1.Pz.Armee*. Busse said that the enemy could not be as strong as was being reported, and that most of his armored units were probably burnt out by now. He ended by stating that a few enemy units will "squeak through," though not in any force to worry about. Therefore, *8.Armee's* corps and divisions should hold fast and simply sit tight until the other corps arrived. Busse had told substantially the same story to Wenck at *1.Pz.Armee* headquarters.

Surprisingly, permission to withdraw to the *Hamsterstellung* was granted by Busse twenty minutes later. The request had been routed back to von Manstein at Rastenburg several hours before and he evidently had gained Hitler's concurrence. Speidel informed Gädke, Stemmermann's chief of staff, that *XI.A.K.* could withdraw to the positions as it saw fit. And not a minute too soon, especially for Hermann Hohn's *72.Inf.Div.* As the sun set, the Soviets finally broke through in front of Kästner's *Gren.Rgt.105*. A last-minute relief attack by Siegel's *Gren.Rgt.266* again saved the day, after it struck the Soviet force in the flank. As it got dark, the German infantrymen withdrew to their new positions, with the enemy following closely.

Confusion reigned. Part of Siegel's regiment was stranded when combat engineers blew the bridge near the village of Popovka too soon. The creek was frozen over, but the troops thought it was too thin to support the weight of a man, much less vehicles towing PaKs and light infantry howitzers. They drove over it anyway and to their surprise and relief, the ice held. During the dark, some units of both regiments got mixed up with one another. Resupply was done only with great difficulty, since no direction markers had been placed at key road intersections. Worse still, Siegel's regiment had lost contact with Kästner's on the right. But at least they had made it back to a position which ought to offer some protection, or so they believed.[24] The next day, the division would hopefully reestablish contact with *389.Inf.Div.* and *57.Inf.Div.* would launch a full-scale division-sized counterattack and restore the situation to their advantage.

Meanwhile, to the north, the bulk of *Wiking* and the Walloon Brigade still manned their old positions along the Dnieper and Olshanka Rivers, and south of the Irdyn Swamp. Nothing had happened there since the offensive began three days before except for occasional enemy patrols. Even the relief in place of *57.Inf.Div.* had proceeded without incident. Except for *Wiking's* armored battlegroup, these two powerful formations, which could have enormously assisted the divisions fighting in the south, were tied down because they had been chosen to hold a portion of the front that had strong propaganda value but little true military value. Leon Degrelle, then serving as an *SS-Hstuf.* in the Walloon Brigade, commented that:

Posted at the easternmost point, the Assault Brigade "Wallonia" escaped the worst of the enemy's clawing during the first few days. As expected, the enemy concentrated its thrust south and west of the Kessel . . . At the Olshanka and the Dnieper, the Red offensive was as yet only by radio. A powerful transmitter, installed just opposite our lines, peddled propaganda every day in a honeyed French. A speaker with a Parisian accent charitably informed us of our situation. Then he tried to seduce us, vaunting the marvels of friend Stalin's regime

and inviting us to come over holding a white handkerchief in our hands, like sentimental aunties . . . [25]

Their period of relative inactivity would soon end and the fight raging to the south would spread to the north and finally engulf them, too.

Throughout the day of 27 January, *8.Armee* and its corps continued to receive reports from the *1.Pz.Armee* detailing the unfolding disaster taking place 100 kilometers to the west. As if having to deal with the crisis in their own sector were not enough, Wöhler's troops would now have to worry about being attacked from the rear as well. Though dire, this situation was primarily the concern of army and corps staffs at this stage of the battle. The combat troops had more pressing concerns, such as preparing to meet another Soviet attack or planning a counterattack to regain lost positions. As the *Landsers* continued to fall back, they would be forced again and again to hack out fighting positions in the frozen ground. Staying alive in this hellish environment was a big enough challenge for the average soldier. Fighting by day and withdrawing and digging new foxholes by night was rapidly sapping German fighting strength and morale. What sleep they got were occasional catnaps they could manage between attacks. As yet, most had no inkling of the noose slowing being drawn about them. That would come later.

The circumstances were hardly better for the average Soviet front-line soldier, or *Frontovniks*. If anything, they were probably worse. Creature comforts was never high on the list of the concerns for most Soviet commanders. Treatment of the wounded was rudimentary, at best, though the Red Army's medical services improved somewhat throughout the war. Any soldier who failed to press an attack vigorously enough or who lagged behind could expect a bullet in the back of the head from his commander or unit commissar. They were driven day and night into the attack with little rest. For the so-called booty Ukrainians, hastily pressed into service without the rudiments of training, things were worse still.

Considered by many of their Russian compatriots as collaborators or, at the very least, shirkers of their patriotic duty to defend the Motherland, they were herded into battle with the utmost callousness. Many of these units suffered appalling casualties from German small arms fire and artillery, which still functioned efficiently at this stage of the battle. Additionally, the weather had begun to grow warmer during the day. Although the rich, black Ukrainian soil or *chernozem* was still frozen beneath, the top layer became a gooey mess during the day that clung to boots and clothing. During the evening, as troops lay in their hasty fighting positions, the temperature dropped below zero degrees centigrade, causing their wet clothing to freeze on their bodies. Fires, of course, were forbidden, being a guarantee of drawing a response from a German patrol or artillery fire. However, Soviet soldiers had one thing in their favor which the Germans did not - they knew that they were now winning and had been doing so steadily since July 1943. And with a string of successes behind them, the troops of both the First and Second Ukrainian *Fronts* were becoming increasingly confident in their own superiority.

Throughout the night of 27/28 January, the fighting continued unabated. The withdrawal of *72.Inf.Div.* to the *Hamsterstellung* was vigorously pressed by the Soviets at many places, though the division made it back intact. Fritz Kruse's much-weakened *389.Inf.Div.*, fighting west of Yekaterinovka, successfully warded off several enemy attacks against its northern flank, where it joined with *72.Inf.Div.* Fighting continued in Ossitnyashka, where the Germans still held the northwest corner of the town. Köller's armored battle group from *Wiking* was tied up in support of the defenders there and did not take part in the counterattack that day. Tinovka was also contested throughout the evening without either side gaining the upper hand. Both *11.* and *14.Pz.Div.* warded off numerous Soviet attempts to penetrate their fighting positions, but were driven off without any major fighting. *XI.A.K.* reported heavy motor vehicle traffic moving east of Ossitnyashka to the north, perhaps a herald of a major attack about to unfold against *389.* and *72.Inf.Div.*

Indeed, the day, which had begun so promisingly, had seen German fortunes unexpectedly reversed. While General von Vormann's two panzer divisions had temporarily cut off the bulk of Rotmistrov's tank army, they had suffered heavy losses in men and equipment. Rotmistrov's decision to commit his tanks to the exploitation now meant that that over 100 tanks with supporting infantry and artillery were loose in the German rear, and there was nothing there to stop them. Even worse, the bulk of Konev's infantry armies had yet to begin their main attack, but intelligence indicators were pointing to signs that such an attack was imminent.

Complicating matters decisively was the absence of von Manstein and the commanders of both *1.Pz.* and *8.Armee*, who also had been called to East Prussia for Hitler's conference. It had been a battle fought that day by chiefs of staffs - Busse, Speidel, and Wenck. Although each had performed well given the circumstances, they did not have the authority to order the major decisions that the situation demanded - the withdrawal of the forces out of the salient before they were encircled. They would have to stand fast pending a decision from Hitler, who was loathe to give up territory, especially if it had any political significance attached to it.

The consequences of Hitler's stand-fast decree had once again bore bitter fruit. The only logical course of action left open to the Germans was to allow the two corps in the Kanev salient to withdraw and reestablish contact with their neighbors to the south, but this request had been repeatedly turned down by Hitler. The frustration felt by commanders is best summed up by Nikolaus von Vormann, who stated that:

> 8.Armee's hands were tied. Hitler's command decree which concentrated power in his own hands had led by 1944 to the point where an army commander had only very little freedom of action. Der Führer dictated the field of battle and the employment and use of individual divisions. The high state of development of communications equipment enabled any kind of questioning [of

commander's decisions] and interference from East Prussia (Hitler's field headquarters) down to the corps level and even further down to small units.[26]

Nevertheless, *8.Armee* would continue its planned counterattack for the following day, 28 January. Although von Vormann's corps had been greatly weakened during the past three days of heavy fighting, the commitment of *Grossdeutschland's* Panther battalion the next day held great promise.

Essentially, the plan was unchanged from that of 27 January. The three aforementioned panzer divisions would continue their counterattack and seal the holes that the Soviets had torn through what was essentially a thin screen line. More artillery would be brought up to pound the narrow corridor still held by the Soviets. In the north, the withdrawal to the *Hamsterstellung* and the division-sized counterattack by Trowitz's *57.Inf.Div.* would throw the enemy off balance and allow a coherent defense to be reestablished. Providing, of course, that the Soviets would cooperate by granting the defenders the required breathing space. After all, nearly a hundred Red tanks had been knocked out and thousands of their men had been killed, wounded, or captured.

Konev, of course, had no desire to conform to German expectations. While Rotmistrov was to continue his exploitation to the west in the direction of Zvenigorodka, 4th Guards, 52nd, and 53rd Armies would launch all-out attacks to crush the Germans' remaining defenses along *8.Armee's* front and begin the creation of the inner ring of encirclement. The southernmost of these armies taking part in the attack, 53rd Army, would strike to the southwest in order to protect the exposed left flank of Rostmistrov's tank army. The Germans, who had yet to feel the full brunt of the Second Ukrainian *Front's* attack, would soon get the opportunity.

While this attack was being prepared, Lazarev's tank corps continued his attack towards Zvenigorodka, pushing his tired brigades and battalions throughout the evening of 27/28 January. He hoped to link up somewhere with the spearhead of Kravchenko's 6th Tank Army, attacking from the west. With luck, Rotmistrov reckoned that Lazarev should get there first.[27] The Soviet's Korsun-Shevchenkovsky Operation appeared to be nearing its long-awaited goal - the encirclement of all of the Germans occupying the Kanev salient, who seemed to be passively content to hold ground that was militarily worthless. Victory was within reach - only a few more kilometers to go! Unfortunately for the Soviets, Army Group South's commander had returned to his headquarters and was not about to permit another Stalingrad to occur along the banks of the Dnieper. This time, both sides would be involved in one of the greatest battles fought on the Eastern Front.

End Notes

[1]   von Vormann, p. 62.

[2]   *8.Armee* KTB entry, 0600 hours, 27 January, 1944, p. 1.

[3]   Kathagen, Fritz. *Chronik der 2./SS Panzer Nachrichten Abteilung 5, 1940-1945.* (Osnabrück, Germany: Munin Verlag, 1989), p. 85.

[4]   Helmuth Spaeter, *The History of the Panzerkorps Grossdeutschland, Vol. 2.* (Winnipeg, Manitoba: J.J. Fedorowicz Publishing, 1995), p. 276.

[5]   *8.Armee* KTB entry, 1005 hours, 27 January 1944, p. 2.

[6]   Armstrong, p. 366.

[7]   *8.Armee* KTB entry, 0910 hours, 27 January 1944, p. 2.

[8]   Armstrong, p. 365.

[9]   Kameradschaftsverband der ehemalige SS-Panzer Division *Wiking, Der Kessel von Tscherkassy: Die Flut verschlang sich selbst, nicht uns!* (Osnabrück, Germany: Munin Verlag GmbH, 1969), p. 6.

[10]   Traditionsverband der 3.Panzer-Division, *Geschichte der 3.Panzer-Division: Berlin-Brandenburg 1935-1945.* (Berlin:Verlag Günther Richter,1967), p. 417.

[11]   *8.Armee* KTB entry, 1220 hours, 27 January 1944, p. 3.

[12]   Letter from Walter Schaefer-Kehnert, Remagen, Germany to the author, 29 August, 1996, p. 2. Original in author's possession.

[13]   Walter Schaefer-Kehnert, *Kriegstagebuch in Feldpostbriefen, 1940-1945.* (Remagen,Germany: Privately published manuscript, 1996), pp. 246-248.

[14]   *Geschichte der 3.Panzer-Division,* p. 168.

[15]   von Vormann, p. 60.

[16]   Armstrong, p. 366.

[17]   Ibid, p. 367.

[18]   Pavel Rotmistrov, "To the Twentieth Anniversary of the Korsun-Shevchenkovsky Operation," in *Selected Readings in Military History: Soviet Military History, Volume I, The Red Army, 1918 - 1945.* (Fort Leavenworth, KS: U.S. Army Command and General Staff College, January 1984), p. 328.

[19]   *8.Armee* KTB entry, 1735 hours, 27 January 1944, p. 3.

[20]   Ibid, 1800 hours, 27 January 1944, p. 4.

[21]   Ibid, 2040 hours, 27 January 1944, p. 5.

[22]   Siegel, p. 7.

[23]   *8.Armee* KTB entry, 1900 hours 27 February 1944, p. 6.

[24]   Siegel, p. 7.

[25]   Leon Degrelle, *Campaign in Russia: The Waffen-SS on the Eastern Front.* (Torrance, CA: Institute for Historical Review, 1985), p. 165.

[26]   von Vormann, p. 61.

[27]   Rotmistrov, p. 328.

Chapter Seven

THE TRAP SLAMS SHUT AT ZVENIGORODKA

"Forward, Kameraden! We must retreat!"
— *Gerhard Mayer, 88.Inf.Div.*[1]

The morning of Friday, 28 January 1944 dawned with freezing temperatures and scattered snowstorms. Another damned day in Russia, many *Landser* must have thought. For the troops of *XI.* and *XXXXII.A.K.*, this day would herald a nightmare that would last for three full weeks. For the soldiers of the First and Second Ukrainian *Fronts*, it would be just as difficult, but their effort would end in victory. Those three weeks, however, would not end until the combatants of both sides had witnessed some of the fiercest fighting they had ever experienced, in a war that was already renowned for its primitive level of ferocity and brutality.

On this day the Soviet forces made the first move. While von Vormann's three panzer divisions were getting ready to renew their own attack to blunt the Soviet assault, at 0800 hours a wave of Soviet infantry with tank support attacked the right flank of *14.Pz.Div.* and the left flank of *3.Pz.Div.*, between the towns of Raymenterovka and Rossoshovakta. *3.Pz.Div.'s* tank regiment launched a counterattack with its *II./Pz.Rgt.8*, commanded by *Hptm.* Koenig, and succeeded in destroying seven Soviet tanks by 1000 hours. Koenig's advance was brought to a halt when his tanks encountered a strong barrier of antitank guns. At least he and his troops had removed, however temporarily, the threat to his division's left flank, though prospects looked dim for continuing with the planned attack for that day.[2] Additionally, more Soviet forces had moved into Tishkovka, making it virtually impossible for *11.Pz.Div.* to reestablish contact with its reconnaissance and engineer battalions which were still cut off in the northern part of the village. The day had already begun inauspiciously.

There was a glimmer of hope, however, with the arrival of the long-awaited *Grossdeutschland* Panther battalion, which had linked up with von Wietersheim's division the previous evening. It moved out to the northeast that morning, attacking towards Ossitnyashka via Pissarevka. Elsewhere, the situation in *XI.A.K.* was mixed. Von Brese's *Pz.Gren.Rgt.108*, cut off the previous day, had established contact with *389.Inf.Div.* and was once again being supplied with food, fuel, and ammunition.[3] To the north, *57.Inf.Div.* had been ordered by Stemmermann to suspend its attack to the south to close up the gap near Pastorskoye for a few hours. Two of its three regiments had been committed to various smaller-scale counterattacks the previous day and the division needed time to regroup its forces before it could launch its attack.

72.Inf.Div. had made it back to the *Hamsterstellung* and its *Gren.Rgt.124* had pulled out of the "rat trap" of Smela, thus freeing it to become the division reserve. In doing so, the regimental commander neglected to tell the *Germania* regiment, their neighbor to the west, that they were leaving. This forced the *Germania*, commanded by *Ostuf.* Fritz Ehrath, to withdraw from its positions too, lest their open right flank suffer envelopment by rapidly advancing elements of 294th Rifle Division. This lack of coordination was to become an increasingly common occurrence as the battle progressed. The withdrawal brought only brief respite; all of *72.Inf.Div.'s* regiments had been closely followed into their new positions by the Soviet 78th and 20th Guards Rifle Corps. How long the *Hamsterstellung* could be held had already become problematic.

To the west, the situation was, if anything, even more dynamic. *1.Pz.Armee* saw the situation quite clearly and was certain that it could not prevent the attacking tank armies from linking up with one another. In its war diary for that day, Wenck noted:

> The powerful movement of the enemy today is clearly aimed at a breakthrough between the two corps (VII. and XXXXII.A.K.) towards Zvenigorodka. He has been attacking ruthlessly through the gap between the two corps with the clearly recognizable intention of linking up at all costs with [his] armored group advancing from the direction of Shpola.[4]

 ❖ ❖ ❖

Vatutin intended to do just that. His infantry armies would continue their attacks to widen the shoulders of the penetration between the boundary of the *VII.* and *XXXXII.A.K.*, while the 6th Tank Army would advance quickly towards Zvenigorodka and arrive there before Konev's troops did. 27th Army would attack in the north to build the western half of the encirclement ring, while simultaneously trying to work its way into the rear of the rapidly forming pocket, in order to carve it up into smaller bite-sized pieces. The neighboring 40th Army would attack to the southeast and establish a defense line facing south in order to protect the exposed right flank of Kravchenko's force from German counterattack. That possibility did not yet worry Vatutin. So far, his forces had encountered no German armor at all, unlike the situation to his east, where Konev had been contending with determined tank-led counterattacks for three days.

There, near Pissarevka, a large tank battle had been underway since mid-morning, pitting the *Grossdeutschland's I./Pz.Rgt.26* against a sizable Soviet tank force situated among the rolling hills northeast of the town. The Panthers, attacking in

Maj. Hans von Brese, *Commander of the lost Kampfgruppe from 14.Pz.Div., Pz.Gren,Rgt.108.*
(Photo: Horst Scheibert)

conjunction with the *905.StuG.Abt.*, ran directly into the path of another Soviet tank attack from the direction of Ossitnyashka. Adding to the Germans' problems was that a large number of Soviet antitank guns had been sited in both Pissarevka and Tishkovka, forcing them to attack through a deadly crossfire. The situation was an ideal one for the Soviet defenders, since the Germans were forced to attack uphill most of the way and were unable to take advantage of their superior long-range tank cannon. By 1100 hours, the Panther battalion had destroyed 12 T-34s, though 15 of its own tanks were knocked out. *Maj.* Glaesgen, the battalion commander, was fatally wounded near Yusefovka while standing in his turret. Though an experienced commander himself, his unit's baptism of fire had come at a high price.[5]

Once again the German counterattack stalled as it had the previous day when it was engulfed by simultaneous Soviet attacks. While the Panther battalion was fighting at Pissarevka, *3.Pz.Div.* came under renewed attack near Raymentorovka. It was forced to pull its left flank further back and was very nearly encircled. The situation was restored after nine of the 14 attacking Soviet tanks were knocked out, but the division had lost contact with *14.Pz.Div.* to its left. This division was now hotly engaged with attacking elements from the 25th and 66th Guards Rifle Divisions, strongly reinforced with artillery, whose goal was to apparently widen the area of the penetration. The historian of *14.Pz.Div.* stated that the troops much preferred this situation to fighting against Soviet tanks; at least the Germans could hold their own against infantry assaults. It would be even better if their opponent stopped and began to build defensive positions.[6] After three days of unremitting combat, Unrein's men had suffered heavy casualties and were exhausted. All of von Vormann's divisions were

in about the same state. How much longer could they hold out before they began to crack?

There was no respite for *XXXXVII.Pz.Korps* that day. A regiment-sized attack against the remaining German positions in Ossitnyashka was reported, as well as renewed attacks against the encircled battlegroup in Tishkovka. Strong enemy forces were resolutely defending Kapitanovka. Both *11.* and *14.Pz.Div.* had suffered such casualties that each had fewer than 300 combat troops left. Despite these adverse developments, the supply line to Rotmistrov's army had been cut once again. In the words of the Soviet after-action report, "During the battles, the populated areas of Kapitanovka, Tishkovka, Zhuravka, and Turiya changed hands several times, which made ammunition and fuel supplies to the tank army difficult."[7] Even Zhukov stated later that the Germans had put up stiff resistance, "fighting back with fire and counterattack."[8]

Stemmermann's corps was also having a hard time of it. A mid-morning attack against *72.Inf.Div.* positions at the Serdjukovko railway station by a Soviet infantry battalion was driven off after heavy fighting. Fighting was also reported near the villages of Popovka and Tenovka. *Gren.Rgt.266* made a surprising report that the inhabitants of Popovka had turned on their German occupiers. Using pitchforks and scythes, both women and men had attacked soldiers in the streets, forcing them to return fire.[9] Even simple peasants had begun to sense the change in the air, as they heard the sound of gunfire, saw the Germans withdrawing, and drew the obvious conclusion - the Red Army was coming. Better strike now rather than be labeled as a collaborator later by a not too sympathetic commissar! Civilians also reportedly rose up against the Germans that day in Ternovka and Tashlyk as well. The German's image of *Ivan* as a cheerful, harmless, simple peasant was in the process of being demolished. Total war had returned to the Ukraine.

In the late morning, the long-delayed counterattack to restore the front line between Pastorskoye and Bogdanovka by Trowitz's *57.Inf.Div.* finally began. By noon, it had nearly succeeded, but his men had to drive off numerous Soviet counterattacks. At the same time, the remnant of *389.Inf.Div.* north of Pastorskoye tried to counterattack south and link up with *57.Inf.Div.,* but the Soviet defenders in its path prevented them from getting far. The other portion of *389.Inf.Div.*, still holding a thin sector running from Ossitnyashka to the northeastern outskirts of Kaptinanovka where it linked up with von Brese's force, reported in mid-afternoon that it had driven off several Soviet infantry assaults.

These forces were evidently trying to turn the division's right flank and get in behind it, but were prevented by von Brese's force, which inflicted heavy losses on the enemy. Although his formation was little more than a reinforced battalion in strength, von Brese's *Kampfgruppe* had already earned quite a reputation, a reflection of the outstanding leadership qualities of its commander. Born 13 January 1914 in Dresden, *Maj.* Heinz Wittchow von Brese-Winiary was commissioned as a *Leutnant* in 1936. He had fought in Poland and the Battle of France, where he earned the Iron Cross, First Class for his leadership of his company during a crossing of the Loire River near Orleans. During the invasion of the Soviet Union, von Brese received his first wound while serving with the *14.Pz.Div.* (one of nine he was to receive during the war in the East) and was awarded the *Ritterkreuz* for his leadership of an ad hoc *Kampfgruppe* during the Stalingrad Campaign.[10]

Named commander of the newly-reconstituted *Pz.Gren. Rgt.108* (the original had been destroyed in Stalingrad) in Spring 1943, he trained it to a very high standard which stood it in good stead upon its return to Russia during the autumn of 1943, in time for the retreat to the Dnieper. Well-liked by his men, von Brese epitomized all of the admirable qualities of the German officer corps - steadfastness, courage, resourcefulness, and concern for the well being of his men. One account of von Brese states, "To look at Heinz von Brese, one would see a mild mannered individual with polished manners that reflect his aristocratic birth. However, as a combat leader, his even temper [turned] to decisive action and positive results."[11]

Von Brese's unit had been fighting steadily for the past several days and had been cut off from its parent unit, the *14.Pz.Div.*, at least twice, forcing him to draw supplies from his eastern neighbor, General Fritz Kruse's *389.Inf.Div.* Fuel and ammunition were beginning to run low that day, since the few remaining supply lines were becoming increasingly stretched as the Soviets made their way further to the west. His group would be cut off again for good that day and from this point onward would be part of the encircled forces. Despite being cut off from their parent division, von Brese and his men would continue to contribute to the German defensive efforts. With an infantry battalion equipped with armored personnel carriers and three to four tanks, they were still a potent force.

Von Brese's *Kampfgruppe* was the only other armored unit under *XI.A.K.* command, besides *Wiking's* armored *Kampfgruppe*. Both were supposed to take part in the German counterattack that day, but now could not due to the enemy pressure. Köller's armored battlegroup from *Wiking*, which was supposed to help counterattack from Ossitnyashka, had been pulled out of the line on Stemmermann's orders and moved north, where it was thrown into a counterattack southwest of Smela to relieve some of the pressure being placed on Hermann Hohn's *72.Inf.Div.*

Here, Siegel's troops were was thrown out of Popovka and flung back to the western bank of the Gniloy Tashlyk River, which the 62nd Guards Rifle Division quickly crossed. A counterattack by *Oblt.* Bork's company met strong resistance and got nowhere. *Maj.* Cluever, the commander of *II./Gren.Rgt.266*, led the counterattack, which succeeded, though barely. With the removal of the battalion's sole remaining 2 cm SP antiaircraft gun to another sector, Cluever's troops were thrown out again. In the words of one witness, "*Ivan* was all over the place…It was a difficult day."[12] The fighting took a heavy toll of Siegel's officers, with six being wounded that day, including Cluever. In the *Wehrmacht*, officers led from the front; the better an officer was, the greater his chance of being killed or wounded.

It went on like this the entire day, as 52nd and 4th Guards Armies pressed their attacks home. *XI.A.K.'s* defenses were simply buckling under the weight of the Soviet assaults. To the west, *VII.* and *XXXXII.A.K.* were not having an easier time of it, either. Here, the gap between the two corps grew larger with every passing hour. As Kravchenko's army barreled towards the link-up with Rotmistrov near Zvenigorodka, 27th Army began pushing back the left flank of *88.Inf.Div.* towards the north, while 40th Army was bending back the right flank of *198.Inf.Div.* Here, the thinner German troop density and lack of armor began to tell in favor of the attacking Soviets, who were clearly trying to get into the operational depth of their enemy.

Although both German divisions were falling back, they at least maintained the integrity of their front-line sectors, despite some rather tense moments. The unit history of *198.Inf.Div.* describes the action that day thusly:

> The enemy . . . ruthlessly attacked on 28 January with all of his troops, including the area of [our division]. In the early morning there arose loud sounds of battle. The division was being attacked along its entire front by enemy tanks (probably from the 5th Mechanized Corps). The continuity [of the front line] was torn asunder. Small individual elements withdrew to the southwest, fighting the whole way. Shortly after the beginning of the enemy attack, about 20 enemy tanks found their way into the rear of Gren.Rgt.326, which had just pulled out of its previous position . . . the regimental staff, which was located in [the town of] Kamenny Brod, wanted to break out and collected the remaining units [of the regiment] in Bushanka . . . the only way out was to reach the heights near Yablonovka and from there seek to regain contact with the division.[13]

The only way the regiment could break out was through a swamp that lay between the tanks, which had in the meantime entered Kamenny Brod, and a forest that was still occupied by elements of the Soviet 136th and 167th Rifle Divisions, which had been encircled there weeks before. A snowstorm that arose in mid-afternoon provided the Germans badly needed concealment. The swamp, which had not frozen over, slowed the movement of the unit's vehicles, which led to the regiment's rearguard being overtaken by five Soviet tanks, which were apparently heading towards the town of Bushanka to link up with the encircled units.

These were soon engaged by the rearguard, which knocked out the lead Soviet tank. The other four pulled back and were seen moving to the east. Fortunately, when the group reached Yablonovka, it was still occupied by the *Feld Ers.Btl.* from *34.Inf.Div.* There, *Gren.Rgt.326* was able to regroup. All that was missing was the regiment's *II.Bataillon*, which found its way back three days later after a roundabout march. Not all of the units made it back so soon. Several straggling groups took several days of movement behind the Soviet line before they could link up with their companies and battalions. Many were captured, such as Heinrich Rentschler, of *Gren.Rgt.305*.

Rentschler, who had been assigned to the regiment's infantry howitzer company, was serving with a gun crew that was busily engaging Soviet tanks when his gun took a direct hit. As he and his comrades were trying to get away, they were suddenly bypassed by a group of tanks. One commander, standing

T-34s of 155th Tank Battalion, 20th Guards Tank Brigade, approach Zvenigorodka for their link up with 6th Tank Army from First Ukrainian Front. (Photo courtesey of Battle of Korsun-Shevchenkovsky Museum, Ukraine)

in his hatch, yelled *"Ruki verch! Davai nasad!"* (Hands up! Move to the rear!), and kept moving. Rentschler and his friends stood there, holding their rifles. There were no Soviet infantry in sight. Quickly making up their minds to make it back to friendly lines, they headed towards a small patch of woods, but were spotted. Shells began bursting in the woods and several men were wounded. His unit decided to break up into small groups and sneak back through enemy lines. Rentschler fell in with six friends and headed west.

Along the way, it began to snow and Rentschler lost his sense of direction. After stumbling around for several hours, they found themselves along a road which they had crossed before. Long lines of trucks, guns, and tanks were moving east along it. They certainly weren't German, Rentschler quickly ascertained. To avoid being spotted, the Germans laid down along the side of the road, camouflaged by their white winter combat suits. Rentschler hoped that they would remain unseen. With nightfall, they would retrace their steps and try again. Suddenly, Soviet soldiers in a nearby field were seen pointing in their direction. Led by a civilian who had spotted them, they began firing upon the small group of Germans.

One man was hit. A large group of infantry was seen running towards them, firing from the hip. One of the Germans, a doctor, shot himself in the head to avoid capture. Since they could not escape, Rentschler and the other survivors surrendered. The Soviet troops surrounded them and quickly rifled through their pockets. They stripped off their winter combat suits, leaving them in just their woolen uniforms and boots. This indignity was soon followed by beatings and interrogations. A Soviet officer, speaking fluent German, demanded to know precise information about his division.

For three days, Rentschler and his other two comrades were held close by the front lines. When they were finally being marched to the rear, they passed their infantry gun, which still lay in the same firing position. As they passed through a town, the inhabitants came out and taunted them, "like we were chicken thieves, not German soldiers." After several days, he and

his friends arrived at a large collecting point, where they had their heads shaved. Finally, far from the front lines, they were put to work in a coal mine. Rentschler survived and returned to Germany several years after the war.[14] He was the one of the first of many who was to become prisoners during the battle.

To the north, the situation in *88.Inf.Div.* sector was just as serious as that of *198.Inf.Div.* While *K.Abt.B* lay virtually unmolested in its original positions, *Graf* Rittberg's troops were being forced back, especially along his division's left flank. There, his troops had pulled back to the northern bank of the Ross River and were engaged in trying to defend the town against attacks by General G.O. Lyaskin's 337th Rifle Division. The left flank stretched a few kilometers further to the east along the river, where the front line petered out before the outskirts of the key town of Steblev. Between Steblev and the right flank of *198.Inf.Div.*, located southwest of Lysyanka, at a distance of over fifty kilometers, there was hardly anything at all, except some training and supply units. The route to Korsun, the logistical hub of the troops in the Kanev Salient, was open to anyone who wanted to use it. And Lyanskin's 337th as well as General S.P. Merkulov's 180th Rifle Divisions wanted to get there very badly. For their commanders knew that if Korsun fell, the Germans would have no choice but to surrender.

While the fighting raged on the eastern and western flanks of the salient, the tanks of the 5th Guards Tank and 6th Tank Armies raced towards Zvenigorodka. With all their troops tied up in the fighting, the Germans had no reserves left to stop them and could now only watch helplessly as the inevitable happened. *8.Armee* had been receiving reports since early that morning from *XI.A.K.* detailing the advance of Rotmistrov's troops. At 0700 hours, three tanks were reported in Topilno, a scant 45 kilometers east of Zvenigorodka. Three hours later, ten tanks were reported in the town of Kazatskoye, 22 kilometers away. All contact with German forces in Shpola had been lost.

At 1500 hours, German supply units reported that they were being forced to detour to the south after fighting was reported near Bagachevka, a mere ten kilometers east of Zvenigorodka. At 1630 hours, the commander of *XI.A.K's* rear services reported that 15 Soviet tanks were in the town, fighting was in progress, and the local defense commander had been killed. He went on to report that "In the town we no longer have any forces."[15] Finally, at 1800 hours, *XI.A.K.* reported that contact to the south had been cut at Zvenigorodka. 60,000 German troops and foreign auxiliaries were now encircled. Stemmermann informed *8.Armee's* chief of staff that supplies were already beginning to run short and that he needed resupply by air to commence immediately!

155th Tank Brigade under the command of Lieutenant Colonel I. Proshin spearheaded Rotmistrov's advance towards Zvenigorodka that day. Proshin had driven his troops relentlessly day and night since his brigade had broken through the day before. Although he knew that he was temporarily cut off, he kept going, stopping his column long enough only to refuel. Then the advance to the west continued. What German resistance they encountered was quickly scattered as their T-34s smashed through the few roadblocks they encountered. Close behind this brigade came the main forces of 20th Tank Corps,

Lieutenant Colonel I. Proshin, *Commander, 155th Tank Brigade, 20th Tank Corps, 5th Guards Tank Army. His tanks were the first to reach Zvenigorodka. (Photo courtesy of Museum of the Battle of Korsun-Shevchenkovsky)*

including 8th Tank Brigade. Rotmistrov reported to Konev that the mission had been achieved but that the encirclement was "thin in spots" where the Germans could attempt to break out of or break into the pocket.[16]

As Proshin's brigade advanced to the west, Kravchenko's forces rushed forward to meet them. His spearhead, 233rd Tank Brigade commanded by General M.I. Savelyev, reached the northern outskirts of Zvenigorodka in the late afternoon and linked up with Proshin's troops.[17] The Germans had now been trapped in what they would term a *Kessel*, or cauldron. Thus was born the *Kessel von Tscherkassy*. For the Soviets, this bold move had not been completely without loss; Captain Nikolai Maslyukov, the commander of the brigade's spearhead, 1st Tank Battalion, was killed at 1300 hours at the northwest outskirts of Zvenigorodka when his Sherman was knocked out by German defenders.[18]

Nonetheless, Kravchenko decided to order the bulk of his tank and mechanized forces to follow 233rd Tank Brigade along the same route, since this seemed at the time to be the easiest way to go. It was a mistake, however, because it gave the Germans time to move their forces in the pocket around without having to worry about a large tank attack into their vulnerable southern flank, where as yet no front line existed. The battle would have ended much sooner had Vatutin and Konev ordered more of their armor to attack into the exposed side of the pocket, at a time when the Germans could not have withstood it. Even with the relatively small number of tanks they

did send against the German open southern flank, the Soviets very nearly succeeded, as we shall see.

The main concern of the Red Army, now that it had cut the supply routes into the pocket, was to build up both the inner and outer encirclement rings in order to keep the Germans inside the pocket from breaking out and to prevent a relief force from getting through, much like a classical siege of antiquity. The Soviets regarded a relief attempt as inevitable, since the Germans always tried to free their forces that had become encircled. To do this effectively, Rotmistrov and Kravchenko would have to wait until the infantry armies had caught up. In the meantime, the tank and mechanized corps would continue their attack to widen the gap between the German forces, block the routes into and out of the pocket, and attempt to strike into the pocket itself in order to splinter it up before a new front could be built in the south, where nothing but 100 kilometers of open country lay.

The breakthrough and link-up at Zvenigorodka had thrown the rear areas of both *XI.* and *XXXXII.A.K.* into chaos. What had heretofore been considered a relative safehaven had now become the front-line. Supply units attempted to escape to the south or to the north along whatever roads were free of Soviet tanks. *Alarmeinheiten* (scratch units drawn from supply and service troops) were hurriedly rushed together in order to block or slow down Soviet attacks. Some 5,000 troops of both corps were cut off from their units in the pocket and would later be incorporated into various *Kampfgruppen* and *Alarmeinheiten*. This applied as well to hundreds of troops from the divisions in the pocket who had just returned from leave in Germany.

Nearly the entire rear services of *389.Inf.Div.* was left outside the pocket, essentially crippling that division for the remainder of the battle. Without trucks, horses, and wagons to move its supplies and without medical, repair, and supply units, the division could no longer function effectively. Its combat performance would markedly decline during the next several days. The same applied to *5* and *72.Inf.Divs.*, though not to such a large degree.[19] Supply would soon become one of the chief limiting factors affecting German combat performance within the pocket.

The commanders of *XI.* and *XXXXII.A.K.* were both well aware that unless they were relieved soon or were allowed to break out, the 60,000 men in the pocket would only be able to hold their positions for a limited time. Aerial resupply, even if it was started immediately, would only serve as a temporary expedient. Stalingrad had taught the lesson that encircled forces could not be resupplied by air indefinitely. In addition, the pocket's size was still too great to be adequately defended with the troops available. A withdrawal to a shorter line needed to be authorized immediately.

With both corps now cut off, the problem of command arrangements arose at the headquarters of both *1.Pz.* and *8. Armee*. Since each corps in the pocket reported to a different high command, coordination between the two would be severely affected unless both were quickly placed under the same headquarters. However, if more effective measures were to be taken to eliminate the Soviet penetration and restore the front line, they would have to be coordinated by Army Group South.

This was necessitated by the fact that the offensive affected elements of two neighboring armies and that any effective German countermeasures had to be controlled by the army group, which had access to more resources than either army possessed. In fact, General Busse, at Army Group South, had already recognized the necessity of such an arrangement and had informed Speidel that morning that he was weighing the need to place Lieb's *XXXXII.A.K.* under the command of *8. Armee*, but did not have the authority to order such a move.[20] Fortunately for the German leadership, von Manstein returned that day and immediately began to restore order and confidence through his decisive leadership.

When he arrived the evening of 28 January from his visit to Hitler's headquarters in East Prussia, von Manstein faced a crisis. Early news was not encouraging. Two of his corps had been encircled by two Soviet tank armies. Follow-on forces were attempting to push back the German front line, increasing the distance between the encircled forces and the rest of Army Group South. Von Manstein acted quickly. His first move was to order that Lieb's corps be placed under Woehler's army command, effective at 1105 hours 28 January. His second move was to authorize the southerly withdrawal of Lieb's troops to a shorter, more defensible line along the Rossava River. With its western flank anchored at the town of Boguslav, the new front line would stretch to the northeast along the line Mironovka-Stepantsy-Kreshatik, where its eastern flank anchored on the Dnieper, next to the *Wiking's* left flank. The troops of *88.Inf.Div.* and *K.Abt.B* would begin movement to this new line at noon the following day. The operation, code-named *Winterreise* (Winter Excursion) would require that some units march more than 30 kilometers in less than 24 hours.[21]

A larger issue was the one which Hitler had been deferring ever since the Kanev Salient had come into being nearly one month before - namely, the fact that it was high time to abandon the salient altogether. Nothing could any longer be gained militarily by holding it. Since mid-January, Von Manstein had repeatedly tried to convince Hitler to give up the salient and withdraw to a shorter line, but Hitler would have none of it. Rather than defending his decision in military terms, Hitler stated that holding on to the Dnieper was critical to insuring the continued political support of Turkey, Bulgaria and Rumania. Von Manstein replied that their attitudes would be better served by preserving an intact German southern front as far to the east as possible from the latter two countries. Hitler declined to heed his advice.[22] Besides, he still harbored illusions of launching a grand attack towards Kiev from the salient. Hitler's appreciation of the situation from a headquarters over 1,000 miles from the front had no connection with reality. Von Manstein realized that the only way to rescue the two corps was to be granted complete freedom of action. Hitler refused.

Pressured by Wöhler throughout the day about the issue, Busse finally declared to him exasperatedly that "I have been trying for five days to get permission to pull back the northern fronts of the *XI.* and *XXXXII.A.K.*, without success."[23] Von Manstein tried again himself to gain Hitler's approval, but got nowhere either. Nevertheless, he instructed both army commanders to begin to assemble forces to effect a relief effort. This would take a few days, since the forces which Hube and Wöhler would use for such an undertaking were currently committed to ongoing operations and would have to pull out, hand their sectors over to other units, and assemble near the front line areas closest to the pocket. Until then, the two encircled corps would have to do their best to maintain the integrity of their front lines and preserve their strength for what was to come.

The leadership in the pocket recognized immediately the seriousness of the situation. Lieb, whose corps was now under the control of *8.Armee*, quickly accepted the new situation. In his personal diary for 28 January, General Lieb commented:

> Communications to the rear along the road Shpola-Zvenigorodka have been cut. We are encircled . . . Our defensive mission remains unchanged. Telephone request to 8.Armee: "Mission requires maintaining northeast front against strong enemy pressure . . . Request authority for immediate withdrawal of northern and eastern fronts. This will permit offensive action toward the southwest and prevent further encirclement and separation from XI.A.K."[24]

His assessment of the situation provided impetus for the launching of Operation *Winterreise*. Without immediate action, his battered corps would soon collapse. In order to preserve any kind of combat power, he realized that he needed to mass his forces as much as possible. The only way to do that was to shorten his front line and free troops to serve as reserve forces.

In fact, as previously mentioned, Lieb had already been denuding his front, to such an extent that by 28 January the area held by *K.Abt.B* was little more than a loosely held screen line. Both *1.Panzer* and *8.Armee* were aware of this, but permitted it, since Hube and Wöhler saw this as a first step towards a future withdrawal from the salient. However, this move brought little consolation to anyone. In his journal entry for that evening, a downhearted Walter Wenck noted that:

> The fate of the brave [men of] XXXXII.A.K. weighs heavily on the hearts of the leadership of 1.Pz.Armee. There is little comfort knowing that 1.Pz.Armee is free of guilt for the events that led up to this development . . . The risk that two corps could be lost [in this salient] was never truly recognized. The Army has never comprehended the decision by the highest level (i.e., Hitler) to hold this "Balcony." One can only obey, even if it fills one with sadness.[25]

While the corps and divisional staffs of the units in the pocket became aware of their encirclement relatively quickly, many front line soldiers would not find out about it for several days. Front line gossip aside, many soldiers had lived so long with the threat of encirclement or had experienced encirclement in previous battles that they had become accustomed to it. Now that it had actually come to pass, many were unconcerned, especially the old *Frontschweine*, the hardened combat veterans of the Eastern Front. After all, if they did get encircled, von Manstein would move heaven and earth to free them, or so many thought. Perhaps the most optimistic of the German troops within the pocket were the men of the *Waffen-SS*. Young, idealistic, and still sure of ultimate victory, they took the news in stride. Leon Degrelle noted that:

> We were beginning to get used to the Kessel. Survivors of a hundred traps on the Donets, on the Don, and in the Caucasus, we felt this was scarcely our first crisis. We all wanted to think that this encirclement would be just one more adventure. The high command wouldn't abandon us here.[26]

Despite the news that they were encircled, the officers of *II./Pz.Gren.Rgt. "Westland"* of *Wiking* celebrated the 27th birthday of their battalion commander, *Hstuf.* Walter Schmidt, nonetheless. Located along the Irdyn Swamp near the town of Buda Orlovetskaya, the battalion toasted their commander's health and proceeded to dine on a birthday meal of roast pork, home-made *Spätzle* (Swabian noodles), and schnapps.[27] It was to be one of their last decent meals for many days to come. One of the men present at this celebration later recalled:

> In the middle of our happily celebrating group came the news from regiment that we were encircled. Naturally, we had not forgotten the drama of Stalingrad the year before. But we did not compare our situation with that faced by the troops [on the] Volga. We had enough supplies and ammunition . . . Our strong desire to do whatever was required to avert such a catastrophe was unshaken.[28]

Other troops of the *Wehrmacht* were more stoic or downright pessimistic. Gerhard Meyer, a radioman in *Art.Rgt.188* of *88.Inf.Div.*, turned down a request by his friends to accompany them on 28 January to a see a gypsy fortune teller in the town of Vasilovka where the regimental staff was billeted. His friends told him afterwards that she told them that "they would return home, but only if they used their heads, but that the trip would take a great deal of time." Instead of relying on the doubtful advice of a charlatan, Meyer decided to trust his own instinct. It seemed to him that she was trying to incite them to desert. Besides, Meyer had survived two previous encirclements at Voronesh and at Kiev. As the saying goes, "all good things come in threes," so he felt that he would probably survive this battle too.[29] He was correct. None of his friends got out alive, but he would.

Adolf Ogrowsky, the *Stabsintendant* (supply officer) for Siegel's *Gren.Rgt.266* had a similar view of things. As an expe-

rienced quartermaster, he had learned the tricks of the trade after nearly three years of fighting in the East. Encirclement did not necessarily mean that his regiment would starve to death. Upon hearing the news that they were now encircled, he recalled that:

> The men [of the supply company] had collected a great deal of experience since the beginning of the Russian Campaign . . . with [seemingly] hopeless situations. They understood as no soldiers before them had, to make necessity a virtue and to provide as much nourishment for the troops as possible. They had to always deal with the possibility - every day and every hour - that normal rations would be cut off.[30]

To provide for his men, Ogrowsky had amassed a considerable store of foodstuffs above and beyond the normal allocation, to include extra *Eiserne Portionen* (canned rations) and even Crimean champagne! Consequently, his ability to keep the regiment fed contributed a great deal towards its continued combat effectiveness, while other units which had not made such arrangements declined in morale and efficiency.

Overall, though, there was sufficient food in the *Kessel*. The problem lay in the even distribution of it. Throughout the days of encirclement, some units ate very well while others virtually starved. However, at the encirclement's early stage, food was less of a problem than the creation of a solid front line. Another problem was determining the whereabouts of the attacking Red Army forces within the pocket itself. One account describes the problems faced by the supply services of the *Wiking*:

> [We] at first tried to drive off the enemy attacks with our own means - mostly with the help of individual small arms (rifles, pistols, etc.) Soon it became clear, and was subsequently verified by neighboring units, that this was no mere raid or partisan ambushes that we were dealing with. Reconnaissance and a stream of reports verified that these were massive enemy attacks, consisting of regular, large combat units of all arms, especially [Soviet] units equipped with armored vehicles and large numbers of tanks. So, there the enemy was, only this time between our homeland and the front![31]

Compounding this issue was the fact that the Soviets were continuing their attack and would evidently not be satisfied with a mere encirclement operation - Zhukov, Konev and Vatutin were after the complete *unichtozheniye* (annihilation) of the forces in the pocket.

For their part, the Soviet commanders believed that they had encircled the bulk of the German *8.Armee*, a force of over 100,000 men. Based on intelligence estimates, they had every reason to think so. The mood aboard Konev's command train was euphoric after the news of the link up at Zvenigorodka was passed along to his staff. This is going to be a second Stalingrad, one of the staff officers later recalled.[32] The Germans would not get away this time, either. Soviet propaganda would continue to play upon this theme, both to the Soviet people, the Germans, and to the rest of the world through their international media. Adherence to this theme would lead to complications later on, but Zhukov had every reason to be satisfied at this early phase of the operation.

The first and second phases had indeed gone according to plan. Although the penetration had taken two days longer than expected, the German defenses had been cleanly ruptured by the two tank armies that had disregarded their flanks and had driven on to effect their linkup on 28 January at Zvenigorodka. While the armored spearheads of the two *Fronts* had indeed met and the German supply routes to the two corps in the Kanev salient had been severed, the Germans were not yet truly encircled. Many lesser routes to the south still lay open. Until the Soviets were able to construct an unbroken ring around the Germans, the threat of a breakout was still a strong possibility. The next phase of the operation was planned to insure that this would not happen.

After the penetration of the German defenses, follow-on infantry armies in the east and west moved to widen the breach in order to push back the Germans and make it more difficult for a relief attempt to reach the beleaguered forces in the salient. Simultaneously, other armies attacked into the rear of the trapped German forces to form an inner ring of encirclement, as well as to try to prevent them from forming a new front in the south. Ideally, according to doctrine, the Soviets would carry out attacks to splinter German forces in the pocket. The Soviets could then reduce and destroy each part at their leisure. However, as the situation developed, the inner ring of encirclement lacked the armored formations doctrinally required to do this.

Konev's *Front*, which had begun its segment of the operation first, aggressively sought to complete the encirclement of the German forces in the eastern portion of the salient. On the outer ring, 4th Guards and 53rd Armies fanned out to the south and southwest. In the northern part of the penetration, 52nd Army began its push to widen the breach to the west and form the inner ring.[33] 5th Cavalry Corps, acting as the *STAVKA* Front reserve for Konev, was to follow in the wake of the 5th Guards Tank Army; in fact, part of it had broken through already. Its mission was to penetrate into the German rear and break up any attempt to form a continuous front in that direction. However, the encirclement formed much more slowly than Konev had anticipated, due to stiffening German resistance and worsening weather.

In the west, Vatutin's infantry armies were experiencing similar difficulties. Although 6th Tank Army's spearheads had broken through on 27 January, the infantry of 40th and 27th Armies had not kept pace. They had quickly been drawn into heavy fighting with bypassed German units of *88.Inf.Div.* 6th Tank Army could do little to help, since it was short of infantry itself. It needed all that it had to establish defenses southwest of Zvenigorodka to ward off the expected German relief attempt. The advance of 40th and 27th Armies was further slowed by the terrain on the western side of the salient and the fact that the

Leader of the *"Reservist Regiment,"* **Major Hans Siegel**, *Gren.Rgt.266, 72.Inf.Div. (Photo courtesy of 72.Inf.Div. Veteran's Association)*

German defensive positions were far more developed than they were opposite Konev's troops. However, Vatutin and Konev soon realized to their amazement that the Germans in the salient were not going to pull back from the Dnieper. As 28 January came to an end, *XI.* and *XXXXII.A.K.* still held on to their positions along the river. A stationary pocket would make the job of destroying the encircled German forces much easier. Hitler's stand-fast directive was continuing to impact upon the Germans' ability to react quickly to events.

That evening however, the Germans believed that the situation, at least in the *8.Armee* sector, was beginning to stabilize. Although fresh movement of Soviet troops and armor had been reported east of Ossitnyashka, *XI.A.K.'s* front-line had been restored by the counterattack carried out by *57.Inf.Div.* The *Hamsterstellung*, though shaky, was holding. True, *XI.A.K.* and *XXXXVII.Pz.Korps* were still separated by over a dozen kilometers, but von Vormann at least thought that this gap could be closed the following day. Wöhler had flown that day to visit von Vormann at his corps headquarters in Novo Mirgorod, and came to the same conclusion. Wöhler also decided to pull the *13.Pz.Div.* out of the neighboring *LII.A.K.* and replace it with an infantry division, and use it to bolster von Vormann's dwindling forces. In addition, the troops from *11.Pz.Div.* encircled in the northern part of Tishkovka had been able to break out. If its corps and division commanders keep their wits about them, *8.Armee* could pull off a victory yet.

SS-Hauptsturmführer Leon Degrelle *of the Walloon Brigade, seen here as an Army Captain before the Walloon Legion was transferred to the Waffen-SS.*
(U.S. National Archives)

Better still was the news from Army Group South that evening that described in broad outlines von Manstein's plans to relieve the encircled corps. Although as yet unsanctioned by Hitler, the plan would consist of a counterattack launched by one of *1.Pz.Armee's* armored corps, most likely Hermann Breith's *III.Pz.Korps*, towards a linkup with *XXXXII.A.K.*, now holding *8.Armee's* left flank. Von Manstein ordered Wöhler to continue his attack, but to be prepared to attack to the west to link up with *1.Pz.Armee*. To do this, he would have to pull his battered panzer divisions temporarily out of the line to refresh them as best as he could. They would be replaced by *320.* and *376.Inf.Div.*, which would be pulled out of the line further to the south. Details would follow, as von Manstein and his staff worked the planning. Unbeknownst to them, Konev still had one more surprise in store.

While Stemmermann's troops had, with difficulty, been able to hold the *Hamsterstellung* throughout the day of 28 January, they were totally unprepared for what unfolded the following morning, when large bodies of enemy troops supported by tanks attacked the southern flank of *57.* and *72.Inf.Div.*, near Pastorskoye and Tashlyk, respectively. Although enemy attacks against these areas had been reported after midnight, the seriousness of the situation did not become manifest until sunrise. Trowitz's division had been attacked that night by the bulk of the 5th Guards Cavalry Corps, which had been unable during the past two days to break through to join Rotmistrov's spearhead. Although one of Seliavanov's divisions

had made it through on 27 January, the day of the dramatic breakthrough, the bulk of the corps, including its armor, had been awaiting a chance to follow. They seized this opportunity on the night of 28/29 January, and before Trowitz's troops knew what was happening, had broken through between Pastorskoye and Kapitanovka and headed west, where the cossack force disappeared. All that *57.Inf.Div.* could report was that "the front line has been repaired, but it is thinly held. Size of the enemy element that broke through is unknown."[34]

That morning, *72.Inf.Div.* was attacked by a force comprising well over 60 tanks and several thousand infantry, which penetrated the front line in two places - near Tashlyk and Yekaterinovka. Hohn reported that one of his own regiments had been reduced in strength to less than 100 fighting troops (probably *Gren.Rgt.124*). Even more serious was Hohn's comment that his division was now beginning to suffer from the effects of ammunition shortages, and that he expected a large breakthrough in the middle of his sector, thus cutting *XI.A.K.* in two.[35] Rudolf Siegel, commander of the division's *Gren.Rgt.266*, was an eyewitness to the day's events and has left a vivid report.

Initially supposed to move to Tashlyk to become the division's reserve, Siegel's regiment had just pulled out of its old positions near Popovka early that morning when its succeeding unit, a battalion commanded by a *Hptm.* Zimmermann from *Inf.Rgt. "List"* (*Gren.Rgt.199* of *57.Inf.Div.*) was attacked. The resulting breakthrough led to Zimmermann's losing contact with *Wiking* on his left flank. The Soviets poured through the gap and caught up with Siegel's regiment near Tashlyk. Quickly sizing up the situation, Siegel led his unit in a counterattack that threw the enemy out of the northern part of town. To Siegel's dismay, Kästner's *Gren.Rgt.105*, his neighbor to the south, had pulled out without telling him. Despite this setback, he ordered his men to occupy the entire town, since it lay atop a commanding height. His men complied gladly, since they would be able to occupy peasant *isbas* and warm up for a change, for they had been living and fighting in the open for nearly a week.

Their respite was short-lived. By mid-morning, the Soviets came back in strength. Reinforced by many tanks, they attacked Siegel's troops again and again. By Siegel's own estimate, the Soviets fired over 1,600 rounds of mortar and artillery fire into Tashlyk. Siegel's division had reported earlier that Tashlyk was lost, based on reports provided by Kästner, whose regiment had hastily departed the town prior to Siegel's arrival. The report by *XI.A.K.* headquarters to *8.Armee* also said that "hardly any fighting troops are left." To personally clarify the situation, Stemmermann and Hohn, drove to Tashlyk to meet with Siegel. It was at this moment that Siegel learned that all German forces in the Kanev Salient were encircled.

Reassured that Siegel's regiment could hold on until dark, Stemmerman informed him that his division was moving out to a new defensive line in the west. Siegel later wrote, "We were able to hold our positions until dark. Had [my regiment] not been able to hold, the entire front would have been in a very serious situation. The *Reservisten-Regiment* (nickname for *Gren.Rgt.266* since it was composed of pre-war reservists) was again "minding the store," an indication of the rivalry that existed between his regiment and Kästner's.[36] Kästner's regiment was recalled and sent back to the front to occupy the heights south of Kusovka. After warding off Soviet attacks from three directions, Siegel's regiment withdrew in good order towards Kusovka, where it once again tied in with *Gren.Rgt.105*, whose troops Siegel's men now held in mild contempt for abandoning their positions earlier in the day.

Part of the sizable Soviet armored force that had broken through near Tashlyk earlier in the day had been encountered by *Wiking's* armored battlegroup east of the town of Rotmistrovka. The tank battalion simply noted in its *Kriegstagebuch* for that day that "In a counterattack enemy forces were encircled in an open field of snow by 2nd and 3rd Companies and totally annihilated. The supporting battery from the artillery regiment supported [our attack] with direct fire."[37] The whereabouts of the other large Soviet force and tanks reported near Yekaternovka was unknown. To the south, the enormous pressure being exerted against *389.* and *57.Inf.Divs.* was forcing them slowly backwards, though the battalions and companies were able to maintain contact with one another and fought effective delaying actions. Zhukov had not expected the Germans to put up such a fight. In his memoirs, he noted that "Clinging to every possible line of defense, to every inhabited locality and every forest and dale, the surrounded German forces continued to put up stubborn resistance."[38]

Indeed, with such strong odds against them, how could the Germans still be offering such a staunch and bitter defense? Part of the reason no doubt is due to the Soviet's underestimation of German morale; after six months of retreat and continued setbacks, their morale was not yet broken. While he may have lost some of his old offensive spirit, the individual German soldier proved himself to still be redoubtable in the defense. In addition, Wöhler had flung three panzer divisions into the effort to close the gap near Kapitanovka. While these divisions were seriously understrength, their continued counterattacks had slowed the Soviet timetable and prevented the bulk of Konev's forces from deploying in the wake of Rotmistrov's tank army.

A more likely explanation of the reason why the Soviets had not brought about the collapse of the German front line is that they were now operating without the accustomed support of their artillery. While the guns provided a tremendous amount of fire during the first two days of the battle, they had been unable to keep pace with the armor and infantry forces. The road network in the area was poor to begin with, and the preceding armor had churned the already bad roads into thick ribbons of slime, forcing the artillery to accompany the assault forces at a snail's pace. Although the roads froze at night and were still relatively solid during the day, the huge ruts brought about by such heavy traffic slowed movement to a crawl. In the words of Zhukov:

What we needed to drive the enemy out of his positions was powerful artillery fire, but road conditions made this impossible to provide. To build up even a minimum stock of shells, mines, and tank fuel, all supplies had to be carried on oxen, on foot, on sacks, or on stretchers -

in short, as best we could. Local Ukrainian villagers gave us great help in getting ammunition, fuel and food to the troops.[39]

Indeed, except for mortar fire and light artillery, the Germans reported very few large-scale artillery barrages during this period. The use of *Katyushas* had also dropped of noticeably, to the relief of the defenders.

Even without artillery support, the infantry of 52nd, 53rd, and 4th Guards Armies were advancing inexorably. By 1800 hours. on 29 January, *8.Armee* informed Army Group South that *XI.A.K's* right flank had fallen back so much that a gap had now formed that was so large that "there are no longer any forces at hand to close it," thus finally stating what had been obvious for at least the past 24 hours.[40] To avoid being enveloped on the right, *57.Inf.Div.* and the remnant of *389.Inf.Div.* on its right (which had been attached to Trowitz's division the previous day) had given up Ossitnyashka and Pastorskoye and withdrew rapidly to the northwest, finally coming to a halt along the rail line that ran from Kapitanovka to Makeyevka. Von Brese's battlegroup, to the right of *57.Inf.Div.* near Zhuravka, was ordered by von Vormann to break out and link up with units of the *11.Pz.Div.* at Zlatapol, but was unable to get that far.[41] From this point onward, von Brese and his men were truly encircled.

Von Vormann's corps was fighting a losing battle that day, and his men knew it. The *Grossdeutschland's* Panther battalion again made a determined effort to link up with *XI.A.K.,* but was brought to a halt by late morning after it had suffered heavy losses. Out of the 61 tanks it had started with, it now only had 17 operational. Of those lost, 20 were totally destroyed. In two days of combat, this unit alone had lost nearly three-fourths of its tanks. Any chance to use this unit as a battering ram were now gone, as well as the hopes to stem the tide. The weight of the second attacking echelons of the Red Army was now being felt.

By mid-afternoon, the bulk of Seliavanov's 5th Cavalry Corps was committed against the thin screenline held by *14.Pz.Div.* near Pisarevka. Over 1,500 cavalrymen supported by 16 T-34s were reported heading towards Tishkovka. All that Unrein's men could do was to engage them with artillery, which hardly had any effect on the mass of men and horses. As if the enemy ground attacks were not enough, many units were reporting constant attacks by fighter-bombers and *Sturmoviks* of the Red Air Force, which made their appearance whenever weather conditions permitted. Of course, "favorable weather conditions" as such, were defined differently by the Soviets - their aircraft would fly even when the ceiling (lowest cloud altitude) was only 100-150 meters (about 328 to 490 feet). Flying in groups of four to eight aircraft in support of ground troops, these attacks, though poorly coordinated and bereft of control by ground forward observers, still provided a significant morale boost to Soviet ground units.[42]

The flood of Soviet units pouring through the gap between Kapitanovka and Raymentorovka was practically unstoppable. German reconnaissance units were now reporting

Soviet tanks moving deep into the rear at Lipyanka. To save his units, Wöhler directed von Vormann to withdraw both *11.* and *14.Pz.Divs.* from their exposed positions in the path of the Soviet advance. The *8.Armee* commander now foresaw that he would need them not for an operation to close a gap or to restore the front line to its previous position, but for a new operation - the relief of the encircled forces in the pocket. Infantry divisions being brought up from the south would fill their place. The panzer divisions would need time to lick their wounds and restore some semblance of combat effectiveness before being thrown into the fray in the near future.

While *XI.A.K.* was pulling its right wing back in order to prevent its flank from being enveloped, and while *XXXXVII.Pz.Korps* was struggling to extract its units from the path of the Konev's accelerating attack, the German units on the western side of the battlefield were having an equally tough time of it. *Gen.Lt.* Hell's *VII.A.K.* was subject to dozens of attacks that day; though pressed, the battered *34.* and *198.Inf.Divs.* held their ground. General Horn's *198.Inf.Div.*, after a particularly hard-fought day on 28 January, was able the following day to reestablish contact between all of its regiments and had been able, with difficulty, to reestablish a coherent *Hauptkampflinie* (*HKL*, or main defense line). The division's eastern flank now lay at the town of Risino, its left flank at Vinograd. Its front now faced towards the east (it had faced towards the west only a week before).[43] Holding this new position would be critical to any effort to reestablish contact with the encircled forces from the outside, and both sides knew it. Despite renewed attacks by the Soviet 167th and 136th Rifle Divisions, *198.Inf.Div.* held its ground and inflicted enormous casualties on the waves of Soviet infantry.

Since his corps was the most exposed and weakest of the two in the *Kessel*, Lieb asked Wöhler to have the main body of *Wiking* attached to his corps so he could use it in order to carry out a coherent defense of his sector, which included the portion of the Dnieper defense line that Hitler insisted must be held. The attachment was approved by 1830 hours and not a minute too soon. For that day, 29 January, the northern portion of Lieb's sector, held by *K.Abt.B*, came under heavy attack by Soviet infantry of 206th Rifle Division, supported by tanks. The sector, which had previously seen little action, was over 75 kilometers long and held only by three German infantry battalions supported by five batteries of artillery.[44]

Fortunately, these units had been authorized to withdraw to the Rossava River line (Operation *Winterreise*) the previous day, so that they were able to pull out in good order, knocking out two T-34s in the process. While *K.Abt.B* and *88.Inf.Div.* withdrew to a shorter line, the SS men of *Wiking* and the Walloon Brigade, in their positions along the Dnieper, were ordered to remain in place. Painfully aware that they were now in a salient at the northeastern-most part of the pocket, they clung steadfastly to their positions, trusting their fate in the hands of their *Führer*.

Leon Degrelle was not so sure. While the men of *Wiking's* reconnaissance battalion patrolled ceaselessly along the muddy trails in their few remaining armored cars, Degrelle's unit had been given the task of holding the northernmost tip of the Dnieper salient, near the town of Moshny. There, he and the men of the company under his command were responsible for holding a bridge that spanned the Olshanka River three kilometers east of the town. Over this bridge ran the road to Cherkassy, where the Soviet 294th Rifle Division lay. Its eastern approaches were held by a strongpoint manned by ten Walloons and two machine guns. Defending the bridge seemed utterly senseless. Should the Soviets attack and seize the bridge, they would have an unfettered approach into the rearward positions of the entire *Wiking*. Degrelle's request to blow the bridge was denied by a *Wiking* staff officer. He was told that his unit "was not to yield an inch of ground or give the enemy the impression that we were losing confidence in the outcome of the battle."[45]

Degrelle, an independent thinker if not a skilled tactician, had convinced his brigade's German liaison officer, *Hstuf.* Wegener, that it was in everyone's best interest to destroy the bridge. Having won him over to the logic of the argument Wegener "effected the blowing of the bridge with all possible discretion." The next morning, 30 January, Wegener called *Wiking's* divisional headquarters and informed the staff that a lucky Soviet shell had scored a direct hit on the bridge, hitting a stockpile of explosives. The bridge was, regrettably, completely destroyed. Degrelle added his regrets and was truly sorry that this had happened. Apparently, so was General Gille, but the question of the bridge was thus resolved.[46]

While both *XI.* and *XXXXII.A.K.* were encircled and were withdrawing into new, shorter defensive positions, the focus of the higher staffs at *1.Panzer* and *8.Armee*, as well as Army Group South, shifted to another series of concerns. First and foremost was the realization that Lieb's and Stemmermann's corps were now, for all intents and purposes, surrounded. A relief attack of some sort would have to be initiated without delay. In fact, preliminary preparations were already underway. An airlift had already been initiated, though would not mature for several days. The shoulders of the penetration had held, luckily, though a 100 kilometer-wide gap now yawned between the two armies.

What the Soviets were doing with the opportunities this offered them, as of yet, was anyone's guess. But a more immediate pressing concern was with the pocket itself. Although the two corps in the pocket had maintained coherent defense lines to the west, north, and east, to the south there was no defense line at all - nothing to prevent the Soviets from penetrating the pocket from that direction and attacking the defenders from the rear. Nothing, that is, but an assortment of supply units, ad-hoc *Kampfgruppen*, and replacement detachments. For the next several days, from 28 January to 4 February, all eyes, both German and Soviet, would be drawn to this area and the towns that lay within it - such towns as Steblev, Kvitki, and Olshana. If these towns could not be held, then the hard-pressed Germans in the pocket had no chance at all.

End Notes

1 Mayer, p. 127.
2 *Geschichte der 3.Panzer-Division*, p. 417.
3 *8.Armee* KTB entry 0820 hours 28 January 1944, p. 1.
4 *1.Pz.Armee* KTB entry 28 January 1944, p. 1.
5 Spaeter, pp. 276-277.
6 Rolf Grams, *Die 14.Panzer Division, 1940-1945*, (Freidberg, Germany: Podzun-Pallas Verlag, 1986), p. 168.
7 *Sbornik*, p. 312.
8 Zhukov, p. 239.
9 Siegel, p. 7.
10 Angolia, pp. 362-63.
11 Ibid, p. 362.
12 Siegel, p. 7.
13 Graser, p. 286.
14 Ibid, pp. 287-88.
15 *8.Armee* KTB entry dated 1635 hours 28 January 1944, p. 5.
16 Armstrong, p. 367.
17 Zhukov, p. 240.
18 Loza, p. 23.
19 Report, *Nicht im Kampfraum XI. und XXXXII.A.K. befindliche Teile, Abteilung Ia, Hauptquartier, AOK* 8, 18 Februar 1944, pp. 1-2.
20 *8.Armee* KTB entry dated 1000 hours 28 January 1944, p. 3.
21 Ibid, entry dated 2400 hours 28 January 1944, p. 7.
22 von Manstein, p. 509.
23 *8.Armee* KTB entry dated 1900 hours, 28 January 1944, p. 4.
24 Oldwig von Natzmer in DA Pam No. 20-234, p. 20.
25 1.Pz.Armee KTB, 28 January 1944, p. 1.
26 Degrelle, p. 163.
27 Fritz Hahl, *Panzergrenadiere der Panzerdivision Wiking im Bild.* (Osnabrück, Germany: Munin Verlag GmbH, 1984), p. 199.
28 Letter from Fritz Hahl, Pentling, Germany to Willy Hein, 27 May 1996, p. 2. Copy in author's possession.
29 Mayer, p. 129.
30 Adolf Ogowsky, *Die Versorgung der kämpfenden Truppen mit Verpflegung im grossen Kessel von Kanew-Korssun.* (Speyer, Germany: Unpublished private manuscript, August 1975), p. 3.
31 Jahnke and Lerch, p. 18.
32 von Vormann, p. 65. Von Vormann quotes as a source a conversation related by a certain Kyrill D. Kalinov in a post-war Soviet publication entitled *Ivan S. Konev, Duke of Kanev.*
33 Sbornik, p. 312.
34 *8.Armee* KTB entry dated 0840 29 January 1944, p. 2.
35 Ibid.
36 Siegel, p. 8.
37 Klapdor, p. 186.
38 Zhukov, pp. 241-242.
39 Ibid, p. 242.
40 *8.Armee* KTB entry dated 1755 hours 29 January 1944, p. 7.
41 Ibid, entry dated 1700 hours, p. 6.
42 Ministry of Defense of the USSR, *The Official History of the Soviet Air Force in World War II* (translated by Leland Fetzer). (Garden City, NY: Doubleday & Company Inc., 1973), p. 233.
43 Graser, p. 288.
44 *8.Armee* KTB entry dated 1600 hours 29 January 1944, p. 6.
45 Degrelle, p. 166.
46 Ibid.

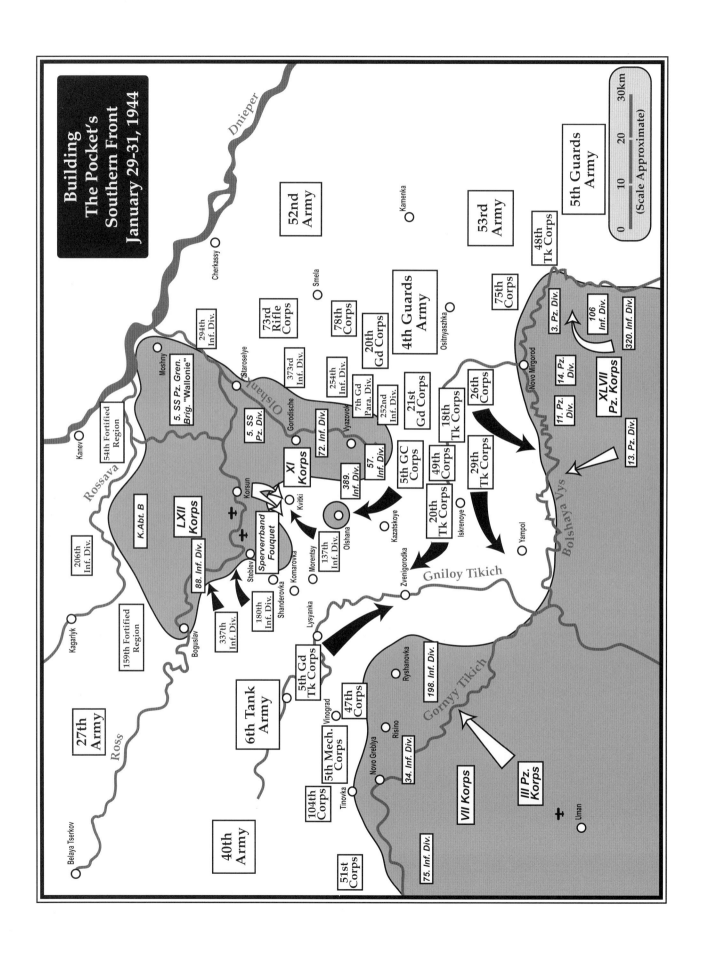

Building
The Pocket's
Southern Front
January 29-31, 1944

30km
20
10
(Scale Approximate)
0

Dnieper

52nd
Army

Cherkassy

Kamenka

53rd
Army

5th Guards
Army

48th
Tk Corps

75th
Corps

Smela

73rd
Rifle
Corps

294th
Inf. Div.

Moshny

5. SS Pz. Gren.
Brig. "Wallonie"

Staroselye

Olshana

373rd
Inf. Div.

78th
Corps

254th
Inf. Div.

20th
Gd Corps

4th Guards
Army

Ositnyaszhka

3. Pz. Div.

106
Inf. Div.

320. Inf. Div.

XLVII
Pz. Korps

14. Pz.
Div.

Novo Mirgorod

11. Pz.
Div.

5. SS
Pz. Div.

Gorodische

72. Inf. Div.

Vyazovok

7th Gd
Para. Div.

252nd
Inf. Div.

21st
Gd Corps

18th
Tk Corps

26th
Corps

13. Pz. Div.

Kanev

54th Fortified
Region

Rossava

57.
Inf. Div.

389.
Inf. Div.

XI
Korps

Korsun

Kvitki

5th GC
Corps

49th
Corps

29th
Tk Corps

Bolshaya Vys

K.Abt. B

LXII
Korps

Sperverband
Fouquet

Morentsy

137th
Inf. Div.

Olshana

Kazatskoye

20th
Tk Corps

Iskrenoye

Yampol

206th
Inf. Div.

Kaganlyk

159th Fortified
Region

88. Inf. Div.

Steblev

Shanderovka

Komarovka

Boguslav

337th
Inf. Div.

180th
Inf. Div.

Zvenigorodka

Gniloy Tikich

Lysyanka

Ryshanovka

198. Inf. Div.

Gornyy Tikich

27th
Army

Ross

6th Tank
Army

5th Gd
Tk Corps

47th
Corps

Risino

34. Inf. Div.

VII Korps

III Pz.
Korps

Belaya Tserkov

40th
Army

5th Mech.
Corps

Vinograd

Novo Greblya

Tinovka

104th
Corps

51st
Corps

75. Inf. Div.

Uman

100

VON MANSTEIN
TO THE RESCUE

Chapter Eight

BUILDING THE KESSEL'S SOUTHERN FRONT

"Not the glow of success, but the purity of the initiative and the true dedication to duty determines the value of a soldier."
— *Field Marshal Graf von Moltke*

The speed of the Red Army's advance not only caught the commanders of the *1.Pz.* and *8.Armee* by surprise, but surprised those in command of the encircled units as well. Faced with the task of trying to reestablish contact with the corps on their left and right flanks, Generals Lieb and Stemmermann had an even more daunting task to carry out - that of creating a new southern flank out of whatever units were available. They now faced the greatest danger of all - that the Soviets would penetrate deep into the pocket from the rear and quickly carve it up into little pieces, rendering any coordinated action by the encircled units impossible. A new front had to be built immediately. Until then, the commanders of *XI.* and *XXXXII.A.K.* had to throw units into the battle piecemeal in an effort to hold several key locations until a more unified front line could be created by a systematic shifting of forces from other portions of the pocket's defenses. It was to prove a desperate race against time (Map 7).

First, the flanks had to be shored up. By 28 January, the day the tanks of the First and Second Ukrainian *Fronts* linked up in Zvenigorodka, a yawning gap stretched nearly sixty kilometers all the way from Shenderovka in the northwest to Kapitanovka in the southeast. Although there were several German units fighting at each of these locations, the space in between lay wide open to the men of Konev's and Vatutin's armies. Faithful to their own encirclement doctrine, the Soviets were busily trying to feed as many units as possible into this vacuum in order to carve up the pocket before the German command could react. Hampering the Soviets at this point were the sheer distances to be traversed over an area that lacked good all-weather roads. The few German units encountered north of Zvenigorodka or Lysyanka were mainly service and supply units, who melted away as soon as the first T-34s appeared. Even a day's hesitation in the construction of a new front facing south could be fatal to the encircled Germans, and both Generals Lieb and Stemmermann knew it.

Stemmermann's solution to the problem on his right flank after 28 January was to continue the counterattack in order to reestablish contact with von Vormann's *XXXXVII.Pz.Korps.* When this attempt failed, as described in the previous chapter, Stemmermann had no choice but to pull his right flank back, causing his embattled units to basically swing to the north. With its hinge at the town of Matusov, *57.* and *389.Inf.Divs.* withdrew step by step, constantly refusing their right flanks as first the 5th Cavalry Corps, followed by 21st Guards Rifle Corps, sought to turn it. This section of Stemmermann's front line did not come to a rest until 31 January, when *389.Inf.Div.* tried to tie in with the German defenders at Olshana.

Two confident-looking Germans from an MG-42 team (known as the "Hitler Saw" by Soviet infantry) pause during an advance. Note soldier on the right wearing a captured Soviet fur cap. (Bundesarchiv 278/890/16)

General Lieb's task was considerably more daunting. On his left flank, where two Soviet divisions from Lt.Gen. Trofimenko's 27th Army were attempting to penetrate to Korsun, Lieb had no reserves to throw in the enemy's path. To shorten his corps' line, Lieb ordered *Gen.Lt. Graf* von Rittberg's *88.Inf.Div.* to pull its left flank across the Ross River during the night of 28/29 January, where it could dig in along its northern bank.[1] Trofimenko's infantry were hot on their heels and attempted to seize a bridgehead at Boguslav during the morning of 29

January. The regiment from *Graf* Rittberg's division holding Boguslav was soon locked in close-quarters fighting with troops from 337th Rifle Division. They were able to throw the Soviets out only after the arrival of seven assault guns from *StuG.Bde.239* borrowed from *XI.A.K.*, though the Germans suffered heavy casualties in the process.

Numerous Soviet truck convoys were spotted from the heights near Boguslav, heading towards Shanderovka and Steblev. Several of these marching columns were destroyed or dispersed by well-aimed artillery fire from batteries of *Art.Rgt.188* from *88.Inf.Div.*[2] The situation in Boguslav slowly began to stabilize. However, between Boguslav and the small German garrison in Steblev, there was nothing to slow or stop the Soviet advance. Worse yet, the area was crisscrossed with decent roads leading eastward into Korsun. The approach to the heart of the pocket from the west lay totally open.

To avert this crisis, Lieb began denuding his northern flank in order to create a reserve, after his new commander at *8. Armee*, General Wöhler, had granted him permission on the evening of 28 January. This force was to be composed of units drawn from *K.Abt.B*, which so far had not been decisively engaged. This unit, to be composed of three battalions from *Div.Gr.255* and *112*, was named *Sperrverband* (Blocking Detachment) Fouquet, after the acting commander of *K.Abt.B*, *Oberst* Hans-Joachim Fouquet.[3] Fouquet's unit was swiftly

loaded up on trucks the next day from their old locations near Kagarlik and Kanev and moved as fast as possible to the open fields southwest of Korsun, where they hastily assembled road-blocks until they could erect a more substantial defense. Although it represented a meager obstacle to the approaching Soviets, *Sperrverband* Fouquet was of sufficient size to stop or slow the first spearheads of 337th and 180th Rifle Divisions. Some of its companies were soon drawn into the fighting in the towns of Shanderovka and Steblev, where the Germans were attempting to delay the Soviet advance.

To defend Korsun itself, the garrison commander, *Oberst* Koft, was ordered by *8.Armee* on 29 January to assembly an *Alarmeinheit* (emergency unit) of drivers, clerks, and mechanics to establish a perimeter, since Soviet elements had been reported only 5 kilometers to the west near the town of Yablonovka.[4] The loss of Korsun, with its railway, ration stores, hospital, airfield, and ammunition dumps, would have quickly spelled the immediate end of an organized German defensive effort, since without this vital support infrastructure, the Germans would soon be unable to offer resistance. On 30 January, to further bolster the town's defense, another battalion-sized *Kampfgruppe*, code-named *Gruppe* Yablonovka, was formed from parts of *K.Abt.B* and sent out to drive off the advancing Soviets and to secure Yablonovka, where an emergency airfield was being constructed.

The Soviet infantry in Yablonovka were quickly thrown out of the warm houses in the village and driven into the woods one kilometer south, where they were kept at bay with mortar and machine-gun fire until a larger unit could be brought up to wipe them out. Slowly but surely, *XXXXII.A.K's* left flank was stabilized, at the price of almost entirely stripping its northern front along the Dnieper River. Now the survival of the encircled Germans would depend on how quickly they could build a southern front. To do this, the *Kesselkämpfer* (cauldron-fighters), as they were soon to be called by their comrades outside the pocket, would have to seize and hold several key locations in order to deny Konev's and Vatutin's forces a quick access into the pocket from the rear.

Three of these key locations on the southern front of the pocket were the towns of Steblev in the northwest, Olschana in the south and Kvitki, which lay between the other two. Until the Soviet offensive, all of these towns were considered to be

During the early stages of battle, both XI. and XXXXII. Armeekorps had to erect a completely new front in the south. Here, troops from an unnamed Kampfgruppe assemble before moving out in the snow. (Bundesarchiv 277/802/29)

Another view of the same unit. (Bundesarchiv 277/802/26)

safely in the rear and were consequently lightly garrisoned, if at all. In Steblev, the *Feld-Ausbildung Bataillon* (*Feld-Ausb.Btl.*, or field training and replacement battalion) of the *Wiking* went about its daily routine of preparing new recruits for the front. Olshana served as the supply depot of *Wiking*, and Kvitki had no garrison at all, except for local Ukrainian auxiliaries. None were prepared in any way for the impending Soviet advance. However, each of these locations was soon forced to serve as breakwaters in the path of the rapidly approaching Soviet flood. Holding them would at least temporarily ensure the continued survival of the encircled forces. First, however, combat troops had to be inserted to set up some semblance of a hasty defense.

Steblev was the first of these towns to be battled for. Situated on the main road between Korsun and Boguslav, Steblev offered a clear avenue of approach into the heart of the pocket, if the troops of General Vatutin's First Ukrainian *Front* were to seize it quickly. They began their attempt to do so early on the evening of 27 January, when reconnaissance patrols from 27th Army's 180th Rifle Division were spotted at its outskirts. Garrisoned at the time only by *SS-Feld-Ausb.Btl.5,* any successful defense of the town was doubtful. Its commander, *SS-Hstuf.* Nedderhof, was a police official in civilian life with little infantry combat experience, having only recently been transferred from *Wiking's* anti-tank battalion. To provide the leadership needed to establish a successful defense of Steblev, on 27 January *Wiking's* commander, *SS-Brigadeführer* Herbert Gille, summoned *Ostuf.* Eberhard Heder to his headquarters in Gorodishche. Heder, a 26-year old aspiring civil engineer from the town of Gross-Kuede who later rose to the rank of *Oberst* in the post-war West German *Bundeswehr*, had been ordered only a few days before to establish a close-combat school for the division's engineer battalion in Steblev. Gille explained to him the situation in Steblev and ordered him to return immediately to serve as the acting commander of *SS-Feld-Ausb.Btl.5.*

This placed Heder in an awkward position, since Nedderhof would still be the official commander. Fortunately, Nedderhof understood the seriousness of the situation and yielded active command to Heder. He knew that he was not up to the task of defending Steblev and although senior in rank, he gave Heder his full support. Upon returning to the town, Heder discovered that he hardly knew any of the men under his command. Only a few days before the Soviet offensive commenced, he had been serving as the company commander of *2.Kompanie* in the Estonian Volunteer Battalion *Narwa* in the area of Teklino, at the northeastern edge of the pocket.[5]

In Steblev, Heder found an organization that lacked heavy weapons, experienced instructors, and worst of all, was manned by a mixture of half-trained recruits and other volunteers from the four corners of occupied Europe who spoke a variety of languages - Swedes, Danes, Belgians, Norwegians, Rumanians, and so forth, but few of whom spoke passable German. A more unlikely group of men who would soon be thrust into the crucible of combat could hardly be imagined. Heder knew that he and his men would soon be in a critical situation. There were alarming reports that Soviet tanks were already in Boguslav, only 20 kilometers away, and the town of Shanderovka eight kilometers to the southwest had already been attacked.[6] Heder sent his own patrols south towards Medvin and towards Boguslav itself, in order to determine the validity of the reports. They confirmed the worst.

The following day, 28 January, Heder's men repelled a number of determined Soviet tank and infantry attacks. However, Heder and his men, who had formed "hedgehog" defensive positions, were soon surrounded. Over the next two days, until reinforced by two battalions pulled from *Div.Gp.255* from *K.Abt.B* on the evening of *29/30* January, the German garrison in Steblev had to hold on against 180th Rifle Division, reinforced by a tank brigade. At several points, the fighting grew especially intense, with hand-to-hand fighting reported in the defensive positions. On the morning of 29 January, Soviet tanks actually broke into Steblev itself.[7] *Waffen-SS* combat engineers and recruits stalked the T-34s in the streets, destroying five tanks and one assault gun, as well as three Soviet anti-tank guns. Two Red Army infantry battalions, supported by 26 tanks, trying to enter the city from the northwest in the direc-

Schenk (*second from left, standing with Soviet felt cap*) and *his battalion command group in an occupied Soviet trench on "Windmill Hill" above the village of Kvitki, early February 1944. (Photo courtesy of Ernst Schenk)*

Willy Hein (*first from left*) *in August 1943 during Wiking award ceremony near Kharkov. (Photo courtesy of Willy Hein)*

The defender of Steblev, **SS-Obersturmführer Ebhard Heder**, *Acting Commander, SS-Feld-Ausb.Btl.5, after being awarded the Knight's Cross. (Photo courtesy of Eberhard Heder)*

Leader of the lone assault gun attack against Soviet antitank company in Olshana, **SS-Obersturmführer Willy Hein**, *1.Abt., SS-Pz.Rgt.5 "Wiking." (Photo courtesy of Willy Hein)*

tion of Chirovka, were driven off by a counterattack. More T-34s were spotted to the west, but were also chased away by fire from an artillery battalion from *K.Abt.B.*, finally brought up to provide badly needed support.

Heder and the defenders of Steblev were constantly harassed by tank and artillery fire from the Soviets forces that had seized the hilltop village of Chirovka approximately four kilometers away. From their positions atop the hill that gradually sloped towards Steblev, the Soviets could easily bring fire to bear on the German defenders below. Heder decided to eliminate this threat by ordering the commander of the Walloon Brigade's *Ersatzkompanie*, a second lieutenant, to seize the town and drive out the offending Soviets. Although the Walloons attacked bravely up the slope in the teeth of intense defensive fire, their attack faltered when, at the moment they had achieved their objective, the lieutenant was killed. Losing heart, the outnumbered Walloons were forced back down the hill into Steblev, having accomplished nothing but adding to their casualty list. Still, the defenders of Steblev grimly held on.

Ten kilometers south, in the neighboring town of Shanderovka, *Div.Gp.323*, hastily pulled from its sector near Boguslav where it had been under the control of *88.Inf.Div.*, had also thrown parts of 180th Rifle Division out and established an all-round defense, warding off numerous tank attacks as well as enduring barrages from a number of *Katyusha* batteries.[8] The defenses of Shanderovka, Steblev, and Boguslav were quickly tied together, forming a coherent front line by 31 January. The westerly approach to Korsun, at least for the time being, was denied to the enemy. Writing about his experiences 53 years later, Eberhard Heder insisted that he did nothing that any other officer in *Wiking* would have done and modestly stated that his men deserved all of the credit for the defense of Steblev, not he. At the time he was ordered by General Gille to defend Steblev, he wrote he felt that his was a mission that offered little hope for success and, at best, was a questionable undertaking.[9] Questionable perhaps, but certainly vital to the survival of his division and Kessel of all the Sothers. With a few hundred raw recruits and determination, he had done far more than what was expected.

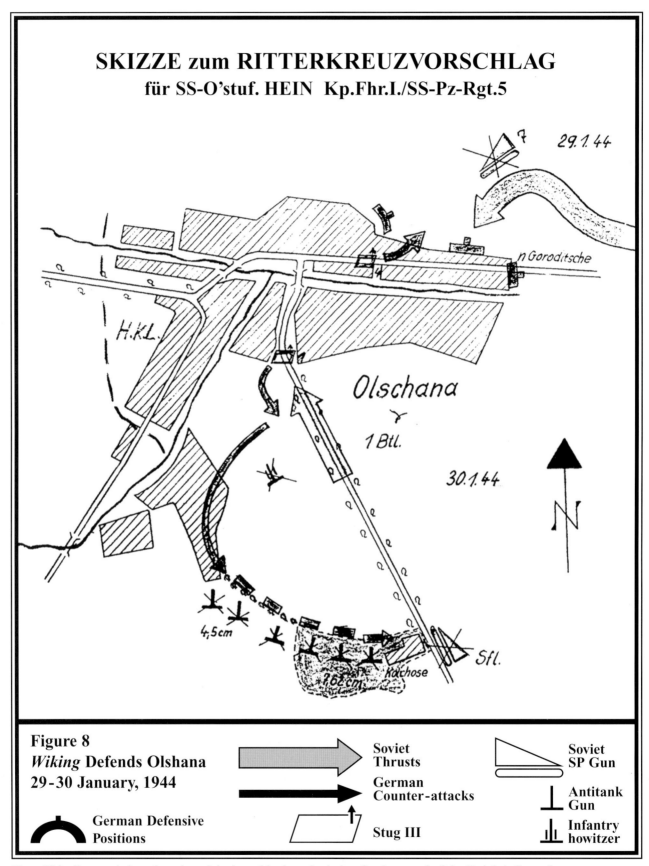

Figure 8
Wiking Defends Olshana
29-30 January, 1944

German Defensive Positions

Soviet Thrusts

German Counter-attacks

Stug III

Soviet SP Gun

Antitank Gun

Infantry howitzer

Note: This diagram is based on the original used in the submission for the award of the Knight's Cross for *SS-Ustuf.* Willy Hein, *1./SS-Pz.Rgt.5.* (U.S. National Archives)

Olshana was next to be threatened. Located some 30 kilometers south of Korsun, it was an important intersection of several key roadways leading to Korsun and Gorodishche in the north to the towns of Shpola and Zvenigorodka in the south. Since it was situated astride the only navigable roads in the area, holding Olshana would delay any attempt by the westward advancing elements of Rotmistrov's 5th Guards Tank Army to seize Korsun and splinter the pocket. It would also buy time as Generals Lieb and Stemmermann frantically sought to organize an all-round defense while they awaited the approaching relief columns of *III.* and *XXXXVII.Pz.Korps.*

Located in a small valley and surrounded on all sides by low hills, Olshana was an ordinary town that lined both sides of the main highway as it snaked its way from the west to the east, paralleling one of the many tributaries of the Olshanka River. Some five kilometers long, Olshana consisted of hundreds of thatched-roof *isbas*, several collective farms, government buildings and a gigantic sugar factory, all laid out in no identifiable pattern. Rather bleak looking, Olshana was like any other typical Ukrainian rural village, except for its tactical significance. It would soon serve as one of the pocket's most important initial cornerposts, to which the early defense of the pocket would soon be tied. In effect, holding the towns of Olshana and Steblev would serve as "corset stays" that would slow down Soviet penetrations until a coherent defensive line could be built. To the east of Olshana, the divisions of Stemmermann's *XI.A.K.* were slowly giving way towards the northwest. But it would be at least a week until *XI.A.K's* right flank unit, *389.Inf.Div.*, could tie in with Olshana's defenders

Soviet patrols radiating northwest out of Shpola towards Olshana were reported as early as the morning of 28 January.[10] At the time, only supply units of *Wiking* garrisoned Olshana. Since the only remaining open supply route for the encircled forces ran through Olshana, its seizure by the Soviets would hasten the destruction of the German forces. The SS men easily drove off these early Soviet patrols, consisting chiefly of armored cars or horse cavalry. However, everyone knew that they would soon be back, only the next time with tanks or infantry. This prediction came true when the light screening force posted south of Olshana by *Wiking's* assistant division supply officer were attacked and chased into the town by Soviet tanks from 20th Tank Corps during the late afternoon. Quickly realizing the danger, General Gille decided that same day to immediately reinforce Olshana in order to help the beleaguered garrison hold the village.[11] At first, all Gille had to send was a company from the Estonian battalion, located at the time some distance away. It would take at least a day or two until they could arrive, since trucks were in short supply. Until then, the mechanics, supply clerks and truck drivers of *Wiking's* supply services would have to make do with rifles, machine guns, and *Panzerfäuste*. Against an armored attack they would be practically defenseless. Help would soon be on its way.

On the morning of 28 January, *Ostuf.* Willy Hein, a company commander in the *Wiking's I./Pz.Rgt.5*, received an order to report to division headquarters in Gorodishche immediately. Leaving his company in the vicinity of Budki where his battalion was engaged in the effort to stem the advance of Marshal

A StuG.III awaiting the next Soviet attack.
(Bundesarchiv 709/303/17)

Konev's Second Ukrainian *Front*, Hein grabbed a ride on a motorcycle and arrived at the division command post at 1100 hours. He was greeted by the division commander himself as well as the division operations officer (or 1a) *Ostubaf.* Manfred Schönfelder. Hein was quickly brought up to date on the tactical situation in Olshana and was given the mission of reinforcing the defenders there.

To carry out this task, he was assigned four ramshackle assault guns belonging to the Army, which were then being repaired by *Wiking's* maintenance battalion. None of the derelict *StuG.IIIs* had functioning radios, thus complicating Hein's task. To crew these vehicles, Hein was provided with four crews of knocked-out tanks from his own battalion. This patchwork force would have to do; the division could spare no other forces for this mission, since all its combat elements were engaged in heavy defensive fighting from the Dnieper River in the north to Smela in the south, a distance of over 50 kilometers. Now its rear area was threatened with a Soviet tank attack and *Wiking* was virtually powerless to stop it.[12]

In many respects, Willy Hein was the ideal man for the job. The son of a renowned painter, he was born in Schleswig-Holstein in 1917 and planned to pursue a career in law enforcement, hoping someday to become a police commissioner. However, the outbreak of war caused him to change his plans, as it did for the overwhelming majority of the young men of his generation. Enlisting in the *Waffen-SS* on 26 September 1939, he quickly rose through the ranks from private to NCO. In the meantime, he fought with SS-Division *Reich* as an infantryman during the short campaign in the Balkans and for the first six months of Operation *Barbarossa*, the invasion of the Soviet Union.

In November 1941, he was posted to the *SS-Junkerschule* at Bad Tölz in Bavaria, in order to attend officer candidate school, from which he graduated in January 1942. Following training as a Panzer officer, he was promoted to *Untersturmführer* in April 1942 and was assigned to the newly raised tank battalion of *Wiking*, *SS-Pz.Abt.5*, commanded by *Sturmbannführer* (Major) Johannes Mühlenkamp, who himself was later to command *Wiking*.

Hein, as a tank platoon leader, took part in his division's campaign in the Caucasus Mountains during the summer of 1942, when the *Wehrmacht's* fortunes were at the high water mark. He proved his worth as a combat commander, earning both the Iron Cross second and first class for valor, as well as the Panzer Assault Badge in Silver. He took part in the retreat from the Caucasus in the wake of the disaster at Stalingrad, and the bitter fighting which took place during von Manstein's successful spring counteroffensive of 1943, when *Wiking* contributed to the retaking of the strategic city of Kharkov. Promoted to first lieutenant in November 1943, he earned mention in the daily *Ehrenblatt des Heeres* (Honor Roll of the German Army) for his bravery and leadership during a tank engagement, wherein his tank company destroyed a much larger number of Soviet tanks. His leadership and daring, observed from the air by Herbert Gille, won him notice, leading directly to his being chosen by name by his division commander to carry out the critical assignment to hold Olshana.[13]

Hein and his makeshift force departed Gorodishche shortly after noon and arrived in Olshana at 1800 hours, shortly after the Soviet tank attack had driven in the weak security screen set up by the supply troops. Upon arrival at the defenders' command post, he was brought up to date on the situation by the assistant division supply officer. While Hein was being briefed, a strong Soviet force equipped with self-propelled guns had gone around Olshana and was attempting to enter the village from the north. Easily driving away the few scattered German pockets, the Soviets had already occupied several houses and were busily fortifying them. Unless they were quickly dislodged, they would soon be reinforced, making it nearly impossible to throw them out and rendering any coherent defense of Olshana impossible.

Hein decided to counterattack immediately. At 1900 hours, with his four assault guns, he attacked the entrenched Soviets head on. Using high-explosive shells, he and his men drove the infantry from the houses and inflicted heavy losses upon them as they fled in disorder into the winter night. For the loss of one of his assault guns, Hein and his men destroyed five Soviet self-propelled guns (probably SU-76s of the 136th Rifle Division of the 5th Guards Tank Corps), temporarily stymieing the Red Army's advance and reestablishing the security screen along the northwest part of the village. Hoping to keep the Soviets attackers off-balance, Hein pursued the Soviets with his guns as far as Kirillovka, stopping only because he had nearly run out of fuel. For the moment, at least, the danger had been averted.

The Soviets attacked again several hours later during the early morning of 29 January. Led again by an infantry regiment from the 136th Rifle Division, the Soviets slipped around Olshana from the north and east, attacking west along the main road from Gorodishche in an attempt to seize the village from behind.[14] Over the next twelve hours, the German defenders, spearheaded by Hein's assault guns, repulsed numerous attempts by the Soviet attackers to gain entry to the town. Time and again, they were stopped by determined counterattacks and repeatedly thrown out of the town's eastern edge. During the course of the fighting, a further seven Soviet self-propelled guns were destroyed, bringing the total thus far to twelve. The battle had not been completely one-sided; the *Alarmeinheit* formed from supply and transportation troops had suffered heavy losses due to repeated hand-to-hand fighting with Soviet infantry. During the fighting, the assistant division supply officer had managed to evacuate the majority of the division's supply vehicles with baggage to Gorodishche using an alternate route, where their loads of food, spare parts, fuel, and ammunition were sorely needed.

The Soviets tried to seize Olshana again the next day, only this time 63rd Cavalry Division of General Selivanov's 5th Cavalry Corps would be used for the task, as well as the additional assignment of closing the German's path of withdrawal and establishing communications with the forces of First

StuG.III assault guns from Wiking during the early stages of battle. (Jarolin-Bundesarchiv 79/59/30)

*A Bandaged **Willy Hein** shortly after being forced to bail out of his burning assault gun, early February 1944. (U.S. National Archives)*

Ukrainian *Front* which had been trying to seize Olshana themselves, but without success.[15] 63rd Cavalry Division consisted primarily of horse cavalry reinforced with a quantity of anti-tank guns and self-propelled guns, as well as light artillery. Its mobility offered a unique advantage to the Soviets in terrain conditions such as they existed during this time of year, because horses could go where armored or wheeled vehicles could not and could move a great deal faster than normal infantry. It had sufficient firepower and flexibility to deal with all but the most heavily armored German forces it would likely encounter. Against lightly-armed "alarm units" consisting mainly of poorly trained supply troops, they were extremely effective. However, the German defenders in Olshana had three remaining assault guns under Willy Hein and elements from the Estonian Battalion *Narwa* were on their way.

The morning of 30 January dawned with a German counterattack led by Hein and his assault guns in a westerly direction towards the neighboring town of Pidynovka, throwing the defending Soviet infantry from the 136th Rifle Division off the heights and keeping them off balance. However, Hein and his men noticed that the Red Army was assembling additional forces a few kilometers further to the southwest. These new units were from 63rd Cavalry Division, only recently having arrived in their assembly areas. Two hours later, elements from this division attacked Olshana from the west with strong tank support. Additionally, Soviet antitank gun batteries were arrayed along their flanks to prevent Hein and his assault guns from attacking. The German defenders withdrew back into Olshana by bounds and braced for the impending attack. With two of his last three assault guns, Hein was able to drive off the attackers, who licked their wounds as they sought to find an easier way into the town. During the move back into town, one of Hein's assault guns had to be abandoned because its steering mechanism had failed. Now he only had two left with which to hold off the next assault.[16]

Fortunately for the Germans, additional reinforcements were available at 1300 hours, when *1.Kompanie* of *Narwa* arrived. The rest of the battalion would arrive later, but for the time being, one company would do. Hein quickly planned another counterattack in a southerly direction towards the towns of Tolstaya and Yukovka with the Estonians' company commander, *Ustuf.* Uhlenbusch. Soviet antitank guns and self-propelled guns had been spotted there south of Olshana, along a wide slope that afforded an excellent commanding view of the center of town, where the German command post lay. Hein ordered Uhlenbusch to have some of his infantry mount his two remaining assault guns, with the remainder of the company to follow. Using the terrain to hide his approach, Hein and his small force crept along a gully at the western base of the slope several hundred meters from the Soviets cavalrymen, who were busily emplacing seven antitank guns along a row of bushes near a collective farm and preparing infantry fighting positions. This threat had to be eliminated immediately, or the Germans would have to withdraw.

Unfortunately, the other assault gun broke down with an unserviceable main gun, leaving Hein and his last gun to carry out the attack (Map 8). Throwing caution to the winds, Hein

attacked the enemy in the flank. The Soviets were taken by surprise, having completely missed the German's approach, since they had thought that the sound of approaching tank engines were from their own tanks. Cavalrymen and antitank gunners were running everywhere, shouting in panic, as Hein and the mounted infantry fired into their ranks. His gunner first knocked out a Soviet light infantry howitzer, then concentrated his fire on two 4.5 cm and four 7.62 cm antitank guns and their crews. While his gunner was engaging these targets, Hein himself was busily throwing hand grenades, firing the loader's MG 34 machine gun, and standing in his open hatch scattering the Soviets with bursts from his machine pistol.

After Hein rolled over the row of parked Soviet halftracks, trucks, and horse teams that had brought the guns into position, the Soviets began to give up. The closely following company from *Narwa* rounded up over 150 Soviet infantrymen hiding in haystacks. After a couple of them were shot, the Soviets put their hands up. The remainder fled headlong towards Tolstaya, two kilometers south. Among the prisoners was the Soviet battalion commander, who, upon interrogation, admitted that there were two additional divisions approaching Olshana. While Hein and his little *Kampfgruppe* was mopping up along the slope, two additional Soviet tanks were spotted rolling towards them from the direction of Tolstaya. Hein quickly engaged and destroyed both of them, but it became obvious that with the approaching darkness, the slope could not be held, since it was too far away from the center of town.[17]

Because of this action, the encirclement of the village of Olshana had been prevented and the splintering of the pocket along the highway from Olshana and Gorodishche had been averted, at least for the time being. The withdrawal of *Wiking's* supply base to Gorodishche had also been made possible, ensuring that the division would be able to maintain its combat power for a least a little while longer. In recognition of his bravery and leadership, General Gille recommended Willy Hein for the *Ritterkreuz,* Germany's highest award for valor. He would not be granted time to celebrate his award, since 63rd Cavalry Division was still intent on seizing Olshana.

The next morning, 31 January, the Soviets reestablished the antitank gun position on the slope south of Olshana and attacked again with two regiments. Rather than leading another counterattack, Hein decided instead to engage them with high-explosive shells from the safety of the town. Later that day, he brought his last remaining assault gun within direct fire range, and destroyed six more antitank guns with armor-piercing shells. A Soviet tank attack from the same direction was also driven off. That same day, the remainder of the *Narwa* Battalion and a company from the division's combat engineer battalion arrived, as well as tanks from Hein's own company.

Leaving the assault gun in which he had inflicted so much damage to the enemy, Hein climbed back into his own command tank, which he had left three days before in the charge of his gunner, *Unterscharführer* (Sergeant) Edgar Schweichler, on the outskirts of Budki. His sense of relief was to prove short lasting, however; during a change of position in a battle with another Soviet antitank gun position, his tank received a direct hit from one of two American-made Sherman tanks, which were part of

63rd Cavalry Division's tank regiment lying in ambush. Although his crew bailed out without injury, Hein received first and second degree burns to his face and hands, forcing him to be evacuated to the division medical treatment battalion in Gorodishche. For Willy Hein, his active role as a combatant in the pocket was over; however, for the remainder of the battle, he was posted to his tank battalion's headquarters to serve as a signals officer while he waited for his wounds to heal. From his position, he was able to witness and record a great deal of the subsequent dramatic events as they unfolded over the next three weeks.

The battle for Olshana did not end with Willy Hein's medical evacuation, however. It was to continue with renewed ferocity for six more days, as General Seliavanov threw more and more forces at the desperately fighting German defenders, who were finally completely encircled on the evening of 31 January. That night, 63rd Cavalry Division finally linked up with 180th Rifle Division of First Ukrainian *Front's* 27th Army, which itself had been trying to seize Steblev to the northwest. Repeated attempts by the Soviets to penetrate into the center of Olshana were beaten back. In the words of the historian of the 5th Guards Cavalry Corps, the fight for the town "took on a protracted and fierce character," so stubborn and effective were the men of *Wiking's* Estonian Battalion, combat engineer battalion, and scratch units from the supply column.[18]

Fighting swirled around the sugar factory, where *3.Kompanie* of *Wiking's* combat engineer battalion were dug in. Since they lacked medium or heavy field artillery, the Cossacks simply could not dislodge them without suffering enormous losses. Anytime they tried to use tanks to blast the Germans at point-blank range, they were knocked out by infantry using *Panzerfäuste.* Without room to maneuver in Olshana's winding streets, the Soviet tanks were sitting ducks. Because of this development, the commander of 63rd Cavalry Division was ordered to cease his attacks on Olshana and concentrate instead on preventing the Germans from breaking out or linking up with any forces attacking to relieve them from outside the pocket, while his division awaited the arrival of 4th Guards Army's infantry.[19]

It had been proven, once again, that although horse cavalry and light armor were superb forces to use during mobile, fluid operations, they simply were not trained or equipped to fight as infantry, especially in house-to-house fighting against a stubborn and skillfully led opponent. Unwittingly, the Soviet decision to delay the attack on Olshana until stronger forces arrived gave the Germans the time they needed to organize an all-around defense of the town, thus ensuring that no Soviet units would be able to penetrate into the pocket from the south via Shpola.

With the arrival of 5th Guards Airborne Division and 62nd Guards Rifle Division of 4th Guards Army, the attack was renewed on Olshana on 2 February. Despite the fact that the Soviets now outnumbered the Germans by a factor of ten to one, by 3 February they had only managed to capture one quarter of the town, a testament to the fierce nature of the fighting. The commitment of 11th Guards Cavalry Division also failed to tip the scales in favor of the Soviets, for the SS defenders were willing to fight to the death to keep the town from falling into the hands of the Red Army.[20] Fortunately for the Germans, the situation outside Olshana had changed enough such that the continued holding of the town was no longer necessary. By 4 February, a continuous defensive line had been established ten kilometers northeast of the town by *Wiking, 57.,* and *389.Inf.Divs.* along the line Viazovok - Petropavlovka - Kvitki. It was time to leave and Gille could not afford to sacrifice his troops if he was no longer required to do so.

During the night of 5/6 February, the *Kampfgruppe* that had held Olshana for the past nine days evacuated its position as ordered and, aided by the attached assault gun company from *SS-Polizei Division*, broke through to the northeast at 0230 hours and linked up with a regiment from *389.Inf.Div.* at Petropavlovka. The survivors of the fighting were then returned to their parent units as planned.[21] The only unit that suffered significant losses during the breakout was a company from the Estonian Battalion *Narwa*, which formed the rearguard. It lost nearly all of its vehicles and suffered heavy casualties when its column was ambushed and shot up by Soviet infantry as the Estonians passed over an elevated causeway northeast of Olshana.

The next day, the Cossacks of 5th Cavalry Corps and the infantrymen of 4th Guards Army entered an abandoned town that was little more than heaps of rubble. This fact did not stop them from claiming in their after-action report that they had completely wiped out the German defenders, which included the *Westland* and *Germania* Regiments, the Estonian Battalion *Narwa*, as well as *Wiking's* entire field training battalion.[22] In effect, they claimed that they had practically wiped out most of *Wiking*, though this was not remotely close to the truth. In fact, *Wiking's* biggest battles in the pocket were yet to come.

Once the Germans had temporarily retained control by 29 January of both Olshana and Steblev, they in effect had secured the shoulders of the pocket's southern flank. Now they had to stitch the gaping hope that still appeared on their situation maps, a gap that invited further incursions. In fact, on 30 January advancing troops of 180th Rifle Division seized the town of Kvitki, only ten kilometers south of Korsun and twelve west of Gorodishche.[23] Although Kvitki did not straddle any major roadway, allowing the enemy to establish himself so close to the Germans' main centers of resistance would invite disaster. Kvitki had to be retaken or at least sealed off from further reinforcement. But where were the forces to carry out this task to come from?

Casting about for a solution, General Lieb of *XXXXII.A.K.,* in whose sector Kvitki lay, performed a quick survey of his already thinly-stretched force. The only area of his front that could afford to give up anything was *K.Abt.B*, which still had elements that were lightly committed. The battalion chosen to carry out the mission of retaking Kvitki was Ernst Schenk's *Rgt.Gr.110*, located at the time at the stockyard in Stepanzy, on the pocket's northernmost line. Thinking that his battalion was about to enjoy a well-earned rest, Schenk and his men were surprised when a column of trucks arrived at noon on 30 January with orders for them to load up immediately and move off in the direction of Korsun.[24] He and his men took this as a signal that

After the attack, Soviet positions are mopped up. Here an Army Grenadier poses with Soviet dead.
(Bundesarchiv 690/219/29A)

the situation in the Kanev salient had grown critical indeed, since trucks generally were not used to transport infantry. No longer could anyone pretend that they were not encircled. In Schenk's words, "it was pretty obvious that we were in a bad way."[25]

The trip proceeded smoothly enough, since the roads were still frozen enough to permit unrestricted traffic. When his battalion climbed out of the trucks, the found that they had indeed arrived in Korsun. They were quickly directed by a staff officer to establish a security screen immediately southwest along the edge of town.[26] Schenk and his men then learned that they were now under the control of *Sperrverband* Fouquet. After occupying bunkers and dugouts for the past several weeks, no one in Schenk's battalion looked forward to a night in the open, especially since the temperature at night still sank below freezing. They did not get the chance to stay there long, though. On the morning of 31 January, Schenk was ordered to attack south towards Kvitki and seize the town of Listvena, then thinly garrisoned by the Soviets.

This he and his men duly accomplished, though the next objective, the town of Petrushki, proved to be a somewhat tougher assignment. After a rapid assault that caught the Soviets by surprise, the fighting degenerated into hand-to-hand combat before the enemy could be thrown out of town. So far, Schenk noticed, his battalion had advanced ten kilometers since leaving Korsun that morning and as yet he had seen no sign of a friendly unit on his left flank or his right. He and his men had been left on their own without any tanks or artillery to carry out one the most critical assignments required for the continued survival of the units in the pocket.

The next morning, 1 February, Schenk was ordered to continue the attack south towards Kvitki, then only five kilometers away. At 1000 hours his battalion had seized Hill 357 south of Petrushki without a struggle. At 1200 hours, he was ordered to initiate the attack on Kvitki, which would involve his battalion attacking uphill in broad daylight to the peak of a featureless 1,500 meter long snow-covered slope that offered absolutely no cover for his soldiers, should they to be pinned down by enemy fire. As for the Soviets, they were observed on the hilltop busily digging in and preparing to give Schenk and his men a warm reception. To make matters worse, artillery support for his attack was still not available. Without support from additional units on Schenk's left or right flank, the enemy would be able to concentrate all of their fire on his men. To Schenk the conclusion was obvious. A daylight attack in such conditions would be suicide and he certainly was not going to do that, no matter what he was ordered to do.[27]

Since refusing to obey an order in battle would be akin to signing his own death warrant, Schenk chose to delay his attack as long as possible. This would not only give him time to carry out a reconnaissance of the enemy positions and make detailed plans, but would possibly enable him to carry out his attack at night, when the Soviets' advantage in firepower would not be as telling. Therefore, Ernst Schenk stalled, demanding artillery and additional troops to support his attack. Over the telephone, he was repeatedly threatened by his superiors with a court martial if he did not attack immediately. While Schenk was buying time, one of his platoon leaders carried out an extensive assessment of the Soviet tactical dispositions and was able to gather enough information to allow Schenk and his staff to compose a hasty battle plan.

Finally, at 1645 hours, just as darkness fell, his battalion was ready for action. Before they jumped off, Schenk's unit was visited by a general officer from corps headquarters, who came by to see what all the fuss was about. Apparently satisfied by what he saw, he observed Schenk's attack on the hill and did not leave until dawn the next morning. Although Schenk did not mention it, he and his men had been visited by *Gen.Lt.* Lieb, his corps commander. Later, Lieb wrote in his diary that he "had a look at the *Gren.Rgt.110* of *K.Abt.B.* Morale of troops very good. Rations plentiful."[28]

Schenk's plan was simple. Using cover of darkness and folds in the terrain as concealment, his battalion would attack the Soviet positions on Hill 357 from the flank, seize them, and immediately advance into Kvitki itself. The surprise attack caught the Soviets totally off guard. Quickly seizing the hill without loss, Schenk led his battalion towards Kvitki, where they rapidly took the northern part of the village. The next morning Schenk continued his attack, hoping to take the remainder of the town before the Soviets could figure out what was happening.

However, Schenk's battalion, now reduced to fewer than 400 men without any heavy weapons to speak of, no longer had the strength to complete the task. The defending Soviet proved to be too deeply dug in to be easily dislodged. On the afternoon of 2 February, Schenk's force was bolstered by the arrival of three assault guns, but they proved to be too unwieldy for use in house to house fighting, which the battle for Kvitki had degenerated into. His force was further weakened when he had to detach a platoon led by *Oblt.* Kreutzer to cover his wide-open right flank near Petrushki.[29]

Kvitki, like Olshana, was built along a narrow valley, straddling several secondary roads which ran alongside a small stream. Like Olshana, it was surrounded on all sides by hills which offered commanding views in all directions. Simply holding the town of Kvitki was not enough. To truly control the area, one side or the other had to hold as many of these hills as possible, which changed hands many times during the course of the fighting. Schenk's *Rgt.Gr.110* simply did not have the number of men needed to do it. What happened over the course of the next week was what he described as the sensation of being caught in a mouse trap, surrounded on all sides by the Soviets who continuously sought to both drive his unit out of the village and cut him and his men off from neighboring German units. In the meantime, the early thaw had set in, forcing him and his men to live and fight in the mud with no opportunity to obtain a change of clothing.

Although Schenk's battalion was reinforced over the next several days by other elements from *Div.Gr.112* and *Wiking*, the Soviets gradually forced the Germans from the center of Kvitki back towards the northern range of hills that overlooked the village. To Schenk, this was a relief, since it was a great deal better than being caught in the "mousetrap" of Kvitki. By 9 February, Schenk's battalion as well as the others had been forced back again to Petrushki, where they had started from eight days previously. That same day, Schenk celebrated his 30th

birthday. He could not help but think that he and his comrades would soon need all of the good luck wishes that they had just given him. They would soon indeed.[30]

Similar scenes played out at other locations along the newly-erected southern front, where hastily assembled *Alarmeinheiten* were rushed to quickly establish a defense capable of blocking, at least temporarily, any Soviet attempts to break up the pocket from the inside. Tiny villages such as Prulitzy, Sselitchya, and Valyava all experienced similar actions. Each of these were faced with encirclement, bravely fought off repeated Soviet attempts to break through, and were eventually incorporated into the new defense line which had finally solidified by 5 February. None of them, however, were as significant or dramatic as the fighting at Steblev, Kvitki, and Olshana.

Today, there are no monuments in these towns honoring the achievements of the desperate German defenders who so resolutely defended their positions, often to the last man. There are no ceremonies held today in Ukraine to commemorate their bravery. But for one critical week, the entire survival of the encircled force of 60,000 men were dependent upon a motley assortment of troops led by men such as Willy Hein, Ernst Schenk, and Eberhard Heder. They and their men had done what was thought to be impossible and that was enough.

How could the Soviets not have succeeded? After all, they did have a clear majority in men and tanks, as well as command of the air. One of the reasons why they did not was due to the composition of some of the forces tasked with carrying out the mission of attacking into the German rear. 5th Cavalry Corps, for example, though highly mobile, lacked enough infantry and heavy tanks to launch coordinated ground assaults, especially against an enemy awaiting their attack in fortified towns and villages. Its cavalry divisions simply lacked staying power. Another unit charged with the mission of taking Olshana, 136th Rifle Division, had only recently been encircled itself and was seriously understrength and lacked a large amount of equipment. Tank units, such as the brigade from 20th Guards Tank Corps which initially tried to seize Olshana, did not have enough infantry. Attacking a town of that size, or a town the size of Steblev, without infantry to neutralize enemy antitank weapons was to invite disaster. 5th Guards Airborne Division, though an elite unit, suffered from a shortage of heavy weapons and transport.

In general, the Soviet attacks were clearly uncoordinated and were designed primarily to accomplish their objectives by relying on speed and surprise. More significantly, though, was the overall shortage of artillery. Without the massive artillery preparations to which they were accustomed, the Soviet infantry had to attack German strong points practically unsupported. This approach worked at first when all the Soviets faced were supply units with little or no combat experience, but failed practically every time when they encountered veteran German infantry. Where was the artillery?

Although the staff officers of both First and Second Ukrainian *Fronts* had planned to provide continuous artillery support, the course of events prevented it. Not only were the artillery units forced to wait until the tanks of 5th Guards Tank and 6th Tank Armies had passed through, they found that the roads, due to the heavy traffic combined with the thaw that set in 3 February, were virtually impassable. Try though they may, the gunners could not get through.[31] Just as the weather was hampering the Germans both inside and outside the pocket, it was affecting the Soviets as well. The few passable roads quickly became endless morasses filled with traffic jams several miles long, requiring the intervention of general officers to bring some order to the chaos. Even the enlistment of the local population in the road repair effort had little effect.

Until construction engineer units could be brought up and repair the roads, from 26 January to 5 February, the artillery had to wait, while Cossacks and guards airborne troops frantically sought to seize towns like Olshana with the few available tanks and by relying on brute force, suffered appalling casualties. Future Soviet offensives, resulting from their experiences in the Battle of the Cherkassy Pocket, would devote far greater care

in the planning, movement, and resupply of their artillery.

Its lack insured that even small and lightly armed German formations, at the beginning at least, were able to stand their ground and fight off numerous Soviet attacks. After both the inner and outer lines of encirclement were formed by their opponents, the Germans began to see once again, to their dismay, the re-introduction of the Soviet's "King of Battle," especially in the form of the *Katyusha* 12.2 cm multiple rocket launcher, the dreaded *Stalinorgel*. Now that the Soviets had completely encircled their hated opponent, they could begin the task of systematically crushing the pocket. However, at this stage at least, the Germans had been able, with great difficulty, to create a solid front. They also realized that they were completely surrounded with no clear way out.

End Notes

[1]   *XXXXII A.K.* KTB entry 0205 hours, 28 January 1944.

[2]   *XXXXII A.K.* KTB entry 2035 hours, 29 January 1944.

[3]   Mehner, p. 51.

[4]   *XXXXII A.K.* KTB entry 1121 hours 30 January 1944.

[5]   Letter from Eberhard Heder, Daseburg, Germany, to Douglas Nash, 22 January 1997. Original in author's possession.

[6]   Strassner, p. 135.

[7]   *XXXXII A.K.* KTB entry 2035 hours, 29 January 1944.

[8]   Schwarz, pp. 40-41.

[9]   Heder letter.

[10] *Truppenkameradschaft Wiking, Die Flut verschlangt sich selbst, nicht uns!,* (Hannover, Germany: H. Botha Hannover, 1963), p. 6.

[11] Strassner, p. 135.

[12] Willy Hein, *Meine Erlebnisse im Kessel von Tscherkassy, 26 Jan. bis 18 Febr. 1944,* private manuscript in author's collection, undated.

[13] Interview with Willy Hein, former commanders, *2.Kompanie, SS-Panzer Abteilung 5,* Lauenburg, Germany, 24 June 1996.

[14] Glanz, "From the Dnieper to the Vistula," Map Study, Situation 29 January 1944.

[15] *Sbornik,* p. 344-45.

[16] Hein, p. 2.

[17] Citation for the award of the Knight's Cross to *SS-Obersturmführer* Willy Hein, SS Panzer Division *Wiking,* 21 April 1944. (Microfilm copy, U.S. National Archives).

[18] *Sbornik,* p. 346.

[19] Ibid, p. 346.

[20] Ibid, pp. 346-47.

[21] Strassner, p. 135.

[22] *Sbornik,* p. 347.

[23] *XXXXII A.K.* KTB entry, 1815 hours, 30 January 1944.

[24] Ernst Schenk, letter to author, 20 August 1996.

[25] Ibid, p. 2.

[26] Schenk, p. 55.

[27] Schenk letter dated 20 August 1996, p. 2.

[28] DA Pam 20-234, p. 22.

[29] Schenk, p. 56.

[30] Schenk letter, p. 3.

[31] *Selected Readings in Military History: Soviet Military History, Volume I - the Red Army 1918-1945.* (Fort Leavenworth: Combat Studies Institute, 1984), p. 334.

Chapter Nine

THE AERIAL BRIDGE

"We are sincerely thankful for the sacrifices of our comrades from VIII.Flieger-Korps, who supplied you from the air and evacuated many of the wounded . . . "
— *General Hans Hube, 19 February 1944*

When the pincers of 5th Guards and 6th Tank Armies met at Zvenigorodka on 28 January, it signaled not only the end of the second phase of the Soviet operation, but also started the clock ticking for the fate of the encircled troops of *XI.* and *XXXXII.A.K..* With nearly all supply routes now cut, it would only be a matter of time when the Germans would run out of supplies and become incapable of further organized resistance. Although both corps had stockpiled quantities of certain items of supply in their depots, such as food and ammunition, these would be quickly used up, especially artillery ammunition, which always demands the majority of the logistical effort in 20th Century warfare.[1] In order to remain combat effectiveness, the units of Generals Lieb and Stemmermann would have to receive no less than 150 tons of supply per day.* Since both corps were denied permission to immediately break out, for the time being they would have to depend on resupply by air.

The *Luftwaffe*, though thinly spread on the Russian Front during this stage of the war, immediately began planning an emergency airlift. Not only would the aircrews of General Seidemann's *VIII.Flieger-Korps*, which directly supported Army Group South, have to support this operation, but they would continue to be required to fly close air support missions and fighter escort as well for the other armies. Resupply efforts quickly began on an ad hoc basis, with aircrews of *1.Staffel, 3.Transportgeschwader*, under *Maj.* Schmidt, flying from their base at the temporary airfield in Korsun to the airfield at Uman, dropping off ammunition and picking up wounded for evacuation. This action, though it demonstrated to the encircled troops that efforts were being made to keep them resupplied, would not work in the long run. In essence, from 28 - 31 January, the existing aerial resupply network which had been in place for several months could no longer meet the demand with the few aircraft available. To preclude a total breakdown of the logistical system, a larger level of effort would be needed.

Fortunately, the *Luftwaffe* had learned from its disastrous performance during the Stalingrad debacle the year before and from its attempt to supply the beleaguered German forces in Tunisia, losing hundreds of transport aircraft in the process.

It now had a much firmer grip on what could and what could not be done. It had learned that it could not resupply a large encircled force indefinitely by air. In order to earn the confidence of the troops in the pocket, the *Luftwaffe* would no longer make a lot of empty promises, such as those made by Hermann Goering, the head of the *Luftwaffe*, to the troops at Stalingrad. Instead of promising a resupply effort that would enable the encircled forces to operate as if they enjoyed a fully functioning logistical lifeline, they would only be resupplied with the absolute essentials - ammunition, medical supplies, and gasoline.

Food was at least available in Korsun, where the local military administrator had evacuated a large store of locally procured foodstuffs, such as flour and grains, in addition to a large *Wehrmacht* food depot that had been moved across the Ross River. Although the troops of *XI.* and *XXXXII.A.K.* would not be dining in luxury, they would at least have enough to eat in order to keep up their fighting strength. According to a remark by General Lieb, at the time of the encirclement, food supplies in the pocket were adequate. His greater concerns were for resupply of ammunition and evacuation of the wounded.[2]

To facilitate the aerial resupply effort, General Seidemann set up an operational staff on 31 January 1944, based at the airfield in Uman. Under the direction of *Maj.* Knapp, this staff was given the sole mission of coordinating the airlift for the Pocket. The arrival of this planning and operations cell was a great relief to *Maj.* Riesch, the commander of *3.Staffel, 3.Transportgeschwader* based in Uman, who until then had been running the operation. His unit was further augmented on 2 February, when *Maj.* Baumann's *2.Staffel* arrived from their base at Golta. These

Ju-52 landing at snow-covered field.
(Bundesarchiv 459/150/29)

---

* During the first week of January 1944, when Army Group South began planning the withdrawal behind the Ross River, the two corps in the Kanev salient had collected all of the food stocks in the hands of the German agricultural administrators and transported them south of the Ross River in the vicinity of Korsun. This made the problem of air resupply much easier. (Earl Ziemke, *Stalingrad to Berlin: The German Defeat in the East*. (Washington D.C.: Center of Military History, United States Army, 1984), p. 231

two units, combined with *Maj.* Schmidt's *Staffel* in Korsun, equipped with *Junkers* Ju-52 *Tante Ju* transports, would fly the majority of the resupply missions during the next three weeks.[3] To carry out their mission, the transport units would fly from airfields at Uman, Golta, and Proskurov (in *8.Armee's* sector). However, only Uman possessed the proper material handling equipment (tractors, forklifts, etc.) needed to insure the rapid turn-around of arriving and departing aircraft, and would eventually become the sole airfield. Uman was also more suitable since it was the closest to the encircled forces (only 30 kilometers at the beginning of the battle) and was co-located near *1. Pz.Armee's* field hospital, also located in Uman.[4] The fact that aircraft had only a 60-kilometer round trip was critical, because this would allow each aircrew to fly several missions each day.

The wounded were quickly becoming a high priority for evacuation. Since all able-bodied men were denied evacuation, resupply missions that landed at the airfield in Korsun or the neighboring airfield at Yablonovka could return with a load of casualties. The wounded began to accumulate quickly. On 29 January, General Lieb reported in his diary that over 2,000 wounded soldiers were awaiting evacuation throughout both corps.[5] The unit that had responsibility for the organization of the wounded at the Korsun airfield, *Sanitäts-Abteilung* (*San.Abt.*) *112* of *K.Abt.B*, was soon swamped. Nevertheless, the medical officer in charge of the wounded there was able to achieve a close working relationship with *Maj.* Schmidt, the commander of the airfield. Shelter for the wounded was found throughout the town of Korsun, with many being placed in the ancient Polish castle on the island in the middle of the Ross River. Despite the efforts of both the medical troops and the aircrews, 750 wounded still needed to be evacuated on 31 January.[6] The number would only climb higher thereafter.

The aircrews of *3.Transportgeschwader* tried several methods to speed up the resupply effort. The first method involved flying low-altitude formations with dozens of aircraft in close formation. Although this made it easier for crews to stay on course and to avoid Soviet fighter aircraft, it did expose them to fire from Soviet anti-aircraft units, which had quickly been emplaced along the flight path of the air corridor chosen for the flight to Korsun from Uman. Occasionally, flights of Ju-52s

Ju-52 "Tante Ju" being prepared to load wounded. (Bundesarchiv 503/223/10A)

suffered losses and many other aircraft were severely damaged, but were able to be repaired. Many wounded soldiers being flown out were wounded yet again during the flight to Uman by the Soviet anti-aircraft fire. Since German fighter escorts were not immediately available at the beginning of the airlift, this was thought to be the best method of insuring the safety of the majority of the transports.

This method backfired on 1 February, when the unit commander on the flight in to Korsun decided to fly back to Uman on the return route at a higher altitude contrary to his orders, in order to avoid particularly heavy antiaircraft fire. As the aircraft were assembling for the return flight over the field at Korsun, they were pounced upon by a group of Soviet fighter aircraft. In the one-sided battle that ensued, 13 Ju-52s, each loaded with over a dozen wounded were shot down, two were forced to make emergency landings, and one overshot the airfield and crashed. The *Luftwaffe* light *Flak* battery flown into Korsun for airfield defense afforded scant protection. This incident aroused a great deal of alarm at Lieb's headquarters, which resulted in Lieb personally contacting *8.Armee's* commander, General Wöhler, and demanding fighter cover for the Korsun airfield.[7] Within several days, aircraft from *Oblt.* Erich Hartmann's *Jagdgeschwader 52* (*J.G.*, or fighter wing) were flying escort, but usually averaged only three Me-109s per mission, flying air cover for up to 36 Ju-52s at a time.[8]

After this disaster, the operations staff at Uman decided to switch to high-altitude close formation flights with the aforementioned fighter protection. These flights, normally flown from 7,640 to 9,550 feet, resulted in fewer losses, though they caused the aircraft to consume more fuel and took more time to arrive in Korsun. Even with only several fighters flying escort, they were usually enough to keep the Soviet fighters at bay. If no fighter escort were available for the return trip, the aircrews would delay their departure until darkness, when Soviet fighters were less likely to spot them. Although this change of flight tactics resulted in the loss of fewer transports, it could not prevent the Soviets from shooting up the airfield during daylight hours with IL-2 *Sturmovik* ground attack aircraft. Any aircraft caught on the ground during these attacks was a sitting duck.

For example, on 3 February, Soviet ground attack aircraft attacked the field at Korsun fourteen times.[9] Fortunately, during this time of year it began to get dark at 1630 hours, allowing more time for nighttime flight operations. Despite these obstacles, the aerial bridge from Korsun to Uman and other airfields continued. From 27 January to 3 February, the aircrews of *3.Transportgeschwader* had managed to evacuate 2,800 wounded soldiers and had kept the encircled troops supplied with between 120 to 140 tons of supplies a day, more or less meeting the requirement.[10] The airfields at Uman, Golta, Korsun, and Proskurov became literally beehives of activity. Hundreds of Luftwaffe personnel were used to help load and unload aircraft around the clock. In order to make the airfield at Korsun more efficient, aircraft salvage and repair crews and their equipment were flown in. In this manner, damaged aircraft were repaired and placed back into operation within the pocket.

From late January to 3 February, the airfields in northern Ukraine had remained usable. Still hard-frozen, they permitted

Wounded in litter racks aboard a Ju-52 during a flight to a field hospital. The Luftwaffe flight engineer will serve as their nurse during the brief flight to safety, while warding off Soviet fighters with the aircraft's sole 7.92 machinegun. (Bundesarchiv 503/224/25A)

aircraft to fly around the clock on their mission to resupply the pocket. On 3 February the weather broke; an early thaw had begun to settle, threatening the continuity of the airlift. Meter-high snowdrifts began to melt, flooding several of the airfields then in use, especially the one at Korsun. Although they usually froze up again at night, when aircrews were able to fly three missions a night, these airfields, little more than hard-packed dirt, turned into a rutted mass of mud during the day. By 4 February, the primary field at Korsun was temporarily unusable and had to be avoided. Despite these conditions, five Ju-52s still managed to land and take off again with their load of casualties, testimony to the dedication of the aircrews, who risked death or injury if their aircraft crashed upon takeoff or landing in the morass. Even so, *Maj.* Knapp and his operations staff began preparations to procure and ship to Uman supply canisters and parachutes and packing materials needed to conduct resupply from the air.

However, he had waited too long - delays in shipment of these items prevented them from being immediately available.[11] In order to conduct resupply missions while the airfield in Korsun was being relocated, aircrews resorted to the novel technique of flying at extremely low altitude - as low as ten feet above the ground - and simply throwing their cargo out the load-

ing hatch. At such low flight speeds, the containers of fuel, ammunition and medical supplies (which were usually packed in boxes filled with straw) normally landed in snowdrifts or mud and were almost always found intact. However, only a fraction of the necessary supplies could be delivered this way. Even this technique had to be temporarily abandoned when heavy fog rolled in on 5 February, forcing the grounding of all aircraft until it lifted.

With the Korsun field out of action, another suitable landing site had to be found immediately. Two were reconnoitered and were in operation by 8 February - one at Korsun (West) and the other near the town of Yablonovka, several kilometers to the west of Korsun. These fields were quickly surveyed and improved as much as time would allow. Although they were little more than large open fields, they were hurriedly graded and marked with a bare minimum of lighting that would allow night take offs and landings. But this was enough. During the following days from 8 to 12 February, over 100 resupply missions were flown into these locations or airdropped. Wounded were flown out until the airfield at Uman became unusable; constant thawing and softening of the surface, as well as constant use, had damaged the airfield there beyond repair.

Even so, 431 wounded were flown out on 10 February and nearly 250 tons of supplies were flown in - the best performance in the airlift to date.[12] One Ju-52 tried to land as late as 12 February, the last day that aircraft were able to land in the pocket, but its landing gear stuck in the mud upon landing, causing the aircraft to flip over onto its back. The few remaining flights were directed out of Proskurov in *8.Armee* sector. By 13 February, the evacuation of wounded by air from Korsun had become academic; by that point, Soviet spearheads had approached the town from the east and north and were within artillery range. Korsun itself was abandoned on the evening of 13/14 February. The wounded, now 2,000 of them, had been evacuated to Shanderovka two days before. From that point on, all resupply for the pocket would have to be dropped by parachute.

The flight into the pocket by the crews of Ju-52s and Heinkel 111s, pressed into service as transports, was a harrow-

A Ju-52 loaded with wounded takes off. Now the nerve-racking return flight could begin. (Bundesarchiv 459/150/130)

ing affair, whether they flew by day or night. First flown in 1932, the *Tante Ju* or "Iron Annie," as she was affectionately called by her crew, was originally designed to serve as a commercial airliner. Its exterior, covered by a layer of corrugated metal, gave it a distinctive appearance, which, combined with its three-motor engine layout, made it one of the most unique looking aircraft in the war. It could carry 18 fully loaded troops or litters for twelve wounded, and could fly at a maximum speed of 189 miles per hour at 18,000 feet. Woefully vulnerable, it was armed with only one 7.9 mm machine gun located in a hatch behind the cockpit.[13] Although it had become obsolete by 1939, it remained until the end of the war the workhorse of the *Luftwaffe's* transport fleet.

Flying the Ju-52 was certainly not like flying a modern aircraft. In addition to its low speed, it was an extremely noisy aircraft. Since each of its three engines were often tuned to different tolerances, the aircraft gave off a distinctive staccato sound, as if each engine was trying to compete against the other two. It was also uninsulated, which required flight crews to wear bulky outer garments during the winter. Nevertheless, it carried the bulk of supplies into the pocket and evacuated nearly all of the wounded. Although it was outfitted with litters for twelve wounded passengers, it was commonly crammed with as many wounded who could possibly be loaded aboard. Care of the wounded for the short flight to Uman or Proskurov was left to the crew chief, who rarely had any medical training whatsoever. In addition to looking after the wounded, the crew chief also had to monitor the engines and man the machine-gun.

The flight from Uman into the pocket was normally conducted in groups of aircraft, ranging from several to two dozen, depending on the availability of fighter escorts. Once airborne, the formation would then either try to fly along the contours of the earth to evade Soviet anti-aircraft fire, or would fly at a much higher altitude to enable escorting fighter aircraft room to maneuver against the agile Yak-9s and LaGGs of the Soviet Air Force. The nap-of-the-earth approach was hair-raising, to say the least. Often pilots flew so low they could see the faces of individual Soviet infantrymen or anti-aircraft gunners, who often took aim at the slow, lumbering transports. Bad weather, such as fog, rain, snowstorms, or low clouds, made

the trip even more nerve-racking. Occasionally, pilots would lose their bearing and crash into hillsides.

Since the Ju-52s had primitive aerial navigation systems, the approach to the airfields in the pocket was usually done by dead reckoning - that is, by using a compass and map, orienting on landmarks along the route of approach. If a formation were lucky, the pilot flying the lead aircraft would know his way around and would be able to find the airfield. Often times, formations would become lost and would fly in circles over the pocket until one of the aircraft would be able to determine their location, then the gaggle would swoop down to the airfield and begin their landing approach. Since the Korsun airfield had only rudimentary air traffic control systems in place, and since aircraft had no tower to talk to during landing and taxiing, aircraft simply landed wherever they saw a clear space. Conditions at these airfields (such as Korsun-West and Yablonovka) were chaotic. Aircraft would often unload their cargo of fuel and ammunition on the spot, forcing other aircraft conducting their approach to avoid these obstacles.[14]

Once loaded with wounded, the aircraft would then take off the best way they could, again avoiding the many obstacles on the airstrip. After each aircraft had taken off, they would circle the airfield until the entire formation was airborne. With luck, there would be another pair of escorting fighters for the return trip; if not, the formation would either wait until darkness or try to make it out by flying at low altitude. The wounded, who had been hurriedly loaded aboard, were often placed in seats or stretchers without seat belts or restraining devices; many would simply be placed on the floor of the aircraft with nothing at all to hold them in place. Exhausted and in pain, the wounded had to endure the 30-minute to hour-long flight back to Uman, while the pilots weaved and dove repeatedly to avoid Soviet anti-aircraft fire, Soviet fighters, or snow-covered hills. The wounded were often thrown against one another during these violent evasive maneuvers. Others would be wounded again as machine-gun fire or exploding shells pierced the thin skin of the transports. Other aircraft were shot out of the sky, carrying its load of wounded to their deaths.

Upon landing safely in Uman or Proskurov, things would finally begin to improve for the wounded. There they would be met by ambulances or horse-drawn *panje* wagons, loaded aboard, and then moved to an evacuation hospital where they would receive further care. Even then, their ordeal would not be over. Many of the more seriously wounded would be evacuated further into Poland or Germany aboard crudely converted rail cars, which often lacked heating and sanitation. At least they knew they were finally out of the Pocket and would probably survive. As for the pilots of the transports, after a quick cup of coffee and perhaps of bowl of soup, they would soon be airborne again, carrying more supplies in to the encircled forces and ferrying more wounded out. They would do this five to ten times a day.

Arranging for the evacuation of the wounded fully occupied the attention of the corps surgeons of both *XI.* and *XXXXII.A.K.* Although they did not have the additional headache of supervising the airlift, they did have to arrange the transport of the wounded from various locations in the Pocket to the air-

A wounded soldier being offloaded at a mud-covered forward airfield, safe for the time being.
(Bundesarchiv 498/32/20)

field. This was not as easy as it sounds - initially, the pocket was as large as the state of Connecticut and the roads became progressively more impassable as the thaw began to set in. The fighting units were widely scattered throughout the pocket. Some units had lost their medical service units during the initial Soviet advance, such as *389.Inf.Div.*, whose medical company had escaped being encircled by fleeing south through Shpola on 25 January. *Wiking* had even disbanded portions of its medical services, and had incorporated its medical personnel into combat units.[15]

Since evacuation flights were often suspended until weather improved, shelter had to be arranged for thousands of wounded, including the digging of slit trenches at the airfield to offer protection against low-flying Soviet ground attack aircraft. Most of the wounded were sheltered in Korsun itself; later, improvised shelter was constructed at the airfield in order to speed up the loading of wounded, since the aircraft could not wait on the ground, completely exposed to Soviet aircraft, while the wounded were moved several miles from the town to the airfield.

The transport of wounded from the eastern front of the pocket, where *XI.A.K.* had established its field hospital at Gorodishche, was greatly handicapped when someone gave the order on 25 or 26 January to destroy the rail line which ran from there to the outskirts of Korsun. Had this order not have been given, thousands of wounded could have been quickly evacuated by rail to Korsun. Instead, these men were forced to ride thirty kilometers in horse-drawn carts along mud-clogged roads, enduring endless traffic jams that transformed a one-hour trip into a daylong affair. Many died along the trip from Gorodishche to Korsun from exposure to the cold, damp weather and from their wounds; these men may have lived had they been able to be evacuated by rail. In the medical officer's report, written by *Oberstarzt* Dr. M. Behnsen on 3 March 1944, this action received a great deal of criticism, since the rail line's destruction had not been coordinated with either corps headquarters.[16] In fact, no one can determine to this day who ordered the demolition. Suffice to say, it made a bad situation worse, for it not only slowed the evacuation of wounded, it also slowed the movement of supplies from the airfield to the fighting units.

The care of the wounded in the pocket was entrusted to Dr. Behnsen, the acting corps surgeon of *XXXXII.A.K.*, who in turn gave the company commander of *1.Kp.,San.Abt.112* from *K.Abt.B*, the responsibility for control of the actual loading and care of the wounded at the Korsun airfield. This officer, *Stabsartzt* (Staff Doctor) von Ohlen, had an enormous task. Not only did he have to provide the immediate care for the wounded awaiting evacuation at the airfield, he had to feed and shelter them as well. Even more importantly, he had to bring some form of order to a situation that had grown completely out of control due to the influx of a horde of unauthorized personnel seeking a flight out.[17]

Control of the airfield was initially placed in the hands of an NCO, who was easily overpowered by throngs of desperate men who surged aboard aircraft even before they had a opportunity to unload. In scenes reminiscent of the last desperate days at Stalingrad's Pitomnik airfield, officers and administrative offi-

Ju-52 dropping a supply cannister. When the airfields in the pocket were forced to close down due to weather or mud, these were the only practical means to get ammunition, fuel, and medical supplies to the encircled troops.
(Jarolin-Bundesarchiv 73/103/66)

cials of the Nazi Party forced their way aboard aircraft at gunpoint. Just as bad were gangs of soldiers bearing legitimate leave passes, who had been denied ground evacuation due to the encircling Soviets. These men, sensing that the Ju-52s were their last ticket out, would sometimes tread upon the wounded, lying in the open air on stretchers. Some wounded soldiers were even taken off of aircraft by these desperate men in order to free seats for those who felt that they had a "right" to fly out first. Even the lightly wounded joined in this unspeakable activity. Clearly, this unauthorized appropriation of aircraft had to stop immediately.

To reassert control at the airfield and to nip this mass psychosis in the bud (a phenomenon known as "*Kesselpsychose*") the corps surgeon directed Dr. von Ohlen to take drastic measures. Von Ohlen decided to use brute force if necessary and quickly rounded up additional medical personnel from Korsun. These men were given the responsibility of supervising the unloading of each individual aircraft and to oversee, with drawn weapons, the orderly loading of wounded. Soldiers with leave passes or the lightly wounded were rounded up and either sent back to their units or pressed into service with ad-hoc *Kampfgruppen* and sent elsewhere in the pocket to serve as reinforcements. Using these brutal yet effective measures, von Ohlen had restored a semblance of order to the airfield by 29 January, the same day when 50 transports flew in with supplies.[18] Working hand-in-hand with *Luftwaffe* personnel, Dr. von Ohlen and his men made the airlift run as smoothly as it could under the circumstances. He even was able to arrange the movement of a four-barreled flak gun (*Flakvierling*) from *Wiking* in order to improve the defense of the airfield against Soviet aircraft.

From all points of the compass, the wounded began to flood into Korsun. Finding space for them while they were awaiting evacuation became a problem, forcing the corps surgeon to commandeer virtually every intact house in the city for sheltering the wounded. Moving and feeding them became increasingly difficult, especially as the weather began to worsen and supplies began to become scarce. In the castle at Korsun, 200 beds for wounded were eventually set up. Due to its status as an easily observed landmark, the castle began to suffer frequent air attacks, despite the red cross painted prominently on its roof. However, its 8-foot thick walls shielded the wounded inside from everything but a direct hit. Even so, dozens of wounded were killed and hundreds more received additional wounds due to the unceasing Soviet air attacks, which began to become a regular event after 1 February.[19] Nothing much could be done about it, since the available German fighters were employed in shielding the transports. Since they had no choice, the doctors and medics of *San.Abt.1./112, 2./188*, and *1./582* grimly went about their business of caring for and sheltering the wounded.

As mentioned previously, the *Luftwaffe* was worried about more than just the evacuation of wounded and resupply of the encircled troops. Increasingly, as the roads became impassable, the aircrews of *VIII.Flieger-Korps* had to provide supplies to the forces attempting to relieve the troops in the pocket. *III.Pz.Korps*, which was to be assigned the mission of attacking to relieve the pocket from the west, soon became bogged down, making resupply by road of its four Panzer divisions and two infantry divisions nearly impossible, was forced to rely on air drops for the essentials it needed to continue its advance. This applied equally to the Panzer divisions of von Vormann's *XXXXVII.Pz.Korps* attacking from the east. Therefore, at a time when all available transports were needed to assist the encircled troops, the air effort had to be further divided into two separate operations - that of supplying both the encircled forces and the relieving forces both of which had separate requirements and were located in three different areas - the encircled forces in and around Korsun, *III.Pz.Korps* near Risino, and *XXXXVII.Pz.Korps* near Zvenigorodka. These Panzer units needed large quantities of gasoline for their tanks and 7.5 cm and 8.8 cm ammunition for their guns, while the encircled forces needed ammunition resupply primarily for the artillery, small arms, and anti-tank guns.

Maj. Knapp's failure to adequately foresee the amount of resupply containers and parachutes led the aircrews to try a variety of makeshift procedures in order to get the needed supplies to the relieving *Panzer* columns. In order to do this, the aircraft would line up with the three and one-half to five mile wide strip alongside the tanks' route of advance and drop the containers of fuel, food, and ammunition from an altitude of only twelve feet off the ground. At such low speeds and altitude, most of the con-

tainers landed safely. The drop zone at night was lighted by an improvised flare path, made up of lanterns and vehicle headlights which were blinked on and off as soon as the Ju-52s or He-111s were heard approaching. Even though a number of these containers burst, enough was retrieved from them to enable the tanks to keep up their advance.[20]

When resupply canisters and parachutes became available, these were used, with mixed success, both in and outside the pocket, which by 13 February was totally reliant upon airdrops for all of its resupply. These were employed with mixed success. Unless they were dropped at a low altitude (from 300 to 400 feet), they risked being carried off course by the wind. Many of these containers landed either far away from the troops who needed them or landed in the laps of the encircling Soviets, who probably appreciated the contents, whether they were medical supplies or food. Additionally, during the ten minutes it took for the transports to carry out their container drop, they were extremely vulnerable to Soviet antiaircraft fire. If conditions were right, some of the more daring and experienced pilots would attempt to land their aircraft on open fields alongside the advancing tanks of Breith's and von Vormann's corps and discharge their cargo right then and there. By landing so close to the tip of the armored spearhead, these pilots risked being hit by Soviet artillery or tank fire, making such landings a high stakes gamble indeed. Despite these difficulties, the resupply operation continued.

The resupply operation for the encircled troops continued until 16 February, the day the breakout from the pocket began. The operation for the relief force continued until 20 February, when they had returned to their initial starting positions, their mission completed. Judged by one authority on *Luftwaffe* airlifts as being one of the few that was truly successful, General Stemmermann's fighting units were able to maintain some semblance of their combat power and mobility for seventeen days thanks to the aerial resupply effort of the *Luftwaffe*.[21] The relieving forces of Breith and von Vormann had been supplied as well. More importantly, a great many of the wounded had been flown out - in all, 4,161 of them had been evacuated by air either to Uman in the *1.Pz.Armee* sector or to Proskurov in the *8.Armee* sector.[22] Besides the wounded who were flown out, an estimated 2,026 tons of supplies were flown or dropped into the pocket, including 867.7 tons of ammunition and 82,948 gallons of fuel airlifted from Uman alone.[23] In addition, over 400 tons of fuel and ammunition were airlifted to the spearheads of *III.* and *XXXXVII.Pz.Korps*. On an average day, the encircled troops received 70 tons of supplies. Although this amount was never enough, it did enable Stemmermann's men to keep fighting and moving. If the relief operation were to fail, it would not be because the *Luftwaffe* did not try hard enough, a charge leveled at it during the Stalingrad airlift debacle.

Seidemann's crews logged more than 1,536 aircraft sorties, of which 832 were flown by the venerable Ju-52s. Although many transport pilots complained about the lack of fighter escorts, Me-109s and FW-190s flew more than 226 individual missions. This success did not come without a price tag. In all, the *Luftwaffe* lost fifty aircraft to a variety of causes, primarily through Soviet fighter aircraft, including 32 Ju-52s. An additional 150 aircraft were damaged. Besides the hundred or so wounded who died when their air ambulances were shot down, 22 Luftwaffe air crew members were killed and 56 were listed as missing in action.[24] These losses contrast starkly with the account offered by the Soviets, who claim to have downed more than 329 German aircraft.[25] This number would have been more aircraft than the *VIII.Flieger-Korps* had operational during this entire period and should be regarded as an example of the degree of exaggeration to which the Soviets were prone. This would not be the last wildly inflated claim they would make. Regardless of the losses each side claims, the airlift succeeded, keeping the encircled German forces with sufficient supplies and providing a highly visible sign that they had not been abandoned, a critical morale boost for the Germans at this stage of the war in the East.

End Notes

[1] Buchner, p. 34.

[2] DA Pam 20-234, p. 20.

[3] Fritz Morzik, USAF Historical Studies No. 167, *German Air Force Airlift Operations*, (Maxwell Air Force Base, Alabama: Research Studies Institute, Air University, 1961), pp 220-221.

[4] Ibid, p. 221.

[5] DA Pam 20-234, p. 20.

[6] *XXXXII.A.K.* KTB entry 1355 hours, 31 January 1944.

[7] *XXXXII.A.K.* KTB entry 1245 hours, 1 February 1944.

[8] Morzik, p. 222.

[9] Ibid.

[10] *8.Armee* KTB entry, 1930 hours, 3 February 1944.

[11] Morzik, p. 222.

[12] *1.Pz.Armee* KTB Morgenmeldung, 11 February 1944.

[13] Alfred Price, *Luftwaffe: Birth, Life and Death of an Air Force.* (New York: Ballantine Books, Inc., 1969), p. 88.

[14] Dr. Behnsen, Martin, *Der Freiwillige*, *"Das Schicksal der Verwundeten im Kessel von Tscherkassy,"* (Osnabrück, Germany: Munin-Verlag, November, 1982.), p. 16.

[15] Ibid, p. 7.

[16] Ibid, p. 6.

[17] Ibid, p. 9.

[18] Ibid, p. 16.

[19] Ibid, p, 18.

[20] Morzik, p. 224.

[21] Ibid. p. 225.

[22] *Abschlussmeldung Gruppe Mattenklott, An der Gruppe Mattenklott, Pz.AOK 1*, 2 March 1944.

[23] Morzik, p. 225 and Report, dated 28 February 1944, from *Oberquartiermeister, Pz.AOK 1, An der Gruppe Mattenklott.*

[24] Buchner, pp. 34-35.

[25] Konev quoted in Sokolov, p. 124.

Chapter Ten

VON MANSTEIN'S PLAN TO ENCIRCLE THE SOVIET

**"But I had much more importants things to worry about
than my personal relations with the Führer."**
— *Eric Von Manstein in "Lost Victories"* [1]

While the battles to complete a unified defense line within the pocket raged at Steblev, Kvitki, and Olshana and while the *Luftwaffe* struggled to resupply the encircled troops and evacuate the wounded, von Manstein and his staff worked to come up with a plan to comply with Hitler's wishes. Hitler, as previously noted, had wanted nothing less than to restore the front line as it had existed on 24 January and to use it as an advanced position to launch his long-desired counterattack aimed at retaking Kiev. Upon his return to his staff in Proskurov on the morning of 28 January from the conference at Hitler's headquarters, von Manstein immediately devoted his attention to reestablishing contact with the two encircled corps.

Once rescued, he envisioned that these corps could then be incorporated into a new, shorter defensive line, freeing additional forces for subsequent operations. Von Manstein never indicated then or in his memoirs later that he ever seriously considered a counterattack aimed at retaking Kiev - it was simply too fantastic to even bother considering. Better than anyone at *OKH*, the Field Marshal knew what his forces were capable of. Von Manstein passed his strong recommendation to Hitler via teletype that operations should strictly be limited to the rescue of the two encircled corps. Hitler, of course, turned the proposal down immediately. He instead ordered his Field Marshal to launch an operation to restore the front on the Dnieper and retake Kiev.

The fact that the units Hitler expected to carry out these ambitious goals were seriously understrength does not seem to have been taken into his calculations. To the *Grösster Feldherr aller Zeiten* (shortened to *Gröfaz*, for "greatest military genius of all time"), flags on a map indicated actual strengths and capabilities, when in fact many of the units represented no longer existed except as remnants. No one on the staffs of the *OKH*, in charge of operations on the Eastern Front, or *OKW*, the German armed forces' high command, and certainly not Keitel or Jodl, had the courage to point out these facts to him, mute testimony to the degree which the General Staff had lost influence over its Supreme Commander. This formerly great institution had now been relegated to the status of merely serving as a conduit for orders from Hitler to the three army groups fighting in the East.

While he believed that Hitler's plan to retake Kiev was, at best, unrealistic, von Manstein saw that this situation did present an opportunity to deal a severe blow to both the First and Second Ukrainian *Fronts*. After all, both Vatutin and Konev had amassed the better part of two tank armies in a relatively small area. If he could smash both of these armies, it would make a continued defense of the Ukraine much easier. His plan would not, how-

ever, be simple. Outwardly, at least, von Manstein would have to appear to be conforming to Hitler's wishes. The first part of Hitler's plan - recapturing Kiev - was thus rejected outright, though to do this would require that Army Group South's commander deceive his *Führer*.

The second part of Hitler's statement of intent - reestablishing the front on the Dnieper - could be used to provide operational cover for the more realistic plan to rescue the two encircled corps. While it would appear to *OKH* Headquarters in East Prussia that Army Group South was trying to restore the Dnieper line by including the appropriate wording in the operations order forwarded for Hitler's approval, the army group would actually go for the much more realistic goal. Thus, von Manstein' plan would have to incorporate elements of two different types of operations. His army group would simultaneously conduct a relief attempt of an encircled force and launch a major counteroffensive with a limited objective.[2] In order to do this, von Manstein quickly ordered *1.Pz.* and *8.Armee* to prepare armored spearheads which would attack simultaneously from the west and east to surround and destroy the forces surrounding the pocket. In effect, von Manstein would encircle the same Soviet forces that had encircled his own men.[3]

But before this could occur, however, he had to have a good idea of what course of action Zhukov, Konev, and Vatutin would follow. For the rescue of the encircled forces was not the only problem the army group commander had to face. Even more ominous was the fact that a hole had been torn in his front line over one hundred kilometers wide between Novo-Mirgorod in the east and the town of Risino in the west. Contact between *1.Pz.Armee* and *8.Armee* had been completely severed.[4] There was absolutely nothing between Zvenigorodka and the Black Sea, a mere 200 kilometers away, to block the Red Army (except postal units, repair depots, and the like), had Zhukov urged Vatutin and Konev to keep heading south. After all, the bulk of 5th Guards Tank and 6th Tank Armies were massed in the vicinity of Zvenigorodka and Shpola and could have easily done so had Zhukov ordered it, which he had the authority to do so, through *STAVKA*. Nor did von Manstein have reserves to throw in the path of the Red Army, except the decimated *2. Fallschirmjäger* (Parachute) Division then in the process of being pulled out of the line preparatory to being shipped to France for reconstitution. From 28 to 31 January, things looked black indeed for the desperate troops of Army Group South.

An indication of Soviet intentions began to emerge when German ground reconnaissance patrols observed engineers laying minefields in the outer ring of encirclement. Signals intelligence

The *"Greatest Military Genius of All Time" and his most capable practitioner of operational warfare,* **Field Marshal Erich von Manstein** *shown here greeting Hitler near Vinnitsa, Ukraine late summer 1943.* *(Bundesarchiv 705/251/5)*

units also intercepted and translated radio messages from various Soviet units discussing requirements to emplace mines, antitank ditches, and other defensive barriers. German aircraft observed that Rotmistrov's and Kravchenko's tanks were being dug in and wire entanglements and antitank defenses were hastily being erected in an arc stretching from Lysyanka in the west, to Zvenigorodka in the south, and to Shpola in the east.[5] These were indicators that Vatutin and Konev were not driving further south after all, but instead were ordering their troops to prepare deliberate defenses. The Soviet after-action report even details these preparations and describes them as preventive measures taken to prevent enemy penetrations from the south to the north, aimed at relieved their encircled comrades.[6]

From the evidence, there seems to be nothing to suggest that Zhukov and his *Front* commanders had any intention of continuing their advance. In fact, the Soviets were busily preparing for the relief attack they knew would come. In his memoirs, Zhukov stated that "Every one of us involved in this operation to encircle the [enemy forces]…fully realized that the Nazi High Command was going to strike a blow from the outside to save the encircled forces."[7] Rotmistrov's and Kravchenko's tanks were staying put. Von Manstein and his commanders could not believe their good fortune.

One can only speculate as to why Zhukov, and by extension, *STAVKA*, ignored this opportunity. Perhaps the Soviet Supreme Command was not willing to reinforce what it saw as a relatively minor operation in order to begin to amass strategic reserves for subsequent larger operations planned for the coming summer campaigning season. Zhukov certainly did not mention this possibility in his memoirs. Another reason could be that

Soviet generals were leery of driving too deeply into the German operational depths and being cut off and wiped out in the manner that Popov's armored group had been at Kharkov the previous winter. Von Vormann stated in his account of the battle that Stalin's generals still "held a healthy respect, even a fear of, German offensive capabilities, which in my opinion no longer existed."[8]

Another reason for Zhukov's reluctance to urge Vatutin and Konev onwards was the Soviet perception that they only had enough strength on hand to liquidate the large German grouping in the pocket. Since they had estimated the size of the German force they had trapped as consisting of over ten divisions with at least 100,000 men (in fact, they thought they had encircled the bulk of General Wöhler's *8.Armee*), the Soviet commanders may have felt that this would be a far better prize than wagering whether their forces could successfully conduct a deep attack. Of the two possible courses of action, destroying the encircled Germans seemed to offer the lowest risk and the highest possible payoff. Both Zhukov's and Konev's memoirs also seem to reinforce this perception.[9] Of course, inflicting the greatest German defeat since Stalingrad would be an enormous propaganda coup, not to mention the awards and promotions that would be bestowed by a grateful Stalin. At any rate, the Soviet armies, corps, and divisions forming the outer ring of the encirclement began to dig in with a vengeance.

Zhukov and the two *Front* commanders were also facing problems that they had not anticipated. The stubborn German defense within the pocket itself was certainly the most distressing problem, but not the only one. The slowness of the Soviet artillery to keep pace with the tanks and infantry was another.

The vast distance to be covered by the attacking troops also was a significant factor. As Vatutin's and Konev's infantry armies began to slowly spread out, their armored forces awaited their arrival anxiously, since Rotmistrov's and Kravchenko's armies were both starved for foot soldiers to protect them against German infantry. As they waited, they continued to improve their own defensive positions facing to the south in order to forestall the expected relief attack.

To offset the shortage of infantry in Rotmistrov's force, Konev directed on 31 January that Galanin's 53rd Army detach three rifle divisions (6th Guards, 84th Rifle, and 94th Guards) and combine them to form 49th Rifle Corps. This new corps, in turn, was then subordinated to 5th Guards Tank Army's commander. Konev gave Rotmistrov the mission of preventing a German relief attempt from the south from linking up with the pocket in the north by holding a line which ran from Zvenigorodka in the west to Lipyanka in the east, where his army would tie in with that of Galanin's.[10] Lazarev's 20th Guards Tank Corps held the front south of Zvenigorodka. To his east lay 49th Rifle Corps and Kirichenko's 29th Guards Tank Corps. Polozkov's 18th Guards Tank Corps was Rotmistrov's reserve. To augment the defensive line, damaged or non-operable tanks were entrenched to serve as armored pillboxes. To further assist in developing his defensive positions, Konev subordinated to Rotmistrov 5th Engineer Brigade, as well as additional antitank and antiaircraft regiments.[11]

Vatutin essentially tried to do the same thing, but had far fewer forces to do it with. To augment Kravchenko's 6th Tank Army, Vatutin had already given him 47th Rifle Corps from Zhmachenko's 40th Army. Kravchenko was also reinforced by the encircled Soviet units that he had successfully relieved the previous week, but these were but shattered remnants, though they did provide some needed infantry support. As of 31 January, Kravchenko's westernmost unit, General Volkov's 5th Mechanized Corps occupied the Risino sector. To its left, 47th Rifle Corps occupied the Vinograd sector. To its east lay General Alekseyev's 5th Guards Tank Corps, which tied in with Rotmistrov's forces west of Zvenigorodka. Vatutin's sole reserve was 233rd Tank Brigade, which lay in the Pavlovka area, northwest of Zvenigorodka.[12]

Kravchenko's mission was to prevent a German relief attempt from the southwest towards Lysyanka, with particular emphasis in the Shubbeny Stav - Ryzhanovka sector, the most likely German avenue of approach. Zhmachenko's 40th Army was given the mission of protecting Kravchenko's right flank. In comparison to Konev's forces, Vatutin's had suffered fewer losses and had gained the most ground in the shortest amount of time. Vatutin's forces had thus far not had to face German armor, but their defensive sector lay upon relatively flat, open ground, which would be hard to defend once the inevitable German relief operation began. Additionally, Vatutin did not have the luxury of denuding other sectors of his front, as Konev was doing, since some of Vatutin's armies were still engaged in battle far to the west with XXXXVI.Pz.Korps. Regardless of the degree of preparation, the Soviets had taken important steps towards solidifying their grip on the Germans in the pocket.

While this improved the defense of the outer ring of encirclement enormously, the redirection of the armor to the outside resulted in an acutely felt shortage on the internal ring of encirclement, now manned almost exclusively by infantry, which normally relied on independent tank brigades to conduct supporting attacks or to lead infantry assaults. Because of extremely heavy losses in tanks (Konev's Front alone lost as many as 205 of them between 24 and 29 January), these brigades were used to augment the strength of the two tank armies.[13] Konev's 4th Guards and 52nd Armies and Vatutin's 27th Army would have to reduce the pocket by themselves. The only mobile force available to help reduce the pocket was Selivanov's 5th Guards Cavalry Corps, though part of it was tied up in the battle for Olshana. Despite the fact that they were not as strong as they felt they needed to be to carry out this mission, the Soviet inner encirclement ring still outnumbered the Germans in the pocket by nearly a two-to-one ratio. This job would be much harder after 4 February, once it became apparent that the Germans had won the race to build up a solid front line. There would be no easy splintering of the pocket, as required by Soviet encirclement doctrine. They would now have to fight for every square foot of ground.

This employment of tanks to form the outer ring of encirclement also went against established Red Army tactical doctrine, since tank corps were supposed to be used on the internal ring of encirclement, as they had been in the Battle of Stalingrad. At the time, Zhukov's, Konev's, and Vatutin's mutually agreed-upon decision seemed to have caused some controversy within the Red Army, as borne out by contemporary Soviet sources.[14] Because they had fewer tanks than they were accustomed to having for this type of operation, Zhukov encouraged the Front commanders to use what they had on the outside, where they saw German armor coming to the relief of the troops in the pocket as the greatest threat.

It was to prove a sound decision. Zhukov's coordination problems were minor compared to what his German counterpart, von Manstein, faced. However, his opponent was drafting a plan that would soon put Zhukov's decision to the test by throwing every available armored division in Army Group South at the Soviet encircling forces. Von Manstein, according to one of his staff officers, Hptm. Alexander Stahlberg, was "Now determined that on no account would he allow a repetition of Stalingrad. His last conference with Hitler and his open clashes with him had obviously…given him more detachment and resolution."[15]

Von Manstein's fear that Zhukov was intent on encircling both 1.Pz. and 8.Armee could be stilled for the time being. This simplified the Army Group's situation somewhat. Instead of having to face a disaster which involved all of Army Group South, von Manstein and his commanders were faced simply with the problem of how to restore the tactical situation and rescue the corps and divisions trapped in the Kessel (cauldron) von Tscherkassy, as it was now being called by German troops both outside and inside the pocket. This would prove to be a much greater challenge than it seemed at the time, for as the great Prussian military philosopher Clausewitz once wrote, "War, in the main, is simple. But in war, the simple things are difficult."

Generalmajor Hans-Ulrich Back,
Commander, 16.Pz.Div.
(from Bender and Odegard, Uniforms,
Organization, and History of the
Panzertruppe)

General der Panzertruppe
Hermann Breith, *Commander,*
III.Pz.Korps, First Panzer Army.
(Bundesarchiv)

Generalleutnant
Karl-Friedrich von der
Meden, *Commander,*
17Pz.Div.
(Photo courtesy of
Andreas Schwarz and
88.Inf.Div. Veterans
Association)

To carry out his plan, in a directive issued 28 January von Manstein instructed *1.Pz.* and *8.Armee* to begin planning the relief operation. Hube would order Breith's *III.Pz.Korps* to disengage from the Vinnitsa area, where it was still carrying out operations, and hand its sector over to *XXXXVI.Pz.Korps,* which would have to further extend its own front to the west.[16] *III.Pz.Korps*, with its two panzer divisions — *16.* and *17.* along with *Schwere Panzer Regiment* (heavy panzer regiment) *Bäke* was commanded by *Gen.d.Pztr.* Hermann Breith. Its mission would be to shift to the far right flank of *1.Pz.Armee* and attack in a northeasterly direction towards the town of Medvin. Two other panzer divisions would follow when they were freed. The overall relief operation was to be codenamed *Unternehmen Heimkehr* (Operation Homecoming) by the *OKH* staff.[17]

III.Pz.Korps was one of the *Wehrmacht*'s most veteran organizations and had taken part in every campaign, except North Africa, since the invasion of Poland in 1939. It had particularly distinguished itself during the Battle of Kursk, where it had successfully protected the left flank of *II.SS-Pz.Korps*, knocking out hundreds of Soviet tanks. Breith, its commander, was one of the German armored force's most experienced corps commanders and had earned the respect of both friend and foe alike. Born in Pirmasens in 1892, he had served in World War One in *121.Inf.Div.* Since 1939, he had commanded, in succession, *5.Pz.Bde.*, *3.Pz.Div.*, and, since 1 March 1943, *III.Pz.Korps*. He had been awarded

the Knight's Cross with Oakleaves on 31 January 1942 for his leadership of *3.Pz.Div.* during the Soviet winter counteroffensive near Tula.[18]

After arriving in its tactical assembly area near the city of Uman, Breith's corps would use the salient still being held by *VII.A.K's 34.* and *198.Inf.Div.* as a springboard to launch its attack to the northeast against 47th Rifle Corps of Kravcheno's tank army. Once it had cut through the Soviet defenses, it would continue until it linked up with Lieb's corps in the vicinity of Medvin, a mere 30 kilometers or so away. After reestablishing contact with the encircled forces, Breith would then redirect his corps to the southeast, and attack into the rear of Kravchenko's tank army, arrayed between Medvin and Zvenigorodka, and wipe it out.

Breith's two panzer divisions, *16.Pz.Div.* under *Gen.Maj.* Hans-Ulrich Back and *17.Pz.Div.* under *Gen.Maj.* Karl-Friedrich von der Meden, were both in relatively good condition at the time, despite being involved in recent heavy fighting. On 28 January, Back's division had 48 tanks operational, including seven attached *Tigers*, as well as seven additional assault guns. His two *Panzergrenadier* regiments were also at 50 percent strength or better, as well as its other divisional units. Von der Meden's division was worse off, with only 29 operational tanks. His *Panzergrenadier* regiments were also in somewhat worse shape than Back's, though von der Meden's divisional artillery was relatively intact, as opposed to his partner's, which had less than half of its authorized howitzers.[19] Von Manstein also

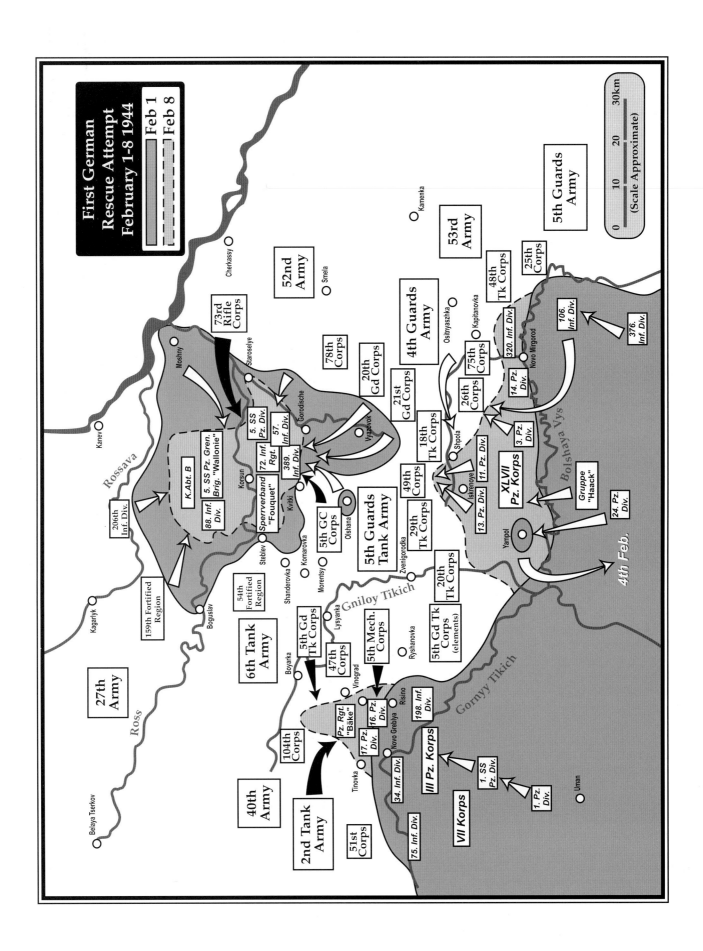

First German
Rescue Attempt
February 1-8 1944

Feb 1
Feb 8

planned on forwarding *1.Pz.Div.* and *1.SS-Pz.Div. Leibstandarte Adolf Hitler* (Hitler's *Waffen-SS* bodyguard division, known simply as the *LSSAH* or the *Leibstandarte*) as soon as they had completed an operation they were involved with against some of Vatutin's units. Rounding out the corps was the heavy panzer regiment, commanded by *Oberstlt.* Dr. Franz Bäke, which provided Breith his offensive punch.

This unusual organization had been formed in mid-January 1944 at the orders of von Manstein to carry out special offensive tasks for the Army Group. It was an extremely powerful *ad hoc* organization for this phase of the war. Assembled from a variety of army-level independent units and battalions "borrowed" from other panzer divisions, it was composed of *Schw.Pz.Abt.503* with *34 Pz.VI Tigers* and *I./Pz.Rgt.23* with *46* Panthers, borrowed from *23.Pz.Div.* It had as well a SP artillery battalion, a combat engineer battalion, and a *Gebirgsjäger* (mountain infantry) battalion.[20] In addition, the regimental armored car platoon from *Pz.Rgt.23* was attached to provide reconnaissance capability.

Schw.Pz.Rgt.Bäke's commander, Dr. Franz Bäke, had been a dentist prior to the war. Born in 1898 in the town of Schwarzenfels, he served in World War One as an enlisted man in *Inf.Rgt.53*, where he earned the Iron Cross, Second Class and was discharged as a sergeant in 1919. Called up again in 1937, he was promoted to the rank of *Leutnant der Reserve* and posted to *Pz.Rgt.11*, where he initially served as the battalion adjutant. When the war began, he was a tank platoon leader and rapidly climbed the ladder of promotion from that point forward. His leadership in battle was recognized when he was awarded the Knight's Cross on 11 January 1943 while serving as a battalion commander in *Pz.Rgt.11* of *6.Pz.Div.* while on the Eastern Front.

After being promoted to *Major* and being named regimental commander, he was awarded the Oak Leaves to his Knight's Cross on 1 August 1943 for leading his regiment during the Battle of Kursk. Bäke had become known for his dynamism and take-charge approach to combat leadership. His bravery was attested to by the fact that he wore three *Panzervernichtungs* (tank destruction) ribbons on his upper right sleeve, proof that he had single-handedly destroyed three Soviet tanks with infantry weapons at close range. A natural leader of armored troops, Bäke skillfully handled his tanks in battle with an intuitive sense possessed by few others.

His skill was attested to by his regiment's performance in battle against five Soviet tank corps which had broken through the boundary between the *4.* and *1.Pz.Armee* near Vinnitsa during the third week of January 1944. In the tank battle at Oratov that followed, Bäke's regiment alone claimed to have knocked 267 Soviet tanks at a fraction of the cost to themselves.[21] In recognition of this spectacular performance, the regiment received special mention 31 January 1944 in the *Wehrmachtsbericht*, the daily communiqué the German Armed Forces initiated in order to recognize outstanding achievements in battle of units of the *Heer, Luftwaffe, Kriegsmarine,* and *Waffen-SS.* Von Manstein and Hube both would harbor great expectations for this unit.

Generalmajor Freiherr von Edelsheim, *24th Panzer Division. (Bundesarchiv 84/78/3)*

The other striking wing of von Manstein's planned attack was to be composed of von Vormann's *XXXXVII.Pz.Korps.* It was directed to assemble *3., 11.,* and *14.Pz.Div.*, to be later joined by *13.Pz.Div.*, and strike due north and link up with Stemmermann's corps in the vicinity of Shpola. Von Vormann was also directed to hold his current positions and prevent any further enemy breakthroughs in the Shpola area. Their current positions would be turned over to several infantry divisions being switched from their own sectors farther to the south.

To do this, von Vormann would have to extend his corps' sector to the west - where there currently was no front line at all - which would entail some degree of difficulty because his divisions would probably have to fight to seize their own front line before they could even begin their attack. To help extend the line, both *320.* and *376.Inf.Div.* would side-step to the west in order to free up the panzer divisions. The condition of *XXXXVII.Pz.Korps* was itself an issue - after being in combat constantly since early January 1944, its three panzer divisions had been given very little time to rest or reform their units.

As noted in previous chapters, the divisions of Vormann's corps had inflicted great damage upon Konev's forces, but they were also much the worse for wear. With the exception of the relatively refreshed *13.Pz.Div.* being transferred from *LII.A.K.*, the other three were practically burnt out. Unrein's *14.Pz.Div.* was

Generalmajor Hans Mikosch, *Commander, 13.Panzer Division. (from Bender and Odegard, Uniforms, Organization, and history of the Panzertruppe)*

the north. This would later bring about serious repercussions. Shortly thereafter on 1 February, Hitler transferred Hollidt's army to Field Marshal von Kleist's Army Group A to the south, partly to prevent von Manstein from transferring additional forces from it without his permission.[22]

This division, commanded by *Gen.Lt.* Freiherr von Edelsheim, was currently located in an assembly area at Apostolovo when it received the order from *6.Armee* on the evening of 28 January to move to join *XXXXVII.Pz.Korps* for the upcoming attack. To get to its assembly area near Yampol would require a road march of over 310 kilometers. Since rail shipment was not available at the time, everything, including the armor, would have to use the roads.[23] Von Edelsheim's men thought that they were up to the challenge and wanted to do whatever they could to free their 60,000 comrades in the pocket. At the time, it did not seem to be an impossible task to carry out - as the roads at the time were still in relatively good condition. Although the road march would be a long one, even by *Ostfront* standards, the men of *24.Pz.Div.* were confident that they could carry out their assignment.

As the divisions that were tasked to take part in the upcoming relief operation began to prepare for their new mission, the staffs of Army Group South, *1.Pz.* and *8.Armee* continued to develop their respective plans. The army group's plan itself was completed and issued to the two armies taking part 29 January 1944. The attack was to begin on 3 February, at the latest.[24] Von Manstein's orders to the armies as spelled out in Army Group South Order number 86/44 dated 29 January, were as follows:

> 1.Pz.Armee: After bringing the battle against the Soviet First Tank Army east of Vinnitsa to a conclusion, disengage III.Pz.Korps as quickly as possible. Transfer this corps no later than 31 January with 16. and 17.Pz.Div. and the SS-Pz.Div. "LAH" as well as Schw.Pz.Rgt. Bäke to the right wing of the army in the area of Uman and assemble it there as the northern attack group. 1.Pz.Div. will follow as soon as possible. 8. Armee: Disengage XXXXVII.Pz.Korps with 3., 11., 13., and 14.Pz.Divs. from the [current] front and assemble them behind your left wing in front of Zvenigorodka as Army Group's southern attack force. 24.Pz.Div. will follow later.[25]

missing one of its two grenadier regiments (von Brese's) and saw little likelihood of ever getting it back. All three divisions had lost most of the few tanks they had remaining, and were little more than tank-supported infantry task forces by this stage of the battle. The Panther battalion from *Grossdeutschland*, attached to von Wietersheim's *11.Pz.Div.*, was now little more than a company in strength. The divisions' personnel were exhausted and much of their equipment had been lost. In short, they possessed very little combat power and were not in themselves up to the task of conducting the relief operation, much less the encirclement and annihilation of Rotmistrov's tank army. Nevertheless, these exhausted men would try their best in the battle which followed.

Von Manstein, for his part, knew that von Vormann's corps was in bad shape. To bolster these forces, he called up *24.Pz.Div.* from *Gen.O.* Karl-Adolf Hollidt's *6.Armee*, which bordered Wöhler's Army southeast of Kirovograd, and ordered it to join *XXXXVII.Pz.Korps* for the relief effort. In exchange for an infantry division., General Wöhler would get the temporary use of one of the Eastern Front's few remaining uncommitted panzer divisions, and a nearly full strength one at that, with over 60 tanks and an assault gun battalion. The deal had been worked out to everyone's satisfaction, except that of Hitler, who was not told of the transfer until the division had already begun its move to

Normally, such a large scale movement would not be difficult to carry out. However, with the exception of *24.Pz.Div.*, all of the other divisions were either engaged in combat operation or reforming a short distance from the front lines. The divisions, especially those of *III.Pz.Korps,* would have to make a road march of several days duration to get to their assembly areas.

For example, part of *III.Pz.Korps* would go by rail. These elements, primarily armored, normally traveled in this manner in order to conserve fuel and lessen the wear and tear on the vehicles' automotive, track and suspension systems, all of which wore out frequently in use. The wheeled elements would travel

German grenadiers prepare to move out to new fighting positions. (Bundesarchiv 241/2173/15)

by road, normally arriving ahead of the elements traveling by rail. *VII.A.K.,* through which these units would pass, was instructed to designate two main routes for the road-bound march elements, as well as to reinforce key bridges in its sector in order to accommodate the fifty-seven-ton *Tiger* tanks. *1.Pz.Div.* had the furthest distance to go and would arrive last, since it had been fighting with General Raus's *4.Pz.Armee,* over 200 kilometers northwest of its designated assembly area for the relief attack.

A great deal of the movement of *III.Pz.Korps'* four armored divisions, with over 50,000 men, was contingent upon the weather - until the end of January, the weather had been favorable, which meant that the primitive road network could bear the weight of thousands of vehicles. This was valid only so long as the temperatures hovered around the freezing point. However, the weather began to change for the worse on 29 January - though not dramatically at first. Temperatures were higher than usual during the day, causing sections of some roads to melt. Although they usually froze up again during the night, allowing the resumption of traffic, a continuation of this warm spell could spell disaster. What if this was not just a brief warming spell, and instead was a herald of an early spring? No one wanted to think about that - especially the *1.Pz.Armee's* chief engineer officer, responsible for road maintenance in the army's area of operations.

Schw.Pz.Rgt. Bäke not only had to worry about how it would move its tanks to the assembly area, but it was also forced to fight for its own railhead on 30 January. Here, at Oratov, Bäke's troops were supposed to load their vehicles on flatcars, but found the railway station and its yards occupied by the enemy. After a sharp, but brief tank battle, his Tigers and Panthers knocked out 46 Soviet tanks without loss to themselves.[26] Once the battle was over, the Germans quickly loaded

their vehicles and were met by their locomotives, which had narrowly escaped immediately prior to the Soviets' attack. Hardly an auspicious beginning for such a decisive operation, it highlights some of the problems inherent in disengaging from a battle while it was still in progress.

As its divisions continued their slow movement to the designated assembly areas, *1.Pz.Armee* continued to receive additional instructions concerning the conduct of the relief operation from the operations staff at Army Group South. These orders concerned the direction of attack and key points to be seized along the route of advance, among other details. General Wenck was informed that after *III.Pz.Korps* had begun its attack from behind the right wing of *VII.A.K.,* it was to attack in a northerly direction and then swing its forces to the east towards the town of Medvin. There, it was to destroy the bulk of the Soviet armor in concert with an attack launched from the opposite direction by *8.Armee,* thereby restoring contact with the two corps in the pocket.

To flesh out the details of this rather vaguely worded order (keeping to the concept of *Auftragstaktik*, or mission-type orders), Hube added additional guidance of his own to General Breith. In his Army Operations Order number 11/44, Hube instructed his corps commander to assemble his divisions as soon as possible. *198.Inf.Div.* from *VII.A.K.* would be attached to Breith's corps to ease the coordination for *III.Pz.Korps'* passage of lines, as well as to cover his left flank during the initial phase of the attack. Furthermore, Breith was to attack in the direction Medvin-Koshevatoye and strike the enemy located between General Hell's *VII.* outside and Lieb's *XXXXII.Armeekorps* inside the pocket. Hube's chief of staff, General Wenck, even came up with a code name for Breith's operation - the relief attack by *III.Pz.Korps* would be called Operation "Wanda."[27]

Other elements of *1.Pz.Armee* would support Breith in his attack, including the artillery of *VII.A.K.*, which was already in position. All other efforts in Hube's sector would be subordinated to Operation Wanda. There was still much for Wenck and his staff to do while they awaited the arrival of Breith's troops and tanks in their assembly areas and begin their attack, such as arranging the supply of ammunition, fuel, food, and medical support. Still, expectations for the operation and morale of the panzer troops were high. Wenck took the time to note his thoughts in the war diary as he reflected upon the current situation, stating that "The highest calling of every soldier is to defend [Germany's] freedom with all his might, with the pride felt by all who are [a part of] the fighting nation of Germany."[28]

Elements of Breith's corps continued to flow into their assembly areas north of Uman according to plan. By the end of 31 January, most of *16.* and *17.Pz.Div.* had arrived, though many sub-elements were still strung along the roads for thirty or forty kilometers. Luckily, the weather was still holding. It snowed sporadically during the day and a strong wind arose, keeping the roads frozen. To crown their good fortune, the Soviets interfered little with the German's movement. To shorten the time it took to reach its assembly area, one wheeled convoy took a direct path through a partisan-infested area that had been studiously avoided by the Germans for several months. To their surprise, they were allowed to pass through undisturbed. General Hell's *VII.A.K.* reported that the front was relatively quiet in its own sector, except for local probing attacks that were easily driven off.

Wenck noted in the war diary that day that the enemy seemed to be devoting his energy to bringing up supplies and regrouping his forces.[29] Aerial reconnaissance confirmed that most of the Soviet movement seemed to be in a northerly direction into the southern portion of the pocket against Olshana, where Willy Hein and the other men of the *Wiking* were fighting for their lives. While Breith's troops seemed to be having a relatively easy time of moving into position, matters were far different in *8.Armee's* sector, where the battle was still raging after over a week.

Here, in *XXXXVII.Pz.Korps'* sector, the fighting never seemed to have stopped. After having failed twice to cut off and destroy Rotmistrov's armor on 27 and 28 January, Wöhler kept pushing von Vormann and his exhausted divisions from 31 January to 2 February to perform what was by then clearly impossible. Wöhler left no written account of his thoughts on the matter, but von Vormann clearly believed that his army commander was being unreasonable. Rather than give von Vormann's corps several days to rest and prepare its divisions for the relief operation to be launched in concert with Breith's forces, Wöhler chose to keep trying to break through before a solid Soviet front was created. Unfortunately, by 31 January Soviet defenses, as related above, were already well developed.

Before von Vormann could do anything, he needed to insert several infantry divisions into line in order to extend his front 60 additional kilometers to the west, where he would launch his attacks. While *11.* and *14.Pz.Divs.* launched diversionary attacks against Rotmistrov's 20th and 29th Guards Tank Corps from 29 to 30 January, *320., 376.,* and *106.Inf.Div.* and

2.Fallsch.Jgr.Div. took up their new positions formerly occupied by the Panzer divisions. With these two divisions released (*3.Pz.Div.* was still tied down in defensive fighting to the east), they could have been taken out for rehabilitation, but Wöhler chose to commit them to his premature relief attack on 1 February instead.

Wöhler directed von Vormann to attack with the two Panzer divisions currently available from their assembly areas southwest of Shpola, seize the town of Iskrennoye, and swing west towards Zvenigorodka, attacking the enemy from the rear and reestablish contact with *XI.A.K.* Once contact was reestablished with the encircled forces, they would reestablish the former front facing east. The other three panzer divisions would be fed into the battle as they arrived. Von Vormann left us his own thoughts on what he was being asked to do:

> This entire grand plan really only existed on paper. For at least five to six days, the initiative rested completely with the Russians. Free and unhindered, [they were] able to do whatever [they] wanted. How the situation would develop after 3 February was anyone's guess.[30]

Had all of his divisions been at full strength, von Vormann later wrote, he would have been able to carry out most of his mission. But they had been worn down so much by the fighting that he saw little chance of success for this attack. The constant retreats since Kursk could not go on forever, nor was there time to build up his forces. Von Vormann informed his army commander that the stubborn defense of a front far too wide to hold was beginning to devour everything. In his opinion, it would have been far wiser to wait until Breith was ready. However, Wöhler believed that his army could not afford to wait for *1.Pz.Armee* to conduct its relief attack. Wöhler felt that the situation demanded that he act now, since it appeared that Stemmermann's "used up" corps could not hold out much longer.[31] He overrode his corps commander's objections and ordered him to attack anyway. Von Vormann reluctantly obeyed.

Nevertheless, von Vormann's divisions began to position themselves from 30 January to 1 February. General Unrein's *14.Pz.Div.* remained in the line, taking over *11.Pz.Div.'s* defensive sector. Lang's *3.Pz.Div.* pulled out of the line on the night of 31 January and moved to the west, where it would establish a thin screen line between *14.Pz.Div.* at Zlatapol and *11.Pz.Div.* at Tolmach, a sector over 20 kilometers wide. Von Wietersheim's *11.Pz.Div.* would make the main effort. To his left, *Gen.Lt.* Hans Mikosch's *13.Pz.Div.* had finally arrived at the town of Nadlak and would cover von Wietersheim's left flank. Hampered by rapidly deteriorating roads, *13.Pz.Div.* would only be able to muster its armored *Kampfgruppe* from *Pz.Rgt.4* and 100 *Panzergrenadiers* for the upcoming attack. The rest of his troops, guns, and vehicles were struggling to get to the front as quickly as possible. Between Mikosch's division there still yawned a gap over 50 kilometers wide towards *1.Pz.Armee.*

Von Vormann still held strong misgivings for this attack. On the evening before it was to begin, he was still debating the wisdom of it with *8.Armee's* chief of staff, General Speidel. Not only did von Vormann believe that his divisions were not ready for the relief attack, but he also believed that his geographical objective and the enemy situation were too vague. He stated that "How could I order an attack to the north with 100 men (from *13.Pz.Div.*) towards an undefined goal?" Speidel retorted that the goal had indeed been clearly stated - the southern flank of *XI.A.K.*[32] It mattered not that no one had a clear idea of where exactly this flank was nor where the enemy forces lay. Wöhler, informed of von Vormann's reluctance to attack, also called him a few hours later to insist that he push forward the next day with whatever he had available without regards to his flanks. It did not matter anyway, since *XXXXVII.Pz.Korps* had no forces left to guard his flanks. Despite von Vormann's vociferous objections to the plan, Wöhler adamantly demanded that he move as ordered. Von Vormann's argumentiveness and annoying habit of seeing the true situation clearly would not stand him in good stead with either Speidel or Wöhler, which would have grave repercussions later.

The attack began favorably enough on 1 February, when *11.Pz.Div.* seized a bridge over the Shpolka River near the town of Iskrennoye, ten kilometers west of Shpola and pressed north (Map 9). The small *Kampfgruppe* holding this bridgehead was unable, however, to go much further and was forced to repel a number of fierce counterattacks carried out by 18th and 29th Guards Tank Corps. Over the next three days, von Wietersheim's troops destroyed 62 Soviet tanks, but the *Kampfgruppe* was itself reduced to a combat strength of one tank and 80 *Panzergrenadiers*.

To make matters worse, they were stranded on the northern bank of the river in the late afternoon of 1 February when rising waters brought on by thawing snow caved in the only bridge, after only four tanks had crossed over.[33] The remaining 26 tanks and the *Panzergrenadier* battalion from *13.Pz.Div.* were unable to cross to provide von Wietersheim's troops the reinforcements which they badly needed. With all momentum now spent, *XXXXVII.Pz.Korps* could only tie up Soviet forces from being used elsewhere while it awaited the arrival of *24.Pz.Div.* Both *11.* and *13.Pz.Divs.* came under incessant attack by the Red Air Force, immensely complicating their relief attack.

In addition to *11.Pz.Div.'s* effort to seize and hold its tiny bridgehead at Ikrennskoye, *14.Pz.Div.* still had not abandoned its efforts to reestablish contact with von Brese's encircled force, which had found itself once again in another tiny pocket north of Shpola. During the fighting from 27 to 28 January, *K.Gr.* von Brese had been repeatedly cut off from its parent division and was finally forced to remain in the pocket, covering the right flank of General Trowitz's *57.Inf.Div.* As this division and the other divisions of *XI.A.K.* reeled back to the northwest from 29 to 30 January, von Brese and his troops had been left behind. On 31 January, *14.Pz.Div.* tried a final time to link up with its "lost battalion" with a force consisting of two assault guns and an armored reconnaissance company, escorting a resupply column of food, fuel, and ammunition. Once they had reestablished contact with von Brese, they were to help him refuel and re-arm his vehicles and lead them south,

where they would break out through the lines of the 21st Guards Rifle Corps near the town of Mokraya Kaligorka.

Despite its best efforts, this tiny force could not get through to von Brese;[34] it was quickly brought to a halt by Soviet tanks and infantry and had to fight to make its way back to German lines. Von Brese, whose rescue had once again been stymied, withdrew to the north where he and his men linked their fate with that of the rest of the men in the pocket. Forced to abandon his tanks due to lack of fuel, his unit was down to a combat strength of 100 infantrymen and one light howitzer battery. When they arrived at the front line of the pocket near Petropavlovka, they were incorporated into *Wiking* for the duration of the battle.[35]

Wöhler's plan to carry out his own independent relief attack had stalled, just as von Vormann predicted it would. Although this would have been a wise idea had von Vormann's forces been at relatively full strength, to do so now with his exhausted divisions only reduced their ranks even further. Wöhler thought that, if nothing else, the fact that a relief operation was being mounted would be enough to give the troops in the pocket a much-needed morale boost. Given the depth of the Soviet defenses along the outer ring of encirclement, Wöhler's plan had little chance of success and, if anything, may have raised false hopes within the pocket. Although he must have been aware of his army commander's actions, von Manstein did not intervene, possibly because he trusted his subordinate's judgment.

Perhaps he thought that the addition of *24.Pz.Div.* would redress the imbalance. Another possibility is that von Manstein had nothing better to suggest, which is certainly hinted at in a conversation between him and Wöhler that took place 31 January. Regardless, for five days, *XXXXVII.Pz.Korps* had frantically thrown its forces against Konev's defenses, with little to show for its efforts except the tiny bridgehead at Iskrennoye. Von Vormann's forces, weak to begin with, were now totally incapable of conducting further offensive operations until *24.Pz.Div.* had been brought up. All von Vormann's forces could do until then was to harass Soviet movement with artillery, and was not to "spare the ammunition" for it. To see the situation for himself, Wöhler flew from his headquarters at Novo Ukraina in a Fiesler *Storch* liaison aircraft to visit von Vormann's corps headquarters in Novo-Mirgorod. What struck him most was the overall shortage of infantry to secure the immense open spaces between the armored formations.[36] Wöhler was to pay another visit the following day, in an effort to patch up relations with his subordinate. In an entry in the *KTB* for 2 February, Wöhler commented on the heated argument the two had had the previous day:

> The [commander's] estimate of the situation must be clear. No more [going] backwards and forwards. The Army is not in the position to issue detailed orders in such a fluid situation. We cannot negotiate whatever assignment we are given. [Our] divisions must be kept intact, not scattered to the four winds. For today and the next few days, all that matters is that we punch through to Stemmermann. Therefore, keep your flank protection as thin as possible.[37]

All of the German commanders involved were under great stress. While von Manstein was not telling Wöhler how he should fight his own battle, his army commander must have felt a great deal of pressure to succeed, and that could not have failed to rub off on von Vormann. At least von Vormann's failure to continue his attack had led Wöhler to reassess the army group's overall plan for the relief attack; he began to realize that, perhaps, even von Manstein's limited counteroffensive was itself too ambitious.

Despite the fact that the Field Marshal's commanders were all united in their desire to rescue the encircled corps, by 2 February von Manstein's concept for the operation no longer had their unanimous approval. Finally realizing that his own forces were too weak to carry out his army's assignment, even Wöhler began to balk. Rather than carry out von Manstein's wide-ranging plan to encircle and destroy the Soviets followed by the relief of the encircled corps, he thought that it would be much more practical to simply take the shortest route towards the pocket. Wöhler felt that a wide encircling movement was simply too great a task for the forces at hand. Rather than have Breith's *III.Pz.Korps* attack towards the north in the direction of Boyarka and Medvin (von Manstein's goal), Wöhler thought it would be much easier if he would just attack northeast towards Morenzy. This route of attack would lead to a more rapid relief of Stemmermann and Lieb's forces that would also help relieve some of the pressure being applied against them by the Soviets.

8.Armee's commander informed von Vormann that he now thought that Army Group South would be much better off to trust in the judgment of commanders on the scene, rather than try to impose unrealistic plans on them from above, thus echoing von Manstein's own sentiments about Hitler's style of leadership.[38] Wöhler and von Vormann had both also come to realize that it now made more sense for *8.Armee* to link up with *1.Pz.Armee's* forces to the west before the main relief attack was launched. But for reasons unknown, von Manstein decided it was better to stick with the original plan, which was to begin at the earliest on 3 February and no later than the following day. Thus the stage was set for the first combined relief attempt by Breith's and von Vormann's panzer corps. If the weather held, that is.

End Notes

1   von Manstein, p. 512.

2   Ibid, pp. 515-516.

3   Ibid.

4   von Vormann, p. 61.

5   Ibid, p. pp. 72-73.

6   *Sbornik*, p. 311.

7   Zhukov, p. 242.

8   Von Vormann, p. 67.

9   See Zhukov, pp. 241-243 and Konev in Sokolov, pp.111-113.

10   *Sbornik*, pp. 312-313.

11   Zhukov, p. 242.

12   *Sbornik*, p. 315.

13   *8.Armee* KTB entry dated 2030 hours 29 January 1944, p. 8.

14   *Sbornik*, p. 313.

15   Alexander Stahlberg, Bounden Duty: *The Memoirs of a German Officer 1932-45*. (London: Brassey's, 1990), p. 327.

16   Teletype message, Army Group South dated 1925 hours 28 January 1944 to Commander, *1.Pz.Armee*.

17   *Oberst Graf* von Kielmansegg, quoted in Glantz, "From the Dnieper to the Vistula," p. 234.

18   Jahnke and Lerch, p. 63.

19   Headquarters, *1.Pz.Armee*, "*Wochenmeldung, Kampfwert der Divisionen, Stand 29. January 1944*" and "*1.Pz.Armee Chefsache, Pz.Div.- und Sturmgeschützlage III.Pz.Div. Korps 29 January 1944.*"

20   *Program zum Appell der Angehörigen der ehem. Deutschen 8.Armee anlässlich des Gedenktages*, Amberg, Germany, 16 February 1974, pp. 25-26.

21   Ibid, pp. 25-26.

22   Ziemke, *Stalingrad to Berlin*, p. 231.

23   Glantz, "From the Dnieper to the Vistula," p. 212.

24   Oldwig von Natzmer in DA Pam 20-234, p. 36.

25   Buchner, p. 21.

26   *1.Pz.Armee* KTB entry dated 30 January 1944, p. 1.

27   Ibid, p. 3.

28   Ibid, p. 4.

29   *1.Pz.Armee* KTB entry dated 31 January 1944, p. 1.

30   von Vormann, p. 69.

31   *8.Armee* KTB entry dated 0900 hours 31 January 1944, p. 3.

32   Ibid, entry dated 1550 hours 31 January 1944, p. 6.

33   Ibid, p. 73.

34   Grams, p. 170.

35   *8.Armee* KTB entry 0810 hours 31 January 1944, pp. 2-3.

36   Ibid, KTB entry 0930 hours 1 February 1944, p. 2.

37   Ibid, KTB entry 1200 hours 2 February 1944, pp. 2-3.

38   von Vormann, pp. 74-75.

Chapter Eleven

CRISIS IN THE KESSEL

"This can not go on much longer."
— *General Theobald Lieb, 4 February 1944*

Despite initial Soviet successes, the encircled Germans had thus far been able to thwart subsequent attempts by the First and Second Ukrainian *Fronts* to split up and destroy the pocket. However, Zhukov, Vatutin and Konev had by no means given up. Nevertheless, by holding the corner posts of the southern front at Steblev, Olshana, and Kvitki, the men of Lieb's and Stemmermann's corps had been able to deny their enemy, at least temporarily, the quick access to the interior of the pocket these crossroads towns afforded. Just as important, the Red Air Force had been unable to shut down the German airlift, although it was making things difficult for the transport pilots of General Seidemann's *VIII.Flieger-Korps*. For the Soviets there was still a ray of hope - the defense line of the German pocket had not yet completely closed up. In fact, there were still great gaps between German units which could be exploited by their attackers if they moved quickly enough.

There were also many lesser routes into the pocket as well. This would assist the division and corps commanders of 4th Guards, 27th, and 52nd Armies, who were supposed to conduct concentric attacks towards the center of the pocket in order to force it into an ever shrinking perimeter, while at the same time forcing the pocket to move away from the assembling German relief forces. These forces would be dealt with by Kravchenko's and Rotmistrov's tank armies, which were busy fortifying the outer ring of encirclement. Success seemed to be within the Red Army's grasp.

The Germans had their own worries. On 1 February, General Wöhler's greatest concern was the right flank of Stemmermann's corps, which had been forced back continually since the Soviet offensive began one week before. It had yet to tie in with the defenders at Olshana. On that day, a gap eight kilometers wide separated the defenders of Olshana from the right flank of Kruse's *389.Inf.Div.*, which was situated near the small village of Verbovka. While another *Kampfgruppe* from the Estonian *Narwa* battalion was being formed to establish a forward position to link up with the encircled troops in Olshana in order to facilitate their breakout, it would still be several days before it would arrive. In the meantime, all Wöhler and Stemmermann could do was to hope that Konev would not react quickly enough to take advantage of this opportunity. An even bigger gap yawned between Olshana and Kvitki to the northwest, where the Soviet 180th Rifle Division had made a deep penetration in a northeasterly direction, which could threaten *XI.A.K.'s* large supply dump at Gorodishche if not dealt with promptly. Clearly, Lieb and Stemmermann had to knit the southern front of the pocket together as quickly as possible.

Lieb's corps was in somewhat better shape than Stemmermann's, since at least it had been able to patch together a solid front in the west. True, it was thinly occupied in many places and under constant attack, especially at Boguslav and Steblev, but Lieb's troops had managed to hold. In all fairness, a far greater number of Soviet divisions were arrayed against Stemmermann's corps, but Lieb's sector had also been under great pressure. By switching battalion-sized units rapidly from one threatened sector of the front to another, *XXXXII.A.K.* had managed to keep disaster at bay, but for how long? Already on this date, ammunition and fuel supplies were running low and would have to be strictly rationed. The senseless order by an unnamed army bureaucrat to blow up the supply trains trapped within the pocket was coming back to haunt the German commanders.

The shortage of supplies led *XI.A.K.'s* chief of staff, *Oberst* Heinz Gädke, to believe that Lieb was unfairly taking the lion's share of what was being flown in by the Luftwaffe. As successful as the airlift had been to date, it would never be able to satisfy all of both corps' requirements. Gaedke did have a point - after all, the airfield at Korsun did lay in the center of Lieb's corps area and it was natural to assume that more supplies than authorized had found their way to some of Lieb's units located in the vicinity of the airfield, whereas the units of *XI.A.K.* were farthest removed from Korsun. Whether *XXXXII.A.K.* was enriching itself at the expense of Stemmermann's corps can no longer be proven with any certainly. Perhaps the time it took for supplies to travel the distance from Korsun to Stemmermann's supply depot at Gorodishche gave rise to this belief by many that *XI.A.K.* was being shortchanged.

To partially satisfy Stemmermann, Wöhler asked Army Group South to conduct additional parachute drops of ammunition in *XI.A.K.'s* sector, since there were no suitable airfields there for the Ju-52s to land. However, Stemmermann and his staff still were not satisfied that they were receiving their fair share of supplies. This finally led to Wöhler being forced to personally intervene in order to resolve the dispute. In an order passed through his Army's *Oberquartiermeister*, Wöhler directed on 2 February that supplies being flown into Korsun were to be divided equally between *XI.* and *XXXXII.A.K.*, but that Lieb's corps would remain responsible for supervising the logistics effort for both encircled corps.[1] Stemmermann's response is not recorded, though he must have felt disappointment. The lack of overall command within the pocket was beginning to cause complications which the German higher leadership had not foreseen, as both corps commanders had begun to compete for their share of increasingly scarce resources.

Antitank gunners attempt to place their 75mm PaK40 antitank gun into position on the wide-open steppes. (Bundesarchiv 69/105/64)

Besides a rapidly worsening supply situation, Wöhler's decision not to fly troop reinforcements into the pocket meant that foxhole strength of the infantry regiments and battalions would only decrease for the remainder of the encirclement. Combined losses of combat troops (killed, wounded, sick, and missing) in both corps were already running at 300 men per day, out of a total strength at the time of encirclement of 60,000 men.[2] For example, on 3 February, Lieb's corps lost 174 men, 105 of those from *Wiking* alone. One did not need an adding machine to calculate that the encircled corps had only two weeks at best to hold out, if supplies did not give out first. All that Generals Lieb and Stemmermann could do at this time was to attempt to hold out with their meager resources until the promised relief force came. Until then, they would have to do the best with what they had and hope that Field Marshal von Manstein would get there in time.

For *XI.A.K.*, this was an open question. Continuously pushed back by Konev's unrelenting attacks since 24 January, Stemmermann's troops had been forced to retreat step by step from its original positions facing east. In constant motion since the beginning of the offensive, his front had swung back like a door on hinges and now faced to the south. The corps' withdrawal had not yet come to a stop, however. At times, some of its divisions and *Kampfgruppen* had seemed on the verge of a rout; only the ruthlessness of their commanders prevented some units from disintegrating. But by 1 February all of Stemmermann's remaining units had finally been able to tie in with each other's flanks. Though its sector was tottering and had yet to tie in with *XXXXII.A.K.'s* left flank near Olshana, *XI.A.K.*

at least had held together. Sorely missed was the transfer of tactical command and control of *Wiking* two days before to Lieb's corps, but at least it limited the area of operations that Stemmermann had to worry about.

Although Stemmermann gladly gave up responsibility for holding the remainder of the Dnieper front to his fellow corps commander which allowed him to concentrate on handling his three remaining divisions - *57.*, *72.*, and *389.Inf.Divs.* - he constantly badgered Wöhler for several days afterwards to give *Wiking* back to his corps. Well aware that Gille's troops possessed the only remaining mechanized capability of all the encircled units, both corps commanders would squabble over its ownership, perhaps to the detriment of other matters which urgently required their attention. Needless to say, both German corps commanders would have their hands full, especially as the Soviet attackers could now concentrate their forces towards the destruction of the pocket. Konev and Vatutin could now do so, especially now since von Vormann's attempt to reestablish contact with Stemmermann's corps had been stymied and Breith's relief attempt had yet to materialize.

XI.A.K.'s situation was indeed serious, but began to improve by 1 February. After a week of being forced out of a series of successive defensive positions, Stemmermann's three divisions finally were able to establish a firm defensive position that they would hold for the next five days. Finally, Stemmermann's troops would be able to build temporary fighting positions, sort out their companies and battalions, and even rest a bit. His strongest division, Hohn's *72.Inf.Div.*, occupied defensive positions facing southeast on the corps' far left, where it linked up with Gille's SS troops south of the town of Orlovets. In the center, facing south, lay Trowitz's *57.Inf.Div.*, which linked up with Hohn's troops near the town of Stanislavchik. On the far right flank was Kruse's *389.Inf.Div.*, the corps' weakest. Although it had been able to gather its widely-scattered regiments back under its own command, most of its battalions had less than 100 men each. Some had even fewer.

Kruse's front faced to the southwest and he had been forced to pull his right flank back between the towns of Vyazovok and Verbovka, so that it faced due west, in order to prevent the Soviet 5th Guards Airborne Division from enveloping him. Foot patrols from the attached *Gren.Rgt.417* had attempted to reach as far as Olshana, where the battle was raging, but were unable to get all the way through. Between the "Rheingold Division" and Olshana lay two deep valleys crisscrossed with creeks and streams, all of them flooded at this stage of the battle. Fortunately, the Soviets had so far been able to penetrate this gap with nothing but infantry and cavalry patrols.

The German's new defenses were soon put to the test. *Oberst* Hohn of *72.Inf.Div.* reported an attack against his troops holding Stanislavchik at 0930 hours on 1 February by infantry, most likely by 252nd Rifle Division, supported by six tanks. *Maj.* Siegel's regiment, *Gren.Rgt.266,* bore the brunt of the attack. An attempt was made by three T-34s using the elevated railroad bed to penetrate Siegel's defenses, but they were quickly knocked out by one of Siegel's antitank guns. The accompanying Red infantry were soon forced to ground by artillery fire from *Ltn.* Bender's infantry-gun company. After several well-aimed salvoes, the surviving enemy infantrymen fled back to their own lines in panic.

Despite the worsening supply situation, Siegel reported that he still had sufficient ammunition on hand to keep fighting, testament to *Ltn.* "Pan" Ogrowsky's prowess as an organizer par excellence. A small penetration by the Soviet 254th Rifle Division on Hohn's left flank near Nosachov was quickly wiped out. Siegel's neighbor to the right, a regiment from *57.Inf.Div.* whose commander Siegel had previously clashed with, had temporarily pulled out during the fighting to Siegel's disgust.[3] It returned later that day, but must have been met with considerable derision by the men of Siegel's regiment. Indeed, the apparent unwillingness of German troops to hold their ground was increasingly becoming a source of concern to other commanders as well.

Hohn's division was not the only one busy that day - in fact, all of General Ryshov's 4th Guards Army had now arrived and his 20th and 21st Guards Rifle Corps appeared to be preparing for a continuation of their attacks against the entrenched Germans. Stemmermann was quickly informed of this development by one of his divisions and reported to *8.Armee* at noon 1 February that a considerable number of Soviet troops, including eight tanks, were observed moving west from Matusov into an assembly area south of Burty in Trowitz's sector. His exhausted troops would have no time to catch their breath after all. Three hours later, German defensive positions south of Burty reported heavy enemy artillery fire. That could only mean a Soviet attack was imminent, but when?

Stemmermann and his division commanders found out soon enough, when a force estimated to consist of five Soviet rifle divisions smashed into German defenses between Stanislavchik and Vyazovok at 1650 hours. All three of *XI.A.K.'s* divisions were quickly caught up in repelling the Soviet attack, which seemed to be focused on nothing less than outflanking their right flank and the destruction of all German defenses between Vyazovok, Burty, and Stanislavchik - in short, most of the corps' sector. In fighting that raged into the early evening, Stemmermann was forced to commit everything he had to halt the attack by Ryshov's men. Stemmermann's reported to *8. Armee* at 1855 hours that "All of these attacks were driven off with the utmost exertion [of our troops]; smaller penetrations have been ironed out or cut off."[4]

The attack must have caused Stemmermann a great deal of concern about his corps' supply situation, since he followed up this report on the tactical situation at the end of the day with no less than three separate requests for more ammunition and fuel. One such request was short and succinct. In a radio report he is quoted as stating to General Speidel, "Thanks for the supply chests (dropped by air). We need more men...Aerial resupply is insufficient. Ammunition. Fuel. More fighter cover."[5] Evidently, the loss of transport aircraft due to Soviet fighter aircraft or miss-drops of aerial bundles had caused Stemmermann to lose faith in the reliability of the aerial resupply effort, for he requested that Wöhler have von Vormann's relief force bring with them considerable amounts of munitions, especially 10.5 cm and 15 cm shells for the artillery.[6] Of course, von Vormann's *XXXXVII.Pz.Korps* was stalled southwest of Shpola and had little chance of breaking through to the pocket that day or the next. To appease Stemmermann, Wöhler requested that Army Group South intensify its efforts to fly additional supplies into the pocket, regardless of losses.

While some of *XI.A.K.'s* regiments, such as Siegel's, kept themselves supplied due to the ingenuity of their supply officers and cooks, others had to make do with what they had. One such unit was *Nachrichten-Abteilung 57* (signal battalion) of *57.Inf.Div.* One of its members, *Offizier-Anwärter* (Officer Candidate) Hans Gaertig, relates that one day he was ordered by a supply officer from the divisional staff to bring a party of men and follow him to a sugar factory that lay in the area. When they arrived, Gaertig was ordered to help himself and his men to as much sugar as they wanted.

When he realized that he had nothing to carry the sugar in, Gaertig improvised by taking an extra pair of long underpants from his pack and tying knots in the legs. He proceeded to fill this homemade sack with as much sugar as he could pour into them. After everyone had taken what they could carry, Gaertig recalled that he and his men were covered with sugar from head to toe. While other rations became scarcer, he and his men relied more and more on their sugar hoard, which they continued to eat until they escaped from the pocket. According to Gaertig, "We were expressly forbidden to drink water from local springs, on account of the danger of them being poisoned. [So we] mixed the sugar with fresh snow, making ourselves a delicacy."[7]

While questions such as logistics and medical evacuation of the wounded occupied the attention of staff officers that evening, holding the enemy at bay and staying alive were the main concerns of the infantrymen in the front line positions. As they had many times before, the men of Stemmermann's divisions strained to see signs of enemy movement to their immediate front. With hand grenades and flare pistols at the ready, men in the advance posts of their companies and battalions struggled to stay awake and as warm as possible, not an easy task when lying dressed in a damp uniform in a shallow hole scooped in the frozen ground by an entrenching tool.

Soviet patrols constantly probed for German defenses throughout the night, as they did every night. A night attack launched by 254th Rifle Division of the Soviet 78th Rifle Corps against Hohn's troops near Nosachov was driven off, as well as another near Verbovka on *XI.A.K.'s* extreme right flank, held by units of *389.Inf.Div.* Evidently, Soviet infantry were probing for the gap between Olshana and the right of the corps, which still had not yet been closed up. If they made a concerted effort the next morning, Konev's troops could still drive a wedge between these two locations and head towards Gorodishche, splitting the pocket in two.

Wednesday, 2 February dawned along the Dnieper Front with warming temperatures and fog, which would conceal the approach of an attacker. Although things had been quiet that morning, the troops of *XI.A.K.* were shocked when it received a report that troops from 180th Rifle Division had penetrated as far as the forest one kilometer south of Vyazovok, where the headquarters of Kruse's *389.Inf.Div.* was located. Evidently, this battalion-sized Soviet unit had crept around the division's far right flank and was preparing to attack the division from the rear. Rear-echelon units from the division were quickly dispatched to deal with this new crisis, successfully wiping out the Soviet battalion by 1050 hours. Until the gap between Olshana and Verbovka was finally closed, this sort of thing would continue.

Although Soviet attacks against Verbovka continued throughout this day and the next, Kruse's division continued to extend its sector to the northwest in order to tie in with the Estonian *Narwa* Battalion, which now held the left flank of Lieb's corps. Unfortunately, the link-up, when it would occur, would be north of Olshana, since pressure exerted by 5th Guards Cavalry Corps and 5th Guards Airborne Division prevented the German forces from raising the town's siege. Olshana's defenders would have to sit tight and hold on for at least two more days. To make coordination easier between Olshana's defenders and the rest of *XI.A.K.* the *Kampfgruppe* from *Wiking* holding the town was attached to Stemmermann's corps on 2 February.

From 2 to 5 February, Soviet attacks against *XI.A.K.* continued without interruption. Tank-supported infantry formations repeatedly flung themselves against the German defenses, with little to show for their efforts. Again and again, Verbovka on the corps' far right and Nosachov on the far left, were attacked by waves of infantry who were mowed down in heaps by mortar and machine-gun fire. Only in the corps' center, occupied by *57.Inf.Div.*, was there relative quiet, though its headquarters in Burty as well as that of *389.Inf.Div.* in Vyazovok reported heavy shelling. The morale of the encircled

troops improved perceptibly, due to reports that von Vormann was mounting a relief attack as well as the evidence of their own tactical successes.

On 2 February, Wöhler issued a proclamation to his troops in the pocket, praising their defensive performance since the beginning of the Soviet offensive. In Wöhler's words, "The performance of the leadership and troops of both corps has exceeded every expectation, in spite of heavy and bloody casualties. The seriousness of the fighting is demonstrated by the impressive numbers of tanks knocked out." In fact, both corps reported that they had knocked out a total of 302 enemy tanks from 24 January to 2 February.[8]

On the right flank of *72.Inf.Div.* near Stanislavchik, Rudolf Siegel's regiment continued to inflict punishment upon their opponent, whose attacks finally began to diminish by 3 February. Although the neighboring regiment from *57.Inf.Div.* on his right flank had fled to the rear, Siegel's men clung steadfastly to their positions. A counterattack carried out by the regiment's reserve company led by Ltn. Maier was able to prevent the attackers from 254th Rifle Division from getting into the regiment's rear area. Ltn. Bender's infantry gun company, nicknamed *Die Bender-Orgel* (Bender's organ, a play on the Soviet *Katyusha* multiple rocket-launcher's nickname, *Stalinorgel*), continued to wreak havoc on Soviet infantry. Finally, *Inf.Rgt. List* from *57.Inf.Div.* was brought out of reserve to restore the situation on Siegel's right flank. With *Btl.* Zimmermann from List on his right, *Oblt.* Giessen, one of Siegel's company commanders who had constantly harped on the fact that their neighbors had the annoying habit of fleeing when the going got tough, had nothing further to complain about.

Both Siegel's regiment and *Inf.Rgt. List* had fought side-by-side in the past and the men of both regiments trusted and respected each other, although they came from different divisions. Despite this, Siegel requested that an officer from corps headquarters personally come to look over the situation to insure that these problems would not occur again. Siegel's concern is understandable, in view of the importance that front-line soldier's attached to flank security. What good would it do, after all, to hold one's own position if your neighbors gave way? Bitter experience in the East had taught that trust in one's adjacent units was a matter of life and death; therefore, it was deadly serious when units frequently pulled out in the heat of combat. After a while, this type of panic would begin to infect one's own troops, who would require the most extreme measures to keep them in line. One message from *XI.A.K.* the following day to *8.Armee* captured the situation succinctly:

> Our troops are facing a crisis on account of the persistently heavy fighting in unfavorable weather. For example, one entire battalion withdrew in the face of an attack by one enemy tank with only a few infantrymen. On account of the exhaustion of our troops and shortage of officers, orders are only very slowly or grudgingly carried out.[9]

Above: *A squad of SS-Grenadiers trying to warm themselves by a fire somewhere near the northern sector of the Pocket, early February 1944. This depicts the hardships endured by troops who had to spend every day in the open during the winter months, with little overhead shelter to keep out the elements. Some of the troops seem to be fortifying themselves with alcohol as well. Note the variety of German and Soviet-issue headgear being worn. (U.S. National Archives)*

Above: *Young SS Grenadiers, wearing what appears to be newly-issued white camouflaged capes over their winter anoraks, enjoying a smoke. Note that three types of headgear are being worn - the summer camouflaged cap, the standard SS side cap (the Schiffchen) and the rabbit fur winter cap. (U.S. National Archives)*

Above: *Three SS Grenadiers asleep in a dugout with several layers of logs for overhead protection. Note the fuel barrel which has been stored in the dugout for safekeeping. Rifles, including a G-43 semiautomatic, stand at the ready. (U.S. National Archives)*

Above: *An SS-Grenadier of Wiking, fully attired in winter combat suit and insulated boots, catches a quick nap from the edge of his dugout, somewhere along the northern sector of the Pocket. (U.S. National Archives)*

Left: *An SS Grenadier taking a healthy swig from a bottle of wine or brandy while standing in his foxhole. He wears the leather fur-lined winter outergarment, which seemed to have been issued in large quantities to SS units. Of particular interest are the hand-made knitted mittens, an item common to Estonia. This could possibly mean that the unit pictured here, or at least this individual, was part of the SS-Volunteer Battalion Narwa, which was attached to Wiking during the Battle of the Cherkassy Pocket. (U.S. National Archives)*

Above: *An SS sentry manning a machinegun keeps a sharp lookout for the enemy in the northern sector of the pocket. (U.S. National Archives)*

Right: *A young SS-Untersturmführer of one of Wiking's Panzergrenadier units about to embark on a patrol in the northern sector of the Pocket. Noteworthy is the fact that he has chosen to arm himself with a Mauser 98K rifle, rather than a machine pistol, perhaps to avoid drawing the attention of Soviet snipers. He is wearing a Wehrmacht manufactured winter overgarment composed entirely of rabbit fur. (U.S. National Archives)*

Left: *An SS Grenadier of Wiking returning to his company with two boxes of ammunition, one of which can be seen hanging from the barrel of his MP-40. (U.S. National Archives)*

On 4 February, the situation of *Gren.Rgt.266* became serious when it was attacked by six T-34s, shortly after its sole remaining antitank gun was moved to the rear for some repairs. One of Siegel's companies grabbed *Panzerfäuste* and molotov cocktails and attacked, knocking out one of the tanks and chasing away the others. Four of them returned at nightfall, but so had *Ltn.* Peters and his 7.5 cm *PaK*. One tank was knocked out by *Obergef.* Harr of I.Bataillon, who was awarded the Iron Cross, Second Class for his bravery.

His action as well as the continued support by the *Bender-Orgel* forced the rest of the attackers to withdraw.[10] By this time, the snow and ice had melted and turned to mud and large pools of water which inundated the landscape. Still, Siegel's regiment, as well as all the others, had no choice but to stand fast and hold off the attackers as long as possible. But Siegel and his men had spent their last day in Stanislavchik; the following day they would pack up and shift further to the right towards Burty, because things were once again in motion.

The shift had occurred because Stemmermann decided that *389.Inf.Div.* was too weak to hold the link between his and Lieb's corps at Verbovka on its own. After three days of enduring continuous Soviet attacks, the "Rheingold" Division had little strength left to hold its position and beginning to crumble. To avert a crisis, Stemmermann decided late in the evening on 4 February to pull most of Trowitz's division out of its sector in the middle of the corps and move it to the corps' far right, where it would take over the Verbovka sector from Kruse's battered division the following day, 5 February. Most of the division's old sector would be taken over by *72.Inf.Div.*, with the exception of *Inf.Rgt. List,* which would remain in place on Hohn's right. This apparently suited *Maj.* Siegel and the men of his regiment just fine. Once Trowitz's division had moved out, the entire southern front of *XI.A.K.* would withdraw later that day to a new defensive line that would shorten up the front and free more men to serve as combat reserves.

Hans Gaertig, from *Nachr.Abt.57*, had in the meantime been incorporated into a scratch *Alarmkompanie* composed of men from various service elements of *57.Inf.Div.* This was the result of the relentless combing-through of support units ordered by von Manstein himself on 3 February, who saw that troops behind the front needed to be reinforced in order to carry out counterattacks to defend against local enemy breakthroughs.[11] Combat strength of the infantry battalions had sunk so low that extreme measures were now called for in order to help fill shortages of fighting troops. Gaertig's new unit of signal troops, cooks, and truck drivers soon set off for their new positions. Led by officers with little front-line experience, Gaertig foresaw that little good would come of all of this. According to Gaertig:

> The seriousness of the situation was made clear to us not only by the shortage of supplies of ammunition and rations, but especially by the order to destroy everything that we could not carry in our assault packs. Except for personal effects and other items such as maps, radio codes, radio sets, and certain vehicles, everything else was to be stripped down, doused with gasoline, and burned.[12]

❖ ❖ ❖

Trowitz's division moved out at dawn, 5 February. The switch came none too soon, since troops from *389.Inf.Div.* holding Verbovka had been attacked the previous day by at least a Soviet regiment supported by 22 tanks.

Although they had managed to keep the attackers at bay, *389.Inf.Div's.* usefulness as a combat unit was obviously coming to an end and it would probably collapse if struck again. Delayed by muddy roads and streams swollen by melting snow, the lead elements of Trowitz's division arrived in their new sector in the early afternoon, just as the Soviets were launching another attack aimed at taking Verbovka. The attackers were swiftly checked, losing four out of the eight attacking T-34s. Trowitz's Bavarians quickly tied in with the survivors of Kruse's division holding Verbovka on the left and with the newly-brought up *Narwa* Battalion on the right. *Narwa*, which still had one of its companies trapped in Olshana, is reported to have fought especially well.

Trowitz had his troops quickly establish a hasty defense facing west, southwest of the town of Petropavlovka, less than ten kilometers from Gorodishche. They had literally arrived in the nick of time. Evidently, 57. and *389.Inf.Div.* with *Narwa* had stopped the largest Soviet effort yet to break into the pocket from the south. Frustrated, the Soviets hurled additional troops at the Germans holding Petropavlovka and Verbovka, but without success. Nor were they able to affect the withdrawal of the rest of *XI.A.K.* to its new positions further north. To the southeast, the rearguard of *72.Inf.Div.* and the rest of *389.Inf.Div.* had only to contend with the mud, which still slowed their movement to the new defense line tremendously.

The Soviet advance towards Verbovka, which was carried out by Cossacks of Selivanov's 5th Guards Cavalry Corps, was supposed to follow the route from Verbovka to the town of Valyava, due west of Gorodishche. Two of the corps' three cavalry divisions were still tied down in Olshana, however, where the German defenders appeared to be making a final stand. Because of this, the Soviet push made little headway, and created conditions that allowed the encircled defenders of that town to break out on the evening of 5 February, as related previously. The move of *57.Inf.Div.* also came as a surprise to Selivanov, since that division was still believed to be holding defensive positions twenty kilometers to the southeast. Once the bulk of the cavalry corps was freed after they had occupied an abandoned town, it would be available to continue the attack.

That attack was planned for the following day, 6 February. Selivanov's corps, in cooperation with elements of 4th Guards Army, would drive on Verbovka and Petropavlovka, seize both villages, and continue advancing towards Valyava. There, his forces would cut the Gorodishche - Korsun road and advance east and seize Gorodishche, with its ammunition and fuel depots. 5th Guards Cavalry Corps would then swing southeast and advance to encircle and destroy *XI.A.K.* To carry out his attack, Selivanov's arrayed 11th Guards Cavalry Division on the right, 12th Guards Cavalry Division on the left, with 63rd Cavalry Division in the second echelon behind it. 11th Division was to make the main effort. Once it had taken Verbovka, Petropavlovka, and Valyava, it would turn to the right and head east for Gorodishche. 12th Division would seize the northern outskirts of Valyava, mop up any remaining resistance, and cut the Gorodishche-Korsun road near the town of Nabokov Khutor.[13] Selivanov's attack would be covered on the right by a supporting attack carried out by 5th and 7th Guards Airborne Divisions of 21st Guards Rifle Corps, part of 4th Guards Army. Their mission would be to roll up the front of Trowitz's *57.Inf.Div.* by attacking to the north via Vyazovok.

The plan looked simple on paper, but took no account of the fact that all three of the corps' divisions had been riding and fighting for over a week and had suffered heavy casualties during their siege of Olshana. The weather and terrain conditions were affecting his forces in the same way they were affecting the Germans. Although the mounted troops could make headway through the mud, the corps' trucks and artillery prime movers were having a harder time of it. Selivanov's plan also did not adequately address the enemy situation - apparently, he thought that the German defenders in that area were at the breaking point. In this, he was completely wrong. Instead of finding a weak and scattered enemy in his path, he encountered a stoutly defended front line. Though thinly held, by 6 February the Germans had finally been able to establish a solid defense line within the entire pocket. To prevent the troops of *389.Inf.Div.* in Verbovka from being encircled, they were withdrawn to the northeast and the new front line was drawn up accordingly.

Selivanov's attack began at 1000 hours that day. 11th Guards Cavalry Division's tanks and cavalrymen were immediately tied down in Petropavlovka by tough German resistance. Nevertheless, the situation created a great deal of concern at *XI.A.K.* headquarters, resulting in Stemmermann's decision to dispatch reserves to the threatened sector. The movement of the reserve battalion, unfortunately, was delayed over an hour when motor transport could not be arranged. Furthermore, the battalion's troops were completely exhausted upon their arrival in Petropavlovka by having to march through the mud. Two Soviet tanks broke into the town of Vyazovok and caused great alarm at *389.Inf.Div.*, until they were knocked out. They tried again a few hours later with three more tanks and an infantry battalion, but they too were driven off after a short battle.

The Soviet pressure against *XI.A.K.* continued throughout the day, with the most serious fighting occurring in Petropavlovka, where Trowitz's Bavarians struggled with Selivanov's Cossacks in house-to-house fighting. Between Petropavlovka and Vyazovok, the Germans were forced to give ground and finally withdrew to another defense line a few hours later several kilometers further to the east. The line had buckled in places, but still held.

While fighting raged in the sector held by *57.* and *389.Inf.Div.*, Hohn's *72.Inf.Div.* on the corps' far right flank did not escape Soviet attention either. At midday, 254th Rifle Division of Soviet 78th Rifle Corps launched a limited probing attack towards the town of Lenina, at the boundary of *72.Inf.Div.* and *389.Inf.Div.* The attack appeared to be aimed at the railway intersection north of the town, but was driven off with relative ease by Rudolf Siegel's regiment. In compliance with an order from divisional headquarters to move his regiment back to the town of Koshmack to serve as corps reserve, Siegel drove his Volkswagen *Schwimmwagen* through the small village of

Troops from 72.Inf.Div. occupying defensive positions near the town of Lenina, early February 1944. (Scanned photo courtesy of 72.Inf.Div. Veteran's Association)

Khlystunovka south of Gorodishche to look for signs of his advance party, led by *Hptm.* Knostmann, but to no avail. After knocking on several doors of peasant *isbas* with no results, Siegel was surprised when a Ukrainian peasant woman finally answered. The ensuing conversation between the German officer and the woman gives some measure of the human impact of the war in the East.

When Siegel asked the woman if there were any German soldiers in the village, the woman, who came to the door with two daughters aged eight and ten years, asked in broken German if he and the other Germans were leaving. When he failed to reply, she fell to her knees, covered her face with her hands, cried and screamed "Oh German, oh German, now comes the *NKVD* (Stalin's secret police)!" Siegel wrote later that he never forgot this scene, so moved had he been by this poor woman's anguish. He surmised that she had probably worked at a German field kitchen in order to feed her children and knew what would happen to her when the Soviets returned.[14] At best, she could hope for a labor camp; at worst, she would be executed by the *NKVD* for aiding and abetting the enemy. But there was nothing that Siegel could do for her - he had a regiment to look after. Thousands of personal tragedies like this one were replayed over and over again throughout this battle, as the civilian population found itself caught between two warring juggernauts.

The fighting in Petropavlovka, Valyava, and Vyazovok continued the following day. The Soviets launched numerous attacks with tanks and infantry against these towns, and their lack of artillery support was plainly evident. Each time a battalion was able to seize a foothold in either town, they were thrown out again by German counterattacks. The artillery, which would have lent the accustomed weight to the Soviet attacks, was stuck in the mud, along with everything else. The after-action report of 5th Guards Cavalry Corps testifies to the stubborn defense of Valyava by *Narwa*, attached to Lieb's neighboring *XXXXII.A.K.* Here, the Estonian battalion's resistance was characterized by the Cossack's commander as "extremely strong."

Only by the end of the following day was 12th Cavalry Division able to take part of the town, after intense street battles against groups of the enemy "stubbornly defending houses and buildings." Actually, they seized the town only after the German defenders had withdrawn, since all of *XI.A.K.* was in the process of moving to a new, shorter defensive line south of Gorodishche. General Stemmermann was still able to exercise enough control over his units to allow such closely timed movements, that time and time again enabled him to order the units to pull out immediately prior to being encircled and destroyed, leaving the Soviets to strike at thin air.

Not all of the withdrawals ordered for 6 and 7 February went according to plan. In addition to having to deal with incessant Soviet attacks, the Germans still had to contend with the atrocious weather and terrain conditions, which had only become worse since the onset of the early thaw 4 February. The roads were so badly rutted and filled with water that a great deal of equipment had to be abandoned. Of all the divisions of *XI.A.K.*, Hohn's *72.Inf.Div.* was affected the most, since it had to withdraw the greatest distance from the old defensive line south of Burty and Lenina to its new positions south of Korsun, where it would become Stemmermann's reserve force.

Rudolf Siegel's account of the conditions encountered by his men are illustrative of what most of the troops of *XI.A.K.* were experiencing when they began their movement to the new defensive line. To his disgust, on the late morning of 7 February, the neighboring regiment to his right, which had still been in position at dawn, had pulled out without informing him. To cover this open flank, he dispatched his antitank platoon and a 2 cm antiaircraft gun. In the meantime, the Soviets had once again attacked the railroad intersection north of Lenina in force, in an attempt to head off his division's withdrawal. The force on Siegel's left holding this critical area, a *Kampfgruppe* from *Gren.Rgt.124* led by *Maj.* Scheerer, was about to crack when Siegel had *Ltn.* Bender with his infantry-gun company direct their full attention to the Soviet force about to overwhelm their neighbor. Once again, the *Bender-Orgel* succeeded in driving the attacking Soviets away.

Meanwhile, *Ltn.* Ohlendorf was reconnoitering a route of withdrawal for the regiment's trucks along the railway bed to Gorodishche, which was virtually impassable due to the log-jam of trucks from his own and other divisions. The entire day he and his men tried to get the trucks out of the mud, but it was impossible to move them. Without four-wheel drive, the under-powered Opel and Mercedes trucks remained stuck in ever-deepening ruts. At dusk, seeing that their retrieval was a hopeless task, Siegel ordered all immobilized trucks to be destroyed. The only things able to get out were antitank guns, infantry guns, and 2 cm antiaircraft guns, pulled either by a team of horses or by half-tracked prime movers.

So far behind schedule had his withdrawal been, that Siegel ordered his regiment to pull out that evening without leaving a rearguard in place. He knew, as did his men, that to leave men behind to delay the Soviets would only have resulted in their needless deaths, and his regiment needed every man. Although *Ltn.* Bender and his company temporarily went astray, the rest of the regiment arrived in their overnight rest area between Khlystunovka and Kratchkovka without incident. The troops were fed by a field kitchen near the division's command post, and were even allowed to sleep a little. Later that evening,

Bender and his men finally staggered in, to the relief of the entire regiment.[15] Left behind were over a dozen vehicles, with their carefully hoarded reserves of ammunition, clothing, and food-stuffs. From now on, the regiment would have to live a hand-to-mouth existence like the others.

The withdrawal to the new defensive line south of Gorodishche, though delayed by the abominable road conditions, went according to plan. By the evening of 7 February, all of *XI.A.K.'s* divisions had closed up and were ready to continue to hold off the Soviets. Many of the withdrawing units, especially *57.Inf.Div.*, were closely pursued by their opponents, who sought any means of achieving a breakthrough into the German rearward positions. Selivanov's Cossack Corps, which had been stymied in Petropavlovka and Valyava that day, was slowed both by the mud and German delaying actions. Most of his units had only been able to register gains of one to one and a half kilometers that day. The following day, 8 February, they were equally unsuccessful and reported many German counterattacks which held them in check. Things began to brighten at dusk, when one of his divisions was able to effect a four to five kilometer penetration along the boundary between *XI.* and *XXXXII.A.K.* southeast of Kvitki. Fortunately, developments outside the pocket finally worked in the German's favor.

Due to the approaching relief forces of Breith's and von Vormann's Panzer corps, Selivanov was ordered by Konev to send 63rd Cavalry Division towards Lysyanka as a reinforcement for the other Soviet forces bracing for the German relief attacks. Selivanov's other two cavalry divisions were to continue their attack across the Gorodishche-Korsun road towards Zavadovka and link up with units from 52nd Army attacking from the north.[16] Hopefully, this would still result in trapping the bulk of *XI.A.K.* in the Gorodishche salient, as well as most of *Wiking*. Selivanov's corps, however, no longer had the offensive punch it had possessed when it broke through the German lines at Kapitanovka nearly two weeks before. With the detachment of 63rd Cavalry Division, the corps' strongest and least worn out, Selivanov had little chance of achieving the decisive breakthrough he had long sought. Nevertheless, his units continued to exert pressure on the Germans as they continued their regroup-

Grenadiers from Korpsabteilung B withdrawing from the northern sector of the pocket.
(Bundesarchiv 277/802/35)

Gunners of Art.Rgt.188, 88.Inf.Div., preparing to fire in support of one of the division's infantry regiments. (Bundesarchiv 277/847/11)

ing, but were unable to prevent the entire *72.Inf.Div.* from being pulled out of line to become the German reserve for a future operation whose success would determine the very survival of all units trapped in the Cherkassy Pocket.

As dramatic as the developments between 1 - 8 February had been for Stemmermann's corps, the situation in Lieb's sector had been no less interesting. In addition to the old sector he had held that ran from Kvitki in the south, to Boguslav in the west, and to Kanev along the Dnieper to the north, on 29 January his corps had the sector held by *Wiking* added to his corps' area of responsibility. This addition, though it increased his combat power mainly through the addition of *Wiking's* armored *Kampfgruppe* with its precious remaining tanks, nearly doubled the amount of frontage his corps now had to defend. This newly-added sector ran from Kanev in the north, along the Dnieper to Losovok (held by the Walloon Brigade), and south to the area east of Orlovets; in all, nearly 80 kilometers. General Gille, the SS division's commander, held the largest sector of any division in the pocket, but was now constantly being forced to detach elements of his division to shore up various parts of *XXXXII.A.K.'s* frontage, especially around Olshana. Nevertheless, Gille remained optimistic that his division was up to the task, though it had yet to be struck with the full force of the Soviet attack. It would not be long in coming.

From the perspective of the corps commander, Lieb's first task was for his corps to hold its positions as long as possible until Breith's relief force coming up from the southwest broke through the ring of encircling Soviets and linked up with Lieb's troops between Medvin and Boguslav. To do this, he would have to constantly shorten his front to free more infantry units needed

to form tactical reserves. These forces would be used to counterattack and close off enemy breakthroughs that would unavoidably occur. Most of all, he had to keep the enemy away from the airfield at Korsun. Should it fall into the hands of Vatutin's or Konev's troops, virtually all resupply for the two encircled corps, except parachute drops, would be cut off and the game would be over quickly.

Lieb had taken a great step towards shortening his line when he had ordered *K.Abt.B* to disengage from its old positions west of Kanev on 29 January and displace to a shorter defensive line to the south along the Rossava River, code-named Operation *Winterreise*. Lieb's second task was to help build the new southern front of the pocket between Steblev and Olshana. His third task was to support the airlift from the airfield at Korsun. While Lieb was able to succeed in the latter two tasks (the southern front had been cobbled together in the nick of time), preventing the collapse of the rest of his long front line would prove to be just as difficult. Despite the addition of *Wiking* to his corps, he still had insufficient forces to hold even this line. With *XI.A.K.* tied down in heavy fighting, Lieb could not expect help from that quarter. Nor could he expect immediate help from the outside, since Breith would not be able to launch his corps' part of the relief operation until 3 or 4 February. It would still take several days more for the troops of *III.Pz.Korps* to effect a linkup near Medvin, if all went as planned. So, from 1 February until 7 or 8 February at the latest, *XXXXII.A.K.* would have to go it alone.

While the addition of *Wiking* and the Walloon Brigade to his order of battle on 29 January greatly strengthened Lieb's corps, his other two divisions were in bad shape. While *K.Abt.B* had as yet suffered relatively few casualties, its regiments and battalions were being parceled out piecemeal throughout the corps sector, making their command, control, and resupply extremely difficult for its acting commander, *Oberst* Fouquet. He now had units, such as Schenk's *Rgt.Gr.110*, fighting in the southern front of the pocket, while other units were fighting in the southwest and northern sectors. The main effort of the corps' fight had shifted to the south between Kvitki and Steblev, so Leib ordered Fouquet to temporarily turn over command of *K.Abt.B* to *Oberst* Wolfgang Bucher and head south to take over the units rapidly assembling near the town of Korsun, the previously mentioned *Sperrverband* Fouquet, to which Ernst Schenk's unit was attached.

Wedged between the two halves of *K.Abt.B* lay the corps' most hardest-hit division, *Gen.Lt. Graf* von Rittberg's *88.Inf.Div.* Although it had somehow maintained a coherent front line, the division had suffered heavy casualties during the initial phase of the Soviet breakthrough. By 1 February, its front actually faced to the south and southwest. With its right flank anchored in the northern outskirts of Boguslav, the division's left flank extended to the east and southeast along the Ross River to the northern outskirts of Steblev, held by Eberhard Heder's *SS-Feld Ausb.Btl.5* from *Wiking*. Along this defense line *Graf* Rittberg's division was able to hold out, though the situation in Boguslav had fluctuated tremendously, as troops from the Soviet 337th Rifle Division and 159th Fortified Region, supported by a few tanks, constantly hurled themselves at the German defensive works from 28 January to 2 February.

Boguslav was critical to the German defensive effort, in that it was situated at the foot of a 219 meter-high bluff that not only commanded all of the approaches into the pocket from the north and northeast, but the river crossings along the Ross River to the south as well. It had to be held at all cost. If it fell into Soviet hands, artillery fire could be directed into the rear area of *88.Inf.Div.* As the Ross River line was strongly held by the Germans (the ice covering the river having melted as well), the division's most exposed position lay to the north and northwest of Boguslav. The unit occupying this critical defensive position was *Sicherungs-Regiment 318* of *213.Sich.Div.* Its line ran from the west, by the village of Missaylovka, to the village of Shupiki, six kilometers north of Boguslav. This regiment, with an additional battalion from the division's *Sich.Rgt.177*, had been attached to von Rittberg's division in early December 1943, while the rest of their division was sent elsewhere. Commanded by *Oberstlt.* Dr. Ernst Bloch, this force had been placed in the most exposed position in the entire sector held by von Rittberg's division. Worn out, this regiment had been withdrawing constantly under enemy pressure since the battle began 26 January.

Dr. Bloch's troops, who were for the most part middle-aged *Landeschutz* (Home Guard) reservists considered unsuited for front-line combat, had so far repelled numerous assaults, often involving exhausting and dangerous hand-to-hand combat. In a report written after the battle, Dr. Bloch wrote that the physical and moral demands on the troops had increased to a critical level and that orders had to be given out by troop leaders three times or more before their men could be roused from their fatigue and apathy. Bloch's men had been forced during the past several days to carry out withdrawals at night, while repelling attacks by the pursuing Soviets during the day.[17] As hard as this constant physical activity was on younger soldiers, it was even more debilitating for the older men of the security regiments.

During this time, Soviet propaganda leaflets began making their appearance, dropped during the night by Red Air Force biplanes, though the effect of such leaflets at this early stage were still negligible. To keep their men going, company and battalion commanders were often forced to take ruthless measures such as corporal punishment or threats of execution to rouse the men. Some men were easily panicked by the mere mention of a Soviet attack, another warning sign of *Kesselpsychose* (Encirclement psychosis), which was becoming more widespread in the other encircled divisions as well.

Besides putting pressure on *88.Inf.Div.* in Boguslav, the commander of 27th Army, General Trofimenko, also began to launch attacks against the rest of the German forces in his assigned sector on 1 February. The night withdrawal by *K.Abt.B* three days before from their old positions west of Kanev to their new ones along the Rossava River had caught the Soviet general by surprise. Trofimenko could not afford to let that happen again, so he began to press the withdrawing German with greater vigor. However, he had to crack the new defense line along the Rossava, while still putting pressure on the defenders of Boguslav and Steblev. The key position of the new German northern defense line was their strongpoint in the town of Mironovka, which lay at the bottom of the plateau which stretched from Mironovka to Korsun, thirty kilometers to the southeast. If the troops from *Div.Gr.332* from *K.Abt.B* could be driven from this town, then Trofimenko would have a clear shot towards the heart of Korsun, along one of the relatively few good roads. Stymied at Boguslav, perhaps 27th Army would have more luck here.

The attack began at 1100 hours on 1 February, when troops from 513th and 493rd Artillery Machine-gun Battalions broke into Mironovka itself as well as the German defensive line south of the town. After several hours of fighting, the troops from *Div.Gr.332* were able to dislodge the attackers and throw them out, though the Red infantry came on again the following morning, also without success. The artillery and machine-gun battalions of the fortified regions were beginning to show their greatest weakness - too few infantrymen. While these units could defend wide frontages, they were particularly unsuited to carrying out sustained offensive operations and lacked sufficient mass to overwhelm the Germans in their foxholes. To the northeast, 206th Rifle Division finally began its attack against *Div.Gr.112's* sector near Sinyavka, north of the bend of the Rossava River held by Hptm. Burgfeld's *Rgt.Gr.258*, as the bulk of *K.Abt.B* began preparations to conduct its withdrawal.

Oberst Viebig, the divisional group's commander, was able to ward off this attack and another one near Sarosava, several kilometers to the southeast, but soon requested that all of his troops be permitted to withdraw to the river's south bank while they still could. Any gains that the Soviets were able to make in this area on 2 February were quickly ironed out by local German counterattacks. So far, the Rossava River line was holding, though Lieb requested and got permission from General Wöhler at *8.Armee* to withdraw to the other side of the river that evening.[18] Once this had been accomplished, Viebig would hand over this shortened sector to von Rittberg's division, while the bulk of *K.Abt.B* would shift to the corps' southern front during 4 to 5 February.

As the rest of *K.Abt.B* withdrew, *Hptm.* Burgfeld and his men conducted a spirited defense along the river bank and launched several counterattacks to keep the Soviets off balance. In a struggle for one nameless village on 2 February, *Gef.* Hans Queitzsch and the remaining 40 men of his company from *Rgt.Gr.258* supported by two assault guns, took their objective without suffering any casualties. On the morning of 3 February, he and the others were ordered by their commander to continue the attack, in order to make the Soviets think that the bulk of *K.Abt.B* was still in its old positions, when in fact most of it had already withdrawn. His *6.Kompanie* was immediately pinned down by heavy enemy defensive fire.

One of Queitzsch's wounded comrades was left laying in the open, screaming for a medic. Despite the entreaties of his sergeant, his training as a *Sanitäter* took over and Queitzsch leapt from cover and ran to his friend through a hail of bullets, but was hit before he could reach the man. Just then, one of the assault guns appeared and suppressed the fire of the Soviets, allowing the Germans to drag Queitzsch and the other man to safety. Soon, Queitzsch and 11 other wounded men were loaded on the deck of one of the assault guns and brought back to a wounded collection point at a *Kholkhoz* (collective farm). There, he was laid on a pile of straw inside a barn until he received rudimentary treatment for his wounds.

The following day, he was brought to the airfield in Korsun to be brought out aboard a Ju-52. After a day's delay due to his evacuation aircraft's mechanical problems, he was finally flown out of the pocket on the night of 7/8 February. Although he was operated on promptly at the field hospital in Uman, his soldiering days were over. Declared unfit due to his severe wounds, Queitzsch was discharged from the *Wehrmacht* in August 1944. He was one of the lucky ones and was able to return to his pre-war civilian occupation, where he sat out the remainder of the war wondering what happened to the rest of his comrades.[19]

However, while the Rossava line was holding, things took a turn for the worse for the Germans holding along the *Rollbahn* south of Mironovka that ran southwest to Boguslav. A renewed attack that afternoon by four Soviet machine-gun battalions supported by 20 tanks reduced the German line between Mironovka and Boguslav to a shambles, forcing troops from *Div.Gr.332* and *88.Inf.Div.* to hastily set up a new line a few kilometers further east. Boguslav had to be given up by that evening, since the danger of encirclement from the north was now too great. *Graf* Rittberg's troops were still able to hold the commanding heights above the town and shell their pursuers with accurate artillery concentrations. After this fighting, the western and northern front of *XXXXII.A.K.* remained stable for several more days, though the fighting along Lieb's southern flank flared up again with a vengeance.

Aware that the Germans were hastily assembling a relief force near Uman, Trofimenko was urged on by Vatutin to finish the job before *1.Pz.Armee* could fight its way through to the pocket. Since Lieb's front had firmed up somewhat in the south-

Gerhard Meyer, *Radio operator of 188.Art.Rgt., at home on leave in Heibronn after escaping from the Cherkassy Pocket. (Photo: Gerhard Meyer)*

west, west and northern flanks, perhaps keeping the pressure on his southern flank might prove to be more promising. Despite the problems the Germans were having in keeping their men's spirits up or in maintaining their supply lines, they were still offering a tough defense, at least from the Soviet perspective. It was not supposed to be this difficult, which perhaps explains why the Soviet after-action report on the battle goes into such detail describing the German's "formidable defensive fortifications," although in reality most of these so-called prepared positions were holes hastily scooped up out of the soggy Ukrainian *Chernozem* that rapidly filled with water.

Surely it was these prepared positions, rather than the men in them, that were responsible for the effective German resistance. For the *Frontovnik*, this battle was not going to be the easy victory that the political officers had said it would be. Despite this lack of decisive success, at a minimum the men of 27th Army could take comfort from the fact that the encircled Germans had been held in check. So far, at least, Trofimenko's men had prevented their enemy from advancing towards the relief force and had even managed to push them further away from their rescuers, who were now still over 32 kilometers away. Hopefully, 6th Tank and 40th Armies would hold them off long enough while 27th Army, 52nd Army, and 4th Guards Army liquidated the Germans in the pocket.

It was still possible for Trofimenko's forces to penetrate the thinly-held German front in the south and perhaps drive towards Korsun, even if the northern approach had been stalled for the moment. This southern route, though, still had not been easy. Trofimenko's troops from 337th Rifle Division had been trying to take Steblev since 28 January, without success, and 180th Rifle Division had been halted at Kvitki as well. Therefore, beginning on 3 February, 27th Army would redouble its efforts to take Steblev, as well as the towns of Shanderovka, Tarashcha, and Selishche. The Germans defending Shanderovka were especially vulnerable, since repeated attacks had reduced the area held by *Div.Gr.323* to a perilously narrow salient connected to Steblev by a single road that had become increasingly vulnerable to being cut. Although Trofimenko's troops from 180th Rifle Division had been unable to penetrate the German defensive lines south of Kvitki, they had been able to keep the Germans from taking the town, as testified previously by Ernst Schenk.

To reinforce 180th Rifle Division, 337th Rifle Division was ordered by Trofimenko to shift from its positions south of Boguslav on 3 February, hand its sector over to newly-arrived 54th Fortified Region, and march to its new assembly area south of Selishche. There, it would conduct a coordinated attack alongside the 180th later that day and drive into the German defenses there, overwhelm them, and march on Korsun from the south, a mere ten kilometers away. The attack would be supported by a few tanks from an independent tank brigade, additional *GHQ* artillery assets, and *Katyusha* batteries. They would be supported by aircraft from *Lt.Gen.* Krassowski's 2nd Air Army, weather permitting. Whether the Germans had constructed prepared defensive positions or not, the attack would not be easy to pull off. In addition to the Germans, the troops of 27th Army would also have to contend with rugged terrain that gave the advantage to the defenders.

The weather had also turned for the worse by 3 February, with heavy fog and thawing temperatures limiting visibility and mobility. Furthermore, the area between Steblev and Kvitki was cut through with many *Balki*, deep ravines that hid numerous enemy artillery batteries, mortars, and command posts. Weather permitting, the Germans would have excellent observation and fields of fire. The barren plateaus which in summer were carpeted with grain and sunflowers would prove to be fertile ground for the hated 8.1cm mortar and MG 42 machine-gun, nicknamed the "Hitler's Saw" by the Soviets. The Germans had hastily converted the many towns and villages in the area into strong points or *Igel* (hedgehog positions), which, though weakly held, could still hold their own against an attacker many times their strength. Here, the men of *K.Abt.B*, *Div.Gr.323*, and *Wiking* would give a good account of themselves.

A radio interception platoon of *Wiking* was able to receive and translate a Soviet signal that provide some measure of just how frustrated some of their commanders had become with the stubborn German defense. At Kvitki, the 337th Rifle Division hurled itself again and again against the troops from *K.Abt.B* holding the northern end of the town as well as the heights above it. One Soviet command post, probably that of a regimental or division commander, was overheard telling a subordinate "I have told you, Kvitki is ours for the taking, but there are still Germans in it." His subordinate replied, "We have had heavy casualties, hardly any food, and then there's the mud…my men can't go any farther!" The commander's response, barely concealing the rage which he probably felt, was "What? they can't do it? Then send a few to the happy hunting ground, so the others will know that

Gefreiter Hans Queitzsch, *shown here as a recruit was wounded after saving the life of another soldier wounded near the Rossava River and flown out of the Kessel. (Photo courtesy of Hans Queitzsch)*

we mean business!"[20] Whether or not his subordinate carried out the threat is unknown. Shooting men out of hand was not unknown in the Red Army of Workers and Peasants, if such was required to spur the men on. If patriotic zeal was not sufficient, then outright fear of their own officers would suffice to spur them to victory. Kvitki was attacked repeatedly, with "fanatical vigor," according to one German eyewitness. Nevertheless, the attacks failed, leaving hundreds of dead and wounded Soviet and German soldiers lying in the town of Kvitki and upon the surrounding hillsides.

The Soviet attack against Lieb's southern front raged from 3 to 6 February, when Shanderovka was finally evacuated by the troops of *Hptm.* Lissl's *I./Rgt.Gr.591* of *Div.Gr.323*. During the bitter fighting which ensued, the men of 180th and 337th Rifle Divisions made numerous penetrations of the German positions, none of them the decisive one for which Trofimenko had long sought after. Many of these breakthroughs were quickly wiped out by German counterattacks. Other key positions or villages that could not be retaken were compensated for by a quick readjustment of the front line a few kilometers to the rear. Despite constant pressure, the German line buckled in many places, but held steady. The Soviet infantry flung themselves repeatedly against the entrenched Germans and gained a village here, a few kilometers of frontage there.

Losses were heavy on both sides. General Lieb, in a diary entry on 4 February, mentioned that daily losses in both corps were still running at an average of 300 men, which amounted to one infantry battalion per day. Ammunition for his corps, particularly for the artillery, was also beginning to run short, with a daily expenditure of 200 tons. To continue to hold out, Lieb sent a request to *8.Armee* for an additional 120 tons of ammunition per day plus 2,000 reinforcements.[21] His request for men was denied, but the Luftwaffe redoubled its efforts to fly in or airdrop the badly needed shells.

The Soviet after-action report, summarized in the *Sbornik* for the Korsun-Shevchenkovsky Operation, mentions that on 5 February, Trofimenko's 27th Army "isolated the encircled German forces into separate groups and narrowed the ring of encirclement."[22] While the ring of encirclement was indeed narrowed (primarily due to a combination of measures taken by the Germans to conserve forces and develop greater defensive densities throughout the pocket, as well as Soviet pressure), none of the encircled German forces were isolated into separate groups, except for the occasional squad or a platoon. In fact, the

Germans constantly thwarted any Soviet effort to cut off significant bodies of troops. Despite their fatigue, hunger, and shortage of supplies, the troops of *XI.* and *XXXXII.A.K.* hung grimly on, fighting a series of nameless, bitter battles and skirmishes around isolated hamlets or hilltops known only by their elevation number on a map, such as Hill 205, or by other distinguishing features, such as "Windmill Hill."

One such nameless skirmish took place along *XXXXII.Armeekorps'* southern front on 6 February near the town of Glushki, situated at that time on the corps' far left flank, two kilometers north of the key town of Valyava. *Obergef.* Gerhard Mayer, a signalman from *Art.Rgt.188* of *88.Inf.Div.*, had been ordered to take his signal section to this "God-forsaken village" to relieve another signal squad from another division and establish communications with an infantry company holding the village in order to provide them artillery support. After a day's march through the mud from their old billet near Yablonovka, Mayer and his men arrived "exhausted near to death." Upon arrival, they discovered that the village was held by a force of 12 to 15 grenadiers, who had no idea where the rest of their company was.

During a discussion with a departing radioman, Mayer was told that the old squad had a man injured when he had tried to light a stove in one of the *isbas*. The stove, it seemed, was packed with explosives, which detonated when a fire was lit inside it. Mayer thought the man was lucky to have only lost a hand; at least he was out of the fighting. Since the village's civilian inhabitants had been evacuated a few days before, Mayer was able to quickly find a suitable *isba* to billet his squad, located near the bridge that spanned a creek on the northern edge of the village that ran through a deep ravine.

While searching the *isba* and the outlying buildings for explosives or booby traps, he and his men were delighted to find a "rather stately sow" in a shack behind the house. The Germans quickly slaughtered the pig, cutting off the best pieces and literally roasting them over the oven "with skin and bristles still attached." While they were enjoying their best meal in over a week, Mayer and his men were surprised when a flurry of rifle shots and grenade bursts rent the air. Sticking his head out of the *isba* door, Mayer saw neither hide nor hair of the enemy, so he resumed his roast pork dinner, unconcerned with what was going on outside. He nevertheless posted a sentry outside their shack, feeling that it was better to be safe than sorry.

The village remained quiet for the rest of the afternoon. Later that day, while Mayer was napping atop the warm stove, he was shaken rudely awake by the sentry. The young man, obviously shaken, stammered that he had just heard a loud "Urrah!," the battle cry of attacking Soviet infantry. Now fully awake, Mayer realized that the whole village of Glushki was alive with the sounds of battle - rifle fire, the rattle of machine-guns, and grenade bursts. Men were yelling and shouting commands. As he exited the shack, men from the infantry squad supposedly holding the town ran past him, fleeing to the north. Mayer ordered the rest of his men to quickly load the *Panje* wagon they had used to carry their equipment and prepare their getaway, while he and the sentry held off the approaching

Oberstleutnant Christian Sonntag, *Commander,Gren.Rgt.248 88.Inf.Div. (Photo courtesy of Anderas Schwarz and 88.Inf.Div. Veteran's Association)*

Soviets with their rifles.

Expecting the worse, Mayer was surprised to see a German officer two hundred meters away rallying the panicked infantry, collecting them for a counterattack to retake the village. Fearing that he and his men would be caught up in a *Himmelfahrts-Kommando* (a "Forlorn Hope" or suicide squad), Mayer decided to take a chance and approached the nearest *Lamettaträger* ("tinsel wearer," slang for a high-ranking German officer) and notified him that he had established radio communications with his artillery regiment and could call for fire to support the infantry, if the officer ordered him to do so.

The officer turned out to be *Oberstlt.* Christian Sonntag, commander of *Gren.Rgt.248* from Mayer's own division. Drawing encouragement from the news, Sonntag ordered Mayer to put a call through immediately for artillery support. Answering the request was *Oblt.* Hans Menedetter, the regimental adjutant, who Mayer knew well. Quickly relaying Sonntag's target information, Mayer was relieved when a few moments later the first shells fell into the village, now occupied by the Soviets. As the firing intensified, Sonntag launched the counterattack with his own *Kampfgruppe* as well as the men he had intercepted trying to leave the town. After a short fight, the Soviets were forcibly ejected from the town and the Germans regained possession. Dead Soviet infantry and abandoned equipment littered the streets of the village.

To his disappointment, Mayer was ordered to move back into his old *isba* and remain in support of Sonntag's unit, finally being allowed to leave several days later. Upon his return to his regiment, Mayer was congratulated by Menedetter for his quick thinking and was told that he had saved many lives by his offer to provide artillery support. Mayer, somewhat sarcastically, recalled years later that he had only been trying to save his own skin. Had he not quickly spoken up to support the infantry attack, he would have quickly found himself and his men "running around like a bunch of idiots, trying to act like infantry."[23]

What had happened in Glushki was typical. Thanks to hundreds of similar actions like Mayer's, the pocket's defensive lines held. At the last minute, a few men rounded up by a resolute officer or *Feldwebel* were able to work wonders, plugging gaps in the line or retaking villages whose possession was critical to the continued survival of the pocket. The names of most of these men will never be known, nor the names of the battles they fought. But their efforts continued to buy time so that Generals Lieb and Stemmermann could hurriedly piece together the front line for a few more days, until the relief forces of Breith and von Vormann arrived.

And so it went. Nameless battles, more names added to the already long casualty rolls. On 3 February, five T-34s

SS-Obersturmführer Heinz Debus, *Acting commander, SS-Pz.Aufkl.Abt.5. He led the Wiking's spearhead during the breakout (seen here after being awarded the Knight's Cross he earned for his role in the battle).*
(Bundesarchiv 81/14/20A)

Wiking. In the Soviet's path lay the 10.*Batterie* from a battalion commanded by *Oberstlt*. Landerer of *Art.Rgt.86*, *Div.Gr.112*, which had remained behind to support the movement of *88.Inf.Div*. into the Masslovka area. Despite engaging the approaching T-34s with direct fire from every piece, the German howitzer crews were unable to score a single hit on any of them and were quickly overrun, their crews scattered, horses machine-gunned in their traces. Although the tanks were later destroyed, Lieb remarked laconically in his diary the following day that "Evidently we have too few experienced gunners."[24]

Despite these and other difficulties, the movement of the bulk of *K.Abt.B* to its new positions along the southern front was completed by the evening of 5 February. Not without difficulty, however, since the combination of Soviet pressure, clogged roads, and incessant enemy air attacks made a movement that should have taken an afternoon to carry out last three entire days instead. Increasingly, there was little that the troops of the encircled corps could do about the increasingly effective attacks by the Red Air Force. Sometimes, though, the *Flak* gunners got lucky - on 3 February alone, gunners from *Wiking*, *88.Inf.Div*., and *K.Abt.B* shot down two *Sturmoviks* and a Yak-9. Not much in real terms, but it did boost the German morale to see Red aircraft go down for a change.

Lieb's greatest concern from 4 to 7 February lay not so much in holding his southern front, but in establishing and maintaining contact with Stemmermann's Corps on Lieb's far left flank. For the determined attack by Selivanov's 5th Guards Cavalry Corps was not only threatening *XI.A.K.'s* rear near Gorodishche, but it threatened to permanently severe contact between the two corps. So, while *XI.A.K*. fought its own desperate battles between Valyava and Petropavlovka from 4-7 February, *XXXXII.A.K*. was doing the same along the line Tarasha - Selishche - Kvitki - Glushki. Many of these towns and villages changed hands several times, such as Kvitki, which was finally given up by the Germans on 5 February after *Katyushas* were brought up to pound the defenders, leaving the village in ruins. After one battle in the hamlet of Shirovka, troops of *K.Abt.B* counted 79 dead Soviet soldiers, though the number of German casualties was not recorded.[25] Neither were the defenders of Steblev ignored, either. Eberhard Heder and his men from *SS-Feld Ausb.Btl.5* were given no time to rest on their laurels after their successful defense of the previous week. During the evening of 5 February, they were attacked by two Soviet infantry battalions supported by tanks. This attack was driven off, but reminded the German defenders that they had not been forgotten by the First Ukrainian *Front*.

Finally, with great difficulty, Lieb's leftmost unit, the Narwa Battalion, was able to link up with *57.Inf.Div*. on the evening of 5 February atop Hill 228.4, one kilometer northwest of Petropavlovka.[26] For the first time since the battle began, a continuous defensive line around the pocket had been established. The cost in blood and materiel had been high. During the past five days of fighting, *XXXXII.A.K*. alone had lost 750 men. Again and again, Soviet armies penetrated the German line in dozens of places. Radio messages from both corps to *8.Armee* headquarters testify to the almost constant nature of these breakthroughs, but none of these turned out to be major in

were destroyed by troops of *K.Abt.B* in the southern village of Turkenzy after their accompanying infantry were driven off. Along the northern rim of the corps' front, 11 Soviet tanks and assault guns harried the withdrawal of Oberst Viebig's men east of Mironovka that same afternoon, as they handed over their sector to troops of *88.Inf.Div*. according to the plan drawn up by General Lieb. Most of these were destroyed, though not before they had flattened several fighting positions, crushing their inhabitants. Later that evening, eight tanks and assault guns were destroyed in the south near Selishche by troops from *K.Abt.B*.

Soviet T-34s seemed to be attacking everywhere, but squads of determined *Panzerknacker* (tank busters) and anti-tank gunners were somehow occasionally able to stop the attacks. That same day, seven Soviet tanks broke through German defenses near Martinovka, where *88.Inf.Div*. had just occupied its new defensive positions adjacent to the left flank of

scope. At the last minute, it seemed, the Germans were able to assemble enough men, often only a handful, to contain or eliminate a penetration.

Sunday, 6 February, passed almost uneventfully for *XXXXII.A.K.*, as both sides seemed to be catching their breath after nearly two weeks of uninterrupted fighting. By that point, most of the Soviet's attention seems to have been occupied by both the attempt to cut off the salient at Gorodishche and by the need to stop the developing German relief attempt from the southwest. The fighting that did take place that day in *XI.A.K.* sector was chiefly limited to the town of Valyava, where the Estonian battalion was holding fast against Selivanov's Cossacks. The village was critical to the successful defense of the pocket's entire southern front, as well as the fact that the inner flanks of both corps joined at the town's southeastern outskirts. Though thrown out of most of the village that morning, the Estonian volunteers were able to retake most of the town the following day, after Köller's *Kampfgruppe* and another battlegroup from *72.Inf.Div.* lent them sorely needed support.

While most of Lieb's corps was fighting a series of pitched battles to the north, west, and south, the rest of *Wiking* and the attached Walloon Brigade, holding the northeastern and eastern right flank of *XXXXII.A.K.*, seemed to be waging their own private war against the divisions of the Soviet 52nd Army. Although the first week and a half since the encirclement had proven to be relatively quiet for most the SS men along the Dnieper and Olshanka River lines, fighting had resumed with a vengeance by 2 February.

While the men of Köller's armored battlegroup, Heder's battalion, and the Estonians had been in constant combat, most of *Wiking's* remaining combat elements - primarily *Germania* and *Westland* - had been involved mainly in minor patrol activity or in intercepting small local Soviet probing attacks along the Dnieper and Olshanka River defense lines. General Gille, at his headquarters in Gorodishche, was determined to hold his ground - after all, the *Führer* himself had declared that holding this position was vital for the conduct of future operations, and as a loyal SS man, it was his duty to carry out this comand. So, his men reinforced their bunkers

and waited for General Konstantin Korotayev and his 52nd Army to make the first move.

On 2 February, 206th Rifle Division finally realized that *Wiking's* defense line along its left flank along the Dnieper between Mikhaylovka, where it tied in with the right flank of *K.Abt.B's* and Kreshchatik, was patrolled by nothing but a few armored cars from *Wiking's* armored reconnaissance battalion and could be broken through with ease. Quickly punching through the flimsy German defenses, the troops of 206th Rifle Division raced into the left rear flank of Gille's division. To keep from being overwhelmed, Gille ordered the reconnaissance battalion, under the temporary command of *Ostuf.* Heinz Debus, to withdraw to a new position starting at 2300 hours while remaining in contact with its neighbor to the west.

With this movement, the Dnieper position was no longer tenable and the troops from the Walloon Brigade holding the rest of the northern sector were now vulnerable to being cut off from the rest of *Wiking*. A withdrawal from this exposed sector was ordered to begin the following day, 3 February, to a new position along the line along the Olshanka River running from Baybuzy in the east to Popovka in the west, where Gille's SS troops would tie in with the troops of *K.Abt.B*, who would also be carrying out a phased withdrawal before handing over their sector to *Graf* Rittberg's *88.Inf.Div.* Without fanfare, the last German defensive positions along the Dnieper were given up.

This movement was carried out from 3 to 4 February, shortening the northern front of the pocket considerably. While the movements of various formations on the *8.Armee's* situation map for this time appear to be neat and orderly, things on the ground were otherwise. The unit most affected by this planned withdrawal, Lippert's Walloon Brigade, was given only one day to prepare this major operation. While the Walloons had evacuated their exposed positions around Lozovok the previous day, they would now have to withdraw over 20 kilometers on roads that had turned into quagmires. Leon Degrelle wrote that "Orders to evacuate Lozovok and the last sector of the right bank to the east of the pocket hadn't been given until the general situation had considerably worsened."[27]

A patrol from the Walloon Brigade moving out through newly-fallen snow,(note the backpack radio carried by the last man). (Photo courtesy of Fernand Kaisergruber)

A MG-34 emplacement of the Walloon Brigade near Moshny. (Photo courtesy of Fernand Kaisergruber)

A Member of the Walloon Brigade at a wintery outpost.
(Photo courtesy of Fernand Kaisergruber)

gone from Baybuzy for barely ten minutes, and already the partisans had slaughtered all of the Ukrainians who had served in the German auxiliary formations."[29] In fact, so close were their pursuers on their heels that in some instances Soviet units were often observed entering a village at the instant the Germans or Belgians were giving it up. Degrelle himself was almost captured in such a situation, when he and his driver became lost after taking a wrong turn. As his Volkswagen passed through a small village, the inhabitants, thinking that the Red Army had come back, hid in their houses and hedges and watched the two Walloons pass through in complete silence, making an eerie impression upon the Belgian Rexist leader.

After several narrow escapes, Degrelle was able to make it back to the safety of his own lines, but he admitted to have been apprehensive about being captured. Not only was Degrelle concerned about his own fate, so was Adolf Hitler. On at least one occasion, he had the *OKH* officer of the day radio an inquiry to *8. Armee* Headquarters in order to determine Degrelle's whereabouts.[30] Apparently, foreign broadcast had made statements to the effect that the Belgian Rexist Party leader had been captured by the Soviets. Of course, this was a deliberate falsehood, but Hitler was truly concerned about Degrelle. His feelings about him arose not only out of his mere presence on the Eastern *Front* being a propaganda boon for the Third Reich's claim to be "fighting for Europe's freedom" in the East, but because Hitler apparently admired the young man as well.

According to one source, Hitler once remarked that if he had a son, he would have liked him to be like Leon Degrelle, since he embodied the type of idealism and faith in a new, national socialist Europe that many of the other European countries lacked in the fifth year of the war.[31] General Lieb had his own opinion of the Walloon Brigade, though not nearly as favorable as Hitler's. In a diary entry for 9 February, Lieb wrote that while he thought that Degrelle and his men were likable fellows, they were "apparently too soft for this business."[32]

As the Walloons occupied their defensive positions stretching from Staroselye along the high ground above the Olshanka River's westward course towards Derenkovets, Degrelle encountered further instances of the war's effect upon the innocent civilian occupants of the area. As he led a group of Walloons to their new positions on the evening of 4 February,

While the Walloons could have withdrawn virtually uncontested had they pulled out as late as 1 February, by 3 February their movements would be disputed, as both the Red Army and partisans operating from the Irdyn Forests, harried them along the entire route back to their new positions along the western course of the Olshanka. The brigade, which had arrived in Russia the previous November with 2,000 men, now had to defend a line that stretched nearly thirty kilometers from the outskirts of Baybuzy to Derenkovets with about 1,200 men. Since the brigade had only three companies of infantry with a total of approximately 300 riflemen, this worked out on the ground to be roughly ten men to defend each kilometer of front.[28] The brigade still had its artillery and heavy weapons, but the individual Walloon in his water-filled foxhole must have felt very alone and outnumbered indeed.

Baybuzy, which the Walloons had occupied since November 1943, was given up on the night of 3/4 February when the Brigade withdrew to a better defensive line a few kilometers south near the large town of Staroselye. When an artilleryman drove back to the town to search for some equipment that had been left behind, he discovered that the battery's *Hiwis*, who had volunteered to guard the town until the evacuation was complete, lay dead, sprawled face-first in the mud, still wearing their white armbands on their right arms marked *Deutsche Wehrmacht*. Degrelle wrote that "Our soldiers had been

Near Baybusy, members of the Walloon brigade use a Ukrainian Panje sled to move supplies through the slush and mud. (Photo courtesy of Fernand Kaisergruber)

Degrelle looked up at the ridge line near Derenkovets and saw that every village along the height was aflame, the result of Soviet air attack and artillery fire. Even from a distance of several hundred meters, he could see "hundreds of women pulling children along or carrying pigs in their arms" as they tried to stay ahead of their advancing countrymen. Their shrill cries for help contributed to what Degrelle described as an "atmosphere of madness," as he observed the peasants' crying, pleading, and stamping their feet to keep warm.

Even though German rule had brought misery and suffering to the people of the Ukraine, it was still preferable to falling back under the control of Stalin. Thousands of fleeing refugees made the movement of the encircled German forces even more difficult, as both groups tried to use the same clogged roads at the same time. The German *Feldgendarmerie* (military police) had their hands full sorting out the mess and exercised rigid control at key road intersections. The so-called *Kettenhünde* (" Chained Dogs," a reference to the gorgets worn by German military police) seldom hesitated to use force to keep things moving. By all accounts, despite the nightmare tableau that existed along the roads in the pocket, the German penchant for order seemed to have ruled the day, until the very end of the battle.

Once the Walloon Brigade had occupied its new positions along the Olshanka facing north, the sector remained stabilized for the next five days. Although the Walloons were attacked along this line numerous times by elements of 73rd Rifle Corps, they held firm. The hastily dug trenches, dotted with firing emplacement, had been dug by Ukrainian civilians impressed into German service the week before. They had been dug so deep that Walloons had to erect firing steps to see over the top of them. Not only that, they rapidly filled with water. Since they had not been reinforced by fascines or other engineer materials to shore them up, they often caved in upon their defenders. To Degrelle, these trenches afforded laughable protection. "Defended here and there by a handful of Walloons who were hopelessly isolated amid the drizzle and the darkness. To the left and right of every post stretched a kilometer's gap."[33] Due to the 30 kilometer width of the defense line, the Brigade no longer had enough telephone line to wire in all of its companies with Lippert's headquarters, leading to a sense of isolation. It also delayed the bringing up of reinforcements and mortar or artillery support, since the individual

companies now had to rely on couriers to pass information between their positions and Brigade headquarters.

The Soviet infantrymen from 294th Rifle Division, supported by a few guns (they, like the Walloons, were also having trouble bringing up artillery) launched numerous attacks against the Walloons from 5 to 9 February. Each time they were thrown back, though the Walloons paid a price in blood for their success. The fights centered around key terrain or villages, and often deteriorated into what Leon Degrelle called "Indian fights," with individual soldiers seeking out and killing each other. On one such occasion near the village of Staroselye, Degrelle himself was wounded in the finger while trading shots with a Soviet sniper. A young 16-year old volunteer standing next to him was shot in the mouth, dying on the spot.

Unable to press his attack forward, Degrelle requested tank support, which arrived a few hours later in the form of two tanks from Köller's armored battlegroup. When the Walloon counterattack finally broke through and relieved the platoon holding a knoll above the town, Degrelle and his men were not surprised to see that the bodies of other Walloons that had fallen into the hands of the enemy had been stripped of their clothes and mutilated.[34] Such indignities against the dead were common on the Eastern Front, though even hardened veterans like Degrelle were still shocked and angered by it.

The fighting had begun to wear on his men as well, who were slowly realizing that their situation was becoming hopeless. According to Degrelle, who commented after this attack:

> We had taken quite a haul of machine guns, but our victory left us skeptical. What did we have more than yesterday? Nothing. In fact, we had lost a number of our comrades. Killing the Soviets didn't do any good. They multiplied like wood lice, kept coming back endlessly, ten times, twenty times as numerous as we.[35]

In the distance, Degrelle could see incessant air attacks being carried out by the Red Air Force at the columns from *Wiking, 72.*, and *57.Inf.Div.* withdrawing along the Gorodishche-Korsun railway bed. The withdrawal's progress could be judge by the

The village of Staroselye, occupied by troops from the Wiking Division and Walloon Brigade, aflame after a Soviet attack. (Jarolin-Bundesarchiv 79/59/20)

Starting to show signs of strain, five members of the Walloon Brigade pose for pictures near Staroselye. (Photo courtesy of Fernand Kaisergruber)

SS-Untersturmführer Leon Gillis, *Walloon Brigade, shown here carrying an MP-44 in a trench west of Beloserye, early February 1944. (Photo courtesy of Fernand Kaisergruber)*

columns of smoke marking burning trucks and other vehicles. In addition to the omnipresent *Sturmoviks* and Yak-9s, the thaw which had begun to set in by 3 February was beginning to make its presence felt as well. Besides making the lives of the Germans and Belgians miserable, it also forced them to increasingly abandon guns and vehicles that had become mired so completely that not even the giant 18-ton Demag half-track recovery vehicles could not pull them out.

While the men of Lippert's Walloon Brigade fought against hopeless odds, the fighting in *Wiking's* sector had intensified as well. Amazingly, most of Gille's defensive sector had been quiet for nearly two weeks. Except for the occasional Soviet patrol or probing attack, the men of *Wiking* had had it relatively easy, while heavy fighting had raged on both their far left and far right flanks. The Soviet records offer no explanation as to why they had left Gille's division alone. In fact, it would have made more tactical sense to have attacked it with sufficient forces to pin it down and prevent it from sending mobile elements to help badly-threatened divisions elsewhere. *Wiking's* front began to awaken on Saturday, 5 February, when Fritz Ehrath's *Germania*, holding the division's right flank, was attacked by elements of 254th Rifle Division. The attack was driven off and, just as important, contact was maintained with

Wiking's right-hand neighbor, *Gren.Rgt.266*.

The Soviets renewed their attack against *Wiking* in earnest on 7 February, timed to coincide with the general withdrawal of *XI.A.K.* to a shorter defense line south of Gorodishche. That day, elements of the Soviet 73rd Rifle Corps launched attacks against *Wiking's* far left flank at Popovka, held by Heinz Debus' *SS-Pz.Aufkl.Abt.5*, the Walloons holding Staroselye, and *Germania*. *Westland*, wedged between the Walloons and Ehrath's troops, reported heavy shelling and reconnaissance activity. All of these positions held, though Debus and his men were temporarily thrown out of Popovka, but were able to retake it in a counterattack late that day. To conform to the withdrawal of *72.Inf.Div.*, *Wiking's* right flank regiment had to fall back step-by-step to the new defensive line southeast of Gorodishche. Though Ehrath's SS men had been able to keep their pursuers at bay, their biggest obstacle turned out to be not Soviet assaults, but the withdrawals routes, which, like everywhere else in the pocket, had become rivers of mud.

Gille's chief concern, from his division headquarters in Gorodishche, was whether or not Lippert's Walloon Brigade could hold its positions. If they caved in, there would be nothing to stop Koroteyev's troops from slicing the pocket in two. To help them somewhat, Gille had already sent two of Köller's tanks to Starolselye to provide Lippert and his men support. He could send no more, since the tank battalion was needed everywhere. Both corps commanders were fighting for ownership of Köller's precious few remaining tanks. What else could Gille do? Even an optimist like he must have begun to have doubts, though his thoughts on the matter are unrecorded.*

Should the Soviets break through and head southeast, they could possibly link up with the attack being launched by Selivanov's 5th Guards Cavalry Corps attacking in the opposite direction from Olshana, thus cutting the pocket in two and isolating *Wiking* and the bulk of *XI.A.K.* Because of this danger, General Wöhler on the evening of 7 February gave tactical control of *Wiking* back to Stemmermann, against Lieb's protest. Though Lieb was unhappy with this decision, the realignment decreased the size of the sector each corps had to defend and would make command and control easier. Stemmermann's sector had shrunk so much since 24 January, that by 7 February, it consisted solely of a minute 20-kilometer long portion of the pocket's total front, while Lieb held the remaining 130 kilometers, a fact which Lieb proudly trumpeted in a daily situation report to *8.Armee*.

From 29 January, the pocket, which had at first resembled the continent of Africa in shape and approximated Belgium in size, had shrunken to a peanut-shaped form the size of the Duchy of Luxembourg. Oriented along a southeast-northwest axis, with the major town of Gorodishche laying in the center of the southeastern pole and Korsun laying in the center in the northwestern pole, the pocket's greatest danger

---

* Gille had kept a personal diary. Its current whereabouts are unknown, since at the war's end it was taken from him by an American soldier when Gille handed over his command to troops of General George S. Patton's Third Army in Austria. While the size of the pocket had indeed shrunk, it's shorter perimeter did at least allow the Germans to build up greater troop densities in the new defensive positions and form additional reserves.

lay in the possibility of being cut in two by the converging Soviet thrust of both 27th and 52nd Armies.

But the pocket had started to "wander." While the encircled Germans had been able to prevent the Soviets from splitting the pocket into individual pieces, they had been unable to prevent their enemy from slowly pushing them away from the approaching relief forces. Another factor that both Lieb and Stemmermann had to worry about were the thousands of wounded men that had collected in the buildings and sheds of Korsun, awaiting their turn to be flown out to safety.

By 7 February, ammunition and fuel were already tightly rationed, and food was beginning to run short. Men were now starting to rummage the bodies of slain Soviet soldiers in hope of turning up a chunk of bread or a handful of *Samishke* (roasted sunflower seeds). The weather had turned against the Germans as well. Rapid movement of reserve forces and supplies, a key advantage supposedly offered by possessing interior lines, was an advantage in name only, as the mud limited all movement of men and logistical support to a crawl. Fatigue and exhaustion were becoming commonplace, and cases of *Kesselpsychose*, the strange type of apathy twinned with unreasoning panic, were continuing to be reported. Certainly, Generals Lieb and Stemmermann both believed the relief attempt had to make it into the pocket soon, no later than 10 or 11 February, or there wouldn't be anything left to rescue.

Neither were the Soviets completely happy. They had counted on quickly destroying the forces in the pocket. While they had squeezed the pocket, it had not cracked. 4th Guards, 27th and 52nd Armies had all suffered thousands of casualties. Hundreds of tanks had been lost to the grimly determined Germans. The Red Air Force, although increasingly effective, had still been unable to shut down the German airlift. The mere appearance by Erich Hartmann and other pilots from his *Jagdgeschwader* would often be enough to scatter the swarms of *Yaks* and *Sturmoviks* that plagued the Germans, lifting the spirits of the miserable *Landser* in his fighting position or the harried *Panje* wagon driver stuck in a muddy traffic jam.

What concerned Zhukov, Vatutin and Konev even more were the approaching German relief forces, which had begun their attempt to fight their way through the Soviet's outer defensive ring and link up with both *XI.* and *XXXXII.A.K.* It must have appeared to the Soviet commanders that the entrapped Germans were not going anywhere for the moment and seemed to be content to await their rescue. This would leave the men of First and Second Ukrainian *Fronts* to focus their full attention on thwarting Breith's and von Vormann's Panzer corps, while simultaneously keeping the pressure on Lieb and Stemmermann.

Surely, they must have thought, echoing the commanders of the encircled German units, the defenders cannot possibly hold out much longer - only a few more days at the most. Once the relief attempt was smashed, the entrapped "Hitlerites" would have no choice but to surrender. But surrendering was the last thought on the minds of Field Marshal von Manstein and his commanders. They would fight with every tank, every gun, and every man at their disposal, no matter what the Soviets threw in their path.

End Notes

[1] *8.Armee* KTB, entry dated 1145 hours 2 February 1944, p. 2.

[2] DA Pam 20-234, p. 21.

[3] Siegel, p. 10.

[4] *8.Armee* KTB, entry dated 1855 hours 1 February 1944, p. 6.

[5] Commander, *XI.A.K.* to Chief of Staff, *8.Armee,* dated 1740 hours, 1 February 1944.

[6] *8.Armee* KTB, entry dated 2155 hours 1 February 1944, p. 7.

[7] Letter from Hans Gaertig, Homburg, Germany to author, 14 May 1997. Original in author's possession, p. 1.

[8] *8.Armee* KTB, entry dated 2030 hours, 2 February 1944, p. 6.

[9] *XI.A.K. 1a radio message to 8.Armee*, 1140 hours 5 February 1944.

[10] Siegel, pp. 10-11.

[11] *8.Armee* KTB, entry dated 1120 hours 3 February 1944, p. 4.

[12] Gaertig letter, p. 2.

[13] "Combat Operations of 5th Guards Don Red Army Cavalry Corps in the Korsun-Shevchenkovskii Operation," *The Journal of Slavic Military Studies.* (London: Frank Cass and Company, June 1994), p. 347-348.

[14] Siegel, p. 11.

[15] Ibid.

[16] "Combat Operations of 5th Guards Don Red Army Cavalry Corps," p. 348.

[17] Adjutant, *Sicherung Regiment 318, Sicherungs-Division 213. Den Einsatz des Sicherung Regiments 318 von Sommer 1943 bis Sommer 1944*, p.5.

[18] *8.Armee* KTB, Entry dated 1915 hours, 2 February 1944.

[19] Queitzsch letter, pp. 6-7.

[20] Fritz Kathagen, *Chronik der 2./SS Panzer Nachrichten Abteilung 5*, 1940-1945. (Germany: Privately Published manuscript, 1983), p. 85.

[21] Lieb quoted in DA Pam 20-234, p. 21.

[22] *Sbornik*, p. 318.

[23] Mayer, pp. 131-133.

[24] Lieb in DA Pam 20-234, p. 21.

[25] *XXXXII.A.K.* radio message to *8.Armee* dated 1715 hours 5 February 1944.

[26] *XXXXII.A.K.* radio message to *8.Armee* dated 2150 hours 5 February 1944.

[27] Degrelle, p. 170.

[28] Ibid, p. 175.

[29] Ibid, p. 173.

[30] *8.Armee* KTB Entry dated 0145 hours 10 February 1944, p. 1.

[31] Andrew Mollo, *A Pictorial History of the SS, 1923-1945.* (New York: Stein and Day, 1977), p. 156.

[32] Lieb diary quoted in DAPam 20-234, p. 22.

[33] Ibid, p. 178.

[34] Ibid, p. 177.

[35] Ibid, p. 178.

Chapter Twelve

Breith Unleashes Operation "Wanda"

"Mud is the greatest enemy of the armored division."
— *Rittmeister von Senger und Etterlin, 24.Pz.Div.*[1]

As the Soviets had anticipated, the Germans would not be able to launch a relief attempt very quickly. Konev and Vatutin put this time to good use, fortifying and improving their already strong defensive positions. When the German attack came, their men would be waiting for them. In the meantime, the Soviet commanders could concentrate on the destruction of the encircled German troops without having to worry unduly about them getting away. The Germans outside the pocket, for their part, still had to assemble enough troops and tanks to punch through the Soviet outer ring and fight their way into the pocket, where the hard-pressed men of *XI.* and *XXXXII.A.K.* awaited. Once they had executed this part of the plan, the relief force then had to turn about and destroy the sizable Soviet forces they had encircled in the course of the relief attempt. It would be a daunting task, even if the German relief force had been the most experienced and well-equipped available.

In order to gather the necessary forces, Manstein would have to concentrate a total of eight panzer divisions from their positions along the entire width of his Army Group. From 31 January to 2 February, the commanders of both *XXXXVII.* and *III.Pz.Korps* struggled to move their forces into position. Although Vormann's corps had been worn down in constant fighting since 24 January, Breith's forces were still relatively fresh. Furthermore, they had just come from a successfully executed counteroffensive that had checked the western advance of Vatutin's 1st and 2nd Guards Tank Armies, and their morale was accordingly good.

Although the wheeled convoys from *16.* and *17.Pz.Div.* and *Schw.Pz.Rgt. Bäke* were encountering bad road conditions due to unusually warm weather, the tanks were arriving by rail on schedule. *1.Pz.Armee* had reported that Soviet activity in the designated breakthrough area was relatively non-existent, except for the occasional foot patrol or attempts to infiltrate *VII.Armeekorps'* front lines, which were easily driven off. *Stukas* also made their appearance, repeatedly attacking and inflicting damage to Vatutin's convoys of tanks and trucks that were observed moving southeast towards Zvenigorodka on 1 February.[2]

The consensus among the officers of *III.Pz.Korps* as they prepared for their attack in their assembly areas northeast of Uman near Mankovka was that they would have no trouble breaking through the Soviet defenses on 3 February and rescuing Lieb's and Stemmermann's troops. With nearly 166 tanks and assault guns, not counting what *1.Pz.Div.* and *Leibstandarte* would later bring, *III.Pz.Korps* represented an enormous concentration of German armor for this stage of the war in the East.

For the relief operation, *17.Pz.Div.* would launch a surprise attack on the right towards Medvin, with *16.Pz.Div.* its left, while *Schw.Pz.Rgt.Bäke* would form the spearhead with its *Tiger* tanks. After Breith's corps had broken through the Soviet line that ran from Chemeriskoye to Roskoshevka, it would strike north for the Gniloy Tikich River, seize a crossing, and punch into the western flank of the pocket near Medvin.

Once it arrived, *Leibstandarte* would follow *16.Pz.Div.* and cover the left flank of the corps' attack. The infantrymen of *34.Inf.Div.,* to the left of *Leibstandarte*, would then extend its right flank to provide a continuous defensive line between it and the relief force as it advanced. When *1.Pz.Div.* arrived on or about 7 February, it would be used however the situation dictated, probably on the right flank of *198.Inf.Div.*, which would cover the attack of *17.Inf.Div.*, while extending its own line further to the east in order to link up with the left flank of von Vormann's *XXXXVII.Pz.Korps.*[3] After both encircled corps had been freed and a new front line built along the Gniloy Tashlyk - Shpolka river line, *III.Pz.Korps* would be available for employment elsewhere. General Wenck's entry in *1.Pz.Armee's* diary for 1 February revealed little trace of doubt about the upcoming mission's chances for success.

Due to bad road conditions which were delaying the arrival of all of *III.Pz.Korps* units into their assembly areas, General Hube asked Army Group South on 2 February for a 24-hour postponement of the attack. He reckoned that, if the attack went forward as originally scheduled, the danger would arise that Breith's divisions would have to go forward without all of their supporting elements, especially artillery. Even worse, this could possibly lead to the corps being forced to fight its way through the Soviet defenses in a piecemeal fashion. To buttress his proposal, Hube informed von Manstein that Breith would welcome a day's delay.

Breith also proposed a slight deviation in the planned route of advance, to take advantage of better trafficability for his armor, since reconnaissance had revealed that the initial route had "especially unfavorable terrain conditions."[4] Rather than following the northeast route to Medvin that led through Shubanny Stav to Bushanka, Breith wanted to go the more direct route due north via the town of Tinovka. The route was not only shorter to the objective of Medvin, but it appeared to have roads far more suited for tanks than the original route did. From a tactical point of view, at the time it seemed to make no difference which route *III.Pz.Korps* took.

Perhaps concerned by this last-minute request to change the timetable and direction of attack, von Manstein drove to Hube's headquarters in Uman that same day to see the situation

A Panzer IV of the relief force laden with accompanying infantry move out to attack the encircling ring of Soviet tank corps. (Bundesarchiv 277/835/4)

for himself. Arriving there at 1315 hours, von Manstein was briefed on the change in plan and concurred with the request to push back the attack a day. Zero Hour would now be 0600 hours 4 February. He also agreed with Breith's proposal to change the route of advance, since it seemed to offer the quickest way to the western edge of the pocket.[5] Although a thaw was beginning to set in, it was not deemed to be serious enough to truly adversely impact Operation "Wanda." Wenck wrote later that evening that he hoped that *1.Pz.Armee's* forces would put this precious additional time to good use. When the attack began on 4 February, he wrote, Breith should be able to make a good start with a powerfully concentrated attack. Soon, however, both the weather and stubborn Soviet resistance, as well as the change in the attack route, would combine to make Breith's achieving his objective nearly impossible.

The following day, both Hube and his chief of staff began to have doubts about the wisdom of von Manstein's plan to encircle the Soviets and relieve the troops in the pocket. Just as General Wöhler had been told earlier, Hube had also been notified by his intelligence staff that strong Soviet formations from both 27th and 53rd Armies were being fed into the southern flank of the pocket in an effort to split it asunder. Time was running out for the men in the pocket. Fearing that Stemmermann's and Lieb's corps would be unable to hold off a major attack for long, Hube proposed to Manstein that his army attack towards the east in the direction of Morentsy, thus completely abandoning an attack aimed at taking Medvin.

There, Hube argued, his troops could link up with Wöhler's forces coming from the opposite direction, both trapping the bulk of 5th Guards Tank and 6th Tank Armies. Once their forces had dealt with the Soviet armor, they would then

unite their forces and attack north in order to free the troops in the pocket. Hube felt, as Wöhler did, that this attack was the only one that could be carried out in the limited amount of time remaining. Von Manstein may have wondered why his subordinates had changed their thinking so quickly at such a late hour. Disregarding his subordinate's suggestions, he ordered Hube and Wöhler to proceed with the original plan and to launch the attack as scheduled. Von Manstein explained to *1.Pz.Armee* that to carry out such an attack in this new direction would require that *III.Pz.Korps* reposition its forces, which would require yet another 24-hour delay.[6]

Manstein evidently believed that his forces could not afford to waste another precious day - he was adamant in his desire to free *XI.* and *XXXXII.A.K.* Besides, he had already given permission for Wöhler to radio both Stemmermann and Lieb and inform them that Breith and von Vormann were headed their way from the southwest and south, respectively. Perhaps haunted by the specter of Stalingrad and Army Group Don's inability to rescue Paulus and his men in December 1942, von Manstein was determined not to let his soldiers down again and would spare nothing in the effort to free them. *1.Pz.Armee's* attack was ordered to commence as scheduled and to use whatever means necessary to insure that *III.Pz.Korps* began its attack on time.

Breith's corps began its attack after a strong artillery barrage softened up the positions held by the Soviet 104th Rifle Corps' 133rd and 58th Rifle Divisions. Despite the fact that they had expected the German attack from this direction, the Soviet defenders in this narrow sector had been caught off guard by the pre-dawn assault and were quickly overrun. Breith's divisions made considerable headway at first, supported by dive-bombing attacks by *Stuka* squadrons under the command of Hans-Ulrich Rudel. On the right of the attacking spearhead, General von der Meden's *17.Pz.Div.*, with *Schw.Pz.Rgt. Bäke* in the lead, had retaken the town of Pavlovka, lost the previous week, by 10:00. That afternoon, von der Meden's troops had fought their way into Votylevka. On the left, Back's *16.Pz.Div.* also enjoyed considerable success that day, recapturing the outskirts of Tinovka and seizing the key intersection southeast of the village of Stanislavchik. By nightfall, Back's *Panzergrenadiers* had seized the southern edge of Kossyakovka, along the south bank of the Gniloy Tikich River.

III.Pz.Korps had performed remarkably well that day. Things seemed to be going according to plan, despite the increasingly bad road conditions. Breith's spearheads had driven a wedge over 30 kilometers deep into the Soviet defensive positions. Both 58th and 359th Rifle Divisions seemed to have been taken by surprise, since the Germans encountered hardly any effective resistance. That evening, as he edited the *Kreigstagebuch*, Wenck noted that:

> These were pretty good results for the first day of the attack. We were only held up by unimaginable terrain difficulties (brought on by the rapidly worsening weather) that demanded unheard-off exertions by [our] exhausted troops, who suffered from the soggy ground, through which they had to march and fight. [Our] leadership had been unable to find anything to offer our troops to fight a battle against nature.[7]

1.Pz.Armee fully intended to continue the attack the following day and exploit Breith's success. The arrival of the first units of *1.Pz.Div.* was expected during the day, as well as *Leibstandarte*. In fact, advance elements of the latter had already begun to arrive in the division's assembly area near Novoya Greblya. The addition of these two powerful divisions would contribute still further to the relief attempt's anticipated success.

The weather, which had warmed considerably since 31 January, was no longer on the German's side. Although the temperature had been hovering around zero degrees Fahrenheit since then, on 4 February it rose above the freezing point during the day, where it remained for the next week and a half. To make matters worse, it alternated between bright sunshine and rain showers; at night it remained cloudy, trapping the heat low to the earth's surface. Snowdrifts, which had lain upon the ground to a depth of up to several feet in places, seemed to melt all at once. The roadways, which even in the best of times were barely trafficable for wheeled vehicles, disappeared beneath rivers of mud. It seemed that spring had come early, after all. As Breith's troops continued their push, they reported increasingly difficult road conditions which were beginning to slow them down.

As *16.* and *17.Pz.Div.* fought their way forward, Wenck was notified that *1.Pz.Div.* and *Leibstandarte's* road-bound convoys were completely stuck and strung along 100 kilometers of

roads between their departure point at *4.Pz.Armee* and their assembly area north of Uman. The only unit of Koll's *1.Pz.Div.* that arrived that day was its advance element, which had moved by rail. This unit, *K.Gr. Huppert*, consisted of one tank battalion from *Pz.Rgt.1*, the division's sole half-track-mounted *Pz.Gren.Btl.*, and its SP artillery battalion that would be used the following day to launch an attack in concert with *198.Inf.Div.* to seize the heights north of the village of Stubenny Stav on *III.Pz.Korps'* right flank. This would create a shorter resupply route for Breith's main effort further north, a critical factor given the increasingly poor road conditions.

In the army's diary for 4 February, Wenck noted his concern for the course of the next day's operation, concluding by stating:

> Normally, the army would be certain that such an operation would be carried out quickly, leading to great success. Now, on account of the onset of the thaw, our difficulties are considerably increased. Therefore, in regards to the encircled corps, we cannot afford to waste any time. Everyone is tensely following the course of the operation.[8]

Despite the mud and delays this caused, Breith and his panzer divisions prepared for the following day. If they could only keep up this pace of attack, they would reach the troops of *XXXXII.A.K.* holding the western rim of the pocket in a couple of days.

The attack resumed the following day. The increasingly muddy terrain and roads slowed the advance to a crawl and heavy fog grounded the *Luftwaffe*, denying both close air support to German spearheads as well as preventing transport aircraft from flying into or out of the Korsun airfield. To assist Breith's attack, *1.Pz.Armee* subordinated to him *Pionier Bau-Bataillon 135*, a road construction battalion, to help improve the roads in his sector. Additionally, a number of horse-drawn supply units were also sent to help *III.Pz.Korps* carry its fuel and ammunition, since they had far better mobility than trucks did in the muddy conditions. Furloughed soldiers, who had been awaiting transportation in Uman, were put to work supervising work details of local Ukrainians equipped with shovels to help repair the roads. Even this was not enough. To complicate matters, the Soviets had begun shifting their own armor from other areas in order to block Breith's advance.

Vatutin, though he had been initially surprised by the sudden German relief attack, had reacted quickly and had reinforced 104th Rifle Corps' sector with as many as 130 tanks from both 5th Mechanized and 5th Guards Tank Corps.[9] This addition to Soviet defensive strength on 5 February was quickly noticed by the Germans. The attack launched by *198.Inf.Div.* on the corps' right flank, after achieving initial success, was struck by a Soviet tank-supported counterattack. Although von Horn's men were able to stop the Soviets, knocking out 10 of the 15 attacking tanks, his own attack stalled. This was the first time that Breith's counterattack had encountered Soviet armor, and more was to come.

The relief attempt begins. Tanks and halftracks of 1st Panzer Division begin movement from Uman towards the pocket, early February 1944. (Bundesarchiv 90/3913/23)

The attack by *17.Pz.Div.* was tied up by strong Soviet tank forces near the town of Votylevka, though von der Meden's own tanks were able to get the upper hand. During the advance, the spearhead from *16.Pz.Div.* at Kossyanovka had lost contact with that of von der Meden's division to its right, so *Schw.Pz.Rgt. Bäke* was sent over to close the gap. En route, Bäke and his men were forced to attack a strong Soviet tank force defending between two *Balki* (ravines) near Tatyanovka, blocking the German's path. Here, the overland maneuverability of his *Panther* and *Tiger* tanks were clearly demonstrated. His tanks were undeterred by the mud and crushed the Soviet defenders with well-aimed shots from their 7.5 cm and 8.8 cm cannon. According to Dr. Bäke:

> The regiment was faced by a massed defensive front of the enemy than ran between two Balki that blocked our attack direction. The length of their front was estimated to be between 800 to 1000 meters. Since a frontal attack would have led to heavy losses, I decided to launch a mock attack at 0600 hours towards their front, in order to tie the enemy down. As the sun rose, I sent the Panther battalion in a great arc around the right flank of the enemy forces at the edge of the eastern ravine, until they had got completely behind him. About 0830 hours., the Panther battalion attacked them in the rear and achieved complete surprise. After this [I ordered] the frontal attack led by the Tiger battalion along with the reconnaissance battalion from 16.Pz.Div.[10]

Bäke's regiment quickly crushed the defenders and was able later that day to reestablish contact with General Back's division. Of the 40 defending Soviet tanks, 31 were destroyed by Bäke's Tigers and Panthers. The way north was temporarily free of the enemy.

His advance was brought to a halt when the only bridge on the Gniloy Tikich capable of holding his 60-ton Tigers was blown up in his face. No bridging material was available, since the engineer's bridging company was stuck in the mud and would not be able to reach Bäke's spearhead in time. Throughout the long day of 5 February, *16.Pz.Div.* was held in check by constant small-scale Soviet counterattacks, which demanded all of its attention. On Back's left, *34.Inf.Div.* reported numerous tank-supported attacks against its positions in Tinovka, but it held its positions and prevented the Soviets from breaking through. Clearly, the advance was not going to get anywhere that day. Against the mud and stiffening Soviet resistance, Operation Wanda had been temporarily brought to a standstill.

After overcoming his initial surprise, Vatutin had indeed reacted quickly to Breith's relief attack. In fact, the evidence suggests that Zhukov, Konev, and Vatutin had all been surprised by the sudden German reaction. It must have made an impression on the great *STAVKA* coordinator, for Zhukov wrote in his memoirs that "In the Risino area, the enemy was able to dent our defenses. The enemy command was sure that this time a successful breakthrough was absolutely certain."[11] In addition, the diversionary attacks which were supposed to prevent von Manstein from bringing up reinforcements from elsewhere had been slow to develop.

This part of the elaborate Soviet *maskirovka* plan was a dismal failure especially in the sector opposite *1.Pz.Armee*,

Soviet prisoners are brought in as von Manstein tries to reestablish contact with the pocket. (Bundesarchiv 277/804/6)

where Vatutin's 2nd Tank Army and 38th Army were supposed to have prevented *III.Pz.Korps* from disengaging. Not only had Breith been able to pull his units out of line, but *Gen.d.Inf.* Gollnick's *XXXXVI.Pz.Korps* was able to deal with the Soviet diversionary attacks quite easily. On von Manstein's right flank, however, the diversionary attacks launched by Third Ukrainian *Front* against *6.Armee* near Krivoi Rog were more successful, though even this attack did not begin until 2 February, four days later than it was supposed to. Despite the temporary transfer of *24.Pz.Div.* to Wöhler's *8 Armee*, *6.Armee* was still able to withdraw in good order from its bridgehead at Nikopol.[12]

Sensing the power of the relief force assembling near Uman, Zhukov ordered Vatutin on 4 February to transfer the bulk of Lt. Gen. S.I. Bogdanov's 2nd Tank Army from First Ukrainian *Front's* far right flank in the west with the utmost speed to an assembly area west of Tinovka. Vatutin also ordered Alexeyev's 5th Guards Tank Corps to move out of its reserve position northwest of Zvenigorodka to block the German advance. Although Bogdanov's army, consisting primarily of 3rd and 16th Tank Corps, was seriously understrength, it would bring 108 tanks, substantially adding to the force Vatutin and Kravchenko had available to block the Germans, since Kravchenko's own tank army had been reduced by this time to a mere 100 tanks.[13] By the evening of 5 February, Bogdanov's troops and tanks had arrived and would balance the scales. This veteran formation would be hurled at the left flank of Breith's forces the next day, with the goal of cutting off the German spearhead and destroying it.

As the sun dawned on Sunday, 6 February 1944, the Ukrainian landscape was covered with fog and low-hanging clouds. It rained throughout the day and the temperature hovered above the freezing point. More unfavorable conditions for fight-

ing could not be imagined. Completely immobilized by the mud, *III.Pz.Corps* got nowhere that day, focusing instead on conducting local operations aimed at mopping up bypassed enemy units and securing its resupply routes. Both *34.* and *198.Inf.Div.* concentrated their attention towards building up their own defenses, particularly in Tinovka and Pavlovka.

The Germans struggled to get fuel and ammunition forward to the tank units, which would quickly be immobilized without these critical supplies. Only tanks and other tracked vehicles, in addition to the venerable horse-drawn *panje* sled could get through. Trucks, jeeps, and motorcycles sat immobilized, either buried up to their fenders in mud or sidelined with mechanical problems. Here, the weaknesses of Germany's wheeled vehicle fleet was again made evident. While Soviet four-wheeled drive two and a half ton trucks obtained via Lend-Lease were able to get through, two-wheel drive German Opel "Blitz" and captured French Citroën trucks fell by the wayside in increasingly large numbers. That evening, General Wenck wrote in despair:

> Unheard of demands have been made on the troops on account of the weather and terrain difficulties. Both men and machines are being slowly tortured by the mud. The leadership is doing everything it can think of in order to guarantee resupply, so that the attacking troops can resume their advance as soon as possible.[14]

To make matters worse, the enemy pressure against Breith's troops constantly increased throughout the day. On his right flank, *198.Inf.Div.* was attacked twice during the day by elements

Lieutenant General of Tank Troops S.I. Bogdanov, *Commander, 2nd Tank Army First Ukrainian Front. (Photo courtesy of the Battle of Korsun-Shevchenkovsky Museum, Korsun, Ukraine)*

from the Soviet 167th Rifle and 2nd Guards Airborne Divisions, though von Horn's men were able to hold their ground, with the help of a counterattack carried out by *1.Pz.Div.'s K.Gr. Huppert.* Von Horn's *Gren.Rgt.305*, which had been tasked with holding the critical towns of Pavlovka and Vinograd on the division's far left flank, prevented the spearheads of *16.* and *17.Pz.Div.* from being cut off when its men halted a determined attack led by 2nd Mechanized Rifle Brigade from Volkov's 5th Mechanized Corps. The Soviets were stopped only after all of the regiment's remaining men, including clerks, cooks, and truck drivers, were put into the line, denying their opponents the bridge that spanned the Svinolovka River.[15]

Von der Meden's *17.Pz.Div.* also had its hands full that day. It wiped out or destroyed numerous tank-supported counterattacks, spearheaded by elements from both 5th Guards Tank and 5th Mechanized Corps, launched against its northern and eastern flank. It even had to defend itself from Soviet attacks on its left flank, which was supposed to be protected by *16.Pz.Div.* The enemy seemed to be everywhere. Nevertheless, von der Meden and his men were able to drive out the Soviet attackers and enlarge the area under their control around Votylevka. Bäke's regiment saw little action that day, but instead was used to provide protection for supply convoys carrying badly-needed fuel and ammunition to the forward elements of *16.Pz.Div.* strung out between Votylevka and Kossyakovka, where Back's troops held a small bridgehead over the Gniloy Tikich in the face of many Soviet counterattacks. Tiger tanks were used to pull several trucks through the mud at a time, since nothing else seemed to work. They were also used to launch an attack south along the main supply route towards Tatyanovka, which had been reoccupied by the enemy after the Germans had passed through two days before.

An extremely serious situation arose when a battalion of Soviet infantry supported by tanks seized two key hills southwest and south of the village of Tinovka. These units, from 3rd Guards Airborne Brigade, evidently had planned to cut off *16.Pz.Div.* and link up with elements of 359th Rifle Division attacking form the east. This would have spelled the end of Breith's relief attack, if these Soviet forces were not quickly wiped out. General Back reacted immediately and launched a counterattack with some of his forces as well as *K.Gr. Weidenhaupt* of *Leibstandarte*, just having arrived in the area.

The arrival of the advance element of *K.Gr. Weidenhaupt* came none too soon. Composed of portions of the division's assault gun battalion and *SS-Pz.Gren.Rgt.1*, it arrived in time to join Back's counterattack at noon. The German force quickly knocked out 18 T-34s and three SU-76 assault guns and retook the two hills. Turning over the defense of Tinovka to *Leibstandarte*, the *Kampfgruppe* from *16.Pz.Div.* headed north to join the rest of its division. On the far left, *34.Inf.Div.* also had a busy day. It, too, drove off many determined Soviet tank-led counterattacks and even had to send a force to wipe out a battalion from the Soviet 133rd Rifle Division, which had seized a road intersection a few kilometers south of Tinovka. Clearly, Vatutin was doing everything possible in order to stop the German relief effort. Breith was also getting reinforcements, which were moving up as quickly as the horrible road conditions permitted.

The single greatest reinforcement Breith got that day was *Leibstandarte*, whose advanced elements were just now arriving in Breith's sector from their forward assembly area near Novoya Greblya. By 4 February, most of the division's combats elements had arrived, though its wheeled vehicle convoys were still struggling to make it through in road conditions that were worse than any ever before encountered. According to one member of the division:

> The fighting began in mud literally knee-deep. The columns trudged their way forward, often struggling along side-by-side. The heavy Ukrainian earth had mixed with snow to create a sticky mess. Even with a light nocturnal frost, it hardened to hold vehicles tight and killed any chance of them moving again. Even tracked vehicles got hopelessly stuck in this lava-like mud. So the Division arrived in the designated area in little groups.[16]

One witness later wrote that the mud was so deep in some places that even their Panthers got inextricably mired. Additionally, some of the bridges along the march route were so bad that the division's columns had to halt from time to time to have its engineer bridging units shore them up enough to bear the weight of the armor. Scheduled to cover the left flank of Breith's drive, *Leibstandarte* struggled throughout the day of 6 February to make it to its scheduled position.

Breith must have welcomed the news when he heard that this well-known formation was to be attached to his corps for the operation. One of the first and oldest units of Heinrich Himmler's *Waffen-SS*, it had carved out a reputation for itself since the beginning of the war as one of the most aggressive and hard-hitting divisions in the German armed forces. During the invasions of Poland, France, the Balkans, and the U.S.S.R., *Leibstandarte* was always at the forefront where the fighting was the toughest. No longer exclusively a bodyguard to the *Führer*, by February 1944 it had evolved into one of the most powerful Panzer divisions in Hitler's arsenal.

Some of the most famous and infamous members of the *Waffen-SS* had passed through its ranks since its founding in 1933, men such as Sepp Dietrich, Kurt "Panzermeyer" Meyer, Jochen Peiper, and Fritz Witt. All of these men's names were synonymous with daring and ruthlessness whenever the situation dictated. Its banners had been crowned with repeated successes, despite the fact that Germany's fortunes had begun to turn for the worse by the summer of 1943. It also carried with it a reputation for brutality, which found its expression in a series of atrocities against both civilian and military enemies, tarnishing its otherwise formidable military reputation. The division was, in the words of historian George Stein, the "hope of the *Führer* and the despair of its enemies."

At the time of the Battle of Cherkassy, it consisted of a panzer regiment with 47 operational tanks (including six Tigers of Michael Wittman's company), an assault gun battalion with 19 *StuG. IIIs*, two *Pz.Gren.* Regiments, a motorized artillery regiment, and an armored reconnaissance battalion, as well as other supporting units. Though authorized well over 18,000 men, its ranks been considerably thinned as a result of the constant fighting it had been engaged in since returning to the Eastern Front in November after a period of reorganization in Italy. Most of its units were between 50 to 70 per cent understrength and its artillery could field but four of its 12 authorized batteries.

Nevertheless, it was still classified by *1.Pz.Armee* on 31 January 1944 as "suited for offensive operations" with the caveat that it urgently required replacements. During the fighting for Radomyshl, Zhitomir, and Vinnitsa, while serving with *Gen.d.Pztr.* Hermann Balck's *XXXXVIII.Pz.Korps*, *Leibstandarte* had once again proven itself as one of Germany's finest combat divisions. Its young division commander, *SS-Brigadeführer* Theodor Wisch, had led it well since assuming the leadership of the division from Sepp Dietrich the previous April.

Born 13 December 1907 in Wesselberener Koog, Schleswig-Holstein, Wisch trained to become an agronomist. Life as an agricultural engineer must not have suited him, for he was one of the first volunteers who joined *Leibstandarte* in the spring of 1933. During the Polish Campaign, in which he served as a company commander, Wisch won both Iron Crosses. While serving as a battalion commander, he led his men through France in 1940, Yugoslavia and Greece in 1941, and in the Soviet Union from the beginning. Wounded severely several times, Wisch led by example and was known as an officer who knew the value of personal initiative when confronted by crisis. He earned the Knight's Cross on 15 September 1941 while commanding the *II./SS-Pz.Gren.Rgt.1* and the German Cross in Gold on 25 February 1943 for his actions in the fighting around Kharkov while commanding the same regiment.[17] Promoted to divisional commander in April 1943, he had led the division during the Kursk offensive, where *Leibstandarte* had played a prominent role, adding to its reputation as Hitler's *Feuerwehr* (Fire Brigade).

Wisch's division was assigned the mission of following the attack of *III.Pz.Korps* and protecting the left flank of *16.Pz.Div.* The task was to prove a daunting one, because as his division arrived over the next several days, its subordinate elements were employed by Breith piecemeal. As his units arrived after their frustrating road march, they were quickly used to plug gaps as they appeared in Breith's front. Although its men, tanks, and guns were a welcome addition to the German relief attack, its piecemeal employment meant that the *Leibstandarte* would not be employed as a unit, but as a group of widely scattered

SS-Brigadeführer Theodor Wisch, *Commander, 1.SS-Pz.Div., "Leibstandarte Adolf Hitler." (Bundesarchiv 87/120/12A)*

Kampfgruppen throughout the battlefield.

These various units of the *Leibstandarte* arrived literally in the nick of time. After *K.Gr. Heimann*, a smaller battle group formed from the bulk of the assault gun battalion and a battalion of infantry, had been dispatched to Tinovka to help *16.Pz.Div.*, it was quickly overtaken by *K.Gr. Weidenhaupt*, riding in half-tracks, with the main body of *SS-Pz.Gren.Rgt.1* and the rest of the assault gun battalion. Another battle group from the division, *K.Gr. Kuhlmann*, was formed from one of the panzer regiment's tank battalions and *SS-Pz.Gren.Rgt.2*. It, too, was dispatched to Tinovka to help Back's troops, but by the time it arrived near nightfall, the fighting was over for the day and *16.Pz.Div.* had moved back to its forward positions.

After establishing his command post in the village of Krassny, Wisch was given additional guidance by Breith that directed him to establish a defensive screen line from Kossyakovka to the northern edge of Tinovka, which would allow *Leibstandarte* to cover the corps' left flank. On the western edge of Tinovka, his division was ordered to link up with forces from the *34.Inf.Div.* The rest of the division's units, such as the main body of the tank regiment and the reconnaissance and engineer battalions, were still struggling to reach the front along the deeply rutted roads.[18] Over the next several days, Wisch would receive a flurry of orders that scattered his command to the four winds, as Breith would continually try to push his units onward.

That day, 6 February, *1.Pz.Armee* received a visit by Speidel. His intention was to discuss with Wenck the measures

A T-34 knocked out in close combat.
(Bundesarchiv 277/802/22)

both armies would need to coordinate in order to punch their way through to both encircled corps. Both Speidel and Wenck were unanimous in their belief that the only way to get through to the troops in the pocket would be to angle their attack towards Morenzy, since it did not appear as if there was enough time to take the longer route via Medvin. Both men were keenly aware that the encircled forces were also running out of time and that the weather and road conditions, not to mention the stiffening Soviet resistance, would only make the situation more difficult. Wenck told Speidel that had the higher leadership taken the measures necessary to withdraw the forces in the salient at the beginning of January, the current situation would not be happening. They all saw at the time that Hitler's decision would lead to a catastrophe. However, although Wenck felt that his Army commander was free of guilt for this decision, it must not have made it any easier for him. Speidel could only agree.[19]

Despite Wenck's own reservations, Generals Hube and Breith were both still confident that *III.Pz.Korps* could break through using the route of advance they were following; that is, to the pocket via Medvin. Hube relayed his confidence to von Manstein, even when the Field Marshal himself had finally begun to have his own doubts about the progress of the attack. Hube told von Manstein that the experience of the past few days had shown that the antitank gun barriers and belts erected by Vatutin's troops posed no real obstacle to Breith's tanks. Hube believed that a powerful attack could simply steamroll right through the defenders and that the only thing limiting his advance was the weather conditions.

Manstein asked whether it would be better to regroup and try the other, shorter direction of attack after all, but Hube countered by echoing von Manstein's own argument that this would take too much valuable time to accomplish, in view of the weather and state of the roads. Hube told him that the terrain was so bad, that areas that would normally require only a few hours to negotiate now took days in comparison. Hube concluded by stating that his staff had reviewed the possibility of taking the shorter route and would continue to see whether a regrouping was necessary. But in the meantime, he would keep attacking. Von Manstein, who perhaps thought it was better to trust his subordinate's judgment, agreed.

Completely overlooked in this argument was the fact that the pocket itself was moving away from Breith's rescue effort. While the route via Medvin to Boguslav would have been the shortest route into the pocket and would have bagged the largest number of Soviet divisions when the plan was drawn up 28 January, by 6 February the plan was no longer truly operable. Boguslav had been given up by 2 February and the entire western edge of the pocket had begun moving eastward, away from the relief force. While part of this movement had been caused by Soviet pressure, another reason had more to do with Stemmermann and Lieb wanting to shorten their lines to free more troops. None of this had been coordinated with *1.Pz.Armee*, since the two corps in the pocket reported directly to *8.Armee*. Even if Breith's forces made it all the way to Medvin, it began to appear that they would strike nothing but thin air. Regardless, Hube and Breith decided to keep going. After all, they had gained over 30 kilometers in just two days and did not want to give up ground they had fought so hard for. Despite the mud and increasing Soviet attacks, they would continue to stubbornly attack as planned the following day.

The German attack resumed on 7 February and quickly stalled. The divisions of *III.Pz.Korps*, attacking across a fog-shrouded landscape, were soon tied down in heavy defensive fighting, as they fought off determined Soviet tank and infantry counterattacks from the east, north, and west the entire day. Bogdanov's 2nd Tank Army had finally made its appearance in a rather forceful manner. His forces, combined with Kravchenko's 6th Tank and Zhmachenko's 40th Armies, battered the Germans relentlessly.

Although mud plagued both sides, the superior mobility of the Soviet tanks and trucks enabled them to move nearly at will across the countryside. Festooned with *tankodesantniki*, the men of 5th Guards Tank, 3rd, and 16th Tank Corps, supported by fresh attacks carried out by 3rd Guards Airborne Division as well as other units, threatened at times to overwhelm Breith's troops. Even *Schw.Pz.Rgt. Bäke* had made no headway, so fierce was the Soviet resistance. Although his tanks had knocked out over 80 of the enemy's since the relief attack began 4 February, Bäke's Tiger tanks could be destroyed at close range by T-34s, as had been so clearly demonstrated at Kursk seven months before. Stalled at the far northern tip of the German penetration, Bäke and his men faced the danger of being cut off from their source of supply. To stay much longer would invite disaster.

Since 4 February, the Soviet defense had been carried out in an uncoordinated fashion, with units from three different armies being freely intermingled. Infantry from Zhmachenko's 40th Army and tank corps from Kravchenko's 6th Tank Army and Bogdanov's 2nd Tank Army resisted stubbornly everywhere or launched numerous poorly-planned counterattacks that tied the Germans down but resulted in far more casualties than had their efforts been properly coordinated by the various staffs. To alleviate this problem, Vatutin subordinated all Soviet units fighting against Breith's spearhead between Kuchkovka and Kossyakovka to Bogdanov, who would exercise command and control of them until the Germans had been defeated.[20]

Essentially, this order required that the less experienced Kravchenko give up Alekseyev's 5th Guards Tank Corps, his largest armored unit. Kravchenko himself was given the order to continue blocking the approach route southwest of Zvenigorodka with the 47th Rifle and 5th Mechanized Corps, as well as the 233rd Tank Brigade. Despite their tanks' maneuverability, the Soviets were suffering from the bad weather as much as the Germans were. Their soldiers, too, were living and fighting in the mud and slush. According to one Soviet account describing conditions encountered by Kravchenko's 6th Tank Army:

> The difficulty of rain and wet snow slowed the supply transports. The [First Ukrainian] Front organized a re-supply of fuel and ammunition with bi-planes, flying into a nearby airfield . . . February 1944 was a wet month. Rain and snow created hazards for wheeled and tracked vehicles which became stuck axle-deep in mud. Even tanks required towing. Fuel and ammunition had to be flown in . . . which could never satisfy the requirement.[21]

Commenting on the fighting between 4 and 7 February, Zhukov later wrote that although the German advance had been brought to a halt, Breith's forces still refused to give up and continued trying to punch their way through.[22] Their enemy's persistence must have begun to worry the Soviet leadership, because Zhukov began to intensify psychological warfare operations against Stemmermann's and Lieb's troops in the pocket, in the hopes that enough of them might surrender before the rescue attempt could reach them.

By nightfall of 7 February, *1.Pz.Armee* had realized that this direction of attack was doomed to fail. The combination of poor weather conditions which grounded transports and close support aircraft, the condition of the roads, and last but not least, the furious Soviet resistance, had made it clear to both von Manstein and Hube that another way into the pocket had to be found - and quickly. It was on this date that von Manstein finally abandoned his concept of encircling and destroying the Soviet forces surrounding *XI.* and *XXXXII.A.K.* Now, the only goal that seemed worth pursuing with the forces available was to simply rescue the men in the pocket.

The fighting on 7 February in *III.Pz.Korps'* sector had been heavy. On the right, *198.Inf.Div.* warded off numerous tank-supported attempts by 2nd Guards Airborne Division to envelop its right flank near Risino and had to pull back so far in that area such that its rightmost regiment's front faced to the south. The division was also being attacked on its left near Vinograd and only the timely arrival of *K.Gr. Huppert* from *1.Pz.Div.* saved von Horn's troops from being cut off from the rest of the corps. Other forward elements from *1.Pz.Div.*, which had been scattered along the roads during the approach march just as those of *Leibstandarte* had been, were hurriedly sent to cover the open right flank of Breith's corps, which still had not yet tied in with the westernmost division of von Vormann's *XXXXVII.Pz.Korps* from *8.Armee*.

A Sdkfz. 251 SPWs of the 24th Panzer Division during their "mud march" to join with von Vormann's relief attack. (Photo from Der Russlandkreig: Fotographiert von Soldaten, Ullstein Verlag, 1968)

Schw.Pz.Rgt. Bäke and *17.Pz.Div.* spent all day tied down in heavy defensive fighting. Von der Meden concentrated his efforts towards retaking the town of Votylevka in the rear area of his division, which had been seized the night before by the Soviets. Bäke's regiment, which had been given the mission of seizing the town of Repki that day, also took part in retaking Votylevka, fighting off Soviet tanks the entire day which were attempting to get back into the town. Dr. Bäke later reported that:

> The movement, especially of tracked vehicles, was especially hindered by the completely muddied roads. As an example of the strength-robbing nature of the men against the mud, many Grenadiers took off their boots and walked barefoot through the morass, as this was easier than taking several steps, each time having to stop to dig one's boots out of the mud.[23]

The story with *16.Pz.Div.* was much the same. Due to strong tank-supported infantry attacks, it was unable to continue its attack north from the Kossyakovka bridgehead as planned. Back's division at one point that day found itself cut off by attacks launched by 5th Guards Tank Corps, and was forced to launch a counterattack towards its rear area to throw the enemy infantry out of Kuchkovka and Vessely Kut, which they had infiltrated into the night before. One battalion from *16.Pz.Div.* destroyed nine T-34s near Tatyanovka and attacked a large depression filled with Soviet infantry which was in the process of forming up to retake the town, wiping them out. So occupied was his division in trying to keep itself from getting encircled, that Back completely gave up any idea of continuing the attack northward.

Help finally came to Back's division later that day when *K.Gr. Weidenhaupt* finally was able to link up at 2130 hours with Back's troops from *Pz.Gren.Rgt.79* holding Kossyakovka. Ordered to protect the exposed left flank of *16.Pz.Div., Oberstuf.* Wilhelm Weidenhaupt and his men had to fight their way through a strong enemy unit holding positions along a stream bed, destroying one T-34 and driving off the infantry. After slogging through the mud and snow, his men were completely exhausted, but at least contact had been restored with Back's division. At the same time, the *Kampfgruppe* commanded by *Stubaf.* Herbert Kuhlmann was able to take up its defensive positions between Tinovka and Votylevsky just before it was hit by a Soviet attack launched by units of the 3rd Guards Airborne Division supported by ten T-34s. In the ensuing battle, Kuhlmann's force, which had 11 tanks attached from *SS-Pz.Rgt.1,* destroyed seven tanks and frustrated the enemy's attempts to prevent the linkup of the SS troops and *34.Inf.Div.* holding Tinovka.[24]

At a conference that evening at *1.Pz.Armee* headquarters in Uman, Hube was forced to concede that his attack could go no further. With time running out, it was no longer possible for *III.Pz.Korps* to make it far enough to reach the pocket. If the attack was maintained in this direction, Breith's troops might make it to Medvin, but they would be striking into thin air. In another week, if this kept up, both encircled corps would have been destroyed or forced to surrender. Neither Hube or von Manstein could allow this to happen. Wenck wrote that night that "The Army no longer has any doubt that every means must now be employed in order to effect the quickest linkup with the cut-off units of *8.Armee.*"[25] Clearly, *1.Pz.Armee* had to find a quicker way to reach Stemmermann; if not, Operation Wanda would be deemed a total failure and the Soviets would have their second Stalingrad.

While *1.Pz.Armee* was fighting its way into the pocket from 4 to 7 February, Wöhler's *8.Armee* had been attempting to carry out its assignment as required by von Manstein's plan. Despite heavy fighting, von Vormann's corps had little success to show for its men's efforts before its attempt also ground to a halt. Weather and road conditions were just as bad as they were with their neighbor to the west. In addition to having to cope with spirited Soviet counterattacks, von Vormann's men also had to battle the elements. In his vivid account, he states that:

> Overnight the weather changed suddenly. For days, snowstorms had howled over the frozen landscape - now it was thawing. The *Rasputitsa* had begun early, with a vengeance. This marked the time of the springtime muddy season, the time of absolute immobility; the time when the local farmers stayed at home by the oven, never leaving the house. He knew how senseless it was to attempt any kind of work outside. Under the effects of sun, rain, and warm wind, the heavy black Ukrainian earth was transformed in one day to sticky, thick mud. There weren't any hard surfaced roads to speak of . . . Wheeled vehicles remained hopelessly stuck. Even our half-tracks had their thin treads ripped [by the mud]. The only means of travel remaining were the huge prime

movers and the tanks, that were able to grind forward with great wear and tear and fuel consumption, though at top speeds of only four to five kilometers per hour.[26]

Infantrymen, panzer troops, and artillerymen, as well as everyone else, had to live in the worst winter conditions imaginable. In conditions every bit as bad as those experienced on the Western Front in World War One, both German and Soviet troops had no choice but to cope with the horrible weather. Von Vormann continues:

> Foot soldiers sank up to their calves, losing their boots and socks after a step or two . . . The number of those reporting sick on account of frostbite rose rapidly, quickly surpassing the number of battle casualties. The infantry suffered especially, since they lay exposed in open terrain. Their damp uniforms, which they had worn day after day, froze on their bodies during the evening. All planning, all calculations gave way. Once again, Russia's climate appeared to have triumphed over the intruders.[27]

Clearly, *XXXXVII.Pz.Korps* was approaching the limit of what its men could accomplish. Despite the enemy's resistance and the atrocious living conditions, von Vormann's men grimly drove off repeated counterattacks by Rotmistrov's tank troops. All hope now rested with the arrival of *24.Pz.Div.*

Since *11.* and *13.Pz.Div.* had been unable to expand upon the bridgehead gained at Iskrennoye, von Vormann also pinned his hopes upon the arrival of *Freiherr* von Edelsheim's division to restore his corps' fortunes. With the addition of this nearly full-strength organization, von Vormann hoped to regain the initiative and finally break through to Stemmermann's *XI.A.K.* As previously described, Edelsheim's division had begun to move out of its positions near Apostolovo near Nikopol on 28 January. Since movement by rail to their assembly area near Novo Archangelsk was not available, the division would have to complete most of its travel by road. To carry this out, the division organized itself into six march groups, with armored vehicles in the first march group, since this would most likely be the first one that encountered the enemy. As the convoys moved out on the first leg of their 300-kilometer journey, the lead march group made it to Krivoi Rog by nightfall. The 75-kilometer movement had taken 15 hours to accomplish, which was not bad considering the poor road conditions. However, the passing of the tanks and assault guns had churned up the unpaved roads so badly that subsequent convoys from the division could only move an average of ten kilometers per day. Just as the thaw was affecting *III.Pz.Korps* further north, it was affecting movement in the south as well.

Just as it had in *1.Pz.Armee's* area, the roads between *6.* and *8.Armee* were adversely affected by warm temperatures, melting snow and rain. They soon became virtually impassable. The *Rasputitsa* had arrived early. Here, as elsewhere, the black, rich soil was transformed almost immediately into a thick, gooey mess that clung to everything, immobilizing man, horses and machine. Wherever the roads passed through stream beds or the bottom of ravines, the roads literally disappeared. Every one of these stream crossings that *24.Pz.Div.* encountered required its combat engineers to quickly erect some kind of emergency bridge in order to keep the convoys moving. Gravel, whenever it was available, was dumped upon the roadbed, where it was quickly compacted into the mud, bringing about no discernible improvement.

During the day, overcast skies alternated with warm sunshine, which made the situation even worse. Layers of earth, which had been frozen up to several feet deep during the winter, thawed, aggravating the situation. Attempts were made by engineers to block off passable sections of road during the day so that they could be used during the night when frost usually fell, but even this was insufficient. At night, the deep ruts which had been made by passing convoys during the day usually froze solid, making them nearly impossible to travel upon, except by tanks. Vehicles which remained stationary during the night usually froze quickly in place, rendering them immobile unless a quick-thinking crew member was able to kindle a fire under it or obtain a blow-torch to thaw out the tank tracks enough for the vehicle to be "rocked out" of the frost's grip. During the day, long sections of the roadway became rivers of mud.

Through this nightmare of mud and ice slogged the march columns of von Edelheim's division, in conditions which even its most grizzled veterans of the *Ostfront* had never imagined possible. Hundreds of vehicles remained stuck in the bottom of ravines or depressions during the march, awaiting a passing tank or half-tracked prime mover to pull them out. Tanks, which often could go as far as 150 kilometers on a tank of gasoline, could only travel a dozen or so, since moving through the thick mud required far more power to accomplish with a correspondingly greater consumption of fuel. Often, roadway intersections became blocked for hours when succeeding march columns tried to gain access to them at the same time.

The division's artillery regiment, which somehow had managed to get a train to carry its artillery to Novo Archangelsk, was ordered to load only its guns and leave its prime movers behind in order to help out stuck vehicles along the route of march. Once the guns arrived at the off-loading point, there was the possibility that there would be no tractors available to tow them to their firing positions, but this was a risk that Edelsheim had to take.

Even the *Panzergrenadiers*, in order to lighten their vehicles, were forced to climb out of their half-tracks and push them through the mud. On level ground, many vehicles were hitched to one another, with one tank providing the towing power. Some participants in the march reported seeing one tank pulling as many as a dozen trucks. In short, from the very beginning of the move any sort of systematic convoy movement was impossible. To make matters worse, the Soviet Air Force carried out numerous ground attacks against the marching columns. Though they affected the movement little, they added to the considerable strain which Edelsheim's troops no doubt must have already felt.

The first elements of the division began arriving in their assembly areas between 1 and 2 February. The first march element with the bulk of the armor had left nearly 70 percent of its men and vehicles strung out the entire distance of the march route. The second march group, consisting of one of the *Panzergrenadier* regiments, was able to get 70 percent of their men and half-tracks to the assembly area near Yampol. Still, 50 out of the regiment's 192 vehicles had been left behind, stuck in the mud or immobilized with broken suspension systems, blown engines, or shattered drive trains. Unfortunately, most of the division's supply convoys had not yet arrived, either. Many still had not yet been able to leave Apostolovo, since the enormous traffic jam began the moment they left their old assembly area. It appeared that *24.Pz.Div.* would have to go into combat with only the supplies of fuel and ammunition their vehicles brought with them. Still, Edelsheim's men were determined to press ahead and launch their attack on time, come what may.

For his part, von Vormann was doing everything possible to help out. To determine how much progress *24.Pz.Div.* was making, he would daily take to the air in a Fiesler *Storch* liaison aircraft to scout ahead and to see where the division's regiments and battalions were located. Without the addition of this "steam-hammer," von Vormann knew that his piece of the planned relief attempt would have no chance of success whatsoever. All of his other panzer divisions were too weak to continue the attack. Von Vormann was therefore understandably anxious that Edelsheim's division arrive in time.

As he established his division's forward headquarters near Yampol on the evening of 2 February, Edelsheim was given the mission of attacking the following day north towards Mali Yekaterinopol, where he was to lead his division in an attack against Lazarev's 20th Tank Corps from Rotmistrov's 5th Guards Tank Army. Edelsheim requested a 24-hour delay in launching his attack, since by nightfall only 12 of his 60 tanks had arrived. Of his artillery, he could muster only one battery of six guns! The infantry was not in much better shape, since both *Pz.Gren.* regiments had become hopelessly intermingled during the road march. To make matters worse, many of the division's radio sets had broken down, rendering effective command and control of his forces virtually impossible. To sum up the past week's activities, the division's First General Staff Officer, *Maj.* Hans-Henning von Christen, noted:

> The intention of the division to push back the enemy . . . with only the weak forces available and to again seize possession of the railroad lines (near Zvenigorodka) by means of a tank attack today had to be abandoned since we have not been able to bring up the tanks, the roads being impassable even for them.[28]

The following day, 4 February, *24.Pz.Div.* began its long-awaited attack. The division's spearhead soon encountered the first Soviet outposts and knocked out three light tanks. The ground was, as of yet, still capable of bearing the weight of the tanks and other armored vehicles, since it had not been churned up by constant movement. With the arrival of this veteran division, many in *XXXXVII.Pz.Korps* must have began to hope that, perhaps, things were finally going to go according to plan.

Edelsheim's division never made it any farther than this initial advance. It had been stopped in the early morning hours of 4 February on direct orders from the *Führer*. Furious that von Manstein had moved *24.Pz.Div.* without his consent, coupled with the fact that Third Ukrainian *Front* had finally began its attack aimed at Nikopol, Hitler ordered Army Group South's commander to send Edelsheim's division back the way it came. To Hitler's way of thinking, holding Nikopol, with its rich nickel deposits and refineries so critical to the Third Reich's armaments industries, was more important than the lives of the 60,000 men encircled west of Cherkassy.

8.Armee received the order to disengage Edelsheim's division with profound disbelief. The initial order to halt the attacked came at 0250 hours, followed by a detailed explanation six hours later after the division's advanced elements had already engaged the enemy. Speidel implored Busse, at Army Group South, to allow *8.Armee* time to comply, since it was senseless to stop now while the attack had begun so favorably. Speidel was clearly deeply affected by the order. He asked Busse over the phone that "had not the Army Group Commander himself ordered *24.Pz.Div.* to take part in the attack? What [are you at] Army Group thinking?" It did not make sense to him, or to anyone else, that the division, which had struggled through hundreds of kilometers of bad roads, rain, and mud, was now being ordered to call off its attack.[29] Even if the division was pulled out and marched south to attack at Nikopol, it probably would not arrive in time, since it would have to travel along the same horrible roads it had used to reach Yampol. It was no use; even von Manstein could not countermand the order, since it had come directly from Hitler. So, *24.Pz.Div.* had to cancel its attack, recall its units, and form up immediately for the return trip. Its eight day-long march had been in vain.

The movement back to its new assembly area at Apostolovo west of Nikopol was just as bad as the movement to Yampol. Except for the tanks, which took a roundabout rail journey, the rest of the division's vehicles traveled by road. The division had lost half of its tanks through mechanical failure alone in the move north. Of the remainder, less than half of these made it to the railhead at Novo Ukraina. Only 15 per cent of the division's armor arrived at Apostolovo - the rest were scattered along a 300-kilometer route stuck in the mud, stranded without fuel, or sidelined with mechanical problems brought about by the constant wear and tear of driving through deep mud. The wheeled vehicles suffered even more. In the movement up and back, over 1,958 of these were lost - 55 per cent of the entire division's complement. Most of these were from the division's logistics, engineer, and signal units, units vital to the operations of any mechanized formation.

The division had been defeated far more soundly by the mud than by enemy action. Typically, Hitler had made a snap decision based more on emotion than a sound grasp of the situation. Once again, he had overridden the advice of his field commanders and tried to impose his own questionable military

judgment upon a situation which should have been left to the men on the scene. Thus, Edelsheim's division did not take part in either battle. Upon its return to *6.Armee* on 8 February, it was a shell of what it had been 28 January. As Speidel had predicted, *24.Pz.Div.* got there too late to affect the outcome of the Battle for Nikopol. The Soviet attack by Third and Fourth Ukrainian *Fronts* had forced the defenders back, liberated Nikopol, and began to advance west before the division had even arrived. Fortunately for the Germans, Generals Malinovsky and Tolbuchin were neither as imaginative as Vatutin nor as ruthless as Konev.

Instead of trapping the Germans in the bridgehead at Nikopol, they opted instead for attacking them frontally, which gave their opponent ample time to delay the Soviets while the bridgehead was evacuated. What Hollidt's *6.Armee* needed for this type of fighting was another infantry division, not a panzer division. According to one member of *24.Pz.Div.* who was present:

> It was a master example of miscalculation. It showed what serious consequences are produced by a false estimate of the situation, an insufficient knowledge of what is technically possible, and a disregard of the factors of terrain and weather by the responsible higher command.[30]

Thus, the planned attack of *24.Pz.Div.* remains one of the greatest "might have beens" of the Battle of the Cherkassy. Had it been allowed to continue its attack from Yampol, it very well could have broken through or at least forced Vatutin and Konev to divert an even greater number of armored units away from *III.Pz.Korps*, thus allowing that unit to break through to the encircled troops more quickly. But it was never to be. The whole episode is best described by von Vormann, who stated that:

> During these critical days, [the division] fought neither at Zvenigorodka nor at Apostolovo. At one point it was prevented from launching a decisive attack, while at the other point it arrived too late to prevent a catastrophe. It was not against an enemy, but against mud and mire that it expended its energy.[31]

With this, *8.Armee's* decisive role in the relief attempt came to an end, before it was even put into effect. Instead of conducting a concentrated surprise attack with five panzer divisions, not a single one was available for the attack planned for 4 February.

Both *11.* and *13.Pz.Div.* were tied up in the Iskrenoye Bridgehead, while *3.* and *14.Pz.Div.* were immobilized near Lebedin by 29th and 18th Guards Tank Corps. Edelsheim's division had been recalled from its line of departure and sent back to where it had started from, 300 kilometers away. According to von Vormann, "The fate of *XI.* and *XXXXII.Armeekorps* was sealed by 4 February. Everything that happened afterwards was marked by desperate attempts by our troops to turn things around in order to save their encircled comrades from doom - regardless of orders."[32]

Von Manstein was now forced to make a decision. With his elaborate plan now falling apart, the only thing left to do now was to get to the encircled troops as quickly as possible. Although von Manstein's failed to mention what happened next in his autobiography, his intentions were clearly spelled out in an order radioed to *1.Pz.* and *8.Armee* on 6 February. This order would alter the concept of operations completely. Not only would the direction of attack change, but the encircled forces, now renamed *Gruppe Stemmermann*, would be required to take part in the endeavor by attacking towards the relief force, something which it had not previously considered within its capability. To do so, it would have to summon the last of its strength - for the first time since they were encircled 28 January, the divisions inside the Cherkassy Pocket would be going over to the offensive. To succeed, the plan demanded that both attacks - from the inside and the outside - reach their goal; if either failed, then the 60,000 men of *Gruppe Stemmermann* were doomed.

End Notes

1 Dr. Fridolin von Senger und Etterlin Jr., quoted in David Glantz, "From the Dnieper to the Vistula," p. 215.

2 *1.Pz.Armee* KTB, 1 February 1944, p. 1.

3 Ibid, p. 2.

4 *1.Pz.Armee* KTB, 2 February 1944, pp. 1-2.

5 Ibid, p. 2.

6 *1.Pz.Armee* KTB, 3 February 1944, p. 2.

7 *1.Pz.Armee* KTB, 4 February 1944, p. 2.

8 Ibid, p. 1.

9 *1.Pz.Armee* KTB, 5 February 1944, p. 1.

10 Dr. Franz Bäke, *"Das Schwere Panzer-Regiment Bäke and der Überwindung der Einschliessung westliche Tscherkassy verdienst-voll beteiligt,* in *Program zum Appell der Angehörigen der ehemaligen Deutschen 8.Armee anlässlich des Gedenktages."* (Amberg, Germany, 16 February 1974), p. 26.

11 Zhukov, p. 243.

12 von Manstein, p. 513.

13 Armstrong, pp. 156-157.

14 *1.Pz.Armee* KTB 6 February 1944, p. 1.

15 Graser, p. 288.

16 Rudolf Lehmann and Ralf Tiemann, *The Leibstandarte, Vol. IV/1.* (Winnipeg, Canada: J.J. Fedorowicz Publishing Inc., 1993), p. 22.

17 Schneider, p. 415.

18 Lehmann and Tiemann, pp. 23-24.

19 *1.Pz.Armee* KTB 6 February 1944, p. 3.

20 *Sbornik*, p. 319.

21 Armstrong, p. 421.

22 Zhukov, p. 243.

23 *1.Pz.Armee* KTB 7 February 1944, p. 3.

24 Lehmann and Tiemann, p. 22.

25 *1.Pz.Armee* KTB 7 February 1944, p. 1.

26 Von Vormann, p. 75.

27 Ibid, pp. 75-76.

28 von Senger und Etterlin, in Glantz, p. 214.

29 *1.Pz.Armee* KTB 4 February 1944, p. 14.

30 von Senger und Etterlin, in Glantz, p. 215.

31 von Vormann, pp. 77-79.

32 Ibid, p. 78.

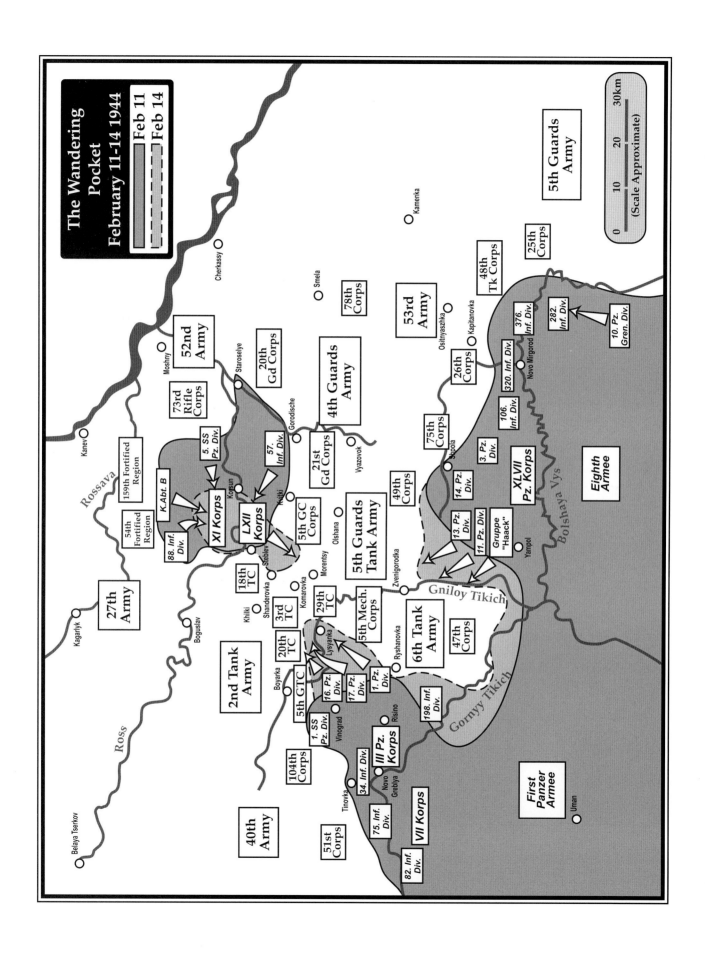

The Wandering Pocket
February 11-14 1944

Feb 11
Feb 14

IV

DAYS OF DESPERATION

Chapter Thirteen
THE WANDERING POCKET

"Even nature seemed to be against us . . . "
— *Oblt. Hans Menedetter, 88.Inf Div.*

As General Breith's relief force slowly ground its way through the mud, it became evident to Manstein by the evening of 6 February that the effort, great as it was, would not be enough to reach the troops in the pocket in time. Except for a few stubborn optimists, such as Generals Hube and Breith, nearly everyone else had come to believe that the continued chances of success were slim if the relief force kept trying to fight its way due north. If *III.Pz.Korps* did not try a quicker, shorter route, the relief attack would culminate far short of the goal. Stemmermann and Lieb's troops had been fighting with a heroism borne of desperation, they could not hold out indefinitely. Supplies were running out and so were men. Worse, the pocket had begun to "wander" away from the relief force due to increasing Soviet pressure as well as the need of the two corps commanders to shorten their lines. What was needed was a radically revised plan (Map 10).

Manstein, as previously related, had already been entertaining such thoughts, as had Generals Wöhler and Wenck. Rather than plowing head-on through increasingly impassable terrain in the face of bitter resistance by Vatutin's First Ukrainian *Front*, the relief force would have to change its direction of attack by nearly 90 degrees. Instead of attacking due north, its only chance of success now seemed to lie in an attack to the east. The Field Marshal's new intent was spelled out in the operations order issued by Army Group South to both Hube's and Wöhler's armies at 1955 hours on 6 February. It instructed *1.Pz.Armee* to halt *III.Pz.Korps'* attack to the north and redirect its forces as soon as possible, so that they would be able to attack in an easterly direction towards the Gniloy Tikich sector in the vicinity of Lysyanka, where it would link up with the encircled forces.

Even so, there was a realization that the pocket would have to be completely evacuated as soon as contact was reestablished with the outside. In the words of General Busse, the men inside the pocket would have to stand ready *mit gepacktem Tornister* (with their packs on their backs) in order to break out immediately upon contact with the relief force.[1] The realization was emerging already that although Army Group South would probably be able to rescue the encircled troops, most of their equipment and heavy weapons would have to be left behind. In a radio message that must have brought a sense of relief to General Wöhler and the rest of his staff, Manstein informed him that he was prepared to order the breakout on his own responsibility, regardless of what Hitler said. In Manstein's words, "Leaving the two corps sitting in the pocket will not even be considered."[2] Previous attempts to secure permission for such a move in advance from *OKH* had failed - Hitler simply could not bring himself to make a decision, for he was still convinced that Kiev could still be retaken.

Broken down and burnt out German trucks litter the Rollbahn from Gorodishche to Korsun, early February 1944. Road conditions had worsened to such a degree that hundreds of trucks, halftracks and other vehicles had become hopelessly mired on the roads leading into Korsun from the east, making them inviting targets for Soviet fighter bombers.
(U.S. National Archives)

The right flank unit of *III.Pz.Korps*, *17.Pz.Div.*, would now become the main effort, while the spearhead, *Schw.Pz.Rgt. Bäke* and the left flank unit, *16.Pz.Div.*, would protect the northern and northwestern flank from a Soviet counterattack. As the length of the exposed left flank increased, *Leibstandarte* would be responsible for moving its units into the gaps as they appeared in order to protect the flanks of the two other panzer divisions. After destroying any enemy armored forces encountered en route, Breith's panzer divisions were to cross the Gniloy Tikich and attack towards the pocket as soon as possible along the route Bushanka-Lyssyanka-Morentzy. Once contact was established, Breith was to evacuate the encircled forces to the rear, while simultaneously tying in with *XXXXVII.Pz.Korps* on his right. Then, both *III.* and *XXXXVII.Pz.Korps* would attack towards each other in order to establish a new front line linking *1.Pz.* and *8.Armee* that faced north.

8.Armee was directed to attack north along the line Olshana-Topilno-Zvenigorodka with at least two panzer divisions of Vormann's corps, conditions permitting, in order to tie up as many enemy forces as possible and to protect Breith's southern flank while it conducted the main effort. More could not be expected; Vormann's corps was almost totally fought out. The two encircled corps were directed by *8.Armee* to plan two different courses of action for their breakout. The first attack was to be with *XI.A.K.* towards the south in the direction

Oberst Karl Baacke, *Commander of Gren.Rgt.266, who was cut off from his troops inside the pocket, led Urlauber Regiment Baacke outside the pocket that attempted to restore contact between both Eighth and First Panzer Armies. (Photo courtesy of 72.Inf.Div. Veteran's Association)*

of *XXXXVII.Pz.Korps*; the second was to be with both corps attacking side-by-side towards the southwest in order to seize favorable positions to break out towards Breith's corps, once the latter had reached Lyssyanka. The first course of action was code-named *Frühlingsglaube* (Belief in Spring) while the second was code-named *Betriebsurlaub* (Bank Holiday). In addition, Manstein ordered that Stemmermann and Lieb should plan to launch their break out under cover of night and to destroy any equipment it could not take along.

Besides the renewed relief attempt, another nagging problem which had vexed Manstein, Wöhler and Hube since the beginning had to be dealt with - and quickly. This problem, the 32 kilometer-wide gap between the two armies, had been put off since the Soviets had broken through the German front lines at the end of January. The Germans had gained some breathing room when the Soviets failed to exploit this opportunity, but the gap remained. The recent efforts of both *1.Pz.* and *8.Armee* had closed this distance somewhat, when their right and left flanks,

respectively, were stretched towards each other, but they lacked the men to completely knit them together. Only so many divisions could be pulled from the opposite flank and thrown into the line before an overextended division gave out elsewhere under Soviet attack. No divisions were forthcoming from *OKH* reserve, either. Therefore, some sort of expedient had to be found somewhere before the Soviets took advantage of the situation and attacked southward towards Uman.

Since both armies were preoccupied with the battle, Army Group South decided to do what it could with whatever forces could be made available to help. On 3 February, Manstein clarified his intentions in an order to both armies that stated that he planned to form an assault group to reestablish contact between the two armies and destroy any Soviet forces that were caught in between.[3] One source of manpower that had recently become available were the thousands of troops on leave status who were cut off from their units when *XI.* and *XXXXII.A.K.* were encircled. These men, who had recently returned from furlough in Germany or Western Europe, had not been permitted to fly into the pocket as reinforcements, on order from General Wöhler. Instead, *8.Armee's* commander was planning to form them into ad-hoc *Kampfgruppen* described in an order to *XI.A.K.* on 4 February. When Army Group South's staff got wind of this, General Busse contacted *8.Armee* and informed Speidel that these units would be used as the basis for the force designed to close the gap between the two armies. Thus, at 2100 hours 5 February, was born *K.Gr. Haack*.

This battle group was named after *Gen.Maj.* Werner Haack, commander of *310.Art.Div.z.b.V. (zum besondere Verfügung* - for special employment). An ad-hoc formation in the fullest meaning of the term, *K.Gr.Haack* was to be composed of a variety of combat and support units thrown together for the operation, which included three artillery *Abteilungen*, one *StuG.Abt.*, a *Nebelwerfer* regiment, one engineer battalion, and a self-propelled anti-tank company. An armored group was supposed to join it later, but never did. The heart of the unit, however, was *Urlauber Regiment Baacke*. Composed of several thousand soldiers recently returned from furlough, its ranks were filled with men from every division trapped within the pocket. It would be employed as infantry, without heavy weapons, communications equipment, or much else. Such essential supply services as it did possess came from that of *389.Inf.Div.*, cut off during the initial breakthrough near Shpola. This hastily assembled regiment would provide the blood and muscle to close the gap.

It was to be commanded by *Oberstlt.* Kurt Baake, commander of *Gren.Rgt.266,* of *72.Inf.Div.*, being led temporarily inside the pocket by *Maj.* Siegel. Left outside of the pocket when he had returned from leave in Germany, Baake was quickly placed in command of an organization that had no staff, no signals equipment, and little cohesion. Control of Baake's regiment and *K.Gr. Haack* would initially be exercised directly by *8.Armee*. Haack's headquarters would initially be the town of Yampol, 45 kilometers due south of Zvenigorodka. The orders establishing it read that it would be "employed on the left wing of *8.Armee*, conduct an attack towards *1.Pz.Armee* in order to close the gap, and win a bridge-head over the Shpolka River at Yerki," some 25 kilometers to the north.[4]

In addition to this task, which would have been enough to strain the capability of a full strength panzer division, *K.Gr. Haack* was also tasked with protecting Vormann's left flank. By 8 February, most of General Haack's newly-minted formation were on the march to their new assembly area. The attack was supposed to begin immediately, but because of the mud and awful road conditions, it had to be postponed to 10 February.

The main focus of Manstein's operation, the relief attack by *III.Pz.Korps*, could now be resumed. But before any of this could come about, Breith had to pull his divisions out of the positions that they had taken by 7 February and return to the line of departure of 4 February. This was not as easy as waving one's hand over a map and expecting it to happen. In addition to the same mud, Breith's troops would have to contend with inevitable Soviet counterattacks led by a sizable number of Red armored units. Since a withdrawal while in contact with the enemy is one of the hardest tactical challenges that exists, careful planning was required to insure that none of the units were attacked and overwhelmed while they were in the process of moving back. In fact, Breith's corps was unable to move either on 7 February or the following day, so fierce were the Soviet efforts to destroy it.

A indicator of just how serious the situation was is borne out by the number of Soviet tanks destroyed on 8 February. On this day alone, 108 Soviet tanks were claimed to have been knocked out by *16.* and *17.Pz.Div., Schw.Pz.Rgt. Bäke,* and *Leibstandarte.* In addition, the Soviet 11th Guards Tank Corps from the 2nd Guards Tank Army made its appearance near Tinovka, where it was halted by *Leibstandarte* and *34.Inf.Div.,* despite the fact that it supported Soviet infantry assaults against that town. Although this force only brought 30 tanks with it, these tanks were the newly-introduced Joseph Stalin IIs, an armored behemoth based on the chassis of the older KV-I heavy tanks and armed with a formidable 12.2 cm gun, making it more than a match for the *Tiger.* Vatutin had moved this corps from the far west in a bid to cut off and destroy the German relief force, an indicator of how worried he was that his enemy would succeed in reaching the troops in the pocket.[5]

Another obstacle to carrying out the new plan was General Hube himself, who still believed as late as 8 February that his army could still slog its way through in the direction it had taken since the beginning of the relief attack. Additionally, he did not want the divisions of Breith's corps to be separated by the Gniloy Tikich, where they would not be able to provide mutual support if attacked, since bridges capable of supporting tanks were scarce. Breith's own chief of staff, *Oberst* Ernst Merk, agreed, imploring *1.Pz.Armee* to postpone the decision for one day in order to see whether the situation improved. Neither Hube or Breith wanted to pull back to the new starting point.

That evening, Manstein made his decision and telephoned Hube to clarify the situation. Hube received rather pointed and detailed instructions from his army group commander in order to help him plan the next attack. No doubt this was helped along by so-called unofficial "back-channel" communications between

For the first time, the monstrous Joseph Stalin II heavy tank, mounting 120 mm guns, were encountered by troops of Breith's III Panzer Corps. Making their debut on the Eastern Front during this battle, they were assigned to Bogdanov's 2nd Tank Army, hurriedly rushed to smash the relief force. Although impressive by any standards, these powerful tanks, too, fell victim to the Tigers and Panthers of Schw.Pz.Rgt. Bäke and 1st Panzer Division. (Photo: von Dörnberg)

Generals Wenck and Busse at Army Group South headquarters. These staff officers had formed a far clearer estimate of the situation days before their commanders had, and had already drafted plans for a new attack before given the order to do so. Overruled by its Army Group Commander, *1.Pz.Armee's* attacking corps would withdraw as ordered to its original starting line and attack eastwards towards Morentzy, regardless of whatever misgivings Hube may have had.

As the Germans struggled back to the line they had started from on 4 February, Soviet counterattacks intensified, but were unable to achieve decisive results. Breith's troops were able to ward off these attacks, though there were many tense moments when it appeared as if the men of 2nd Guards and 6th Tank Armies would succeed in breaking through. German strength was also rapidly eroding; many of Breith's tanks and other vehicles which had broken down or were stuck were deliberately destroyed by their crews to prevent them from falling into enemy hands. The infantrymen were exhausted and worn down from five days of heavy fighting in the mud. The combat strength of the leading panzer divisions (not counting *1.Pz.Div.,* which had yet to be fully committed to battle) had declined alarmingly; on 9 February, *III.Pz.Korps* could only field 62 tanks and assault guns, less than half of what it had started with five days before. Meden's *17.Pz.Div.* had only four tanks operational. For all of their efforts, Breith's men had little to show, except for the fact that they claimed to have knocked out or disabled nearly 300 enemy tanks in five days of combat.

However, from the point of view of Zhukov and other Soviet leaders, it appeared as if Vatutin's *Front* had actually achieved a victory. They seemed to have believed that they had pushed back the Germans, or at least they reported that they had done so afterwards. According to Zhukov, "In the Rizino area the enemy was able to dent our defenses…The enemy was checked and partially thrown back to the areas he had attempted to leave."[6] Whether Zhukov or Vatutin realized that their opponents were deliberately withdrawing is unknown. However, when the Germans attempted their next relief attack, the Soviet defenders appear to have been taken completely by surprise when they were caught between two converging attacks - one from the outside of the pocket and the other from the inside.

In truth, Breith's and Vormann's initial relief attempt had achieved very little. The hundreds of destroyed Soviet tanks would quickly be replaced by more, rushed from other areas of the front or from reserves assembling far to the rear. The Germans had suffered heavy losses in men and material, as much from the elements as from the enemy. Instead of realizing that continuing their attack to the north was fruitless since the pocket had wandered to the east, Breith and Hube instead stubbornly slogged onward, despite the advice of their Army Group Commander. Vormann's troops achieved even less, seizing a bridgehead over the Shpolka River at Iskrenoye, that they were unable to exploit. Instead of charging ahead, *XXXXVII.Pz.Korps* was forced to endure a week of ferocious counterattacks by 5th Guards Tank Army that kept them from getting anywhere.

Even Manstein had clung to the concept of an ambitious combined large-scale encirclement and relief operation far longer than the situation warranted. To his credit, he ignored Hitler's demand to keep going and had ordered Hube to pull back Breith's corps and try a shorter course once he realized that *III.Pz.Korps'* attack would strike nothing but thin air. When Hitler was informed of the change of direction after the new attack was already underway, he feebly acquiesced. Far better to seek forgiveness than permission, Manstein must have thought. Furthermore, all of *1.Pz.Div.* would now be available for the renewed thrust. But while the new avenue of approach appeared to provide certain advantages, five precious days had been lost, time which the two encircled corps could not afford to lose.

To better exert his influence over events as they unfolded, Manstein ordered his command railroad car and his staff moved to Uman on 7 February, virtually within range of the fighting. He tried several times during the battle to be driven in his *Kübelwagen* to the front lines to see the situation for himself, but each time was forced to turn back on account of

the mud. During one of these trips, Manstein noticed once again the advantage that the broad tracks of Soviet tanks had over those of his own.[7]

Besides changing the direction of the relief attack, there was another matter that had to be attended to. The issue of command and control within the pocket had been festering ever since 28 January, when Lieb's corps had been attached to *8.Armee*. While this was a logical move, it left no one in overall command of the encircled forces within the pocket. As previously related, both corps commanders were competing against each other for allocation of scarce resources, such as fuel and ammunition, as well as the tactical control of *Wiking*. On 6 February, Stemmermann sent a secret radio message to Wöhler demanding that he make a decision in regards to appointing someone to be the overall commander of the encircled forces, that the situation demanded nothing less.[8] Therefore, by 7 February it had become evident to both Wöhler and Manstein that unity of command had to be established immediately in order to guarantee that one commander, and one commander alone, had the authority to direct all of the activities within the pocket itself.

Who that should be proved an easy decision, because it was based on common universal precepts which were shared by nearly all of the members of the officer corps who had been in the service since World War One. Namely, command should go to the senior officer. Not only did *Gen.d.Art.* Stemmermann outrank *Gen.Lt.* Lieb, but his date of seniority in grade was 1 December 1942, as opposed to Lieb's, which was 1 June 1943.[9] Therefore, in an order issued by *8.Armee* headquarters on the morning of 7 February, Stemmermann was placed in command of all troops in the pocket, including those of Lieb's *XXXXII.A.K.* The encircled forces would henceforth be called *Gruppe Stemmermann* (Task Force Stemmermann).[10] In his diary entry for that day, General Lieb recorded no objections to this turn of events. In truth, Lieb was to be spared both a crushing responsibility and a bitter fate.

However, Wöhler, for one, must have had his doubts about whether Stemmermann was capable of handling the strain that this appointment entailed. Certainly, Stemmermann's nervous-

A wounded SS grenadier is being evacuated by akja (sled), late January 1944. (U.S. National Archives)

Artillerymen help push a horse-drawn 105mm howitzer along a snow-encrusted road. (Bundesarchiv 278/883/36)

ness during the first week of the battle had perhaps given the former cause to wonder, when it seemed that *XI.A.K.'s* commander had fired off anxious teletype messages every few minutes describing some calamity or the other. To be fair, it was Stemmermann's first corps-level command and his sector had been hit with a major attack, so it would be natural to assume that he be overanxious during his first real test. Even so, Wöhler ordered that a *Maj.* Bittl from *8.Armee's* operations staff fly in to the pocket aboard a Fiesler *Storch* on at least two separate occasions, in order to conduct assessments of both corps commanders in the pocket, as well as to determine actual conditions. In fact, Wöhler himself tried to fly in to meet with his two subordinates at least once, though was forced to cancel on account of the foul weather.

The result of one of Bittl's assessments is illuminating, for it illustrates the effects that nearly two weeks of fighting had wrought upon both Stemmermann and Lieb. On 5 February, Bittl and the Army's assistant *Oberquartiermeister* (supply officer) flew into Korsun, where he met with General Lieb and *Oberst* Gädke, Stemmermann's Chief of Staff. In addition to bringing instructions concerning what both corps were to do in order to support the first relief attempt, he also was instructed to report on the two men's mental condition, as far as he could determine.

In regards to Stemmermann, Bittl noted that he seemed deeply affected by the number of casualties his corps had suffered and was well aware of the general situation of the encircled forces. To emphasize that Stemmermann understood the gravity of their current predicament, Bittl noted that the general spoke in a "very serious manner." Lieb, on the other hand, appeared calm and confident and seemed to have a positive view of events. However, Bittl noted, Lieb did not seem to truly recognize just how serious the overall situation was.[11] Bittl was also brought up to date on the fighting capabilities of the two corps as well as the supply situation, which did not appear favorable - both corps had at most only three days of fuel and ammunition left.

Upon his return to Army headquarters, Bittl briefed Wöhler and Speidel in detail as to what he saw. His evaluation no doubt contributed to Wöhler's belief that while Stemmermann was capable of exercising overall command of the troops in the pocket, only Lieb's corps had the strength and motivation to serve as the *Sturmbock* (battering ram) to lead a breakout towards the approaching relief force, should that be called for, and informed Manstein accordingly. In a teletype message, Manstein replied that it was up to Wöhler to decide when a breakout should be made, but that whatever the case, Wöhler should let him know immediately.[12] By 7 February, such a breakout had become a necessity. When the order came, it would be Lieb and his men who would lead the breakout.

In addition to these matters, Manstein had upper level meddling to worry about. Perhaps to bolster Stemmermann's and Lieb's spirits and boost the morale of the encircled troops, Wöhler had forwarded a message to both men notifying them that he was submitting their names for the award of the Knight's Cross. Wöhler was preparing to actually confer the awards with his hearty congratulations when Manstein, having been notified of what was afoot, stepped in.

Through the battle, the encircled German forces were able to maintain direct radio communications with forces on the outside, which made coordination between forces inside and outside the Kessel much easier. Here, troops from a signal battalion erect the mast antenna for the teletype. Note panje wagon in background with portable generator aboard.
(Bundesarchiv 241/2173/11)

In a teletype message the same day he conferred with Wöhler in regards to whether or not a breakout should be ordered, Manstein also stated that he was of opinion that the awards should not yet be proffered upon Lieb and Stemmermann, in order to avoid any comparisons between the current situation and January 1943.[13] What he meant, of course, was that he did not want the awards given out, simply as a morale boost to the generals and the troops, since that is exactly what Hitler had done with Paulus at Stalingrad the year before. Manstein wanted to prevent such an incident from reoccurring as long as he had a say

Enigma encoding keyboard for standard radio teletype communications system. (Bundesarchiv 241/2173/9)

in the matter. Rather than improving morale, he thought, such awards would instead signal to the commanders and men in the pocket that they would be expected to fight to the death, just as Hitler had expected of Paulus. This, in Manstein's opinion, would lower morale, not raise it. Therefore, he ordered that the awards be deferred until the encircled troops had been freed.

Wöhler relayed his best wishes instead and informed Stemmermann that he had submitted his name for the award, but that it would be presented after the battle was over. Stemmermann radioed back to Wöhler and thanked him for the compliment, adding that the *Führer* could count on *XI.A.K.* to fight to the last round, if need be.[14] Manstein's thoughts on the matter are not recorded, but he must have inwardly winced when he heard about this remark. That was just the sort of *Kadavergehorsam* (blind obedience) that had sealed Paulus' fate and Manstein detested that manner of thinking.

Such communications between Hitler, Manstein, the two army commanders, and the commanders of the corps concerned in the battle were possible thanks to technological breakthroughs. Although both the German and Soviet Armies relied on field telephones for the majority of their routine communications requirements, advances in radio and radioteletype could now allow orders and reports to be transmitted nearly instantaneously. In this manner, Hitler and Stalin could remain at their command posts thousands of kilometers away, yet be in constant, real-time contact with commanders. This was, as is today, both a blessing and a curse. Stalin, who was increasingly less likely to interfere

with ongoing operations, allowed *STAVKA* to use these means to exercise more direct control of *Fronts*, armies, and corps. For Hitler, as previously related, it granted him the means to meddle in operations at increasingly lower levels, limiting the flexibility of his commanders and sacrificing the initiative to the enemy.

Improved encryption devices, using the *Enigma* system, allowed orders and reports to be sent by radio teletypewriter or by encrypted voice communications. Many such orders were sent back and forth between the two encircled corps and *8.Armee* throughout the battle. The standard item of equipment for corps headquarters and above, such as those used during the Battle of the Cherkassy Pocket, was the *Feldfernschreiber* T36 Teletypewriter/Tape Teleprinter. With its associated transmitter, repeater, and receiver components, it could send encrypted teletype messages using *Enigma* codes to receiving stations at distances ranging from 155 to 207 kilometers. Powered by a portable gasoline-driven generator, this system could be placed into operation by three or four men, who were required to emplace the set, erect the antennae, and maintain the equipment (See photograph). With equipment such as this, Generals Wöhler and Hube could remain in constant contact with each other and with the leaders of the encircled corps, as well as with Manstein at Army Group South Headquarters.

The troops of the signal regiments or *Abteilungen* attached to both *XI.* and *XXXXII.A.K.*, as well as *Pz.KorpsNachr.Abt.447* of *XXXXVII.Pz.Korps*, received high praise from General Vormann after the battle. In addition to keeping their sets

Above: *By now, the aerial relief effort was in full swing. Completely cut off, all the units of Gruppe Stemmermann, including Wiking, had to rely for all of their resupply on the Luftwaffe. Here, an SS-Grenadier of Wiking recovers 10.5 cm artillery shells from a aerial delivered canister, dropped by parachute at low level by a Ju-52 near Gorodishche, early February 1944. (U.S. National Archives)*

Above: *Three NCOs of the Germania Panzergrenadier Regiment, including Knight's Cross wearer Hauptscharführer Gustav Schreiber (center) inspect a new G-43 semiautomatic rifle near Gorodishche. (U.S. National Archives)*

Above: *SS-grenadiers of Wiking huddle in the snow for warmth as they occupy hastily-prepared fighting positions scooped out of the melting snow, which had began to thaw in earnest on 4 February 1944. (U.S. National Archives)*

Above: *Without overhead cover or a place to escape from the elements, men quickly succumbed to frostbite or a variety of other ailments if forced to occupy positions in the open for long. (U.S. National Archives)*

Above: *A battery of self-propelled 10.5 cm Wespen of SS-Pz.Art. 5 Wiking fire on the attacking Soviets. Having modern, mobile weapons systems like these went a long way towards delaying and thwarting repeated Soviet attacks. Photo taken near Gorodishche, early February 1944. (U.S. National Archives)*

Above: SS-Gruppenführer Herbert Otto Gille, *commander of Wiking, in conversation with his 01 prior to the breakout. (U.S. National Archives)*

Right: SS-Sturmbannführer *and Knight's Cross with Oakleaves wearer* **Hans Dorr**, *commander of 1st Battalion, SS Panzergrenadier Regiment Germania, at his battalion command post near Gorodishche. He is wearing the standard SS-issue fur-lined anorak with a rabbit-fur covered winter cap. His battalion led the attack that seized the crucial town of Shanderovka several days after this picture was taken. (U.S. National Archives)*

Above: Hans Dorr *in conversation with one of his officers near Gorodishche. (U.S. National Archives)*

operational up until the very last stages of the breakout, they also relayed thousands of messages despite the great distances involved, Soviet air attacks, artillery barrages aided by radio-direction finding, wet weather (the bane of all radio operators) and shortages of equipment.

The logs of all radio broadcasts from both encircled corps to *8.Armee* still exist in the *Bundesarchiv* (German Federal Archives) and provide a practically hour-by-hour account of events in the pocket. Considering the number of divisions and corps involved that had to remain in contact with one another, the accomplishments of the signal troops in the battle are nothing short of extraordinary. Without their ability to keep Stemmermann in touch with his higher headquarters throughout the battle, it is doubtful today whether any kind of breakout could have been successfully executed.[15]

It was thus over the airwaves that the new orders were received at Stemmermann's headquarters in Gorodishche on the morning of Monday, 7 February. The order informed him of the direction of attack of the relief forces - Vormann's corps would attempt to attack north towards Olshana via Zvenigorodka, while Breith would change his direction of attack towards Morentsy. *Gruppe Stemmermann* was directed to effect the initial breakthrough of the Soviet inner ring of encirclement, then concentrate its entire strength in an attack across the line Shenderovka-Kvitki towards Morentsy, where it would conduct the linkup with the relief force of General Breith.

The final decision of whether or not to conduct the breakout would depend upon the progress of the relief force. The order ended with the telling remark that "situation does not permit further delay."[16] The initial date set for the breakout was to be 1700 hours, 9 February, but Stemmermann requested permission to change that to 10 February, since the poor weather and traffic conditions was causing innumerable delays and his forces would not be able to be in position in time.

To help Stemmermann and his staff conduct their planning, *8.Armee* had previously determined on 4 February that there were two possible courses of action to follow if a breakout attack was necessary and tentative plans had been made. Now detailed planning began in earnest. The first option, *Frühlingsglaube* involved an attack from the southern rim of the pocket by *XI.A.K.* towards Vormann's corps. The other, *Betriebsausflug*, involved a combined attack by both *XI.* and *XXXXII.A.K.* in a southwesterly direction towards Breith's corps in the vicinity of Lysyanka.[17] Breith's relief attack retained its prior code-name of *Wanda*. Initially, Manstein was inclined to proceed with *Fruehlingsglaube*, since *XI.A.K.*, on 7 February at least, was the nearest of either corps to one of the rescue forces, although Vormann's corps was by then almost completely fought out and could only hope to tie up further Soviet forces.

On 7 February, however, *Gruppe Stemmermann* was not properly positioned as yet to carry out such an attack from the inside. On that date, the pocket was shaped like a figure eight around the two key towns of Korsun and Gorodishche. Its 45 kilometer-long axis pointed from the northwest (where Korsun lay) to the southeast. While this had been the best disposition of the encircled forces for the first unsuccessful relief attempt, by 7

Oberst Kurt Hummel, *Commander, Gren.Rgt.124, 72.Inf.Div. (Photo courtesy 72.Inf.Div. Veteran's Association)*

February it was no longer so. By giving up ground along the southern front near Shanderovka and Olshana, the pocket had actually moved away or "wandered" from the best positions to launch its newly-ordered breakout attack. Stemmermann would have to change the shape and direction of the pocket from one running northwest to southeast, to a new shape and longitudinal axis running from east to west - "rather like turning a battleship in the midst of an enemy sea."[18]

Newly-sized positions would have to be given up and old positions retaken from the enemy. Gorodishche would have to be abandoned and the forces holding the salient around the town, in danger of being cut off anyway, would have to be evacuated. This movement would apply to virtually all of *XI.A.K.* - both *57.* and *72.Inf.Div.* and *Wiking*. General Kruse's decimated *389.Inf.Div.* would be temporarily disbanded on Stemmermann's orders on 9 February, when its combat strength had sunk to a mere 200 infantry and three batteries of artillery, making it combat ineffective as a division and no longer a factor in the battle. These remnants were attached to Trowitz's *57.Inf.Div.* for the remainder of the battle.

As for Kruse and his staff, they were to be employed in various "special assignments" as a movement control staff at

Korsun and later at Shanderovka. In two short weeks, the *Rheingold* Division had lost at least 75 percent of its effective strength. But its desperate resistance in the path of Konev's main attack slowed the Soviet timetable and enabled Stemmermann and Lieb time to patch together a semblance of a southern front.

The new defensive line in the east would be located initially on the western outskirts of Gorodishche. Actually, it was planned not to be a formal defensive line at all, but rather *XI.A.K.* would carry out a phased withdrawal towards Korsun. The bulk of this fighting would be carried out by Trowitz's Division, with help from the remnants of *389.Inf.Div.* as well as the bulk of *Wiking. Oberst* Hohn's *72.Inf.Div.*, the Walloon Brigade and part of *Wiking* would go into reserve near Korsun to be used for the next phase of the operation. *Gruppe Stemmermann's* headquarters were moved from Gorodishche to Korsun on 8 February, which by then was crammed with thousands of troops from all branches of the *Wehrmacht*, as well as civilian officials, *Reichsbahn* railway employees, and foreign auxiliaries. Korsun was bombed by the Red Air Force daily, its packed streets and alleyways a tempting target for *Sturmoviks* and fighter bombers.

In the pocket's northwest corner, *88.Inf.Div.* would have to pull out of the sector it was occupying along the arc stretching from Tagancha-Ivanovka-Moskalenki and displace to a much shorter front line five kilometers to the south. The division and the elements from *K.Abt.B* that had been placed under *Graf* Rittberg's command had to hold firm against the renewed assaults being launched by troops of Trofimenko's 27th Army. Gerhard Meyer, back again with his regiment, *Art.Rgt.188*, which was located on 9 February in the small village of Yablonovka several kilometers southwest of Korsun, found things not to his liking:

> [Here] everything is the same as it was when we left. The weather is still lousy. When it clears up, the fighter bombers return and we lose a few more vehicles and horses. Our shack on the edge of the village remains untouched . . . [our positions] lay outside in the cold and in the muck of the melting snow and the fields. We are freezing just like a poor tailor. Often we see fleeting figures appear out of the fog like ghosts, and grab another drum for the machine gun, but the Russians haven't been up to anything here . . . [19]

The fighting in *XXXXII.A.K.'s* sector elsewhere, though, was heavy. On 9 February, the positions of *Div.Gr.323* west of Vygravev were attacked by several battalions from the Soviet 159th Fortified Region. Some of the enemy troops broke through and penetrated as far as the German rear service area, destroying or scattering some supply and service units before a counterattack restored the breach in the lines.[20]

The constant withdrawals had begun to wear down everyone in Lieb's corps, especially the artillerymen. With the snow and mud, mere horsepower was no longer enough to move the guns into and out of their firing positions. To arrive in time to support the infantry, gunners had to manhandle their guns and howitzers into position. According to *Oblt.* Hans Menedetter, an Austrian who was serving as the adjutant of *Art.Rgt.188,*

> During this phase of the battle, the mud allowed hardly any movement at all. The regiment's battalions stayed in their firing positions as long as they possibly could. When a change of position became unavoidable, the guns had to be moved meter by meter into their new positions with everyone lending a hand, in order to provide fire support to the infantry in their increasingly exposed defensive positions. We were nearly at the end of our strength; even nature seemed to be against us.[21]

Despite these and other difficulties, *XXXXII.A.K.* and its subordinate units slowly positioned themselves for the breakout.

The central axis of the pocket would remain Korsun, for here was the lifeline to the outside world - the airfield. Regardless of cost, the airfield had to be kept out of the range of Soviet artillery - a distance of from 15 to 20 kilometers - lest the evacuation of wounded and the delivery of fuel and ammunition

Oberleutnant Hans Kurt Menedetter, *Regimental Adjutant, Art.Rgt.188, 88.Inf.Div., (shown here as Hauptmann). (Photo courtesy of Hans Menedetter)*

Bottomless mud. Supply troops of the Rollbahn inside the pocket try to wrest their truck free of the gooey muck and ice. (Bundesarchiv 710/356/6A)

be brought to a halt. This new line would have to be held until a day or two before the breakout commenced - after that, Korsun and its airfield would no longer be needed.

A day or two later than that, any chances for success would be doubtful - by 9 February, *Gruppe Stemmermann* reported that the average rifle strength of its infantry regiments had sunk to as low as 150 men - about ten percent of their authorized number.[22] On 8 February alone, the Germans suffered 350 casualties and 1,100 wounded were awaiting a flight out. The already decimated ranks of the infantry battalions and companies had been augmented somewhat by the addition of service and supply troops from the *Trosse*, but these men became casualties quickly and hardly represented a real increase in combat power. In addition to casualties suffered, Stemmermann estimated that he only had about one-third of the fuel and ammunition needed to launch the breakout.

The most important part of this scheme of maneuver required that the most favorable positions in the southwest from which to launch the breakout towards the relief force would have to be recaptured. These positions had been given up to the Soviets a week earlier - a goose egg-shaped area encompassing the villages of Novo Buda, Komarovka and Khil'ki. The even larger and more important crossroads town of Shanderovka, which also needed to be retaken, had only been evacuated on the morning of 9 February. A few days before, these villages were thought by the German leadership to be no longer needed since the relief forces would not be approaching from this direction, but rather more to the west or southeast. Because of this, the men of *Div.Gr.323* and *Sperrverband Fouquet* had evacuated them in the dead of night without firing a shot. Now, they would have to be retaken, regardless of the amount of blood shed doing so.

To carry out this maneuver, Stemmermann would use his last remaining units that were still capable of offensive action - Hohn's Division, which was now located in Koshmak after having been pulled out of the Lenina area beginning on 7 February, *Germania*, Köller's tank battalion, and the Walloon Brigade, as well as a *Kampfgruppe* from *K.Abt.B*. Although these units had been in action for weeks, they still had enough strength and, more importantly, the offensive spirit needed to carry out the task assigned them. They were allotted a few days to reorganize and replenish their thinned ranks as much as conditions permitted in their new assembly areas near Korsun. For example, Köller's battalion received the order at 0830 hours 9 February to move all of its available tanks and assault guns from their positions south of Gorodishche near Valyavskiye to the town of Korsun.

Moving out immediately, the armor arrived in Korsun at 1400 hours, with the wheeled vehicles arriving later that evening. The muddy roads from Gorodishche appeared not to have posed a serious problem for Köller's tanks, though this was an exception. While tanks could travel cross-country, wheeled vehicles of *Wiking* and other divisions were mired in an almost unending convoy stretching from Gorodishche all the way to Korsun, offering an inviting target to the Red Air Force. Once in Korsun, Köller put the rest period to good use, ordering his crews to perform as much maintenance on their vehicles as time permitted.[23] By this point, he still had over a dozen tanks and assault guns operational, including the vehicles and troops from *K.Gr. von Brese*, which had been attached to Köller's battalion since the early days of the encirclement.

Köller was ordered on 10 February by General Gille, then located in Korsun, to form an infantry company from all of his tank crews and truck drivers who had lost their vehicles and place them under the control of division headquarters as a reserve force. This company, commanded by *Hstuf.* Wittmann (no relation to the famous Tiger ace), was to be employed wherever the situation required. Untrained as infantry, this ad-hoc company, consisting of four platoons, totaled 220 men led by four officers. Armed solely with light machine-guns and small arms, they were to prove their worth time and time again during the next week.

The following day, this small *Kampfgruppe* was thrown into battle when they were used to repel a Soviet attack by 294th Rifle Division that threatened the Korsun rail station, the end of the line for the Gorodishche-Korsun *Rollbahn*. That night, they were ordered to conduct a forced march towards Arbusino, where they counterattacked and wiped out a Soviet penetration that threatened to rupture the defenses there.[24] Once Wittmann and his men marched off, they were not to see the rest of their battalion until after the breakout was over.

Although the armored units of *Wiking* and the Walloon Brigade had been able to move to their designated positions in time, the initial attack to seize the breakout area set for 10 February had to be postponed once again until 11 February because the withdrawal from the Gorodishche salient was not going fast enough. The thaw that had bedeviled Breith and Vormann had now struck the troops inside the pocket with a vengeance. In a diary entry, General Lieb wrote "Artillery, heavy weapons, and horse-drawn vehicles of *72.* and *389.Inf.Div.,* and the *Wiking* Division, as well as hundreds of motor vehicles of *Wiking* carrying many wounded, are stuck in the mud at Gorodishche."[25]

In Lieb's and Stemmermann's opinion, adhering to the time-line laid out by *8.Armee* and Army Group South's Headquarters would involve heavy losses in men and equipment, so they pleaded for more time. Confronted with the reality of conditions that were affecting the units outside the pocket as well as those inside, both Wöhler and Manstein assented. Even then, Lieb thought that the date arrived at, 11 February, was still optimistic. "Much as we would like to," he wrote in his diary, "we cannot do it by then. In this mud the infantry cannot possibly cover more than a thousand yards per hour."

Maj. Siegel and *Gren.Rgt.266* knew exactly what Lieb meant. When his regiment moved out on 8 February from Klystunovka to its assembly area near Koshmak, the only hard-surfaced roadway in the pocket was the one that ran along the Gorodishche-Korsun railway bed, which had been filled in with gravel in spots or had planks laid across it. The railway and road running parallel to it, according to Siegel, was "completely blocked with traffic." His infantry kept moving around the vehicles. Many men had to stop with every other step to retrieve their boots from the deep mud which had sucked off both their footgear and their socks. Others went barefoot. Frustrated, Siegel ordered his mounted platoon to reconnoiter forward in order to bring back information on which roads could be taken and which to avoid.[26]

Complicating the situation were the incessant Soviet air attacks that shot-up the densely-packed columns of vehicles, which often sat immobile for hours at a time. At first, according to one eyewitness, the Soviet fliers flew perpendicular or diagonally to the railway when they conducted their bombing and machine-gun attacks, hitting only one or two vehicles at the most. After a few days, they seemed to have finally deduced that attacks against a linear target, such as a railroad, was best carried out when one flew directly above or parallel to the *Rollbahn*. German losses in trucks and other motor vehicles skyrocketed. Siegel and his men were more fortunate, noting that "despite all the bombs being dropped, we came through without a scratch."

Trapped within this endless column sat Willy Hein, who had been serving as the acting signals officer for his tank battalion since being wounded at Olshana the week before. Suffering from burns to his face and hands which had become infected since being forced to bail out of his burning tank, he wrote in his diary as he sat in a truck along the Korsun-Gorodishche *Rollbahn* . . . "under heavy air attack. Bottomless mud makes all movement difficult. My own condition very bad. Unable to sleep. Hungry and lice-ridden . . ."[27] In a recent interview, he mentioned how glad he was to finally rejoin the rest of the battalion, which had moved from Korsun to Yablonovka on 10 February. With rescue so seemingly close, he remembered how his spirits soared despite his pain and suffering. Unknown to him, he would have to hold on for another week, not two more days.

When Siegel and his regiment arrived at their new assembly area for units of *72.Inf.Div.* in the village of Koshmak that afternoon, they found things in disarray. Somehow, *Oberst* Hummel and his *Gren.Rgt.124* had lost their way. The division's headquarters did not seem to know where its units were. After an overnight's rest, Siegel and his men were informed that they were now the combat reserve for *Gruppe Stemmermann* and were to depart that day, 9 February, for Korsun immediately. During the briefing by *Oberst* Müller, the division's 1a, Siegel grasped the full implications of *Gruppe Stemmermann's* situation. "Things did not look rosy," he noted. During their short stay in Koshmak, Siegel observed a dogfight between a He-111 and a group of Soviet fighters. To his surprise, the German aircraft shook off its pursuers and was able to escape, a rare feat indeed for the slow, poorly-armed bomber.

Much to his relief, Siegel and his men were given several day's rest upon arrival in Korsun. Although the supply column had gotten lost on the way from Koshmak, they arrived later on the morning of 10 February, just in time for most of their stores to be destroyed on order of division headquarters. Siegel even found time to hand out Iron Crosses to deserving men. Though he and his men were called out to form a screen line to the east when a Soviet attack was rumored, they were able to go back to the houses they had occupied after it was proven to be a false alarm. The next day, Siegel found out why his regiment and Robert Kästner's rival *Gren.Rgt.105* had been permitted to remain idle while fighting raged elsewhere. That night the two regiments were to lead the initial attempt to break the inner ring of encirclement at Novo Buda. The days of relative rest and relaxation for *72.Inf.Div.* were over. That night, they would find themselves in pitched battle against troops of General Selivanov's 5th Guards Cavalry Corps.

According to Leon Degrelle, the withdrawal from the *Gorodishche* "noose" went according to plan. In his account,

HELL'S GATE

written long after the war, he praised the manner in which the German command within the pocket was able to maintain control of the situation during this critical period. *Gruppe Stemmermann,* he wrote:

> kept the situation in hand with incomparable sang froid. Despite the frightful situation of the fifty to sixty thousand survivors in the pocket, we couldn't detect the least trace of agitation or hurry in the orders. The maneuvers were accomplished methodically and calmly. Nowhere did the enemy manage to seize the initiative.

❖ ❖ ❖

Charged with forming the rearguard for the withdrawal from Gorodishche, the Walloon Brigade could only retreat at the same pace as the convoys stalled on the Korsun-Gorodishche *Rollbahn.* Acutely conscious that a peremptory withdrawal would endanger the lives of thousands of others, the Walloons struggled to hold their designated positions long enough for the convoys to withdraw a few more kilometers. Whenever the pursuing Soviets of 294th and 373rd Rifle Divisions managed to penetrate their defensive positions and seize a key hill or village, the Walloons would immediately mount a counterattack and throw them back, "regardless of the price," according to Degrelle.

On 9 February, Lippert and his Walloons were forced to withdraw from the Staroselye-Derenkovets defense line, after their neighbor on the right, the young SS men of *I./SS-Pz.Gren.Rgt. Westland,* gave way in the face of a strong attack launched by 78th Rifle Corps. According to Degrelle, the Soviets launched a dawn surprise attack and quickly drove the battalion from *Westland* from its fighting positions near the village of Skiti and routed the survivors. "We saw them drifting back from the Soviet tide and they gathered behind our positions. They had nothing more to give. Some of them were crying like children." On their behalf, Degrelle noted, most of these SS troops had been with *Wiking* for less than a month and had "barely received the rudiments of military instruction amid the bustle of January. These unfortunate boys were worn out with fatigue and emotion."

Through this breach vacated by the battalion from *Westland* poured two Soviet columns of infantry. Lippert, without requesting permission, ordered his brigade to pull back to the forest before they were enveloped. There, he rallied his men and braced for the worst. This unauthorized withdrawal, though probably necessary based on the local tactical situation, drew condemnation from General Stemmermann, who noted acidly in a radio message to General Wöhler that evening:

> The Wiking Division along with parts of the Walloon Brigade, against orders from corps, withdrew from the line Derenkovets-Nabukov-Chutor. This had led to an unforeseen dire situation along our southeast flank with wide-ranging consequences. Cause of withdrawal: Shortage of leadership and supervision.[28]

A Waffen-SS grenadier toting a Panzerfaust as he makes his way to another defensive position. (U.S. National Archives)

No doubt that General Lieb was not the only one to hold the Walloon Brigade in low regard, though in retrospect it seems that Lieb's and Stemmermann's condemnations were unfair.

To General Gille, this message must have stung bitterly; regardless, orders went out to the Walloon Brigade and a *Kampfgruppe* from *72.Inf.Div.,* which had been sent by Stemmermann to provide assistance. These units were to launch a counterattack and retake the town of Skiti that evening and hold it long enough so all of Gorodishche, with its depots and field hospitals, could finally be evacuated. The attack, led by *Stubaf.* Lippert himself, commenced later that evening. "Fighting tooth and nail," wrote Degrelle, "we pushed the Soviets back into the woods. Once again the situation was temporarily saved." With this crucial position retaken, the evacuation of Gorodishche could continue in relative safety. When the chastised troops of *Westland* returned that night, they tied in their defenses on the left with those of their Belgian neighbors. For the next two days, Germans, Belgians, Dutch, Swedes, Danes, and Norwegians of the *Waffen-SS's* most multinational division struggled to keep the Soviets at bay and to buy additional time for General Stemmermann.

Finally, on the evening of 10 February, the last German position along the Olshanka line was given up. With the roads before them totally impassable except for tracked vehicles and *panje* wagons, the Walloon Brigade destroyed the rest of its wheeled vehicles and headed out towards Korsun on tracked vehicles, by foot and by panje wagons. The Soviets were slow to mount a pursuit, since the thaw had caused the Olshanka to swell to twice its normal width. One of the last Walloons to die in the brigade's old positions was Walloon *Hstf.* Anthonissen, a brigade staff officer who had been a manufacturer from Ghent in more peaceful times.

When it was reported that a large group of Soviet troops had crossed the river and were attempting to cut off the Walloon Brigade's route of withdrawal, he led a small *Kampfgruppe* in a counterattack to clear the road of the enemy. When he and his men were ambushed by a much larger Soviet force, most of the men in his group, many of whom were *Volksdeutsche* (ethnic Germans) recruits from Yugoslavia and Rumania, fled, leaving Anthonissen and a few others to continue offering resistance. Eyewitnesses reported that he was last seen alive shouting at the oncoming Soviets, firing his machine pistol from the hip. A counterattack, carried out an hour later by *Wiking*, was able to dislodge the Soviets and throw them back across the river. They then found Anthonissen's body in a thicket 30 meters to the east of the road. "It was [the body of] a very tall man bearing the Belgian colors on his left sleeve," a German officer later reported.[29] At least this was one Walloon who was not "too soft for this business."

As the units of *Gruppe Stemmermann* slowly began to change the shape of the pocket and reorient themselves in accordance with the orders relayed from above, General Wöhler, for his part, also tried to stay abreast of the changing situation. On 10 February, he sent a message to both Lieb and Stemmermann and inquired whether a breakout in the direction of Morentsy-Zvenigorodka was still feasible or whether it would be better if it were to be aimed along the line Dzhurzhentsy-Pochapintsy towards Lysyanka. Stemmermann replied that it would be better if the relief force launched a tank attack immediately towards the Shanderovka-Steblev area, since his corps was tied down in heavy fighting and Lieb's corps had been reduced to the effective combat strengths of two weak battalions (an incorrect assessment).

When queried by *8.Armee's* chief of staff, Lieb replied with a much more thorough assessment than he had expressed a few days earlier. Rather than wait for the relief attack to approach the pocket, Lieb stated that changing the route from Morentsy to Lysyanka would be more attainable - it was now the shorter route with an easier route of approach for the relief force. Furthermore, in a backhanded criticism directed at Stemmermann's corps, Lieb stated:

> Situation on east front critical. Several enemy penetrations. For the past forty-eight hours, XI.A.K. has been unable to establish a new defense line. [Its] troops are badly depleted and battle weary. [My] corps front intact. We are attacking south of Steblev. Serious danger if east front not brought to a halt . . . [My] troops are well in hand. Early advance of Breith towards Lysyanka decisive.

Evidently, Lieb felt that he had a far better grasp of the situation than his commander and events were to prove him correct. General Speidel replied, thanking Lieb for the comprehensive information about the overall situation and informed him that, based on discussions between Wöhler and Manstein, *III.Pz.Korps* would attack on 11 February in the direction of Lysyanka.

Speidel closed with "Will do all we can. Good luck." But *Gruppe Stemmermann* now had to meet them halfway-provided that its forces could break through the inner ring of encirclement defended by the Soviets and seize the towns of Shanderovka,

Khilki, Komarovka, and Novo Buda. However, the forces available to carry out such an attack were dwindling rapidly. Could his men take and hold these villages long enough? And, just as important, would the morale of the troops hold out? For, just as they were preparing their final attack to wipe out the pocket, the Soviets were also preparing a propaganda offensive designed to break the German's will to fight.

End Notes

[1]   *8.Armee* KTB entry dated 0905 hours, 3 February 1944, p. 2.

[2]   Ibid.

[3]   Ibid, entry dated 1120 hours, p. 3.

[4]   *8.Armee* KTB, entries dated 1700 hours 6 February, p. 5 and 1140 hours 7 February, 1944, p. 4.

[5]   Glantz, "From the Dnieper to the Vistula," p. 154.

[6]   Zhukov, p. 243.

[7]   Manstein, p. 516.

[8]   Radio message, Commander, *XI.A.K.* to Headquarters, *8.Armee*, dated 1940 hours 6 February 1944.

[9]   *German Order of Battle, 1944: Directory Prepared by the Allied Intelligence of Regiments, Formations, and Units of the German Armed Forces.* (London: British War Office, 1944), pp. K11, K16.

[10] *8.Armee* KTB, entry dated 0930 hours 7 February 1944, p. 2.

[11] *8.Armee* KTB, entry dated 1530 hours 5 February 1944, p. 4.

[12] Ibid, entry dated 2335 hours, 5 February 1944, p. 8.

[13] Ibid.

[14] Radio message from Commander, *XI.A.K.* to Commander, *8.Armee* dated 2144 hours 7 February 1944.

[15] Vormann, pp. 86-87.

[16] *8.Armee* KTB, entry dated 1140 hours 7 February 1944, p. 3 and Lieb Diary, entry for 7 February 1944, quoted in DA Pam 20-234, p. 22.

[17] *8.Armee* KTB entry dated 1900 4 February 1944, p. 6.

[18] Carell, p. 482.

[19] Mayer, p. 133.

[20] Schwarz, p. 42.

[21] Menedetter, p. 68.

[22] Radio message from Headquarters, *XI.A.K.* to Headquarters, *8.Armee* dated 0935 hours 9 February 1944.

[23] *Kriegstagebuch Nr. 1, 1st Battalion, SS Panzerregiment 5*, 9 February to 30 November 1944, entry dated 9 February.

[24] Klapdor, p. 188.

[25] Lieb diary quoted in DA Pam 20-234, p. 22.

[26] Siegel, p. 8.

[27] Hein manuscript, p. 3.

[28] Radio message from General Stemmermann to General Wöhler, *8.Armee* dated 2050 hours 9 February 1944.

[29] Degrelle, pp. 178-184.

Chapter Fourteen
THE PARLEY ATTEMPT

"I have only one thought, one wish to convey to you that you recognize your completely hopeless situation and cease the senseless sacrifice of German blood. Save yourselves and come across to serve the German people!"
— *Surrender leaflet from Bund Deutscher Offiziere*[1]

With the German relief attack apparently having stalled by 7 February, Zhukov and Konev seemed to believe that the time to offer surrender terms had arrived. To them, the desperate Germans in the pocket were clearly doomed - it must have seemed to them that it would be only a matter of time before the inevitable *unichtozhenye* would take place. The airlift appeared to have completely failed, the two-pronged relief attack had been brought to a standstill by the combination of a stoutly-conducted Soviet defense and the *Rasputitsa*, and the encircled force had suffered appalling casualties. True, the troops of the First and Second Ukrainian *Fronts* had suffered even greater losses, but these were acceptable in light of the great victory about to be won.

The time therefore seemed ripe for the Soviets to offer the Germans what appeared to be generous terms of surrender. In addition, the Germans had been subjected to a propaganda barrage ever since the beginning of the battle which hopefully lowered their morale and will to resist. There was not much evidence that the psychological warfare campaign was working, because few German deserters came across. Nevertheless, hundreds of thousands of surrender leaflets had been dropped by air and by artillery shell. Loudspeakers had harangued the Germans day and night with music and detailed descriptions of the relative comfort of prisoner of war camps that awaited them if they would only come to their senses and desert. They were constantly reminded to come across with a surrender leaflet serving as a ticket to ensure safe passage of the Soviet front line positions. They promised that those who did so would receive good treatment in captivity and would return home early when the war was over, they promised.

One particularly ingenious Soviet technique was that of staging photographs with German prisoners (or possibly Soviet soldiers in captured German uniforms) sitting down to sumptuous banquets in their prisoner of war camp, printing these images on leaflets, and disseminating them by aircraft. All of this will be yours, so the leaflets went, if you only realize that we are your friends! Another original idea was that of sending individual recently-captured German soldiers back to their old front lines with their pockets full of cigarettes and chocolates. When they encountered their former comrades, they were instructed by their captors to tell them all about the friendly reception that had received from the Red Army. Whether or not they did as they were told is unknown; however, no one in their former unit probably trusted them afterwards, although the offers of warm food, comfortable living conditions, and cigarettes must have been tempting.

To carry out such a closely orchestrated psychological warfare campaign, the Soviets brought with them two and a half years of experience fighting the Germans, as well as nearly three decades of conducting propaganda against their own people. When the war started in June 1941 though, the Red Army had no such organized capability and had to build it up from scratch. Politically reliable German area experts had to be found. German expatriates were used, but were considered untrustworthy. A great deal of the early Soviet psychological warfare literature directed towards the Germans was both crude and hamhanded, and did not resonate with prisoners. In the words of Konstantin Krainyukov, political commissar of Vatutin's First Ukrainian *Front*, "At first our propaganda against the Germans had little success. Sometimes it was incorrectly applied at the front; other times it was insufficiently clever." Most German soldiers did not even take notice of it, welcoming the arrival of propaganda leaflets because they came in handy as toilet tissue when one had to visit the *Drückeberg*, or field latrine.

In order to revamp the Red Army's psychological warfare capability, the Main Office of the Red Army's Political Indoctrination Bureau issued a decree on 27 June 1942 which stated that propaganda directed against the Germans would in the future concentrate more on things that affect the lives of ordinary soldiers, rather than on political concepts that they were unlikely to understand. Instead of using propaganda materials such as leaflets and broadcast messages that dwelt on themes that stressed moral issues like humanity, justice, and conscience, the Main Office instead urged field operators to use a different approach, since it was believed that the Germans had no concept of these lofty ideals. What would be far more effective, the decree stated, would be the use of psychological themes designed to spread terror and apprehension in the ranks of the enemy.[2] Krainyukov claimed that this approach was proven during the Battle of Stalingrad the year before, but the facts cast his claim in doubt. Few Germans deserted during that epic battle, with most units holding their cohesion to the very end, long after any hope of rescue had disappeared. Both types of propaganda - persuasive and terror - were used during the Battle of Cherkassy.

During the battle, the troops of Gruppe Stemmermann were bombarded continuously by Soviet propaganda leaflets. One example shown here, tried to depict the number of German soldiers who were doomed to surrender.
(From Peter Strassner, Europaeische Freiwillige)

One Soviet leaflet that got the German's attention in the pocket was one that depicted a map signifying locations and identities of all encircled units as well as the number of Soviet formations drawn up on the outside. The accompanying German text stated that the troops of the Red Army had created a ring of steel around the pocket on the Dnieper, just like they had at Stalingrad on the Volga. And just like the troops of Paulus' ill-fated *6.Armee*, they too were doomed. The statement ended with a sentence that read "Choose surrender and live; or continue to resist and die." Many German troops who were able to break out still have this leaflet in their possession today. Visually effective, it cannot but have helped to make many soldiers of *Gruppe Stemmermann* wonder if the relief attempt was merely a sham to make them more readily fight to the death.

Contrary to all expectations, the results of the intensive Soviet psychological warfare campaign had thus far been disappointing. The Germans, despite their individual feelings about the matter and the obvious hopelessness of their situation, were nonetheless continuing to resist stubbornly. The dismal showing of the propaganda troops attracted the attention of the Red

Army's Political Indoctrination Bureau in Moscow, which dispatched a delegation to the headquarters of Konev's First Ukrainian *Front* in early February to investigate. To the surprise of Krainyukov and the rest of Konev's staff, this delegation was led by Lt.Gen. J.W. Shikin, the Bureau's chief. Even more surprising, Shikin had two German officers in tow. Evidently, they were to be used as some sort of propaganda secret weapon, but who were they?

The mysterious German guests were *Gen.d.Art.* Walter Seydlitz-Kurzbach and *Gen.Maj.* Dr. Otto Korfes. Both men had surrendered at Stalingrad the year before; Seydlitz while commanding *LI.A.K.* and Korfes, commander of *295.Inf.Div.* Deeply disillusioned by the needless suffering, defeat and surrender of *6.Armee*, both men had embraced a cause that sought nothing less than the overthrow of Hitler's regime and the return of Germany to a nation and social order founded upon democratic principles. To do so, they allied themselves with the Soviets, who used them for their own ends. While in captivity, Seydlitz and Korfes and many other German officers (Paulus abstained) were encouraged to form their own organization to help both themselves and the Soviets attain their goals of fostering the end of the war. Of course, their methods were vastly different - the Germans wanted to convince their countrymen of the error of their ways, while the Soviets saw the turncoats as yet another weapon in their arsenal to weaken and defeat the armies of the Third Reich.[3]

Seydlitz had been elected by fellow officers to serve as the president of the *Bund Deutscher Offiziere* (League of German Officers), while Korfes had been chosen to be the Director of the League and *Oberst* Luitpold Steidle had been appointed chief of staff. This organization originally consisted of three generals captured at Stalingrad as well as 100 officers of lower rank, though the organization had been growing as the tide began to turn against the Germans in the Fall of 1943. Seydlitz's League had been formed in September 1943 at the Lunyovo prisoner of war camp near Moscow in the wake of the German defeat at Kursk. In addition to conducting political indoctrination sessions in POW camps, the League also put out a weekly newspaper, the *Wochenblatt*, and broadcast messages to German troops by radio designed to convince them to surrender and join the Free Germany Committee.[4] During this visit to the front, Seydlitz and Korfes were accompanied by the Vice President of the *Nationalkomitee "Freies Deutschland"* (Free German Committee), of which Seydlitz's organization was a subsidiary.[5]

The Free Germany Committee was founded on 12 July 1943 with Soviet support at Prisoner of War Camp 27 in Krasnogorsk near Moscow. Composed primarily of expatriate Germans living in the Soviet Union, most of whom were Communists who had fled Hitler's purges in the early 1930s, the organization actively conducted agitprop activities within the camps in order to gain converts to their cause, which was the establishment of a Communist Germany under Soviet supervision. The Committee's president was author and Communist activist Erich Weinert, who later served as the vice president of the League of German Officers. The League, on the other hand, was primarily voluntary in nature and non-communist. By force of circumstances, both organizations were forced to work together, not always harmoniously, always aware that the Soviets, and not they, were calling the tune.

The effects of Seydlitz and his organization's attempt to set his errant countrymen straight soon became evident. Radio broadcasts of Seydlitz and others exhorting the troops of *Gruppe Stemmermann* to surrender were picked up by German radio interception units; if they could receive such broadcasts on their equipment, so could the troops in the front line. Despite the stringent ban on listening to foreign broadcasts, some units probably tuned in anyway. Another tactic that the Germans reported was the appearance of mysterious officers in German uniforms who appeared out of nowhere, asking units questions about their weapons, strengths and objectives, and so forth. One such officer appeared at the headquarters of *Pz.Aufkl.Abt.1* of *1.Pz.Div.* on 11 February and began to ask about the unit's strength and tactical dispositions. When the unit checked with division headquarters in order to ascertain the man's identity, they were ordered to immediately arrest him, but by then the man was gone.[6]

Even senior officers within the pocket were not exempt from Seydlitz's and the Soviet's attention. On 10 February, General Lieb received a letter addressed to him by Seydlitz dropped on top of his command post by a Soviet aircraft. In the letter, he urged Lieb to go over with his entire command to the Soviets, much as General Yorck had done in 1812 when his Prussian corps concluded an armistice with the Russians when it had been fighting under Napoleon. Later that day, 50 German prisoners of war were returned to Lieb's corps, each one bearing letters to their commanders and instructed to convince their comrades to go over to the enemy. Flabbergasted, Lieb wrote in his diary that evening "I cannot understand Seydlitz. Although the events at Stalingrad must have changed him completely, I am unable to see how he can now work as a sort of intelligence officer for Zhukov."[7]

A few days later, Lieb again received Seydlitz's attention, when a letter addressed to the commander of *198.Inf.Div.* was dropped on his headquarters with a black, white and red pennant attached. Lieb took this as a good sign, since that division was not even in the pocket. Perhaps, thought Lieb, the Soviets think we are stronger than we really are. Despite their error, Lieb was still frustrated by the note's aerial accuracy, which meant that the Soviets knew exactly where his headquarters was. "These people never fail to find my headquarters," he wrote later that day in exasperation.[8]

As impressive as the combined Soviet propaganda effort was, it bore little fruit. Few Germans deserted and most did not take the leaflets and radio broadcasts seriously. By all accounts, the men of *Gruppe Stemmermann* were grimly determined to hold on as long as possible and, if need be, to break out to freedom on their own. According to Alex Buchner, himself an Eastern Front veteran, "the German soldier had long known what awaited him in Soviet captivity - a pitiful life of hunger, degradation, and forced labor. This was no propaganda slogan."[9] In addition, many German officers and enlisted men considered Seydlitz and Korfes as traitors to their country, cowards who would do or say anything to survive Soviet captivity. The constant barrage of leaflets and loudspeaker broadcasts wore on the nerves, but not nearly as much as artillery barrages or strafing runs. Despite their honest intentions, the words of their former comrades failed to resonate with their encircled countrymen.

Both the League of German Officers and the Free Germany Committee were disbanded on 2 November 1945. After the war, many of the members of the Free Germany Committee and the League of German Officers settled in East Germany and found employment there in the new Communist government. In a speech during the dedication of the new East German Ministry of Defense building in 1959, Walter Ulbricht, serving as president and virtual dictator at the time, stated that the state had much to thank the Free Germany Committee for, because it had recruited and inculcated a considerable number of men who had laid the foundations of the Communist German state in the period immediately after the war.[10] While many of these men today are gaining increasing respectability in the newly reunified Germany of the present, where they are being depicted by the German media as men of principle and honor, to the average *Landser* who fought in the pocket, these men will forever be *Vaterlandsverräter* - traitors to their own country and deserving only scorn and derision.

After their failure to bring about any significant German defections during this battle, Seydlitz and his organization lost favor with their Soviet masters and found themselves in less demand at the front than before, though they were still a useful propaganda tool that could be used to politicize the increasing numbers of German prisoners the Soviets began to gather from the Summer of 1943 onward. After the war, a decidedly ungrateful Soviet Union had Seydlitz tried for war crimes in 1950 by a military tribunal in Moscow and sentenced him to 25 years of imprisonment. Released in 1955, he died in 1976.[11]

Nevertheless, the East Germany Ministry of National Defense issued a glowing account of the efforts of Seydlitz, Korfes, Steidle and the others in 1959, entitled *They Fought for Germany*. The book, an effort to rehabilitate the reputation of the League of German Officers and the National Free Germany Committee, provided a rather detailed account of their efforts which gives the impression that their contribution to the outcome of the Soviet's offensive was far greater than originally thought. Of course, at the time the East German government was trying to build a new army, the *Nationale Volksarmee,* and needed to establish some precedent for loyal German service under the Soviets. While the book, a thinly veiled pro-Communist treatise, fails in this regard, it does show the uncommon length to which Seydlitz and the others went to convince their countrymen of the error of their ways.

The combined Soviet and League of German Officers propaganda had absolutely no effect whatsoever on another group of soldiers in the pocket, who made up 25 percent of *Gruppe Stemmermann* - the 14,000 or so members of the *Waffen-SS* in both *Wiking* and the Walloon Brigade. More than any one else in the pocket, these men knew that a particularly bitter fate awaited them should they fall into Soviet hands. The atrocities of the *SS-Einsatzgruppen* who had murdered hundreds of thousands of Jews, partisans, and other innocent civilians since the beginning of the war in the Soviet Union had brought about their organization's collective condemnation by the Red Army. This led to a feeling that death was preferable to capture.

According to Franz Hahl, who served with *II./Westland*, then located at the northeast corner of the Pocket:

> The soldiers were continuously urged in [Soviet] leaflets to surrender. In the companies, plans were secretly drawn up as to how they could fight their way through if the situation became worse. Captivity? No! Everyone had seen and experienced too much in this country.[12]

Other members of *Wiking* laughingly compared the quality of the Soviet-prepared propaganda leaflets with those drafted by Seydlitz and the League of German Officers. The Soviet ones were found to be crude in comparison to the fairly well-done ones of Seydlitz, but both types were found to be totally lacking in believability. The men of *Wiking* and their Walloon brethren would rather die than surrender, as long as there was a chance they could fight their way out.

This attitude, however, did not keep the League of German Officers from trying. A letter addressed to Herbert Gille, signed by *Gen.Maj.* Korfes, was dropped by air on *Wiking's* headquarters. It began by restating the same theme that all the other leaflets had used - that the German's hope of breaking out with the help of a relief attack from outside was a delusion. Korfes then went on to state that one possible reason why Gille's SS troops had kept on fighting was the fact that they feared being charged with war crimes by the Soviets, should they be captured. To ease any such fears they may have had, Korfes stated that both Seydlitz and he would give assurances that the Free Germany Committee and the League of German Officers were in the position to have any legal proceedings being drawn up against them struck down. Of course, this was only on the condition that they would voluntarily lay down their weapons and join the Free Germany Committee.[13]

To add emphasis, Korfes wrote that "Today, many officers and soldiers of the *Waffen-SS* are already fighting in our ranks," a statement which must have caused many of the hard-bitten SS men to laugh. Why on earth, they thought, would anyone want to surrender to a pack of traitors who were merely fronting for the hated Communists? None of the several *Wiking* division unit histories mention any of their men who took Korfes or Seydlitz up on their offer, and it is unlikely that there were any, for they saw this as an ideological fight to the death. The men of the *Waffen-SS* were the shock troops of the Third Reich and would not admit defeat easily. If anything, these ineffective attempts to win them over probably intensified their desire to keep fighting. Certainly few SS were taken prisoner during the battle.

There is evidence that Soviet front-line troops were beginning to become perplexed by the German's continuing stubbornness. After all, any rational man would have long surrendered by now, many Soviet officers and men must have thought. Clearly, the Germans' position was hopeless, anyone could see that. One incident that illustrates this increasing frustration took place in the sector held by *Oberstlt.* Dr. Ernst

Bloch's *Sich.Rgt.318* at the beginning of the second week of February, when men holding a forward outpost spotted a Soviet officer galloping full-tilt towards their position. When he approached to within fifty meters of their foxhole, they let loose with their machine gun, killing the horse and unseating the rider, who landed unhurt after tumbling head-over-heels through the snow. Immediately, he threw his hands up and walked slowly while shaking his head towards the Germans and surrendered. He was then taken to Dr. Bloch's command post to be interrogated. Dr. Bloch's adjutant wrote later that the officer, a young major, smelled strongly of alcohol. At first, he refused to speak to his captors and seemed satisfied to glower suspiciously at them. After being proffered a cigarette, which he accepted, he began to loosen up a bit. It seemed that he was the commander of the Soviet rifle battalion that lay opposite the German's front line. He also revealed that he was 25 years old and a student of literature, who felt that he had been promoted to command a battalion before he was ready.

When asked why he had ridden towards the German defensive positions in such a suicidal manner, he stated that he and his staff had been celebrating the pending Soviet victory in his command bunker. He had told his officers that it was high time for his battalion to continue attacking, since the fascists had already withdrawn from their positions. His staff disagreed with him, stating that the Germans were indeed still there, just as they were the day before. He then called his subordinates a bunch of old ladies and cowards, and said that he was going to set an example of how a Soviet officer leads by example. They did not try to stop him, inebriated as he was, when he ordered his horse to be saddled and took off at a gallop towards the German's positions.

For several hours, Dr. Bloch's adjutant and the Soviet major conversed over a variety of topics. As soon as he smoked one cigarette, he was offered another. To the Germans, he seemed to be a vain, insolent man, hardly suited for the study of literature, despite what he claimed. Finally, he began to explain why he had ridden across the lines, at great risk to his life. He knew that the German's situation was hopeless, but had wanted to tell Dr. Bloch and his men that their continued defense did not make sense any more. To the Soviet major's way of thinking, it was high time for the Germans to end it all. He could not understand how they could sit around so calmly waiting for the arrival of the relief force, when the chances of it reaching them were so slim. That evening, he was led away by guards to the headquarters of *Graf* Rittberg's *88.Inf.Div.* Dr. Bloch and his adjutant never learned what happened to him afterwards.[14]

The Germans tried their hand at counter-propaganda on their own troops and against the Soviets, but were unable to devote as many resources to it as their enemy was able to. Virtually all of it consisted of radio broadcasts to the two encircled corps' headquarters, which was then handed down to the subordinate divisions and regiments as part of their daily situation briefings. Some of the broadcasts were intentionally bombastic, a tendency which Manstein tried to play down, but with little success. One such broadcast by General Hube is a good example. In an order of the day for 10 February, Hube closed with the encouraging words to the encircled troops of *Gruppe*

On 8 February, Zhukov ordered emissaries to carry a capitulation demand to Gruppe Stemmermann. The two men chosen to carry the ultimatum, a **Lieutenant Colonel I. Savelyev** *(left), and his translator,* **Lt. Smirnov** *(middle), were treated to brandy and escorted back to their lines witht their offer unanswered. After the failure of the parley attempt, the battle renewed with unmatched ferocity. (Photo courtesy of the Battle of Korsun-Shevchenkovsky Museum, Korsun, Ukraine) The Parliamentarians were escorted by* **Major Johannes Sepauschke** *(right), the operations officer of Korpsabteilung B (shown here in Bundeswehr uniform). (Photo courtesy of Andreas Schwarz and 72.Inf.Div. Veterans Association)*

Stemmermann, "We will break through the ring and carve you out!"[15] Besides statements like this, the German high command tried to boost morale in other ways, such as Wöhler's attempt to confer the Knight's Cross on Lieb and Stemmermann before they had even broken out.

The encircled troops could also pick up radio messages from the individual tank companies and infantry battalions on the outside, as they fought their way slowly through the Soviet defenses. They could certainly hear the impact of artillery shells and see the muzzle flashes from tank battles 20 or 30 kilometers away. Additionally, the airlift was still working, an important morale factor. By 5 February, 3,000 wounded had been flown out safely and enough ammunition and fuel had been flown or dropped in by parachute into Korsun to keep them supplied with a minimum of what they needed.[16]

But perhaps most effective of all was the constant flow of situation reports from Breith's and Vormann's corps that were typed out by the encircled corps' teletype machines.These reports allowed staff officers to mark the relief force's daily rate of progress on situation maps tacked up on the wall of some peasant *isba* in Korsun or Yablonovka. These lines in red and blue pencil told everything. It also told them that by 7 February, the relief attack had stalled. Nevertheless, most of *Gruppe Stemmermann* were blissfully unaware of these difficulties and remained confident that Manstein would get them out. Admittedly, reported cases of *Kesselpsychose* were on the rise, but that was a sickness that seemed to affect the troops of the rear services the most.

Thus, a disappointingly small number of Germans deserted or surrendered voluntarily. Since Zhukov did not expect

that the psychological warfare campaign being carried out would be enough to bring about the mass surrender of the encircled Germans, he had also decided to offer them terms of surrender as well, a time-tested technique with deep antecedents in military history. During the present war with Germany, it had a mixed record. *6.Armee* had certainly surrendered at Stalingrad, but its situation had become so clearly hopeless that even Paulus had no choice but to submit. On the other hand, proffering terms of surrender to the garrisons of the Demyansk Pocket, Cholm, and Velikiye Luki had not worked. As long as a chance of rescue existed, the Germans would hang on and keep fighting. With the armored spearhead of Breith's relief column stalled only 30 kilometers away, the Germans would cling to the possibility that they would be relieved in few more days, at worst. Hopefully, the psychological warfare campaign would help dampen their spirits, while a surrender request might yet bring the Germans to their senses.

In accordance with Zhukov's orders, parliamentaries were dispatched by General Vatutin towards the German lines on 8 February. Whether the Soviets were motivated by the desire "to avoid unnecessary bloodshed" in Konev's words (hardly likely, in his case) or to speed up the operation, they came back empty handed. The envoys, Lt.Col. I. Savelyev, his translator, Lt. Smirnov and a bugler, Private Kuznetsov, arrived forward of the front line positions of *K.Abt.B* at 1100 hours in an American jeep. After the parley attempt, Savelyev wrote:

The point of departure for our mission was a hill about 300 meters north of the line Chirovka-Steblev. From there to the enemy front lines was approximately 1,000 meters.

A strong wind was blowing . . . it was clear to me, that the Fascists under these conditions and at this range would not be able to hear our attempt to hail them by loudspeaker. We still hoped that our white flag, which we were waving conspicuously, would be seen. They couldn't even hear our bugle, at least at the beginning.[17]

Opposite them were troops of *Rgt.Gr.258* of Viebig's *Div.Gr.112*, with attached troops from Eberhard Heder's *SS-Feld Ausb.Btl. 5.*

When the commander of the *Regimentsgruppe*, *Hptm.* Burgfeld, reported to Viebig that some Soviet parliamentaries had been spotted forward of the *Hauptkampflinie* (*HKL*, or main defense line) blowing a bugle and waving a white flag, Viebig immediately telephoned the headquarters of *K.Abt.B* and asked what he should do. Since the commander, *Oberst* Fouquet, and his deputy was further to the east where they was controlling the fighting along the southern front of the pocket with *Sperrverband Fouquet,* his operations officer, *Maj.* Johannes Sepauschke answered the phone.[18]

Savelyev, as quoted in Krainyukov's account, stated that as soon as he and his tiny delegation approached the German front lines, they were fired on by a machine-gun after they had only gone 30 or 40 steps. Halting, he had Kuznetsov blow the bugle again, while his translator kept waving the white flag. Then they advanced another 20 steps, and were fired on once again, with the bullets narrowly missing them. All three men took cover in a shallow depression, holding the flag high above their heads as bullets continued to whistle past them. Finally, they were approached by an SS patrol from Heder's unit that had been sent out to verify their identity. Quickly blindfolding them, the Germans led the party to Viebig's headquarters in Steblev. There, they were met by Sepauschke, the senior officer on duty at the *Korpsabteilungs'* headquarters, and a German military translator of Baltic descent.

Upon being led into a typical Ukrainian hut, the party's blindfolds were removed by the patrol and they were met by a German officer, whom Savelyev thought was *Oberst* Fouquet. The Soviet officer demanded to know to whom he was speaking because he had a message to deliver to the two German commanders in the pocket, Generals Lieb and Stemmermann. When Sepauschke told the Soviet officer who he was, Savelyev seemed disappointed. Instead of being brought to Korsun, he was only to get as far as the forward defensive positions of *K.Abt.B*.

Savelyev peppered Sepauschke with questions, which the German staff officer believed was an attempt to gain information about the status of *Gruppe Stemmermann*. He also complained that he and his party had been fired upon even though they had approached under a white flag of truce. Sepauschke apologized, stating that on account of the wind direction his men had not heard the bugle at first and that the outposts had fired at him because they were not used to seeing officers of the Soviet General Staff running around the battlefield in their best uniforms. Although Sepauschke gave the parliamentarian no definite answers, he did take the two white envelopes which the

Soviet officer extended to him. Sepauschke excused himself to make a telephone call, ordering the Soviet party to be led outside under armed guard.

Sepauschke made a telephone call to General Lieb at his corps headquarters in Yablonovka and informed him that he had two envelopes addressed to both him and General Stemmermann. Lieb ordered Sepauschke to open both letters and to read the contents. Both letters, signed by Zhukov, Konev, and Vatutin, started with an introduction which summarized their present situation in the most pessimistic of terms. It stated that "Your situation is hopeless and further resistance is senseless. It will only lead to a colossal sacrifice of German officers and soldiers." In order to avoid unnecessary bloodshed, the Soviet leaders demanded that Stemmermann and Lieb accept the following terms:

> 1. All surrounded German troops led by Lieb and Stemmermann's staffs were to immediately cease combat operations;
>
> 2. Both commanders were to surrender to the Red Army the complete complement of personnel, weapons, all combat equipment, transport and all of the Army's goods in an undamaged condition.

Furthermore, Zhukov and the two *Front* commanders guaranteed that all officers and soldiers who cease fighting would be unharmed and would be repatriated as soon as the war was over. In addition, all personnel who surrendered would be allowed to keep their uniforms, decorations, rank insignia, personal property and any valuables. Officers would be allowed to keep their swords and wounded personnel would be provided prompt medical attention.

In addition to being showered with surrender leaflets, the encircled Germans also had to contend wih organizations composed of Germans who had previously surrendered to the Soviets, such as the Bund Deutsche Offiziere of the Free Germany Committee, consisting of German communist emigrees who had settled in Germany. Here, Oberst Steidle from BDO is shown meeting with Germans who had supposedly deserted during the battle. (Photo courtesy of the Battle of Korsun-Shevchenkovsky Museum, Ukraine)

In closing, the ultimatum demanded that the German forces trapped in the pocket return a written reply to the ultimatum no later that 1100 hours the following day, 9 February. The German emissary carrying the reply was directed to drive towards the Soviet front lines along the Steblev-Chirovka road in a staff car draped with white flags and would be met by a "fully empowered Soviet officer" at the east end of Chirovka. Ominously, it concluded with the remark "Should you reject our suggestion to lay down your weapons, the units of the Red Army and its air forces will begin operations to destroy the surrounded German forces, but you will bear the responsibility for their destruction."[19]

Sepauschke told Lieb that this could be a ruse. Both men knew that Breith and his four panzer divisions were not far off; in fact, German troops had heard the sounds of heavy fighting in the southwest for several days. Their rescue was only a matter of time and each day brought them closer to freedom. Sepauschke proposed that he, Lieb, could ask the parliamentaries for more time and ask them to add some conditions that were more favorable to the Germans. Lieb immediately disapproved, stating that this was nothing more than a deception which might prove dangerous later should Sepauschke be captured. Sepauschke agreed and concluded the conversation. Calling Savelyev and his party back into the hut, he told the Soviet officer that he had just spoken to General Lieb, commander of *XXXXII.A.K.,* and had informed him of the contents of the envelopes as well as the time which a reply was expected. As for the ultimatum itself, it remained unanswered. Sepauschke informed the emissary that the negotiations were at an end.

Lieb, of course, did not have the authority to surrender, even had he wanted to - that was something only Stemmermann could order, and only then if he had been granted permission by Manstein via *OKH* - in other words, by Hitler himself. And that would never be an acceptable proposal for Hitler to agree to. Had the *Führer* known that Lieb had parlayed with a Soviet emissary at the time, he would probably have been relieved from command and placed under arrest, since Hitler had issued very strict orders forbidding any of his generals or soldiers from ever negotiating with Soviet *untermenschen*. However, Lieb's humanity and courage ensured that he would at least give Savelyev's message a hearing. Savelyev, for his part, felt frustrated. Despite his protestations, he was unable to get a direct answer from General Lieb via Sapauschke. The best he could get was Sepauschke's rejoinder that the Soviets would know the answer to their demands tomorrow.

The Soviet officer asked in what manner would the Germans let their reply be known and was told that it would be in accordance with what was laid out in the ultimatum.[20] On this point, Savelyev was incorrect - the Germans had no intention of making any form of reply, for that matter. Their answer would be in the form of continued, bitter resistance. With the negotiations at an end, Sepauschke decided to play the host towards his guests, offering them brandy and sandwiches, not only as a sign of hospitality, but also to demonstrate to the Soviets that his command, at least, still had sufficient food to hold out much longer than their enemy had thought. Savelyev declined

Sepauschke's proffered cigarette, a German-made "Atikah," choosing to smoke his own hand-rolled *papyrossy* instead.

When brandy snifters could not be rounded up, Sepauchke's orderly found four small glasses the Germans normally used for tooth brushing and filled them to the brim with brandy. Sepauschke toasted the health of Savelyev and his party, who drained their glasses with one gulp. He reported later that they liked the brandy so much, that they asked for another drink. Sepauschke gladly complied, and they all drank another round. Both men departed with a friendly handshake. Savelyev and his men bowed deeply towards their host and said their good-byes. They were then blindfolded again for their return trip and were then led to the exact spot where they had entered the German lines nearly six hours earlier. Later, Sepauschke noted, "this was the most memorable event of my entire military career."[21]

A witness to the departure of the emissaries was Eberhard Heder, who had also watched them arrive. As the blindfolded Soviet soldiers were led away by their escorts back through the gap in the German defense, Heder overheard Savelyev say to one of his escorts in a threatening manner "You're really going to catch it tomorrow!" On that score Savelyev was to be proven prophetic. Savelyev described the rest of the trip back to his own lines in an account written after the war. In it, he recalled:

> We were quickly brought back to our Jeep to the same place where the Germans had first found us. It was already late, about 1830 hours. We had to hurry back. The officer, who escorted us, made us fold the white flag we were carrying. White-knuckled, we drove back to our lines, escorted to the left and right by German soldiers, as quickly as we could. The officer demanded that we not look back after his men had removed our blindfolds, so we couldn't again find the same spot. When we arrived back at our trenches, it was pitch black. One of our soldiers welcomed us back with merry laughter.[22]

All in all, it was a sad ending to an enterprise that Savelyev had set out on a few hours earlier with such hope. Soon, no doubt, many German soldiers would wish that General Lieb had given the emissary a lengthier hearing. Now *Gruppe Stemmermann* would have no choice but to fight.

Hoping to salvage something from the failure of Savelyev's parley attempt, Zhukov ordered thousands of leaflets printed up the next day, detailing the surrender terms offered to Lieb and Stemmermann, and had thousands of them dropped by air over the German positions. Perhaps, according to Krainyukov, the individual officer or soldier might realize the futility of their situation and take advantage of such generous terms. After all, who would not want to survive the war and return home to their loved ones? Had not the defeat at Stalingrad taught the Germans anything? Apparently not, for few Germans crossed over the lines with copies of the ultimatum in their possession, though more and more *Landser* secreted them on their persons, even veterans such as *Oblt.* Menedetter. After all, one never knew. . .

On 9 February, Zhukov sent a coded message to Stalin that stated, based on Savelyev's report, that his surrender terms had been rejected. He also reported, based on recent prisoner of war interrogations, that *Gruppe Stemmermann* had sustained heavy losses and that their officers and troops "are now in a state of confusion bordering on panic."[23] Clearly, the end was in sight, or at least both Zhukov and Konev must have thought. However, they had learned enough from fighting the Germans over the past two and half years to know that their enemy rarely gave in if there was still any chance of rescue, no matter how desperate their situation was. The failure of the propaganda campaign had reinforced this belief. There was, besides, an increasing amount of evidence to indicate that the Germans were going to make an effort to break out on their own.

By 10 February, Soviet intelligence had detected the movement of *Wiking* and *72.Inf.Div.* to the Korsun area, a significant development - these two units were the only ones that still seemed to have much fight left in them. To Zhukov and his *Front* commanders, this could mean only one thing - the Germans were preparing to break out towards the southwest, where the stalled relief columns of *III.Pz.Korps.* were drawn up. To be on the safe side, Zhukov advised Konev to move a tank brigade from Rotmistrov's tank army to the Lysyanka area and 340th Rifle Division from Zhmachenko to the area between Krasnogorodok and Motayevka. Meanwhile, they would sit back and wait for the Germans to make another try; the victorious troops of First and Second Ukrainian *Fronts* would smash this attempt too, just as they believed they had smashed the first one. To their chagrin, the Soviets would relearn the bitter lesson that the Germans had taught them during the opening days of Operation Barbarossa - never underestimate the *Wehrmacht*.

End Notes

[1]   Lewerenz, Hermann. "*Die Tätigkeit der Bevollmächtigen des Nationalkomitees Freies Deutschland am Kessel von Korsun-Schewtschenkowski,*" from *Sie kämpften für Deutschland: zur Geschichte des Kampfes der Bewegung, Freies Deutschland bei der 1. Ukrainischen Front der Sowjetarmee.* (Berlin: Verlag des Ministeriums für Nationale Verteidigung, 1959), p. 231.

[2]   Krainyukov, Konstantin. *Vom Dnepr zur Weichsel.* (East Berlin: Militärverlag der Deutschen Demokratischen Republik, 1989), p.122.

[3]   Lewerenz, pp. 47-49.

[4]   Ziemke, *Stalingrad to Berlin*, p. 149.

[5]   Ibid, p. 124.

[6]   Carell, p. 415.

[7]   Lieb quoted in DA Pam 20-234, p. 23.

[8]   Ibid, p. 24.

[9]   Alex. p. 26.

[10] Jahnke and Lerch, p. 49.

[11] Ibid p. 51.

[12] Hahl, p. 199.

[13] Strassner, p. 256.

[14] Feisthauer, Günther. "*Der Einsatz des Sicherungs-Regiment 318 von Sommer 1943 bis Sommer 1944.*" (Hamburg: Unpublished Private Manuscript, 1997), pp. 49-50.

[15] *1.Pz.Armee* KTB, entry 10 February 1944, p. 1.

[16] *8.Armee* KTB, entry dated 1605 hours, 5 February 1944.

[17] Krainyukov, p. 126.

[18] Johannes Sepauschke, quoted in Jahnke and Lerch, p. 48.

[19] Strassner, pp. 257-258.

[20] Krainyukov, p. 127.

[21] Sepauschke in Jahnke and Lerch, pp. 47-48.

[22] Krainyukov, p. 127.

[23] Zhukov, p. 243.

Chapter Fifteen

STEMMERMANN ATTACKS

"There is no need to worry, Comrade Stalin.
The encircled enemy will not escape."
— *Ivan Konev in "Battles Hitler Lost"*

Now that Army Group South had finally issued orders for *Gruppe Stemmermann* to make preparations to break out under its own power and link up with the relief force, events began to unfold rapidly. While the men of *III.* and *XXXXVII.Pz.Korps* began yet another attempt to reach their encircled comrades, the troops inside the pocket began the laborious effort to reorient the pocket to the southwest, the direction which appeared to offer the greatest chance for salvation. The assault position most favorable to launch the breakout, encompassing the towns of Shenderovka, Novo Buda, Khilki and Komarovka, had to be recaptured from the Soviets.

This area lay astride the shortest route into the pocket from the southwest and offered good defensive positions to hold out until Breith and his tanks had drawn close enough. The eastern, southeastern, and northern sectors had to be drawn in like a collapsing paper bag, all the while under steady Soviet pressure. General Lieb had already remarked upon the precipitous speed of withdrawal of *XI.A.K.,* who seemed to be offering only token resistance against 4th Guards and 52nd Armies. Troops, guns, and other vehicles of six divisions had to be moved over a totally inadequate road network while subjected to constant Soviet air attack. All of this had to be carried out in the worst weather imaginable, with rainshowers and sunshine intermixed with freezing temperatures and snow. The resulting difficulties experienced by of both sides were indescribable.

Simultaneously, the Soviets were making preparations of their own which involved the movement of dozens of major and minor units. At this stage of the battle, events were in flux and neither side had a true picture of what their opponent was doing. For their part, Zhukov, Konev and Vatutin knew that the Germans were very likely planning to launch some type of breakout, but evidence seems to indicate that they did not have a clear idea of where such an attack would take place. Zhukov thought that the two German forces - Breith's corps and *Gruppe Stemmermann* - would probably try to link up in the Lysyanka area. But whether the commanders of both First and Second Ukrainian *Fronts* could move enough of their forces there in time was questionable, since they, too, were affected by the road conditions.

Meanwhile, 4th Guards, 27th, and 52nd Armies continued to apply steady pressure against the Germans, while the Red Air Force bombed and strafed everything that moved. Despite their increasing numerical and materiel superiority, Soviet accounts admitted that the pursuit of the withdrawing Germans was anything but easy. "Under difficult conditions," according to the

The Soviets suffer from the mud as well. Here a mobile field kitchen and its truck are being wrestled from the muck by a gang of Red Army troops. (Photo courtesy of the Battle of Shevchenkovsky Museum, Ukraine)

Soviet after-action report, "units advanced, fighting stubborn battles and subsequently occupying several populated areas."[1] Despite their best efforts, 52nd and 4th Guards Armies were unable to cut off the German troops occupying Gorodishche, despite the noose being drawn about them. At the last minute, *57.Inf.Div.* and *Wiking* were able to pull out their troops and most of their supplies, although some wounded were left behind and subsequently believed to have been murdered by the Soviets. Adolf Salié, who was serving as an sergeant with *Wiking's* signal battalion, intercepted a Soviet radio message that described which captured Germans should be executed and who should be spared. According to Salié, an order from Stalin was broadcast to Soviet troops in the northeast corner of the Pocket on 30 January, which stated, in part, that "Only lightly wounded [enemy soldiers] are to be taken prisoner. Seriously wounded and *Hiwis* are to be shot immediately."[2]

Soldiers of the Red Army, for their part, claimed that the Germans frequently shot their own wounded rather than allow them to fall alive into enemy hands, though this cannot be substantiated. After Gorodischche had been liberated, according to Alexei Fyodorovich, a soldier who served with a rifle regiment from 373rd Rifle Division, he and his comrades found an abandoned German field hospital where dozens of wounded German officers lay dead, all with a bullet wound in the head.[3] Whether or not one may be tempted to conclude that the Soviet account is true, one must also bear in mind that the Germans, thus far,

Along the Rollbahn, Germans chip in to lend a hand freeing a Volkswagen Kübelwagen from the mud. (Bundesarchiv 278/859/18)

had demonstrated great concern for the care and evacuation of their own wounded and such cold-hearted conduct on their part must at the very least strike one as inconsistent. The Soviet record in regard of their treatment of German wounded was certainly not beyond reproach; there are numerous substantiated cases at least where *NKVD* troops shot German wounded out of hand, even going so far as to mutilate their bodies. Such incidents no longer surprised the Germans, a factor which, if anything, contributed to their intense desire to keep fighting in hope of the promised relief thrust.

Regardless, through a combination of deliberate German withdrawals and Soviet tactical success, by 10 February, the ring of encirclement about *Gruppe Stemmermann* had shrunk to an area encompassing only 450 square kilometers, reduced from its original size 28 January of 1,500 square kilometers - every square meter of it increasingly subject to Soviet bombing, shelling and strafing.[4] Although the smaller area made it somewhat easier to defend since it allowed *Gruppe Stemmermann* to concentrate its meager remaining combat power, the equation worked both ways. With a smaller area to attack, the Soviet armies, corps, and divisions making up the inner ring of encirclement could now achieve truly overwhelming numerical superiority, while at the same time being able to detach units to the outer ring, now busily preparing to repel yet another relief attack from the outside. The Soviets were having difficulties moving up supplies and reinforcements, but most of these had arrived by 10 February and were now in a position to inflict a tremendous amount of punishment upon the Germans.

The order to conduct the breakout towards *III.Pz.Korps* was relayed by *8.Armee* to *Gruppe Stemmermann* on the evening of 8 February and must have been received with great relief. Stemmermann's staff quickly completed preparations on Operation *Betriebsausflug* and passed it back to *8.Armee* head-

quarters located in Novo Mirgorod, which received the draft early the following morning. By now, the *Frühlingsglaube* plan had been abandoned since *XXXXVII.Pz.Korps'* chances on making its way all the way up to the pocket seemed unlikely. Only *III.Pz.Korps'* thrust appeared to offer any chance of success.

For *Betriebsausflug* to succeed, the northern, eastern, and southeastern flanks of the pocket would first have to be drawn in tight, in order to concentrate the German's remaining combat strength. Then, once the relief force had approached to within a certain distance of the pocket, the encircled force would conduct an attack to break through the Soviet ring and conduct a link up. Like all such tactical plans, it was based on a number of assumptions, such as whether the remaining fuel and ammunition would hold out, whether the Soviets could be prevented from cutting the pocket in half, or whether Breith and his troops could get close enough, and so on.

Another critical assumption was whether *Gruppe Stemmermann* could seize favorable positions from which to launch their breakout; as of 10 February, they had not yet done so. Therefore, Gädke and the rest of the staff had to plan a preliminary operation to seize this area bounded by the towns previously mentioned. This operation was to prove to be nearly as difficult as the actual breakout and would involve the hardest fighting yet experienced by either side during the battle.

The operation to change the orientation of the pocket, i.e., to cause it to "wander" - would unfold in four phases. At the time of receipt of *8.Armee's* execution order, the first phase of the plan, the withdrawal of *57.* and *389.Inf.Div.* and the left flank of *Wiking* to the line "Red," had already taken place the previous evening. This line, which ran from the town of Valyava in the south to the northern outskirts of Gorodishche then to the Olshanka River line, was only intended to serve as an intermediary position for two days but had already begun to crumble.

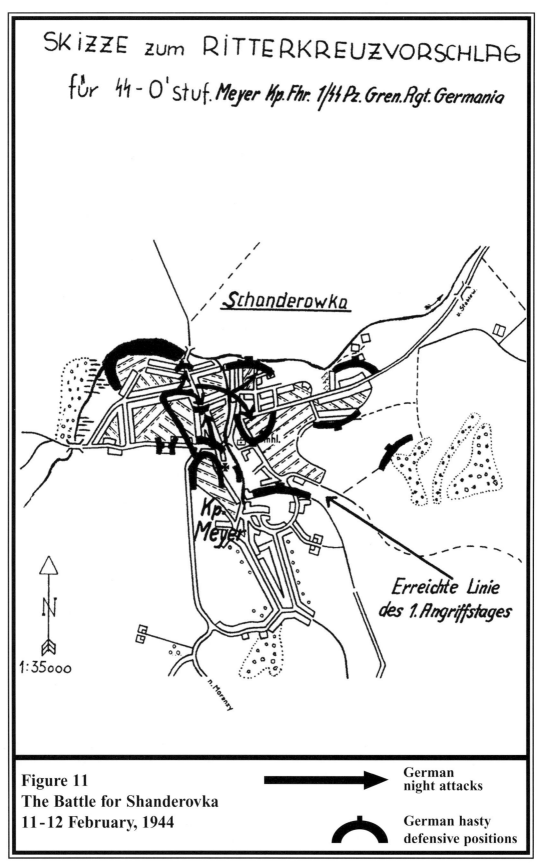

Figure 11
The Battle for Shanderovka
11-12 February, 1944

→ German night attacks

⌒ German hasty defensive positions

Note: This diagram is from the original Knight's Cross award recommendation for *SS-Ustuf.* Werner Meyer. (U.S. National Archives)

The next phase involved the pulling back of the entire southeast front during the night of 9/10 February to the line "Blue" , which ran from Glushki to the town of Derenkovets. Phase III involved pulling the bulk of *Wiking* out of the line on 10 February and moving it to an assembly area near Korsun, joining *72.Inf.Div.* The final phase involved an attack directed southwest against Shanderovka and the other key towns, supported by diversionary counterattacks launched by elements of Lieb's *XXXXII.A.K.* on 11 February.[5]

The attack had to be delayed a day due to the repositioning of troops for the preliminary phase of the breakout. The abysmal road conditions and the fact that the units tasked to carry out this mission were moving into position very slowly were the primary reasons given by Stemmermann for this postponement. It, at least, gave his staff an additional day to improve the plan. In the meantime, the northern part of Gorodishche still in German hands was given up precipitously by late afternoon of 9 February, when the rearguard, consisting of a *Kampfgruppe* from the soon-to-be dissolved *389.Inf.Div.* pulled out of its positions, leaving Trowitz's division and *Wiking* to hastily plug the gap.

General Trowitz had to deal with a dangerous penetration of his own sector the following day, when an attack by elements of Selivanov's 5th Guards Cavalry Corps broke through between Valyava and the Gorodishche railway station. Since his division was no longer strong enough to eject the Soviets, *57.Inf.Div.* was forced to pull its line back several kilometers. Like Trowitz's regiments, most German regiments in the Pocket now had an average combat strength of 150 men, a far cry from their authorized establishment of 2,008 men.[6] Stemmermann informed Wöhler that some regiments had suffered so many casualties, that they had an effective combat strength of only 50 men!

Slowly, from 9 to 11 February, the pocket turned on its central axis, the town of Korsun, and began to point towards the southwest. Towns which had been defended at great cost for weeks were given up one by one, such as Glushki and Derenkovets. Kvitki, which Ernst Schenk's troops had tried for so long to take, was given up for good on 9 February. His men, who had been holding a defensive line on a ridge above the town for a week, withdrew north under Soviet pressure to the town of Petrushki, where they had begun their assault on Kvitki on 31 January.[7] In other places within the Pocket, troops fought as ordered and pulled out at the appointed hour. Sometimes, when an escape route was cut off, some units were forced to fight to the death. A few units fled their positions, providing a closely pursuing Soviet infantry battalion, tank platoon, or squadron of Cossacks the opportunity to break through and cause a great deal of mischief before being wiped out or thrown back by a last-minute German counterattack.

For example, *Westland's I.Bataillon*, commanded by *Hstuf.* Günther Sitter, once again lost its nerve and pulled out precipitously when its defensive positions near Cherepin were subjected to a Soviet tank and infantry attack during the late afternoon of 10 February.[8] This prompted yet another complaint cabled to *8.Armee* by Stemmermann's 1a, *Oberstlt.* Hans Schiele. To remedy the situation, Stemmermann was yet again

forced to commit part of *72.Inf.Div.,* the reserve slated to provide the offensive punch for *Betriebsurlaub*, to eliminate the penetration, which it did only after marching several hours and conducting an assault late that evening. If the morale of even the vaunted *Waffen-SS* could crack at a time like this, what did it spell for the "ordinary" infantry of the Army?

While the fighting raged at nearly every point along the perimeter of the pocket, Ju-52s continued to land supplies, and pick up wounded, despite the swarms of *Yaks* and LaGGs that hovered above the airfield. Even Erich Hartmann's squadron could not keep them at bay all the time. His Me-109s had to return to base to rearm and refuel; in the meantime, any German aircraft parked on the airstrip near Korsun were sitting ducks. Many were shot up and set afire by constant ground attacks by the Red Air Force. Although the light flak battery set up at the airfield shot down a *Sturmovik* or fighter nearly every day, it hardly deterred the persistent attacks. Despite this carnage, wounded were still flown out. On 9 February, for example, 566 wounded were evacuated; in addition, 100 tons of badly-needed ammunition and 8,450 gallons of gasoline were brought in. An additional 135 supply containers of ammunition and fuel were also dropped into the pocket by parachute, an impressive performance in any case, but there were still an additional 1,100 wounded awaiting evacuation.[9]

The significance of the renewed movement and withdrawals was lost on the average German soldier, who at any rate had no time to worry about such things. What mattered was that the bulk of the encircled troops were still willing to fight and do whatever it took to survive. According to Gerhard Mayer of *88.Inf.Div:*

> It was a good thing, that we actually knew quite little about the overall situation. No one had any idea how much the pocket had shrunken in the past few days…It was quite surprising, how good our morale was. Certainly, each had his doubts and misgivings, but we had an overriding respect and trust in our leadership. None of us gave any thought to giving up.[10]

The *Rollbahn* built on the rail bed from Gorodishche to Korsun was still clogged with bumper-to-bumper traffic, and now even this area of the pocket was beginning to come under artillery attack, so close had the front line approached.

According to Mayer, whenever German troops needed to move urgently from one place to another on such clogged roads, traffic jams seemed to be the most insufferable. As part of his unit moved from Yablonovka to Steblev, it seemed to Mayer that the town was overrun with fellow soldiers; every *isba* was packed to capacity with troops trying to keep warm, leaving no quarters for him or his fellow radiomen. Stragglers or shirkers were everywhere and many had given up trying to find their units. Soviet aircraft constantly bombed and strafed the town. There was no longer much difference between the "rear" and the "front" any more, except that the dying in the front line was more personal, less random.

Above: SS-Hauptsturmführer Hans Drexel, *German Operations Officer of the Walloon Brigade, clad here in a fur-lined short jacket and carrying a hand-carved walking stick, near Derenkovets 9 or 10 February 1944. In the background, a German half-tracked prime mover hauls away a captured Soviet antitank gun. (U.S. National Archives)*

Above: *Here, both* **Drexel** *and* **Degrelle**, *as well as another unidentified officer of the Walloon Brigade, watch the withdrawal from the Derenkovets defensive position, 9 or 10 February 1944. Note by this point, all of the snow had melted, exposing the grass and soil beneath. The officer with the MP-40 machine gun pouches may well be Lucien Lippert commander of the the Walloone Brigade. (U.S. National Archives)*

Above: *A bare-headed* **Leon Degrelle***, then deputy commander of the 5.SS-Sturmbrigade Wallonien, surveys a captured Soviet 7.62 cm antitank gun during the fierce fighting that took place 9 - 10 February along the Olshanka defense line near Derenkovets. (U.S. National Archives)*

Above: *Halftracks of the Walloon Brigade, including one towing a 2 cm antiaircraft gun and another towing a 10.5 cm howitzer, withdrawing from the Derenkovets defensive position towards Korsun, 9 or 10 February 1944. Only halftracks or tanks, as well as the horse-drawn panje wagon, had much success in navigating the horribly muddy roads at this stage of the operation. (U.S. National Archives)*

SS-Sturmbannführer Hans Dorr, *Commander, 1.Btl., SS-Pz.Gren.Rgt. "Germania" sometime during the battle.* *(U.S. National Archives)*

Ever so slowly, these skeletons of battalions and regiments shifted from their old positions and occupied new ones. Finally, the assault troops were ready. The preliminary attack to the southwest to seize the jump-off positions bounded by the three towns was to be carried out on 11 February by *Germania* and *72.Inf.Div.* from *XI.A.K.* and a *Kampfgruppe* from *K.Abt.B* from *XXXXII.A.K.* On the left of the attacking wedge, *72.Inf.Div.*, with Kästner's *Gren.Rgt.105* in the lead, would seize the town of Novo Buda, then press on to take Komarovka, followed by Siegel's *Gren.Rgt.266.* In the center, Ehrath's *Germania* would retake Shanderovka, abandoned only two days before. On the far right, the *Kampfgruppe* from *K.Abt.B*, led by *Oberst* Wolfgang Bucher, would take Khilki and cover the right flank of the attack.

Once these objectives had been seized, their positions would be taken up by troops from the Walloon Brigade and other units of *K.Abt.B*. Next *Germania*, still a relatively fresh force, would hold Shanderovka, while *72.Inf.Div.* would move on and seize the town of Komarovka. Once these towns were in German hands, the northern defense line held by *88.* and *57.Inf.Div.* would then cross over to the southern bank of the Ross River, giving up the town of Korsun by 12 February, at the latest. After this initial phase of *Betriebsausflug* was completed, the final breakout could be delayed no more than a day or two at the most. So many troops concentrated in such a small area would invite a massive Soviet counterstrike; certainly, every square meter of the pocket would certainly be subject to artillery fire. The Germans would have to act soon; their strength was steadily ebbing away and they would soon lack the combat power to even conduct a limited breakout.

On the morning of 11 February, *Gruppe Stemmermann* provided *8.Armee* its first strength report since the encirclement began, which gives some idea of the severity of the fighting thus far. After seventeen days, the personnel count of *XI.* and *XXXXII.A.K.*, including attached units, stood at 56,000 men, including nearly 2,000 wounded.[11] Since 24 January, the encircled Germans had lost perhaps five to eight thousand men, most of them troops from the combat branches. For instance, as it prepared for the upcoming attack, *72.Inf.Div.* could field only 450 infantrymen in three greatly understrength regiments. While it was true that several thousand men had been left outside the pocket when the Soviet jaws slammed shut at Zvenigorodka, the decision not to fly them in as reinforcements had already been made and most of them in fact had already been incorporated into *Gr. Haack*. Several thousand wounded had already been flown out and an unknown number had been killed or captured.

Although thousands of support personnel had been assembled into scratch units, their effectiveness as infantry was limited. It was thus left to the few remaining combat troops to do the bulk of the fighting that lay ahead. From the perspective of the staffs at corps and army level, the manpower situation did indeed look bleak. General Speidel, for one, recognized how desperate things really were when he remarked in a telephone conversation on the evening of 10 February with General Wenck at *1.Pz.Armee*, that *Gruppe Stemmermann* had only enough strength for "one last push." Actually, it had a great bit more than that left, as the Soviets were soon to experience.

For the first time since the encirclement began, the troops inside the Cherkassy Pocket would be launching a major attack of their own, and not a hastily conceived counterattack to restore some line or to throw the Soviets out of a position. This, added to the knowledge that they were finally given a clear-cut goal of fighting their way out had lifted the men's spirits, as relayed in one account.[12] Now it was the Soviet's turn to be the anvil, and the troops of *Gruppe Stemmermann* would be the hammer. The

Leutnant Bender, *Gren.Rgt.105, whose infantry gun company was known in his regiment as the Benderorgel, a play on the nickname for the Katyusha (Stalinorgel).*
(Photo courtesy of 72.Inf.Div. Veteran's Association)

Once the German leadership had decided to break the encirclement with combined drives by both the encircled troops and the relief force, the forces inside the pocket had to regroup in order to attack to the southwest. Here, a Panzer IV from Wiking during a short pause on the outskirts of Korsun.
(Photo courtesy of Kaisergruber)

fact that Breith's corps was known to be steadily approaching from the south also contributed to a sense of confidence that many men began to feel, for the first time in weeks. Perhaps, some thought, we will make it out of this hell after all. But first, they would have to fight harder than at any time since they had been encircled, for the Soviets would not let them escape without a severe struggle.

Throughout the day of Friday 11 February, the units chosen to seize the breakout area moved into their positions in the area between Steblev and Shanderovka. There would be little artillery preparation, since ammunition would be scarce and would be saved for emergencies. This unpleasant news was mitigated somewhat by the fact that the weather that day, which had threatened to clear, had actually turned to a light snowfall in the early evening hours, thus providing some concealment for the attack. Once they crossed the line of departure, the assault units would be on their own until the follow-on forces caught up with them. Originally scheduled to begin at 2100 hours, one of the three assault elements' attack had to be delayed for two hours, while the other two went ahead as ordered. A platoon from *Stubaf.* Hans Dorr's *I./Germania* had gotten lost on its way to the assembly area, to the chagrin of *XI.A.K.'s* staff. Finally, Dorr's unit crossed the line of departure at 2300 hours as the wind whipped the falling snow from the northeast into the eyes of the defending soldiers from Trofimenko's 27th Army.

Dorr's battalion, since it was the strongest in *Wiking*, had drawn the assignment of seizing Shanderovka, which had been lost two days before to troops from two battalions of the 54th Fortified Region of 27th Army. These units, 22nd Flame-thrower Battalion and 200th Artillery Machine-gun Battalion, had quickly consolidated their positions in and around Shanderovka. Taking the town would not be easy, especially since intelligence indicated that elements of Selivanov's 5th Guards Cavalry Corps were on their way to reinforce it.

After briefing his company commanders behind a large haystack east of the village of Shanderovka, Dorr asked them for

suggestions as to how they thought the attack might best be prosecuted. When Dorr asked for a company to volunteer to lead the attack, he was surprised when his request remained unanswered; no one appeared enthusiastic to take on the mission. Startled and perhaps angered by his subordinate commanders' lack of "SS-spirit," Dorr ordered *Ostuf.* Werner Meyer's *1.Kompanie* to lead the attack and told him that he would accompany Meyer's troops.

To carry out their night attack, Dorr's battalion approached the southern outskirts of Shanderovka using a large *balka* that ran east of the town, thus concealing them from view. After exiting the ravine, they would then turn right and attack the center of the objective and take it street by street. Snow and wind muffled the sound of their approach. When the battalion reached the edge of the ravine closest to the town's southern edge, Dorr and Meyer went forward to scout out the enemy positions. As they returned, they were spotted in the darkness by two Soviet sentries, who were immediately shot by some of Meyer's troops.

Since they had lost the advantage of surprise, Dorr immediately ordered his men to attack. With a roar, the men from *Germania* burst forth from the cover of the ravine and rushed into the Soviet defensive positions on the edge of town. Two additional sentries were shot when they challenged the group of men moving towards them. A couple of bunkers were dealt with by hand grenade bundle charges. Leaving *Ostuf.* Sören Kam's *2.* and Otto Klein's *3.Kompanie* to roll up the Soviet positions on the left and right, Meyer's men crossed the main road and stopped on the edge of the town, where they briefly reassembled.

Several minutes later, Meyer and his men continued their attack towards the town, whose defenders had in the meantime been thoroughly awakened. When they approached the first row of buildings, one man stumbled over a trip wire, setting off an emplaced flame-thrower that sent a fountain of burning jellied gasoline a few feet above their heads. Although momentarily panicked by this unexpected booby-trap, no one was harmed. Meyer and his men quickly began the battle for the town, fighting house to house. Joined by Kam's company, Dorr and Meyer's troops were engaged in heavy street fighting for most of the night, finally ejecting or killing most of the Soviet defenders in southern Shanderovka before daybreak.[13] At 0700 hours the next morning, 12 February, Dorr reported to a relieved General Stemmermann, who had not received any situation reports since the attack began eight hours before, that at least part of Shanderovka was again in German hands. Several individual pockets of Soviet troops in the town's southern outskirts continued to resist until they were wiped out later in the morning (Map 11).

The remainder of Shanderovka, however, had yet to be taken. The defenders were resisting so fiercely that Dorr had to rule out a daytime attack, and instead chose to conduct a night assault beginning at 2215 hours with Kam's company in the lead. After penetrating several blocks in house-to-house fighting, Kam's troops were pinned down three hours later by heavy machine-gun and antitank gun fire. With a stalemate at hand, Meyer, whose *1.Kompanie* was several houses behind Kam's, decided to act on his own, since waiting for orders from his battalion commander could prove fatal to his entrapped comrades.

Using an abandoned Soviet trench line that ran in a westerly arc for cover, Meyer and his company approached the enemy positions from behind without being detected. Once he had discovered that his company was immediately adjacent to the Soviet defenders who were pinning down Kam's unit, Meyer and a few other men leapt up from the trench and ran towards the first Soviet position. Unfortunately, most of his company remained where they were, preferring not to risk their lives it what seemed to be a suicidal endeavor. Using two hand grenades, Meyer quickly knocked out one antitank gun and kept going. Watching from the trench, the rest of his company, inspired and perhaps shamed by this personal example of bravery, jumped out of their shelter shouting "Hurrah!" at the top of their lungs and joined in the fighting.

They quickly reunited with their company commander and the few brave souls who had accompanied him and began systematically to reduce the Soviet's positions, eventually freeing Kam and his men. Both companies, soon joined by Otto Klein's, then began to assault the remaining positions in the enemy stronghold. After 11 hours of fighting, all of Shanderovka was finally in German hands by 1000 hours the following day. Once again, the effectiveness of German night attacks against Soviet defensive positions had proven their tactical worth. There remained a few bypassed enemy snipers and other holdouts, which Dorr's battalion spent the next day rooting out, but most of the fighting was over. While Dorr's losses were not insignificant, the defending Soviets suffered heavy casualties.

In fact, nearly all of the defenders were either killed or captured. There were so many enemy dead that no one even bothered counting them. The second night's attack alone had netted ten antitank guns, two infantry guns, and several heavy machine-guns, as well as 48 prisoners. In one house, some of Meyer's troops surprised an enemy regimental staff at work and captured three officers. The Soviet regimental commander killed himself rather than be taken prisoner by the SS. For the key leadership role that Meyer had taken in the assault on Shanderovka and the house-to-house fighting that followed, his name was submitted for the award of the *Ritterkreuz*.[14]

As Dorr's troops consolidated their hold on Shanderovka that afternoon and prepared to ward off any enemy counterattacks, the rest of their regiment joined them. Köller's tank battalion was supposed to have joined them earlier that day, but had instead been rushed the previous day back to the northeast to repel a Soviet breakthrough near the Korsun railway station, along with *Ostuf.* Wittmann's infantry company. While Wittmann and his men remained behind, Köller turned his tanks around and headed back to Shanderovka where he hoped to join the rest of *Wiking* engaged there, but was instead diverted to Sawadski to repel yet another Soviet penetration.

Their absence was sorely felt that afternoon, when Shanderovka was attacked by an enemy infantry battalion of perhaps 200 men and a T-34, supported by a great deal of artillery, which pinned the startled men of *Germania* in their fighting positions. This attack, probably launched by 202nd Rifle Division from the direction of Skripchintsy, actually carried into the village, where German and Soviets were soon fighting hand to hand. The situation was in doubt until nightfall, when the Germans finally gained the upper hand, though they suffered heavy casualties in the process. Finally, the key position of Shanderovka, little more than a minor agricultural town in peacetime with its brick factory as the sole landmark, was in German hands.

On the right flank, the attack by *Oberst* Bucher's battlegroup from *K.Abt.B* had an even more difficult time of it. Instead of having to work with regiments from a single division, he had to piece together an ad-hoc assault force from four separate *Regimentsgruppen*. These units, from *Div.Gr.255, 323,* and *332* had never worked together before and Bucher had the unenviable job of setting up a command and control structure by the evening of 11 February before he set out to take the villages of Skripchintsy, Khilki and Petrovskoye. He was only able to assemble his units at the last possible minute as well, since *Rgt.Gr.678* arrived just hours before the attack, fresh from the fighting near Vygravev, where it had been replaced by elements from *88.Inf.Div.*

This particular *Regimentsgruppe* had distinguished itself in the fighting to retake Vygravev, wiping out several Soviet infantry companies from 337th Rifle Division that had tried to hold onto the town. Even better, from the perspective of its troops, was the fact that its men captured a Soviet field kitchen, a truckload of winter clothing, and another one full of rations. The men from *Rgt.Gr.678* could certainly put these items to good use in the fighting that lay ahead. They had not had a good meal in weeks and were short of winter clothing. The report that detailed the *Regimentsgruppe's* accomplishments also mentioned that three captured Soviet officers were "shot while trying to escape," adding a sour note to an otherwise successful operation.[15]

K.Gr. Bucher departed on schedule at 2200 hours from its assembly area one kilometer northeast of Shanderovka. Moving

SS-Hauptsturmführer *and Knight's Cross wearer*
Hans Drexel, *German Operations Officer for the
Walloon Brigade and the brains behind the operation,
mid-February 1944. In this picture, he has traded in his
fur-lined jacket for a leather overcoat.
(U.S. National Archives)*

*His unit broke the ring at Schanderovka in a daring
night attack.* **Oberstleutnant Robert Kästner**,
*commander of Gren.Rgt.105, 72.Inf.Div. (Photo cour-
tesy of 72nd Infantry Division Veteran's Association).*

silently through a two-kilometer long valley that ran from the northern outskirts of Shanderovka to their first objective, Skripchintsy, Bucher and his men were able to take the village from the south almost without having to fire a single shot. By 0700 hours it was in German hands. Interrogation of Soviet prisoners, many of whom had been roused from their sleep by shouts of *Ruki Verch,* disclosed that Bucher and his troops were facing 202nd Rifle Division, previously unreported. Leaving *Rgt.Gr.676* to hold Skripchintsy, Bucher and the remainder pressed on southward towards their second objective, the village of Khilki, two kilometers away.

Again, catching the Soviets napping, Bucher's force walked nearly unopposed into the village and rounded up the sleepy enemy troops, who seemed bewildered and amazed that they were in German captivity. A T-34, sitting in the middle of the village with its crew asleep inside, was knocked out by a bundle of hand grenades. Unbeknownst to them, Bucher and his men had broken through the Soviet's "ring of steel" around the Pocket. Certainly it had all seemed too easy. It must have been with a certain sense of confidence that Bucher and his men set out for their third and last objective of the day, the little village of Petrovskoye, where both Generals Wöhler and Hube hoped that *Gruppe Stemmermann* and Breith's *III.Pz.Korps* would effect their linkup. And it was here that Bucher and his men literally ran into a brick wall.

As they continued their attack uphill towards Petrovskoye an hour later, Bucher and his men initially seized the eastern entrance to the town. Before they could consolidate their positions in the hilltop village however, the Germans were counterattacked unexpectedly by two Soviet rifle battalions, which drove them back down the hill for nearly a kilometer.[16] Back in Khilki, Bucher's command hastily organized their defense line for the evening and made plans to try to seize Petrovskoye again the following day. *K.Abt.B's* relatively successful action, for that day at least, was over. Although it had not seized Petrovskoye, it had at least taken Khilki, which would help secure the breakout area. However, to the south, an even greater battle was in progress, one that featured one of the most successful small-unit actions fought during the entire Battle of the Cherkassy Pocket. While troops from the *Wiking* and *K.Abt.B* were fighting isolated garrisons in Shanderovka, Khilki, and Skripchintsy, men from *72.Inf.Div.* were about to do battle with 5th Guards Cavalry Corps.

Although it had done its share of the fighting to date, *Maj.* Robert Kästner's *Gren.Rgt.105* had drawn the scorn of one of its sister regiments, Siegel's *Gren.Rgt.266.*, for pulling out from its defensive positions too hastily during the course of several planned withdrawals earlier in the battle. Perhaps stung by the ribald comments and insults hurled at them by the men of the "Reservist Regiment" over the past several weeks, the

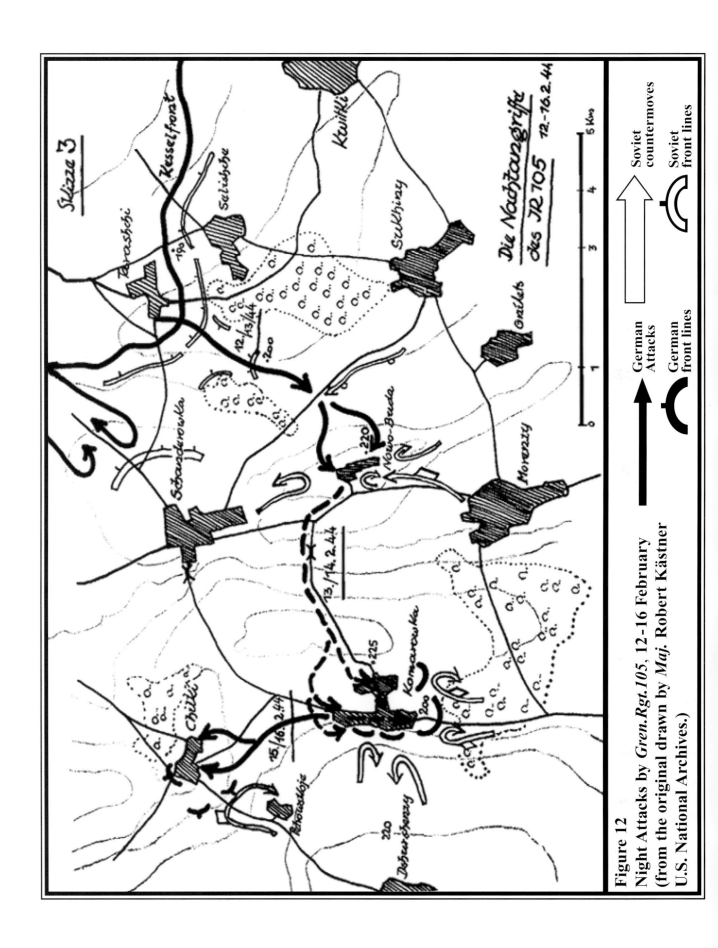

Figure 12
Night Attacks by *Gren.Rgt.105*, 12-16 February
(from the original drawn by *Maj.* Robert Kästner
U.S. National Archives.)

A column of SS vehicles from either Wiking or the Walloon
Brigade plowing through the mud enroute to Korsun from
Gorodishche. Most likely they have just departed the main
Korsun rail station, located on the northern edge of the town,
and are headed uphill to the town's center, where the bridges
over the Ross River lay, mid February 1944.
(U.S. National Archives)

The regrouping was carried out in the worst road conditions
imaginable. The walking pace of the infantry was reduced to
one kilometer per hour. (Bundesarchiv 711/435/33)

men from Trier, where the regiment had been raised in 1936,
would soon give a good account of themselves. In Robert
Kästner, *Gren.Rgt.105* had a robust, outgoing leader who
radiated confidence wherever he went. A stocky, powerfully-
built man, he towered over his men and seemed to them to be a
pillar of strength, a commodity in increasingly short supply
during the last few days of the battle. In twelve short years,
he had risen from the rank of private to major, an impressive
feat in any army.

After enlisting in the *Reichsheer* in October 1931, Kästner
was commissioned an officer in the infantry in 1937 and fought
in Poland in September 1939. By 1943, he had risen to the
rank of *Major* after serving on the Eastern Front for two years
and had already been given command of the regiment on
1 April 1943. He received the Knight's Cross on 11 December
1943 for his leadership during the defense of the Dnieper
River line and would soon add the Oak Leaves for his role
in the coming action.

Kästner's regiment had been assigned the mission of
taking the two key villages of Novo Buda and Komarovka. Novo

Buda, the first objective, lay along a north-south running ridgeline that would serve to protect the breakout area's eastern flank
against any Soviet attacks from the direction of the town of
Morintsy. After Novo Buda had been taken, it would be handed
over to Siegel's regiment, which would follow closely
behind, and Kästner and his men would press on and take
Komarovka. Possession of that village, which lay two
kilometers west of Novo Buda, would enable the Germans to
set up a strong east-west defensive position along a string of
low lying hills that stretched between the two towns. Meanwhile,
within the area bounded by these towns as well as by Khilki and
Shanderovka, the men of *Gruppe Stemmermann* could
prepare to launch their final breakout while protected by a 360-
degree defense perimeter.

The main problem, as Kästner saw it, was not with the
magnitude of the assignment - but the fact that the ground
between his assembly area near Tarashcha and Novo Buda
favored the enemy. In a situation similar to the one faced by
Ernst Schenk near Kvitki two weeks before, Kästner and his
men would have to attack uphill without any cover. Worse, his

The only passable roadway from the major town of Goro-dishche to Korsun lay atop the railroad bed connecting the two towns. From about 6 February, elements of 57th and 72nd Infantry Divisions, as well as Wiking, were forced to use this one route to conduct their withdrawal.
(Bundesarchiv 241/2187/13)

This elevated railroad bed was soon named "the highway of death" due to the constant attacks by Red Air Force fighter bombers. Here a supply truck of Wiking burns as soldiers try to save as much material as they can.
(Photo by Adolf Salie courtesy of Willy Hein)

scouts had determined that the Soviets had erected well camouflaged and constructed defensive positions along the ridgeline one kilometer southwest of Tarashcha. There were few *balkas* or depressions which Kästner and his men could use for cover as they approached the Soviets, who would see them as soon as they left their assembly area. He had ruled out any reconnaissance in force to determine the enemy's strength, since he felt that he could not afford the casualties that would necessarily result.

In his estimate of the situation, Kästner also realized that his supporting artillery, suffering from a shortage of ammunition, would only be able to give limited support, and then only in short concentrations; Therefore, any rolling barrage in support of his attack was totally out of the question. How to approach the first line of Soviet positions weighed heavily on his mind. According to Kästner in a report written after the war, these facts, as well as his own personal estimate, led him to decide that a daylight attack was simply not practical.

Kästner was not the only one that reached this conclusion, General Stemmermann had already ordered that all of the attacks would be conducted at night on 11 February starting at 2100 hours. In his report written after the war in an American prisoner of war camp, Kästner was only stating the most sensible course to follow in carrying out such an attack. A night attack offered several advantages over a daylight attack. Although it would be harder to control than a daylight attack, since units could get lost or fire on friendly units accidentally, a night attack would limit the enemy's ability to direct the fire of their weapons, would increase the likelihood of surprise, and allow the attacker to mass and direct the bulk of his forces against a single point in the enemy's defenses. The disadvantages of a night attack were mitigated by Kästner's belief that his officers and men were up to the challenge, for they were experienced in night combat and had trained for this eventuality. This, coupled with the realization that the subsequent breakout of *Gruppe Stemmermann* was dependent upon the success of their attack, probably reinforced his men's desire to succeed.

To guarantee the success of the attack, Kästner decided to provide the leading platoons with as much firepower as they could carry. To do this, the attacking echelon would be organized as a *Feuer und Bajonett-treffen* (Firepower and Bayonet Wave), with nearly every man equipped with a machine pistol. They would be heavily reinforced by MG-34 and MG-42 machine-gun crews who would accompany the assault. Behind this initial assault wave, the regimental staff would follow with a self-propelled 2 cm antiaircraft gun. Artillery support would be provided by *1.Batterie, Art.Rgt.72* as well as the two remaining infantry guns the regiment possessed. To insure that the guns could keep up with the infantry through the snow and mud, a double team of horses would be harnessed to each piece. Behind the guns the rest of the battalion would follow; the rear would be brought up by the regiment's other self-propelled 2 cm antiaircraft gun.

After seven months of constant action since the Battle of Kursk and after two weeks of encirclement, *Gren.Rgt.105* had only 346 officers and men fit for duty. The rest lay in field hospitals and makeshift cemeteries that stretched from the Orel salient to the Dnieper. Weak though it was, it was one of the few regiments left that was deemed capable of conducting limited offensive operations. To lead the understrength regiment, Kästner had only two other officers besides himself - the regimental adjutant, *Ltn.* Hoppe, and acting battalion commander, *Leutnant* Matthias Roth. To strengthen Kästner's assault force, *Oberst* Hohn ordered that *Feld Ers.Btl.72* be attached to it, nearly doubling it size.

These 343 officers and men, most of whom had been clerks or truck drivers a few days before, were a welcome addition. This force was led by none other than *Ltn.* Bender, the redoubtable commander of *Gren.Rgt.266's* infantry gun company (of *Bender-Orgel* fame), who had been loaned out since he had lost all of his guns during the withdrawal to Korsun. Assisting him was *Oberzahlmeister* (Senior Pay Master) Schaefer, who had been adjudged a "good troop leader" by Kästner. With this patchwork force of 689 men, Kästner was about to embark on one of the most dramatic battles before

A column of Wiking stuck in the mud near the Korsun rail station, 10/11 February, 1944.
(Photo by Adolf Salie courtesy of Willy Hein)

Battered trucks of Wiking upon arrival at the Korsun rail station. (Photo by Adolf Salie courtesy of Willy Hein)

the breakout, with his force pitted against thousands of Soviet troops and dozens of tanks. Nothing less than the survival of *Gruppe Stemmermann* would depend upon the success of Kästner's mission.

Shortly after dark, Kästner moved his regiment into an attack position on the southwestern outskirts of Tarashcha. Although it was a moonless night, the starlight reflecting off the newly-fallen snow provided enough illumination to enable the troops to prepare themselves for the attack and to make any last minute plans. As they had done so often before, the men checked their machine pistol magazines, insured that their grenades were tucked properly into their waistbelts, and adjusted the straps on their equipment harnesses. Perhaps a bite or two, if one had something to eat. Most of the men were relatively well rested though, since they had an opportunity to get some badly-needed sleep during the two days they spent in reserve in Koshmak.

Kästner spent a few moments coordinating a passage of lines with the unit already holding this sector, a *Kampfgruppe* from Christian Sonntag's *Gren.Rgt.248* of *88.Inf.Div*. While they were waiting, a patrol that had crept up to the Soviet defensive positions to determine their locations returned and informed Kästner which was the best manner in which to approach them unnoticed. Based on this intelligence, he determined that his regiment would be initially attacking a relatively weakly-held position. Finally, at 2030 hours (half an hour earlier than he was supposed to), he and his men left the relative safety of their own positions and moved out towards the Soviet front line (Map 12).

Silently, the first assault wave in their white camouflage suits moved up the long slope that lay one kilometer ahead and approached the first line of Soviet fighting positions. The defenders did not see them until it was too late. Then, the Germans were in amongst them, swiftly dispatching the defenders without firing a shot. As the main body of the regiment pushed through the breach in the Soviet positions, additional platoons fanned to the left and right to roll up the enemy flanks. With relative ease, the regiment broke through the deeply echeloned Soviet positions, testimony to the effectiveness of their

surprise attack. Most of the Soviet troops died before they knew what had happened. As the spearhead pushed on, the motorized and horse-drawn heavy weapons followed closely behind. By that point, the Soviets had awoken and tried to impede their advance by firing into the flank of Kästner's regiment from a small forest west of Selishche, but without effect. Most of his force had already passed through. Siegel's regiment, moving up behind Kästner, mopped up any bypassed Soviets and protected his ever-lengthening left flank.

Pressing on to the next objective, Hill 200, Kästner and his troops encountered unexpected difficulties when the horse-drawn 10.5 cm howitzer battery from the artillery regiment barely made it through deep snowdrifts that lay on the hill's northeastern slopes. Both men and horses strained to haul the big guns up the hill. After struggling for over an hour, the assault force reached the top of Hill 200 near midnight and found it unoccupied. From this position, Kästner's regiment could observe Soviet traffic to the south moving northwest along the road running from the village of Sukhiny to Shanderovka. This was probably a convoy of Selivanov's Cossack moving into their new positions.

Counting 30 trucks and several truck-mounted *Katyushas*, Kästner ordered that the two 2 cm antiaircraft guns be brought forward into position. From a range of only two hundred meters, the *Flak* gunners poured fire into the lead vehicles in the column, setting them ablaze and illuminating the snow-covered landscape. Methodically, the German gunners worked their way towards the rear of the column, shooting up everything. The *Katyusha* gunners attempted to fire their rockets at the Germans, but due to the close range, the 12.2 cm projectiles shot harmlessly over their heads. These, too, were quickly destroyed by the accurate fire from the *Flak* troops. Buoyed by this success, Kästner's men were eager to keep going - perhaps things were finally going to go their way!

After a short pause to sort out their tactical formation and to wait for the units in the rear to catch up, the Germans moved out quickly with a renewed sense of purpose. Swiftly covering the two kilometers from where they had ambushed the Soviet convoy, the spearhead spotted the outline of their next objective, Novo Buda, at 0100 hours. Rather than launch a direct assault on the village, Kästner decided to carry out a pincer movement, sending elements to attack the village from the north and the south. As the Germans silently crept forward, not a single shot rang out from the defenders, who were evidently fast asleep. Completely surprised by the enemy's night attack, most of the defending Soviet troops gave up without a fight. An hour and a half later, the entire village and its outlying areas were in German hands.

With a bare minimum of actual fighting and with few casualties of their own to report, *Gren.Rgt.105* had advanced five kilometers to take a key objective and had captured 250 Soviet troops, 24 trucks, and five anti-tank guns. A few Cossacks and some wagons, however, did escape to the south and southwest to warn their headquarters of the new German attack. The rest of the evening passed uneventfully. Kästner, aware that a Soviet response would not be long in coming, ordered that his men establish an all-round defense of the village. To ward off any Soviet forays from the direction of Shanderovka or Morenzy, he ordered that the artillery emplace two guns to cover each likely avenue of approach. The two 2 cm *Flak* guns would be held in reserve to serve as a mobile counterattack force. Morale was high. While inspecting his men's positions in the early morning hours, Kästner noted that the night attack "had awoken the men's confidence in the inevitable success of the planned breakout."[17]

Maj. Siegel, whose regiment followed closely behind Kästner's, had also noticed that his men's morale had perceptibly improved. Although his regiment was not in the lead, he and his men still managed to claim their share of the attack's success, since they had mopped up bypassed Soviet troops left in Kästner's wake. Siegel's regiment also took part in the later stages of the attack on Novo Buda, if only for the last few moments.[18] His regiment tied in with *Gren.Rgt.105* that evening, protecting its left or northern flank from attack. To its north, connecting Novo Buda with the troops holding Selishche, lay *Oberst* Hummel's *Gren.Rgt.124*, the weakest of Hohn's three regiments. To exercise command and control over his regiments, *Oberst* Hohn moved his command post from Korsun to Steblev, where his staff sought shelter for their headquarters amidst the chaos. Thus, a thin line of field gray now stretched from the old defensive line to the southwest - the direction where salvation lay. As the Germans dug new fighting positions within and around Novo Buda, they could hear the sounds of gunfire from Shanderovka, two kilometers to the north, where Hans Dorr's SS troops were fighting house to house. Everywhere else was silence.

Siegel, like Kästner, knew what the next day would bring. Once Zhukov and Konev realized that their inner ring had been pierced, they would no doubt throw as many troops and tanks at the Germans as they could possibly lay their hands on. At least Siegel could take brief pleasure in the setback that his and Kästner's regiments had dealt their enemy. For a change, the Soviets had been taken by surprise by *Gruppe Stemmermann* - at least, they hardly expected an attack from the inside of the pocket at this spot.

While the Germans rejoiced in their good fortune, the reaction within the Soviet camp was exactly the opposite when the loss of Shanderovka, Novo Buda, and Khilki was reported. If the encircled Germans could get this far without outside assistance, what did this portend? The unexpected turn of events would soon evoke the wrath of Stalin. For the time being though, Soviet reaction to the German attack was limited to what the local commanders could carry out, while the news filtered up the Red Army's chain of command.

The morning of 12 February began with temperatures slightly above freezing. Later that day it began to rain, turning the battlefield once again to muck, creating a suitable backdrop for the fighting that raged throughout the day. It began uneventfully enough, at least for the troops in Novo Buda. While fighting continued in Shanderovka, Khilki, and Petrovskoye, dawn found the men of Kästner's and Siegel's regiments wondering where the inevitable Soviet counterattack was. They had not long to wait. At 1000 hours, German outposts reported a Soviet attack from the direction of Shanderovka consisting of an infantry battalion supported by three tanks. It was quickly broken up and driven off, with the loss of two of its tanks to the emplaced German artillery, firing over open sights.

This Soviet attack apparently was not carried out with the intent of retaking Novo Buda, but seemed to be an attempt by some of the forces trapped in Shanderovka by *Germania's* attack to escape to the south. They came back up the hill again with another battalion and more tanks and attacked *72.Inf.Div.* during the afternoon, losing four more tanks. An attempt by the Soviets to penetrate the northern outskirts of Novo Buda held by Siegel's troops was thwarted when *Feldwebel* (Sergeant) Albers and his platoon of truck drivers counterattacked and prevented the Soviets from breaking through the German defenses. The assault unit, led by a commissar, was wiped out.

Kästner's men, holding the southern part of the town, had to contend with several attacks that day from the south, where Morentsy lay. At 1100 hours, the Soviets succeeded in penetrating into the town itself with a battalion of infantry and two tanks. After half an hour of fighting, this attack was driven off and both tanks were destroyed in close combat by the use of hand grenade bundles and *Panzerfäuste*. Things were getting lively indeed. Relief, fortunately, was on the way. Earlier that morning, the division had been notified that *Wiking* was sending the Walloon Brigade to Novo Buda to bolster German defenses there, and would arrive in the early afternoon. Siegel's regiment would move out of the town completely and construct a regular defense line running from Novo Buda to Selishche. Kästner's troops would take over the northern half of the town, while Lucien Lippert's Walloons would defend the southern and southwestern portion of the village.

Siegel was not very pleased with his new assignment; once again, his troops would be forced to occupy defensive positions in wide-open terrain. It would be almost impossible to keep his men supplied with ammunition and food during the day, since anything moving along his five-kilometer wide sector would draw the attention of the enemy and be shot up. Nor was Siegel impressed with the Walloons. He remarked that, upon meeting Leon Degrelle at the German command post in Novo

Buda later that afternoon, the only thing the Belgian Rexist Leader kept asking was "When are we going to make it out of this pocket?," instead of where was the best location to emplace troops, heavy weapons, and so forth.[19] Everyone else probably had similar thoughts. There was only one way out of the trap, and that was by fighting.

Of course, the Walloons had been in action continuously for over a week and had fought well during their occupation of the Olshanka River defense line. In the vicinity of the town of Derenkovets, they had withstood a number of determined Soviet attacks led by 294th Rifle Division, retaking the town each time they had been forced out. But even their optimism had begun to crack, as evinced by Degrelle's anxious demeanor. Realization seemed to have dawned upon Degrelle when, on 10 February, he was informed of a message from *Wiking's* headquarters to his commander, Lippert, that the Germans' chances of "escaping total annihilation" was estimated to be only four or five in a hundred. Upon receipt of this message, according to Degrelle, "We looked at one another, [and] our blood ran cold. We saw the faces of our children, far away, as in a mirage. The hour was not far off when all would be lost."[20] Even this stalwart optimist had finally begun to realize the magnitude of the Germans' predicament. The only thing unusual about this realization is that most of the other German officers had come to the same conclusion a week before Degrelle did.

Degrelle and the rest of the Walloons must have felt relieved when they received orders on the evening of 11 February to hand their sector around Derenkovets over to the *Westland* and proceed the next morning to Novo Buda, where the brigade would take part in the fighting to take and hold the breakout area. Disengaging from the enemy with some difficulty, the Walloons were on the road near Arbusino by 1330 hours and had completely pulled out of their old positions two and a half hours later. When about to pass through the center of Korsun, Lippert ordered his men to dismount their vehicles and parade through the town in close order, singing at the top of their lungs. To the many Germans still holding the town, if must have been a fantastic sight. Imagine, singing martial tunes in a situation like this! On the southern edge of the town, the Walloons reformed and boarded their few remaining vehicles, crossing the Ross River over the temporary bridge erected over the hydroelectric dam.

During their brief halt at the headquarters of *Wiking* in Korsun that morning, Degrelle and Lippert witnessed General Gille's anger when the divisional commander was informed over the field telephone that Heinz Debus' *SS-Pz.Auflk.Abt.5* had been thrown out of Arbusino shortly after the Walloons had passed through during the early morning hours. Its fall would place the Soviets only three kilometers away from Korsun and allow them to shell the airfield southwest of the town. To their amazement, Gille grew red in the face, grabbed his gnarled *Knotenstock* (hiking stick), jumped into his Volkswagen and drove off in the direction of Arbusino, which was retaken when *Hstuf.* Wittmann's infantry company was thrown into the counterattack. No doubt relieved to have been spared the mission of turning about and taking part in this attack, Lippert, Degrelle, and the rest of the Walloons reached the outskirts of Novo Buda by 1130 hours.

Oberleutnant Matthias Roth, *Gren.Rgt.105,72.Inf.Div. His specialty was conducting night reconnaissance patrols through Soviet lines. (Photo courtesy of 72nd Infantry Division Veteran's Association).*

Lippert and most of his brigade had not had any sleep for days and had been exhausted by their early morning movement along the muddy roads. To keep awake, Degrelle and many others resorted to Pervetin pills, an artificial stimulant developed to allow pilots to stay away during long flights. While Degrelle may have thought that the Walloon Brigade was at the end of its strength, *Maj.* Kästner thought otherwise. When the leading columns of the brigade began arriving in the early afternoon, he noted that the Walloons still possessed six assault guns, four self-propelled anti-tank guns, and four rifle companies with an average strength of 50 men each - thus, amounting in Kästner's opinion, to "a considerable addition to [our] combat power in Novo Buda."

Their arrival precipitated the movement of Siegel's regiment to the aforementioned exposed position and the switching of Kästner's regiment to the northern part of the town later in the afternoon, even while the Soviets kept up their probing attacks against the village. However, *Gren.Rgt.105* would not have much longer to worry about it. During the early evening, its commander received a new set of orders from division that instructed him to prepare to disengage from Novo Buda that night and advance on the village of Komarovka, his regiment's next key assignment. His men would hand their sector over to the Walloon Brigade, who would then be responsible for the defense of this key village.[21] The Walloon's fighting ability

SS-Grenadiers of either Wiking or the Walloon Brigade taking a break from the withdrawal from the Derenkovets Gorodishche defensive line, mid-February 1944. One has even found an accordion and is putting it to use. Note that the weather during this stage of the operation was so warm, that many troops had discarded their winter combat suits. They would soon regret having done so. (U.S. National Archives)

In this picture, two SS-Grenadiers wearing fur-lined anoraks have enterprisingly carved out a shelter inside a haystack in their assembly area somewhere southwest of Korsun, 10 or 11 February 1944. While one writes a letter, rifles and hand grenades lay within close reach. (U.S. National Archives)

would once again be put to the test. For by that evening, the Soviet leadership had finally realized the magnitude of the German's overnight successes and had already placed troops in motion to regain the initiative.

The Soviet chain of command did not determine what exactly had happened for nearly a day. It took time for the word about the Germans' advance to filter up from the various companies, battalions, regiments, and divisions that had been routed or defeated by the unexpected series of night attacks. Certainly, none of these lower-level commanders - captains, majors, and colonels - wanted to be the ones who broke the news that the Germans may have escaped from the pocket on their watch. After all, General Konev had himself said that "The very idea that the Nazis could get through at the juncture of the fronts…was inadmissible."[22] However, it was hard to ignore the battlefield reality. In Konev's own words, "The Nazis succeeded in breaking through the defenses of the 27th Army, which unfortunately was understrength and held a broad front…It was the most critical phase of the operation."[23] Indeed, it was. But what happened next has been a source of contention between Soviet historians that resulted in the poisoning of the relationship between Konev and his erstwhile protector, Georgy Zhukov, as well as an unnecessary shuffle of the Soviet chain of command at this critical juncture.

Somehow, Stalin had been notified during mid-morning on 12 February (possibly via political officer channels) that the Germans had broken out of the inner ring of encirclement and had taken several villages. Who notified him remains unknown to this day. This knowledge must have angered the Soviet dictator all the more, since Zhukov and the two *Front* commanders had apparently been sending forth a steady stream of reports to Moscow that purported to show the Germans on the verge of total collapse and victory within their grasp. With the relief forces stalled and the pocket disintegrating, how could it be that they had almost broken out on their own?

The first to feel Stalin's wrath was General Konev, who received a call over the high frequency *STAVKA* radio network

around noon on 12 February. In his account, Konev relates Stalin's anger:

> [Stalin] said we had loudly announced for all the world to hear that a large enemy grouping was surrounded in the area of Korsun-Shevchenkovsky, and yet STAVKA had information that the encircled Germans had broken through the front of the 27th Army and moving towards their own forces. "What do you know about the situation on the neighboring front?" he demanded.[24]

Konev knew Stalin well enough to know that he was deadly serious; he had to weigh his words very carefully. Whoever had contacted Stalin, Konev thought, must have evidently given him a "slightly inaccurate report" (actually, the report was quite accurate, though in his memoirs Konev did not admit this). To assuage Stalin's anger and to show him that he was well aware of the situation, Konev told him that his *Front* had already taken the necessary steps to insure that the enemy's escape path would be blocked by ordering Rotmistrov's 5th Tank Army and 5th Guards Cavalry Corps to the sector of the breakthrough and to "drive them back into the trap and secure a linkup with First Ukrainian *Front*."[25] He also told Stalin a great deal more than that, as Zhukov and Vatutin soon found out.

Actually, the troop movements that Konev described to Stalin had been ordered in the early morning hours that same day by Zhukov, though they had nothing to do with the actual German attack. It was precautionary in nature, since it was obvious to nearly everyone on the various Soviet staffs that the Germans would try to break out either to the south or southwest, the direction from which the relief forces were approaching. Although no one could predict the exact spot were the breakout would occur, Zhukov probably felt that by cramming as many forces as possible in the corridor between the German forces inside and outside the pocket, sheer numbers

Along the highway of death. Trucks of Wiking burn in the distance. (Photo by Adolf Salie courtesy of Willy Hein)

Wounded of Wiking being loaded aboard a truck in Gorodishche. (Photo by Adolf Salie courtesy of Willy Hein)

alone would decide the issue. In Zhukov's own words, "…we could feel that the enemy simply did not have the strength to effect a linkup."[26]

An examination of Zhukov's order shows that he was concerned chiefly with stopping Breith's and Vormann's relief forces and was not overly worried about the Germans breaking out. The move of Rotmistrov's and Selivanov's units had already been ordered long before Konev's radio conversation with Stalin, leading one to conclude that Konev was simply covering up the fact that he had been caught napping and wanted to avoid blame by denying the anonymous report's essential veracity and informing the dictator that he was already "on top" of the situation.

Zhukov was also caught by surprise by a call from Stalin, who must have just ended his conversation with Konev. On the morning of 12 February, he was in bed with an attack of the flu. Suffering from a high temperature, he had only just fallen asleep when his adjutant, General L. Minyuk, shook him roughly awake. "What's the matter?" asked a sleepy Zhukov. "Stalin's on the phone," Minyuk replied. Zhukov leapt out of bed and raced to the radio. It was Stalin, who demanded angrily "I was just told that during the night the enemy broke through in Vatutin's sector from the Shanderovka area to Khilki and Novo Buda. Do you know anything about it?" Of course, Zhukov did not, and was ordered to check on the situation and report back to him. Zhukov immediately telephoned Vatutin, who informed the *STAVKA* coordinator that the Germans had indeed "pressed forward two or three kilometers," but had been stopped. Zhukov gave Vatutin some additional advice as to how to deal with this new situation, then called Stalin back.[27] What Stalin then said must have shocked and angered him.

Evidently, Konev must have told Stalin a great deal more than he mentioned in his postwar account of the battle. Before he could even give Stalin his report, Zhukov was told that Konev had spoken with him and that he had proposed to Stalin that control of all the units responsible for destroying the encircled Germans be immediately subordinated to Konev's Second Ukrainian *Front*. In effect, this meant that Trofimenko's 27th Army would be subordinated to Konev. Zhukov protested, stating that with the end so clearly in sight, such a last-minute transfer of control from one headquarters to another would only "retard the progress of the operation," a mild way of telling

the dictator that this proposal made no sense. But Stalin had already made up his mind to follow Konev's advice and he was not finished.

He also had ordered, based on Konev's suggestion, that Vatutin be relieved of any responsibility for the further conduct of operations in this area and instead "personally supervise the operations of 13th and 60th Armies in the Rovno-Lustk-Dubno area," nearly 100 kilometers further to the west.[28] Perhaps Konev had placed the blame for the loss of the towns in question squarely upon Vatutin; the evidence would seem to suggest so. When the entrapped Germans were finally liquidated, Konev would be able to claim the credit for himself and his *Front*. Before Zhukov could protest, Stalin then told him that he, Zhukov, would now assume command of the units arrayed in the path of Breith and Vormann's relief forces and would henceforth be responsible for insuring that any further breakthroughs be prevented at all costs. With that, Stalin hung up.

Before Zhukov could draft any orders of his own, he was sent a radio message which contained a detailed operations order drafted by General Antonov of the *STAVKA* and approved by Stalin. It laid out in writing the suggestions that Konev had given to Stalin, as well as detailed information in regards to troop movements. Control of Trofimenko's 27th Army, including 180th, 337th, and 202nd Rifle Divisions, as well as 54th and 159th Fortified Regions, would pass to Second Ukrainian *Front* by midnight. Vatutin's Front would still be responsible for supplying them and relaying orders from Konev. Zhukov would be released from "supervising" the operation and would be charged with coordinating the actions of the units resisting the approaching German relief forces, thus, giving him *de facto* command of 1st, and 2nd Guards Tank Armies and 6th Tank Army, as well as 40th Army.[29] For the first time since 1941, Zhukov and Konev would be serving as equals.

Any thoughts of gratitude Konev must have felt towards Zhukov, for his intervention of Konev's behalf in 1941 when Stalin wanted to have him tried and executed for incompetence are not recorded. That time was long past and Konev was quickly becoming one of Stalin's most effective generals. As for Vatutin, one of the Red Army's rising stars and Konev's rival, he had been humiliated for his alleged poor performance

An SS-Grenadier taking a cigarette break during the hard-fought delaying actions near Gorodishche, mid-February 1944. (U.S. National Archives)

Crouching behind a low hill, an SS-Grenadier loads another magazine into his MP-40, somewhere near Gorodishche. (U.S. National Archives)

not only for his inability to stop the German breakout attack on 11/12 February, but also for his *Front's* poor showing against Breith's approaching relief force. He had essentially been fired by Stalin and was ordered west to take charge of secondary operations well away from the main battle.

It was an angry Vatutin, who, upon hearing the news of his being ordered out of the battle, called Zhukov immediately after receiving this order. Vatutin, who Zhukov claimed to be an "extremely emotional man" when circumstances dictated, accused Zhukov of orchestrating this seeming demotion and stated angrily:

Comrade Marshal, you of all people surely know I've had no sleep for several days on end and [have] given every ounce of strength to [this] operation. Why then have I now been brushed aside from the completion of this magnificent operation? I am proud of my troops too and I want Moscow to salute the soldiers of the First Ukrainian Front!

Zhukov told his hot-headed subordinate that the orders came directly from Stalin and that he, too, thought that the order was unfair. In closing, Zhukov told him "Nikolai Fedorovich…You and I are soldiers, so let us carry out our orders without argument." Vatutin, with some reluctance said "The order will be obeyed."[30] Zhukov concluded his account of this incident by stating that after this date (12 February) all of the enemy's

attempts to break through from Shanderovka to Lysyanka were thwarted, but this is not the case. Simply stating that no Germans would escape, however, would not suffice, no matter how much both Zhukov and Konev wanted to please Stalin.

Zhukov, Konev, Vatutin, and *STAVKA* had simply been caught napping. Focused on the approaching relief forces of Breith and Vormann, they had not anticipated the German attempt to break through the inner ring of encirclement would happen so soon or in the exact area where it occurred. They had also believed that the Germans in the pocket were far weaker and in greater disarray than was the case. This underestimation of German capabilities, coupled with their opponent's logical choice of conducting a night attack, ensured that the Germans would have the element of surprise in their favor. Except for Shanderovka, the towns of Novo Buda, Skripchintsy, and Khilki had been taken with hardly a shot being fired. The going had indeed been surprisingly easy thus far for the assault units of *Gruppe Stemmermann*. But that situation was about to change.

The first Soviet unit affected by the change in plans was Selivanov's Cossack Corps. At 0430 hours 11 February, before the German attack commenced, Selivanov had already received orders to move his corps from the Kvitki-Valyava sector, where they were fighting Trowitz' *57.Inf.Div.*, towards Steblev. The night march towards their new positions had not been an easy one, for in addition to a snowfall during the night, it had rained that day. Their overtired ponies became even further exhausted. The Cossacks also were not expecting to encounter any Germans along the line of march and they commenced their movement towards their new positions at roughly the same time the Germans began their night attack. As previously related, elements from Selivanov's corps had been ambushed late that evening by Kästner's troops as they moved along the road from Sukhiny to Shanderovka. On the morning of 12 February, 63rd Cavalry Division had taken up new positions along the Gniloy Tikich, with its guns oriented towards Breith's corps. The rest of the corps was still on the road between Selishche and Morentsy. It was thus disposed when Selivanov was first informed on the magnitude of the German attack during the early afternoon of 12 February.

Selivanov was instructed by Konev, his *Front* commander, that his corps would be assigned the mission of encircling and destroying the German forces that had broken through and taken Shanderovka and Novo Buda. In accordance with these orders, his 63rd Cavalry Division was ordered to turn over its new positions along the Gniloy Tikich to another unit and rejoin the rest of the corps, which was subordinated to Ryshov's 4th Guards Army. Selivanov was not quite sure that his corps was up to the task. In his corps' after action report, he stated that it was in bad shape. Not only had his men and their mounts been in action for almost three straight weeks, they were suffering from supply shortages as well from the impassability of the roads intensified by the intermittent thaws.

Resupply had practically ceased, especially in regards to ammunition and fuel. He described how tanks, assault guns, artillery pieces, and trucks were scattered along the path of the battles his corps had fought, destroyed, broken down, or stuck in the mud. Regardless, he issued the appropriate orders to his divisions. Their first object of attention would be Novo Buda, which would be attacked during the afternoon and evening of 12 February by 11th and 12th Guards Cavalry Divisions, in many instances directly from the line of march without any preparation.[31] It was these units that Kästner's and Siegel's regiments had driven off that day. They would be back, along with a third division.

The Germans, for their part, were unaware of the developments within the Soviet camp. Even had they known that powerful forces were being arrayed against them, they would have had little choice but to continue attacking as ordered. There was only one way out, and that was to keep advancing. *Oberst* Bucher and his battlegroup from *K.Abt.B* were ordered on 12 February to continuing their attack towards Petrovskoye. Kästner and his grenadiers were ordered to continue their attack and seize Komarovka during the night of 12/13 February. *Germania* was still occupied in mopping up Shanderovka. True, the Soviets had already initiated counterattacks, but so far these had not proven worrisome. While the defenders of Khilki and Shanderovka seemed to have been satisfied with what they had accomplished so far and dug in for the night; Kästner was not. He had to take Komarovka, and the sooner, the better.

To help *Gren.Rgt.105* carry out its attack, *Oberst* Hohn gave Kästner the division's last three self-propelled 7.5 cm PaKs. Otherwise, Kästner chose to use the same tactical formation that had proven so successful the night before.

Before launching his night attack, he ordered his *Truppführer, Hptm.* Matthias Roth, to carry out a reconnaissance towards the objective. Upon his return, Kästner learned that the road that led from Novo Buda to Komarovka was free of the enemy. The question as to whether or not the self-propelled antitank guns could accompany the attack was answered when Roth replied that a bridge along the route that spanned a small creek could support the weight of his three light armored vehicles. As for Komarovka, it was occupied by the enemy and Roth had observed a considerable amount of vehicle traffic that ran along the road from the town to Shanderovka, where sounds of fighting could still be heard.

Since the enemy in Komarovka appeared to have occupied the town in force, the only hope for success seemed, once again, to lie in a night surprise attack. The objective itself actually seemed to be two smaller towns jammed up next to one another. The eastern part of the town was a tightly compacted cluster of houses that had been built next to a hill crest. The eastern, or lower part of the town, was far more spread out where it straddled the road to Shanderovka. A frontal assault was out of the question. Once again, Kästner decided to use a pincer movement - part of his force would attack the western part of town from the north, while the other part would attack the eastern part of town from the east.

The two-phased attack would begin at 2100 hours. The infantry battalion under Roth would attack the western part of the town from the north. Once this attack seemed to be gathering momentum, he would signal to Kästner and the rest of the regiment, to commence their own part of the attack from the east. Both forces would then roll the Soviets up until both met in the town's center. The artillery battery and infantry gun company would follow close behind and prepare to lend their weight against the enemy's defenses with direct fire, if necessary. The three self-propelled antitank guns and the motorized 2 cm *Flak* cannons would remain in concealment until the attack had progressed, since their engine and track noises would alert the enemy about their approach.

Soundlessly, Kästner's and Roth's men moved out. All metallic items, such as gas mask containers or entrenching tools, had either been tied down or discarded. Smoking had been forbidden. Through the snow and mud, they slowly advanced. Two and a half hours later, the hill overlooking Komarovka was reached, where they split into two assault groups. Roth and his men, using the folds of the terrain to mask their approach, moved out to the northwest, initiating their envelopment from the north. In the moonless night, Kästner could barely make out the outlines of the eastern part of the town; the western part, which lay in a hollow, could not be seen at all. To provide immediate fire support, he ordered two of the accompanying artillery pieces to take up hasty firing positions. Kästner watched and waited anxiously as the minutes slowly passed. Finally, at 0100 hours, Roth notified Kästner by radio that he and his men had reached their attack position. His regimental commander gave him the order to go in.

Roth's scouts, moving ahead of the main body of his battalion, spotted and quickly dispatched eight Soviet sentries before they could give out a warning. Storming into the village, Roth and his men were surprised when they encountered a Soviet infantry battalion boarding a long row of trucks. Immediately sizing up the situation, Roth ordered two of his heavy machine-guns into position. At point-blank range, the MG-42s and accompanying infantrymen poured automatic weapons fire into the Soviet troops that were standing around the trucks, which burst into flames. Those few remaining survivors not mowed down by this intensive fire were either killed in hand-to-hand combat or taken prisoner. Once Roth had seized the western part of the town, Kästner commenced his part of the attack from the east. The few remaining Soviet troops who had fled to this part of the town to escape Roth's attack were caught by Kästner's men and killed. Mopping up lasted until 1030 hours that morning.

Like the previous night's attack against Novo Buda, Komarovka had fallen to the Germans readily. Kästner's regiment counted 196 enemy dead for less than a dozen casualties of their own. They had also captured 51 of the enemy, four trucks, and a large number of mortars, small arms, and other heavy weapons. The Soviet battalion, which evidently belonged to 7th Guards Airborne Division, had been virtually wiped out. Kästner duly notified his division commander of the success of the attack, who then relayed the information to Stemmermann's operations officer. At 0740 hours., *Gruppe Stemmermann* radioed *8.Armee* laconically, "Since 0400 hours [our troops] have penetrated into southern and eastern Komarovka."[32]

Taking Komarovka was not the same as defending it. Kästner was experienced enough to know that a Soviet response would not be long in coming. However, defending the town posed a number of problems. The western part lay in a hollow, offering poor fields of fire and observation. He decided to place Roth's infantry battalion and the three self-propelled antitank guns in this part of town. If the enemy came over the hill that lay immediately to their west, the defenses would have to be strong. The defense of the southern part of the town, where the road led towards the village of Potchapintsy, was entrusted to the regiment's reserve company, supported by the 2 cm *Flak*. The infantry howitzer company (two guns) and the artillery battery (four guns) was positioned in the upper or eastern part of the town, where they could support against an attack coming from either the west or the south.

To connect the troops holding Komarovka with those holding Novo Buda, *Feld Ers.Btl.72*, commanded by *Ltn.* Bender, was placed in position. Although this force, which had accompanied Kästner and his regiment since the evening of 11 February, had few heavy weapons of their own, they would be able to hold their own. Here, the terrain would be extremely unfavorable for the attackers, since the Soviets would have to attack uphill to reach the Germans, who were dug in along the crest of the hill that spanned the distance between both towns. As fighting flared around them to the north, west and east (Shanderovka, Khilki, and Novo Buda, respectively), the men of *Gren.Rgt.105* spent the remainder of the day in relative peace. It would not last long. As Kästner later recalled, "We would soon find ourselves in the hardest fighting we had heretofore experienced."[33]

This sentiment was echoed by General Lieb, who paid a visit during the afternoon of 12 February to Khilki, shortly after *Oberst* Bucher was mortally wounded while leading another attempt to take Petrovskoye. "So goes one after the other," remarked Lieb in his diary. Things in Khilki looked bad, he wrote, noting that "nothing gets done anymore unless officers are constantly behind [the troops]." Lieb had moved his headquarters from Steblev to Shanderovka to be closer to the fighting. So close, in fact, that Lieb decided to get rid of any extra baggage he was carrying.

He instructed his orderly to give away any of his extra uniforms, burn most of his personal papers (except his diary, of course), and to keep his horses inside the hut where he was staying, noting that "they are in better shape than I."[34] He knew that the next few days would be marked by heavy fighting and wanted to travel as light as possible. Unlike Stemmermann, Lieb seems to have kept a positive attitude, providing encouragement to his subordinate commanders and their troops, trying to keep their spirits up by appearing in their fighting positions as often as was prudently possible. He was also, of course, attempting to keep abreast of the actual conditions in the front line and to determine the capabilities of his battalions and regiments, a hallmark of good leadership.

With the breakout area for the most part in German hands by the morning of 13 February, Stemmermann now had to "collapse" the northern and northeastern area of the Pocket and move the troops holding these defense lines south of the Ross River. Korsun would have to be given up, the airfield abandoned. But at least, the hard part seemed to be over; now all the troops of *Gruppe Stemmermann* had to do was await the arrival of Breith's relief force. The pocket had wandered halfway to its rescuers - now it was up to the tanks and troops of *III.Pz.Korps* to come the rest of the way.

End Notes

1 *Sbornik*, p. 322.

2 Kathagen, p. 85.

3 Interview with Alexei Fyodorovich, Korsun-Shevchenkovski, Ukraine, 29 June 1996.

4 *Sbornik*, p. 331.

5 *8.Armee* KTB, entry dated 0445 hours 9 February 1944, p. 1.

6 Radio message, *1a, XI.A.K.*, dated 0935 hours 9 February 1944, to *8.Armee* Headquarters.

7 Schenk, p. 56.

8 Radio message from Headquarters, *XI.A.K.* to *8.Armee* dated 1650 hours, 10 February.

9 *8.Armee* KTB, entry dated 0750 hours 9 February 1944, p. 1.

10 Mayer, p. 134.

11 *8.Armee* KTB, entry dated 0903 hours 11 February 1944, p. 2.

12 Siegel, p. 13.

13 Strassner, pp. 144-145.

14 Recommendation for the award of the Knight's Cross to the Iron Cross, *SS-Untersturmführer* Werner Meyer, dated 24 March, 1944, pp. 4-5. (Washington, D. C.: U.S. National Archives),

15 *Tagesmeldung, XXXXII.A.K.* to Headquarters, *8.Armee*, radio message dated 2044 hours 11 February 1944.

16 *Tagesmeldung, XXXXII.A.K.* to Headquarters, *8.Armee*, radio message dated 1900 hours 12 February 1944.

17 *World War Two German Military Studies,* (Vol. 1, p-143d). "Breakout from Encirclement in the Cherkassy Pocket by the 105th Infantry Regiment, 72nd Infantry Division, February 1944" by Robert Kästner. (U.S. Government: U.S. Army Europe Historical Division, 1954), p. 11. Text from this manuscript is virtually identical to that written by Matthias Roth, *Bericht über der Ausbruchs der Kessel von Tscherkassy,* undated manuscript courtesy of 72nd Infantry Division's Veteran's Association.

18 Siegel, p. 13.

19 Ibid.

20 Degrelle, p. 188.

21 *World War Two German Military Studies,* (Vol. 1, p-143d), pp. 11-12.

22 Sokolov, p. 119.

23 Ibid, p. 121.

24 Konev in Sokolov, p. 121.

25 Ibid, p. 122.

26 Zhukov, p. 245.

27 Ibid, p. 247.

28 Ibid, p. 248.

29 Ibid, p. 248.

30 Ibid, p. 249.

31 "Combat Operations of 5th Guards Don Red Army Cavalry Corps in the Korsun-Shevchenkovsky Operation," *The Journal of Slavic Military Studies*, Vol. 7, No. 2. (London: Frank Cass, 1994), p. 350.

32 Radio Message from *1a, XI.A.K. to 8.Armee* Headquarters, dated 0740 hours 13 February 1944.

33 *World War Two German Military Studies*, (Vol. 1, p-143d), pp. 13-18.

34 Lieb in DA Pam 20-234, p. 23-24.

NOW OR NEVER

Chapter Sixteen

BREITH TRIES ONCE AGAIN

"Bravo! In spite of the mud and Russians, you have almost made it!"
— *Field Marshal Manstein, 13 February 1944*

Friday, 11 February, proved to be a decisive day for both *1.Pz.* and *8.Armee.* Not only had the Germans been able to break out of the Soviet's inner ring of encirclement that evening at Novo Buda and Shanderovka, but Breith and Vormann had been able to steal a march on them as well. Ironically, part of *Gruppe Stemmermann's* success that day and the next were due to the Soviet's having focused on the relief attempt's approach, leaving them vulnerable to a surprise attack from the opposite direction.

The troops of 6th Tank, 5th Guards Tank, 4th Guards, 53rd, and 40th Armies were prepared to repulse Breith and Vormann, but when those attacks came, they were caught by surprise as well. The wrath of Stalin, when informed of the German's tactical successes of 11/12 February, is quite understandable. He no doubt felt somewhat misled; after receiving positive reports for the past two weeks, the report of the sudden turn of events in the German's favor must have shocked and angered him. For the first time during this operation, his armies had lost the initiative; initiative which Zhukov and Konev had to regain at all costs.

As stunned as Stalin had been when he received the news, the effect upon the army, corps, and division commanders of both the First and Second Ukrainian *Fronts* must have been just as great. While the loss of Shanderovka, Novo Buda, Khilki and Komarovka were unexpected, the sudden energy displayed by the German relief forces that day must have been just as surprising. By 7/8 February, with Vormann stalled at the Iskrenoye bridgehead and Breith stymied north of the Gniloy Tikich at Vessely Kut, it seemed to the Soviet leadership that the German relief attack had culminated. Indeed, with Breith's withdrawal back to his forces' original line of departure in full swing on 9 February, it must have seemed to the Soviet leadership that the crisis was past.

With enough tank and infantry armies crammed in the area between the encircled Germans and the relief forces to ensure that no link up would occur, many Soviet generals undoubtedly felt that they could now turn their full attention towards the *unichtozhenye* of the entrapped Fascists. However, just as they had underestimated the fighting ability of *Gruppe Stemmermann*, Zhukov, Vatutin, and Konev also seemed to have discounted the determination of the men of *III.* and *XXXXVII.Pz.Korps* to break through and rescue their encircled comrades. For Breith's corps had not departed from the battlefield at all; in fact, his divisions were rallying for one more

The thaw sets in. As roads turn to ribbons of mud, the individual vehicle crewman must struggle to keep their vehicles from becoming immobilized. Here, a panzer soldier tries to scrape mud from the running gear of his tank. (Bundesarchiv 69/117/28)

attempt to reach the men in the pocket, nor would Vormann remained bottled up in the Iskrenoye bridgehead. This time, the Germans would come via a much shorter, direct route where the Soviets did not expect them and in much greater strength than they thought possible. Operation Wanda would continue with renewed vigor, beginning at dawn on 11 February.

By 9 February, most of *III.Pz.Korps'* divisions had managed to withdraw to their original starting point from which they had begun their assault on 4 February. Although *16.* and *17.Pz.Divs.* as well as *Schw.Pz.Rgt. Bäke* had been decimated by the mud as much as by the enemy, the relief force had been reinforced by the arrival of the rest of *Leibstandarte* and *1.Pz.Div.* Now, they could try one more time to reach the pocket - this time, towards the east via Bushanka and Lysyanka. Aside from the fact that this route was the shorter one, *1.Pz.Armee's Ic* had determined that there were only one Soviet tank corps (5th Guards Tank) and one to two rifle divisions from 47th Rifle Corps barring their way, which led him to conclude that "This enemy situation reinforces the hope, that the attack of *III.Pz.Korps* would not find the [enemy's] defense of this area as great as what it had encountered in the north."[1]

As the staffs of *1.Pz.Armee* and *III.Pz.Korps* applied themselves to planning for this renewed thrust, Manstein paid a visit to Hube in Uman on 9 February, where the commander of Army Group South had just moved his headquarters in order to

The going gets tough. Panzer Mark IVs fight melting snow and mud as much as the Soviets, early February 1944. (Bundesarchiv 277/844/14A)

be nearer to the fighting. At 1100 hours, Manstein and members of his operations staff arrived at *1.Pz.Armee's* headquarters. The Field Marshal, after having been briefed by Wenck on the overall situation and the concept of the upcoming operation, proceeded to give Hube additional guidance regarding the planned attack of *III.Pz.Korps*. Manstein thought that Hube's plan for the attack would force Breith's panzer corps to advance along an insufficiently broad front. Since Hube was averse to having his units separated by the Gniloy Tikich, he had planned that all four of the attacking divisions move north of the creek through a very narrow corridor, thus limiting their freedom of movement. Hube and Wenck disagreed, thereupon igniting a vigorous debate with their army group commander, who, to his credit, heard them out.

Manstein thought that it would be better if *16.Pz.Div.* attacked on the right along the southern bank of the Gniloy Tikich, while *17.Pz.Div.* attacked along the left on the northern bank. Hube and Wenck argued that this would insure that the attack would not be able to go forward as scheduled, since *16.Pz.Div.* could not move that far south in time in order to comply with its instructions to attack by 11 February. Furthermore, Wenck stated that by requiring the two lead divisions to fight in this manner, each would be fighting in isolation, unable to provide mutual support should the other one encounter a Soviet counterattack. They would also be vulnerable to Soviet attempts to cut them off by attacks on their left and right flanks. After a heated debate of over an hour's duration, Manstein finally gave in, and approved *1.Pz.Armee's* original plan, with some modifications.[2]

The amended plan, *Armeebefehl* (army order) Number 116/44, went out that evening. The aforementioned *16.* (to which *Schw.Pz.Rgt. Bäke* had been attached) and *17.Pz.Divs.* would

attack side-by-side north of the creek, *1.Pz.Div.* would conduct a supporting attack along the south of the creek, guarding the corps' right flank, and *Leibstandarte* would protect the corps' left flank. The attack itself would pass through the *HKL* held by *198.Inf.Div.*, which was holding a defensive sector between Risino in the south to Vinograd in the north.

As the attack progressed, Horn's division would have to stretch to the north in order to retain contact with the panzer divisions, while at the same time lengthening its southern defensive line to help cover the gap that yawned between *1.Pz.* and *8. Armee.* General Hell's *VII.A.K.* would hold its current position and prevent the Soviets from breaking through and cutting off Breith's corps, which would necessarily be advancing along a narrow front and hence vulnerable to envelopment. The key position of Tinovka, on *VII.Armeekorps'* right flank, would continue to be held by *34.Inf.Div.*, which had repelled literally dozens of Soviet counterattacks over the past two weeks.

The Army's *Oberquartiermeister* was instructed to devote the priority of his office's effort towards the resupply of *III.Pz.Korps*, even if it meant that other corps went without key items of supply. General Seidemann's *VIII.Flieger Korps* would provide *Stukas* for close air support and fighter cover for the attack. So far, except for supply missions, his aircraft had been conspicuously absent, grounded by mud and poor flying conditions. The Red Air Force had been able to keep flying in support of its own troops in the same conditions, however, leading many Germans on the ground to wonder whether the *Luftwaffe* had let them down yet again.

By 9 February, most of the salient that had been created by the previous relief attempt had been evacuated. All that was left was a small bulge occupied by *16.Pz.Div.* that ran from

First Panzer Division troops awaiting a traffic jam to be sorted out. (Bundesarchiv 277/844/14A)

Tinovka in the west to Tatyanovka in the north, turning to the south near Repki, where it linked up with *17.Pz.Div.* This salient, too, would be largely evacuated by the following day, since an attack could not be conducted to the east from this location, owing to the unfavorable terrain. During the next two days, *Leibstandarte* would take up this sector, allowing *16.* and *17.Pz.Divs.* to concentrate their forces in assembly areas near Rubanny Most and Vinograd, respectively. Fortunately, the previous day's fighting had forced the Red Army to order a pause in operations; the loss of so many tanks on 8 February, combined with the impression that the Germans seemed to be withdrawing probably accounts for this, though the Soviets undoubtedly put this breathing space to use to bring up more reinforcements.

The 9th of February passed relatively uneventfully for *III.Pz.Korps*, except for isolated sporadic local counterattacks that were easily repulsed. Breith's biggest concern that day was reassembling and supplying his units, as well as evacuating the wounded from the previous week's fighting. The best news of all was the arrival of the bulk of General Koll's *1.Pz.Div.*, which had finally closed up after struggling against the *rasputitsa* and weather for nearly a week. By 10 February, most of the division had assembled north of Risino, bringing with it 48 Panthers and 18 Pz.IVs, almost doubling the amount of armor Breith had at his disposal. The division's forward detachment, *K.Gr.Huppert*, organized around *Pz.Aufkl.Abt.1*, was ordered to rejoin its division, after supporting the right flank of *198.Inf.Div.* for the past five days. Despite this welcome addition to the German's combat power, Koll's division would still carry out a secondary effort - a supporting role, that of guarding *III.Pz.Korps'* right flank against any counterattacks launched by either Kravchenko or Rotmistrov.

Tuesday, 10 February also passed relatively uneventfully, allowing *III.Pz.Korps* even more time to prepare for the resumption of Operation Wanda. Even so, 19 Soviet tanks were knocked out that day, when infantry and tanks from 6th Tank and 40th Armies attempted uncoordinated attacks against Tinovka and Votylevka, where troops from *34.Inf.Div.* and *Leibstandarte* received them with stout resistance. Elsewhere, German tank recovery teams attempted to retrieve both battle-damaged and broken down tanks, all of which were stuck in the viscous Ukrainian muck. Hundreds of trucks were simply abandoned on the roads where they where, since the priority of effort was directed towards placing as many combat vehicles back into operation as possible.

Mechanics were busy repairing what they could; by day's end, for example, Bäke's heavy panzer regiment had nearly forty tanks operational; the *Leibstandarte* had twenty-three. Back's *16.Pz.Div.* managed to get 24 tanks and assault guns back into operation. Von der Meden's worn-out *17.Pz.Div.* only had 12 serviceable tanks and assault guns, two of which were Tigers from the attached company of *Schw.Pz.Abt.506.*

What concerned Breith at this point was not the number of tanks that he had at his disposal, but the amount of artillery (or lack thereof). Although there were artillery pieces aplenty scattered over his sector, the fact that the tractors that pulled them were in short supply rendered a large part of his guns useless.[3] Many of the artillery's prime movers were engaged in the tank recovery effort, since they were one of the few types of vehicles that could still move about in the mud. Both *16.* and *17.Pz.Divs.* were also short of infantry, particularly Back's *16.Pz.Div.*, since he had been instructed to leave *II./Pz.Gren.Rgt.64*, in support of *Leibstandarte* near Tatyanovka.

Leibstandarte, even on 10 February, was rated "especially weak" by *III.Pz.Korps*. On that day, it reported only 180 infantrymen present for duty. Nearly all of its heavy weapons and vehicles had become stuck along the march routes leading to Uman, along with hundreds of troops who had remained behind with orders to extricate them and place them back into operation. All that the *Waffen-SS'* premier armored division had left to offer was a few infantrymen, as well as its tanks and assault guns, many of which could not be moved due to lack of fuel. To provide *Leibstandarte* more offensive firepower, Hube ordered that two independent army-level artillery *Abteilungen* be attached to Wisch's division, but it was doubtful whether they would arrive in time.

Breith expressed his fear to Hube that, if attacked, *Leibstandarte* and the entire northern flank would collapse and the relief attempt planned for the following day would be threatened with disaster. In fact, Wisch's sector was held together by a series of widely-spaced, weakly held strong points, focused on holding the towns of Votylevka, Tatyanovka, and Repki. From 9 to 11 February, Hitler's bodyguard division had warded off a series of small Soviet probing attacks. Although these actions barely rated a mention in the daily journal at *III.Pz.Korps* or *1. Pz.Armee*, they are illustrative of the bitter nature of the fighting that the men the *Leibstandarte* had to endure.

On the night of 10 February, for example, a *Leibstandarte* outpost that lay atop Hill 246.3, four kilometers northwest of Tinovka was attacked by three T-34 tanks and 60 infantrymen. This Soviet force was attempting to turn the right flank of the division's *II./SS-Pz.Gren.Rgt.2* and attack Tinovka from the east, held by *34.Inf.Div.* The outpost protecting the right flank was held by four men, the sole survivors of the battalion's *6. Kompanie.* When the T-34s approached the crest of the hill, the accompanying *Tankodesantniki* dismounted and rushed towards the four SS men in their foxholes. With their machine-gun, *SS-Rttf.* (corporal) Westrich and *SS-Strm.* (private) Bauer were able to kill many of the attackers. In hand-to-hand combat, they themselves were killed by the enemy only after they had expended all of their ammunition.

As the Soviet attack rolled on, they came up against the foxhole occupied by the acting company commander, *Rttf.* Gawlik and *SS-Grenadier* Leniker, the company medic. Armed only with pistols, both men put up such a fight that, in the darkness, the Soviets thought that they were dealing with a far larger force and hesitated. As the Soviets were rallying to attempt another thrust, a counterattack launched by *II.Bataillon's* reserve threw them back down the hill in disarray. For their heroism, all four men were mentioned in the daily Honor Roll of the German Army, a considerable honor to be bestowed upon men of such junior rank, although Bauer and Westrich were no longer alive to hear their names read in the order of the day.[4] To fight their way towards their encircled comrades, all of the troops of *III.Pz.Korps* and the neighboring *XXXXVII.Pz.Korps* would have to show an equal amount of determination and an even greater amount of skill, as well. But Hermann Breith was not so sure that would be enough.

Despite the problems Breith had in reassembling his forces and the worries he and his staff had about their overall weakened condition, his greatest concern was with keeping them supplied, no easy task with such bad road conditions. In a

discussion with Wenck on 10 February, Breith expressed his growing doubts about Manstein's and Hube's decision that his corps make the main effort for the upcoming attack. With his already long supply lines increasingly vulnerable to interdiction by the enemy on the ground as well as in the air, Breith felt that the attack should not be carried forth unless continued logistical support could be guaranteed. To ensure that his tanks would have enough fuel, he had already ordered that his tanks be loaded with as many jerrycans of gasoline as they could carry. Although this was a dangerous expedient, there was no other recourse. If fuel could not be brought up in the wake of the advance once this fuel was used up, Breith believed that the attack would fall short of the goal of reaching Lysyanka.

Another concern was his belief that Lysyanka had to be taken at all costs, since everyone, from Army Group South headquarters down to division level, knew that this was the only suitable route into the pocket from the southwest. If his troops could not take Lysyanka and its two bridges which led across the Gniloy Tikich, then there was absolutely no chance that his men could fight their way into the pocket, since the corps heavy bridging assets were stuck in the mud far to the south near Uman. Furthermore, Breith felt that *1.Pz.Armee's* statement that the route into the Pocket through Morentsy via Lysyanka,

Troops from 1st Panzer Division advance along the icy roads towards Lysyanka. (Photo courtesy of Rolf Stoves, Die 1.Panzerdivision 1935-1945)

Meanwhile, the relief force slowly fought its way forward. Here, escorting infantry from a Jäger battalion slog through the mud. One such battalion was attached to Schw.Pz.Rgt. Bäke during the battle. (Bundesarchiv 69/117/28)

Clearing up newly retaken villages is left up to the accompanying Panzergrenadiers. Note the officer in the old-style peaked cap with the MP-43 assault rifle slung over his shoulder. (Bundesarchiv 90/3904/25)

"offered the most favorable terrain" reflected the Army Headquarter's poor appreciation of the situation.

In his opinion, based on a terrain study, the area from Lysyanka to Morentsy was especially unfavorable for armor, and should be totally ruled out as a route of advance. Most of it would be uphill from Lysyanka and it was not known whether any bridges existed over the Gniloy Tikich along that route. Moreover, Lieb had informed *1.Pz.Armee* by radio the day before that the route from Lysyanka to Shanderovka was far better. The overall unfavorable situation led a discouraged Breith to advise Wenck to study the alternative of having *XXXXVII.Pz.Korps* make the main effort. The terrain in that direction, in his opinion, was far more favorable.[5] Breith was overruled his attack would go forward "without tanks, if necessary" according to Hube, who had sworn in a radio message to the encircled corps that he would rescue them. The attack would begin as scheduled, 0700 hours 11 February.

Prior to this attack, Hans Hube issued a general order that was to be read by radio to all troops taking part in the relief attack as well as to the troops of *Gruppe Stemmermann*. It illustrates both the hope he must have felt at the time as well as the realization that the mission would be a difficult one. In order Number 117/44, Hube stated:

On 11 February, III.Pz.Korps will conduct a renewed attack as the Army's main effort, in conjunction with elements of 8.Armee, in order to relieve the encircled corps, who are surrounded by a strong enemy force. I am aware, as are the troops concerned, of the difficulty of this

attack that I have ordered, which will be going against a heavily entrenched, numerically superior enemy force as well against unfavorable terrain. In spite of this, we must overcome both the enemy and the mud.

Despite the unfavorable circumstances we face, every troop leader must be clearly motivated by one guiding thought in every minute and in every action - the reestablishment of contact with our encircled comrades, who are threatened with destruction by the enemy who bars our path. With or without vehicles, we have only one thought: Forwards to our hard-pressed comrades. I demand from every individual soldier his last measure of devotion. Then we will achieve our goal. I trust in the leadership of III.Pz.Korps, who have in the past few days overcome many great challenges, I trust in the heroic courage continuously displayed by the proven divisions assigned [to your corps]. We will break through the ring and cut our comrades free.[6]

The same order was intercepted by Soviet radio intelligence, which, after the battle, mocked Hube's bombast and ridiculed him for demanding the impossible. One German observer after the war even criticized Hube for raising false hopes among the troops of *Gruppe Stemmermann*. Such statements, according to Edgar Röhricht, amounted to nothing less than wishful thinking and conflicted with the oft-spoken Prussian General Staff motto, "deeds, not words."[7] More likely, such examples of

Befehlsoptimismus reveals the degree of emotion Hube felt at the time and how personally he empathized with the troops in the Pocket. After all, Hube himself had commanded a Panzer division at Stalingrad and knew first hand how it felt to be encircled. Whether spoken in bravado or in sincerity, Hube's order left no doubt in anyone's mind that this would be a hard fight.

The question of whether or not the terrain favored Vormann's corps or Breith's was, by 10 February, irrelevant. Breith's corps would make the main effort. Vormann's corps simply lacked the power to fight its way up to the Pocket and nearly everyone, including Manstein, knew it. By 11 February, *XXXXVII.Pz.Korps* was little more than a group of tank-supported infantry *Kampfgruppen* with little hope of reaching the encircled troops of *Gruppe Stemmermann*. The German leadership nevertheless thought that, even in its greatly weakened state, Vormann's corps could still accomplish something. Manstein and Wöhler hoped it would tie up as much of Rotmistrov's 5th Guards Tank Army as possible in order to prevent this powerful tank force from being used against Breith's southern flank. If Vormann hit the Soviets hard enough near Zvenigorodka, he could perhaps fool the Soviets into believing that his attack was equally as dangerous as Breith's, forcing Konev to divert even more of his forces away from the Lysyanka corridor.

Vormann was even more pessimistic than his counterpart at *III.Pz.Korps*. He had long felt that any offensive action in the direction of Morentsy by his corps in cooperation with Breith's corps was impossible, for he knew that *XXXXVII.Pz.Korps* was too weak. The impact of the recall of *24.Pz.Div.* the week before was now being felt throughout his corps. In continuous action since 24 January (actually, since the Battle of Kirovograd even earlier), his divisions were simply burnt out. His troops, Vormann felt, had done all that could be expected of them and that they should feel free of guilt for what he saw as a looming disaster. Afterwards, he wrote,

> . . . willingly, they sacrificed themselves and literally gave everything they had. There was no means to describe what it was like to someone who had not spent their nights in the open, lying in the frozen mud. No one had reckoned with how much of a mental and physical burden we had imposed on our troops, with the effect of the enemy [attacks] and the spiritual burden this entailed.[8]

Regardless, *XXXXVII.Pz.Korps* was expected to do its part and attack the same day as *III.Pz.Korps*. When Vormann asked Speidel at *8.Armee* headquarters in Novo Ukraina, how he was supposed to accomplish this with his battered force, he was told in no uncertain terms that "You will fight your way through to the two [encircled] corps even if takes the last man or the last tank to do so."[9]

The main effort of *8.Armee* would now be an attack towards Zvenigorodka, which lay some twenty-five kilometers to the northwest of *XXXXVII.Pz.Korps'* current location. Accordingly, most of *13.Pz.Div.* still holding the Iskrenoye

Bridgehead was evacuated during 10 February, and the point of main effort was moved further west, where both *11.* and *13.Pz.Div*, shadows of their former selves, would now be required to make the main effort. *14.Pz.Div.,* the weakest of the corps' four panzer divisions, would be placed in reserve once it was relieved in place by *106.Inf.Div.*

As it was, it was only suited to holding a screen line that connected to the east with *3.Pz.Div.*, also in a very weakened state, born out by the fact that between 10 and 12 February, three of the corps' four panzer divisions could only muster between them 17 operational tanks and assault guns. None of these divisions were truly capable of conducting any type of offensive action, since they had received no replacements since the battle began 24 January, but Vormann had nothing left to commit. Although *106., 320.,* and *376.Inf.Div.* had been brought up and put into line, they were only suited to hold a thinly-spaced series of strong points. Thus, it was up to the battered panzer divisions to make one last, supreme effort.

While Hube was publishing his order of encouragement on 10 February, *11.Pz.Div.* had already taken up its attack positions east of Yerki. It would have to conduct the main attack without the bulk of *13.Pz.Div.* on hand, since *Gen.Maj.* Hans Mikosch was still trying to extricate the rest of his division from the bridgehead at Iskrenoye, though he had been ordered to leave a token force behind in case the bridgehead might be needed at a later date. This portion would follow along the badly rutted roads as soon as possible, but for now all that Mikosch had available to help Wietersheim was an armored *Kampfgruppe* and the divisional reconnaissance battalion.

If they could somehow be freed from holding a sector of the front line, *3.* and *14.Pz.Div.* would be sent their way too, but Vormann did not believe that was very likely. That evening, he was paid a visit by his army commander, who again urged him to press his leaders and troops as hard as possible. As a consolation, Wöhler promised his corps commander that he would attach to him *StuG.Abt.203*, though both men must have known that it would not arrive for at least another day or so. It was small consolation, but Vormann would have to be satisfied with that for the time being.

Surprisingly, the attack from the south on 11 February, the same day that *Gruppe Stemmermann* reported its remaining strength in the pocket at 56,000 men, began promisingly enough, even though the units slated to take part in the battle were far from ready. *K.Gr.Haack*, attached to *XXXXVII.Pz.Korps* the previous day, attacked first, seizing the town of Romanovka at 1630 hours. Late that morning, Wietersheim's *11.Pz.Div.* launched an attack towards the west and seized the town of Yerki in cooperation with *K.Gr.Haack* against light Soviet resistance. Pushing on, the Germans seized an intact bridge over the Shpolka River and pressed onwards in the direction of Mali Yekaterinopol, encountering a Soviet antitank gun barrier near Yurovka that had been swiftly put into position. Here, the Germans halted in mid-afternoon, stopped as much by a shortage of fuel as by enemy resistance.

As if battling the Soviets, the terrain, and shortage of supplies was not enough to occupy his attention, Vormann had to deal with the meddling of *8.Armee's* chief of staff, who kept constantly radioing *XXXXVII.Pz.Korps* demanding to know the exact location of his divisions and their activities. To alleviate the fuel situation, Vormann told his own staff to inform *8.Armee* that the corps needed air delivery of gasoline urgently. In response, he was told that he needed to move his command post to the far left flank of his corps and to prepare to continue the attack and seize Hill 204.5, five kilometers southeast of Zvenigorodka, the next morning. Fuel would be airdropped during the night to enable the tanks to keep going.

Later that day, elements of *13.Pz.Div.*, which had conducted a grueling night march after pulling out of Iskrenoye, joined in the attack. Making steady progress against the troops of the Soviet 49th Rifle Corps, Vormann had his two attacking panzer divisions execute a right turn, which led them north along the eastern bank of the Gniloy Tashlyk. Everything that *8.Armee* had left was sent in that direction to reinforce this unexpected success, even to the point where other sectors of the Army's front were dangerously denuded of troops.

At the time, this seemed an acceptable risk, since it appeared as if the Soviets were doing the same. To hold this ground so the two panzer divisions could take advantage of the little amount of momentum they possessed, Wöhler decided to give control of *K.Gr.Haack* to Vormann, who then attached it to *11.Pz.Div.*, where it protected that division's exposed western flank along the Gniloy Tashlyk.[10]

When Wöhler was told that Vormann would move forward the following day and lead his corps from the inside of an armored half-track on account of the poor road conditions, he issued his subordinate a stern rebuke, stating that muddy roads or not, he, as the corps' commanding general, had to find himself a suitable command post. Evidently, the *8.Armee* commander felt that his corps commander could best control the movement of his troops from a stationary command post. Wöhler's frustration with Vormann would subsequently increase during the next several days.

The attack pressed on the following morning, aided by a light frost that evening which made the ground more passable for the German tanks. During the night, the *Luftwaffe* dropped enough fuel and ammunition by air to keep the two attacking panzer divisions reasonably well supplied. However, the defenders reacted first. A dawn attack by Soviet tanks of 20th Guards Tank Corps against the bridgehead at Yerki was driven off after the defenders of *K.Gr.Haack* knocked out 13 T-34s. More would soon follow. With their western flank securely in hand, both panzer divisions pressed on towards Zvenigorodka. By the evening of 12 February, both *11.Pz.Div.* on the left and *13.Pz.Div.* on the right had occupied the towns of Skalevatka and Yurkovka, and knocked out 18 Soviet tanks in the process

K.Gr.Haack, with *Urlauberregimet Baake* in the lead, seized another bridge over the Gniloy Tashlyk and was ordered by Vormann, accompanying *13.Pz.Div.* in his *SPW*, to build a bridgehead to be used as a springboard for an attack to tie the two fronts of *8.* and *1.Pz.Armee* together. The attack towards the north pressed onwards. Supported by an effective *Stuka* attack launched by Hans-Ulrich Rudel's famous *2.Sturzkampfgeschwader* (Dive Bomber Wing) *"Immelmann,"* a welcome sight for an army that had seen very little evidence of

the *Luftwaffe* up to that point, the tanks and *Panzergrenadiers* seized the heights overlooking Zvenigorodka from the south and the commanding point of Hill 204.8 by 1600 hours.[11] During one such mission in support of *XXXXVII.Pz.Korps'* attack, Rudel and his wingman encountered a swarm of Soviet ground attack aircraft and managed to down one *Sturmovik* with a burst from his underwing-mounted 3.7 cm antitank cannon, quite a feat of marksmanship for the ungainly, slow-moving dive bomber.

Slowly, the Germans pressed forward. Zvenigorodka, which had fallen into Soviet hands 28 January, lay a mere five kilometers away. Some German tanks had even approached within two miles of the city before they were forced to turn back by a Soviet counterthrust. To keep his two attacking divisions supplied, Vormann requested that the armored train operated by *1.Pz.Armee* be sent in his direction from its base in Talnoye, thirty kilometers away, since the route had been cleared almost all the way up to Yerki. *K.Gr.Haack* was ordered to send a battalion in that direction to ensure that the rail line was free of the enemy, but was forced to turn back when its men encountered strong Soviet artillery fire on their exposed positions along the rail line, so the train never made it all the way. Wöhler was even sending *2.Fallsch.Jgr.Div.* from its assembly area near Kirovograd as reinforcements. These successes lead Vormann at the time to believe that perhaps things were, for once, turning in his favor.[12] But it was to be the last offensive success of *XXXXVII.Pz.Korps.*

The expected Soviet reaction was not long in coming. That evening, German ground and aerial reconnaissance had determined that four infantry divisions of 4th Guards Army were moving in Vormann's direction, as well as the bulk of 20th Guards Tank Corps and another unidentified tank corps from 5th Guards Tank Army. Besides having to contend with overcoming prepared Soviet defensive positions, *11.* and *13.Pz.Div.* now had to deal with a series of ferocious counterattacks. The Soviet reaction here had been far swifter than anticipated, despite the fact that Zhukov, Konev and Vatutin were having to counter three separate German attacks - two from the outside (both *XXXXVII.* and *III.Pz.Korps*) and one from the inside.

General Konev seems to have prepared his defenses in the Zvenigorodka area much more thoroughly than Vatutin. As a result, Vormann's attack got no further than the heights south of Zvenigorodka and the towns of Skalevatka and Yurkovka. From 12 to 15 February, elements of 20th Tank Corps and 49th Rifle Corps hurled themselves at the Germans, whose attack had ground to a halt. Soviet artillery fire also noticeably intensified. Although *11.* and *13.Pz.Div.*, as well as *K.Gr.Haack* had knocked out 58 enemy tanks by 15 February, it was still not enough to break the Soviet defense.

Another Soviet unit that was directed to stand in Vormann's path was 18th Tank Battalion of the 29th Tank Brigade, detached from 18th Tank Corps. One of the battalion's company commanders, Captain Mikhail Yakolevich Hadai, who had fought in the Battle of Kursk, recalled later that this type of armored warfare had nothing in common with what he had experienced the past summer, when literally hundreds of tanks had been involved in engagements that covered an area encompassing a few square kilometers. Here, the nature of the terrain dictated that the fighting would be individual tank against tank, or against a group of several tanks, but nothing so grand as what happened at Kursk. In his words, "We respected the German tankmen. They were tough fighters, but we trusted our own tanks and we believed that we could stop them. We made sure that their advance would go no further. And we were fighting to liberate our Motherland."[13]

The Soviet tank crews endured the same privations as their German counterparts did. At night, Hadai would order his tanks to move to defensive positions in the nearest forest or wood, where they would form a circular position. Then, he would have them dig a hole to sleep in and park their tank over it for protection against artillery. "Fires to warm ourselves with were forbidden, for the German tankmen fought very well at night," he stated. To keep warm, the Soviet tank crews would huddle together in their crude shelter using every blanket they possessed, while one crewman stood watch outside. It was not very comfortable, but it increased one's chances of staying alive. Against such determined men as Mikhail Hadai, Vormann and his troops had little chance of advancing any further.

Nevertheless, Vormann was ordered in no uncertain terms again and again by Wöhler to keep driving north. Wöhler again found time to scold his subordinate in regards to where he should place his forward command post. Wöhler thought that his corps commander should be where the main effort was being directed, not on the western flank, where *K.Gr. Haack* and parts of *11.Pz.Div.* were busy repelling numerous assaults. If the attack towards the north was to have any chances of success, Wöhler notified him by radio, then Vormann would have to be at the spearhead, leading by example. This last message must have puzzled the commander of *XXXXVII.Pz.Korps*, since he had just been criticized for being too close to the front only two days before.

To be fair, Wöhler himself was feeling the heat from Field Marshal Manstein, whose staff kept stressing the absolute importance of pressing ahead. The only noteworthy combat that *8.Armee* was engaged in was in the sector of *XXXXVII.Pz.Korps*, so it was natural for Wöhler to direct his attention to the hills south of Zvenigorodka. In addition to the enemy and meddling from his higher command, Vormann had an even more serious problem - keeping his troops resupplied with fuel, ammunition, and food.

While the temperature during the night continued to fall below freezing, during the day, the combination of snow, rain, and warm temperatures made the roads in the corps' sector even worse. The mud had become so bad that even the giant 18-ton half-tracked prime movers could not make it through. The tanks were affected as well. Vormann noted that a Panther used up its entire load of fuel after going a mere 18 kilometers, so deep and thick was the mud.[14]

On 14 February, *11.Pz.Div.*, including the remnants of the attached Panther battalion from *Grossdeutschland*, had only three tanks in operational condition: an additional 55 lay broken down or stuck in the mud along the route from Kapitanovka to hill 204.8.[15] Since there were no airfields, fuel

and ammunition had to be dropped by air. Due to a shortage of aerial delivery canisters and parachutes, barrels of fuel or crates of ammunition were often dropped out of the open cargo hatch of JU-52s at altitudes of less than ten meters, many of which burst on impact. In these conditions, only the infantry could make any headway, but without tanks, they had no hope of dislodging the Soviet troops defending the industrial area northwest of Yurkovka, a key objective that had to be taken if the Germans were to drive on Zvenigorodka.

Troops were also going hungry and had neither bread nor the butter to spread on it. Uniforms were becoming torn and ragged and both infantrymen and tank crews were covered with lice. Morale was being affected as well, for no one could maintain a positive attitude in such conditions. Vormann himself was deeply affected. Later, he wrote:

> This was the last success of 8.Armee in this battle. Its strength was finally spent. In the mud and frost, drizzling rain and snow storms, the troops had performed superhuman feats during the past few days despite insufficient rations - now it had come to an end. Only with tanks, that is, with machines, was it possible to carry out any kind of offensive action in this muddy ground. More was demanded of them than [the tanks] were capable of doing, and they simply broke down without warning, as opposed to men and horses, who gradually reached the limits of their endurance before collapsing.[16]

The disappointment that Vormann felt was also being experienced by the staff of the *OKH*, which had been following events closely. On 12 February, *Oberst Graf* Kielmannsegg wrote in his diary, "The attack 'Heimkehr' [has come] to a standstill." Two days later he wrote, "The nervous strain becomes agonizing if one becomes aware of it. A distance of only eight kilometers separates Gruppe Stemmermann from liberation and today it looks as if they would not make it. There is not much time left."[17]

By 15 February, both Army Group South's and *8.Armee's* headquarters had finally realized that Vormann's attack was not going anywhere. Consequently, Wöhler notified him that he was to hold his ground and tie up as much of the enemy as possible, thereby drawing away as many of the enemy from *III.Pz.Korps.*[18] All Nikolaus Vormann could do now was watch from afar as the truly decisive action unfolded some 25 kilometers to the northwest.

Like *XXXXVII.Pz.Korps'*, the attack of Breith's corps that Friday went well at first. The night before, the temperature dropped below freezing and a light snow fell, helping to harden the ground and conceal German preparations. A 15-minute barrage by corps artillery and *Nebelwerfers* from *II./Schw.Werfer-Rgt.1* hit the Soviet front line positions, followed by a *Stuka* attack against key positions.[19] With *Gren.Rgt.308* in the lead, Horn's *198.Inf.Div.* attacked first and took the important town of Shubeny Stav, *Gren.Rgt.326*, with tank support, took the town of Kutchkovka. The divisional history describes the attack as follows:

> For all of us, who had been fighting a "poor man's war"
> up to this point, the tanks were a guarantor of success.
> Now we would do it, now we would be able to free our
> encircled comrades! There was a break in the weather,
> the ground froze a little during the early morning, so that
> tanks and grenadiers could advance easily. Then our
> attacking companies ran up against the defensive fire of
> the enemy. Stalin organs [explosions] burst between the
> attackers; machine-guns, including our new MG-42, rat-
> tled away. But our tanks stopped abruptly and shot up the
> nests of enemy resistance. The enemy on the right and in
> the middle of our attacking columns were overrun. Our
> grenadiers were surprised to see how the Russians, like
> busy bees, had dug in and developed such strong posi-
> tions in such a short period of time. But they could not
> stand up against our artillery fire and the point-blank fire
> of our Panzers.[20]

The seizure of both of these towns by *198.Inf.Div.* enabled
both *16.* and *17.Pz.Div.* to push through the Soviet defensive
positions without having to worry about their flanks.
Achieving complete tactical surprise, they broke through at
0700 hours on a wide front between Chizhovka and Tolstyye
Rogi, crossed the elevated railway embankment, and headed
east. The defenders from 47th Rifle Corps' 359th Rifle
Division were quickly overrun.

By late morning, the spearhead of *16.Pz.Div.,* consisting
of the Tigers and Panthers of *Schw.Pz.Rgt. Bäke* had overcome
three successive Soviet defensive belts and had raced ahead 15
kilometers to the outskirts of Bushanka, seizing a bridge on the
town's western outskirts near the hamlet of Frankovka that
spanned the Gniloy Tikich. This bridge fell into the hands of Dr.
Bäke's panzer troops before it could be blown up, though a companion bridge in Bushanka itself was destroyed just as the
Germans were approaching. When notified of this success, Hube
awarded the tank crew that had first reached the bridge eight
days of "Special Leave" to recognize their achievement.[21] Even
with the loss of the bridge in Bushanka, the Germans were still
able to get across the flooded creek and establish a hasty bridgehead. Fleeing remnants of 359th Rifle Division "came under the
barrels" of *Schw.Pz.Rgt. Bäke* as they tried to pass through the
outskirts of Bushanka and were shot to pieces.

To the north, *17.Pz.Div.* was able, in conjunction with a
Kampfgruppe from *Gren.Rgt.305* of *198.Inf.Div.*, to seize the
towns of Stepok and Tolstyye Rogi. By 1700 hours, *17.Pz.Div.*
was able to reach and seize the town of Bessovka and defended
it that night against a number of tank-supported Soviet counterattacks. *K.Gr.Blömecke* from *16.Pz.Div.*, consisting of
I./Pz.Gren.Rgt.64, followed in the attack's wake, mopping up
bypassed pockets of Soviet resistance in Shubanny Stav and
Vishnevka. While clearing the town of Vishnevka, *Uffz.* Freitag
of *3.Kompanie* knocked out a T-34 with a hand grenade bundle.
The seizure of these towns would enable the Germans to protect

Generalmajor Richard Koll, *Commander, 1.Pz.Div.*
(Photo courtesy of Rolf Stoves)

their ever-lengthening supply routes.[22] This was critical, for
without a continual flow of fuel, ammunition, and food, the
spearheads of *III.Pz.Korps* would quickly come to a halt. To
keep the tanks and half-tracks running, the supply services had
to work 24 hours a day.

The portion of *Leibstandarte*, holding the northern, or left
flank of the corps (the bulk of the division had yet to arrive),
ordered *K.Gr.Kuhlmann* to conduct a counterattack northwest of
Votylevka, where it smashed a battalion-sized Soviet unit that
had penetrated the division's defensive positions. *K.Gr.
Weidenhaupt*, holding the town of Tatyanovka, was thrown out
and forced to withdraw 800 meters to the southwest where it
faced, throughout the day, waves of regimental-sized Soviet
attacks launched by 58th Rifle Division supported by armor
from 3rd Tank Corps.[23] No further counterattacks were
attempted; Weidenhaupt's unit was too weak to launch an attack
against such a strong enemy force.

Not only were the SS affected by the heavy losses they
had suffered, they also suffered, like everyone else, from
extreme fatigue, a combination of little sleep, poor rations,
physical exertion, and the stress of prolonged combat. One
member of the *Leibstandarte* left us an account of how it
affected his own performance. *SS-Rttf.* Fritz Gottzman, an
artillery forward observer from *II./SS-Pz.Art.Rgt.1*, had
accompanied *Kampfgruppe* Weidenhaupt in its march
northwest of Vinograd. Before night fell on 13 February, he
had helped dig a foxhole for himself and several infantrymen
that measured 1.5 meters wide by 1.2 meters deep. Before
moving in, he telephoned back the artillery registration
coordinates for the night and ordered preparatory fires along
the likely enemy avenues of approach in his assigned sector.

Once this had been done, he and the others crawled into their holes and prepared to spend another night in the open.

Soon, he and the others were shivering, despite the fur-lined parkas they had been issued. For this particular evening, however, Gottzman had brought along a small acetylene torch he had taken from one of his regiment's half-tracks. Covering his foxhole with his shelter quarter, he adjusted the flame to its lowest setting and soon began to feel it growing warmer. As he became comfortable for the first time in several days, he quickly nodded off. While he slept soundly, the Soviets launched a night attack against the German positions. The infantry company that Gottzman was supposed to be supporting immediately shot off the pre-arranged red flare to signal the artillery to commence firing. The German artillery, combined with small arms fire, soon drove the enemy off. Gottzman slept through the whole thing and did not wake up until the next morning. According to Gottzman, "But then, battle noise, even at night, was hardly uncommon. The battery commander heard about it pretty quickly and offered me his 'praise' with the words, "I wish I had your nerves.""[24]

Though outnumbered, *Leibstandarte* hung grimly on, denying the enemy the breakthrough he needed in order to cut off *III.Pz.Korps*. To the left of *Leibstandarte*, *34.Inf.Div.* of *VII.A.K.* held on against repeated attacks that day against Tinovka. At one point, a Soviet push, supported by 18 T-34s, threatened to overrun the defenders, but this, too, was warded off by a last-minute counterattack.[25] Breith could continue on without having to worry about his northern flank.

The biggest surprise that day was not the rapid advance of *16.* and *17.Pz.Div.*, but the startling success of Koll's *1.Pz.Div.* This division, which had only been able to mass most of its regiments and battalions the day before, led off with a *Kampfgruppe* consisting of the division's panzer regiment commanded by *Oberstlt.* Frank. This powerful battlegroup has been especially reinforced for this mission and consisted of *I./Pz.Rgt. 1* (Panthers) under the command of *Hptm. Graf* Wedel., *II./Pz.Gren.Rgt.113*, under the command of *Hptm.* Ebeling, and *II./Art.Rgt.73*, under the command of *Hptm.* Kublitz, as well as supporting *Flak*, infantry gun, and antitank platoons.[26] Quickly penetrating Soviet defenses, the infantry-laden tanks of *K.Gr. Frank*, with *Oblt.* Seeman's *1.Kompanie* in the lead, found the route towards Bushanka wide open, except for an antitank belt laid along the road junction east of the town of Chizhovka.

Initially assigned the limited task of protecting the corps' right flank, the division surged ahead, taking the town of Chizhovka by 1000 hours, before moving on. Momentarily stopped near the village of Yablonovka by a counterattack launched by the Soviet 5th Mechanized Corps, *K.Gr. Frank* quickly knocked out five T-34s and pressed forward. West of Bushanka, a Soviet infantry battalion tried to make a stand, but was shelled "with vigor" by *Hptm.* Kublitz's artillery. Ebeling sent his *Panzergrenadiers* in to attack the Soviet position, but the Soviets already had the fight knocked out of them. Several hundred surrendered; these were quickly disarmed and later led off to Bushanka, where they were placed in a church under guard. By 1230 hours, *K.Gr. Frank* had seized the southern portion of Bushanka and quickly established contact on the left

with *Schw.Pz.Rgt. Bäke*, which had taken the western part of the town two hours earlier. *Hptm.* Ebeling ordered his men across the Gniloy Tikich, where they quickly established a small bridgehead.

Bringing up the rear was *II./Pz.Rgt.1*, commanded by *Hptm.* Düntsch with 20 Pz. IVs. His mission was not to engage in the attack, but to serve as an armed escort for the *Kampfgruppe's* 18-ton prime movers and supply trucks, which would allow Frank to keep moving should his supply routes be severed. Long experience had taught him that the Pz. IV was no longer a match for the improved versions of the T-34, but was still useful as a defensive weapon; therefore, he had previously decided that the Panther-equipped tank battalion would lead the attack.[27]

Local Soviet reaction to this unexpected German success was slow. General Kravchenko, commander of 6th Tank Army which had the responsibility for defending the approaches to the pocket from the southwest, ordered 5th Guards Tank Corps and 5th Mechanized Corps that afternoon to counterattack and wipe out the German bridgehead over the Gniloy Tikich and bar the route to the pocket.

This attack was carried out, but without success. Attacking from the southeast, 5th Mechanized Corps lost 21 tanks to *K.Gr. Frank* in less than an hour. An attack from the north by 5th Guards Tank Corps against the bridgehead held by *Schw.Pz.Rgt. Bäke* was equally unsuccessful, losing 12 tanks to Bäke's Tigers and Panthers. In the defense, the Tiger was virtually impregnable, while the incredibly accurate long-barreled 7.5 cm cannon of the Panthers easily penetrated the T-34's armor at ranges over 1,000 meters.

Despite the success of *III.Pz.Korps'* attack that day, Wenck was concerned. It had been a busy day for him. To check on the actual conditions at the front, he commandeered a *Ketterkrad* and drove from army headquarters in Uman to Breith's headquarters in Buki to speak to the corps commander. Intercepted Soviet radio messages clearly spelled out the Soviet's concern about the German advance and indicated that reinforcements were being rushed towards the area where a breakthrough towards Lysyanka was feared. A Guards Rifle Division, the 62nd, was on the move, as well as 22nd Tank Brigade from 5th Guards Tank Corps.

Aerial reconnaissance had spotted some 250 Soviet vehicles moving towards the southwest from the area between Tarashcha and Zvenigorodka, the area encompassed by Rotmistrov's 5th Guards Tank Army. To stay ahead of the enemy's moves, Breith would have to quicken the rate of his advance, lest the enemy reinforcements arrive in time to block his path. Wenck stated that evening in the Army's daily journal that "In order to take advantage of our initial success, [Breith's] Corps must ruthlessly and rapidly press his advance towards the east." To ensure that Breith got the point, this demand was expressed in an order that evening. Wenck stated further that:

> We must be prepared to do everything it takes to keep our momentum going. The fighting and the unimaginable terrain difficulties (at the cost of at least three times the normal rate of fuel consumption) will compel us to halt

for resupply. [However], the organization of supplies on the battlefield at the present time is being carried out using expedient methods.[28]

To maintain the rate of advance, Hube ordered that the attack be continued that evening, taking advantage of the hardening ground and the Soviet's lack of experience in night fighting. Since the best route towards Lysyanka at this time seemed to be along the southern bank of the Gniloy Tikich, Hube ordered that *K.Gr. Frank* of *1.Pz.Div.* make the main effort that evening and the following day. Hopefully, Frank would be able to drive all the way to Lysyanka that night and block the Soviet main supply route that ran from Zvenigorodka to Medvin, cutting off any attempt by Rotmistrov's army to reach the battlefield on 12 February.

As ordered, Breith's divisions continued the attack throughout the evening of 11/12 February, the same time that the assault units from *Gruppe Stemmermann* were seizing Shanderovka and Novo Buda within the pocket. On the left, *K.Gr. Finck of 17.Pz.Div.* fortified the defense of Bosovka in the north and defended it throughout the day against a series of tank attacks launched by elements of 5th Guards Tank Corps. The rest of the division was engaged in clearing the northern part of Frankovka and improving the bridge over the Gniloy Tikich. In the center, *16.Pz.Div.'s* reconnaissance battalion, *Pz.Aufkl.Abt.16,* pressed forward five kilometers towards the village of Dashukovka, where it was brought to a halt in the face of a well-emplaced line of Soviet antitank and assault guns of 259th Rifle Division.

After losing several vehicles, the divisional commander, General Back, ordered a halt until the rest of the division could catch up with him. This did not occur that day, due to a number of events over which Back had no control. For example, on account of the fuel shortage, *Oberstlt.* Dr. Bäke's Tigers had to remain in the Frankovka bridgehead until fuel could be air-dropped. The situation in the division's rear area that evening became serious when several bypassed Soviet units attacked supply convoys, forcing the division to divert combat units towards their elimination. Equally serious was a Soviet attack against the *Kampfgruppe* from *Leibstandarte* that was holding Repki, to the rear of *16.Pz.Div.*

At 1630 hours, a sizable Soviet attack launched by 58th Rifle Division forced *Leibstandarte's* weakened reconnaissance battalion out of the village, compelling it to fall back several kilometers to the east, where it finally came to a halt at the sector held by *SS-Pz.Gren.Rgt.2* east of Votylevka, which soon came under attack as well. Though the Soviet force attacked Votylevka all day with infantry, artillery, and tanks, all of the attacks were repulsed by *II./SS-Pz.Gren.Rgt.2,* led by *Ostuf.* Wald, who had assumed command only the day before. Vinograd, now held by a regiment from *198.Inf.Div.,* also came under attack by 3rd Guards Airborne Division.

Just as the northern edge of the village appeared ready to fall, *Leibstandarte's* sole reserve, a force consisting of only one Panther and 12 infantrymen, counterattacked. Caught unexpect-

edly in the flank, the Soviet airborne unit were thrown back by this tiny force, which then took up position in the woods that covered the northern edge of the town.[29] They were not, however, able to affect fighting in the town's eastern edge, which fell to the airborne troops that afternoon. The town's defender's, from *Gren.Rgt.305* of *198.Inf.Div.,* were being "bled white" as a result of their unsuccessful attempts to retake lost ground. Until another reinforcing regiment from General Horn's division could arrive, *17.Pz.Div.* had to divert part of its forces in an attempt to throw the enemy back. Despite this infusion of forces, the eastern edge of Vinograd remained in Soviet hands.

Later that evening, the bulk of *Gren.Rgt.326* arrived on foot, after marching all day from Yablonovka, which it had taken from the enemy the night before. Exhausted, the men had been marching non-stop for six hours and were given only half an hour in which to prepare for their counterattack. In the words of the division historian:

> The men of Gren.Rgt.326 were still totally exhausted from the previous evening's fighting. For weeks, the men had lived without a roof over their heads; always marching, fighting, marching! The route [to Vinograd] was in an unimaginably bad condition. The land had been totally plowed up by tanks. And now [the men] were not even to receive a rest.[30]

The attack began at 2330 hours, with the new moon providing scant illumination as the Germans approached. It had rained all day, forcing the exhausted Germans to advance through the ankle-deep mud. Slowly, the attack pushed forward as the Germans were forced to fight for every house. As the regiment reached the stream that cut the town in two, it seemed as if the attack had lost its momentum. The regimental commander was surprised when reinforcements arrived in the form of five assault guns that had been sent by *III.Pz.Korps.*

Heartened, the men renewed their attack. The engineer platoon under *Fw.* Straub climbed aboard the assault guns and roared off towards the northern part of Vinograd, which had just again fallen to the Soviets. Pushing through the Soviet positions, they then turned right. After completing a wide arc around the village, the assault guns attacked the enemy from the rear. Surprised, the Soviet fire against the main body of the regiment slackened, allowing it to press its attack home.

Caught between two German pincers, the remaining airborne troops died where they were, surrendered, or fled. By 1000 hours on 13 February, Vinograd was back in German hands and the northern flank of Breith's corps was secure. The combined forces of *Gren.Rgt.305* and *326* counted 200 enemy dead, three knocked-out tanks, and 20 captured cannon and antitank guns. Both regiments were now in an extremely weakened state, but their accomplishment had been significant enough to warrant mention in the 15 February *Wehrmachtsbericht.*[31]

Again, *1.Pz.Div.* was more successful that day. Frank and his troops, after a brief pause in Bushanka to replenish supplies of fuel and ammunition from the supplies that *Hptm.* Duentsch had brought up, set off for Lysyanka shortly after dark. The decision to provide a heavy escort for the supply convoy had been a sound one, for one group under *Oblt.* Mischke had several encounters that night with cut-off Soviet units along the road from Chizovka to Bushanka, causing them to engage and destroy them at close range with machine-gun and tank cannon fire.

Fortunately, the nights had grown colder, causing the ground to harden. With *Oberstlt.* Frank leading the attack in his Panther, his *Kampfgruppe* advanced eastward in darkness shortly after midnight. Frank intended to capture the bridge on the eastern edge of Lysyanka before it got light, and speed and surprise was the best way to accomplish this. With their left flank protected by the unfordable Gniloy Tikich, Frank and his men surged ahead, unimpeded by the Soviet defenders, reaching the main road leading to the southwestern outskirts of Lysyanka by 0300 hours, 12 February.

Several hundred meters from the outskirts of the long, spread-out town, which had been in Soviet hands since 27 January, Frank ordered a halt to enable his tanks and infantry to close up. Knowing that it would be suicide to attempt to conduct an uncoordinated night attack with tanks against a defended locality the size of Lysyanka, he quickly shuffled his tank and infantry companies around in order to make the most of their capabilities. With a tank company on each side of the road and a third one behind the other two, *K.Gr. Frank* set off towards the enemy. When the regiment's *1.Kompanie* got within 25-30 meters from the first house, it encountered a well-laid out anti-tank defense line consisting of some 20-25 T-34s with a 7.62 cm antitank gun emplaced between each tank.

Incredibly, the German attack caught the Soviet defenders, most likely from 20th Tank Corps of 5th Guards Tank Army, completely by surprise. Only one or two antitank guns at the most got off a shot at the onrushing Panthers before being over-run. Over a dozen T-34s were knocked out in rapid succession at point-blank range before the others backed away into the darkness. With the most experienced tank commanders, including *Oberstlt.* Frank, in the lead, the Germans stormed into the town's southern outskirts. Antitank mines immobilized several Panthers from *2.Kompanie*, but the attack rolled irresistibly onward into the heart of the town. *Panzergrenadiere* dismounted the Panthers and engaged in bloody house-to-house fighting. The sound of battle reached an indescribably crescendo; the light from burning houses, flare pistols, and parachute flares showed the following echelon of tanks from Frank's battlegroup the way towards the town.

After a few moments, the German attack began to lose momentum when the spearhead ran upon yet another barrier of antitank mines near the town's center. *Oberstlt.* Frank, deeply concerned about the status of the Gniloy Tikich crossing, called *Oblt.* Ciliox, commander of *1.Kompanie*, on the radio. His order was succinct: "Ciliox - quickly, get to the bridge!" As morning dawned, Ciliox's remaining tanks with a few infantrymen aboard moved down the main street of the village, heedless of the Soviet defenders on their flanks, who tried to block their path. One of Ciliox's platoon leaders, *Ltn.* Mankel, was felled by a shot to the head by a concealed antitank rifle, but the Panthers kept going.

In Ciliox's wake followed the rest of the *Kampfgruppe*. Still feeling the shock of the unexpected German tank attack, the defenders were unable to mount a coherent defense, although they vastly outnumbered their attackers. Just when Ciliox had approached the bridge, it literally blew up in his face. Debris rained down upon the tank, forcing Ciliox to duck inside. Unfortunately, he had arrived one minute too late - all that was left of the bridge was a few burning timbers.[32]

Nevertheless, the southern part of Lysyanka was in German hands. The bridge could be rebuilt, if the heavy bridging company could make its way forwards. In the meantime, *K.Gr. Frank* spent the rest of the day consolidating what they had seized the night before. Batteries from *Pz.Art.Rgt.73* moved forward and established firing positions within the town. *Hptm.* Ebeling and his *Panzergrenadiere* drew the unenviable tasks of combing the southern part of the town for bypassed Soviet troops and wiping them out. The tanks, for the most part, were quickly positioned along the eastern and southeastern edges of the town in order to defend against the inevitable Soviet counterattacks.

Now that south Lysyanka was in German hands, Frank quickly returned in his tank that morning to Bushanka to confer with Koll in order to sort out the supply situation. Most of his

Oberfeldwebel Hans Strippel, *Pz.Rgt.1, 1.Pz.Div. He led his division in the number of Soviet tanks destroyed during the fighting in the Lysyanka bridgehead.*
(Bundesarchiv)

tanks were low on fuel and ammunition and he required immediate replenishment. After a brief meeting, Frank turned around and headed back to Lysyanka with *Ltn.* Wall's *4.Kompanie* and a supply column in tow. When the tank-escorted supply column was less than 300 meters from the town's outskirts, it was taken under fire by Soviet antitank guns which had crept forward under cover of a sudden snowstorm.

A glancing blow on Frank's Panther killed or wounded several of the *Panzergrenadiere* perched atop the tank and knocked them to the ground. *Oberfeldwebel* Hans Strippel, one of the division's most experienced tank commanders, recognized the danger immediately and moved out in his tank to a concealed location on the edge of the town. There, covered by *Ltn.* Wall's tank, Strippel dismounted from his tank and worked his way slowly forward in order to locate the antitank guns' position. Spotting their location, he raced back to his tank and had his driver move forward out of defilade, where he methodically engaged and destroyed four 7.62 cm antitank guns. With the way ahead now clear, Wall and the supply column were able to enter Lysyanka without further loss.

Now that he had enough tanks, Frank ordered a 360-degree defense of south Lysyanka, while he figured out a way to cross the Gniloy Tikich and take the northern part of the town. However, the fuel and ammunition that Wall had brought with him were not enough to resupply the battalion; fuel was still in short supply and the special ammunition for the Panther's 7.5 cm cannon was critically short. Despite this, in less than thirty-six hours, *1.Pz.Div.* had advanced thirty kilometers and had knocked out over forty T-34s. When notified of Breith's success that day, Wöhler radioed Stemmermann, stating that "Breith has taken Lysyanka. Vormann is advancing from the bridgehead at Yerki towards Zvenigorodka…Best wishes for your success."[33]

Despite this, the atmosphere that evening at *1.Pz.Armee's* headquarters in Uman was anything but positive. In a gloomy evaluation of the day's events that he wrote that night in the army's daily combat journal, Wenck worried openly about the crisis that loomed in the days ahead. Both the weather and the road conditions seemed to be conspiring against the Germans, hampering the army's and *III.Pz.Korps'* ability to keep the five divisions of Breith's corps supplied with the necessary fuel and ammunition to maintain the relief attack's momentum. Just as the mud had adversely affected *XXXXVII.Pz.Korps*, so was it hampering "Relief Group West." Wenck wrote that:

> The continuation of the attack today was greatly hindered by renewed difficulties with weather and terrain, which has led to a crisis in the resupply situation. We have lost the momentum that our surprise attack afforded us . . . on our side, our weak assault spearheads have been so hindered by the power of nature and the enemy, that, as of today, a continued advance cannot be reckoned on. The Army, the corps, and the divisions have done everything in their power to master these difficulties . . . [34]

Wenck was also keenly aware of the situation faced by the troops inside the pocket, and that their survival depended upon *III.Pz.Korps* linking up with them as soon as possible.

Each division did what it could that day and the next to get supplies to their forward units. Koll's *1.Pz.Div.,* stymied by its inability to get enough of its supply trucks forward, hit on the solution of loading barrels of fuel and crates of ammunition atop the hulls and turrets of the Pz.IVs of *II.Abteilung.* While this somewhat increased their vulnerability, it provided an effective means of getting the needed supplies safely forward, where *Oberstlt.* Frank's Panther battalion was warding off Soviet armored counterattacks in and around Lysyanka.

The supply officer of *Leibstandarte*, *Ostubaf.* Günter Stoltz, hit upon an even more ingenious idea. At first, he had commandeered 150 *panje* wagons from the local population to carry supplies from the railhead at Uman to the division's forward supply base. Each *panje* was loaded with a barrel of fuel and ammunition. Even that was not enough; in its weakened condition, the division still required several trainloads a day of food, fuel, water, medical supplies, ammunition, and spare parts to function properly.

Casting about for a solution to *Leibstandarte's* supply problem, Stoltz found a large number of narrow-gauge railroad tracks the previous day, lying unused in a local brickyard. Taking advantage of a disused railway bed that ran through his division's sector up to the front line, Stoltz press-ganged a number of local inhabitants into quickly laying the tracks as far forward as the supply allowed. Soon, Stoltz had coal hoppers, each pulled by a team of confiscated horses, carrying supplies to the beleaguered troops of the battle groups led by Weidenhaupt and Kuhlmann.

Despite this feat, Stoltz felt that his division was not being provided the proper amount of supplies it needed. He seemed to believe that since his division had been assigned the task of "only" protecting the flank of the battle group, it had drawn a lesser priority in the allocation of needed supplies.[35] This can no longer be proven; no doubt, every division in Breith's corps probably felt that it was not receiving its fair share of fuel and ammunition. To make matters worse, a supply drop planned for that night was called off due to high winds that blew the first parachuted canisters far off course.

Just as Wenck had predicted, the Soviets were rapidly taking forces away from other locations and assembling them preparatory to launching a massive counterblow. Stalin's anger had engendered a sense of urgency in both Marshal Zhukov and General Konev. Both men knew that Stalin would not tolerate failure a second time, especially when the goal of annihilating the encircled enemy grouping appeared so close. For his perceived failure to block *III.Pz.Korps'* attack on 11/12 February and the breakout of *XXXXII.A.K.* towards Lysyanka, Vatutin had been sent back west to Proskurov in disgrace. Neither Zhukov nor Konev wanted that to happen to them, not when both had struggled so hard to get to their current positions of power and prestige.

For example, the commander of 47th Rifle Corps, which had been surprised and overwhelmed by the German tank attack that day, was strongly criticized for his corps' performance. One

Oberstleutnant Dr. Franz Bäke, *(third from right) holding a lighthearted conversation with some of his commanders.* *(Bundesarchiv 706/399/20A)*

Soviet source latter stated that the commander, General Shmygo, had poorly positioned his units to stop any German attack, despite the fact that he had nearly two weeks to prepare for it. According to Viktor Matsulenko, Shmygo's positions "had no depth, the combat formations were extended into a line, and there were no prepared trenches towards the rear," a outright violation of Red Army tactical doctrine.

As a result, *III.Pz.Korps* was able to punch through the Soviet defensive line held by 47th Rifle Corps with relative ease, although bypassed units of Shmygo's corps continued to harass the Germans for days afterwards, forcing them to divert combat forces to about turn and deal with these threats to their supply lines.[36] Fortunately for the Soviets, they were quick to recover from this initial setback and would forge a powerful response to the German thrust with astonishing speed. As previously related, to coordinate the battle against Breith, Stalin had entrusted to Zhukov all of the armies that lay in the Germans' path. Konev, for his part, was given command of all the armies that were assigned the task of ensuring the *unichtozhenye* of the Germans in the pocket.

1.Pz.Armee got an indication that night of what was in store the following day, when it intercepted Soviet radio messages that indicated that 57th Mechanized Brigade of 5th Mechanized Corps was now en route, as well as another unidentified tank brigade. Yet another tank brigade was spotted five kilometers north of Lysyanka, heading south towards *K.Gr. Frank.* That meant that the following morning, at the earliest, Breith's troops would be faced by no less than two tanks armies (2nd and 6th, plus parts of 5th Guards Tank) and one infantry army (40th) composed of no less than six tank or mechanized corps as well as two rifle corps. None of these units were at full strength, but they still represented an enormous amount of com-

bat power once one calculated the additional artillery regiments, *Katyusha* batteries, and antitank brigades that accompanied each army. Wenck knew that there would be tough fighting that Sunday, but nevertheless, the attack would continue .

Accordingly, Wenck drew up orders that night for the following days' operations. The next morning, 13 February, both *16.* and *17.Pz.Div.* would continue their attack towards Dashukovka, with the goal of pressing forwards and seizing the town of Khizhintsy. There, *16.Pz.Div.* would be able to reach Khilki, only ten kilometers away from *K.Abt.B.* At the same time, *17.Pz.Div.* would take up positions along the northern flank of the attacking armored wedge and block any attack by the Soviets from the direction of Medvin. In Lysyanka, *1.Pz.Div.* would cross the Gniloy Tikich, seize the town's northern district, and prepare to drive towards *Gruppe Stemmermann* via Hill 239 through the town of Zhurzhintsy. *Leibstandarte* and *198.Inf.Div.* would hold their current positions and prevent the enemy from breaking through and cutting off Breith's spearhead.

A question came up concerning the need to hold the bulge around Tinovka, Repki and Votylevka, currently held by *Leibstandarte* and *34.Inf.Div.* Although holding this salient at such cost afforded little military advantage, it would allow tank recovery units to evacuate the "graveyard of broken tanks" that had been collected a few kilometers to the rear during the previous week's fighting. Although these tanks, assault guns, and other heavy weapons could not be used in the days ahead, they could be placed back into operation in a relatively short period of time. Therefore, *Leibstandarte* would remain in place and bleed, as ordered by Breith, who commanded that "The *Führer* expects *Leibstandarte* to hold fast under all circumstances. The continuation of *III.Pz.Korps'* thrust is not possible otherwise."[37]

Wisch's division had no choice but to dig in and await the next round of Soviet counterattacks.

The Germans renewed their advance the following morning, another cloudy day that grounded the *Stukas* of the *Luftwaffe*. Just before dawn, *16.Pz.Div.* with its 29 remaining operational tanks advanced from the bridgehead at Frankovka, with the attached *Schw.Pz.Rgt. Bäke* in the lead. Replenished the previous day with fuel and ammunition, it ranged ahead of the rest of the division, destroying dozens of Soviet tanks which vainly attempted to stop its Tigers and Panthers. By 1100 hours, Dr. Bäke's tanks had reached Dashukovka, which the reconnaissance battalion had tried to take the previous day without success.

There, they ran up against the arrayed antitank guns on the town's southern outskirts and brushed them easily aside, knocking out 20 guns in the process. as well as 15 assault guns and 16 T-34s. By that afternoon, *Schw.Pz.Rgt.Bäke* had knocked out a total of 31 tanks that day, bringing their total since the unit's formation on 24 January to 400 destroyed Soviet tanks, an amazingly high number, but understandable when one considers the numbers of enemy tank units it had faced since it was first engaged near Proskurov.[38] Unfortunately Bäke's crews had little time to rest on their laurels.

The infantry units of *16.Pz.Div.*, *K.Gr. Blömecke*, composed of *Pz.Gren.Rgt.64* and *K.Gr. Hesse* from *Pz.Gren.Rgt.79*, followed in Dr. Bäke's wake. By that afternoon, Blömecke's men had occupied Dashdukovka after killing or capturing most of the town's defenders from a mechanized rifle brigade of the Soviet 3rd Tank Corps. The divisions reconnaissance *Abteilung* and a battalion from *K.Gr. Blömecke* attacked and seized the neighboring town of Chesnovka, extending the line that protected the division's left flank. Dr. Bäke and his tanks, accompanied by *K.Gr. Hesse*, pressed on, crossing the important Medvin-Lysyanka road at 1300 hours, after fighting a tank battle with counterattacking T-34s from 3rd Tank Corps.

Leaving part of his force behind on hill 239.8 to block this road, Dr. Bäke kept going, knowing that he only had a few hours of daylight left. Finally, his leading tanks approached the outskirts of the small village of Khizhintsy, only ten kilometers from the troops from *Gruppe Stemmermann* holding Khilki. Now short of infantry, Dr. Bäke could not take the town, since his tanks were vulnerable to Soviet infantry attack, especially at night. A powerful counterattack launched late that afternoon by 5th Guards Tank Corps ended *16.Pz.Div.'s* attack for the day, forcing Dr. Bäke to withdraw a few kilometers to the west, where it sought the protection of *K.Gr. Hesse's* infantry. Despite this, Bäke's advance was a major achievement - whether he knew it or not at the time, his unit had gotten closer to the pocket than any other German unit that day. In fact, it was the closest that both forces were ever to get. Only ten kilometers, a mere three hours on foot.

A few kilometers to the west, Meden's men of *17.Pz.Div.* had a much easier day of it, where they focused most of their effort consolidating the defenses of Bosovka and Frankovka. One regiment launched an attack to clear the woods east of Bosovka of enemy, but otherwise it was quiet. So quiet, in fact, that Breith ordered Meden to send his armored *Kampfgruppe*

A dispatch rider and his passenger from a heavy tank battalion aboard a BMW R75 motorcycle await orders as a Tiger I passes by in the background. By 12 February, it had started to snow again and temperatures had dropped noticeably. (Bundesarchiv 279/946/20)

consisting of one operational Pz.IV and four Tigers from the attached *Schw.Pz.Abt.506* forward to conduct an attack against the northwest outskirts of Lysyanka to relieve enemy pressure being exerted by waves of Soviet tanks against *K.Gr. Frank*.

While Bäke was conducting his successful attack of that morning, *K.Gr. Frank* had been conducting a detailed ground reconnaissance of Lysyanka in order to locate suitable crossing sites along the Gniloy Tikich. Once such a site - either a place suitable for bridging or fording - had been found, then Koll, who had arrived in Lysyanka early that morning along with *Oberst* Söth, the division's artillery commander, was to order his division to cross the stream, seize northern Lysyanka, and keep driving north towards the pocket. Although his division had lost a number of tanks due to mechanical problems and minefields, it still had a total of 30 operational Panthers and Pz.IVs with which to continue the advance.

Even while Frank's infantry were reconnoitering a crossing point, Soviet counterattacks from the south and southwest by a hastily reorganized 47th Rifle Corps, supported by a few tanks from 5th Mechanized Corps, attempted to drive out them out. Two of Frank's tank companies, supported by a few infantrymen, forced the Soviets to break off their attacks each time, driving them back to seek safety behind the hilltop town of Orly or the village of Budishche around a bend in the Gniloy Tikich, out of range of Frank's Panthers, who themselves awaited the news of when the attack would continue.

That morning, one German dismounted patrol, composed of seven men led by *Ofw.*Strippel, had scouted ahead through the side streets and back alleyways of Lysyanka. On the map, Strippel had spotted two possible fording sites in the vicinity of the destroyed north bridge and set out with his patrol to find them. Undetected by the enemy, he and his patrol discovered that these two sites were unsuitable, especially since the rain and melting snow had swollen the Gniloy Tikich beyond its normal depth and width. Changing directions, the patrol moved out silently towards the half-destroyed eastern bridge, still in the hands of a regiment from 359th Rifle Division. There, Strippel found a suitable ford and discovered that the bridge near the church was not in as bad of condition as had been reported by another patrol. Quickly returning to his company, the news of the tank sergeant's discovery was quickly passed up the German chain of command.

Koll ordered Frank to attack immediately and seize the fording site. Shortly before noon, five Panthers, with *Ofw.* Strippel in the lead and one company from *Hptm.* Ebeling's *Panzergrenadier* battalion in support, approached the eastern bridge. Carefully taking advantage of the terrain and neighboring houses to conceal their approach, the tanks and infantry crept forward as unobtrusively as they could. Incredibly, the Soviet defenders appeared to not have noticed their approach, since the sounds of tank engines reverberated throughout the town, masking their true location. *Oberstlt.* Frank established his command post nearby, in order to observe the operation. There, the attacking force waited. A *Stuka* strike that was supposed to support the attack was abruptly canceled due to the overlying fog and bad weather, but Frank decided to go ahead with the forces at his disposal, since Koll had run out of patience. With a battery from divisional artillery firing in support, the attack began shortly after 1400 hours.

The tank platoon rolled forward to the stream's bank, where it ran through the town's eastern outskirts. With Strippel in the lead, the Panthers quickly picked out enemy targets on the opposite bank and began to knock them out one by one. Supported by the other tanks, Strippel waded his Panther into the stream, which at that point was 20 to 30 meters wide. Water surged up to the top of the tank's treads, but Strippel kept going until he reached the other side. A well-camouflaged T-34 fired at point-blank range, but missed. Reacting quickly, Strippel had his gunner fire a round into the Soviet tank, which exploded in a ball of flames.

With Strippel across, *Fw.* Hofmeister drove his tank into the ford next. Just as both tanks were about to continue the attack, they received the order to halt where they were - the canceled *Stuka* attack was en route after all. Both tanks quickly sought cover along the stream's higher eastern bank, only to be told that the air attack had been canceled yet again. With that, Frank decided to send the rest of the tanks over anyway - he could not wait for the *Luftwaffe* to make an appearance. As it turned out, Strippel did not need air support

anyway and continued cautiously ahead.

In the tank's wake came *7.Kompanie* of *Hptm.* Ebeling's battalion, protected against enemy fire by their tanks as well as covering fire from *Oberst* Söth's *Pz.Art.Rgt.73*. Led by *Oblt.* Leben, they had been ordered up to support the tanks before the advance into the northern part of Lysyanka could resume. Since there was no bridge for them to cross, they had no choice but to wade through the ice-cold water of the creek which came up to their necks in some places. With their weapons over their heads, Leben's men slowly made their way over the ford and seized the opposite bank in the face of Soviet small arms fire.

Motivated by the thought of breaking through and rescuing their comrades, the men of *Pz.Gren.Rgt.113* set out to accomplish the nearly impossible, and had succeeded. Other grenadiers made it across the creek after checking the damaged bridge for demolitions. Everywhere, company and battalion commanders were leading their men from the front, inspiring and urging their men forwards. After a few hours, the Germans secured their newly won bridgehead over the Gniloy Tikich and began sending more troops and tanks across, while combat engineers attempted hasty repairs to the bridge before the Soviets could react.

A Soviet response was not long in coming. The Germans in the bridgehead had already warded off the first uncoordinated enemy counterattacks. Several burning T-34s sat in mute testimony to the firepower of the Panther. However, *K.Gr. Frank* could not afford to wait for the Soviets to come to them - he, like Koll, realized that their best chance for success lay in a continuation of the attack. Now the grenadiers were amongst the houses that lay along the stream's northern bank.

When a nest of enemy resistance could not be overcome with rifles or grenades, tanks were brought forward to eject the Soviets from their positions. Antitank guns and T-34s lay in ambush, awaiting the approach of an unwary Panther. Close cooperation between Frank's tank troops and Ebeling's grenadiers was an absolute necessity for survival. One by one, the Soviet defenders were killed or captured. Finally, most of the northern part of Lysyanka was in German hands by 2300 hours that evening, 13 February.

1.Pz.Div.'s seizure of the one-kilometer deep bridgehead had not been without loss. Though the defending Soviets had been roughly handled and thrown out of town by the veteran German division from Erfurt, Ebeling's battalion had suffered heavy casualties, especially during the house-to-house fighting. Three Panthers had been totally destroyed and several veteran tank commanders, such as *Fw.* Hofmeister and *Uffz.* Platt had been killed in action. The tank regiment's surgeon, Dr. Feuerbach, had set up a medical clearing station in south Lysyanka and set about treating the wounded of both sides, until they could be evacuated to the rear along the hazardous route to Bushanka, where Dr. Koenigshausen, the division's surgeon, could provide more appropriate care.

That night, *Oberstlt.* Frank ordered his battalions and companies to consolidate and improve their defensive positions before the attack could resume the following day. To protect the northerly approach to Lysyanka during the evening, Frank ordered *Oblt.* Ciliox with four Panthers to establish a thin screen line. An attempt by the regimental staff of *Pz.Rgt.1* to ford the Gniloy Tikich misfired when they failed to find the fording place in the darkness. Thinking that he was following the same route that Strippel had followed earlier that day, the commander of *I./Pz.Rgt.1*, *Hptm. Graf* Wedel, was startled when his command tank, a Pz. IV, got stuck when the water surged over its fenders and into its fighting compartment which should have come as no surprise, since the Panther had a much greater fording capability than the older, smaller Pz. IV. In his eagerness to rejoin the forward units of his battalion, Wedel had forgotten this limitation. No matter, *1.Pz.Div.* had now seized all of Lysyanka and would continue the attack the following day.

Not everyone in *III.Pz.Korps* had the opportunity that day to bask in the offensive success of *1.* and *16.Pz.Divs.* To the south and west, the widely-separated regiments of *198.Inf.Div.* were tied up in costly defensive fighting. Throughout the day, *Gren.Rgt.305* and *326* holding Vinograd, fought off a series of half-hearted Soviet counterattacks supported by a few tanks, but were easily able to hold their own. Besides this, both regiments were also able to tie in their left flank with the right flank of *Leibstandarte*, still holding the Repki-Votylevka-Tinovka salient.

On the far right of the Division, *Gren.Rgt.308* was forced that night to carry out a counterattack against a large Soviet contingent from 167th Rifle Division holding the town of Tikhonovka. Earlier that day, this enemy force had ambushed one of *1.Pz.Div.'s* supply columns and had destroyed its entire cargo of badly-needed fuel and ammunition. As the Germans assembled in neighboring Yablonovka, they were joined by six Pz.IVs from Koll's division.

The objective lay two kilometers away across a wide-open steppe. Approaching in the daytime would be suicidal, especially since the Soviets seemed to be liberally equipped with antitank guns and even had a couple of their own tanks. Therefore, the regimental commander decided upon a night attack, hoping that his forces would be able to approach the Soviet positions without being discovered until the last possible moment. With the stars obscured by clouds, the grenadiers set off across the wet, soggy ground. Many men sank up to their knees in some places, requiring the assistance of friends to free them from the mire.

To guide the tanks through the darkness, each had been detailed an infantryman to serve as a guide, using the green lenses of their pocket torches to show the way. After nearly an hour of marching, the outline of Tikhonovka came into view. Following a prearranged signal, the six tanks pulled up on line and began shooting into the town with their machine-guns. Tracers rounds soon caused the roofs of several *isbas* to alight, illuminating the objective for the attacking grenadiers and tanks, which slowly and methodically began their work with their 7.5 cm guns. The Soviets appeared to have been caught completely by surprise, making the Germans' work that much easier. Most of the defenders ran off into the night or were made prisoner.[39] For the time being, the threat to *1.Pz.Div.'s* flank from that direction had been quelled.

Leibstandarte also had a rough time of it that day, especially in Votylevka, where *K.Gr. Kuhlmann* of *SS-Pz.Gren.Rgt. 2*, repelled numerous attempts by 58th and 74th Rifle Divisions to surround the town. The attack, according to *Leibstandarte's* daily journal, were brought to a halt "only with extraordinary effort." By 1710 hours, the Soviets were able to break into the northwestern edge of the town. A counterattack by the regimen-

Generalmajor Höchbaum, *Commander, 34.Inf.Div. (Photo: Andreas Schwarz and 88.Inf.Div. Veterans Association).*

tal reserve force augmented by tanks from *SS-Pz.Rgt.1 "LAH"* succeeded ten hours later in throwing them out again, only after having to root them out, house by house.

During the fighting, *Hstuf.* Roehwer, who had just returned from convalescent leave to resume command of *II./SS-Pz.Gren.Rgt.2,* was again seriously wounded. In the early morning hours, the exhausted SS men counted 220 enemy dead. The following morning, *SS-Pz.Gren.Rgt.2* only had 309 men left standing out of its original authorized strength of 3,242, which obviously represents a considerable bloodletting.[40] In the four short months since the division had returned to the Eastern Front after its brief stay in Italy, the regiment had lost 90 percent of its men due to deaths, wounds, accidents, and sickness. *SS-Pz.Rgt.1* itself* only had 13 tanks and assault guns still operational. Remarkably, this division, as well as the others in *III.Pz.Korps*, was still determined to break through and rescue Stemmermann and his troops. They would not quit until ordered to do so, a trait they shared in common with *Ivan*, "their comrade from the opposite field post address."

To *Leibstandarte's* left, the German defenders were hotly engaged in Tinovka, where *Gen.Lt.* Friedrich Höchbaum's *34.Inf.Div.* held firmly against the strongest Soviet attacks his troops had yet faced, which began with a powerful artillery barrage that lasted over an hour. One Soviet attack, pressed home by troops of 133rd Rifle Division supported by elements of 11th Guards Tank Corps, actually managed to penetrate all the way to the town center before a counterattack threw them back out again, leaving behind two destroyed tanks. In special recognition of its defensive achievements, Hoechbaum's division was recommended for mention in the *Wehrmachtsbericht*.

In the recommendation penned by Hube, he stated that *34.Inf.Div.* had presented an exemplary model of soldierly conduct, as illustrated by the fact that during the past four weeks of defensive fighting, without mobile antitank support (in the form of tanks or assault guns), the division was able to knock out 90 enemy tanks - a large proportion in close combat.[41] Brave words, indeed, for in many respects *34.Inf.Div.* was little more than a regiment in strength - but now it would have to assume even greater duties besides holding Tinovka - now it had to ensure the continuity between its own corps and *III.Pz.Korps.*

---

* Incidentally, *SS-Stubaf.* Jochen Peiper, the famous commander of the Leibstandarte's tank regiment, had departed for Germany on medical leave the second week of January and did not take part in the relief attempt.

In discussions that evening at their command post in Uman, both Generals Hube and Wenck were heartened by the day's developments, though they knew that they were operating on borrowed time. To assess the situation, Wenck himself had once again gone forward in a *Kettenkrad* at great risk to himself, to speak in person with Koll at his forward command post at Bushanka. While the attack had managed to forge ahead that day and reached to within ten kilometers of the pocket, if only momentarily, both men knew that Breith's corps was rapidly reaching the end of its strength.

More worrisome was the realization that, while *1. Pz.Armee* had been able to ruthlessly denude its center and western flank in order to free up forces to reinforce the right flank, the army would be extremely vulnerable to attack on its opposite flank once the relief operation was over. The Soviets, Hube and Wenck believed, would quickly take advantage of the imbalance of forces this represented and would attempt to carry out once again a large-scale envelopment of *1.Pz.Armee* similar to the one they had tried the previous November. The army's left flank was even further weakened when *4.Jg.Div.* was pulled out to be switched to the Uman area to serve as a badly-needed reinforcement, though it would take nearly a week to arrive.

Manstein also knew this, and urged his commanders and troops to keep driving ahead. With Vormann's spearhead blocked by strong Soviet forces south of Zvenigorodka, Breith's attack was *Gruppe Stemmermann's* last chance. As happens frequently in war, when both sides feel as if they are about to lose, victory would go to the opponent that admits defeat last. The battle was clearly nearing its climax. Certainly, the men of *III.Pz.Korps* felt anything but defeated. Buoyed by the successful seizure of Lysyanka, Manstein sent a radio message on the evening of 13 February to keep *III.Pz.Korps'* spirits up: "Bravo! In spite of mud and the Russians you've almost made it. Now its down to the last few steps. Clench your teeth and keep going! It's now or never. We will make it!"[42]

For 14 February, Breith planned to continue the attack. Khizhintsy, to the north, would be retaken by *16.Pz.Div.,* while *1.Pz.Div.,* in the south, would attack towards the pocket via Hill 239 and Zhurzhintsy. Meden's *17.Pz.Div.* would protect the northern flank, while supporting Koll's division in Lysyanka. Hube had decided to pull *Leibstandarte* out of the salient north of Vinograd, so that this division would be available to support the attack. By then, most of the disabled armored vehicles that had been collected south of their position would have been evacuated. As Manstein commented, panzer divisions were not suited to hold static defensive positions in any case. This withdrawal, code-named *Mondschein* (Moonshine), would take place during the night of 14/15 February. The front would then be pulled back to a line running roughly from Vinograd in the east to Tinovka in the west and would then be occupied by *34.Inf.Div.* from *VII.A.K.,* which would have to stretch its sector nearly ten kilometers to the east to cover the empty space created by *Leibstandarte's* departure. Meanwhile, the attack would continue.

Monday, 14 February, marked the fourth day of Breith's relief effort. It began with a change in the weather, which, for once, would work in the German's favor. The warm, spring-like weather of the past ten days gave way once again to winter. The

wind rose up from the north, bringing snow and sub-freezing temperatures. Slowly, the plowed-up roads began to harden, making it somewhat easier for the wheeled vehicle supply convoys to make their way towards the forward units. While it grounded most of the *Luftwaffe's* close support aircraft, the cloudy sky also made it more difficult for the fighter bombers of the Red Air Force to hit the Germans. Despite the foul flying weather, waves of Ju-52 transports and He-111 bombers laden with parachute canisters passed over the heads of Breith's troops in a continuous stream back and forth towards the Pocket, where they deposited their needed loads of supplies, thus keeping the chances of the men of *Gruppe Stemmermann* alive for a few more days.

In ground action that day, *III.Pz.Korps* made only small gains. The attack was losing momentum, but Breith's division commanders thought that if only the troops of *1., 16., and 17.Pz.Divs.* could make it a few more kilometers, success, so it seemed, would be guaranteed. Koll's *16.Pz.Div.,* with *Schw.Pz.Rgt. Bäke* in the lead, tried once more that day to seize Khizhintsy, which commanded the high ground and provided relatively easy access to the Pocket at Khilki, where troops of *K.Abt.B* awaited their relief. Easy, that is, if Bäke's force had not been faced with the bulk of the Red Army's 3rd Tank Corps from 2nd Tank Army, which had conducted a forced march during the night to take up defensive positions in the town, as well as 259th Rifle Division.

At first, Bäke's attack went well. *Hptm.* Walter Scherf's *Abteilung* attacked the town that morning with its eight remaining Tigers and five accompanying half-tracks with *Jägers* from the attached light infantry battalion. Seven T-34s that launched a counterattack, as well as five hidden antitank guns, were quickly knocked out and Khizhintsy was in German hands by mid-afternoon. Later that evening, the Soviets launched a concerted counterattack, but Scherff's tanks and troops knocked out six more tanks and eliminated the advancing infantry. To Sherff, it seemed, the route to *Gruppe Stemmermann* via the neighboring town of Zhurzhintsy, which seemed to be occupied only by a company or two of Red infantry, lay wide open.[43] But it was not to be.

The reason for the decision not to go that route had been made earlier that afternoon by Generals Back and Breith, who had flown in to the outskirts of Khizhintsy aboard a Fiesler *Storch* to meet with Bäke. Counterattacks against *16.Pz.Div.'s* northern flank near Chesnovka by Soviet tank brigades barreling down the Lysyanka-Medvin road had almost broken through several times that day, illustrating the vulnerability of continuing the attack from the northeast towards the pocket. In addition, the supply route from Frankovka to *16.Pz.Div.'s* spearhead was completely impassable, making it virtually impossible to get any supplies forward or to evacuate the wounded, much less the withdrawal of Stemmermann's entire force once they had broken out.

Furthermore, and even more worrisome, was the fact that the bulk of 20th Tank Corps had slipped in between Lysyanka and Khizhintsy with an estimated 80 tanks and 52 antitank guns, where they were busily preparing a counterattack. The only remedy to the situation, as Breith saw it, was to detach Scherff's Tiger *Abteilung* early the next morning and have it moved south to counterattack the mass of Soviet armor. Khizhintsy, only ten kilometers from the anxiously waiting troops of *Gruppe Stemmermann*, was to be given up the following day.[44]

Meden's *17.Pz.Div.* had a relatively quiet day. The only exception was the division's small armored *Kampfgruppe*, which had been sent to link up with *K.Gr. Frank* on the northwestern outskirts of Lysyanka. Establishing contact with Frank that afternoon, the five tanks from *17.Pz.Div.*, accompanied by a few armored infantrymen, set up a defensive position atop Hill 216.7, one kilometer northwest of Lysyanka and awaited the next day's developments. Except for some half-hearted Soviet attempts to push foot patrols into the outskirts of Tikhonovka, the rest of *198.Inf.Div.'s* sector was quiet as well.[45] Even *Leibstandarte* had a relatively easy day of it, though a regimental-sized enemy attack against Votylevka from Fedjukovka was reported, which was broken up by artillery and *Nebelwerfer* barrages. Small penetrations of the division's front line near Pavlovka were also reported, but were quickly ironed out by local counterattacks.

General Wisch's greatest concern that day was the scheduled withdrawal from the salient his division had occupied the past four days that was to occur that evening. He had already moved his division command post back to Shubiny Stav, where the entire division would assemble later on. The mud on the roads was still so bad that it took *Leibstandarte* 36 hours to travel the 21 kilometers to its assembly area.[46] Even in *VII.A.K.'s* sector, things were quiet. The massive bloodletting in Tinovka the previous day had resulted in a relative reprieve for *34.Inf.Div.* A few feeble attempts were made to penetrate the eastern district of the town, but these were easily warded off. The relief in place of *Leibstandarte* by *34.Inf.Div.* would take place uneventfully.

The real locus of the fighting that day, however, was Lysyanka. Koll planned to push his division out of Lysyanka and up the long slope towards Hill 239, where his division would be in a commanding position from which they could continue their attack to free their encircled comrades in the ever-shrinking pocket encompassing Shanderovka, Novo Buda, Komarovka, and Khilki. Fierce Soviet counterattacks throughout the day held *K.Gr. Frank* in check, though, as well as the increasingly worse supply situation.

The day dawned inauspiciously, when the security screen of Panthers arrayed along Lysyanka's northern outskirts spotted a line of T-34s with *Tankodesantniki* aboard coming towards them out of the mist. *Ofw.* Strippel and *Fw.* Bohlken, awakened by grenadiers in forward listening post, went into action, knocking out two tanks and damaging a few others before the rest turned about and fled back from whence they had come. They would be back soon. In another attack later that day, *Oblt.* Ciliox, who had led the initial tank attack into the center of Lysyanka, was severely wounded when his tank was knocked out by a T-34.

Another piece of bad news was the fact that the damaged bridge that had been captured the day before could not be made strong enough to bear the weight of tanks. Worse yet was the fact that divisional engineer battalion's *Brückenkolonne-K* (heavy bridging company) was still stuck in the mud far to the

rear near Uman along with most of the division's other wheeled elements. The grenadiers and a few combat engineers from *Pz.Pio.Btl. 37* would have to do the best they could with the few building materials at hand, which meant that they would have to tear apart native *isbas* in order to get the beams, planks, and stringers needed to build an temporary bridge. Furthermore, not all of Lysyanka was in German hands yet. A small area in the northeast was still held by the Soviets, so *Hptm.* Ebeling, with 70 men from his battalion, set out to rid the town of the last vestiges of the enemy.

Supported by three tanks, Ebeling were able to slowly clear out the enemy in costly house-to-house fighting. Meanwhile, to the north, other Panthers and grenadiers of *K.Gr. Frank* held off another series of Soviet tank-led counterattacks, which included elements of 20th Tank Corps' 8th and 155th Tank Brigades. Finally, by 1745 hours, Ebeling's little force had almost cleared the entire town of the enemy, and had received quite a surprise as a reward for his efforts. To his amazement, he spotted an undamaged 40-ton bridge across the Gniloy Tikich at a previously unknown location at the town's far northeastern tip.

To seize it before it was destroyed, Ebeling ordered Hans Strippel, who had participated in the attack, to move forward immediately with a few infantry aboard his tank. As he neared the bridge, Strippel saw two well-camouflaged T-34s tracking him. Reacting quickly, Strippel trained his gun on the two tanks and destroyed them at point blank range, his 59th and 60th consecutive tank kills. With the bridge now in German hands, the little force stormed ahead 500 meters and seized a commanding hill that overlooked the town's northern outskirts and held it in the face of bitter Soviet counterattacks, which failed to dislodge them.

That evening, Frank ordered his *Kampfgruppe* to form *Igel* (hedgehog) positions in order to defend Lysyanka during the night. With several batteries from the divisional artillery regiment now in position, each tank and infantry company were wired into the fire directional control network and received artillery forward observers to direct the fire. The badly-needed artillery support would provide the Germans the edge they would need to hold off the forces of their numerically superior enemy. Also that day, *K.Gr. Frank* received a visit when Breith himself flew into the town's southern outskirts aboard a Fiesler *Storch* to meet with Koll, who had pushed the division headquarters forward.

Breith, who had just met with Back of *16.Pz.Div.* a few hours before, first complemented Koll and Frank on their division's outstanding performance in the relief operation so far. He then told them that their division would now make *III.Pz.Korps'* main effort. All the hopes of "Relief Group West" and the success of Operation Wanda would now ride on *1.Pz.Div.* Koll and Frank must have felt a crushing weight being laid on their shoulders. The rescue of some 56,000 men of *Gruppe Stemmermann* was now their responsibility.

That night Marshal Zhukov, who was now responsible for preventing the linkup from occurring, threw everything he could against Lysyanka. This, after all, was not supposed to happen - how could the Fascists have broken through so far? He had already ordered General Bogdanov to move his 2nd Tank Army towards the endangered area, and two of Rotmistrov's tanks corps were already there or en route. In his postwar memoirs, Zhukov admitted that the Germans were able to "press forward to Lysyanka, but lack of strength forced the enemy to pass over to the defensive."

He also thought that his forces were facing over 160 German tanks, but by 14 February that number was closer to 63.[47] In contrast, Zhukov had several hundred at his disposal, with many previous losses already made up for by the transfers of new crews and vehicles as well as the wholesale denuding of independent tank brigades and battalions from other areas of the sectors held by both First and Second Ukrainian *Fronts*. Zhukov and Konev would do whatever it took to keep their promise to Stalin.

That night, Hans Strippel helped fight off one of the most desperate attempts made by the Soviets thus far to wipe out the defenders of Lysyanka. Later, Strippel wrote "An entire battalion of mostly drunken [Soviet] soldiers waltzed up to the sector held by our Panthers later that night shouting "Hurrah!" They rolled right up to our strong points, but we were finally able to drive them off at close range."[48] Although they were slaughtered, they kept coming, fighting with admirable toughness and enthusiasm, if not skill.

The fact that the lower-level Soviet commanders felt compelled to resort once again to the old tried and failed use of human-wave attacks illustrates the fact that not only the Germans were getting desperate. Their motivation, however, was entirely different; the Germans were doing everything in their power to rescue their encircled comrades, while the Soviets were doing everything they could to keep from disappointing Stalin. Both the Soviet's Korsun-Shevchenkovsky Operation and the German's Operation Wanda were rapidly reaching a culminating point, resulting in an incredible effusion of blood on both sides.

That night, Wenck wearily made his entries in the army's daily journal. Even this extremely talented, energetic officer was beginning to see that the end was in sight. He wrote pessimistically:

> Strong enemy counterattacks and muddy streets and roads have brought the attack of III.Pz.Korps once again to a halt. K.Gr. Frank of 1.Pz.Div. reports that it is engaged in bitter fighting against constant counterattacks against the northern portion of Lysyanya carried out by our opponent from the north and northeast. The tanks of Bäke's group are unable to break through the strong defensive barriers east of Khizhintsy despite numerous attempts to do so. This recent halt has placed a heavy burden on our leaders and troops, whose willpower to fight their way through to their cut-off comrades had been strengthened by the fact that goal finally seems to be in sight; this adverse turn of events will sap their inner [moral] strength, which will be badly needed in the stormy days to come.[49]

Wenck also had noticed that the Soviets were now beginning to cram as many tank and infantry corps within the narrow neck of land that separated Breith's corps from the corps of *Gruppe Stemmermann*.

In addition to his own problems, Wenck noted that the weight of the enemy's attacks against the now-tiny Pocket had grown to unimaginable proportions, especially against the south and southwest corner of the egg-shaped pocket. *1.Pz.Div.* would renew its attempt to reach the pocket the following day, but the desperate troops of *Gruppe Stemmermann* would have to hold on for at least two or three more days. Had Walter Wenck only known the true extent of their plight, his report that night would have been even more pessimistic. For inside the pocket, the battle for the survival of *XI.* and *XXXXII.A.K.* was rapidly approaching its climax.

End Notes

[1] *1.Pz.Armee* KTB, entry dated 9 February 1944, p. 1.

[2] Ibid, pp. 1-2.

[3] *Tagesmeldung, III.Panzer Korps* to *1.Pz.Armee* dated 2000 hours 10 February 1944, and *Besprechungpunkte, Besuch bei III. Panzer Korps am 10.2.1944,* p. 1.

[4] Lehmann and Tiemann, p. 30.

[5] *Besprechungpunkte, Besuch bei III.Panzer Korps am 10.2.1944,* p.3.

[6] *1.Pz.Armee* KTB, 10 February 1944, p. 1.

[7] Röhricht, Edgar. *Probleme der Kesselschlacht.* (Karlsruhe, Germany: Condor Verlag GmbH, 1958), p. 158.

[8] Vormann, p. 86.

[9] *8.Armee* KTB, entry dated 0815 hours 10 February 1944, p. 2.

[10] Ibid, KTB dated 11 February 1944, pp. 1-6.

[11] Ibid, KTB entry dated 1605 hours 12 February 1944, p. 5, and Rudel, Hans-Ulrich, *Stuka Pilot.* (New York: Ballantine Books, Inc., 1958), p. 110-111.

[12] Vormann, p. 92.

[13] Interview with Mikhail Hadai, Korsun-Shevchenkovsky, Ukraine, 29 June 1996.

[14] *8.Armee* KTB, entry dated 1915 hours 14 February 1944, p. 6.

[15] Ibid, entry dated 2100 hours 15 February 1944, p. 7.

[16] Vormann, p. 92.

[17] Kielmannsegg, in Glantz, "From the Dnieper to the Vistula," p. 234.

[18] *8.Armee* KTB, entry dated 2100 hours, 15 February 1944, p. 6.

[19] Graser, p. 289.

[20] Ibid.

[21] Werthen, Wolfgang. *Geschichte der 16. Panzer-Division, 1939-1945.* (Friedberg, Germany: Podzun-Pallas Verlag, 1958), p. 200.

[22] Ibid.

[23] Lehmann and Tiemann, pp. 30-31.

[24] Ibid, pp. 32-33.

[25] *1.Pz.Armee* KTB, 11 February 1944, p. 3.

[26] Stoves, Rolf. *1.Panzer-Division, 1935-1945: Chronik einer der drei Stamm-Divisionen der deutschen Panzerwaffe.* (Bad Nauheim, Germany: Verlag Hans-Henning Podzun, 1962), p. 497.

[27] Stoves, p. 500.

[28] *1.Pz.Armee* KTB, 11 February 1944, p. 2.

[29] Lehmann and Tiemann, p. 31.

[30] Graser, p. 289.

[31] Ibid, pp. 289-290.

[32] Stoves, pp. 503-505.

[33] Stoves, p. 506.

[34] *1.Pz.Armee* KTB, 12 February 1944, p. 1.

[35] Lehmann and Tiemann, p. 32.

[36] Matsulenko, Viktor. *Encirclement Operations and Combat.* (Moscow: Voyenizdat, 1983), p. 152.

[37] *1.Pz.Armee* KTB, 12 February 1944, p. 2 and Lehmann and Tiemann, p. 31.

[38] *III.Pz.Korps* KTB, entry dated 1950 hours 13 February 1944.

[39] Graser, pp. 290-291.

[40] Lehmann and Tiemann, pp. 32-33 and War Department Technical Manual TM-E 30-451, *Handbook on German Military Forces.* (Washington, D.C.: War Department, 15 March 1945), p. II-28.

[41] *1.Pz.Armee* KTB, 13 February 1944, p. 4.

[42] Radio Message, Headquarters, Army Group South, to Headquarters, *III.Pz.Korps,* 2010 hours, 13 February 1944.

[43] Ruebbel, Albert. *Erinnerungen an die Tigerabteilung 503 1942-1945.* (Bassum, Germany: Privately Published, 1990), p. 220.

[44] Ibid, p. 221.

[45] *1.Pz.Armee* KTB, 14 February 1944, pp. 2-3.

[46] Lehmann and Tiemann, p. 34.

[47] Zhukov, p. 160 and Report, *III.Pz.Korps* to *1.Pz.Armee, Panzer und Sturmgeschützlage III.Panzer Korps,* report dated 1110 hours 15 February 1944.

[48] Stoves, p. 512.
[49] *1.Pz.Armee* KTB, 14 February 1944, p. 1.

Chapter Seventeen
THE BATTLE FOR NOVO BUDA

"Breith will have to arrive soon . . . "
— *General Theo Lieb, 14 February 1944* [1]

Although the men of *Gruppe Stemmermann* had been able to seize the breakout area encompassing Novo Buda, Shanderovka, Khilki, and Komarovka, they would have little time to congratulate themselves. Nor would they be able to sit passively and await the arrival of Breith's relief effort, the sounds of which could be heard by 13 February, less than 30 kilometers (18 miles) away. In fact, the crack of tank cannon from the Lysyanka area was plainly audible to the troops in Khilki and Komarovka. Their long nightmare, which had begun 21 days before, now seemed about to end.

General Stemmermann was not so sure, nor was General Lieb. While most of the breakout area had indeed been captured, the failure of *Oberst* Bucher's *Kampfgruppe* to take Petrovskoye meant that any breakout towards the southwest, or the approach of the relief force from that direction, would both have to go uphill. With the Soviets in possession of the high ground between the German forces, any attack from either direction would be a difficult one. To stress the critical nature of the situation, Lieb even sent a message to General Speidel on 12 February, in a circumvention of the commander of *Gruppe Stemmermann*, which stated in part that "I consider it absolutely necessary, that Breith reach Petrovskoye as quickly as possible, in order to reestablish contact. Speed is required. My corps' assault spearhead is in Khilki." [2] Wöhler's staff, in response, informed Lieb of Breith's and Vormann's current location and told him that Breith was going to try to attack towards the pocket via Dzhurzhentsy the following day.

Both Lieb and Stemmermann also knew that the breakout of their forces would have to be postponed another day or two, since units were being delayed by heavy Soviet flank attacks and final mopping up in Shanderovka. The earliest that both *XI.* and *XXXXII.A.K.* could break out was 15 February, and even that was in doubt. Lieb was very concerned with the increasing number of Soviet air attacks, especially in view of the growing congestion in the ever-narrowing pocket. Theo Lieb wrote in his diary that night that "Have requested strong fighter protection for 14 February…I am most afraid that [*8.Armee*] cannot comply with this oft-repeated request." [3]

Stemmermann also had realized that the Soviet ground forces, though initially surprised by the successes of both his and Breith's force, were quickly recovering and were in the process of moving sizable forces into the narrow neck of land that separated the two German commands. In addition, units holding defensive positions around the perimeter of the pocket

Despite the worst, the troops in the pocket refused to give up. (Bundesarchiv 277/803/21)

reported that the Soviets were continuing to apply steady pressure, forcing the Germans to keep half of their remaining forces tied up in static defense. This meant that Konev's and Zhukov's troops were not only positioning themselves to prevent a German linkup, but would continue their efforts to wipe out Stemmermann's encircled force.

The challenge that this posed to Stemmermann and Lieb was twofold; first, they had to pull the rest of their units into the breakout area encompassed by the four towns and hold it at all costs until Breith's forces linked up with them. Fortunately, the breakout area had been chosen with defense in mind; Shanderovka, in the center, lay in a long, broad bowl-shaped valley bounded on all sides by hills or ridgelines that denied observation to enemy ground forces. All of these areas, with the exception of Petrovskoye, had been taken on 11 and 12 February.

Now, all that the Germans had to do was hold them long enough for *III.Pz.Korps* to arrive, then give up those positions too once the rest of the forces inside the valley had been evacuated.

The casualty rate had increased perceptibly as well. In three short days (between 11 and 14 February), *XI.* and *XXXXII. A.K.* had lost 2,000 men. By the evening of 13 February, *Gruppe Stemmermann* had 54,000 men left, including wounded.[4] Any manpower saved by shortening the line only meant that the Germans would have enough men to replace losses elsewhere in the pocket, which precluded assembling additional forces that could be made available for conducting an attack.

The withdrawal of the rest his forces towards the breakout area would be more problematic and would involve not only ordering *88.Inf.Div.* and *Wiking* to cross over to the south bank of the Ross River, but the evacuation of Korsun and its neighboring airfield as well. This, of course, meant the end of air evacuation for the thousands of wounded (as of 12 February, *8. Armee* headquarters was notified that both corps were caring for a combined total of 2,000 wounded).[5] The movement of the wounded to the new collection areas in Steblev and Shanderovka would begin that day; by 13 February, at the latest, Korsun was to be completely evacuated.

Another problem vexing the troops of *Gruppe Stemmermann* was the intensifying activities of the Red Air Force against the ever-shrinking pocket. The larger towns of Korsun, Shanderovka, and Steblev appeared to be the primary targets, whose streets were crowded with men, horses, guns, and vehicles from six divisions and assorted corps troops. Stemmermann constantly begged *8.Armee* for air support, but his requests were seldom satisfied. Seidemann's *VIII.Flieger-Korps* could not work miracles - the weather, Soviet flak and fighters, as well as muddy airfields had greatly reduced the numbers of sorties that could be flown.

Unconvinced as he watched the Yak-9s and *Sturmoviks* of the two Soviet air armies harass and bomb his troops, Stemmermann could only ask "Why isn't our *Luftwaffe* attacking?"[6] Intermittent snow and rainshowers had provided some concealment against Soviet air attacks, but whenever the skies cleared, Soviet aviators would pounce and shoot up supply columns, medical clearing stations, and even front line positions. *57.*, *88.Inf.Div.* and *Wiking* began their movement to the south and southwest during the night of 12/13 February. To the northwest, *88.Inf.Div.* with the attached *Sich.Rgt.318* gave up their positions between Sotniki and Vygrayev and took up a new line a few kilometers south by 0700 hours on 13 February, while both Generals Gille and Trowitz held the eastern perimeter between Arbusino and Glushki (to the north and south, respectively) against several minor Soviet attacks. They only had to hold this sector until nightfall, while *Graf* Rittberg's division would have to hold north of the river for another day. Korsun itself would be abandoned during the night of 13/14 February - Stemmermann had decided not to defend the town, since at this stage he could no longer afford to spare the men and ammunition to hold it anyway.

It was to prove a long, anxious day for the German troops holding the eastern sector of the pocket. Though the Soviet 52nd Army made no concerted effort that day to break through this thinly-held defense line, its 294th, 373rd, and 254th Rifle Divisions continued to apply steady pressure against the Germans. North of Arbusino in the sector held by *SS-Pz.Aufkl.Abt.5*, a battalion from 294th Rifle Division achieved a breakthrough that afternoon, but was ironed out after the German commander, Heinz Debus, launched a counterattack with the assistance of Wittman's makeshift infantry company from Köller's tank battalion. The previous day, the Soviets had actually taken over part of the town, weakly held by troops from *7.Kp./Westland*. A counterattack led by *Ustuf.* Fritz Hahl's *6.Kompanie*, as well as remnants of two other companies, were able to throw the Soviets out after house-to-house fighting.

The fighting netted Hahl's company several enemy light and heavy machine guns, as well as a 7.62 cm antitank gun, which his men put to use in their retaken defensive positions. Hahl noted afterwards that:

> Our success through such decisive combat buoyed the men's spirits . . . but there were gloomy periods of time where we asked one another how much longer could we hold out in the face of such pressure from the numerically superior Soviets? Could we hold out, would we come through it all?[7]

To the south of *Wiking*, an assortment of different units under the control of *57.Inf.Div.* warded off numerous Soviet attempts to seize Karashin, Koshmak, Glushki, and Petrushki that same day. Trowitz's men would not have to pass through Korsun or worry about having to cross a river, since the Ross ran north of their position (in fact, it served as the boundary between *57.Inf.Div.* and *Wiking*). They would just have to withdraw due west instead, a much shorter, easier route, and take up new defensive positions west of Korsun along the Ross River near Yablonovka on the evening of 12/13 February.

According to *Oblt.* Erwin Witzer, the battalion surgeon for *Pi.Btl.57*, the Germans discovered much to their surprise upon arriving that several Soviet tanks and some infantry had slipped past them and had set up positions in a grove of trees two kilometers south of Yablonovka, necessitating a hasty withdrawal by Witzer's engineer battalion and *Inf.Rgt. "List"* (*Gren.Rgt.199*) to new positions further to the west.[8]

Meanwhile, the airfield at Yablonovka west of Korsun had been shut down. Apart from its poor condition and with the enemy so close, it could easily be bombarded by Soviet artillery. Besides, the condition of the airfield was so bad that only the bravest pilots dared to try to make a landing upon its muddy surface. With no other suitable location within the ever-shrinking pocket to lay out another temporary airfield, most of *Gruppe Stemmermann's* supplies were being airdropped anyway. With the airfield gone, the 2,000 remaining wounded would have to be evacuated by road during the breakout itself.

One of the last to be flown out of Yablonovka on 12 February was *Ltn.* Karl Schierholz, from *Pi.Btl.112* of *K.Abt.B.* Two days before, Schierholz had been wounded in the leg when his battalion had been sent to an area east of Korsun, where it

ing on his payload of nine wounded passengers one more time, the pilot started the engines. Unbeknownst to the pilot or Schierholz, the German driver of the *Panje* wagon had sneaked aboard the aircraft and secreted himself in the aft cargo area. Evidently, he did not want to be left behind either! Feverishly, Schierholz and the others waited as the aircraft slowly gathered speed, the damaged engine coughing as if it would quit at any minute. As the aircraft rose into the air, he felt as if "a great stone had been lifted from my heart."

The aircraft quickly gained altitude to evade the Soviet antiaircraft belt, banked left, and headed southwest towards Uman, where it landed undamaged half an hour later. It was the last load of wounded to be flown out of the Cherkassy Pocket.[9] Another aircraft tried to take off later that day, but flipped over upon its back during takeoff when the wheels got stuck in the deep mud at the end of the runway. Now there was only way out for the wounded, the same as everyone else - by the land route from Shanderovka to Lysyanka.

As night fell 13 February, *88.Inf.Div.* and *Wiking* began their phased withdrawal. While all of Gille's division would cross that evening, *88.Inf.Div.* would have to occupy an intermediate line for another day. In most places, they were pursued closely by the men of 27th and 52nd Armies, though the Germans were able to avoid becoming decisively engaged by pulling out of successive defensive positions at the last moment, leaving their pursuing enemy to strike at thin air. The withdrawal of rear echelon units, such as combat support companies and battalions, as well as the artillery, hit a snag earlier in the day when a lucky hit by a bomb dropped by a Soviet aircraft detonated the explosive charges set to destroy the bridge that lay over the top of the hydroelectric dam across the Ross in Korsun. Fortunately, another smaller bridge near the old Polish castle in the center of the town enabled the harried *Feldgendarmerie* to detour traffic across the river, thus ensuring that there would still be a means by which the German troops could reach the breakout area.

The bridge had been prepared for demolition earlier by sappers from *Eisenbahn Pionier Einheit* (Railroad Engineer Unit) *0*, who had been ordered to destroy both the hydroelectric dam and the bridge constructed on top of it once the last German troops had crossed over. *Uffz.* Walter Notz and his men had arrived at the dam a few days earlier, and had taken up residence in one of the generator rooms. Here, for the first time in weeks, they had been able to remove their boots and sleep in a dry place that seemed safe from random artillery fire or strafing from Soviet fighters. Able to dry their feet for the first time, Notz remarked later that everyone in his platoon had blisters, abscesses, or frostbite. His unit, which normally was engaged repairing damaged railroads, had been since employed as infantry when all trains within the pocket were destroyed during the initial stages of the encirclement.

Provided with explosives and other demolition materials, Notz and his men set about placing them in key places about the dam and bridge. When the Soviets scored the lucky hit on the bridge thus setting off the demolitions, Notz and his men were out of a job. Although the bridge was destroyed and the dam itself heavily damaged, they did not complete its

Leutnant Karl Schierholz, *Pi.Btl.112, Korpsabteilung B. He flew out of the Kessel in the last Ju-52 before the airfield was abandoned. (Photo courtesy of Karl Schierholz)*

was to blow up the railroad bridge on the western outskirts of Gorodishche. When someone in his battalion accidentally stumbled and discharged his rifle, the alert Soviet guards at the bridge opened fire, wounding Schierholz and his battalion commander, *Hptm.* Harry Schlingmann. The battalion was quickly surrounded; just when all seemed lost, a counterattack launched by headquarters personnel of *Div.Gr.112* drove away the enemy, rescuing Schierholz and his comrades.

After receiving first aid for their wounds, Schierholz and Schlingmann as well as others from their battalion were brought to Korsun, where they were billeted in a private home and cared for by a Ukrainian woman and her daughter until they could be flown out. Finally, in the early morning hours of 12 February, they were picked up by a *Panje* wagon operated by *San.Abt.112* and brought to the airfield, where they were loaded aboard a waiting Ju-52. When the crew began to start the engines, it became quickly apparent that something was wrong with the center motor - in fact, upon landing that morning, the aircraft had hit a loading platform while taxiing, damaging the propeller. Dire thoughts swam in Schierholz's head, as he envisioned having to be left behind to fall into the hands of the Soviets. To complete the scene, it began to snow.

After a short conversation amongst his fellow crew members, the pilot decided to try and take off anyway. After check-

destruction, but were ordered to join up with *Wiking* instead as it withdrew across the river.[10]

By the morning of 14 February, all of *Wiking* was across and *57.Inf.Div.* had completely withdrawn to the new eastern defense line near Tarashcha as well, though Trowitz's division was very weak. In fact, it was reported that *Inf.Rgt. "List"* only had 50 infantrymen left, while the engineer battalion had practically ceased to exist.[11] *88.Inf.Div.* had an easier time of it and had been able to withdraw without much difficulty. A well-timed counterattack by *Hptm.* Burgfeld's *Gren.Rgt.258* stunned the pursuing Soviets from 206th Rifle Division when the German battalion threw them off the *Eierhügel* (Egg Hill), a bald knob one kilometer west of their old positions near Vygravyev. The Soviets certainly had not expected the Germans to conduct an attack this far north, and were caught off guard.

The Soviets facing them seemed to have lost their eagerness to attack, and were content for the time being with merely closely pursuing the Germans as they withdrew. After three weeks of bitter combat, had the Red Army lost its willingness to fight? It must have seemed strange indeed to have gotten away from their enemy so easily. Had the Germans only known, there was an explanation for this change in events, and it was due to the Germans' own successes of 11/12 February. The Soviets were simply pulling troops away from the northern and eastern positions around the pocket and were sending them towards the Lysyanka area, where they would be used both to thwart Breith's attack as well as destroy the Germans in the recently recaptured breakout area.

Opposite *Wiking* and *57.Inf.Div.*, three Soviet rifle divisions - 5th Guards Rifle, 62nd Rifle and 254th - had moved out during the evening of 12 February, significantly decreasing the pressure being applied against the eastern face of the pocket, while 202nd Rifle Division was in the process of moving away from *88.Inf.Div.* towards Khilki (in fact, part of this division had already been in contact with the assault force from *K.Abt.B.*).

This meant that the battle had shifted away from most of the rest of the Cherkassy Pocket and had begun in earnest further south. Over the next four days, German troops both inside and outside the pocket would be involved in heavy fighting to take or hold several key localities—Lysyanka and Oktyabr on the outside, Shanderovka, Komarovka, and Khilki on the inside. But nowhere was the fighting more fierce than that for the control of the town of Novo Buda, which would soon bear the brunt of the counterattacks launched by both 5th Guards Cavalry Corps and a tank corps from 5th Guards Tank Army. To maintain the integrity of the breakout assembly area's defensive perimeter, the town would have to be held at all costs. It was to become the grave yard of large numbers of Walloons.

This small farming community, laid out along both sides of the road like most Ukrainian towns, lay atop a plateau that was bounded to the east by a large ravine that ran from the north to the south. Its position atop the plateau dominated all avenues of approach into the Shanderovka basin from the east and southeast. The town itself was long and narrow, with most of its *isbas* and outbuildings laying on either side of the road that ran from Morentsy to the south and to Shanderovka to the north, where the road itself ran through a long, steep-sided ravine. To the

south, the town was bounded by wide-open fields where sunflowers and corn grew during the summer. Fields also stretched to the north and west, where the plateau gave way after half a kilometer to a steep-sided *balka* that descended to the towns of Shanderovka and Komarovka. Should Novo Buda fall into Soviet hands, the Red Army would have a commanding position from which to blast the increasingly packed valley.

After the town had been taken by Kästner's *Gren.Rgt.105* on the night of 11/12 February, *XI.A.K.* ordered that its defenses be handed over to the Walloon Brigade, which just arrived after a grueling night march from its old positions near Arbusino. The lead elements of *Ostubaf.* Lippert's unit began arriving at noon on 12 February, with the rest of the brigade arriving later that afternoon and evening. By 0500 hours the following day, the handover would be complete and Novo Buda's defense would be the responsibility of the Belgians, since the town's previous defenders had moved out for other assignments - Kästner's regiment, which had moved out during the evening of 12/13 February to take Komarovka and Siegel's, which had stayed long enough for its commander to brief Lippert and his staff about the town's defenses before Siegel ordered his men out to positions north of the town, where they would form a defense line that would link Novo Buda with the town of Tarashcha.

Although, according to Rudolf Siegel, the Walloon Brigade appeared to be a relatively powerful force, to Leon Degrelle, it appeared to be anything but. In his memoirs, he described the brigade as consisting of "…a nondescript army of cooks, accountants, drivers, mechanics, quartermasters, and signal troops, flanked by the legal officer, the dentist, the pharmacist, and the postman, all transformed into reinforcements for our skeletal companies."[12] Casualties had been so high that the brigade had been forced to disband its headquarters and support units and incorporate them into the infantry, though it reported over 1,000 men still in its ranks.

Throughout the afternoon and evening of 12 February, the Walloons staggered into the village, which was still relatively quiet after the initial Soviet counterattack had been driven off by the two regiments from *72.Inf.Div.* Most of the Walloons were caked with mud and soaked to the skin after their march. All were exhausted. Upon arriving in the village, they crowded into the town's few remaining intact *isbas*, where many soon fell asleep. A few tried to dry out their wet clothes in front of fires kindled from corn stalks, while the officers attended the orientation briefing being provided by Käster and Siegel.

At 0200 hours on 13 February, Lippert's men were roused from their sleep and ordered to form up in companies along the water-logged streets of the village. Few had even bothered to clean their weapons properly and most had not eaten a solid meal for two days. They were then led by squads to their new defensive positions, where the equally tired and hungry men from *72.Inf.Div.* relinquished their foxholes and marched off to their own new assignments. Thankfully, the Soviets chose not to attack that evening. By 0500 hours, the handover was complete.

Degrelle and Lippert hurried back to Siegel's headquarters (Kästner had already departed by then), where they found him

German troops engaging Soviets with rifle fire. (Bundesarchiv 88/3742/18A)

and his officers waiting impatiently, glancing at their watches. With the sound of approaching Soviet tanks reverberating in the background, Siegel and his staff scooped up their maps, bid a hasty goodbye, and hastened to rejoin their regiment, already in its new positions With an enemy assault imminent, Siegel could not afford to be cut off from his troops. All Lippert and Degrelle could do was stare at one another. The town was now theirs to hold at all costs.[13] But no attack took place; it seemed as if the enemy tanks were merely being repositioned.

Two hours later, Cossacks and 15 tanks from 11th and 12th Guards Calvary Divisions commenced their attack against Novo Buda. For the Walloons and neighboring *Gren.Rgt.266*, Sunday, 13 February would be anything but a day of rest. Supported by fire from artillery and *Katyushas*, the Soviets emerged from their positions in the woods north of Morentsy one kilometer to the south and stormed the village. Caught off guard, the Walloons watched in amazement as the T-34s and two battalions of Cossacks roared towards their positions. The six German assault guns from the *SS-Polizei Division* backed into positions behind the northern edge of town, as if to hide from the attack. Lippert and Degrelle, in the brigade command post, were knocked flat when no less than three tank shells ripped through their *isba*, showering them and their staff officers with roof timbers and straw. Three T-34s were already in the town, rumbling up and down its narrow streets, machine-gunning anyone who they came upon.

As Degrelle and his commander crawled out of the wreckage, two tanks raced past them. Other T-34s were busily engaged in crushing the Belgian's defensive positions. Hundreds of Cossacks, on foot, followed in the tank's wake. One German assault gun, braving the Soviet assault, crept forward into the town and found itself nose-to-nose with a T-34; both fired simultaneously and destroyed each other.

Degrelle watch in horror as one of the Brigade's German liaison officers, *Hstuf.* Wegener, was blown into the air, landing head-first in the mud with his legs protruding. Soviet artillery and rocket fire fell indiscriminately throughout the village, killing friend and foe alike. Seeking cover, Degrelle dove into a water-filled ditch, but was wounded by a jagged piece of shrapnel that pierced his jacket, breaking two ribs and leaving a shallow but painful wound on his abdomen. A Walloon antitank gun crew tried to get their 7.5 cm PaK40 into position, but were killed when their half-track was blown up by a Soviet shell. After a few more minutes of this, the Walloons decided they had been punished enough, and began a panicked rout to the slopes west of the village. Degrelle mounted a horse and attempted to rally his men. It had all happened in less than ten minutes.[14]

On the town's northern edge, *Maj.* Siegel watched the unfolding events in Novo Buda with ill-disguised disdain. Once again, a neighboring unit had departed without asking his permission! In his diary, Siegel wrote that "Hardly had we taken up our new positions, when *Ivan* attacked [the town] with tanks and the whole bunch (the Walloons) cleared out. It was terrible."[15] Siegel knew that he had to act quickly, since Lippert's Brigade appeared to be incapable of offering much resistance. If all of Novo Buda fell, the route to Shanderovka and the rest of the breakout area would be wide open, thus sealing the fate of *Gruppe Stemmermann,* which was still moving into the valley below.

Grabbing as many *Panzerfäuste* as he could lay his hands on, Siegel led a portion of his regiment in a counterattack that drove the Cossacks to the southern outskirts of the town. In the fighting, Siegel's troops and two Pz. IVs from *Wiking's* tank battalion that had hurried over from their positions behind Siegel's, knocked out 12 T-34s and chased the rest back to Morentsy. Even

Siegel's adjutant, *Ltn.* Peters, knocked out a tank with a *panzerfaust* as Siegel watched from the opposite side of the street.

The appearance of the two tanks from Köller's *SS-Pz.Abt.5* gave a tremendous boost to the defense. Initially ordered to established a protective screen on the high ground due east of Shanderovka, his battalion (which at that point still had between 17-18 tanks and assault guns) had just finished refueling using captured Soviet gasoline when they heard sounds of battle in Novo Buda. Köller, after conferring with one of Siegel's staff officers, ordered two tanks, led by *Ustuf.* Gerd Schumacher, to head out immediately towards the town, a mere kilometer south of the SS tank battalion's headquarters. Schumacher's and the other tank arrived in the town at roughly the same time that Siegel's regiment was preparing to counterattack.

Moving out ahead of the infantry, Schumacher waded into a group of eight T-34s. With the help of the other tank commanded by *Oscha.* Fiebelkorn (who himself accounted for three), all eight enemy tanks were destroyed, most of them at point-blank range. When Fiebelkorn's tank was knocked out by a hit in its engine compartment (he and the rest of his crew were wounded when they crawled out of their tank under Soviet machine-gun fire), Schumacher continued alone and knocked out two more T-34s in the town's southwest corner, thus personally accounting for seven of the 12 Soviet tanks destroyed that day.[16]

With the situation well in hand, Siegel then went to the ravine at the town's western edge and fetched the demoralized Walloons, urging them, with Degrelle's help, to return to their hastily abandoned fighting positions. Degrelle later estimated that his brigade lost over 200 men in two hours of fighting that morning, nearly 20 percent of its remaining strength. Although their troops had been driven out of most of the village, the Soviets continued their artillery and rocket barrages, which, in Degrelle's words, "…threw up a spray shaped like an apple tree. Gray orchards…which scattered bloody fruits of torn human flesh."[17] Having regained their composure, the Walloons

German soldier, with Soviet Ppsh submachinegun slung over his shoulder, interrogates a prisoner.
(Bundesarchiv 88/3743/15)

set grimly about their business and would hereafter give a good account of themselves.

Although Degrelle was too injured to actually carry a weapon, he moved about his fellow Walloons, cajoling and inspiring them, as did his commander, Lucien Lippert. Just as Lippert arrived at Siegel's temporary headquarters at an *isba* in the town's center, he was shot in the chest by a Soviet sniper, collapsing and dying on the doorstep after uttering an ear-piercing scream.[18] Leon Degrelle, politician-turned-soldier, was now in command, a position for which he was hardly qualified, but as the senior officer in the brigade, there was no other course. His German staff would have to take up the slack, since none of the other Belgian officers had the training or experience to exercise effective command and control.

Degrelle then ordered that Lippert's body be buried beneath an *isba* in order to prevent it from being discovered and mutilated by the Soviets. As the Walloons returned, Siegel and his men went back to the positions they had held north of the town before they launched their counterattack. For his role in the successful counterattack, Siegel learned that he had been nicknamed "Novo Buda" by his division commander, *Oberst* Hohn. During the remainder of the day, the Soviet corps commander, General Selivanov, was content to shell the town while he awaited the arrival of 63rd Cavalry Division. He had not expected such strong German resistance.

As the Walloons crouched in their muddy foxholes, they were racked by chills, as the weather had turned cold once again. Many of them had cast off their heavy winter parkas, felt boots, and overcoats when the weather had turned warm the previous week. They had not noticed the change during the battle that morning, when they were exerting themselves and sweating profusely. Now, they regretted their decision, as the cold wind whipped snow in their faces. Throughout the long night of 13 February and into the next morning, Selivanov's troops kept up pressure against the Walloons and Germans. The artillery fire rarely slackened and more tank noises could be heard in Morentsy. The Soviet troops holding the town's southern outskirts were reinforced and tried to infiltrate into the town, but each time were killed by Degrelle's men. Whenever the sky cleared, fighter bombers and *Sturmoviks* would strafe the village with machine-gun fire, forcing its defenders to stay in their foxholes.

The battle for Novo Buda continued unabated the next day. However, the Soviets decided not to send large numbers of tanks into the village again until more infantry had arrived. Once again, the Cossacks had shown their weakness in house-to-house fighting, especially now that the Walloon Brigade had regained its composure. Besides the Walloons, Selivanov now knew that the Germans had armor in the town as well, which dictated caution on his part. Selivanov tried again the next morning with eleven tanks and had no luck this time either.

As the tanks and Cossacks approached the southernmost tip of Novo Buda, which was still held by some of their own troops who had gained a foothold a few hours earlier, Gerd Schumacher and another tank which had arrived to replace Fiebelkorn's conducted a flank attack against them from the

A panje wagon of the Walloon Brigade on the outskirts of Korsun, February 1944. (Kaisergruber)

A Raupenschlepper Ost full-tracked supply vehicle, as well as many panje wagons of the Walloon Brigade, upon arrival at the Korsun rail station. (Kaisergruber)

west. As the two German tanks approached the unsuspecting Soviets, an alert antitank gun crew fired and hit the barrel of the other Pz.IV with a lucky shot. Again, Schumacher decided to go it alone.

At a range of less than 100 meters, he picked off the T-34s one by one, destroying seven in all before the rest turned around and fled back towards Morentsy. Since he had used up the rest of his armor piercing rounds, he was forced to shoot at the last three with high-explosive shells, which caused their crews to bail out. Although these were relatively undamaged, the noise of the resulting explosions against armor plate so unnerved their crews that they abandoned their vehicles anyway, only to be mown down by Schumacher's co-axial machine-gun. While covered by the other damaged Pz.IV's machine guns, Schumacher dismounted his own tank with grenades and personally completed the destruction of the three derelict T-34s, which were soon in flames.

Another T-34 which tried to escape past his position was knocked out by a armor-piercing shell from a Pz.III which Schumacher had left inside the town. At such a range, even the 5 cm gun on the Pz.III could penetrate the armor of the T-34. For his independent decision to continue his attack in the face of overwhelming odds, Schumacher probably prevented the fall of Novo Buda on two occasions and contributed towards the continued survival of *Gruppe Stemmermann*. For this feat of arms, he was awarded the Knight's Cross. Köller's tank battalion destroyed 32 T-34s from 13 to 16 February while defending the area in and around Novo Buda, Komarovka, and Shanderovka, while losing five of their own.[19]

In the meantime, *Maj.* Siegel learned that he would hand over his own sector to the *Germania* Regiment on the night of 13/14 February. Fritz Ehrath's Hamburg-based SS regiment, including Hans Dorr's *1.Bataillon*, had finally secured Shanderovka, and had been ordered to hand over the town and relieve both Siegel's *Gren.Rgt.266* as well as *Oberstlt.* Hummel's *Gren.Rgt.124*, one of Siegel's sister regiments. Now the defense of Novo Buda was to be almost entirely an SS affair. *Oberst* Hohn, on orders of Stemmermann, directed Siegel to move the

bulk of the regiment to the ridge west of Novo Buda, where it would reinforce the positions held by *Feld.Ers.Btl.72* led by *Ltn.* Bender, that covered the gap between Novo Buda and Komarovka.

Furthermore, Siegel was ordered to turn over the command of his regiment's sole battalion temporarily to *Ltn.* Peters and to make his way to Shanderovka, accompanied only by his regimental command post and engineer platoon. There, Siegel was to serve as that town's *Kampfkommandant* (battle commander), an assignment that elicited little enthusiasm from this battle-wise officer, since he would have to accomplish this thankless task with few troops of his own.[20]

At a last-minute conference that night in Novo Buda between Siegel, Hummel, and Degrelle, the officer representing *Germania* was none other than *Maj.* Heinz von Brese, whose *Pz.Gren.Rgt.108* had been attached to *Wiking* since the beginning of the encirclement. His soldiers and the SS men had been *Waffengefährten* (brothers in arms) for two weeks and Brese himself had earned the respect of men like *Germania's* battalion commanders, Hans Dorr and Kurt Schröder. Siegel could depart knowing that the defenses of the northern outskirts of Novo Buda were in good hands. The movement of *Germania* to its position north of Novo Buda was cause for some controversy the following day, when *Oberst* Hohn of *72.Inf.Div.* complained to Stemmermann that *Germania* was not holding its "fair share of ground."

Apparently Hohn, whose division command post was situated in Shanderovka (while Gille's had been moved to Steblev from Korsun) had seen a great number of idle troops on the morning of 14 February, which apparently was an affront to him, since his own troops at that time were engaged in heavy fighting near Novo Buda and Komarovka. Hohn singled out *Germania* for particularly harsh criticism, stating that Ehraths' regiment had taken over its new defensive positions near Novo Buda with only a small proportion of its available forces, with the rest camped out in Shanderovka.

Hohn's report was endorsed by Stemmermann, who was in Steblev at the time and unable to evaluate the situation in person, and forwarded it by teletype to *8.Armee* headquarters. In Stemmermann's opinion, based on Hohn's report, the failure of *Wiking's* leadership to control its troops was hindering the ability of *72.Inf.Div.* to continue its planned attack to the west. Adding to the controversy was the fact that *Wiking* was supposed to have relieved Hohn's division by 12 February at the latest and that Gille had disobeyed Stemmermann's order to disband his service and supply elements to provide more infantry. The situation was further exacerbated by the feeling of enmity between Gille and Stemmermann's chief of staff, *Oberst* Gädke, who later described the SS commander as a "difficult and headstrong man."[21]

To remedy the situation, Stemmermann ordered Gille to personally attend to the situation by moving his divisional headquarters to Shanderovka, reform the Walloon Brigade, and comb out all of his drivers and support personnel in order to strengthen *Germania* enough to "carry out its assigned mission."[22] This must have been quite an affront to the highly professional SS commander, whose own division had been fighting as hard as any other for the past three weeks. Tempers were fraying. Lieb, who had heard about the affair, noted laconically in his diary the next day that "Since this morning there is trouble at the SS Division. The Walloons and the *Germania* Regiment are getting fidgety. They must hold out only until tomorrow night."[23]

Later that day, Degrelle was told to report to Gille, who had arrived in Shanderovka a few hours before to carry out Stemmermann's order. As Degrelle passed through the sunken road that led to the town, the Walloon leader noted the dead bodies of several German couriers laying along the way, victims of Soviet snipers who prowled the area. Degrelle, perhaps expecting to be congratulated for assuming command of the brigade, was instead surprised to receive a curt command that forbade any retreat from Novo Buda. With steely eyes, the SS commander informed Degrelle through clenched teeth that "The officers are responsible for the troops, and you are responsible for the officers!"[24] Whether or not Gille had been informed of the precipitous flight of the Walloons earlier that

day (he probably had), Degrelle accepted the rebuke.

At least Gille had provided Degrelle with 50,000 rounds of rifle and machine-gun ammunition to take back with him, enough to allow his brigade to hold on another day or so. As for food, there was not much to go around any more. What there was had already been eaten and troops, were now depending upon bread and chocolate rations that were being dropped by the *Luftwaffe* inside supply canisters. Upon his return, he informed his officers that they had to hold on as long as possible, since the continued survival of *Gruppe Stemmermann* was dependent upon them. Degrelle described the situation thus:

> My orders to the officers were firm. Poor lads, all so devoted and so courageous, their skin sallow, their faces gray, their hair unkempt, their eyes hollow, their nerves raw, they had to keep sending hundreds of men back into combat. They really had come to the limit of human endurance . . . The worst hardship was the lack of food. There was not another forkful of meat or a thin slice of bread. There was nothing. The [Wiking] Division had expended its last supplies at Korsun. [My] shivering sleepless men had not been fed for three days. The youngest would faint [from hunger], their faces on their submachine guns.[25]

It is also unknown what Gille told Ehrath, Dorr, or Schröder about the scathing report. Doubtless they would have shrugged off the criticism, though they, too, promptly complied with the order. Dorr, for one, had no cause to feel any shame. Of all the battalion commanders in *Wiking*, he was unanimously considered to have been its most dedicated. A prudent officer who seldom sacrificed the lives of his men needlessly, he was not one to shirk battle.[26]

In retrospect, Hohn's and Stemmermann's assessments seem unduly harsh, though understandable. *Germania* had been involved in house to house fighting in Shanderovka for the past three days against at least three Soviet battalions and dozens of

Horse-drawn supply columns of Wiking line up outside the Korsun rail station. (Jarolin-Bundesarchiv)

On 12 February, Korsun and its airfield was abandoned. Here, some of the last wounded of Wiking to be flown out of the pocket being evacuated. (Photo by Adolf Salie/Willy Hein)

tanks, and had suffered hundreds of casualties. Novo Buda and the surrounding area was vital to the overall German plan and had to be held; similarly, *72.Inf.Div.'s* mission to continue attacking to the west was an important one, but Ehrath had at least two battalions already in position north of the town, not to mention almost all of Köller's remaining tanks, which *Germania's* commander probably felt was enough to carry out his mission. The Walloon Brigade, after recovering from its initial panic, had also fought well, though it still seemed to be held in low esteem by its German Army counterparts, probably due to the fact that not only was it a foreign unit, but an SS unit as well. Degrelle felt that his brigade had been unduly blamed by another unit for "reverses in its own sector . . . as is the custom in the Army"[27]

Despite nearly five years of war and a record of impressive military achievements, many German officers still did not consider the *Waffen-SS* the equal of the *Wehrmacht* in professional ability or social standing. Some SS veterans, after the fact, believed that a certain amount of antipathy or jealousy may have been behind Hohn's report; certainly, they felt that this affair did not deserve to be elevated to attention of the Army commander while all parties to it were still involved in heavy fighting. To those SS officers who knew and respected Hohn, his report at the very least seemed out of character. Some of the junior officers and enlisted men of the *Wiking* saw the matter in an entirely different light.

Officers such as Fritz Hahl saw it merely as a way for the Army to denigrate his division's reputation with falsehoods, since he felt that it was Gille who was strengthening Stemmermann's spine, and not the other way around. He even apparently believed the rumor that was going the rounds of the frontline positions that Stemmermann had tried to surrender earlier but had been prevented from doing so by Gille.[28] Though there is no evidence to support this contention, it does show how some of the troops of the *Waffen-SS* saw themselves in comparison to the Army - they were the tough ones, the reliable ones, who would not flinch in carrying out their *Führer's* orders.

However, Hohn had been right about one thing - Shanderovka was full of a great number of troops who seemed to be doing nothing except trying to find shelter until the relief force approached. Most of them were a mixture of Army, *Luftwaffe*, foreign auxiliaries, *Reichsbahn* workers, Nazi Party administration officials, and even a troop of entertainers, including many German women, who had been trapped 28 January. Thousands of Ukrainian civilians were trapped in the town as well. Again, Degrelle provides an illuminating account:

> We were reduced to an area no greater than 60 square kilometers, into which a human tidal wave flowed. For every man who was fighting, seven or eight men were waiting, crammed into this last valley. There were the drivers of thousands of trucks, sunk into the mud during the withdrawal. There were the personnel of the auxiliary services: administration, supply, hospitals, motor pools, the Feldpost . . . The village of Shanderovka was the capital of this army, hunted for the last eighteen days. This microscopic capital, pounded by sixty hours of fighting, had been reduced to crumbling isbas and broken windows.[29]

Rudolf Siegel's reactions, when he arrived in Shanderovka on the night of 14 February, were similar. He described the "unimaginable concentration of troops and clogging [of the streets].[30]

Even Gille's command post was not immune from the chaos. Degrelle remarked that the headquarters of *Wiking*, *Germania*, and the Walloon Brigade were crammed into one dirt-floored *isba* that had but two rooms. Eighty people were packed into this hut, including the staffs, messengers, wounded personnel, and other soldiers who had been separated from their units.[31] In the middle of this mess stood Gille, receiving a continuous stream of pessimistic reports.

Selivanov's tanks and troops attacked Degrelle's force throughout the day of 14 February, but without success. The continued presence of Gerd Schumacher and his tiny armored force stiffened the Walloon's resolve to hold Novo Buda and enabled them to ward off all of the Cossack's attacks. When the *isba* in the town's center that housed Lippert's body was captured by a group of Cossacks, *Ustuf.* Thyssen led a counterattack and retook the hut. Thyssen had the body dug up, placed on some planks, and dragged back to safety. He had made the decision to carry the corpse along with the brigade during the breakout, a decision which Degrelle fully supported, a measure of the great deal of esteem in which the brigade still held its fallen commander.[32]

Degrelle also did his best to feed his troops and to care for the increasing number of wounded who were being placed in a *kolkhoz* (collective farm) barn on the western edge of town. His medical officer had run out of medicine and had been forced to tear strips of cloth to use in making bandages. The barn provided some protection from the snow and freezing rain which fell intermittently, but none against a hail of shrapnel from nearby artillery bursts. After a direct hit, the roof collapsed, killing dozens of wounded or wounding others afresh. Degrelle organized a convoy to bring as many as could be saved to safer quarters in Shanderovka.

There, carts and wagons full of wounded clogged the streets of the town, since there was no longer any space in Shanderovka's few undamaged buildings to house them. Harried surgeons worked around the clock, but could little to ease the suffering. Many wounded lay in horse-drawn carts covered with blankets, which soon were covered by a layer of snow. Those who died in the carts while awaiting medical attention were removed and laid alongside a street or in a snow bank. Many died from their wounds or from exposure before they could even receive rudimentary treatment.

The fate of the wounded greatly burdened the two corps commanders, who knew that the chances of bringing them out were slim. The breakout would be a risky undertaking as it was; most of the carts carrying wounded probably would not be able to make it through. Rather than condemn these men to certain death, Generals Lieb and Stemmermann decided to leave the non-ambulatory wounded behind in Shanderovka with doctors and medical personnel and hand them all over to the Soviets once the breakout began. Both commanders felt that chances for their survival was better in Soviet hands, as dubious as that was, rather than condemn them to certain death; certainly, it was the

Despite their precarious situation, these Walloons can still find something to laugh about.
(Jarolin-Bundesarchiv 81/16/25A)

only humane thing they could do. There were no longer enough medical supplies, since these essentials, as well as food, had been given a low priority during the airlift, which concentrated primarily on ammunition and fuel. Although there was not much he could do for his wounded, Degrelle did at least manage to get some food to his troops, who had not eaten a full meal since leaving Arbusino four days before. He dispatched several of his more resourceful men on horseback with orders to bring back anything that could be used to feed his men. Several hours later, they came back with bags of flour slung across their saddles. Where they had found them, he did not ask. An oven in a damaged *isba* in Novo Buda was placed into operation, and several bakers were rounded up, while fighting raged on the southern and southeastern corners of the town. All they had to leaven the bread with was sugar, though that was better than nothing.

After a few hours, enough round, flat loaves were made to give each man in his brigade a quarter of a loaf; not much, but better than nothing. Foragers also brought in several "stray" cows, which were promptly butchered with bayonets and hatchets. These chunks were par-cooked over open fires using bayonets and pitchforks as spits. According to Degrelle, "We had neither salt nor spices, but twice a day each man received his chunk of beef, more or less cooked, which he tore with his teeth like a tiger."[33] Degrelle even tried to get soup to his men, though the effort miscarried when the tractor carrying it took eight hours to haul the soup (which had been placed in empty barrels) the three kilometers from Shanderovka to Novo Buda. By the time it arrived, most had sloshed out and the remainder was ice cold. After this experience, Degrelle decided to stick with bread and meat.

As admirable as Degrelle's efforts to feed his men were, it contributed little in actual terms towards the defense of Novo

Buda. Degrelle's greatest contribution to the battle was his driving energy. He frequently visited the men in the forward positions in and around the village. His mere presence among his men, who admired and respected him, helped instill in them the desire to keep fighting and to hold out. Most of the actual direction of the battle had been left to the Walloon Brigade's German staff, with *Hstuf.* Hans Drexel serving as the brigade's operations officers.

Drexel, a 25-year old professional soldier who had formerly commanded *II./Westland,* had his hands full trying to coordinate the actions of the Brigade, the attached tanks from *Wiking,* supporting artillery, and nearly everything else. Drexel was short handed, since his assistant, *Hstuf.* Wegener, who also served as the brigade's liaison officer to *Wiking,* had been killed two days before.

The Soviets, who were exhorted by Konev to take back Novo Buda at all costs, renewed their attack again on the morning of 15 February. Selivanov's Cossacks of 11th and 12th Guards Cavalry Divisions, who were also approaching exhaustion, had been reinforced by 29th Tank Brigade from 18th Tank Corps of Rotmistrov's tank army. After a tremendous artillery barrage, they assaulted the village once again from the south. Unable to overcome the German tanks and assault guns arrayed against them, the brigade commander, Lt.Col. I. Mishenko, ordered one of his officers, Junior Lieutenant Balakin to try and get around the town's defenses from behind. Approaching the town from the west, Balakin and several other tanks carefully crept forward through some gardens and outbuildings.

After driving slowly through the town's outskirts, Balakin spotted a German tank, which fired at him from a range of 200 meters, but missed. Knocking it out with a well-placed shot of his own, Balakin ordered his driver to speed up. As he rounded a corner, he spotted another German tank firing in the opposite direction. He knocked this one out as well. Suddenly, Balakin's T-34 was being fired on from behind. When he turned around, he spotted several German half tracks firing at his tank with machine guns. Shrugging off this insignificant threat, his gunner soon destroyed two of them in rapid succession, though Balakin beat a hasty retreat, since he had been spotted by enemy infantry toting *Panzerfäuste* who were approaching his tank among some *isbas*.[34] Balakin had managed to disrupt the German defense and enable Soviet infantry to seize more of the southern part of the town.

Another Soviet tank commander that fought in Novo Buda that day was Capt. Mikhail Hadai, whose 18th Tank Battalion repeatedly attempted to penetrate the Walloon positions. Hadai, whose own company of T-34s had been hurriedly ordered northward from defensive fighting near Zvenigorodka, recalls that the fighting was exceptionally bitter and that the enemy put up a stout resistance, despite the fact that the town had been virtually obliterated by repeated artillery barrages. This veteran of Kursk later expressed his admiration for the tough Walloons who bravely knocked out his tanks with bazookas and explosive charges, though he could not comprehend why they would fight for Adolf Hitler. During an interview he stated "What did Belgians want from Russia?"[35]

Meanwhile, Gerd Schumacher, the object of Balakin's daring attack, had been able to knock out two T-34s. Several others were knocked out by the Walloons or by the assault guns loaned from the *Polizei* Division. Slowly, the Germans and Belgians were driven back, so that by nightfall, they held only the northern part of Novo Buda. Despite this setback, they still controlled the plateau upon which the village lay. The Walloon Brigade and its attached units bought the time that *Gruppe Stemmermann* needed to concentrate its forces in the valley below for the final breakout attempt.

The Walloons, from their freezing water-filled fighting positions, withheld numerous assaults that day and the next. However, they could not hold out indefinitely, for the brigade would soon run out of men. According to Leon Degrelle:

> The surrounded troops had held out as long as there was hope. Now everything was falling to pieces. We were down to our last cartridges. Since Sunday, the quartermasters hadn't [been issued] any food. The wounded were dying by the hundreds from exposure and loss of blood. We were suffocating under the enemy pressure.[36]

Fortunately, they would not have to hold out much longer. *Gruppe Stemmermann* had reached a decision point.

Fighting raged that Monday and Tuesday not only in Novo Buda, but in Komarovka as well. Selivanov, whose corps was assigned the responsibility of retaking both towns, decided to assign the task of throwing the Germans out of Komarovka to 63rd Cavalry Division. Prior to the attack, the Soviets pounded the village with heavy artillery fire and Katyushka volleys, forcing *Gren.Rgt.105* to seek cover. Then the Soviets attacked. The

Captured Soviet 8.5 cm anti-tank gun manned by troops of Walloon Brigade, on the outskirts of Novo-Buda several days before the breakout. (Jarolin-Bundesarchiv)

cavalry division was reinforced for this attack by elements of General Kirichenko's 29th Tank Corps with 19 tanks and 202nd, 254th, and 62nd Rifle Divisions.[37] Robert Kästner described the fighting which followed as "the hardest that the regiment ever experienced."[38] The Soviets attacked without pause throughout that day and into the night, until the afternoon of 15 February, when their attacks finally abated somewhat.

At one point, when Kästner's troops were in danger of being overrun, a well-timed counterattack spearheaded by four tanks from *Wiking* led by *Uscha*. Schweiss knocked out four T-34s and threw the Soviets out of the village.[39] In 24 hours of fighting, *Gren.Rgt.105* and Schweiss's tanks knocked out 21 Soviet tanks and captured 240 prisoners.[40] They did not even bother to count the enemy dead. The German's own losses had been heavy as well, the price for holding on to this critical area which was to serve as the jump-off position for the breakout attempt.

Meanwhile, to the north where *XXXXII.A.K.* was holding Khilki, the situation had deteriorated alarmingly. While the attack of *XI.A.K.* to the southwest had been an almost uninterrupted series of successes, that of Theo Lieb's corps had stalled 13 February when *Oberst* Bucher had been mortally wounded leading the attack to take Petrovskoye. Lieb still had to worry about pulling back *88.Inf.Div.* to the southern bank of the Ross, which was to take place 15 February. From 13 to 15 February, he would have to contend with numerous penetrations by elements of the Soviet 27th Army along the entire perimeter his troops had established on the evening of 11/12 February.

Towns such as Khirovka, Sklimentsy, and Skripchintsy, which marked the northern perimeter of the breakout area, changed hands numerous times. With each counterattack, Lieb's few remaining combat elements, most of which were from *K.Abt.B.*, grew steadily weaker. With the loss of Bucher, *Oberst* Fouquet was recalled to resume command, since he had been able to hand over the positions held by his *Sperrverband* to *57. Inf.Div.* So far, at least, Lieb had not to worry about tank attacks, which seemed to be directed primarily against Novo Buda and Komarovka.

On the night of 13/14 February, the situation took a turn for the worse, when the Soviets began a concerted effort to

After passing through Korsun, Wiking crossed over the bridge erected upon the top of the hydroelectric dam to the south, where it would occupy assembly areas for the breakout. Town of Korsun in the background. (Jarolin-Bundesarchiv)

retake Khilki, the town closest to the German relief force, whose Tiger tanks and *Jägers* from *Schw.Pz.Rgt. Bäke* were only 12 kilometers away in Khizhintsy. Whether the Germans knew or not that the two forces were so close to establishing contact, the Soviets apparently did and began to switch units to that region in earnest to prevent a linkup. Long convoys of trucks and other vehicles were heard moving from the vicinity of Boguslav towards the Sidorovka area west of Steblev. The Soviet 337th Rifle Division, previously unidentified, made its appearance when it launched an assault that night against the troops of *Rgt.Gr.591* from *Div.Gr.323* holding Chirovka.[41]

Despite these indications of a renewed Soviet effort to block him, Lieb made one more effort the next morning to take Petrovskoye. This attack which got nowhere when the assault battalion became pinned down by heavy machine-gun fire that came from the forest just west of Khilki. After suffering heavy casualties, the Germans beat a hasty retreat to the safety of their positions in the town below. Acknowledging his defeat, Lieb wired Wöhler and requested that he direct a tank attack from the outside towards Petrovskoye, an attack which neither Wöhler nor Breith had the means of carrying out.[42] Stemmermann ordered Lieb to try to reach Petrovskoye one more time that evening, but Lieb only sent out a reinforced reconnaissance patrol to determine if they could establish contact with Breith's armor. They came back several hours later without having found anything but thousands of Soviet troops.

Lieb's corps was also feeling the effects of chronic ammunitions shortages. An attempt by the *Luftwaffe* the night before to drop supplies miscarried when the parachute containers landed behind enemy lines. The *Luftwaffe* blamed Lieb's corps for not properly illuminating the drop zone with search lights, a ludicrous statement, since Lieb's quartermaster officer had been forced to abandon those days ago when the airfield at Yablonovka was given up. The *Luftwaffe* demanded that Lieb then have fires lit that night in a 50 meter long triangular pattern as an expedient, to which he glumly assented.[43] Even doing that was not going to be easy, since the only thing that would burn in the wet, muddy ground was gasoline, which was understandably in short supply. He had no choice but to comply, since his corps badly needed the supplies.

Out of the morning mist on Tuesday, 15 February the troops holding Khilki were surprised when a large attacking Soviet force supported by tanks stormed out of the forest east of the town and quickly penetrated the German defenses. Hand-to-hand combat raged throughout the town and seven T-34s were knocked out with *Panzerfäuste* and grenade bundles. By late morning, Lieb had no idea of the situation in the village, as a wave of troops from 180th, 202nd, and 33rd Rifle Divisions assaulted the troops from *K.Abt.B.* holding Khilki and the surrounding hills as well as *Rgt.Gr 676* holding Skriptchentsy.

Two kilometers to the south, Komarovka was also under attack, as Kästner's troops warded off 63rd Cavalry Division's attack. By late afternoon, most of Khilki had been given up. The position from which the attack towards Breith would be launched had almost been entirely lost. Unfortunately, Lieb no longer had forces available with which to retake the village, forcing him to turn to Stemmermann for help.

Once again, Stemmermann called upon Kästner's *Gren.Rgt.105*. At 1600 hours that afternoon on 15 February, Kästner received a message from division headquarters informing him that his regiment would hand over the defense of Komarovka to elements from *Oberstlt.* Hummel's *Gren.Rgt.124* and move out no later than 2000 hours that night to retake Khilki. Hohn's message stated that "The retaking of Khilki is absolutely decisive for the breakout from the pocket."[44] Despite the knowledge that they probably were going into a hard fight, Kästner wrote that his men were in high spirits because they would soon break out of the *Hexenkessel* (Witch's Cauldron). As usual, Kästner chose to conduct a night attack.

Kästner's regiment was no longer as strong as it had been when it launched its attack against Novo Buda four days before. He had lost 30 percent of his infantry, as well as two self-propelled antitank guns in the fighting for Komarovka. He had also lost one of his two 2 cm self-propelled antiaircraft guns, as well as two of the four artillery pieces from *Art.Rgt.72*. To carry out this next attack, he would only have a total of 255 men, only 180 of which were infantry. Despite their heavy casualties, Kästner described the morale of his men as excellent, who had great trust in their leadership as well as their own fighting ability compared to that of their opponents.

After a brief patrol by *Ltn.* Matthias Roth showed that the territory between Komarovka and Khilki were free of the enemy, Kästner decided to approach Khilki again using a pincer attack from the southwest and southeast. Fortunately, unlike Komarovka, Khilki was relatively small and compact, which would make taking it somewhat easier. The preparations for the assault took place smoothly. The first assault element entered the town at 0130 hours 16 February, finding it to their surprise to be only lightly defended. The sleeping defenders were easily rounded up and sent off towards Shanderovka under a light guard. The regiment quickly oriented itself towards the north and southwest edge of the village to await the inevitable Soviet counterattack, which came from the direction of Petrovskoye at dawn.

This attack was easily smashed. The attackers, after suffering heavy casualties from the fire of the regiment's sole remaining 2 cm *Flak* gun, its artillery and infantry guns, beat a hasty retreat. They came back a few hours later, this time augmented by six tanks with *tankodesantniki* aboard. These, undoubtedly, were from a brigade of General Polozkov's 18th Tank Corps, which had been sent around the pocket from its old positions near Zvenigorodka to lend weight to Konev's efforts to liquidate the encircled enemy before Breith could rescue them.

This attack carried into the village, where Germans and Soviets fought with submachine guns, bayonets, and hand grenades. Four of the tanks were destroyed by the last remaining self-propelled antitank gun or with *Panzerfäuste*. During this battle, which lasted long into the night, Khilki was finally secure, though the self-propelled antitank gun from *Pz.Jäg.Abt. 72* was destroyed, as was the 2 cm *Flak* gun.[45] Attacks during the day failed to so much as dent Kästner's defenses, but by then, he and his men knew that they had only more night in the pocket. The decision to break out had been made.

It had become apparent to Generals Hube and Wöhler since 12 February at the earliest that neither Breith's nor Vormann's relief spearheads would be able to fight their way all the way up to the pocket. Vormann's tanks and troops were stalled just south of Zvenigorodka and had over 28 kilometers to go before they could reach Novo Buda or Komarovka, an impossible distance given the weakness of *11.* and *13.Pz.Div.* Similarly, *1.Pz.Div.* seemed to be held in check at Lysyanka, despite their initially promising seizure of a bridgehead over the Gniloy Tikich, the last river barrier between *III.Pz.Korps* and *Gruppe Stemmermann.* Only 12 more kilometers had to be traversed in order to reach the pocket, but between Breith's men and their objective lay the better part of three tank armies. Looming above Lysyanka was the commanding height of Hill 239, which dominated the area for several kilometers in all directions. Although General Koll and *Oberstlt.* Frank of *1.Pz.Div.* were holding their own against constant Soviet tank attacks, they could not do so forever. Fuel, ammunition, tanks, and men were running short.

Even Field Marshal Manstein, at his command train in Uman knew this, for Hube and Wöhler had kept him fully informed of the battle's development. He saw only one course left - Stemmermann and Lieb would probably have to keep attacking towards Breith. If they sat there any longer in the Shanderovka valley, they would only get weaker warding off repeated enemy attacks and would invite certain destruction, since aerial reconnaissance had confirmed that Zhukov and Konev were assembling their forces to both crush *Gruppe Stemmermann* and cut off and destroy Breith's corps, which now occupied a very narrow finger of land pointing to the pocket. Manstein simply could not afford to let this happen, since he needed both corps for his defense of the Ukraine. Besides which, the field marshal had already vowed that he would not allow another Stalingrad.

What clinched his decision to order Stemmermann to break out on his own was the fact that the situation in *III.Pz.Korps'* sector had deteriorated so alarmingly. The four panzer divisions appeared to have completely expended the last of their offensive capability. If Stemmermann and Lieb's corps were to make it out, they would now have to meet them halfway. Appraised of *III.Pz.Korps'* weakness, Manstein ordered Wöhler

on the morning of 15 February to inform Stemmermann of the change in plans. Wöhler radioed Stemmermann at 1105 hours that day that "Capacity for action by *III.Pz.Korps* limited by weather and supply situation. *Gruppe Stemmermann* must perform breakthrough as far as the line Zhurzhintsy - Hill 239 by its own effort. There link up with *III.Pz.Korps.*"[46]

Wöhler had to make a decision in regards as to whose force would lead the actual breakout attack. Though it may have hurt Wilhelm Stemmermann's professional pride, Wöhler chose Lieb to lead the attack, since he was adjudged, based on reports, to be the "fresher" of the two. Stemmermann, in Wöhler's judgment, lacked the sufficient "inner energy" to take the "necessary measures" that such an assault would require. Manstein disagreed, stating that Stemmermann was used to the pressure of command and that he was confident that he would rise to the occasion, but his army commander won out. Lieb would lead the assault spearhead. Later that day, Manstein called Wöhler again and told him that the moment was quickly arriving for Stemmermann to breakout. In Manstein's words, "Stemmermann must break out under any circumstance."[47]

Wöhler's commander then detailed explicitly how Stemmermann should conduct the attack, even going so far as to tell him how to employ his artillery, how to comb the *Tross* for more troops, and how to employ each division in the breakout so as to concentrate his forces for the actual breakout. He concluded by stating that each general must accompany the assaulting troops in order to insure that each task would be accomplished. The following day, 16 February, Manstein would send another message to Stemmermann that emphasized the importance of achieving surprise and the need for maintaining centralized control over artillery and heavy weapons so that they could be quickly employed at the main point of effort.[48]

Wöhler must have felt somewhat frustrated, since he was unused to being told how to fight his individual divisions by his army group commander. Manstein does not mention in his memoirs how much pressure was being placed upon him by Hitler, commanding "by wire" at his headquarters in East Prussia over 1,000 kilometers away. Hitler certainly was accustomed to doing so - this order from Manstein certainly seems out of character, considering his past record of confrontations with Hitler over the same issue.

When Wöhler passed on the order to Stemmermann, the latter replied exasperatedly "When and with what forces am I supposed to do this?" Stemmermann emphasized the absolute necessity for the *Luftwaffe* to provide air cover for the breakout, a fact that nearly everyone recognized, otherwise the breakout had no chance. Whether Seidemann's pilots could take to the air in the prevailing weather conditions was questionable at best. The die had been cast. *Gruppe Stemmermann* would fight its way out. The date chosen for the attack was Wednesday, 16 February. When asked what password he wanted to use when his assault spearheads encountered the first troops of *III.Pz.Korps*, *Oberst* Gädke, Stemmermann's chief of staff, replied *Freiheit* (Freedom).[49]

After three weeks of encirclement, this word had assumed enormous significance, for it symbolized what the men of *Gruppe Stemmermann* had so longed for since Konev's artillery began thundering on the morning of 24 January. But before the promise that this word signified could be fulfilled, a great deal had to be done. To many men inside the pocket, the distance to overcome seemed paltry in comparison to the road they had already traveled to Shanderovka over the past three weeks. What was twelve more kilometers, after all?

End Notes

[1] Lieb in DA Pam 20-234, p. 24.

[2] Radio Message, *XXXXII.A.K.* to General Speidel, *8.Armee,* dated 2030 hours, 12 February 1944.

[3] DA Pam 20-234, p. 24.

[4] *8.Armee* KTB, entry dated 1805 hours 14 February 1944, p. 5.

[5] Ibid, entry dated 1250 hours 12 February 1944, p. 4.

[6] Ibid, p. 3.

[7] Fritz Hahl, "Die 6.Kompanie/ Panzergrenadier Regiment Westland im Kessel von Tscherkassy." (Pentling, Germany: unpublished private manuscript, 28 March 1996), p. 3.

[8] *Sbornik*, pp. 331-332.

[9] Letter, Karl Schierholz, Butjadingen, Germany, to author, 19 August 1997, pp. 3 - 7.

[10] Letter, Walter Notz, Reichenbach, Germany, to author, 9 July 1997, p. 5.

[11] Erwin Witzer quoted in *Sbornik*, p. 332.

[12] Degrelle, p. 196.

[13] Ibid, pp. 197-198.

[14] Ibid, pp. 198-199.

[15] Siegel, p. 13.

[16] *Gefechtsbericht, I./SS Panzer-Regiment 5*, entry dated 13 February 1944, p. 2.

[17] Degrelle, p. 199.

[18] Ibid, p. 200. In his account, Degrelle insists that before he died, Lippert placed his cap back on his head, so as to die fittingly. While this sounds noble indeed, Siegel's account is more believable.

[19] *Gefechtsbericht, I./SS Panzer-Regiment 5*, p. 2.

[20] Siegel, pp. 13-14.

[21] Pierek, Perry. *Hungary 1944-1945: The Forgotten Tragedy.* (Nieuwegein, The Netherlands: Aspekt b.v., 1998), p. 160.

[22] Radio message, *XI.A.K.* to *8.Armee*, dated 1300 hours 14 February 1944.

[23] DA Pam 20-234, p. 25.

[24] Ibid, p. 202.

[25] Ibid, p. 203.

[26] Letters, Willy Hein, Lauenburg, Germany to author, 27 February 1998 and Günther Jahnke, Munich, Germany, to author, 6 February 1998 (note: Jahnke was serving at the time as General Gille's adjutant and was in training to become a *Generalstabsoffizier*).

[27] Degrelle, p. 202.

[28] Hahl, *Panzergrenadiere der Panzer Division "Wiking,"* p. 197.

[29] Ibid.

[30] Siegel, p. 14.

[31] Degrelle, p. 202.

[32] Ibid, p. 201.

[33] Ibid, p. 203.

[34] Rotmistrov, pp. 330-331.

[35] Interview, Mikhail Yekolevich Hadai, Korsun-Shevchenkovsky, Ukraine, 29 June 1996.

[36] Degrelle, p. 206.

[37] "Combat Operations of 5th Guards Don Red Army Cavalry Corps in the Korsun-Shevchenkovsky Operation," p. 350-351.

[38] MS No. P-143d, p. 17.

[39] *Gefechtsbericht, I./SS Panzer Regiment 5*, entry dated 14 February 1944.

[40] MS No. P-143d/17, p. 17.

[41] Radio Message, *XXXXII.A.K.* to Headquarters, *8.Armee* dated 2247 hours 13 February 1944.

[42] Ibid, message dated 1040 hours 14 February 1944.

[43] Ibid, message dated 1340 hours 14 February 1944 and Lieb's diary, quoted in DA Pam 20-234, p. 24.

[44] MS No. P-143d, p. 17.

[45] Ibid, pp. 18-20.

[46] *8.Armee* KTB, entry dated 1105 hours 15 February 1944, p. 4.

[47] Ibid, p. 3.

[48] DA Pam 20-234, p. 38.

[49] Ibid, entry dated 2155 hours 15 February 1944, p. 7.

Chapter Eighteen
DEADLOCK ON HILL 239

"All of us are expecting the successful arrival of your tanks with confidence."
— *Oberst Gerhard Franz, 15 February 1944*

"When are they coming?" was the question *Hptm.* Ernst Schenk began to hear with increasing frequency. Over 200 of his men had been killed or wounded since they left their fighting positions along the Dnieper. Only a few days before, it had seemed, judging from radio reports emanating from both *1.Pz.Armee* and *III.Pz.Korps*, that the embattled corps and divisions of *Gruppe Stemmermann* were on the verge of being rescued.

Indeed, where were Breith's tanks? A fair question to ask, thought Ernst Schenk, of *Rgt.Gr.110*, located north of Petrushki at what was now the pocket's eastern defense sector. Schenk also wondered what lay in store for him and his men after receiving a message on the morning of 15 February from his acting division commander, General Trowitz. To his surprise, Trowitz ordered that Schenk march his battalion that morning from its current defensive positions to a new position somewhere in the vicinity of Khilki, fifteen kilometers away. He would then report back to his old unit, *Div.Gr.112*. After holding off a series of determined Soviet attacks for the past two weeks, Schenk and his men welcomed the opportunity to vacate their positions and move closer towards the direction where the rescue force of General Breith was expected.

Accordingly, his unit moved out later that morning as part of *57.Inf.Div's* overall withdrawal from the pocket's southeastern flank, leaving the Soviets to be content with searching through their muddy dugouts for momentos. After slogging through the congested streets of Shanderovka in the mud and slush, Schenk and his men collided with another German unit several kilometers southwest of the town. To Schenk and his men, the unit appeared to be fleeing from the fight then going on in Khilki, which had just fallen to the enemy, an incident that led to *Gren.Rgt.105* being ordered to retake the town. Was the breakout plan beginning to fall apart?

After positioning his men where they were in a hasty defensive line, Schenk expected to encounter a Soviet attack at any moment, but no attack came. In the distance, the sound of tank cannon could be clearly heard. But this was not the breakout he thought his *Regimentsgruppe* was being ordered to carry out. Instead, he was issued orders from *Div.Gr.112* directing him to retake Hill 226.8, one kilometer to the north, which commanded the approaches into the towns of Khilki and Skripchintsy. The defending unit from *K.Abt.B, Gren.Rgt.676*, had been thrown off of its summit several hours before, creating a gap in the defenses of the ever-shrinking Pocket. Without further ado, Schenk ordered his troops to attack. Panting heavily as they slogged up the hill, his men reached the hilltop late in the afternoon just as a Soviet unit was forming up on the other side to continue its own attack. His men quickly placed the unit's few machine-guns and mortars into operation and opened fire on the enemy, scattering them.

Schenk promptly ordered his men to dig in. Over the next 24 hours, *Rgt.Gr.110* held off every attack the Soviet 337th Rifle Division launched in their direction. Schenk, for his part, was shocked to find the defenses of the pocket in such disarray. He had expected to find the relief attack only hours away, but now he saw no sign of Breith. To make matters worse, it had begun to snow heavily and there was no shelter at all for him or his men. However, they had little choice but to stay and shiver in their hastily scooped out foxholes. His group of less than 300 men had just been ordered to hold this hill at all costs until relieved. Had he had an inkling of just how desperate the situation actually was, he would have been even more disheartened, for things had begun to deteriorate badly for the German forces both inside and outside the Cherkassy Pocket.[1]

Oberst Gerhard Franz, General Lieb's chief of staff, was certainly under no illusions about what lay ahead for the two encircled corps. He knew that, unless the tanks of *III.* or *XXXXVII.Pz.Korps* could fight their way up to the edge of the pocket, the chances that *Gruppe Stemmermann* could break out on its own were slim. Franz, who had been Lieb's operations officer when the latter had been the commander of *112.Inf. Div.* believed that, with a little luck, they could still succeed if both forces continued to attack towards each other. In a personal message to General Speidel, an old friend of his, Franz stated "All of us are expecting the successful arrival of your tanks with confidence. It is a long way to go, but you can make it if you try."

When Speidel radioed back a note of encouragement on the morning of 16 February, Franz replied "Thanks for the best wishes. We are getting ready [to go]. We are awaiting expectantly the approach of our forces towards Breith."[2] But where was Breith and his panzer divisions? Unless he could advance far enough to seize Hill 239, the successful breakout of *Gruppe Stemmermann* would be in jeopardy. No one inside the pocket had any ideal of the difficulties that Breith and Vormann, his counterpart from *8.Armee*, would face that day and the next. If they failed, even Franz's expectations would be little more than fantasy.

A frost and snow enshrouded Tiger I awaits the Soviets from an ambush position. (Bundesarchiv 279/946/20)

Both Generals Breith and Vormann had both been urging their men forward since the second German relief effort had begun in earnest on 11 February. However, by 15 February, both panzer corps seemed to have run out of steam altogether. Vormann's assault units from *XXXXVII.Pz.Korps* were stymied along the hills south of Zvenigorodka and still had thirty kilometers to go before it would reach the southern flank of the pocket near Novo Buda. Clearly, his attack was going nowhere and by this point could only tie up Soviet units that could have been used against Breith's attack, though this was bitter consolation. General Breith's force had been somewhat more successful, having seized a bridge over the Gniloy Tikich at Lysyanka on 12 February, but *III.Pz.Korps* also seemed to have run up against a brick wall, only twelve kilometers from the pocket's southwestern corner at Komarovka.

Marshal Zhukov and the tanks from 2nd, 5th Guards, and 6th Tank Armies personified the brick wall. Giorgy Zhukov and his rival for Stalin's attention, Ivan Konev, had both sworn not to let a single German escape. To make matters worse for the Germans, General Konev, now solely responsible for the *unichtozhenye* of *Gruppe Stemmermann* (an honor he had enthusiastically sought), was now placing renewed pressure upon the pocket's shrunken perimeter and had begun to exert his considerable energy towards insuring that he would be able to keep his word to Stalin. This would be an achievement that would net him the honors and accolades that would accompany such a glorious victory. But the victory would not be an easy one, Konev realized, as he observed the Germans within the pocket grimly holding off his forces as well as those on the outside struggling forward to rescue their encircled comrades. According to one Soviet source:

From 13 to 16 February there were several exceptionally intense battles in the Lysyanka and Shanderovka regions. The enemy, having committed large tank groups (up to 200 vehicles on a narrow front from the direction of Lysyanka), attempted to link up by means of a simultaneous attack from the Lysyanka region northeast and the Steblev region southwest. All of his attempts were, however, unsuccessful; our energetic counterattacks threw the enemy back to his initial position and inflicted serious losses on him.[3]

This was not exactly true, in that the Germans were able to maintain their positions, and had even managed to approach to within 12 kilometers of the pocket.

General Konev, for his part, was doing his utmost to keep his own promise to Stalin that he would not let a single fascist escape. In his memoirs, Konev wrote that he issued orders to strengthen antitank defenses throughout the narrow corridor separating the two German forces and ordered that thousands of land mines and other obstacles be laid in Breith's path. "Tankproof" areas, under the control of rifle division artillery regiment or antitank brigade commanders, were set up at all vital road junctions, populated centers, and hills. In Konev's words, "The antitank brigades gave an exceptionally good account of themselves…"[4] It now had become obvious to everyone on the Soviet side as to where exactly the Germans would try to accomplish their breakout - from the line Komarovka-Khilki to Lysyanka, making the task of the Soviets much easier.

Zhukov and Konev decisively set about insuring that every available unit they could lay their hands was moved to the Lysyanka area, in order to stymie the Germans. In fact, so much

Oberst Franz, *Chief of Staff, XXXXII.Armeekorps.*
(Shown here as Generalmajor). (Bundesarchiv)

so that the rest of the front held by units of both First and Second Ukrainian *Fronts* had, by 15 February, become strangely quiet, as they had been nearly stripped bare. The same, of course, was true of the Germans, who were forced to denude their own front to build up their relief force, but they had fewer available units to work with. Whoever concluded the battle first would have a decisive advantage over their opponent, since the victor would be able to conclude operations and move them to their enemy's weakest point in order to maintain the initiative.

However, it now had become apparent to both sides that the battle would soon have to conclude in two or three more days at the most; by 15 February, the pocket had shrunk so much that General Lieb stated that he could see the entire defensive perimeter of the pocket from his command post in Shanderovka.[5] It had begun to snow again, a development which Lieb and others welcomed since it would help conceal their preparations for the breakout, now scheduled for 2300 hours 16 February. Fortunately for Generals Lieb and Stemmermann, neither Breith nor Vormann had given up in their attempts to get through the Soviet defense line with their few remaining tanks. The Soviets, for their part, believed that the Germans still had hundreds of tanks involved in this effort, but in actuality, *III.Pz.Korps* had only 59 tanks and assault guns operational as of noon 15 February.[6] Vormann's corps had only ten tanks and assault guns in fighting condition that day as well.

The explanation for the much larger number of tanks the Soviets credited the Germans as having available is due to the fact that the Red Army routinely inflated the number of enemy tanks it faced, as it tended to magnify the scale of their own achievement and partially explain why the Germans almost succeeded in breaking through to Stemmermann's force from the outside. From reading their official reports, one is almost led to believe that the Soviets themselves were outnumbered, but this is not the case - in fact, by 15 February, the Soviets were still able to put two or three times as many tanks into the battle as the Germans, even if their crews were untrained and the tanks had literally just rolled off the production line.

Captain Mikhail Hadai of 18th Tanks Corps stated that his tank company received replacement tanks and crews throughout the battle, and found itself with more tanks on hand at the end of the Korsun-Shevchenkovsky Operation than it did at the beginning! Of course, his company had lost over 100 percent of its original vehicles and a large percentage of its original crews, but his company's experience was not uncommon.[7] Regardless of the number of Soviets tanks they would have to face, both panzer corps would continue their efforts to break through the Soviet ring. But by 15 February, only *III.Pz.Korps'* effort had any chance at all of carving its way through the stubbornly resisting Soviets.

Though the attack of *1.* and *16.Pz.Div.s* had stalled by the evening of 14 February due to lack of ammunition and fuel, as well as by the effects of Soviet tank-led counterattacks, both divisions were able to receive an adequate supply of both gasoline and tank ammunition later that evening when transport planes of Seidemann's *VIII.Flieger-Korps* dropped dozens of containers in and among the houses of Lysyanka. Guided by the headlights of vehicles lined up along the roadway, Ju-52s, flying at rooftop level, wobbled overhead as anxious crewmen kicked crates and fuel drums overboard. A shortage of jerry cans to carry the fuel to the waiting tanks proved to be an unexpected problem, forcing tank crews to pour gasoline from 50 gallon drums into buckets or other handy containers, which were then hoisted up to the tank's deck and poured into fuel tanks.[8] It was not a technique called for by regulations, but this crude field expedient method worked. Ammunition was still in short supply as well. The roads were in such bad of a condition that not even half-tracks could get forward any more.

The roads were, of course, partly to blame for the shortage, but the men of *K.Gr. Frank* and the neighboring *Schw.Pz.Rgt. Bäke* were expending 7.5 and 8.8 cm ammunition at a phenomenal rate. Breith's corps had knocked out over 100 Soviet tanks since the second attempt began on 11 February, but by 15 February, they had to ration every round. With this late-night airdrop, however, both of these spearhead divisions would be able to make another attempt to get up to the pocket the next day. Despite General Wenck's gloomy estimate that Breith's corps no longer had the strength to get through to Khilki or Komarovka, the tank crews and *Panzergrenadiers* of *1.* and *16.Pz.Div.* and *Schw.Pz.Rgt. Bäke* would try their best anyway.

While fighting raged at Komarovka, Khilki, and Novo Buda on 15 February, *K.Gr. Schiller* and *K.Gr. Blömecke* from General Back's *16.Pz.Div.* struggled to block the approach of

Troops from SS-Pz.Aufkl.Abt.1 of the Leibstandarte pause during their approach march to free the troops in the Cherkassy Pocket. (Photo courtesy of Bernd Lerch)

A self-propelled 5cm PaK of the Leibstandarte's armored reconnaissance battalion during a pause in the action. (Photo courtesy of Bernd Lerch)

5th Guards Tank Corps from Medvin along their defensive line between the outskirts of Khizhintsy and Chesnovka. At the same time, it was ordered to lend a helping hand to *1.Pz.Div.* in the latter's effort to break out of Lysyanka towards the line Khilki-Komarovka via Hill 239. To carry out this task, the division was ordered by General Breith to detach the Tiger battalion of *Schw.Pz.Rgt. Bäke*, which had been attempting to break through to the pocket via Khizhintsy, towards the south. The Panther battalion of *17.Pz.Div.* was still struggling to protect the northern flank of Operation "Wanda" between Dashukovka and Bosovka, where it linked up with the grenadiers of General von Horn's *198.Inf.Div.*

The left, or western shoulder, of the German penetration at Tinovka was firmly in the hands of *34.Inf.Div.*, while the right, or southern shoulder, of the penetration towards the pocket was protected by a combination of troops from both *198.Inf.Div.* and *Pz.Aufkl.Abt.1* of *1.Pz.Div.* Twenty-eight kilometers to the east, *K.Gr. Haack* of *XXXXVII.Pz.Korps* was attacking towards them in the hope that it could close up the gap that still separated the two armies.

All of the divisions of *III.Pz.Korps* were in bad shape, but despite their losses in men and materiel, the units guarding the flanks were still able to keep the Soviets at bay and prevent them from cutting off the narrow salient which contained Breith's corps. In the words of *Hptm.* Rolf Stoves, then serving in *1.Pz.Div.*, "There were a number (sic) of infantry divisions (*34.* and *198.)* which were actually the strength of reinforced battalions with infantry strengths of only between 100 and 150 men...but they kept our [flanks] clean."[9] To *1. Pz.Armee's* consternation, the Soviets began to exert pressure against *III.Pz.Korps'* right, or southern, flank on 15 February. "Vigorous" reconnaissance activity was reported near Tikhonovka, defended by *Gren.Rgt.308* of *198.Inf.Div.*

Several probing attacks, most likely carried out by 359th Rifle Division, and were warded off. General Wenck recognized the threat that this renewed enemy activity posed towards *1.Pz.Armee's* open right flank, but after discussing the situation with General Breith, and Hube, decided that they had no

choice but accept the risk since they could not spare any more combat units to shore it up. It would have to wait until *Gruppe Stemmermann* was relieved before any units could be freed up for a counterstrike.[10]

More help for Koll's *1.Pz.Div.* was on the way. During the night of 14/15 February, *Leibstandarte* had pulled out of its old defensive positions between Vinograd and Tinovka and moved its forces, including eight battle-worthy tanks and assault guns, a dozen kilometers to the town of Shubiny Stavy. There, it would serve as Breith's reserve force, although a large part of that division was scattered or intermixed with other units of *III.Pz.Korps*. Nevertheless, *Leibstandarte* was ordered to prepare two battalion-sized *Kampfgruppen* for immediate employment, as soon as they could get sorted out from the interminable traffic jam between Vinograd and Shubiny Stavy. *2.Gebirgs-Division* was also en route, but when it would arrive was anyone's guess. Regardless of whether it was reinforced or not, *1.Pz.Div.*, still bottled up in Lysyanka, would try again that day to break out and continue its advance to the northeast.

Aside from having to worry about how his division was going to break out of its bridgehead in Lysyanka, General Koll had to constantly worry about getting supplies up to his forward units. While the *Luftwaffe's* delivery of fuel and ammunition on the evening of 14/15 February had been adequate, it could not guarantee continued delivery the following evening if the weather once again were to prove unfavorable. Therefore, Koll was forced to try to get additional supplies through on the ground. In order to guarantee that the supplies would get forward, however, Koll was obliged to divert additional combat elements to provide security for the trucks and prime movers. Previous expedient methods had not been enough - the Soviets were still continuing to interdict the division's long supply route which stretched now all the way from Chizhovka to Lysyanka, a straight-line distance of over 17 kilometers (on the ground, the route was more like 30). Carcasses of burned out trucks and *Raupenschlepper* (tracked supply vehicles) littered the route, victims of roving Soviet tanks or infantry ambushes.

BMW motorcycle of the Leibstandarte during the approach towards the pocket. (Photo courtesy of Bernd Lerch)

A Hummel 15cm SP howitzer of the Leibstandarte during the approach towards the pocket. (Photo courtesy of Bernd Lerch)

To deal with this menace that threatened his division's ability to keep fighting, Koll ordered *Maj.* Feig, commander *of* the division's *II./Pz.Gren.Rgt.1,* to take charge of *Gruppe Feig.* To carry out his task of guaranteeing the division's supply routes, Feig had not only his own battalion, but other powerful elements of the division as well, such as seventeen Pz.IVs of *II./Pz.Rgt.1* and a battery from *Pz.Art.Rgt.73.* That General Koll was forced to detach such a powerful combat group to protect his supply lines illustrates the magnitude of the threat posed by the Soviets, many of which were from units that had been bypassed several days before. For the next several days, *Maj.* Feig and his troops were kept busy repelling numerous Soviet attempts to block *1.Pz.Div.'s* lines of communication. His force also had to retake villages in the rear that had fallen to the enemy, even after the battle was over and rescued troops of *Gruppe Stemmermann* were trudging back along these same routes towards their assembly areas. So dangerous was this supply route, that *1.Pz.Div.* convoys evacuating wounded from the fighting in Lysyanka even received an armored escort, usually consisting of four to six Pz.IVs and one or two halftracks.[11]

Meanwhile, in Lysyanka, the combat engineers attached to *K.Gr. Frank* had been able to repair the northern bridge in the town enough so that by the morning of 15 February, it would bear the weight of tanks. They also began work on repairing the eastern bridge as well, though it would only allow trucks to cross, so badly had it been damaged by the retreating Soviets two days before. Throughout that day and through the several that followed, both bridges were attacked every ten minutes or so by the Red Air Force, which tried to cut these lifelines for the elements of *K.Gr. Frank* that occupied the northern part of the town. Although there were many near misses that killed or wounded dozens of men from *Pz.Pi.Btl.37,* these dedicated men would quickly go about their work putting things right again, using planks from *isbas* or telegraph poles as construction material.

As the day progressed that Tuesday, the weather became foggy and hazy, a sign that more snow was on the way. It also concealed attack preparations being made by 11th Guards Tank Brigade of General Kirichenko's 29th Tank Corps, which had

recently arrived in the area. Shortly after noon, the anticipated attack came. With *Tankodesantniki* aboard, a dozen T-34s attacked the northern outskirts of the town. These attacks, which seemed to lack the determination of the those launched against the bridgehead during the past three days, were easily broken up by the Germans, who also suffered losses, though not nearly as great as those of the Soviets.

A small group of T-34s caused a great deal of consternation when they were able to penetrate into the town and race towards the northern bridge. If it fell, the part of *K.Gr. Frank* holding northern Lysyanka would be cut off. A Panther and a rifle squad detailed to protect the bridge were ready for them, quickly knocking out several T-34s and driving the rest away, where they were soon destroyed by other tanks from *Pz.Rgt.1.*[12] Oddly, the attacks petered out by mid-afternoon, but had achieved their purpose of delaying *1.Pz.Div.'s* own attack. The five-tank *Kampfgruppe* from *17.Pz.Div.* holding Hill 216.7 one kilometer northwest of Lysyanka was also attacked that day, but was able to stop the Soviet tanks from 8th Tank Brigade with ease. Were the Soviets regrouping for a more determined and better-planned attack for the following day?

By early afternoon, the Tiger battalion commanded by *Hptm.* Scherff from *Schw.Pz.Rgt. Bäke* had arrived at the southwestern outskirts of the town and linked up with *1.Pz.Div.* Originally detailed to reinforce Frank's battle group for the attack scheduled to take place later that day, the Tigers, at 57 tons each were too heavy for the small bridge over a northern tributary of the Gniloy Tikich and were unable to cross. In order to take part in the attack, Scherff's battalion would have to take a roundabout course that circumvented the small stream to the north, requiring a detour of several kilometers. Their long-range 8.8 cm cannon would be sorely missed elsewhere, for later that day, the eastern outskirts of Lysyanka, defended by a Panther platoon commanded by *Ltn.* Tonn, was fired upon by Soviet tanks in the village of Budishche, nearly two kilometers away. Several Panthers were knocked out, including Tonn's, and several men were killed or seriously wounded. Surely these tanks were not T-34s, the old Eastern Front veterans thought, since they knew that the T-34's gun did not have such range or penetrating power. To their surprise and consternation, *1.Pz.Div's* troops had made their first encounter with the new Joseph Stalin II tank, mounting a powerful 12.2 cm gun. In the words of Rolf Stoves, "[This] tank became a dangerous opponent for our own Panzer IVs and Panthers."[13] These tanks most likely were from a brigade of General Lazarev's 20th Tank Corps, which had been partially re-equipped with this behemoth during their short stay in reserve north of Zvenigorodka. It was a bad omen.

The Soviet tank attacks carried out earlier in the day had cost the Germans time, time that had to be made good. Not waiting for the Tigers to make their appearance, *Oberstlt* Frank launched his attack early in the afternoon. By 1400 hours, his troops and tanks had been able to advance in the face of tough enemy resistance only as far as the rail line that ran in an arc north and northeast of Lysyanka. By mid-afternoon, Scherff's battalion, part of the attached *Jäger* Battalion, and the command group from *Schw.Pz.Rgt. Bäke* had arrived after their detour around the creek and linked up with the leading elements of *K.Gr. Frank.*

Frank, in cooperation with Scherff, planned to seize the small village of Oktyabr that day and continue the attack in order to seize the critical commanding heights dominated by Hill 239. By dusk, the Germans were able to advance only as far as the southern outskirts of Oktyabr and the small forest east of the village, after encountering a large number of Soviet tanks reinforced by an antitank barrier. Here, Frank and Scherff were tied up in heavy fighting that prevented them from advancing any further that day.[14] After stopping to refuel and replenish ammunition, they would try and push through to the pocket the following morning, 16 February.

That evening, General Wenck surveyed the discouraging results of the day's fighting. Well aware of *Gruppe Stemmermann's* critical situation, he was also becoming increasingly pessimistic that *III.Pz.Korps* would be able to break through in time. In a discussion with Generals Hube and Breith, Wenck decided to notify both Army Group South and *8.Armee,* to include *Gruppe Stemmermann,* that *III.Pz.Korps'* future offensive capability was limited, which meant that Stemmermann and his troops would have to break out on their own and link up with Breith's spearhead. This resulted in the message that was issued a few hours later, as discussed in the previous chapter, which directed *Gruppe Stemmermann* to break out on the evening of 16/17 February and link up with *K.Gr. Frank* along the line Zhurzhintsy-Hill 239. In the Army combat journal for that day, Wenck wrote despairingly:

> The attack of *1.Pz.Div.*, reinforced by [K.Gr.] Bäke, gained ground today with great difficulty. It is now clear to everyone that the only hope for success now rests with 1.Pz.Div.... All eyes today rests upon Koll and Bäke. Through mechanical loss of weapons and vehicles, a consequence of the severe weather conditions, the combat powers of the divisions are further diminished. The loss of men and material due to enemy action is considerable. In spite of this, our tough Panzergrenadiers and tanks are punching their way grimly forward and are pushing the

enemy back to the east and northeast meter by meter. . . Against the rest of the [corps] front the enemy made only a few weak attempts to advance. Apparently, he is regrouping so that he can continue his counterattacks and is awaiting the approach of further reinforcements. . . We can assume, that the [enemy's] preparations will be concluded shortly and further attacks are expectedly to take place directly. . . [15]

In fact, Zhukov, controlling all Soviet units defending against *1.Pz.Armee's* relief attempt, was both bolstering the defense as well as gathering forces for a counterattack.

The defenses in the Lysyanka area received special attention. According to one account, both 3rd Tank Corps from 2nd Tank Army and 20th Tank Corps from Rostmistrov's 5th Guards Tank Army, reinforced by two rifle divisions and an antitank brigade, were arrayed against *1.Pz.Div.* and *Schw.Pz.Rgt. Bäke.* In real terms, this worked out to a density of 8 to 10 tanks, 30 to 36 artillery and mortar tubes, and one-half to eight-tenths of a rifle company per kilometer of front, a fairly dense grouping of forces. Soviet combat engineers reportedly laid 20,000 antitank mines in the German's path. According to this account, Lysyanka changed hands several times and that:

> Despite of this troop density, the overall ratio of forces favored the Germans.* Only through the heroic resistance of the Soviet officers and men. . . were the German troops prevented from advancing further, forcing them on 18 February to finally go over to the defense along their entire breakthrough sector.[16]

The Soviet after-action report for the Korsun-Shevchenkovsky Operation also does not credit the Germans with making any advance at all that day; in fact, it states that "our energetic counterattacks threw [the enemy] back to his initial position and inflicted serious losses on him."[17]

Perhaps the best description of the fighting in and around Lysyanka is summed up by General Pavel Rotmistrov, who stated that "The battles in the Lysyanka region became extremely fierce, during which the enemy was bled white."[18] It might be added that a large portion of 5th Guards Tank Corps was bled white as well. *1.Pz.Div.* had indeed suffered heavy losses during the past four days of fighting, with its tank companies down to three to four tanks each and *Panzergrenadier* battalions down to 50 to 100 men, at the most. But *1.Pz.Div.*, the *Wehrmacht's* most senior armored division, still had some fight left in it, as the Soviets were to discover the following day.

Wednesday, 16 February 1944 began with a further worsening of the weather situation. The temperature stayed below

---

* This is not supported by the facts. At this time (15 February), *1.Pz.Div.* had no more than 27 tanks operational, including those engaged in the supply convoy effort.

freezing most of the day, accompanied by a heavy frost the night before. Snow began to fall heavily, once again carpeting the ground with up to a foot of powder in some places and drifted to a depth of three feet in ravines or *balki*. To prevent their tank's treads from freezing to the muddy ground, crewman placed logs or boards from nearby *isbas* under their treads. Failure to do so would cause damage to the tank's engine, drive train, or running gear, as the tanks strained to break free from the ground's icy grip. Three Pz.IVs of *1.Pz.Div.* were damaged in this way, and could not be recovered, forcing their crews to prepare them for demolition. In the meantime, they would serve as static pillboxes.[19]

But the men of *K.Gr.Frank* and the Tiger crews from *Schw.Pz.Rgt. Bäke* had no time to worry about the weather – they were fixated on the attack planned for that day instead. At least the snowfall grounded the Red Air Force. As they prepared to resume their attack towards Oktyabr and Hill 239, Frank's and Bäke's troops could also hear the sounds of heavy fighting to the north, where both *16.* and *17.Pz.Div.* and *34.* and *198.Inf.Div.* were involved in heavy fighting against Zhukov's renewed attempt to cut off *III.Pz.Korps*.

Attacks of regimental strength with strong tank support were launched against *16.Pz.Div.'s* positions at Chesnovka and Dashukovka by the Soviet 3rd Tank Corps, supported by 206th and 340th Rifle Divisions. *K.Gr. Collin* and *II./Pz.Gren.Rgt.64*, protecting General Back's division eastern flank, were tied down in heavy fighting just west of Khizhintsy. The battle swung back and forth all day, but nightfall found 16th Panzer in possession of the battlefield. During that day's fighting, General Back's division had destroyed 19 Soviet tanks and assault guns.

One Soviet attack in company strength, on *16.Pz.Div.'s* western flank, was able to break through and cross the road connecting Dashukovka and the division's supply base in Frankovka and shot up several supply trucks. A quick-thinking officer, *Ltn.* Larsen, collected a few troops from the *Tross* and launched a counterattack that quickly drove off the enemy. Sixty dead Soviet infantrymen were counted. The troops of *16.Pz.Div.* that day counted 400 enemy dead in front of their positions, mute testimony to the ferocity of the fighting, characterized by one witness as the end result of "Resistance of a fanatical opponent who was prepared to pay any price to prevent the freeing of [our] encircled troops."[20]

Soviet attacks launched against *17.Pz.Div.* were also unsuccessful, though it led to several tense moments. *198.Inf.Div.* was heavily engaged that day as well. That morning, two battalions of 9th Motorized Brigade attacked Vinograd and were able to achieve a breakthrough in the sector held by *Gren.Rgt.326*. The commander responsible for the town's defense ordered his reserve force, the regiment's combat engineer platoon, to counterattack. Supported as it had been a few days before by several assault guns, the platoon was once again able to surprise the Soviets and eject them from Vinograd at small cost to themselves. In Tolstyye Rogi, another one of *198.Inf.Div.'s* regiments had to counterattack and force back a Soviet battalion from 3rd Guards Airborne Division. In the words of one eyewitness, "The enemy paid for this advance with very bloody losses."[21] On *198.Inf.Div.'s* left flank, *34.Inf.Div.*

held fast, despite renewed attacks against Tinovka and Pavlovka by 104th Rifle Corps and inflicted heavy losses on the enemy, including the destruction of tanks.

Wisch's *Leibstandarte* spent most of the day on the march towards its new assembly area in Frankovka. Shubiny Stavy was deemed to be too far away for the division to be of immediate use, so after only a few hours after arriving there, it was ordered off by *III.Pz.Korps* towards Frankovka, to be put at the disposal of the corps for possible employment in either Lysyanka or Oktyabr, in order to bolster *K.Gr. Frank*. The division's lead element, *K.Gr. Sandig*, drawn from its *SS-Pz.Gren.Rgt.2*, consisted of only three officers, eight NCOs, and 76 men. It had been somewhat larger before the *Kampfgruppe* departed Shubiny Stavy, until the commander had ordered a health inspection, forcing him to leave behind 44 men because of illness.

Reduced in size almost by half, this tiny *Kampfgruppe* set out towards Frankovka at 1500 hours. Upon arrival, *Ostubaf.* Rudolf Sandig, the regimental commander, was ordered to proceed to Lysyanka, report to *K.Gr. Frank*, and prepare to launch an attack that evening. Here, he received a more detailed set of instructions, which specified that:

> The LSSAH is to send its advance detachment (K.Gr. Sandig) immediately and the bulk of his forces as soon as possible, to Oktyabr. These forces are to attack across Hill 239 in close cooperation with [K.Gr. Frank] of 1.Pz.Div. This attack will create the necessary conditions for a reunification with the encircled elements. The LSSAH and 1.Pz.Div. are to hold the terrain reached and they should improve their position toward the front as circumstances allow . . . The physical condition of the forces coming out of the encirclement will be such that they cannot be put into battle immediately. The [Leibstandarte] is to assure care for these elements and the safe return of their wounded behind the front.[22]

Sandig's troops, already exhausted from their march from Votylevka-Tinovka salient, trudged towards their new assignment. *K.Gr. Heimann*, formed from perhaps 120 men of *SS-Pz.Gren.Rgt.1*, was also sent to Lysyanka and departed Frankovka at 1800 hours.

Both *Kampfgruppen* arrived by 2300 hours, the same time that *Gruppe Stemmermann* was scheduled to begin its breakout. Not much in terms of overall combat power, they still represented a significant addition to the forces available to General Koll. That same day, the *OKW* awarded the Oak Leaves to the Knight's Cross to Teddy Wisch. He had earned this higher grade of Germany's highest award for valor in recognition of his leadership of his division during the previous November's offensive to retake Kiev.[23] Although this was a great honor indeed, he was unable to receive the award that day due to ongoing operations.

The main action that day revolved around *K.Gr. Frank* and the attached Tiger battalion from *Schw.Pz.Rgt. Bäke*. In the early morning hours, low-flying Ju-52 transports were able to drop enough 50-gallon drums of gasoline and crates of tank ammunition an area directly north of Lysyanka. Although many of these burst upon impact, Frank's and Dr. Bäke's troops, for once, had enough of both to see them through the fighting that day. While most troops had not seen warm food for days and had not shaved or bathed for nearly a week, they were determined to give a good account of themselves. Nearly everyone who took part in the fighting that day remarked later how the very air around him seemed to crackle with the intensity of the fight.

While most written accounts of the events that followed give some sense of the dramatic nature of what *K.Gr. Frank* experienced, the actual fighting was much more intense for the actual participants. The fighting that Wednesday was the worst many veterans of *1.Pz.Div.* had ever seen. Frank and Bäke, accompanied by 150 or so remaining infantrymen from Ebeling's *II./Pz.Gren.Rgt.113*, began their combined attack early that morning across the snow-covered slope stretching uphill towards Oktyabr and Hill 239. They were immediately confronted by a Soviet counterattack consisting of 20 T-34s launched by a tank brigade from 5th Guards Tank Army's 20th Tank Corps from the direction of Oktyabr. The Germans immediately halted and returned fire.

Aided by well-directed artillery support being provided by *Oberst* Söth's *Pz.Art.Rgt.73*, the German tanks poured a withering fire into the ranks of the onrushing Soviet tanks, forcing them to turn around before they reached the rail line that ran north of Lysyanka. *I./Pz.Rgt.1* (minus one company) under *Hptm.* Cramer continued their attack towards the northeast and reached the outskirts of Oktyabr by 0630 hours. The rest of the German force under Frank and Bäke temporarily took up defensive positions orienting northeast towards Hill 239 when they came under heavy Soviet tank and anti-tank fire.

As the main attack was unfolding on the northern bank of the Gniloy Tikich, the eastern part of Lysyanka came under renewed attack, when the few tanks left there providing security reported a strong tank-supported attack coming from the direction of Hill 222.5, due east of their position. To deal with this serious threat, Cramer dispatched *Ofw.* Strippel with three Panthers towards the threatened sector, where they joined the other four that were anxiously waiting their arrival. Picking good hiding positions among the *isbas*, outbuildings, and hedges on the town's eastern outskirts, Strippel and his companions made good use of the Panther's formidable range and accuracy. During the next several hours, 27 T-34s were destroyed, of the 30 that took part in the attack, against the loss of only one Panther, *Fw.* Zies'. For the time being, at least, this serious threat had been averted. At the same time, 20th Tank Corps launched an attack against the southern part of Lysyanka, held by several Pz. IVs of *Oblt.* Mischke's company from *II./Pz.Rgt.1* and a platoon of combat engineers. Here again, German tank gunners, ably supported by the artillery, were able to ward off any successful penetration of the division's long right flank.

While the battle raged north of Lysyanka, General Koll paid a visit to the staff of *K.Gr. Frank* at 1230 hours. He was joined a short while later by General Breith, who made yet another flight to the town aboard his Fiesler *Storch*, and Frank, who had only just begun his attack. Leaving *Hptm. Graf* von Wedel in charge of supervising the attack, Frank and his staff

were told of the heavy defensive fighting involving both *16.* and *17.Pz.Div.* to their north, as well as the efforts that were underway to get more fuel and ammunition up to their position. Breith remarked that he had been informed that it was the view of the *OKH* that "The pocket had to be liberated from the outside, no matter what the circumstances dictated."[24]

Both Generals Breith and Koll must have been under tremendous pressure to achieve results. Despite the fact that General Hube had already determined that *1.Pz.Div.* was not strong enough to break through to Stemmermann's force on its own, Hube perhaps believed that Koll and Breith, if pushed hard enough, could still make it. If *1.Pz.Div.* had been the same unit as one week before, and had the ground been firm enough to support his division's wheeled supply vehicles, it probably could have done so. But by 16 February, *1.Pz.Div.* more closely resembled the decimated *16.* and *17.Pz.Div.* than it did its former self. At least *Leibstandarte* had two *Kampfgruppen* on the way to lend a hand.

Shortly before noon, Cramer of *I./Pz.Rgt.1* and Ebeling, of *II./Pz.Gren.Rgt.113*, received the order from Frank to take Oktyabr – this time, for good. To do so, Cramer's Panthers and Ebeling's grenadiers - that is, the last 50 or 60 men of his battalion, augmented by another two dozen men from *II./*

Oberleutnant Freiherr von Dörnberg, *Pz.Rgt.1, 1.Pz.Div. (shown here as a private). His tank company held firm in Oktyabr despite dozens of Soviet tank attacks. (Photo courtesy of Freiherr von Dörnberg)*

Oberleutnant Dörnberg *in his Panther during the advance towards Lysyanka. (Photo courtesy of Freiherr von Dörnberg)*

Panther of 1st Panzer Regiment in assembly area near Lysyanka. (Photo courtesy of Freiherr von Dörnberg)

Pz.Gren.Rgt.1 - would have to cross the wide-open snow-covered slopes leading up to the village, which offered no cover at all. Under the covering fire of a platoon of four Panthers commanded by *Ltn. Freiherr* von Dörnberg, Ebeling's men braved the heavy defensive fire coming from the village.

The grenadiers were able to race the last few steps up the hill and seize a north-south running ravine a hundred meters west of the town, from which they were able to find cover from the rather heavy enemy fire. Ebeling's losses were not inconsiderable; nearly a dozen of his men lay dead or writhing upon the open slope behind the ravine in which they crouched. Worse, three of the accompanying Panthers got mired when they ventured out across a snow-covered swamp, leaving only Dörnberg's tank to accompany them the rest of the way.

Fortunately for Ebeling and Dörnberg, the main body of *K.Gr. Frank* had pushed ahead at the same time several hundred kilometers east of Oktyabr, using the road that ran due northeast from Lysyanka to Hill 239. This road, which passed through a deep cut in the side of the hill, provided sufficient cover for Wedel and the dozen or so tanks he had with him that allowed his force to approach the town unobserved from the east. The T-34s protecting this avenue of approach had fled when *K.Gr. Frank* began engaging them with accurately directed artillery fire, leaving their comrades in Oktyabr unaware of what was about to hit them. In addition, the nine remaining Tigers of Bäke's regiment were approaching Oktyabr from the northwest, where they drew the immediate attention of the defending Soviets long enough to allow Ebeling to begin his attack.

Ltn. Dörnberg used the moment to good effect. Ordering his driver to move forward from his tank's concealed position in the *balka*, he and his gunner quickly sighted and knocked out four T-34s with their 7.5 cm gun. Supported by Wedel's force approaching from the east, Ebeling's men let out a loud "Hurrah!" and stormed out of the ravine towards the village. In a few moments, they quickly overran the surprised defender's first line of defense. The fight quickly degenerated into a house-to-house struggle.

Ltn. Leben, Ebeling's last remaining company commander who had led his men across the icy Gniloy Tikich several days before, was killed in action and all of his other platoon leaders were killed or wounded. By noon, Oktyabr was in the hands of what remained of Ebeling's battalion.[25] Losses had been heavy; companies had been reduced to an average of ten to twelve men each. Ebeling's only remaining officer was his adjutant, *Ltn.* Katzmann, who was now serving as his second-in-command. With this small force of less than 100 men, Ebeling was supposed to defend Oktyabr.

Despite its losses, *K.Gr. Frank* was able to set up a defensive line that now stretched in a ragged line from Oktyabr to northern Lysyanka. Just as the Germans were getting settled into Oktyabr, a Soviet counterattack against their positions was observed approaching from the northeast. In the nick of time, the three Panthers that had gotten mired had extricated themselves from the swamp and rejoined Dörnberg. The counterattack quickly evaporated, when the leading Soviet tanks were shot up or damaged. To cover the road that led to the intersection atop Hill 239, Dörnberg advanced up the hill and positioned his tank alongside the road to serve as a roadblock should the Soviets attempt to use this route to launch another attack.

Shortly afterward, he was joined by several other Panthers of Wedel's force, as well as by several badly needed squads of grenadiers and combat engineers. During their approach, Dörnberg's battalion commander, *Hptm.* Cramer, was mortally wounded when the rest of *K.Gr. Frank* crested the long slope and encountered a strong enemy antitank barrier. Several other veteran tank commanders and their crews were killed or wounded during this engagement as well, which kept the tank regiment's medical personnel busy with emergency medical treatment and the evacuation of wounded to the aid station in Lysyanka. *I./Pz.Rgt.1,* which had provided the backbone for the seizure of Lysyanka and the advance towards Hill 239, was now reduced to a total of twelve operational Panthers. Others that had suffered battle damage or mechanical failure were left in Lysyanka to serve as stationary antitank positions. The regiment's mechanics

During a pause in the fighting, tank crewmen from 1st Panzer Regiment discuss the situation.
(Photo courtesy of Freiherr von Dörnberg)

Signpost showing the way for 1st Panzer Division.
(Photo courtesy of Freiherr von Dörnberg)

labored unceasingly but could never get enough tanks back into operation to redress the balance.[26] A bypassed enemy position in the small forest 200 meters east of Oktyabr gave the Germans a great deal of trouble; several attempts to take the woods broke down in the face of determined Soviet tank and antitank gun fire. Unless *K.Gr. Frank* could destroy or neutralize its defenders, any attempt to continue the approach would be vulnerable to flanking fire and possible destruction. Finding any way around the problem was hopeless; the position had to be taken.

After communicating with the division's attached *Luftwaffe* forward observer, Wedel requested an air strike. A short while later, several waves of *Stukas* from Rudel's *Immelmann Geschwader* made their first appearance in two days. *Stuka* after *Stuka* rolled in on the target for perhaps 15 minutes and dropped their bombs, which nearly obliterated the little forest and the larger one due south of the road intersection atop Hill 239. Secondary explosions from red-hot shells shook the air and filled the sky with plumes of black smoke. With this pocket of resistance finally eliminated, *K.Gr. Frank* could rest and count its losses.

After Oktyabr had fallen, the remaining nine Tigers of *Schw.Pz.Rgt. Bäke,* accompanied by nine half-tracks carrying infantry from their attached *Jäger* battalion, pressed forward the attack towards Hill 239 and the village of Zhurzhintsy, two kilometers away. *Hptm.* Scherff, standing in the open commander's hatch of his Tiger, led the advance another kilometer and a half against light resistance. His tanks actually reached the road intersection at the summit of Hill 239, thus opening the way for their regiment, as well as the rest of *K.Gr. Frank,* to fight its way through to *Gruppe Stemmermann*, a scant ten kilometers away. Never had their liberation been so close. As Scherff's command tank reached the hilltop, he noticed that the road that led northwest to Zhurzhintsy, one kilometer away was free of the enemy. If he could seize that town quickly, the escape route of Stemmermann's force would be secured.[27]

However, Scherff noticed that the *Stuka* attack had not completely subdued the enemy. Despite the pounding, the tough Soviet antitank gun crews, probably from 41st Guards Rifle Division, manhandled four 7.62 cm antitank guns into position, less than 100 meters away from Scherff's Tiger. To his amazement, the Soviet gunners calmly loaded and aimed their guns at his and the other tanks. Reacting first, Scherff's tank and several others fired at their enemy, but none of their shots had any noticeable effect - they discovered that they were shooting armored piercing ammunition instead of high explosive shells, which were better suited for "soft" targets such as guns or unarmored vehicles.[28]

The Soviets fired; even at this close of a range, their shells caromed of the bow armor of the 57-ton behemoths. Scherff's and the other Tigers responded with machinegun fire; simultaneously, he ordered his *Jägers* to withdraw further down the hill where their *SPWs* would not be as vulnerable. Suddenly, three T-34s appeared from a stand of trees on the northern side of the road intersection several dozen meters away. These Soviets tanks were soon flaming hulks, victims of the Tiger's powerful 8.8 cm gun. Scherff ordered his tanks to take up a 180 degree defensive arc that covered the westerly approach route from Zhurzhintsy, to the north, and along the road where it lead east towards the village of Pochapintsy, which lay at the bottom of the slope two kilometers away.

Scherff and his men soon became the object of attention for a large number of enemy antitank guns and tanks firing in concealed positions from the direction of the two villages. Shells bounced off the turret armor and flanks of the Tigers. *Fw.* Fendesack's Tiger took a direct hit in the engine compartment by a shell fired from the direction of Zhurzhintsy. The engine quickly caught on fire, forcing the five-man crew to bail out and seek safety inside two neighboring tanks, as their tank's ammunition began to "cook off," sending bits and pieces of its interior flying into the air. A T-34 that was hiding in the woods behind them was chased out of its position by the accompanying *Jäger* and was quickly destroyed by Scherff's tank. Grudgingly, he had come to the conclusion that it was too dangerous to remain much longer in this position; it would be better to seek safety by joining up with the rest of *K.Gr. Frank* further down Hill 239's southwestern slope.[29]

Scherff's battalion (only eight tanks were left out of the 34 he had started with three weeks before) had done enough for one day. Just as his unit began its withdrawal, it was attacked by five T-34s, again from the direction of Zhurzhintsy. These were quickly spotted and engaged by the three Tigers on the left flank. Three of the T-34s were destroyed in short order, while the two survivors turned around and headed back at top speed to the safety of the village. Shortly thereafter, Scherff's tanks and his half-tracks full of *Jägers* were safely back within their own lines, several hundred meters down the long, open slope that stretched towards the Lysyanka valley. They would try and retake the hill again the following day. Had they known what would soon unfold, they would have held on to Hill 239 regardless of their losses.

As Scherff made his way back to Bäke's command post in a *balka* located on the northern edge of Oktyabr to make his report, his regimental commander greeted him with a plate of fried potatoes and wished him "*guten Appetit*" (bon appetite). Bäke's orderly had found the potatoes and bacon fat in a root cellar of one of the *isbas* that had been occupied by the Soviets a few hours before. Scarcely had he finished his meal (the first hot one he had eaten in over a week) when the air was torn by the sound of tank cannon firing nearby. Running out of the house, Scherff stumbled and fell face-first onto the snow-covered ground. As he rose, a bypassing soldier asked him if he was wounded, though he was only stunned. Reaching his tank, he found *Fw.* Fendesack, whose own Tiger had been destroyed atop Hill 239, standing in his commander's hatch. Less than 100 meters away burned four T-34s.

After he had recovered from his initial shock and surprise, Scherff asked what had happened. His gunner, *Fw.* Mueller, told him that Fendesack had spotted the Soviet tanks approaching along the upper edge of the *balka*. Fendesack, an experienced veteran of Russia, quickly jumped into the turret, gave the command to fire, and all four tanks were in flames in less than two minutes. Where the T-34s had appeared from, nobody knew, but the Soviets appeared to be able to infiltrate the German's lines at will. Bäke, who had approached while Scherff was speaking to Mueller, praised the crew's performance.

Scherff then rejoined Bäke for a continuation of their previous discussion. *1.Pz.Div.* had instructed Bäke and his two tank battalions (the eight remaining Panthers had in the meantime been ordered to rejoin Bäke's regiment) to hold their current positions, while a *Kampfgruppe* from *Leibstandarte* retook the forest due south of Hill 239 that night. Then, once the hill was securely in German hands, Dr. Bäke's remaining Tigers and Panthers would move up and occupy defensive positions atop the heights while they awaited the arrival of *Gruppe Stemmermann*. Scherff was also told that General Koll had placed Bäke in command of all German forces that lay on the northern bank of the Gniloy Tikich because *Oberstlt.* Frank had been seriously wounded by a Soviet shell a few hours before. "Should the breakout of the encircled units fail to succeed," Bäke told Scherff, "we will lead a combined tank attack of both *1.Pz.Div.* and our regiment towards Komarovka." That was all the instruction that Scherff needed, as he set about preparing his few remaining tanks for the next day's action.[30]

Ju-87D Stukas flying over the wintry Ukrainian landscape. Unfortunately, clear flying conditions like this seldom prevailed, forcing the troops of Gruppe Stemmermann to do without close air support. (Photo courtesy of Bernd Lerch)

Twenty-eight kilometers to the southeast, *XXXXVII.Pz.-Korps* had not given up in its effort to take Zvenigorodka and to tie down as much of Zhukov's forces as possible. By Tuesday, 15 February, both Wietersheim's *11.* and Mikosch's *13.Pz.Div.*, at the end of their strength, vainly kept trying to break through the defensive positions stoutly held by five rifle divisions of 49th Rifle Corps. Nor was Vormann's corps able to "bind up" many of the Soviet armored and mechanized reserves by this point either. Except for a tank brigade, nearly all the other Soviet tank units had departed the field to add to the forces being hastily assembled to block *III.Pz.Korps* at Lysyanka. The four Soviet rifle divisions (375th, 110th Guards, 233rd, and 94th Rifle) and one airborne division (6th Guards) positioned in the Zvenigorodka area, supported by several artillery and antitank regiments, were proving themselves to more than enough forces to keep Vormann from going any further.

The two attacking German divisions had fewer than five tanks and assault guns apiece and simply did not have the power to punch through this array of forces, much less lead a successful assault on Zvenigorodka. Even the addition of *3.* and *14.Pz.Div.* would not do much to redress the balance. Dissatisfied with this state of affairs, General Wöhler ordered Vormann to have Wietersheim's division send a force ahead in order to cut the Soviet supply route than ran atop hill 208.9, several kilometers north of *11.Pz.Div.'s* present positions. There, large numbers of Soviet tanks and trucks could be seen heading west almost undisturbed. If *XXXXVII.Pz.Korps* was supposed to tie up as many of the enemy's forces as possible with its limited attacks, it did not appear, at least to Wöhler and his staff, that it was doing a very good job of it.

Wietersheim's division was too weak to do even that, since it would have to overcome at least one defensive line held by 110th Guards Rifle Division. To add to the corps commander's troubles, Wöhler was continuing to lecture Vormann over the radio about spending so much time away from the front line, since he believed that a visible display of his "determination and willpower would be sufficient to urge his weary troops ahead to victory." The friction between the two commanders appears to have come to a head during the final stage of the battle, leading, it seems, to the point where General Wöhler was far more concerned with criticizing Vormann's performance as a corps commanders than with the actual battle in progress.

How Vormann felt at the time is unknown. He did not criticize Wöhler in his monograph about the battle he wrote after the war, though he must have felt unfairly singled out for criticism. On 15 February, for instance, Wöhler, when told by the corps staff that Vormann could not be reached again because he was en route from his forward command post back to his main corps command post at Yerki, radioed back in frustration to *XXXXVII.Pz.Korps'* Chief of Staff, *Oberst* Walter Reinhard, "You must make it undoubtedly clear [to Vormann] that he had better find himself at the front again!"[31]

In addition, Wöhler told him in no uncertain terms that the corps would make a renewed attempt to continue its advance that evening, since the experiences of the past few days (such as the attack against Novo Buda by *Gren.Rgt.105*) had shown that a night attack had a better chance of success against the entrenched Soviets than one carried out during the day. This was only restating the obvious, since accurate Soviet artillery fire and ground attacks by alert Red Air Force pilots had made any daytime movement of Vormann's divisions foolhardy. It is doubtful whether Wöhler would have allowed Vormann's forces to sit idle until nightfall. The commander of *XXXXVII.Pz.Korps* must have certainly felt that regardless of how he carried out his assignment, he would have been criticized for the manner in which in did it.

Vormann wrote afterwards that he was far more concerned with keeping his divisions from being destroyed than with continuing the attack north. He knew better than anyone else did that his divisions were no longer capable of carrying out any sort of effective attacks. Besides, he was more concerned with what would happen when the relief of *Gruppe Stemmermann* was completed. With his corps of ten weakened divisions holding a 150-kilometer long sector, he knew that his units were too thinly manned to resist a renewed Soviet drive, which was expected shortly. In addition, he also had to concern himself with his other assignment, that of reestablishing contact with neighboring *1.Pz.Armee*, a mission which had been given to *Gruppe Haack.*

To help Haack's attack, Vormann had temporarily attached the five remaining tanks from *11.Pz.Div.* in support, making any renewed drive north by the bulk of this division unlikely that day at all. Mikosch's division itself was tied down cleaning up after a Soviet attack that on Yurkovka, where a Soviet force had managed to break through *13.Pz.Div.'s* sector, requiring virtually all of that division's resources to contain. Wöhler's orders to keep attacking towards Zvenigorodka and to seize Hill 208.9 therefore made little sense to him.

General Wöhler persisted. By nightfall on the 15th, Vormann still had not attacked. Had there been a misunderstanding? He had his *1a* send another message at 2100 hours. Vormann could not be reached because he was observing the fighting taking place in *Gr. Haack's* sector, where the men of *Urlauber Regiment Baake* were attempting to seize Hill 204.8 on the western bank of the Gniloy Tikich. The corps *1a* responded, stating

that Vormann had "every intention of continuing his attack," once the one being carried out on his left flank was completed. When lectured about the need to redirect *11.Pz.Div.s'* tanks towards the attack that had been ordered to sever the supply route leading atop Hill 208.9 at Zvenigorodka, Vormann's *1a, Maj.* Hans-Wilhelm Weise, responded that the corps was trying its best, but that it no longer had enough tanks. *11.Pz.Div.* alone had lost 55 tanks to various causes since the battle had begun. Weise closed by stating that he would notify Vormann of *8.Armee's* concern.[32]

Less than half an hour later, Wöhler's chief of staff was on the line, demanding to speak to Vormann's Chief of Staff, *Oberst* Reinhard. Speidel ordered Reinhard to cease all other attacks immediately and launch the attack against Hill 208.9 without further delay. Reinhard demurred, stating that he would have to relay the message first to his superior, who could not be reached at the time by radio from *8.Armee's* command post in Novo Mirgorod. Reinhard stated that he would insure that Vormann had returned to oversee *11.Pz.Div.s* attack, but that both he and Vormann doubted that the attack could not be carried out until the following morning.

Forty-seven minutes later, Speidel radioed back, having evidently spoken with General Wöhler, and told *Maj.* Weise that only Vormann in person could categorically rule out the attack ordered for that night and, furthermore, that he was to use both *13.* and *14.Pz.Div.* (the latter division was 20 kilometers away holding part of the defensive line and not attacking itself) if the situation required it. Again, Vormann could not be located. Finally, *8.Armee* realized at midnight that any further operations would have to be postponed until the next morning. To guarantee that *XXXXVII.Pz.Korps* had enough fuel and ammunition for the attack, Speidel insured that sufficient supplies were airdropped to *11.* and *13.Pz.Div.* by the *Luftwaffe* that night.

Whether Vormann was being deliberately non-responsive can no longer be determined. Suffice to say, he never received this order directly, though he certainly knew about it. But by being temporarily out of direct contact with *8.Armee* headquarters, he at least had an excuse for what followed. The next morning, 16 February, began unfavorably enough. Though obscured from Soviet aircraft by the snowstorm that was blanketing the entire area, *XXXXVII.Pz.Korps'* attack that began at 0800 hours got nowhere.

As both *11.* and *13.Pz.Div.* began their advances, Mikosch's division was counterattacked and forced to give up ground, while Wietersheim's division limped ahead a few kilometers, managing to cross a road at the foot at of Hill 208.9, but got no farther. To complicate matters for Vormann, watching the attack unfold from Wietersheim's command post, the Soviet 375th Rifle Division attacked *Gruppe Haack* to the southwest and pierced its front line, necessitating Vormann to send help its way from *11.Pz.Div.* When informed that *XXXXVII.Pz.Korps'* attack had been halted, Wöhler had an order relayed to his corps commander that the attack to seize Hill 208.9 would go forward as ordered at all costs. Vormann was ordered to disregard his flanks, and throw everything into one final attack. Wöhler stated that "It is a matter of honor that we do everything in our power to free our fighting corps [in the pocket]."[33]

A few minutes later, Wöhler received a radio message from General Busse at Army Group South stating that *8.Armee* must do its utmost to seize this important objective in order to ease the pressure being felt by Breith's corps and *Gruppe Stemmermann*. Wöhler, ironically, now found himself in the same position as he had placed his corps commander! Army Group South was following the battle just as closely as he was. Having given army group headquarters his assurances, General Wöhler flew to Verbovets, where the headquarters of *Gr. Haack* was located, then took a *Kübelwagen* to Yerki, *11.Pz.Div.* headquarters, to see what was going on.

There, he encountered not only Vormann, but Generals Wiestersheim and Mikosch as well. After briefing the three generals on the situation of *Gruppe Stemmermann*, he then explained why the attack to seize Hill 208.9 was so important and why they should continue to tie up as many of the enemy's forces as possible. It is unknown today whether or not Wöhler gave Vormann a public dressing down for his alleged failure to always remain in the right place at the right time, but he did leave for posterity an evaluation of each man in the Army's *Kriegstagebuch* that day, that speaks volumes about how he had assessed each man's condition and abilities at that point in the battle.

Weitersheim of *11.Pz.Div.* had only just returned to duty after spending several days in bed with Vohlhynin Fever, a viral infection similar to flu, and was able to stand "only with the aid of an innoculation," though he had improved somewhat from the previous day. His *1a, Oberstlt.* Werner Drews, was also sick with the fever. Therefore, to him the lack of offensive spirit by this veteran division was understandable. *Gen.Maj.* Mikosch, commander of *13.Pz.Div.*, was "healthy and steady," but he deemed him to be more of a "long distance runner than a sprinter." Therefore, he was not the bold commander that the situation required either. But Wöhler saved his invective for Vormann. In his report, Wöhler stated that he was,

> Evidently strongly affected by the cold and nervous strain. I do not have the impression that he is a Führer (leader) whom the troops feel comfortable with. He lacks the vigor and confidence [in himself] and the . . . [required] shot of optimism, - all properties that are necessary for a sound constitution. By every reordering [of battle plans] he sees insurmountable difficulties.[34]

Thus, it had become evident by 16 February that Wöhler had completely lost confidence in his subordinate, who had served under him now for well over two months, months which had been marked by heavy fighting, beginning with the withdrawal from Kirovograd.

Rather than acknowledge that Army Group South and *8.Armee* had given Vormann an impossible assignment to carry out, Wöhler chose to shift the blame for his army's failure to relieve *Gruppe Stemmermann* to a man who had tried harder than anyone else to do just that. Not only had Vormann been forced to lead his corps through some of the fiercest engage-

ments, but he had also been required to maintain an extremely overextended sector. It would have been far better had Wöhler done what General Hube had done - give the relieving corps one mission, which it could exclusively focus on. This had made General Breith's mission somewhat easier.

There, holding the shoulders of the relief effort was left up to General Hell's *VII.A.K.*, leaving Breith's corps free to concentrate only upon breaking through to the pocket. At the very least, Wöhler should have turned over most of Vormann's static sector between Schpola and Gruzkoye to another corps headquarters, even if this meant temporarily standing up a provisional corps from an existing division. Instead, most of the strain and responsibility had been left to fall upon Vormann's shoulders. It is no wonder that he seemed to be under a great deal of "nervous strain." Now, should the breakout of *Gruppe Stemmermann* fail, at least *8.Armee* would have a convenient scapegoat, if the need arose.

Something positive at least had been gained by Wöhler's trip to the front line. For the first time in nearly two weeks, he had been able to see exactly what conditions in which the men of *XXXXVII.Pz.Korps* had been living and fighting. Perhaps it brought about a new appreciation of the difficulties that Vormann and his division commanders faced. For example, he saw how the resupply of the corps had been made "extraordinarily difficult" by the deep mud. Not only had the bringing up of fuel and ammunition been affected, but supplies of bread, boots, and socks as well. The troops, according to Wöhler, seemed to have not been well taken care of (under the circumstances, an unfair accusation), and were noticeably crawling with lice. The demands of the fighting had caused the two divisions' combat power to sink to their lowest point. He saw how losses of tanks and recovery vehicles, due to lack of maintenance, had skyrocketed.

Wöhler, affected by what he had seen, was finally convinced that *XXXXVII.Pz. Korps* had done everything possible. He ordered *11.* and *13.Pz.Div.* to ease up their attacks to take Hill 208.9, but instructed Vormann to keep exerting pressure on the Soviet forces opposite his corps by carrying out limited attacks.[35] Perhaps they could still tie down enemy forces and prevent them from being moved to the north. But Vormann had no intention of carrying out any further attacks at all; he was convinced that it would serve only to bleed his units for no attainable goal.

Towards this end, he had already ordered Wiestersheim and Mikosch to only conduct counterattacks if they lost ground.[36] The greatest danger to his corps now came from the west, where the Soviets were beginning to exert considerable pressure upon *Gr. Haack*. All efforts by Wöhler and *8.Armee* staff to get Vormann moving again were complicated by the fact that Wöhler's errant corps commander, as instructed, had moved his command post so far forward that all communications had to be relayed between *8. Armee* staff and Vormann's staff before it could finally be relayed to him, thus delaying the exchange of messages.

Although he knew the risk his actions would pose to his career, Vormann stood his ground because he knew his corps would need its strength for the battles that would quickly follow once the relief operation was over. Wöhler's insistence on attacking no longer made sense. But with this halt in offensive operations, all that *XXXXVII.Pz.Korps* could do now was to listen to radio messages being sent back and forth between *Gruppe Stemmermann* and *8.Armee* 28 kilometers to their north. Vormann and the men of his corps had done everything humanly possible to get through to their encircled comrades, and had suffered immeasurably in consequence.

Despite this, many of the men of *3., 11., 13.,* and *14.Pz.Div.* felt pangs of guilt for not succeeding in their task. They had fought as well as anybody and had knocked out several hundred Soviet tanks during the past three weeks, upsetting General Konev's timetable in the process. Despite their impressive performance, it was up to Breith's and Stemmermann's troops, who would now attack towards each other and link up in the middle. With that, the German relief attack from the south finally came to an end.

Fighting continued along *XXXXVIIPz.Korps'* front throughout 16 February and afterwards, though by this point it had little to do with the larger battle raging to the north. On the corps' left flank, *Gr. Haack* labored to seize Hill 204.8 and to extend the front line closer to *III.Pz.Korps.* Once *2.Fallsch.Jg.Div.* arrived, both units would then attack in concert to close the gap separating *8.Armee* from *1.Pz.Armee.* Until then, *Gr. Haack* would be fighting in isolation. Facing General Haack and his hastily thrown together-formation of corps units and *Urlauber Rgt. Baake* was 375th Rifle Division, which had entrenched its units along the slope of the hill. Previous attacks had failed when Baake's troops were pinned down by Soviet artillery. To Vormann, this attack was far more important than any attempt to continue the advance towards Zvenigorodka, since it would serve to both protect his corps' left flank and to seize a commanding position from which to commence the drive to link up with *III.Pz.Korps.* For this reason, Vormann had attached *11.Pz.Div.'s* remaining Panthers to *Gr. Haack*, in hopes that their addition would tip the balance in Haack's favor.

The battle for Hill 204.8 was every bit as bitter as the fighting in the pocket and continued for several days after the breakout of *Gruppe Stemmermann* was over. One of the participants in this fighting was *Hptm.* Schaefer-Kehnert, who had taken part in the fighting with *11.Pz.Div.* since the beginning of the encirclement, three weeks before. He had seen the rise and decline of German fortunes in the many failed attempts to relieve the troops in the pocket. Now he was supporting a unit that did not even have a number - an ad-hoc formation of men from nearly a dozen different divisions together for less than a week. It did not matter - his artillery battalion, *II./Pz.Art.Rgt.-119* would support them.

To provide better observation for his battalion's guns, Schaefer-Kehnert had been loaned a Panther from his division's panzer regiment. This would allow him to move much closer to the front line than an observer normally would, since its armor would protect him from all but the most powerful Soviet anti-tank guns. Quickly acquainting himself with the tank's crew, he marveled at the technical sophistication of the vehicle and dubbed it a suitable "machine of death." Positioning the Panther next to some *isbas* in a small village that straddled the *HKL*,

Schaefer-Kehnert proceeded to spot targets to the west and call for artillery fire in support of an infantry attack by *Urlauber Rgt. Baake*, which would come out of the wood line to his immediate left. While directing the fire of his battalion, Kehnert noticed two well-camouflaged Soviet anti-tank guns through the tank's commander's scissors binoculars. Since he did not know how to shoot the 7.5 cm gun, he decided to revert to artillery indirect fire procedures instead, just to see if he could do it, much to the amusement of the crew.

Ordering his driver to move the Panther behind a small rise, so that only the commander's hatch could look over the top, Kehnert calculated the range and direction to the target. Then, he ordered the tank's gunner to elevate and traverse the main gun to the approximate setting and to fire one round of high explosive ammunition at the enemy position. This shot missed. Correcting for the error, Kehnert ordered the gunner to fire again; this time, the first anti-tank gun and crew received a direct hit. After another short correction, the second one was hit too. He saw both gun and men fly into the air, spinning slowly as they fell back to earth. With this serious threat to his tank removed, Kehnert ordered the driver to gun the engine and advance.

As the Panther moved up the slope, young *Komsomol* (volunteer communist youth) were seen scrambling away along a trench line perpendicular to the tank's route of advance. Kehnert opened fire on them with the machine-gun at the tank commander's position, then in a leisurely manner called artillery upon their heads. At that moment, the infantry from *Gr. Haack* supposed to lead the attack finally caught up with him. After a short pause, Kehnert continued the attack. He remembered "I'd never realized what a feeling of security you get when you are in such a steel colossus and not have to worry about machine-gun and mortar fire, safe in the knowledge that you were protected against all but a direct hit from an anti-tank gun."[37]

The assault carried to the hill's summit. The Soviets, stoic as always, waited until the last moment to pull out of their positions. Many of them were observed crawling away from the Germans along their trench lines before they could be mopped up. Kehnert, quickly ordering his artillery battalion to cease fire, cut off the escape route by ordering his driver to position the tank at the opposite end of the trench. Then, as they exited the trench one by one, he mowed them down with the commander's MG-34. "Like a cat before a mouse hole," he wrote, "we waited at the exit of the trench for others to appear." Meanwhile, the accompanying grenadiers joined in, assaulting the enemy trench frontally with hand grenades and submachineguns. Kehnert longed for a camera to record the scene, since he had never seen an infantry assault carried out so perfectly. The last surviving Soviet troops surrendered to *Urblauber Rgt. Baake* and Hill 204.8 was now in German hands once again. As for the 100 or so enemy dead, they were left where they had fallen.

The attack to clear both sides of Hill 204.8 continued the rest of that day. In the fighting that followed, Kehnert knocked out two more anti-tank guns using indirect fire, a skill that is rarely practiced today. He also assaulted several more trenches, using the same technique that he had tried the first day, though he admitted feeling uncomfortable about running over the "brown-clad forms of the scrambling enemy" with his 45-ton tank. Later that night, he called blocking artillery fire upon Soviet reinforcements that were seen approaching the area, handed the tank and crew back over to the tank regiment, returned to his battalion's headquarters, and went to bed, greatly satisfied that he had done his part in the fighting.[38] While he had undoubtedly fought well, a far more serious battle was set to begin 28 kilometers away that very evening, pitting thousands of German infantry against tanks and artillery of the Second Ukrainian *Front*. This time, it would be the Germans' turn to feel the effects of massed tanks and overwhelming firepower on unprotected infantry, as the 50,000 remaining men of *Gruppe Stemmermann* prepared to make their bid for freedom.

End Notes

[1] Schenk, p. 56 and letter, Ernst Schenk to author, dated 26 July 1996.

[2] Radio message from *XI.A.K.* to *8.Armee* Headquarters, 1350 hours 16 February 1944.

[3] *Sbornik*, p. 320.

[4] Sokolov, p. 122.

[5] DA Pam 20-234, p. 25.

[6] *Panzer und Sturmgeschützlage III.Pz.Korps,* dated 1110 hours 15 February 1944.

[7] Interview, Mikhail Yakolevich Hadai, Korsun-Shevchenkovsky, Ukraine, 29 June 1996.

[8] Bäke, Franz. *"Bericht über die Verbindungsaufnahme der westlichen Tscherkassy eingeschlossenen Korps am 17.2.1944,"* dated 24 February 1944, p. 2.

[9] Glantz, "From the Dnieper to the Vistula," p. 188.

[10] *1.Pz.Armee* KTB entry, dated 15 February 1944, p. 1.

[11] Stoves, pp. 513-514.

[12] Ibid, p. 515.

[13] Ibid, p. 517.

[14] *1.Pz.Armee* KTB, entry dated 15 February 1944, p. 2.

[15] Ibid, p. 1.

[16] Aue, A. *"Die Handlungen der sowjetischen Panzertruppen in der Kesselschlacht von Korsun-Tschewtschenkowki," Militärwesen,* Volume 4, April 1964. (East Berlin: Militärverlag der DDR, 1964), p. 671.

[17] *Sbornik*, p. 320.

[18] Rotmistrov, p. 332.

[19] Stoves, p. 518.

[20] Werthen, p. 202.

[21] Graser, p. 2.

[22] Lehman and Tiemann, p. 35-36.

[23] Ibid, p. 36-37.

[24] Stoves, p. 518.

[25] Ibid, p. 519.

[26] Ibid, p. 522.

[27] Scherff, Walter. *"Die Tiger-Abteilung 503 im Schweren Panzer-Regiment Bäke: Angriffsoperationen im Rahmen des III.Panzer-Korps im Februar 1944 zum Entsatz des Tscherkassy-Kessels," Erinnerungen an die Tigerabteilung 503 1942-1945.* (Bassum, Germany: Alfred Rubbel Selbstverlag, 1990), p. 223,

[28] Ibid.

[29] Ibid, p. 225.

[30] Ibid, pp. 225-226.

[31] *8.Armee* KTB, entry dated 0840 hours 15 February 1944, p. 2.

[32] Ibid, entry dated 2100 hours 15 February 1944, p. 7.

[33] *8.Armee* KTB. entry dated 0850 hours, 16 February, p. 2.

[34] Ibid, entry dated 1000 hours, 16 February, pp. 3-4.

[35] Ibid, entry dated 1830 hours, 16 February, pp. 6-7.

[36] Ibid, entry dated 2150 hours, 16 February, p. 7.

[37] Schaefer-Kehnert, *Kriegstagebuch in Feldpostbriefen 1940-1945*, pp. 251-253

[38] Ibid.

THE BREAKOUT

Chapter Nineteen
WAITING AT SHANDEROVKA

"This is going to be one giant snafu."
— General Theo Lieb, 15 February 1944

Inside the pocket, events were also approaching a climax. In a six by eight-kilometer area, the troops, tanks, trucks, carts, artillery, and wounded from two corps — a total of between 49,000 and 50,000 men awaited the order to break out. During the night of 15/16 February, the pocket had become even more crowded when *88.Inf.Div.* evacuated Steblev and pulled back to a shorter defensive line that stretched in an arc from the southernmost edge of Steblev towards Khilki.

Fittingly enough, the last unit to pull out of Steblev was Eberhard Heder's *SS-Feld Ausb.Btl.5*, which had been attached to the division on 14 February. Heder's unit took up its new position that straddled the road to Steblev, facing north. On their right, Heder's SS recruits, by now veterans, were flanked by the remainder of *57.Inf.Div.* which had given up Prutiltsy the night before. Trowitz's troops had taken up their final defensive sector between Savadsky on the left, where they tied in with Heder's battalion, and on the right, towards the outskirts of Novo Buda, with *Germania*.

The Soviets followed the Germans closely, seeking to take advantage of the fluid situation, but were unable to break through anywhere. That night, the Soviets launched a determined attack to retake Komarovka, but were driven off with heavy losses by the troops of *72.Inf.Div.* and *Westland*, which had moved into the town earlier that evening. Khilki was back in German hands after Kästner's attack and Novo Buda was still held by the Walloons. Soviet artillery ranged throughout the pocket; every round fired was guaranteed to find a target.

Shanderovka was the focus of the Soviet gunner's attention. Aptly nick-named *Höllentor* (Hell's Gate) by German troops, the town was pummeled again and again by volleys of shells and *Katyushas*. General Stemmermann had no more maneuver room for his divisions. He still doubted whether his force could make it out of the pocket on its own. In a radio message early that morning to General Wöhler, he stated that:

> For the successful completion of the breakout, it is absolutely necessary that Breith smash the enemy forces to his direct front (atop Hill 239). Gruppe Stemmermann can break through the enemy forces in front of its position, but the second breakthrough cannot be managed without Breith's help.[1]

❖ ❖ ❖

At that time, of course, *K.Gr. Frank* was just beginning its attack against Oktyabr and had not yet seized Hill 239, though both *1.Pz.* and *8.Armee* seemed to have expected that it would be taken in time. It had to be - the direction of the breakout described in the order issued the day before presupposed that the line Hill 239 - Zhurzhintsy would be firmly in the hands of *III.Pz.Korps* before the breakout could even begin.

Throughout the day, Stemmermann continued to inquire *8.Armee* exactly where *1.Pz.Div.'s* leading units were and the status of their attack, but he was continuously reassured by General Speidel that everything was going according to plan. Had Stemmermann been under the direct control of *1.Pz. Armee,* he may have been told differently. At the very least, he would have received more timely information, since everything that *8.Armee* knew had to be routed from *1.Pz. Armee's* headquarters in Uman before it could be forwarded on to Stemmermann. Thus, the seeds of a fatal misunderstanding had been sown.

Throughout Shanderovka, there was a frenzy of activity. The staffs of five divisions and two corps vied for room in the remaining peasant huts with thousands of wounded. General Fritz Kruse and the staff of *389.Inf.Div.*, which had been detailed as a traffic control element since the division was temporarily disbanded the week before, vainly tried to regulate the movement of thousands of men and hundreds of vehicles. Many units had ignored the order to destroy unneeded vehicles and were still driving hundreds of staff cars, postal trucks, and buses. The streets of the town were hopelessly jammed; any movement was practically out of the question anyway. Tanks and half-tracks waiting repair were parked in the streets or in garden plots. Abandoned or unused artillery pieces were strewn haphazardly about. Horses, still hitched to their traces, snorted as they sought hay or straw in the drifting snow.

The leaden, snow-filled skies at least protected them somewhat from all but the most determined attacks by *Sturmoviks*, though it contributed to the overall depressing atmosphere. Whenever the Red Air Force's attacks diminished, the sky was filled with the droning sound of German transports, seeking to blindly discharge parachute bombs over the town. While the supplies they contained were badly needed, several men were crushed when containers landed on them. The snow was so heavy that in some places it drifted to depths of up to three feet in gullies and shallow depressions. The mud, which heretofore dominated every

*German troops and Ukrainian civilians en route to the final assembly area.
(Bundesarchiv 89/3754/20)*

attempt at movement, froze solid, leaving iron-hard ruts. Any vehicles which had remained stationery in the mud when the frost set in became impossibly stuck.

Thousands of dispirited stragglers, many of them victims of *Kesselpsychose*, and walking wounded swarmed through the streets. Heaps of abandoned materials burned throughout the town, adding to the smoke produced by dozens of buildings that had caught fire during a barrage. Dead bodies still lay where they had fallen in previous fighting. Ringing the town were a series of low ridges that shielded it from direct observation by the enemy. Held by a thin line of troops, they must have observed the activity in the town below with a combination of disdain and horror. From their perspective, Shanderovka must have truly looked like a gate to Hell. According to Gerhard Mayer of *88.Inf.Div.*, the pocket had so shrunk by this point that it had assumed the proportions of the city center of his hometown, Heilbronn. "This," Meyer later wrote, "was the end of the line."[2]

Fuel and ammunition, which always had been in short supply since the encirclement began 28 January, became even scarcer. General Stemmermann demanded another supply drop that evening as a prerequisite for the success of the breakout planned for that evening. Many troops had not eaten for days. Even *Wiking* had begun to run short. Many of its field kitchens had been destroyed or abandoned during the many withdrawals of the past week. *Uscha.* Schorsch Neuber of *SS-Pz.Nachr.Abt.5*, vividly remembered that:

We were tortured by hunger. For days we hadn't anything to eat. Snow was our only sustenance. The last ration we received, laughingly small, we got issued in Steblev and that was a small frozen-together handful of rice for eight men. . . a comrade from a supply unit brought us a few scraps of pickled meat, that we tried to roast over a fire.[3]

Even at this stage, many young German soldiers, such as Neuber, still had no idea of the seriousness of their situation. Even after three weeks of constant combat and changes of position, many still trusted their leadership. According to Neuber, "I believe that us youngsters - I'm including myself - did not see the great danger. We were moving around like sleepwalkers."

Gerhard Mayer, who had arrived in Shanderovka earlier that day, felt lucky to find a place in a root cellar to catch a quick nap. Although the roof of the cellar appeared rather shaky, being merely a hole in the ground with a few boards laid atop it, he felt fortunate to have this much. After a few moments, he was rudely snatched from his nap by a comrade, who informed him that he had been summoned to his artillery regiment's command post. Against his will, Mayer left his cover and trudged through the streets in search of the command pennant of *Oberst* Böhm, the regimental commander of *Art.Rgt.188*.

Upon arrival, he was informed by a staff officer, *Ltn.* Pfortner, that the breakout from the pocket was planned for that night. Mayer, who had thought that he had been summoned to "wash the general's laundry," was told instead that he was being placed in an ad-hoc escort unit being assembled to protect the corps staff of *XI.A.K.* during the breakout. Mayer did not know

Staff cars from Wiking trying to move cross-country in order to avoid the roads get mired anyway.
(Photograph by Adolf Salie courtesy of Willy Hein)

A horse-drawn unit moves to its final position immediately prior to the breakout. (Bundesarchiv 711/438/5A)

any of these officers except one - his regimental commander, *Oberst* Böhm, who he decided to keep an eye upon if things began to get too hot during the breakout.[4]

At Stemmermann's headquarters on the southwestern edge of Shanderovka, his staff worked feverishly to implement the breakout order, which was issued to all units during a commander's meeting late in the evening on 15 February. The breakout order for *Gruppe Stemmermann*, entitled *1a Nr. 236/44 Befehl für den Durchbruch,* was a model of brevity at only three pages long including the map indicating the breakout route. Typewritten, its distribution was limited to only nine subordinate headquarters — *XXXXII.A. K., 72., 57., 389.Inf.Div., SS-Wiking, Arko* (Artillery Commander), *Korpspionierführer* (Corps engineer officer), *Korpsnachrichten Abteilung* (Signals) and *Quartiermeister.* Upon receipt of a copy of the order from *Gruppe Stemmermann's* staff, General Lieb's staff at *XXXXII.A.K.* would draft their own order, after quickly conducting an analysis to pick out the specific tasks assigned to their corps.

To summarize (for a complete copy of the order refer to the appendix), the order directed that the breakout attack of *Gruppe Stemmermann* would begin at 2300 hours 16 February. General Lieb's *XXXXII.A.K.*, code-named *Angriffsgruppe Lieb,* would lead the assault wave, which would consist of (from right to left) *K.Abt.B, 72.Inf.Div.,* and *Wiking* (minus the *Germania* Regiment). This echelon would attack in a southwesterly direction from the line Khilki-Komarovka, break the enemy's resistance with a bayonet assault, and throw them back in continuous attack toward the southwest in order to reach Lysyanka, where it would link up with elements of *III.Pz.Korps.* To orient the attack, troop leaders were to use Compass Heading 22 (roughly southwest; on an American compass, equivalent to a direction of 236°), a heading which was to be made known to each individual soldier. The password to use when encountering the relief force was *Freiheit* (freedom).

For the attack and breakout each division was to be organized into five successive waves. The First wave was to consist of one infantry regiment reinforced by one battery of light artillery (at least eight horses per gun) and one engineer company. The Second wave was to consist of anti-tank and assault gun units. The Third wave was to be composed of the remainder of the

infantry (minus one battalion), engineers, and light artillery. The Fourth, and most vulnerable wave, was to consist of all wounded that were able to be transported, accompanied by one infantry battalion. The Fifth, and last wave, was to consist of supply and service units, those considered to be least able to conduct any sort of organized attack.

The rearguard, which consisted of both *57.* and *88. Inf.Div.*, would be under the direct command of General Stemmermann himself. This force would protect the flanks and rear of Lieb's corps as it conducted its breakout. By 2300 hours, Stemmermann would order these units to withdraw to a previously determined defense line on the northern and eastern edge of Shanderovka upon receipt by radio of the command *Absetzen* (disengage). Once the breakout had begun, it could not be stopped. To support the assault element, all of the remaining medium and light artillery batteries would be brought to bear, though it had been decided at the last minute that the initial attack would go in without artillery preparation in order to hopefully achieve surprise. After the battle had commenced and the first units had linked up with the outside, the artillery would fire its remaining ammunition and the crews would destroy their pieces to prevent them from falling into the hands of the enemy. General Stemmermann's last ace in the hole, Köller's tank battalion from *Wiking*, was to serve as a reserve force, prepared to counterattack whenever the breakout was threatened by enemy tanks.

To keep in touch with Lieb's attacking corps and the rearguard, the order specified that the radios of all divisions would be brought along on packhorses. Each division was ordered to keep at least one radio set in operation at all times and to report every hour on the hour. Both corps would keep their radios operating constantly. Lieb's command post initially would be at Shanderovka until 2000 hours 16 February, after which he would move it to Khilki. Stemmermann would remain in Shanderovka in command of the rearguard until he judged a suitable time to withdraw it and join the rest of the force along the same route Lieb and his force had taken previously. To succeed, the breakout had to be timed precisely and only radio could provide a rapid medium for the transmittal of the necessary orders. However, the vacuum tube radios used by the Germans, as well as all the

Although snow has fallen, the roads still have not firmed up. Trying to free a horse-drawn supply wagon. (Bundesarchiv 89/3751/16)

other combatants, tended to be easily broken. Whether they would hold up to rough jostling was an open question.

The ten-kilometer long route chosen for the breakout would force *Gruppe Stemmermann* to leave most of its vehicles behind, since there were no roads running from Khilki-Komarovka to the line Hill 239 - Zhurzhintsy. Only tracked vehicles or horse-drawn *panje* wagon would be able to negotiate the many ravines and *balki* that lay perpendicular to the German's line of march. Most of the route lay in the open, though there were two large wooded areas along the way. The first one lay at the halfway point, also perpendicular to the chosen route. Bounded to the north and south by deep *balki*, this first forest was approximately three kilometers long, though only eight hundred meters wide at its widest point. The other small forest was the one hundred meters south of Hill 239, where *Hptm.* Scherff's attached *Jäger* were to briefly seek shelter on 16 February. Both of these forests would soon figure prominently in the fighting. The exact dispositions of the enemy were unknown, though it was expected that they would have constructed at least two defensive belts between the encircled force and *III.Pz.Korps.*

Units were ordered not to evacuate any civilians as they withdrew, since they would prove burdensome. However, hundreds, perhaps thousands, of Ukrainians decided to take their chances and escape with the Germans, since many were convinced that they would be treated harshly as collaborators by the Red Army. A more vexing worry than what to do with civilians was the disposition of the wounded. Those wounded during the breakout, the order read, would be carried along either by *Hiwis* or the wounded soldier's comrades. More problematic was the issue regarding the thousands of wounded laying in Shanderovka.* Many of these could not be moved. To take them

along would surely result in their death. Stemmermann, after consulting with Lieb, had to make a difficult decision. In the past, the Soviets had been known to murder captured German wounded or had failed to provide them medical treatment. To be sure, the Germans had mistreated or killed thousands of prisoners as well, though at least front-line troops as a rule provided initial medical treatment for wounded enemy soldiers who had fallen into their hands.

To Lieb, this was a bitter decision. Both men decided that the only humanitarian thing to do was to leave the non-ambulatory wounded, about two thousand in number, behind in Shanderovka with four doctors and twelve other medical personnel to be handed over to the pursuing Soviets. In a typewritten note addressed to the first Soviet commander they encountered, the names of all of these medical personnel were listed as well as a statement testifying that these personnel had been ordered to remain behind in Shanderovka to care for the wounded. Signed by General Stemmermann himself, a copy of the note still exists.[5] What the Soviets did with the note is unknown, though what happened later served as an indication. As an additional safeguard, the houses and barns housing the wounded were ordered to be draped with flags bearing the red cross, though in the past this internationally recognized symbol had often been disregarded on the Eastern Front by both the Red Army and the Red Air Force.

Some units, such as *Wiking*, disregarded this order entirely. To leave wounded SS men to the Soviets would, their comrades thought, mean their certain death. At the main dressing station of *Wiking* in Shanderovka, *Ostubaf.* Dr. Thon, the division's medical officer, had 240 of the division's wounded

---

* One source states that the number of both ambulatory and non-ambulatory wounded in the pocket at of 16 February 1944 was in excess of 4,000.

loaded up into two convoys - one of tracked vehicles and one of *panje* wagon. To provide escorts, Werner Meyer's *1.Kp./ Germania* was attached to Dr. Thon and his assistant, *Hstuf.* Dr. Isselstein.[6] Other units did the same. In all, only 1,400 German wounded actually were believed to have been turned over to the Soviets, out of the 2,000 previously counted. Had they known what was in store for them, their comrades would gladly have left them all behind.

Aside from the wounded, by 16 February Generals Stemmermann and Lieb had approximately 45,000 troops left to launch the attack, reflecting the fact that the encircled units had lost a total of 15,000 men killed, wounded, or missing since the battle began. To insure that the assault echelon commanded by Lieb would succeed, Stemmermann had given him the three strongest units in the pocket, a total of 22,930 men, minus corps troops. With 11,500 men (including the Walloon Brigade), *Wiking* was still the strongest division in the pocket. It also still had thirteen operational tanks and assault guns.* *K.Abt.B* was his second strongest, with 7,430 men, while Hermann Hohn's *72.Inf.Div.* had only 4,000 men.

While the total number of remaining artillery for *Gruppe Stemmermann* on 16 February is no longer known with certainly, *XXXXII.Armeekorps'* records still exist. Surprisingly, after three weeks of heavy fighting, Lieb's corps was still able to field 61 light and medium howitzers (10.5 cm and 15 cm, respectively), four 10 cm cannons (for artillery counter-battery fire), as well as 26 infantry guns of various caliber. In addition, *Wiking* still had nine 10.5 cm self-propelled *Wespen* operational and three 15 cm self-propelled *Hummeln*. All told, Lieb had 83 guns and howitzers.[7] Compared to what the Soviets had in the field, this amount was ludicrously small, but it would be enough to provide support for one more day, providing that the ammunition held out long enough. Even more incredible was the fact that their crews had managed to drag or drive them this far. But more important than numbers of men, tanks, or guns was the assessment that these divisions still possessed unbroken combat spirit, which may have seemed unfair to the other two divisions which had been chosen to protect the breakout's flanks.

Both *57.* and *88.Inf.Div.*, which would form the rearguard, were in far worse shape than Lieb's three divisions. Trowitz's division, which had been weakened even before the encirclement, now had only 3,534 men, while *Graf* Rittberg's had been reduced to 5,150 men, which included the attached *Div.Gr.323.* and *332.*, with 650 and 500 men, respectively.

Also attached to *88.Inf.Div.* were the two security regiments from *Sich.Div.213* that had exceeded all expectations during their determined defense of Boguslav two weeks before. Some of the other encircled divisions bore little resemblance to what they had been three weeks before. For example, *K.Abt.B's* commander, *Oberst* Fouquet, had chosen *Oberst* Viebig's *Div.Gr.112* to spearhead his own attack, but also under his command was *Rgt.Gr.593* (from *Div.Gr.323*), *Gren.Rgt.417* (from *168.Inf.Div.*), *Rgt.Gr.678* from *Div.Gr.332*, and *Rgt.Gr.465* from *Div.Gr.255*.

It is a wonder that Fouquet was able to make any headway with this arrangement at all. In fact, it is a tribute to the tactical skill of the *Wehrmacht*, even in the third winter of the war in the East that this kind of ad hoc organization worked as well as it did. Certainly the Red Army was never able to approach the Germans in terms of tactical flexibility, especially at division level and below. While the command arrangement described above would have given pause to any British or American commander, to a German one, such as Fouquet, it did not. In fact, his *K.Abt.B* was nothing more than a division-sized *Kampfgruppe*. According to German doctrine, units usually fought at the tactical level as *Kampfgruppen* anyway, and Fouquet had acquired a great deal of experience leading such an amalgam of forces during the past three weeks. Certainly the existing records do not depict any problem with this arrangement. To the average soldier, who only knew the men in his immediate squad or platoon anyway, it mattered little whether the company on his right or left was from his division or not. What mattered was that his own little *Haufe* (gang) held together.

Included in the total number of Germans in the pocket were over 10,000 troops from independent corps units that make the functioning of large military formations possible, but have little combat value in terms of actual fighting capability. Despite the ruthless combing-through of rear echelon units, there were still thousands of these men who now, for the most part, found themselves unemployed.

The combat value of these units was practically nil, so placing them in the middle of the formation as it fought its way out was probably the best that could be done with them. After all, most of them were not in the prime age bracket to serve as combat troops anyway and would not last long in any sort of fire fight if it came down to that. In regards to the women, they were divided up into small groups and parceled out to combat units who would do their utmost to bring them out safely. No one wanted to imagine what would happen to himself in Soviet captivity, though it would have been even worse for female captives.

Soldiers of the Wiking receiving hot food in Shanderovka from a Ukrainian cook immediately prior to the breakout. (Photo by Adolf Salie from Der Russlandkrieg: Fotografiert von Soldaten, Ullstein Verlag, 1968)

---

* The numbers listed in *I.Abt.,SS-Pz.Rgt.5's* report were 2 Pz. Mk. IVs, 4 Pz. Mk. IIIs, 6 *StuG.III*, and 1 *Befehlspanzer* (command tank).

Troops from Wiking awaiting orders while resting in a roadside ditch, shortly before the breakout.
(Bundesarchiv 279/946/20)

General Lieb knew that the breakout would not be an easy one, regardless of how optimistically *8.Armee* viewed the situation. In his diary he sarcastically commented that his corps was being asked to "perform a miracle" the following night. Breith had yet to fight his way through, that was plain enough, which could mean that the encircled troops might have to fight their way out without any assistance. Lieb had summoned the three division commanders who would participate in the breakout to a briefing at his headquarters in Shanderovka on the evening of 15 February.

Of the three divisional commanders, only Gille of the *Wiking* was taking part in a breakout for the first time; the other two, Hohn and Fouquet, Lieb rated as "old hands." By coincidence, all four men were artillerymen. Lieb left no doubt in their minds that, in his opinion, this [operation] was going to be one giant *Durcheinander* (snafu) and that they should not get rattled, no matter what happens. In closing, Lieb stated that "You need a guardian angel to bring you through this kind of thing."[8] A detailed briefing by *XXXXII.Armeekorps' 1a, Maj.* Hermani, followed. Illuminated by a flickering candle, the map showing the divisions' assigned attack sectors, marked in red and blue, was tacked against the wall of the *isba* that served as Lieb's corps headquarters. Hermani spoke tersely, running his hand lightly over the map as he spoke.

The scheme of maneuver was simple. The three divisions of *Angriffsgruppe Lieb* would attack abreast in deeply echeloned columns. Eschewing artillery preparation, Lieb chose to rely on the bayonet and spade instead of firepower. On the right, *K.Abt.B* would take up an assembly area on the southwestern outskirts of Khilki and would attack towards Zhurzhintsy via Petrovskoye. In the center, *72.Inf.Div.* would take up an

assembly area in a depression between Khilki and Komarovka and would attack parallel with *K.Abt.B* towards Lysyanka over Hill 239. On the left, *Wiking* would occupy an assembly area on the southwestern outskirts of Komarovka and would advance towards Lysyanka via the town of Pochapintsy. All three divisions would break through in one swift movement, and be met along the line Hill 239 - Zhurzhintsy, then believed to be held by *III.Pz.Korps.*

Troops were instructed to attack with unloaded weapons, lest an errant shot awaken the Soviet defenses. Cigarettes were strictly forbidden. Any noisy items of personal kits, such as gas mask canisters and mess kits, would be discarded or securely fastened. The troops would also have to travel light, so extraneous equipment and personal baggage was to be left behind. The total width of the three attacking columns was approximately two kilometers, which represented probably the densest grouping of forces the Germans had ever achieved since they had been encircled. It would prove to be an irresistible battering ram against the Soviet's inner defensive ring, especially since General Lieb had chosen the strongest of his remaining regiments to lead the assault. Hermani closed the briefing with a few sobering words about how the leaders' and troops' comradeship would undergo its "supreme test" during the next few hours.[9] No one present had any idea how severely it would be tested over the next two days.

The last briefing of *Wiking's* commanders took place the next morning, after General Gille had his staff cobble an order together. Huddled into the shack in Shanderovka that served as a division headquarters, Gille briefly read Lieb's order. Leon Degrelle remembers it being very short. No stirring speeches on National Socialism or duty to the *Führer* were heard. Instead,

Gille stated that:

> Only a desperate effort can save us now. Waiting is pointless. Tomorrow morning. . . the 50,000 men in the pocket must charge towards the southwest. We must either break through or die. Troop movements begin this evening at 2300 hours. According to Degrelle, Gille took pains not to describe the situation to his regimental and battalion commanders too realistically. It all seemed as if "all we had to do was cross a zone of five and a half kilometers to reach the liberating army. . . . our 50,000 men charging at once would be able to overrun the enemy."

Degrelle, ever the realist, accepted Gille's words with skepticism. Despite his doubts, the sense of urgency and the knowledge that the relief force was quite near was enough to "light the burning fire of inspiration" in the breast of the Walloon Brigade's new commander, who raced back to Novo Buda in order to motivate his troops and urge them forward for one last heroic effort.[10]

To lead the attack, General Gille had chosen *Ostuf.* Heinrich Debus's *Kampfgruppe* from *SS-Pz.Aufkl.Abt.5.*, augmented by a battery of self-propelled 10.5 cm *Wespen.* In his wake would follow *II./SS-Pz.Gren.Rgt. Westland*, commanded by *Hstuf.* Walter Schmidt. Next would come the division's main body, including the engineer battalion, antitank battalion, and the artillery. *Germania*, along with *Pz.Gren.Rgt.108*, would constitute part of the rearguard, and would not withdraw until ordered to do so by General Stemmermann.[11] Willy Hein, still recovering from wounds received in Olshana nearly three weeks before, was traveling with Köller's tank battalion, positioned as a general reserve in the middle of the pocket so that it could be employed quickly in any direction, should the Soviets penetrate the pocket's perimeter. Still serving as the battalion's signal officer, he would have a ringside seat from which to observe the breakout as it unfolded.

Hans Köller, Willy Hein's commander, had only received orders detailing his tank battalion's role in the breakout at 1500 hours that afternoon, when Ehrath's adjutant from *Germania* showed up at his headquarters in Novo Buda with instructions from General Gille. Köller was instructed to move his few remaining tanks and assault guns at 1900 hours to Shanderovka. Rather than wait, he went at 1700 hours in a half-track to Shanderovka to speak to Gille personally and to personally tell other elements of his battalion that were quartered in the town to prepare themselves for the breakout. Upon arrival at division headquarters, he met with Gille, who gave him his precise instructions, which read in part that his tank battalion would march to the western side of Shanderovka after the withdrawal of the *Kampfgruppe* from Novo Buda. It would then place itself in readiness for the breakout. At 1920 hours, Köller's unit began pull off of the hill north of Novo Buda and pass through Shanderovka, which his men found to be nearly completely stopped up with other vehicles from the infantry divisions, which forced his tanks to detour around fields or roadsides. During the descent down the hill, Hans Fischer's Pz.IV became immobilized when a worn-out caterpillar tread slid off of the road wheels, causing it to careen into a roadside ditch. Fischer, who had led the "Hussar ride" in early January against the first group of Soviet tanks that had broken through in early January, had to walk the rest of the way.

While *Wiking* was preparing for the breakout, both *72.Inf.Div.* and *K.Abt.B* were doing likewise. *Oberst* Hohn had chosen *Gren.Rgt.105* to lead the attack, a wise choice, since it had more experience in night combat that any of his other remaining units. *Gren.Rgt.105* would be followed by *Gren.Rgt.266*, then the remnants of *Gren.Rgt.124*. Once he had been given his assigned mission early on the morning of 16 February, Kästner ordered a thorough reconnaissance be undertaken as far as possible along their planned route of advance. To carry out this dangerous assignment, he turned once again to *Ltn.* Bender, who had proven his ability as a scout many times before. Bender took several men with him and headed towards the southwest, concealed somewhat in the murky early morning hours by falling snow. Wrapped with peasant shawls and blankets, the Soviets could easily have mistaken Bender and his men for civilians.

Alternating between advancing forward slowly at a crouch and crawling through the snow, he and his men were able to work their way through the Soviet lines south of Khilki undetected. Carefully, Bender located the main Soviet positions along the route planned for that night's attack and marked them on his map. The patrol was even able to approach to within five hundred meters of the most forward element of the relief force - probably *Hptm.* Scherff's Tiger battalion, when it briefly had possession of Hill 239 before it was forced off by tanks from 5th Guards Tank Army. Unfortunately, Bender was unable to proceed further; had he been able to do so, he would have had a far better idea of what the actual situation along the line Hill 239 - Zhurzhintsy that would have proven to be critical the following day.[12] Bender's patrol, its mission accomplished, then began to make its way back to regiment, arriving at the outskirts of Khilki at 1800 hours. Leaving his patrol at the regiment's front line outposts, Bender and his translator briefed Kästner on what they had seen. With this key information, the regimental commander was now able to develop a plan to conduct his attack. He decided to use the same tactical formation that had worked so well at Novo Buda, Komarovka, and Khilki - automatic weapons up front with the assault wedge, followed by heavy weapons and the rest of the infantry. Although the division had assigned him several hundred men from disbanded units as reinforcements, Kästner decided not to use them in his attack formation, since he deemed these men to be of no practical value, since few of them had any infantry experience.

The morale of *Gren.Rgt.105* that night was very high indeed, for the men knew that they would break out that night towards freedom. Each man was confident that the breakout would go just as well as the other night assaults had, and were loaded up with as much ammunition as they could carry. Despite the positive attitude displayed by his men, Kästner knew that this breakout would be harder than any other they had previously attempted. In all, the regiment would have to traverse a distance of between fourteen and seventeen kilometers before they reached safety, after breaking through both an inner and an outer encircling ring. The only means at hand to orient the attack's direction was a captured Soviet 1:10,000 map and Kästner's *Marschkompass* (military compass). Lying in the hollow south of Khilki, his men used the rest of their time to prepare themselves and their equipment for this last battle. Those who could napped; others wrote letters home and distributed them to their comrades.

In Khilki, *Oberst* Fouquet had chosen *Oberst* Viebig's *Div.Gr.112* to spearhead *K.Abt.B's* attack that evening. It was the only organization Fouquet had left that was still tactically capable, with most of the rest of his units being little more than remnants. Viebig decided to lead off his attack with *Hptm.* Burgfeld's *Rgt.Gr.258*, closely followed by Ernst Schenk's *Rgt.Gr.110*. Three hundred meters or so behind the spearhead, the artillery and anti-tank gun crews would follow, then the infantry howitzer company. *Feld-Ers.Btl.112* would bring up the rear. Since Viebig's artillery had been lost in previous fighting, a battery of 10.5-cm howitzers from *Oberst* Böhm's *Art.Rgt.188,* commanded by *Maj.* Landerer, was attached. Viebig stressed that Burgfeld's and the other units should approach the enemy silently. To help his commanders and troops mentally prepare for what was to come, Viebig stated:

> I entrust this [attack] into the hands of the regiment's founding members and their leaders . . . The forwardmost assault troops must attack ruthlessly with unloaded weapons. You have only two choices [of weapons to use]: the bayonet or the spade. Any unnecessary shooting is a grave offense that could endanger the entire breakout. Every man, down to the lowest ranking soldier, must know that what is at stake is more important than one man's [fate].[13]

His order closed, appropriately, with a speech originally given by a Prussian general during the time of Frederick the Great. "Beginning, middle and end, may the best man win!" For his part, Ernst Schenk was relieved to get the news. After spending the night in a blizzard atop Hill 226.8, he and his men were half-frozen and only too glad to receive the order to attack. Anything was better than another night on that barren hilltop! Things would soon get hot enough for the men of *Rgt.Gr.110.*

While the corps and divisions of *Gruppe Stemmermann* spent the rest of 16 February preparing for their breakout that evening, the situation inside the pocket grew increasingly tense. Worse yet, the *Führer* had not yet granted Manstein permission

As the day for the breakout approaches, more and more units are crammed into an ever-shrinking perimeter. At least the snow conceals the Germans from the omnipresent Red Air Force. (Bundesarchiv 711/438/5A)

to order the breakout. At a time when he should have implicitly had trust in one of his most talented subordinates, Hitler chose to reserve all decision making authority to himself. As was the case with many similar crises, he hesitated. Would he, as he had at Stalingrad, wait until it was too late to order a breakout? Would he veto an order by Manstein? Even more serious for the Germans in the pocket, a breakout could no longer be delayed, since the units no longer had room to maneuver. Every square inch of the pocket was now under artillery fire and air attack. Further delay would prove fatal, since the Soviets were only a day or two away from launching a final, crushing attack. If ordered to break out by Manstein, would Stemmermann waver, just as Paulus had?

Manstein was determined, in the words of one of his staff officers, that on no account would he allow another repeat of Stalingrad. According to *Hptm.* Alexander Stahlberg, his aide-de-camp, "His last conferences with Hitler and his open clashes with him had obviously - at last - given him more detachment and resolution."[14] With the fate of 50,000 men resting in his hands, the field marshal made a decision. Assuming full responsibility for what he was about to do, he radioed General Stemmermann directly on 16 February and issued him a laconic but clear order, "Password Freedom, objective Lysyanka 2300 hours."[15] Stahlberg wrote later that after that moment "We breathed sighs of relief." The breakout was on - with or without Hitler's permission. Now at least Lieb's and Stemmermann's corps would have a fighting chance. All that Manstein and his staff could do now was to sit and wait.

The Red Army was equally determined to prevent the encircled Germans from escaping. The German's direction of attack and troop dispositions were now known with utter certainty. In order to present to Stalin and *STAVKA* a Stalingrad on the Dnieper on schedule, General Konev had been forced to redouble his efforts to destroy Stemmermann's force before it got away. In fact, he was in the process of repositioning forces for a final, crushing attack which would take place the following day, 17 February. Konev planned to carry out an attack against the northwest sector of the pocket by 18th Tank Corps from 5th Guards Tank Army combined with another one against the southeast by elements of 4th Guards Army. Selivanov's 5th Guards Cavalry Corps would take part in the attack as well. Leaving 63rd Cavalry Division in place in the Komarovka-Novo Buda area, Selivanov was ordered to move 11th and 12th Guards Cavalry Divisions along a circuitous route so that they would be able to attack the western side of Shanderovka. This movement would require the Cossacks and their tired horses to march 40 kilometers along a rutted, snow covered road before they could occupy their assault positions and would not be completely in place until 2000 hours on 17 February.[16]

Both Soviet armies would attack towards each other and cut the pocket in two, while the Cossacks would mop up the survivors. However, since this plan necessitated that many of each army's corps and divisions reposition themselves prior to the start of the attack, many of Konev's troops and tanks would be in transit during the evening of 16/17 February. This proved to be to the Germans' advantage, since some of these forces could not be committed to the fight until late the following day. Had they remained in their original positions, the breakout would have been much more difficult. However, Konev seemed to have been little concerned. The defenses of the inner line of encirclement appeared to be quite strong. In his account of the battle that followed, he stated that "It was impossible for the Nazis to burst through four defense lines: two on the inside and two on the outer one, and to bypass tank-proof areas and artillery in the center of the corridor." He also apparently felt that he had assembled enough mobile reserves of tanks, infantry, and cavalry to cut off and destroy any of the enemy attempting to escape.[17] But the inner ring was not quite as solid as it appeared, as would soon be proven.

Nor was the Red Air Force dormant. Although in the past both air armies had carried out night attacks, these had been poorly planned and coordinated, with little to show for their efforts. But with so many enemy troops crammed into such a narrow area, it presented a golden opportunity for the Soviets to carry out effective aerial bombardments of the Shanderovka area, and Konev wanted to use every weapon at his disposal to make good his promise to Stalin. Therefore, Konev ordered that General Goryunov redouble the efforts of his 5th Air Army to destroy the encircled Germans, including the prosecution of night attacks. Goryunov turned to the 392nd Night Bomber Air Regiment, flying ancient U-2 aircraft, and ordered it to carry out the attack. Using incendiaries, the Soviet aviators bombed Shanderovka during the night of 16/17 February, just as the Germans were completing preparations for their breakout.[18]

Despite falling snow and strong, gusty winds, the Soviet pathfinder aircraft, piloted by Captain V. A. Zayevsky, was able to successfully start several fires in the town that served as a beacon for following strikes. The resultant fires added to the Germans troubles and illuminated the landscape, providing a beacon for unobserved Soviet ground artillery to focus on, thus increasing the effectiveness of their bombardment, as attested to by German survivors. However, such effective cooperation between Soviet aerial and ground units was the exception rather than the rule, but it emphasized to Soviet com-

Oberst Viebig, *Commander, Divisionsgruppe 112, Korpsabteilung B. (Photo: Andreas Schwarz and 88.Inf.Div. Veterans Association).*

manders just how effective such attacks could be, lessons that the Red Army took to heart for subsequent operations carried out in the summer of 1944.

Nor did Konev intend to give the Germans a rest on 16 February. While he had ordered the repositioning of his major units, he had already ordered that attacks would continue to be made against the southeast and northeast sector of the pocket in order to maintain pressure of the enemy and force them to continue to use up their remaining reserves. The first attack, carried out by two hundred paratroopers of 5th Guards Airborne Division supported by tanks from a battalion from 29th Tank Corps, hit Komarovka at 1130 hours that Wednesday. Though they managed to achieve a small penetration for the loss of four tanks, they were held in check by troops from *Westland* as well as *Gren.Rgt.124* of *72.Inf.Div.* Other attacks were launched against troops of *57.Inf.Div.* holding the northern part of Tarashcha and a position one kilometer southeast of Steblev. A few hours later, the Soviets carried out a much larger attack from the direction of Dazki. Launched by divisions of 20th Guards Rifle Corps, estimated to consist of over 1,000 men, the attack hit General Trowitz's sector and jostled the *HKL* back to the west a distance of one kilometer.[19]

The attacks by Selivanov's 5th Guards Cavalry Corps against Novo-Buda had also not diminished. The Walloon Brigade, by this point down to less than 800 men, was still holding its positions in and around the town, though its defensive sector was nothing more than a series of widely-spaced foxholes inhabited by two or three men. Companies were down to 20 men. Degrelle's headquarters no longer had any field telephones or radios to remain in contact with his companies' positions. Regardless, Degrelle vowed to stay and hold off the pursuing Soviets as long as possible. Retreat was out of the question. Any attempt to withdraw north towards Shanderovka during daylight would be greeted by a hail of artillery anyway, since the town's defenders would have to cross an open field one kilometer wide.

That afternoon, Degrelle succumbed to despair. He felt that by the time Breith's tanks had arrived, they would all be dead. Neither Degrelle nor anyone else knew why the relief attack had stalled. Carefully nurtured hopes had been dashed once again. In his mind, all of the optimistic radio messages from General Hube:

had been nothing but fiction. The tanks hadn't come. The surrounded troops had held out as long as there was hope. Now everything was falling to pieces. We were down to our last cartridges. Since Sunday the quartermasters

Inside the pocket, things are reaching critical mass. Fewer than a dozen tanks are left to hold the encircling Soviets at bay in an ever-shirinking perimeter. Here, a StuG. III and a Panzer III of Wiking. (Jarolin-Bundesarchiv 78/22/1)

hadn't any food. The wounded were dying by the hundreds from exposure and loss of blood. We were suffocating under the enemy pressure.[20]

Degrelle had received his brigade's orders for the breakout during General Gille's briefing at *Wiking's* headquarters the night before. He realized that they would not be easy to carry out, for his brigade had been designated one of the rearguards for the operation. Once the initial breakthrough by Lieb's corps had been carried out, the rearguard, composed of *57. and 88.Inf.Div.,* as well as *Germania,* would fall back to an intermediate position. The Walloon Brigade would continue to hold Novo Buda until its northern neighbor, *Germania,* had evacuated its old positions. Then, once this had been accomplished, they would pull out according to plan and link up with Ehrath's regiment near Komarovka, where it would join that regiment for the escape of the rearguard across the Gniloy Tikich. In the meantime, the Walloons fended off a number of Soviet probing attacks, which ceased by nightfall. Where had the Soviets gone?

Lieb's corps also had its hands full that day holding the line until the attack could begin. The Soviet 294th Rifle Division, attacking from Steblev, twice attempted to seize Hill 197.5, one kilometer due north of Shanderovka, but its attacks, each consisting of approximately one hundred and fifty men, were driven off by counterattacks launched by *Füs.Btl.112* from *Oberst* Viebig's *Divisionsgruppe.* Khilki's defenders were also under pressure the entire day by 180th Rifle Division. By 1800 hours, troops from *Gren.Rgt.417* and *Rgt.Gr.465* (Kästner's regiment had already moved to its assembly area for the night attack) had

managed to ward off several attacks, knocking out three Soviet tanks and one assault gun during the day's fighting.

By mid-afternoon, the eastern and southern portions of Komarovka had fallen to the enemy after the defenders from *Westland* and *Gren.Rgt.124* were forced out in hand-to-hand fighting. When Lieb asked Gille whether his division could retake the village that night, Gille replied that he did not consider it possible, since the Soviets had heavily reinforced the part of the town they had recaptured. He did not want to sacrifice his men at this late of a stage in the operation, so Lieb assented. The loss of this part of Komarovka affected the breakout plan, since the assembly area chosen for *Wiking* lay in that town.

To compensate for the loss, a new assembly area was drawn on the map north of the town, forcing *72.Inf.Div.* to shift its assembly area a few hundred meters to the northwest. One disadvantage of this last minute shifting of forces was that it would force three divisions to use a single bridge on the western outskirts of Shanderovka to reach their assault positions. Another risk was that the entire left flank of *Wiking* would be subject to Soviet fire or counterattack from Komarovka. Lieb feared that this development would slow the movement of troops into their assembly areas, but in this case, his fears proved unfounded. By 2230 hours, the spearheads of the three divisions chosen to lead the attack of *XXXXII.A.K.* were in position.[21]

Not so with the units following in their wake. An unimaginable traffic jam nearly two kilometers long had developed on the western outskirts of Shanderovka, along the road than ran southwest towards Komarovka and Khilki. Here, literally thousands of vehicles and carts had become immobilized three or four abreast, as each driver awaited his turn to move forward when the break-out commenced. Stemmermann's orders to reduce the number of non-combat vehicles to a minimum had seemingly been ignored. Thousands of support personnel and stragglers from every unit in the pocket were to be found. All the while, the column was under sporadic Soviet artillery fire. Soldiers were yelling at each other, gesticulating wildly, or accepting their fate stoically. The few remaining *Feldgendarmes* cursed and swore to no avail. Yet no one relinquished his place in line, lest he lose his chance of riding out of the pocket.

Into this chaos waded the tanks of *SS-Pz.Abt.5*, which arrived on the town's western edge at 2100 hours. Cutting into the line, the tanks were just about to cross the single bridge that spanned a creek that bordered the town when the lead vehicle, Köller"s command tank, crashed through the wooden bridge that had collapsed under its weight. All traffic came to a standstill, as Köller"s tank recovery specialists and combat engineers labored to pull the tank out of the creek and to repair the bridge. Finally, the battalion's 18-ton *Famo* prime mover, a giant *Sd.Kfz.9*, was able to make its way forward through the traffic jam.

Attaching tow cables to the tank, the crew of this behemoth was able to winch it out of the ditch as engineers labored with heavy beams and planks pulled from nearby *isbas*. Finally, by 0145 hours, the bridge was repaired sufficiently for the tanks to cross.[22] One by one, each tank or assault gun slowly crossed over, aided by the winch of the recovery vehicle, and formed up again several hundred meters west of the bridge. After their passage, the enormous tide of waiting vehicles began to flow across again, as if freed from a high-pressure container. The drivers of these vehicles would soon find that their road ended at the outskirts of Khilki and Komarovka and any further progress, by wheeled vehicles at least, would be absolutely impossible. By then, the attack was already in progress.

As the clocked ticked towards 2300 hours, every man in *Gruppe Stemmermann* must have instinctively looked towards the southwest. Only a few hours and a few kilometers separated them from freedom. During these last few moments, the Soviet artillery fire seemed to intensify. *Katyusha* rockets were impacting every few moments, all the more dangerous because they hit targets randomly, without pattern. On the doorstep of *XXXXII.A.K.* headquarters lay the body of a staff officer whose head had been torn off by a shell splinter. Men who had been wounded while standing in the streets of Shanderovka were dragged into an *isba* to receive hasty first aid. In middle of this noise and chaos, *Maj.* Hermani, *Ia* of the corps, sat and waited for the clock to strike 2300 hours. In his journal, he wrote:

> We are sitting in our battle HQ, silent. There are no more orders to be given and no directives to be issued - for the first time since the encirclement twenty days ago. Every man is thinking of home. The last letter from "outside" has been burnt and all those other things one had become so attached to in over four years of war – photographs of one's wife and children, Goethe's Faust or Eugen Roth's Women in World History.[23]

SS-Untersharführer Adolf Salie, *SS-Nachr.Abt.5. He took some of the most dramatic photographs to survive the battle. (Photo courtesy of Willy Hein)*

Half an hour before zero hour, the sound of low-flying He-111s could be heard, as they flew at tree-top level dropping cases of small arms ammunition and artillery shells. Bursting as they hit the ground with an enormous crash, they narrowly missed hitting huts full of wounded or the many vehicles still clogging the streets. In his diary, General Lieb wrote, "Ample supply of ammunition dropped in aerial delivery containers…In this respect we are now well off — if we can take it along."[24]

Lieb had one last meeting with Stemmermann before he went up to the front to lead the breakout. After exchanging a few words about some tactical necessities, they bid each other farewell. It was the last time that Theo Lieb would ever see Wilhelm Stemmermann again. Lieb then returned on horseback to his forward command post, which he had ordered moved to Khilki to better supervise his three divisions. Deep in his musings, *Maj.* Hermani was surprised to see General Lieb enter the hut where Hermani had set up the corps staff. Wearing his favorite white fur cap, Lieb was accompanied by *Oberst* Gädke, Stemmermann's chief of staff, who had come to discuss last minute details of the breakout with Lieb and his staff; after a few minutes, he departed. Outwardly, Lieb appeared to be calm and optimistic, qualities that would soon be needed. Privately, however, even he had his doubts. To insure that his personal diary would get out, even if he did not, Lieb had entrusted it to his orderly, "…a crafty fellow [who] will get it through somehow."[25]

Finally, after three weeks of waiting, the hour had come. Everything that had gone before had now come down to these last few moments. Hermani wrote:

> The time was 2300 hours. H-hour. The night was pitch dark. No moon. No stars. The thermometer stood at four degrees below zero Centigrade. But an icy wind was blowing form the northeast. Fortunately, it was a tail wind for the marching columns and a head wind for the watching enemy. At times it was so fierce that it carried the snow before it. Favorable weather for an enterprise which hoped to escape the enemy's eyes and ears.[26]

Now the embattled troops of *Gruppe Stemmermann* knew only one phrase: Password Freedom; Objective: Lysyanka! During the next 48 hours, both freedom and Lysyanka would prove to be out of reach with the hardest fighting still ahead.

Until then, all hope rested on the three assault columns from *72.Inf.Div., Div.Gr.112,* and *Wiking,* who were nervously eyeing their watches as their minute hands ticked the last seconds off towards 2300 hours. As for Manstein, at whose command the entire train of events had been set into motion, all he could do now was to sit anxiously in his command train at the railroad siding in Uman with his staff and await news of whether the breakout had succeeded or not.[27] Things were now truly out of his hands — *Gruppe Stemmermann* was now the master of its own fate. That night, many thousands of kilometers away at *OKH* headquarters in East Prussia, Kielmannsegg wrote in his diary, "Tonight at 2300 hours the last attempt to reach Stemmermann will be made."[28]

End Notes

[1] Radio Message, *XI.A.K.* to *8.Armee*, dated 0825 hours 16 February 1944.

[2] Mayer, p. 135.

[3] Kathagen, p. 90.

[4] Mayer, p. 136.

[5] *Zur Betreuung der im Kampfraum Schanderowka verbleibenden Verwundeten,* Gruppe Stemmermann, Anlage 1 zu Gen. Kdo. XI. A. K. 1a 19/44 g. Kdos., 16 February 1944.

[6] Strassner, p. 146.

[7] *Gefechtsbericht, Generalkommando XXXXII.A.K.,* Chef des Generalstabes. Meldung zu Pz. A.O.K. 1 Abt.1a Nr. 370/44 geheim vom 19. 2. 1944, dated 24 February 1944, p. 1.

[8] DA Pam 20-234, p. 25.

[9] Carell, pp. 418-419.

[10] Degrelle, p. 207.

[11] Strassner, p. 145.

[12] *World War Two Military Studies*, Vol. 1, p-143d, p. 21,

[13] Div.Gr.112, *Befehl für den Durchbruch am 16.2.1944*, dated 1500 hours 16 February 1944, p. 1.

[14] Stahlberg, p. 327.

[15] Carell, p. 417, and Stahlberg, p. 328.

[16] *Combat Operations of 5th Guards Don Red Army Cavalry Corps in the Korsun-Shevchenkovskii Operation*, pp. 351-352.

[17] Konev in Sokolov, p. 123.

[18] Wager, Ray, ed. *The Soviet Air Force in World War II:The Official History, Originally Published by the Ministry of Defense of the USSR.* (Garden City, New York: Doubleday & Company, Inc., 1973), p. 235.

[19] *Tagesmeldung, XI.A.K.* to *8.Armee*, dated 1730 hours 16 February 1944.

[20] Degrelle, p. 206.

[21] *Gefechtsbericht, Generalkommando XXXXII.Armee Korps, Meldung zu Pz. A. O. K. 1, Abt.1a Nr. 370/44 geheim vom 19.2.1944*, dated 24 February 1944, p. 3.

[22] *Kriegstagebuch, 1.Btl. SS-Pz. Rgt.5*, entries dated 1500 and 2100 hours, 16 February 1944.

[23] Carell, p. 419.

[24] DA Pam 23-234, p. 25.

[25] Ibid.

[26] Carell, pp. 419-420.

[27] Von Mastein, p. 517 and Stahlberg, p. 328.

[28] Von Kielmannsegg in Glantz, 1985 *Art of War Symposium*, p. 234.

Chapter Twenty
GRUPPE STEMMERMANN BREAKS OUT

"The enemy pressure on us had become unbearable . . . "
— *Uffz. Werner Hilss, 389.Inf.Div.*[1]

Finally, the hour of deliverance had arrived. As the clocked ticked away towards 2300 hours, the first attacking wave lay in the snow anxiously waiting to move out. Thousands of others in the second and other subsequent waves were still moving into final position. Over 47,000 soldiers, including 2,000 ambulatory wounded, looked hopefully towards the southwest, where the spearheads of *III.Pz.Korps* were supposed to be awaiting their arrival. Thousands of lips repeated the words "Password Freedom, Objective Lysyanka" like a mantra, as if by merely saying them would effect their release. Between Stemmermann's weary troops and freedom was a thin, ten-kilometer long bottleneck in which were positioned two encircling Soviet rings - an inner one facing against them and an outer one that held back Breith's troops and tanks. Fortunately for the Germans, there does not appear to be any indication that the defending Soviets had an inkling of what was about to befall them, for they too, like their enemy, were exhausted, hungry, cold, and battle weary. Besides, Konev and his armies expected that they, and not the Germans, would make the first move.

In broad outlines, the dramatic breakout that followed devolved into three distinct phases. The first, the initial breakout by the assault groups, went roughly according to plan. The second phase, which involved the movement of the mass of troops in the center of the pocket, quickly became a disorganized rout. The third and final phase, the withdrawal of the rearguard, also went more or less according to plan. The breakout itself was to last nearly 48 hours - from the time of the departure of the first assault wave until the last of the rearguard staggered back into German lines near Lysyanka.

From 16 to 18 February 1944, the two encircled corps of *Gruppe Stemmermann* experienced the greatest challenge either corps had ever known before and saw both of them crushed as organized military formations. Those 48 hours bore witness to thousands of acts of individual heroism and sacrifice, as well as acts of cowardice and despair. To understand what happened during the breakout, it is not enough to merely read the official reports and post-war histories; rather, one can only begin to understand what happened to *Gruppe Stemmermann* by examining the individual accounts of its survivors. In its emotional and psychological impact, the breakout from the Cherkassy Pocket was to prove for many of them to be the one battle that they would never forget as long as they lived.

The breakout began promisingly at 2300 hours, despite the last-minute shuffling of *Wiking's* spearhead to the right,

At 2300 hours 16 February, the breakout begins. The first wave of troops break through easily. For the rest, the going is much tougher. Here, a member of Wiking moves out during the snowstorm which blanketed the steppes and helped to hide the German breakout. (Bundesarchiv 691/229/24)

where it had been forced to share an assembly area with *Gren.Rgt.105* after the loss of the southern portion of Komarovka to the Soviets earlier that evening. Silently, the assault elements moved out, concealed by their white camouflaged winter combat uniforms. Aided by snow blowing directly into the eyes of the defenders, they crept up unnoticed upon the infantrymen of 27th Army. On that moonless light, the temperature hovered below freezing. As ordered, all weapons were unloaded with bayonets fixed. Entrenching tools, as well as trench knives, hung at the ready. Almost every other piece of equipment except ammunition pouches with their precious few remaining rounds had been flung away, all personal papers burnt. Any remaining food was passed out to be shared by all. Only one thought remained: *Vorwärts! Vorwärts! Voran, voran!* (forward and onwards).

At the same time the breakout was to begin, the small *Kampfgruppe* from *Leibstandarte* had reported to *Oberstlt.* Dr. Bäke in Oktyabr and began preparations to retake Hill 239 as ordered. Once taken, the Tiger battalion from *Schw.Pz.Rgt. Bäke* was supposed to reoccupy its positions from the previous day. The seizure of this hill and its commanding terrain was absolutely vital for the breakout's success. As of yet, Stemmermann did not know that it was not in German hands - in fact, he predicated the success of the breakout on the condition that the relief force had taken the hill and established a linkup point there. Had he known that it was not in German hands, Stemmermann might have conducted the breakout differently. Otherwise, his forces would not be strong enough to overcome any Soviet defenses that he knew would be emplaced there.

This battlegroup, *K.Gr. Heimann*, which consisted of less than 120 infantrymen from *SS-Pz.Gren.Rgt.1*, departed Oktyabr on schedule and moved forward on foot through the snow to take their intermediate objective, the small forest due south of the road intersection atop Hill 239 that had been bombed by *Stukas* earlier that day. They found the defending Soviets alert and ready for them. Several times the SS attacked, but each time they were driven back by stout Soviet resistance. Completely exposed on the bare icy slope leading up to the forest, *Hstuf.* Heimann and his men were subjected to intense enemy machine-gun fire and driven to ground.

After over an hour of this, Heimann felt that he and his men had endured enough and gave the order to pull back into Oktyabr, where they established defensive positions around Bäke's tanks.[2] Without tank support, *Leibstandarte's* attack had no chance of success. A mere 120 men were not enough to wrest control of the hill from elements of two Soviet armies. Had it been present, the entire division would have undoubtedly succeeded, but it, too, had been bled white in the fighting of the previous two weeks and could spare nothing. The only other combat unit available, *K.Gr. Sandig* was still on the march and would not arrive until mid-morning.

The failed effort to seize Hill 239 that night was to have grave consequences, which soon became evident. Apparently, *III.Pz.Korps* attempted after midnight to notify Stemmermann by radio that it had been unable to seize Hill 239 that evening and establish a forward receiving area. According to *Oberst* Merk, Breith's operations officer, the message had been sent, but *Gruppe Stemmermann* failed to acknowledge receiving it - in fact, all radio contact had quickly been lost with the encircled force. Whether it was ever received or not, by then it was too late, since the breakout had already been set into motion.[3] *Angriffsgruppe Lieb* would soon enough find out that the hill was not in German hands, but there was nothing more that Breith nor *K.Gr. Frank* could do about it. After the fight for the woods south of Hill 239 died down, an eerie silence descended upon the snow-covered battlefield.

Unaware of what was happening ten kilometers to the southwest, the troops of *Angriffsgruppe Lieb* completed their final tactical preparations. The three assault columns quickly moved out into the darkness and at first seemed to have encountered little difficulty. Stemmermann radioed a message to *8.Armee* at 0100 hours on 17 February to notify Wöhler that *Angriffsgruppe Lieb* had crossed the line of departure on schedule and had begun its attack (Map 13). It was the last radio message that Stemmermann was to send.[4] On the right, the spearhead of *K.Abt.B, Hptm.* Burgfeld's *Rgt.Gr.258*, departed its assembly area on the southern outskirts of Khilki. His men quickly overcame a thin Soviet outpost line a kilometer southwest of that village. Pressing on, Burgfeld and his men quickly overran the next line of Soviet positions atop his battalion's intermediate objective, Hill 234.1 immediately south of Petrovskoye.

Realizing, all to late, that the approaching column consisted of German troops, and not their own, the Soviet defenders were quickly subdued and the way to Lysyanka was clear once again. Burgfeld's battalion pushed on to the southwest, moving through the deep *balka* south of Zhurzhintsy and up the steep slope towards Hill 239. Avoiding Zhurzhintsy, he and his 300 remaining men crossed the road that ran between the town and Hill 239 and soon encountered the outer Soviet encircling positions, which faced to the west and southwest. Catching them completely by surprise, Burgfeld's battalion killed or captured these men too. A few minutes later, the Germans marched into the northern outskirts of Oktyabr, where they encountered the first tanks of the relief force at 0410 hours.[5] Incredibly, Burgfeld's men had not fired a shot.

The first unit to spot the arrival of Lieb's troops were the Tiger crewmen of *Schw.Pz.Abt.503* of *Schw.Pz.Rgt. Bäke*, which were positioned several hundred meters to the southwest of Hill 239. *Hptm.* Scherff had just received a resupply of gasoline for his eight remaining tanks when he saw two white signal flares rise up into the air half a kilometer away from his position south of Hill 239, which his battalion had been unable to hold on to the previous day. As prearranged, *Ofw.* Sachs, commander of the attached *Jäger* company, fired two white flares in return. Were these the men they had fought so long to set free from the Soviet trap?

Cautiously, Scherff ordered Sachs to drive his half-track a few meters forward to take a look. A few minutes later, a long line of silent troops, marching single file, could be seen approaching. According to Scherff:

> Those in front still carried machineguns or rifles; then came those who were without weapons. Some limped along or were supported by comrades, or had some sort of a walking stick as a support. They all looked bedraggled, yet they moved with a firm and steady sense of purpose . . . [They] must have had many terrible trials behind them by the time they encountered us. A few of them cried from exhaustion. I had begun to cry [from joy] as well. They had made it![6]

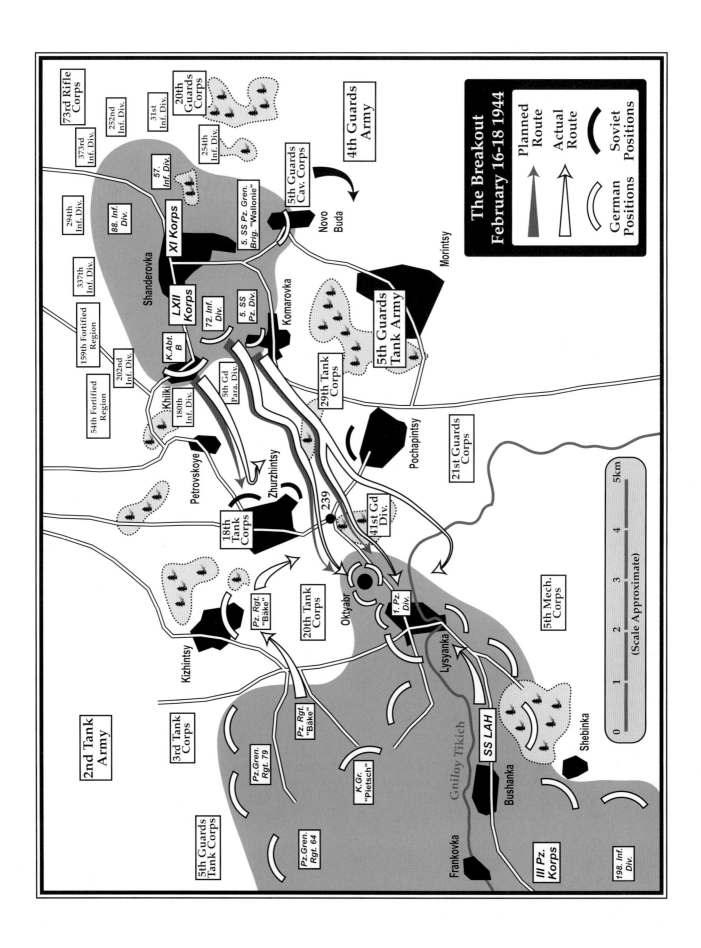

The Breakout
February 16-18 1944

Planned Route
Actual Route
Soviet Positions
German Positions

Some of the *Jäger* climbed out of their half-tracks and helped those who needed it the most. Scherff notified Bäke of their arrival by radio. Not waiting until they reached his command post, Bäke ordered a half-track to take him to Scherff's location so he could supervise their movement. While waiting his arrival, Scherff was surprised to see that the troops who had just broken out still had crackers and *Schoko-Kola,* (a type of substitute chocolate) which they were sharing with his men, who had not eaten a decent meal in over a week.

While Scherff was talking with an *Oberleutnant* from the group, escaping soldiers dressed in white camouflage smocks kept moving past him. Another heavily armed group of soldiers was seen marching towards Scherff's positions a few minutes later, evidently the vanguard of another group.[7] In all, he estimated that from 400 to 600 men made it out from this first wave of *K.Abt.B.* The news of Burgfeld's arrival was immediately radioed to headquarters, *III.Pz.Kps.*, where *Oberst* Merck passed it on to *1.Pz.Armee* and attempted to notify Stemmermann at 0445 to inform him of his attack's progress. Merck asked Stemmermann's headquarters to inform him where the rest of his elements were, but received no reply - by this time, Stemmermann had been separated from his radio section and could not answer.[8]

The approaching group was Ernst Schenk's *Rgt.Gr.110*, which had followed in the wake of Burgfeld's unit by a ten-minute interval. His battalion was also just as lucky as Burgfeld's. He lost only one man during the entire breakout, a weary *Landser* who had fallen asleep in the snow during a halt. He remained unnoticed when the rest of his battalion continued on and is still missing in action to this day. According to Schenk, this was understandable, since he reckoned that no one in his battalion had slept during the last 60 hours. During the breakout, Schenk took a Soviet captain prisoner, who had approached the German column, thinking that it was some expected reinforcements. Shocked to see that the encircled Germans were suddenly breaking out, he was quickly bundled up and taken along. "Now," Schenk wrote later, "he would have to break out with us too!" His ghostly column continued marching, passing several Soviet sentries in the night, who seemed immobile as "pillars of salt," neither firing nor raising the alarm.[9] Perhaps they, too, thought that Schenk and his men were fellow Red Army soldiers.

After several hours of uneventful marching through the deep snow, Schenk and his men arrived in northern Oktyabr shortly after Burgfeld's battalion. He later wrote "After the terrible nerve-wracking tension we had finally arrived at the German tanks, which had come to pull us out and had gotten stuck in the mud. Everyone in the ranks breathed a sigh of relief."[10] There, they were greeted personally by Bäke, acting commander of *K.Gr. Frank,* who had watched them approach in the darkness. Men from both the relief force and Schenk's battalion whooped with delight. After three weeks, Schenk had managed to bring nearly 160 of his men to safety.

To their shock and dismay however, instead of being led to the rear where a warm *isba* and a bowl of soup awaited them, Bäke instead ordered both Schenk and Burgfeld to immediately place their battalions at his disposal. Both men were

At first, the breakout goes smoothly. At dawn, the Soviet defenders awaken to discover the magnitude of the German attack and begin to direct concentrated fire upon the escaping columns. Suddenly, all order and discipline vanish, as the troops commense a panicked rush for safety.
(Photo by Adolf Salie courtesy of Willy Hein)

further directed to position their units along the northern flank of the relief force in order to reinforce it against further Soviet attack, since *Hptm.* Ebeling's *Pz.Gren.Rgt.113* was down to a mere 118 men. Schenk's and Burgfeld's battalions, after all, still had most of their weapons and enough ammunition to keep the Soviets at bay. As Bäke headed back to his command post in Oktyabr, he instructed both men to report to him once they had placed their battalions into position east of Oktyabr where they could cover the road from Zhurzhintsy to Lysyanka.[11]

However, neither Schenk nor Burgfeld had any intention of doing so. The last orders they had received from *Oberst* Viebig, their commander, was that they were not to stop until they had arrived in Lysyanka. Since that town still lay two kilometers to the southwest, both commanders ignored Bäke and continued on towards their objective, crossing the northern bridge and entering Lysyanka by 0600 hours. Here, both battalions halted and sought lodging in nearby *isbas*, where they would wait for Viebig and the rest of their unit to arrive. Their ordeal, as far as they were concerned, was over. In fact, it had been far easier than they had imagined.

Uphill in Oktyabr, Bäke was peeved that both men had yet to report to him, so he sent his signals officer out to look for them, but without success. In the early morning darkness, he still had not noticed that both battalions had departed without his permission until the Soviets launched a counterattack an hour later that penetrated all the way into the village, even threatening his own command post. After mustering all available headquarters personnel, Bäke was able to throw the enemy out once again, but at the cost of heavy casualties. By pulling out of their designated positions without telling anyone, Burgfeld and Schenk had unwittingly created a gap several hundred meters wide through which poured a Soviet infantry battalion supported by tanks. Bäke was furious, but in the present circumstances there was little he could do about it except complain angrily to General Koll.[12]

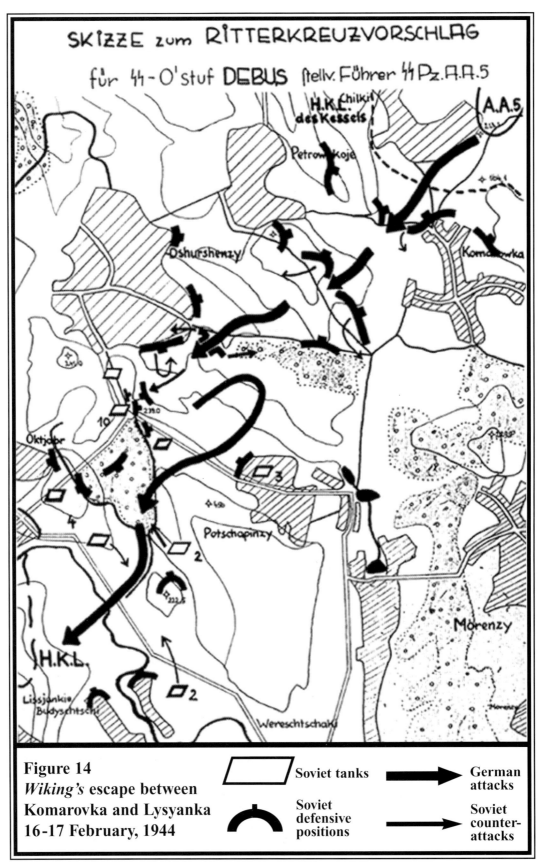

Figure 14
***Wiking's* escape between Komarovka and Lysyanka 16-17 February, 1944**

Soviet tanks

Soviet defensive positions

German attacks

Soviet counter-attacks

Note: This diagram is from the original Knight's Cross award recommendation for *SS-Ustuf.* Heinz Debus. (U.S. National Archives)

Close-in tank fighting in the hamlet of Oktyabr. Both T-34s were destroyed by von Dörnberg in his Panther (see arrow for location) at point-blank range.
(Photo courtesy of von Dörnberg)

One of the two knocked-out T-34s in Oktyabr.
(Photo courtesy of von Dörnberg)

The attack of the center assaulting column from *72.Inf.Div.* also went well initially. The spearhead, consisting of Kästner's *Gren.Rgt.105*, moved out soundlessly as they had so often before. Moving several hundred meters to the left of Burgfeld's battalion, Kästner and his men easily broke through the forward Soviet positions with bayonet and spade. A few men had to resort to using machine pistols on the startled defenders, but it was over so quickly that the Soviets had no time to raise a general alarm.[13] Kästner's battalion kept moving on, but somehow got disoriented in the darkness and swerved to the north several hundred meters, unwittingly crossing the route of the third echelon unit of *K.Abt.B, Feld-Ers.Btl.112,* cutting it off from both Schenk's and Burgfeld's units. Now out of his assigned attack sector, Kästner marched his men onwards, swerving back to the southwest an hour later once the error had been detected. Navigating at night in a snowstorm with only one captured Soviet map as a reference was proving to be a greater challenge than Kästner had first thought.

Approximately halfway through their escape, *Gren.Rgt. 105* encountered two Soviet artillery battery positions, which they quickly destroyed before their crews could train their guns in the German's direction. Kästner later wrote that it was the only significant fight he and his men experienced during their breakout. Moving on, he realized that he and his men had now completely broken through the enemy inner ring of encirclement and were halfway to their goal of Lysyanka. About 0330 hours, his regiment reached the deep *balka* immediately south of Zhurzhintsy, where he ordered his men to take a quick rest while *Ltn.* Bender and a few men conducted a reconnaissance to their immediate front, a copse of trees atop Hill 239, a mere 400 meters away. The battlefield was totally quiet. To Kästner, it seemed as if the war had come to a standstill. Upon Bender's return half an hour later, Kästner, Bender, and *Ltn.* Roth held a quick discussion of their situation as the regiment continued its march up the side of the *balka*. The report did not sound encouraging.

Along the road running from Zhurzhintsy to Hill 239 (crossed an hour before by both Burgfeld's and Schenk's *Regimentsgruppen*), Bender had spotted the outlines of five tanks – and they were definitely identified as T-34s, not German models. Most likely, these belonged to a brigade from 29th Tank Corps of 5th Guards Tank Army. In the woodline paralleling Hill 239 that ran east to the town of Pochapintsy, Bender had spotted two more tanks and silhouettes of other vehicles as well. Kästner informed his commander that he was going to push on regardless. He and his men had come too far to turn back now. Using the rolling terrain and the deep gullies that ran down the hillside as cover, Kästner and his men, organized in a narrow, deeply echeloned column, slowly approached the ridge upon which the road and the T-34s lay. A quick peek over the top of the slope revealed that they had not, as yet, been discovered. Kästner ordered his men to rise and move out as quickly and as silently as possible.

The leading squad quickly crossed the road unnoticed, followed by the rest of the regiment. As the regiment was halfway across the road, a column of trucks and tanks coming from the direction of Pochapinsty was seen heading along the road in their direction. One quick-thinking soldier left the column, approached the trucks and shouted *Stoi!* (Halt!). The Soviets drivers, thinking that these were their own men, dutifully stopped and waited until the rest of Kästner's men, including the regiment's remaining horse-drawn infantry howitzer, crossed over.[14] Not so fortunate were the regiment's horse-drawn *Tross* (supply column), which was bringing up the rear. It was quickly shot up by tank and machine-gun fire, its horses killed, the drivers forced back down the hill. These men would have to find another way out.

At the same moment, some 200 meters west of the road, the spearhead, led by *Ltn.* Roth, suddenly encountered the foxholes of 180th Rifle Division, which formed the outer ring of encirclement at this point. The Germans knew that they were almost out of the pocket now. Incredibly, the Soviets had not noticed their approach - most were in fact fast asleep. Roth and his men quickly jumped into the Soviet foxholes, but enough of the surprised defenders were soon awakened to put up a fierce, though brief, show of resistance. Shooting blindly in the dark, the remaining Soviets were soon overcome, but the noise soon attracted the attention of the tanks along the Zhurzhintsy road, which turned on their searchlights. The tanks quickly spotted the Germans as the regiment's rear element, the infantry howitzer company, crossed the road. They then opened fire on Kästner's supply column and the one following it, which consisted of *Gren.Rgt.266.* Fortunately, by then Kästner and his men had made good their escape.[15]

After breaking through, Kästner assembled his regiment in a deep ravine two kilometers northeast of Oktyabr and counted heads. Most of his men had made it through safely, including a number of the last-minute replacements. After its men sorted themselves out, *Gren.Rgt.105* continued moving southeast. Marching now at the head of the column, Kästner spotted the outlines of three tanks arrayed upon a hilltop a few hundred meters away. Crawling through the snow, he slowly approached the tanks to determine whether they were friend or foe. To his relief, all three were Panthers, bearing the *Balkenkreuz* of the *Wehrmacht.* They were the outpost tanks of *1.Pz.Div.* Kästner and his men shouted the password - "Freedom, Freedom!" Finally, Kästner's regiment had made it out - they were free!

The hatch cover of the nearest tank swung open and out jumped its commander, *Ltn. Freiherr* von Dörnberg, acting commander of *1.Kp./Pz.Rgt.1,* who greeted Kästner.[16] Somehow, the latter had swung his regiment to the north of Oktyabr, which placed them far off course from their original line of march. After being given directions by Dörnberg, he and his regiment continued their march, arriving in Lysyanka at 0630 hours, which lay under heavy artillery fire. To the northeast, Kästner could hear the sounds of heavy fighting, where the rest of his division had drawn the attention of a now fully awakened enemy.

Kästner's was now the third unit to make it out of the pocket. Like Schenk and Burgfeld had done, he had brought out all of his remaining small arms and heavy weapons, and even some of the wounded he had refused to leave behind in Shanderovka. In all, some four officers and 216 men of *Gren.Rgt.105* made it out that morning, along with 12 MG-42s, one mortar, and their last remaining 15 cm infantry howitzer. These were all that was left of a regiment that had numbered 27 officers and 1,082 men present for duty when the encirclement began three weeks before.[17] The remainder was dead, wounded (either flown out or left behind), and missing, a casualty rate of eighty percent. During the breakout itself, the regiment lost fewer than a dozen men, a testimony to Kästner's leadership, skill, and determination. After a brief pause to reorganize, the survivors were placed under the control of *K.Gr. Frank,* and directed to the southeastern corner of the town, where he and his men took up defensive positions on the edge of Lysyanka without incident.

In Lysyanka, Schenk and Burgfeld's battalions were greeted by the commander of *1.Pz.Div.* Although General Koll was sympathetic to their situation, he ordered them to immediately take up defensive positions along the northern edge of Lysyanka to defend

Oktyabr was destroyed during the fighting. Here, ruined peasant huts and Soviet dead litter the snow-covered landscape. (Photo courtesy of von Dörnberg)

against Soviet counterattacks. Since Bäke's radios were malfunctioning, Koll had no idea of what had transpired in Oktyabr - if he had, he might have placed both officers under arrest. Dutifully, Schenk and Burgfeld obeyed, though without much enthusiasm. They had believed that they and their men were out of harm's way, yet now they had to go back into the line again. In fact, they would soon discover that no place was safe - whether inside the pocket or outside.

Schenk and his men moved to their designated position along the town's northern outskirts and tried to dig in, but the ground was too frozen. Instead, they took up positions inside deep ruts made by passing tanks, which had once again solidified in the freezing temperature. It was better than no cover at all. While Schenk's adjutant attempted to round up some warm food and perhaps some coffee for the battalion, the rest of his men glumly prepared to repel the next Soviet attack. If tanks attacked them, they would be hard-pressed indeed to defend themselves, for *Rgt.Gr.110* no longer had any antitank weapons.[18] Meanwhile, the rest of *Div.Gr.112* had become involved in heavy fighting, which could be heard coming from the direction of Hill 239.

In comparison to the right and center assault columns, which had made good their escape, the leftmost assault column, *Ustf.* Debus' *SS-Pz.Aufkl.Abt.5,* had a much tougher time of it (Map 14). Debus' force was a powerful one, but it now consisted primarily of infantry - all of his armored cars and half-tracks had either been abandoned or destroyed due to lack of fuel, except for one Pz. III. Reinforced by a company from *SS-Pz.Jäg.Abt.5* (without their antitank guns) and two batteries of self-propelled 10.5 cm *Wespen* from *SS-Pz.Art.Rgt.5,* it was still a potent force.

At first, his attack went well. On the right, his *3.Kompanie* kept in contact with *Gren.Rgt.105.* On the left, *1.Kompanie* protected his open flank. *2.Kompanie* was in the lead, silently moving towards the Soviet defensive line. The *Wespen* and antitank gunners, acting as infantry, brought up the rear. To Debus' surprise, the line of low hills two kilometers south of Khilki were unoccupied, allowing his unit to pass through unhindered. Then things began to unravel. Because they were unable to cross an ice-covered lake south of Khilki, the *Wespen* had to detour to the south, where a bridge was reported, separating them from the rest of Debus' force. Since he could not spare the time to wait for them to catch up, he ordered the rest of his unit to push on.[19]

Marching ahead rapidly through the snow, Debus and his men made good progress until they encountered the first weak Soviet outposts south of Petrovskoye, which *2.Kompanie* overcame after a brief firefight. Continuing on to the southwest, his troops ran up against a much stronger enemy position, estimated to consist of at least two antitank guns and four machine-guns on the ridge of hills three kilometers southwest of Petrovskoye. Now when they were needed, the *Wespen* were nowhere to be seen. Ordering a brief halt in the bottom of a *balka* so that his force could conduct a deliberate attack, Debus ordered his men to storm the ridge. After a few minutes, he and his men drove the Soviets off of the hill and destroyed two 7.62 cm antitank guns and their tractors. Before they could catch their breath, mortar rounds from the direction of another *balka* to the southwest began to rain upon their position, forcing them to take cover. Suffering heavy losses due to the mortar fire, Debus ordered his battalion forward and in a few minutes it had overrun the enemy's mortar firing positions as well.

While they regrouped, some of the *Wespen* caught up with them. After a few minutes, Debus ordered the advance to continue, reaching the southeast edge of Zhurzhintsy without enemy interference. Here, another halt was ordered in order to carry out a more thorough reconnaissance. It confirmed the worst. Not only was Zhurzhintsy occupied by the enemy, but the Soviets appeared to be present atop the ridgeline dominated by Hill 239 as well. Debus decided to press on, skirting to the south of Zhurzhintsy and coming to a halt in the large *balka* at the foot of Hill 239. It was still quiet. Unaware of the location of Kästner's neighboring unit to his right (in fact, Debus had lost contact with it early on), Debus decided to launch a frontal attack against the Soviet positions.

By that point, Debus's battalion had been joined by a company from *II./Westland*, which he had requested be sent as reinforcements. The attached antitank company had somehow gotten lost in the darkness and was nowhere to be seen. With "great energy," Debus led his small force up the hill and seized a section of the highway between Hill 239 and Zhurzhintsy at bayonet point, at about the same time that Kästner's unit was crossing the road, several hundred meters to the right, where heavy firing was soon heard. Alerted by the passage of Kästner's regiment, the rest of the Soviet units occupying the ridgeline were now wide-awake. As Kästner's unit made good its escape, Debus' battalion was caught in intense enfilading fire from Zhurzhintsy which forced them to fall back to the northeast, reaching the safety of the large *balka* at the foot of Hill 239 at 0430 hours. While he reorganized his battalion for another attempt, Debus was told that scouts had spotted several Soviet tanks atop the ridgeline. After a brief preparation, Debus launched his attack.

As his men surged up the slope shouting "Hurrah!," they were met by a hail of fire from Soviet positions in the woods that fringed the southeastern edge of the ridgeline. Dozens of Germans fell, killed or wounded. The attack collapsed, forcing Debus and his men to retreat down the hill. The *Wespen*, which

accompanied the attack, fired upon the enemy positions with their 10.5 cm howitzers using open sights, but were unable to negotiate the steep hillside. One of these top-heavy vehicles, when it attempted to turn, rolled over on its side, pinning its crew inside the fighting compartment. The battery's Pz. III artillery spotter's tank, which had only a dummy gun, pulled up, attached a tow cable, and righted it so the crew could be pulled out of the wreck. The rest of the SP guns were blown up by their crews to prevent them from being captured by the enemy.[20] Soon it would be daylight, and Debus would have to attack up the exposed slope, where his men would in all probability be shot to pieces.

By that point, any further attempt to seize Hill 239 from the inside had become problematic. Additionally, other battalions and regiments from his division that had been following his column began to arrive, piling up inside the *balka*. Soon, there were hundreds of soldiers from other units seeking shelter there as well. Rather than continue the attack towards the southwest, Debus decided instead to go around the Soviet positions towards the southeast, breaking through the gap between Pochapintsy and Hill 239 rather than tackle the Soviet defense head on.

As dawn approached, the German breakout plan began to fall apart. The successful passage of Kästner's, Burgfeld's and Schenk's forces had now thoroughly awakened the Soviets, who soon realized that the Germans were escaping from their grasp. Luckily for Marshals Zhukov and Konev, *1.Pz.Div.'s* inability to take and hold Hill 239 was now beginning to alter the entire course of the battle, with unfavorable consequences for the Germans. Instead of finding the relief force waiting atop the ridgeline, Stemmermann's troops now found dozens of tanks and thousands of troops of 5th Guards Tank Army and 27th Army. What had initially been an orderly movement now began to disintegrate into chaos as dawn approached.

As more and more units ran up against the impregnable tank barrier atop the ridge dominated by Hill 239, they began to shift their direction of march towards the south and southeast, where Debus' unit lay pinned down in the deep *balka*. Soviet artillery fire began to noticeably increase, though at first most of their batteries were firing blind due to the snow and mist that concealed the battlefield. There were so many German units moving in the valley below, however, that it was almost impossible to miss. Not only did the shift in direction put the desperate troops of *Gruppe Stemmermann* further away from the relief force, it also placed them on the wrong side of the Gniloy Tikich. This error would not be discovered until a few hours later.

One of the first units to suffer from the Soviet's attention was *Gren.Rgt.266*, which had followed closely in the wake of Kästner's regiment. When *Gren.Rgt.105's* supply column was shot up immediately in front of his column, Siegel called a halt. Dawn was still two hours away, but Soviet parachute flares and tank searchlights had illuminated the escape route. To go that way would be suicidal, Siegel thought. Somewhere to the left was Debus' column, where Siegel could clearly hear the sound of gunfire. During the halt, the unit behind Siegel's, Hummel's *Gren.Rgt.124,* began crowding in. Siegel ordered *Ltn.* Ohlendorf to peer over the hill and see if there was any chance the regiment could slip by the tanks, but upon his return, Ohlendorf reported that more tanks were heading in their direction from Zhurzhentsy.[21]

Since neither his nor Hummel's regiment had any anti-tank weapons, Siegel decided after a hasty discussion with his fellow regimental commander that he had no choice but to detour to the south, about the same time that Debus made the same conclusion. As both regiments moved along the edge of the *balka*, they drew small arms and mortar fire from Soviet infantry positions in the woods that ran along the edge of the ridge. The Germans panicked and began to run in all directions. Siegel yelled out, "Regiment 266, rally on me!" Soon, he was surrounded by troops from his own regiment, as well as troops from *Wiking* and *K.Abt.B.*

Restoring some semblance of order, Siegel ordered his men to attack the southeastern edge of the woodline. Better to break through now while it was still dark! Unbeknownst to him in the darkness and chaos, one of his battalion commanders, *Hptm* Knostmann, led a group of men directly up the hill, overcame several Soviet defensive positions, shot up several trucks loaded with Soviet infantry they encountered on the road, and crossed the top of Hill 239. Knostmann pushed on into the woods that *K.Gr. Heimann* from *Leibstandarte* had tried to take several hours before. After a brief but sharp fight, Knostmann overcame Soviet resistance in the woods and led his small group to safety, crossing the northern bridge into Lysyanka shortly before dawn. *Ltn.* Ohlendorf, who had accompanied Knostmann, was wounded in this action and taken prisoner. Siegel did not know what happened to Knostmann or his men until after the battle was over, when he met up with him in Lysyanka.

Siegel's and Hummel's regiments, along with hundreds of other troops, continued moving south along the ridgeline, vainly trying to find a point where Soviet defenses were weak enough to break through. Along the way, the mass of troops merged with Debus' group from *Wiking*. Finally, they reached the southern edge of the woodline and crossed the road running from Zhurzhintsy to Pochapintsy, approximately 500 meters northwest of the latter town. Siegel urged the group across the road and the open slope, aiming for the southern edge of the forest south of Hill 239. Cloaked by the darkness and concealed by the falling snow, he ordered a halt when several Soviet troops pulling sleds were spotted heading in their direction. Unnoticed by enemy, who passed within 100 meters of his group, Siegel next observed a Soviet mess truck that was driving along the edge of the forest approximately 70 meters to his front.

This, no doubt, marked the positions of the outer Soviet encircling ring. The mess truck kept moving along the edge of the woods, dropping off containers of hot soup at some gun positions and bunkers, which pointed towards the west. Concealed by a row of bushes, Siegel and a few others crept slowly towards the enemy, who seemed more intent on eating than maintaining local security. It appeared to be an antitank gun position, protected by infantry. At his signal, the Germans rose up and charged the Soviets, who returned fire.

Siegel's men quickly overran the Soviets, chasing them out of their bunkers, which were soon destroyed with hand grenades. A quick-thinking *Leutnant* from *14.Kompanie* removed the breech-blocks from the guns and threw them into the snow, rendering them useless. Soon joined by several hundred other troops which had followed his regiment, Siegel decided to keep pushing on before daybreak, when the chances of being discovered and fired upon would increase. Although he and his regiment had broken out of the Pocket, they were not yet free, for they still had to cross the Gniloy Tikich and reach Lysyanka.[22]

Lieb, travelling with the command group of *72.Inf.Div.*, was hard put to stay in touch with the assault units. Mounted on horseback with his staff, several aides and radio operators, Lieb planned to travel with the leading unit in order to exercise close command and control of the breakout. Shortly after the leading attack columns departed at 2300 hours, he and his staff observed their passage from their tactical headquarters at the edge of Khilki. Lieb anxiously awaited news of the breakout's progress. "Any news from up front?" he asked his chief of staff, *Oberst* Franz. "Nothing," Franz replied. Lieb then asked Franz what he made of the silence. Franz replied that "It can mean only one thing - the first wave has got through and has opened the pocket at bayonet point." "Then let's go, gentlemen," Lieb replied. Pushing his white fur cap tightly upon his head, Lieb mounted his awaiting horse and prepared to move out.[23]

Just then, the sounds of heavy fighting could be heard coming from the northern edge of Khilki, which formed the right shoulder of the German breakout corridor. It had to be held at all costs. The southern part of Komarovka had already been lost earlier that day - if Khilki fell too, then the Germans would be trapped. Lieb hurriedly dismounted and, accompanied by his chief of staff, strode back into the *isba* that served as his command post to see what was going on. He asked Franz, "I need a reliable combat group to hold up the Russians. Whom have we left?"

At that moment, an Austrian officer, *Oberst* Neufellner of *Art.Rgt.86 (K.Abt.B)* stepped forward to the map table, illuminated by candlelight and said calmly "Herr General, I have only a hundred men left, but I'll cover the army's back with them, come what may. Send my best wishes to my homeland - I'll hold Khilki." Neufellner then led a counterattack that threw the Soviets out of the village and chased them as far as Hill 226.8, where they were shot by *Rgt.Gr.593*, which still held the hill. As he had promised, Neufellner and his men defended Khilki until the very end, and even managed to get themselves out.[24] The whole success of the entire endeavor was now dependent upon officers like Neufellner and NCOs who were willing to take responsibility and carry out their duty to the last.

With the situation in Khilki well in hand, Lieb and his staff could now join the breakout. As the leading units silently moved out, Lieb and his mounted headquarters group followed. After a few hours, it had become evident to him that his troops had broken clean through the enemy's inner ring of encirclement. However, Lieb had received no reports from either *K.Abt.B* on the right or from *Wiking* on the left. He could only gauge their progress by the sounds of fighting and vehicle noises, but things seemed to be going according to plan, at least so far. Nor could he raise Stemmermann's headquarters by radio. Lieb summoned

Hptm. von Meerheimb, his corps intelligence officer, and ordered him to ride to Stemmermann's command post in Shanderovka and notify him that the attack had commenced. Meerheimb, an experienced steeplechase rider from Mecklenburg, silently saluted and moved off in the snow. Wheeling his piebald mare round, he was seen a few moments later galloping back towards Shanderovka through several bursts of Soviet artillery fire.[25]

Lieb kept moving with the rest of his staff and the bulk of *72.Inf.Div.* towards the southwest. As he later recalled, movement of the main column was proceeding excruciatingly slow, due to the broken terrain. The lack of any decent connecting roads within the route of advance was beginning to extract its toll. Numerous gullies, *balki* and steep hillsides, which were far steeper than the maps indicated, caused frequent halts. Often, men and horses suddenly disappeared as they stumbled into deep snow-filled holes. Vehicles got stuck and had to be dug out by hand, but more and more of them had to be abandoned.[26]

According to *Maj.* Hermani, the corps operations officer, the entire procession looked like a Napoleonic nightmare, a later-day version of the retreat from Moscow. Ahead, the sound of small arms firing could be heard. *Maj.* Ganschow, the corps quartermaster, told Hermani that he had experienced a premonition of his own death. "Give my love to my wife," Ganschow said. "I won't get through…look after my dog - I don't want him to become a stray." Hermani tried to convince him that the would make it through, but was haunted by Ganschow's words as he watched him canter alongside the marching column astride his powerful grey, with his dog, a huge German mastiff, running beside him.[27]

As Lieb recalled, the firing gradually died down by 0200 hours. Two hours later, the bulk of *72.Inf.Div.* had drawn abreast with Zhurzhintsy, yet he still had not received any messages from the two divisions on the left and right. Somehow, the pack animals with his headquarters signals unit and its precious radios had strayed off course and could not be located. Lieb was now helpless to influence the events that followed. At 0400 hours, he heard the sounds of fighting along the road running from Zhurzhintsy to Hill 239, signifying the breakout of *Gren.Rgt.105*. The Soviet fire began to increase noticeably. Sounds of fighting could now be heard from the south, where the SS troops were vainly trying to seize the ridgeline. At 0600 hours, Lieb was then swept up in the general movement of units away from Zhurzhintsy towards Pochapintsy. As each successive assault wave reached the base of the slope between Zhurzhintsy and Hill 239, they recoiled in the face of Soviet tank and artillery fire and shifted towards the path of least resistance.

Lieb soon found himself in the large *balka* directly at the foot of Hill 239. Sounds of firing could be heard coming from all directions, which increased as it began to get lighter. He could hear the sounds of firing from the far left or south, where he adjudged the location of the main body of *Wiking*. Of *K.Abt.B*, there was no trace. Lieb had no idea that the bulk of *Div.Gr.112*, his old division, had already broken through, nor did he know the fate of *Gren.Rgt.105*. As Siegel led the general movement out of the *balka* towards the south, Lieb

joined in. There was now little that he could do anyway, since part of his staff had been scattered and he no longer had any radios to control anything with. Lieb watched helplessly as tanks, heavy guns, and horse-drawn carts tried to negotiate the steep hillside under fire.

Most of them slipped, rolled over and had to be blown up. Only a few, as he later recalled, were able to make the steep ascent. As the sun slowly rose in the misty wintry sky, all order seemed to collapse. Units, which had been under the control of their officers until now, disintegrated rapidly into disorder. At about the same time, Lieb observed troops from *Wiking* appearing on his left, probably the bulk of *Westland*.[28] As he watched, elements of *72.Inf.Div.*, including Siegel's regiment, made several attempts to break through via Hill 239, but without success. Each time they were bloodily repulsed. By noon, even these were discontinued and the bulk of the division turned to the south, as the other units already had.

After being separated from their corps commander in the crush and confusion, Lieb's staff struggled to find him in the chaos. Artillery fire upon their position began to increase, scattering them in all directions. Hermani's roan horse was hit by a shell fragment and collapsed. Stunned by the burst and the fall from his horse, he staggered on. His enlisted aide had disappeared, and he had lost his map case and binoculars as well. Machine-gun fire was now coming from the hill to Hermani's right. *Oberst* Franz also had his horse shot out from under him, causing Franz to fall heavily to the ground. Men and horses seemed to be running everywhere in panic. If he wanted to survive, he had to get off the open slope at once. Having lost his pistol, he quickly picked up a sniper rifle that someone had dropped. As an artillery horse trotted by, Franz reached out and grabbed its harness, pulling himself into the saddle, and rode towards the south, along with the rest of the troops.[29]

Lieb, with a few other staff officers, had decided to push on. Gathering a battalion composed from troops from several different divisions, he headed for the gap between Hill 239 and Pochapintsy, the same route that Siegel had taken shortly before. As they marched onwards, they were attacked by several Soviet aircraft, which fired and missed before disappearing again into the clouds. It appeared to Lieb that all command and control had vanished. He later wrote that "There were no regiments, no battalions. Now and then small units appeared alongside us…my staff still kept up with me, but the aides who had been sent on various missions did not find their way back."[30] After a short while, he fell in with a large group from *72.Inf.Div.* There, at the eastern edge of the large field west of Pochapintsy Lieb met up with the division's *1a, Oberstlt.* Müller, who informed him that one of his regiments (Siegel's) had already penetrated the enemy positions along the woodline. Their way, however, was barred by at least ten Soviet tanks.

Up to this point, the breakout had more or less gone according to plan. True, while only a few hundred to a thousand of Lieb's attacking force had reached Oktyabr along the planned line of attack, most of the assault forces had managed to stay together and reach the area immediately west of Pochapintsy. What would happen over the next dozen hours had not been planned or accounted for by any of the German leadership. It would prove to be the greatest challenge that Lieb's and Stemmermann's troops would face. Now, there was only one way out and that was barred by the enemy. Lieb and Müller decided to attack. They were to now encounter an awakened and enraged enemy.

End Notes

1   Hilss, Werner. " Ein Reitpferd zog mich durch den Fluss," *Alte Kameraden*, Vol.2, 1990. (Stuttgart: *Alte Kamerad*, 1990), p. 25.

2   Lehman and Tiemann, pp. 36-37.

3   Carell, p. 419.

4   *8.Armee* KTB, entry dated 0100 hours 17 February 1944, p. 1.

5   *1.Pz.Armee* KTB, entry dated 17 February 1944, p. 1.

6   Scherff, p. 227.

7   Ibid, p. 228.

8   Radio Message, *III.Pz.Kps. to XI.A.K.,* dated 0445 hours 17 February 1944.

9   Letter, Ernst Schenk, to author, dated 26 July 1996, p. 3.

10 Ibid.

11 Bäke, Dr. Franz. *Bericht über die Verbindungsaufnahme der westlich Tscherkassy eingeschlossenen Korps am 17.2.1944*, Rgts.Gef.Stand, den 24.2.1944, p. 1.

12 Ibid, p. 2.

13 *World War Two German Military Studies*, Vol 1, p-143d, p. 24.

14 Ibid, p. 25.

15 Ibid, p. 25 and 1a, 72.Inf.Div., *Gefechtsbericht, Anlage 3 zu Generalkommando XI.A.K.,* 1a Nr. 19/44 g. Kdos., Div. Gef. Std., den 23.2.1944.

16 Carell, p. 421.

17 Buchner, p. 42.

18 Schenk letter, p. 4.

19 Strassner, pp. 260-261 and *Vorschlag für die Verleihung des Ritterkreuzes des Eisernen Kreuzes, 5.SS-Pz.Div. Wiking*, 21.4.1944, p. 4.

20 Interview with Günther Lange, former member, *SS-Pz.Art.Rgt.5,* Korsun-Shevchenkovsky, Ukraine, 27 June 1996.

21 Siegel, pp. 1-2.

22 Ibid, p. 2.

23 Carell, p. 423.

24 Ibid, p. 424 and Hermani quoted in Jahnke and Lerch, p. 95.

25 Ibid.

26 Lieb in DA Pam 20-234, p. 27.

27 Carell, p. 424.

28 Ibid, p. 29.

29 Carell, pp. 424-425.

30 Lieb in DA Pam 20-234, p. 29.

Chapter Twenty One
KONEV'S WRATH

"There was no time to take prisoners."
— *Maj. Kampov, Second Ukrainian Front* [1]

lthough the breakout had been underway since 2300 hours the night before, it took Second Ukrainian *Front's* commander several hours to fully realize what was taking place. However, once Konev sensed the magnitude of what was occurring under his very nose, he and his commanders reacted aggressively. As it grew lighter, the now fully-alerted Soviets began to pummel the German columns with direct and indirect fire, forcing the mass of troops to increasingly turn to the left or south, away from Oktyabr and the escape hatch bounded by Zhurzhintsy and Hill 239.

To the far right, *Oberst* Fouquet's *K.Abt.B* had run into difficulty. Although most of the advance column had managed to break out without difficulty, the rest of the attacking column had been cut off when *Gren.Rgt.105* swerved across its path. By the time the column was back on course, the Soviet defenses near Zhurzhintsy had been alerted, much to the dismay of *Feld Ers.Btl.112*, which suffered heavy losses from a company of T-34s. Even division commanders were becoming casualties. *Oberst* Fouquet had been wounded while personally leading an attack against an antitank gun position and was reported missing in action by his staff.

The withdrawal of the supporting artillery, *Oberst* Böhm's attached *Art.Rgt.188* from *88.Inf.Div.*, was hindered by the deep *balki* and steep slopes of the hillsides, finally forcing Böhm to blow up the remaining guns. After shooting off the rest of its ammunition, the guns of the 15 cm *Abteilung*, which had remained behind on the western edge of Shanderovka to provide fire support, were also destroyed by their crews. Böhm's artillerymen now joined the stream of troops moving to the south, away from Hill 239. Some individual groups, however, pushed on and detoured north of Zhurzhintsy, arriving at the western edge of Oktyabr throughout the day. Böhm's adjutant, *Oblt.* Hans Menedetter, was able to break through south of Zhurzhintsy with a group from *Div.Gr.112*. After crossing the ridge, Menedetter's group encountered trenches and bunkers manned by troops from 41st Guards Rifle Division. His group rushed the Soviets and were soon locked in hand-to-hand combat, where both sides suffered heavy casualties. After overcoming enemy resistance, the group pushed west and reached the Gniloy Tikich by mid-morning, where they encountered hundreds of men from other units who had somehow arrived before them. Menedetter crossed the swollen creek on a log and soon reached the safety of Lysyanka, where he rejoined the remnants of his regiment.

Scattered Walloons, including a Ukrainian woman with child, steadily head towards saftey. (Photo courtesy of Kaisergruber)

After the artillery marched the *Korpsabteilung's* rearguard, the two security regiments from *213.Sich.Div.* Organized as *Gruppe Hellbach*, the middle-aged home guardsmen were supposed to constitute the fifth wave of Fouquet's divisional column. As they struggled forwards, *Oberstlt.* Hellbach and his men collided with the rear of the artillery column, marching now without their guns. As they halted, additional groups of marching troops from *72.Inf.Div.* and *Wiking* ran into them from behind. As these disorganized units marched by, Hellbach attached his unit to the rear of a much larger column from *Wiking* and followed them to Hill 239, where the advance halted in the face of heavy enemy fire. Hellbach and his men, as so many others had, gave up and sought shelter in the cover of the large ravine at the foot of the hill.[2] Any organized action by his unit became impossible, as his two regiments became mixed with the troops of three different divisions. Soviet artillery fire, now joined by rockets from *Katyushas*, increased perceptibly.

As the Soviet gunners determined the range to their targets, some crews even fired directly at individual Germans. Every meter of the escape corridor, barely three kilometers wide at its greatest point, now seemed to be directly targeted by the enemy. As the hazy sun rose into the sky, there was no sign of the *Luftwaffe* to provide the flank protection that Stemmermann had demanded as another prerequisite for the breakout - heavy snow and fog had grounded *Maj.* Rudel's *Stuka* squadron and *Oblt.* Hartmann's Messerschmidts. The Red Air Force, which attempted to bomb the escaping German columns during the day, had to do so blindly and with little effect, unlike their night attack on Shanderovka the previous evening. Overhead hummed the engines of Ju-52s, which still tried to drop bundles of ammunition along the planned route of advance, in hopes perhaps that the troops of *Gruppe Stemmermann* would be able to find them. In all likelihood, most landed within Soviet lines. The Soviet high command itself did not discover the magnitude of the German breakout effort until later that Thursday morning. Konev claimed that he knew about it as early as 0300 hours, because he had moved his *Front* headquarters close to the scene of the action to supervise the fighting.[3] However, by that time, *Angriffsgruppe Lieb's* attack had been underway four hours and the two *Regimentsgruppen* from *K.Abt.B* had already reached safety in Lysyanka. The two Red Army divisions in Lieb's path, 206th Rifle and 5th Guards Airborne, had been simply overrun by the mass of German troops and were busy fighting for their own survival, so the late notification is understandable.

Soviet wire communications were also hampered because the German assault columns had been cutting every telephone cable they found as they passed through the escape corridor. Additionally, the German's choice to forego an artillery barrage and to rely on the bayonet to cut their way out also contributed to the surprise and confusion the Soviet leadership must have experienced. Their total lack of tactical preparation indicates that they had not expected the attack to be so sudden nor so powerful. According to available evidence, it appears that Konev did not actually discover the magnitude of the breakout's initial success until much later that morning, despite what he claimed afterwards.

German radio interception units of *III.Pz.Korps*, which were monitoring Soviet radio broadcasts, indicate otherwise. One logbook shows that the first radio message reporting the breakout was sent by a tank battalion of 5th Guards Tank Corps at 0815 hours 17 February, over nine hours after the breakout had begun. In it, the officer reports:

> The enemy has broken through the sector encompassing the southern exit of Khilki and is moving in columns along the ravine in the direction of Oktyabr. In the long, narrow forest [between Khilki and Hill 239] he has been partially brought to a halt. Southeast of me as well as the southeastern corner of Khilki the enemy is (still) concentrating his forces. In the long forest he has concentrated about 200 vehicles. I am shooting uninterruptedly with my two tanks. Twice I have shot at the southern entrance of Khilki . . . [4]

Nor was that the only report. Others soon followed on its heels, as each message appeared more worrisome than the one before. Another one sent 15 minutes later from an artillery unit of 22nd Guards Tank Brigade, attached to 27th Army, to its higher headquarters of 5th Guards Tank Corps reported that "The enemy is breaking out of the ring with powerful forces. Fighting has been reported in the vicinity of our observation post."[5]

Fifteen minutes after that, 5th Guards Tank Corps had been able to gather enough information to determine what was going on, though many details were still lacking. This was the moment the First and Second Ukrainian *Fronts* had been waiting for, the climax of the battle, and its leaders had been caught by surprise. The commander of 5th Guards Tank Corps sent the following report to his higher headquarters, 27th Army, at 0845 hours "The enemy has broken out of the ring. [He is] marching in large groups with tank and artillery support in the direction of Pochpintsy, suffering heavy casualties."[6] Another report stated that the Germans had seized Hill 239 and were advancing towards Zhurzhintsy, though this report was contradicted a few minutes later. Reflecting the fate of the subsequent columns' attempts to break through via Hill 239 - Zhurzhintsy, a subsequent message reported that Hill 239 was in fact in Soviet hands and that the Germans were moving south one and a half kilometers from the observer's present position (towards Pochapintsy).[7] Another message sent by the same headquarters five minutes later, its sender baffled perhaps by the German's determination, reported that the enemy was attacking like "drunken maniacs, like men possessed..."

This information, once it had been received by Lt.Gen. Trofimenko's headquarters at 27th Army, must have been passed rapidly up to his *Front* commander, Konev. By 0900, Konev began framing his response, which chiefly consisted of ordering all of the armor and artillery that he controlled to move immediately towards the pocket and attack. To do so, 206th Rifle Division and 18th Tank Corps, on the northwestern edge of the pocket, were ordered to attack towards the southeast; 5th Guards Airborne Division and 5th Guards Cavalry Corps were ordered to attack from the southeast towards the northwest. Both attacks would slice across the German axis of advance and cut *Gruppe Stemmermann* in two. At the same time, portions of 5th Guards Tank Army's 29th Tank Corps was ordered to attack Khilki and Komarovka from the east through Shanderovka, while 2nd Tank Army from Zhukov's command was ordered to keep *1.Pz.Div.* boxed in at Lysyanka.[8]

By conducting such a concentric attack, Konev hoped that it would quickly crush the Germans before they could escape by destroying their tactical cohesion, achieved by chopping their combat elements into little groups and rendering them helpless in the face of tank attacks. The stopper in the bottle, that is, the units forming the defensive line along the line Pochapintsy-Hill 239-Zhurzhintsy was 41st Rifle Division as well as companies, battalions and brigades from three tanks corps-18th, 20th, and 29th, all of which seem to have become intermingled by this point, so confused had the situation become. This indicated the haste in which units had been flung into the narrow neck of land between the two German forces. All they had to do was to hold their positions against thousands of desperately determined German soldiers and block their path - which was to prove a difficult task.

Konev's corps and divisions should have been able to do this, but the actual execution of the plan proved to be far more complicated. His units were mixed up badly; the inner encircling ring of his *Front* was literally back-to-back with the outer encircling ring of Zhukov's command. Communications were poor. The two infantry divisions in the Germans' path had been smashed, leaving the tank units short of their accustomed infantry support. Konev had more than enough artillery available, perhaps more than he could effectively employ.

Indeed, as previously mentioned, artillery coordination had degenerated to the point where 15.2 cm howitzers were firing directly at individual infantrymen, when it would have been far more effective to mass fires and attempt to throw up a curtain of steel in the Germans' path, thus effectively trapping them so that tanks and infantry could mop them up at their leisure. This does not seem to have occurred. Additionally, 5th Guards Cavalry Corps would have to carry out a 40 kilometer forced march, which would not put all of its horsemen into position until 2000 hours that evening, so that force, ideally suited for attacking infantry columns, would not be available for employment until most of the fighting that day was over.[9]

At first, as German survivors later recalled, Soviet tanks along the breakout corridor seemed satisfied to shoot at them with cannon and machine-gun fire from a distance of 500 meters to one kilometer - hardly a serious threat, unless one was unlucky enough to be hit. As it began to grow light, their fire became more accurate. Since the tanks appeared to be unsupported by infantry, the T-34s and JS IIs seemed to respectfully keep their distance. The artillery fire was another matter, though it seemed to be poorly directed. Indeed, one's chances of being hit appeared small. As the day lengthened, the snow kept falling. There was no sign of either the *Luftwaffe* or the Red Air Force. By mid-morning, the situation began to change. Reports began to filter in that seemed to indicate that the Germans were getting away. One message sent out by 22nd Guards Tank Brigade at 0955 hours stated that "The enemy is approaching in large columns from the ravine east of Zhurzhintsy…individual groups and pushing onwards towards Oktyabr and Lysyanka."[10] Fearing that his prize was slipping from his grasp, Konev urged his tanks and troops onwards - no Fascists could be allowed to escape! After all, he had promised Stalin as much and he knew what happened to those who displeased the dictator, from his own bitter personal experience.

Groups of Soviet tanks, which had hugged the woodline or had stayed out of range of German antitank weapons, began to move forward from the northwest and southeast. The long columns of German troops, horse-drawn sledges, and the few motorized vehicles were hard for them to miss. While the initial attacking columns had been able to punch their way through, the large group of troops in the center - the columns

of wounded, artillery, headquarters units, corps units, and so on - were relatively defenseless. After initially hesitating, the Soviet tanks plunged into the long lines of troops. What had begun as an orderly movement quickly became a rout. Just as the troops had veered to the left in panic at the foot of Hill 239 several hours before, now the mass of the German non-combat units in the center of the breakout formation panicked as well. The results were some of the bloodiest carnage ever seen on the Eastern Front.

One witness of what transpired next was *Oberst* Franz of *XXXXII.A.K.* As he moved on horseback towards the southern end of Hill 239, Franz spotted 15 T-34s approaching from the direction of Pochapintsy. As the tanks bore down upon a narrow gorge close by, he noticed that it was filled with columns of peasant carts blazoned with Red Cross flags - one of the units that had decided not to leave its wounded behind. First, the tanks stopped and machine-gunned the wagons, horses, and their contents. Then, they moved forward and crushed the wagons with their treads, smashing horses and men into a bloody pulp. To his horror, Franz watched as the tanks drove back and forth over the bloody mess, until nothing was left alive. "The swine, the swine!" Franz shouted in frustration, but it was no use.[11]

The column of wounded had belonged to *Wiking*, which consisted of 130 wounded men of that division plus a few dozen others from *K.Abt.B*, led by Dr. Thon. As Franz later related, "The war for them ended right there." Somehow, Thon was able to rescue a dozen of the wounded and escape from the tanks. Another column of wounded, consisting of 140 men from *Wiking* led by Dr. Isselstein were ambushed by tanks as their column passed through the western outskirts of Shanderovka. Isselstein, who had tried to save as many of the wounded as possible, was himself killed by a tank shell. Increasingly, troops began to leave their wounded behind, as they had become impediments to their own survival. The wounded's pleas of "Take me with you! Don't leave me behind!" failed to dissuade men whose hearts had hardened after three weeks of debilitating combat. Hundreds, if not thousands, of wounded were left behind on the escape route to either make it out on their own or await the approach of the Soviets who would administer the *coup de grace*.

Packs of T-34s and JS IIs then began to wade into the infantry columns and attack the defenseless troops. Virtually all antitank guns and howitzers had been abandoned by this point, after becoming stuck in the steep ravines or *balki* that crisscrossed the escape corridor. Thousands of men leapt into snow-filled ditches or ravines to escape from them, hoping that they would be able to exit after the tanks had passed by. In some cases, the Soviet tanks appeared satisfied to play cat and mouse until someone finally gathered the courage necessary to fight back. Two men who refused to give up were *Ofw.* Krause and *Gef.* Fritz Hamann of *3.Kp./Pz.Jäg.Abt.389* of *389.Inf.Div.* Only 97 men remained of their battalion, which had been attached to *Wiking* nearly two weeks before. Krause, Hamann and the 30 men that remained of their company were hauling a handcart loaded with 12 *Panzerfäuste* which they soon put to good use.

When their unit and soldiers from other units were forced to take cover in a ravine north of Pochapintsy because of Soviet tanks approaching from the direction of Komarovka, the anti-tank gunners soon found that they were trapped. Two T-34s had been positioned at the top of the ravine, where they began to fire leisurely into the pack of massed troops. Krause ordered Hamann to follow him. Scooping up armloads of *Panzerfäuste,* both men cautiously crept forward, taking advantage of the dead space in front of the tank where its crew's vision was limited. Suddenly, both men rose up from the ground, took aim, and fired. Two explosions reverberated across the snow. Soon, both T-34s were on fire with smoke pouring from the hatches. Using the two burning tanks as cover, Krause and Hamann continued their daring attack - men pitted against tanks. Hamann soon knocked out two more, while Krause bagged another. The commander of the Soviet tank unit finally decided that he had had enough and ordered the remaining five tanks to withdraw. Now that their escape route was cleared, hundreds of men surged out of the ravine and continued marching towards Pochapintsy.[12] Thanks to the heroism of a few dozen men like Krause and Hamann, the German breakout, as disorganized as it was, continued to build momentum.

With or without infantry, the Soviet tanks continued their attempt to cut off the German columns. By 0930 hours, a combined infantry and tank attack had managed to wrest control of all of Komarovka from the defending troops from *Westland,* narrowing the bottleneck between that town and Khilki even further - now it was only one kilometer wide and only half of the Germans had yet passed through the gap. *Westland* was immediately ordered to carry out a counterattack in order to regain the northern half of the village. They seized it, but soon were forced to give it up again. Throughout the day, additional Soviet units tried to retake Khilki as well, but were repeatedly repulsed. *Oberst* Neufellner was good to his word - his artillerymen held firm.

Eight kilometers to the west, the battle raged. Despite their confusion and disappointment, the Germans still had not given up their attempt to break out. In fact, it seemed to only increase their determination to make it through. Having given up their efforts to make it to Lysyanka via Hill 239, the mass of disorganized troops began to shift towards the south. Following in the wake of Siegel's successful escape, thousands of men pushed onwards. Having noticed Siegel's passage, the Soviets began to shift tanks to the south in order to block any further attempts to break out between Hill 239 and Pochapintsy. *Oberst* Franz, who had followed the tide of troops away from the *balka* at the base of Hill 239 towards Pochapintsy, was surprised to hear a sound he had not heard in a long time, the sound of thousands of voices shouting "Hurrah!" at the top of their lungs. Turning around, he saw a mass of between 3,000 to 4,000 German soldiers pouring out of the *balka* at the base of the hill, where he had just left minutes before. It was now midmorning and the breakout had been underway for 11 hours.

Franz stood there, mesmerized by a spectacle that perhaps had not been seen since the Napoleonic wars, a massive column of men charging the enemy with fixed bayonets. Led by an officer on horseback, the formation raced towards the line of Soviet tanks and antitank guns arrayed along the clearing in front of the woods where Siegel had passed with his men several hours before. The officer leading the charge was *Oberstlt.* Johann Müller, the *1a* of *72.Inf.Div.,* who had taken command of the division when its commander, *Oberst* Hohn, was wounded and presumed missing. Accompanied by General Lieb, Müller's column was composed of men from several divisions - *Wiking, K.Abt.B,* and his own *72.Inf.Div.* Once they reached the woods beyond the tanks, they would be safe, or so they thought. This attack by the determined German infantrymen against tanks was a spectacle that Franz never forgot. Recovering from his astonishment, Franz spurred his mount onwards and joined the column as it passed by. Soon, the Soviet tanks and guns began to shoot at the onrushing column with machine-gun fire and high explosive shells, and men fell by the score, yet on they came through the driving snow.

As Lieb galloped onwards, he noticed that small groups of German soldiers had begun to surrender, but the main body of troops kept pushing onwards until they reached the safety of the woods, where they threw back the defending Soviet infantry from 41st Rifle Division. Lieb recalled later that the entire area was littered with dead horses, destroyed wagons, and abandoned guns. He could not differentiate between the wounded and the fit; their white camouflaged clothing blended in with their bandages. Although the situation was characterized by extreme confusion, Lieb wrote later that " . . . one could still recognize the determination in the minds of the troops to break through toward the southwest, in the direction of *III.Pz.Korps.*"[13] After reaching the woods, Lieb and the remaining members of his staff pressed on along the wood's edge towards the Gniloy Tikich.

Near Lieb, Franz, spotted a 50-meter gap between a T-34 and a JS II tank, and spurred his horse in a bid to get through before he was noticed. To his relief, he and his horse rushed by both tanks before they could react and raced towards the woodline, only a scant distance away. Suddenly, his horse was hit by a hot splinter from a shell bursting nearby, causing it to somersaulted as its forelegs collapsed. Franz was thrown, rolling end over end in the snow, but was amazingly unhurt. Picking up his sniper's rifle that lay next to his dead horse, he ran for the cover of the woods, where he was soon joined by hundreds of other men who had made it through the line of tanks.[14] Although the T-34s and JS IIs had killed or wounded dozens of men, without supporting infantry they could only slow the escaping Germans. Some tanks were even destroyed by *Panzerfäuste* or by molotov cocktails. One tank was knocked out in the melee when a quick-thinking soldier of *K.Abt.B* leaped up on its engine compartment, poured gasoline over it, and lit a match. As the crew bailed out of the flaming vehicle, they were taken prisoner and forced to accompany their captors.

Meanwhile, *Maj.* Siegel and his regiment had approached the Gniloy Tikich. After breaking through the Soviet antitank gun position in the woods two kilometers west of Pochapintsy, Siegel and his men kept pushing to the southwest, where by mid-morning they encountered a steep slope that descended into a swampy meadow bordering the creek. On the opposite bank, there were no signs of a relief force, no signs of any German troops at all. Worse yet, there appeared to be no bridge over the

Troops from Wiking move out through the snowstorm toward the supposed safety of Hill 239.
(Jarolin-Bundesarchiv 81/16/29A)

Troops of the Walloon Brigade, intermingled with men from other regiments, move steadily southwest across the open steppe between Shanderovka and Lysyanka.
(Photo courtesy of Kaisergruber)

creek as far as the eye could see. At this point, the creek, fed by melting snow of the previous two weeks, had rose to flood stage. Two to three meters deep and up to 30 meters across, its waters rushed swiftly past the Germans who had not expected such an obstacle at the end of their ordeal. Three kilometers away in the hazy distance lay Lysyanka, where salvation was still thought to be awaiting them. Suddenly, a salvo of *Katyusha* rockets burst nearby. Evidently, the Soviet unit that Siegel had previously swept aside had sounded the alarm and was now bringing artillery and rocket fire to bear upon their position. Fortunately, it was impacting upon the Soviet antitank gun positions, and not near enough to cause any harm to his men.

Of more concern were five Soviet tanks that had taken up positions on a hillside to the north of Siegel's location, between 400 and 500 meters away. Siegel feared the worst, since his men no longer had any heavy weapons. Incredibly, nothing happened. Quickly gathering together the remnants of his and *Oberst* Hummel's regiments, Siegel then moved his force to the bank of the creek. Along the way, they flushed a group of Soviet infantry out of a thin line of foxholes who gave up without much of a fight. Finally, after crossing the bed of an abandoned railroad, they were at the creek. Still there was no sign of any relief force. Siegel quickly decided to form a bridgehead on his side of the river in order to prevent the crossing site from being overrun by the enemy.

Summoning the company commanders of his and Hummel's regiment, as well as Debus' remaining SS men, Siegel briefed them on the overall situation, as much as he knew about it, and assigned each unit defensive sectors in the bridgehead. He expected the Soviets to attack momentarily, and wanted his troops to be able to hold them off long enough for a bridge to be built. For the next several hours, Siegel and his men held this tiny bridgehead, which measured a mere 300 meters wide by 200 or so meters deep. Fortunately, it was sheltered from all but direct fire from the steep bluffs on his side of the creek. Since most of the units in the bridgehead (more troops kept arriving throughout the morning) were without any leadership, Siegel briefed his own officers and sergeants that the success of their little enterprise was up to them - all "alte Hasen"

(old hares). Later Siegel recounted that "It was heroic, the way these grenadiers comported themselves in this situation."[15]

Siegel assigned *Ltn*. Gross, of *Gren.Rgt.124,* control of the right (or southern) flank of the bridgehead, while Siegel took command of the left. He assigned an unnamed SS officer the task of constructing some kind of emergency bridge using whatever materials he could lay his hands upon. Siegel did not visit the crossing site, since he was more concerned with insuring that his men stayed in their foxholes, so he had no idea of what was happening along the banks of the creek. Several times over the next few hours, the Soviets tried to mount uncoordinated infantry attacks against the bridgehead, which was constantly swelling as thousands of German troops and hundreds of *panje* wagons loaded with wounded sought refuge there. Each time the Soviets were beaten back by rifle and machine-gun fire. Siegel moved back and forth between the flanks to keep abreast of the situation and to reassure his men.

Through the bare trees between his position and the creek, Siegel could observe groups of German soldiers climbing the bank on the opposite side and marching towards Lysyanka, so he assumed that the crossing was progressing in an orderly manner. Siegel remembered that his main concern at the time was with the town of Vsemirnyye, one kilometer to the southeast, where Soviet troops and could plainly be seen with binoculars. He was also concerned about a row of bushes to his left, through which the Soviets could approach undetected until the last moment. Except for intermittent artillery harassing fire, most of which was observed landing on the opposite bank of the creek, it seemed to be quiet. Even the Soviet tanks, which had backed further away, were keeping a respectful distance. About an hour later, the first armored vehicle of *Wiking* arrived, probably the Pz.III *Beobachtungspanzer* from *SS-Pz.Art.Rgt.5*. How it had gotten through was a mystery.

Less than an hour after the arrival of the tank from *Wiking*, a Soviet tank suddenly charged from the left flank and fired point blank into the masses of horse-drawn vehicles that had collected along the creek's eastern bank. As it continued its advance, it quickly became stuck in a deep gully on the left flank of the German position. Its crew, described by Siegel as consisting merely of *blutjunge Bengels* (young little rascals), quickly bailed out and were taken prisoner. The other tanks on the hillside, perhaps dissuaded by their comrades' fate, decided to remain where they were and lob shells intermittently into the mass of German troops, which still kept arriving. Despite the chaos which surrounded them, both *Gren.Rgt.266* and *Gren.Rgt.124* remained in their foxholes, exhibiting, in Siegel's words, "exemplary conduct." Around 0830 hours, a large group of German horsemen arrived at the bridgehead, among whom were many officers.* None of them asked Siegel what was going on - they seemed concerned only about their own fate. After what had happened on the slopes of Hill 239, it seemed to Siegel that the new password, instead of "Password Freedom, Objective Lysyanka" had now become "Every Man for Himself!"

While the main body of German troops had dissolved into disorganized groups of soldiers under the leadership of whomever shared their determination to fight his way out, the rearguard kept withdrawing in an orderly manner under the control of their officers. Stemmermann, who had moved his headquarters from Shanderovka to Khilki during the evening, was at first able to control their withdrawal by a combination of radio and couriers. That evening, both *57.* and *88.Inf.Div.* had already withdrawn to phase line "Green" by 2230 hours, the first phase of their covering action. By 0300, both divisions and attached elements had begun to withdraw to phase line "Black," on the eastern outskirts of Shanderovka.

The command to withdraw to the last defensive positions, phase line "Red," reached *88.Inf.Div.* at 0445 hours. The movement was supposed to occur at 0600 hours and the division was able to comply. The courier carrying the same message for *57.Inf.Div.* could not deliver it, since the messenger could not find the divisional headquarters in the darkness. Trowitz finally got the command to withdraw to "Red" two hours later, after the message was relayed to him by radio from *88.Inf.Div.*, thus delaying his division's rearward movement by two hours. By that point, Stemmermann had lost almost all contact with his units, as his radio sets had been irreparably damaged by the constant shifting of positions and the unloading and loading of the fragile equipment from truck to horseback. The withdrawal to phase line "Red" would also be the most difficult to accomplish, since it lay to the west of Shanderovka and both Trowitz and *Graf* Rittberg would have to move their divisions through the bottleneck formed by that town at roughly the same time. If the enemy attacked during this critical movement, the result could be disastrous.

The evacuation of Shanderovka proved to be difficult. Not only were the streets still jammed with abandoned vehicles and equipment, it was under heavy artillery fire. Many of the wounded who had been left behind on Stemmermann's order begged the rearguard to take them along as they withdrew to the southwest. The few guns remaining in position fired their last few rounds of ammunition, then were spiked by their crews, who joined the mass of soldiers marching through the town. Fires burned throughout Shanderovka, giving full meaning to the term

"Hell's Gate." It would soon become the front line once again. The forward elements of both divisions were further delayed by the traffic jam that still held sway at the small bridge west of the town, where Trowitz reported that vehicles were still lined up four abreast waiting their turn to cross. After ruthlessly pushing many of these unnecessary wheeled vehicles out of the way, Trowitz's men were able to restore some logic to the traffic flow. Precious hours had been lost in the meantime.

Meanwhile, Stemmermann moved his headquarters again, displacing with rear elements of *K.Abt.B* from Khilki to a location one and a half kilometers south of Petrovskoye at 0400 hours, inadvertently making it difficult for the various couriers and battle commanders to locate him. According to *Oberst* Gädke, Stemmermann decided to move his headquarters so that he would have a better view of the unfolding battle when it had become light enough to see. By accident, Stemmermann and his adjutant, who had both proceeded on foot, had become separated in the darkness and confusion from the rest of *XI.A.K.* staff during the march from Khilki, where he had apparently mixed in with the unending flow of traffic heading southwest. Gädke and the rest of the staff searched for him in vain, but without success. By 0500 hours, he had arrived at the agreed upon location, but Stemmermann was nowhere to be seen.[16] Now, at the time when his men most desperately needed their commander, he could not be located. The confusion which followed that day is partially due to the fact that no one could exercise overall command and control of troops escaping the pocket, with fateful consequences.

At one point during the rearguard's withdrawal, it appeared as if the Soviets might actually succeed in breaking through the thin defensive line. Spurred on by Konev, 73rd Rifle Corps carried out an attack by mid-morning which threatened to slice down the division boundary shared by *88.* and *57.Inf.Div.* Rolling south out of Steblev along the Steblev-Shanderovka road, this attack, consisting of units from 294th and 273rd Rifle Divisions supported by thirty-four tanks from 29th Guards Tank Corps, threatened to cave in the rearguard before it could complete its withdrawal to phase line "Red." Despite the best efforts of the rearguards, who were using howitzers to engage tanks with direct fire, the line began to give way. Where was Stemmermann to find reserves at a time like this? Fortunately, he still had one ace in the hole remaining-Köller's small armored force from *Wiking*, now reduced to 13 tanks and assault guns. This force had taken up an assembly area west of Shanderovka, where it would serve as a general reserve for the breakout, poised to counterattack any Soviet tank assaults. Köller and his tanks leapt into action. He knew what had to be done - wipe out the enemy penetration that threatened to split the Pocket in two. Leaving his wheeled vehicles behind on the outskirts of Khilki, Köller and the rest of his tanks hit the Soviets hard, knocking out several tanks and sending the rest reeling back into the town. With the line thus temporarily restored, both *57.* and *88.Inf. Divs.* could complete their withdrawal to phase line "Red" unmolested.

On the return trip to Khilki, Köller's tanks were attacked in the flank by a number of T-34s attacking from the direction of Komarovka. At nearly point-blank range, the two tank forces fired upon each other. *Uscha.* Hans Fischer, riding in a Pz. IV that he had commandeered after his own tank had broken down

---

* Several survivor's accounts state that this group of horsemen was composed of officers from *XI.A.K.'s* staff, including its chief of staff, *Oberst* Gädke.

311

earlier, knocked out one tank in the melee. One German tank was lost when a T-34 fired a shell into its crew compartment, causing an explosion that sent its commander hurtling into the air. Incredibly, he landed in a snowbank, unhurt. *Ustuf.* Schumacher, who was following Fischer's tank, destroyed this Soviet tank with an accurate shot of his own. At virtually the same time, the infantry company formed from tank crews without vehicles from Köller's battalion were fighting but a short distance away. Had Köller known they were so close, he probably would have invited them to come along and join the rest of their battalion, but it is just as well that they did not, for Köller was killed a short time later.

During the tank melee south of Khilki, several wheeled vehicles of the battalion were shot up and destroyed. Riding in one of these was Willy Hein, who had been serving as the battalion's acting signals officer near Nova Buda since being wounded in Olschana nearly three weeks before. His radio vehicle was hit and began to burn, forcing Hein to bail out of a flaming vehicle for the second time during the battle. Seeking protection in a ditch on the side of the road, Hein was spotted by his fellow company commander Schumacher, who was passing by after the remaining Soviet tanks had been chased away. Schumacher ordered his driver to halt and shouted at Hein to hop aboard. Sitting on the tank's engine compartment, Hein had the opportunity to size up the situation. "Things did not look very pleasant," he later wrote, and asked Schumacher to let him off after the tank had proceeded a couple of kilometers. Hein did not want to hinder his friend or the crew.[17] As Hein walked on, he joined a large group of marching soldiers and noticed that several Soviet prisoners had rearmed themselves with castoff weapons and were fighting their former captors a few hundred meters away, creating, in Hein's words, an "unforesee-ably desolate situation."

West of Khilki, Köller realized that the remaining wheeled vehicles could not make it across the rugged landscape and ordered them destroyed. When Köller's command tank's running gear was damaged by a shell, he ordered it blown up. Then, he and his adjutant briefly took over Schumacher's tank and directed the fighting, but shortly afterwards turned it back over to Schumacher, whom he entrusted with commanding the few remaining tanks and assault guns. Köller chose instead to ride with the wounded, whose ambulance was being towed by the big 18-ton recovery vehicle, to ensure that they were delivered to safety. During the next few hours, most of Köller's tanks and assault guns were destroyed by enemy fire or had become hope-lessly stuck in ravines or gullies. Only one or two at the most were able to run the gauntlet.

Köller tried to keep his battalion together, but it quickly became impossible due to the terrain, the weather, and the chaos which swirled about them. As the recovery vehicle in which he was riding was climbing the northern slope of the tree-covered hill due east of Zhurzhintsy, it was fired upon by a Soviet 7.62 cm antitank gun. Striking behind the driver's seat, the shell scored a direct hit, riddling Köller with shrapnel, killing him instantly. Many others were wounded for a second and third time. Köller's body was removed under enemy fire by survivors and his death was confirmed by one of the battalion's physicians. Since he

could not be buried in the frozen ground, *Ostuf.* Frels, an eyewitness, helped cover his body with pine boughs.[18] It is only fitting that he died while picking up individual wounded off of the battlefield, for he had been dedicated to the welfare of his men. Never mentioned as being one of the *Waffen-SS'* tank heroes, like Michael Wittman or Max Wünsche, Hans Köller nonetheless had led his battalion well during some of the sever-est fighting it had ever experienced and undoubtedly deserved the Knight's Cross he was never awarded.

A few tanks and assault guns had managed by midday to get as far as the eastern slope of Hill 239, but were unable to climb it due to the ice and steepness of the grade, except for one or two that managed to make it to the banks of the Gniloy Tikich.[19] These, too, were destroyed by the Soviets or blown up by their crews. Like all the other units that had gone before them, *SS-Pz.Abt.5* had ceased to exist as a coherent organization, as its survivors individually or in groups sought to escape. After fighting against hopeless odds for over three weeks and after destroying over 100 Soviet tanks, the battalion had fought its last fight of this battle. Leaderless, the tank crewmen fled south of Hill 239, joining the masses of other men who had collected in the giant ravine at the bottom of the hill. Now, each man would fight his own individual battle.

As the rearguards withdrew as planned, the units holding the northwestern and southeastern flanks began to withdraw as ordered as well. As the battalions and regiments of *57.* and *88.Inf.Div.* slowly withdrew west of Shanderovka, troops from *K.Abt.B* holding Khilki and Skripchintsy in the north and the SS holding the south disengaged and moved towards the center of the pocket, where they joined the stream of troops moving out in the early morning hours. All the while, *K.Gr. Neufellner* held the line north of Khilki, warding off repeated tank and infantry assaults. Line "Red" ran through Khilki, and it had to be held until the last possible moment. To the south, *Germania* and the Walloon Brigade held on along the arc encompassing eastern Schanderovka, Novo Buda, and the eastern outskirts of Komarovka.

One unit holding a position along the southeastern rim of the pocket was *II./Germania*, commanded by *Stubaf.* Kurt Schröder. He had been informed the night before by *Wiking's 1a, Ostubaf.* Manfred Schönfelder, that his battalion would form the division's rearguard, holding its position along the line Novo Buda - Khilki starting at 0600 hours 17 February, until the bulk of the division, including the Walloon Brigade and the Estonian *Narwa* battalion had been withdrawn. When he asked Schönfelder how long he would have to hold his positions, Schröder was told that he had to hold his position until relieved. Understandably, he was not very reassured by this response, for he was keenly aware of what was going on and did not want his battalion to be left behind. He had only 140 men left and intended to get every one of them out.

After destroying whatever equipment he could not bring with him, Schröder had his men on the road to Khilki shortly before dawn. Setting up his headquarters in a shack on the hill-side to the east of Khilki, he watched as endless columns of German troops and horse-drawn wagons passed on the road below. His outposts on the southern edge of Khilki reported large numbers of Soviet troops approaching, while Soviet artillery fire began to increase. Soviet tanks appeared at various locations, firing a few rounds before disappearing again. It all seemed so chaotic, yet the Soviets had yet to mount a concerted attack. He asked himself why was he still holding a line, if the rest of the rearguard had finally moved out? Growing impatient, Schröder sent his aide to the regimental command post in Khilki at 1000 hours to ask for permission from his commander, Fritz Ehrath, to begin pulling his men back from their exposed positions. The officer never returned, so he decided on his own initiative to withdraw his battalion and set them in motion towards Hill 239. Merging with the trickle of troops still withdrawing through Shanderovka, Schröder, with ten other men, formed his battalion's rearguard.

As he marched his unit to the southwest, it merged with the giant disorganized mass of men that had collected in the valley north of Pochapintsy. Here, Schröder was separated from his battalion, which had disappeared into the large group of troops of all branches and ranks. With his remaining men, he pushed and shoved his way forward. No one he asked had any information or knew what was going on. Approaching the head of the group of men, where the valley ended at the base of a steep slope that led up to Hill 239, he spotted three Soviet tanks that were shooting at anything that moved. There was no sign of his battalion. Schröder and the other ten men tried to get past the tanks anyway, successfully reaching the safety of a woodline before they were discovered.

As they caught their breath, the Germans heard the Soviet battle cry "Urrah," soon followed by a fusillade directed in their direction. Returning fire, Schröder and his men scattered in all directions. The Soviets did not pursue them, but instead disappeared back into the woods. The small group reassembled and pushed on. A short while later, they encountered three sleds being pulled by teams of Soviet troops. *Ruki Verch!* one shouted, and the Germans responded with rifle fire and hand grenades, which pinned the Soviets down long enough for Schröder and his men to make good their escape. Like many other men, he and his troops decided that their chances were far better if they moved in small groups rather than with larger formations, since they would attract less attention.[20] Such groups became increasingly successful at punching their way through as the day lengthened.

Other flank guard units did not even wait as long as Schröder's had. One of these units, *Westland's* 6.*Kompanie*, commanded by 21 year old Fritz Hahl, had been posted along the corridor on a hilltop a few hundred meters in front of Komarovka. Hahl was not quite sure that he welcomed this "special assignment." Although he had been ordered to hold the position ostensibly until the rearguard had disengaged, he viewed it rather more as a suicide mission than an opportunity to distinguish himself. But, an order was an order. Expecting to find the hilltop occupied by the enemy, he and his men were astonished to find it deserted when they arrived a few hours later, except for a solitary *Ivan* whom they captured while he was inspecting telephone lines.

As they stood there on the barren hilltop in the snow, his men gathered about him questioningly. He knew what they were thinking. His tactical sense told him that holding this hill had little military value, since there was no enemy as far as he could see, but he had been given an order to hold it, which he could not ignore. Fortunately for Hahl and his men, his battalion commander, *Hstuf.* Walter Schmidt, one of *Wiking's* most highly decorated soldiers, came by on horseback a few hours later to inspect their positions. Hahl reported to him and described his company's troop dispositions. Then, he asked his superior how long he was expected to hold his position. With a great smile, Schmidt spontaneously replied "Lad, I'll leave that to your own discretion!" and rode away. With that, Hahl assembled his company and marched off of the hill.

His unit, like Schröder's, headed towards the southwest and the illusory safety of Hill 239. Joining the mass of men on the road, Hahl and his men were frustrated when they received small arms fire from the vicinity of Komarovka. When a massive group of up to a thousand German soldiers impetuously charged the town, Hahl and his men joined in. Quickly overrun, the Soviet defenders abandoned their defensive positions and fled to the east, where they soon rallied and came back a few hours later with tank support. By then, Hahl and his company had made good their escape.[21]

The next flank protection unit to withdraw as ordered was the Walloon Brigade, which was still holding the northern outskirts of Novo Buda. Leon Degrelle and his men had been ordered to follow after the Estonian Volunteer Battalion *Narwa*, which would itself withdraw after *Westland* had moved out. The Walloons would then form part of *Wiking's* assault column, with *Germania* bringing up the rear. In preparation for this mission, Degrelle ordered all of his brigade's remaining walking wounded evacuated from Novo Buda towards Shanderovka during the night of 16/17 February. At 1300 hours on 16 February, he ordered his infantry to begin disengaging from their forward positions to a shorter line running through the northern outskirts of the town itself, except to the north, where one of his companies still tied in with Hans Dorr's battalion along the forest that stretched in an arc towards Shanderovka. Degrelle's brigade would continue its planned withdrawal early the next morning, when it would give up its positions in Novo Buda entirely.

One group of Walloons withdrawing that morning carried a special burden - the body of their commander, *Oberstuf.* Lippert, who had been killed in the fighting four days previously. According to the commander of the brigade's 1.*Kompanie*, *Ostuf.* Jules Matthieu, Degrelle planned to bring Lippert's corpse back to Belgium, where he intended to bury it with full military honors. Two days before, two men, *Ustuf.* Henri Thyssen and *Hscha.* Pascal Bovy were ordered to dig up the body and place it in a coffin of rough pine boards for transport aboard an antitank gun carriage. Once this was completed, Thyssen and Bovy, who were both wounded themselves, then hitched the carriage to a team of horses and transported the coffin to Shanderovka with the rest of the brigade's wounded.[22]

At 0500 hours that Thursday, Degrelle and his Walloons began to slip out of Novo Buda by platoons and companies and marched towards Shanderovka. As he and his men descended the hill that commanded the town from the south, Degrelle noticed that there was "a column of trucks and carts two kilometers long and 50 meters wide [that had] pushed up very close to the line of attack." By this point, most of these vehicles would not progress much further, and would remain stuck until the Soviets overcame them. To signal his men, who had collected in the valley below, Degrelle climbed aboard a truck, from which he hailed his men at the top of his lungs. Degrelle noticed that it had grown lighter, illuminating the "inextricable mass of tanks, automobiles, horse-drawn vehicles, combined battalions, Ukrainian civilians, and Soviet prisoners."

Suddenly, Soviet artillery fire began to increase, followed by the appearance of tanks. Degrelle and his troops then witnessed the last tank battle of Köller's battalion, which threw the attackers back one last time.* According to Degrelle, who saw them as they drove their tanks towards the Soviets:

> The faces of those young tankers were admirable. Clothed in short black jackets with silver trim, their heads and shoulders protruding from their turrets, they knew that they were going to die. Several proudly wore the tricolor ribbon and the large black and silver Knight's Cross around their necks, a glittering target for the enemy. Not one of those marvelous warriors seemed nervous or even moved . . . as they ploughed up the snow with their treads as they departed through the tangle of the retreating army.[23]

The tank battle finished, the way was cleared once again. Degrelle's unit then joined in the general movement of *Wiking*, as it began its drive, spearheaded by Debus' battalion, to the southwest. No one, certainly not Degrelle, had any idea that the breakout was not progressing as favorably as it seemed. The failure of communications and the inability of couriers to get through with urgent messages had left virtually every commander of the encircled forces in the dark.

That became apparent once his brigade cleared the safety of Khilki and headed southwest across the broken terrain, where he and his men were surprised to find themselves under heavy artillery and tank fire. To Degrelle, it seemed as if all order among the escaping columns had vanished.

Due to the many ravines, ditches, and *balki*, he was soon forced to order his remaining vehicles to be destroyed, except for the remaining *panje* carrying the wounded of his brigade. By mid-morning, his brigade reached the relative safety of the large *balka* at the foot of the wooded ridgeline east of Zhurzhintsy. It was already full of troops seeking shelter. According to Degrelle:

> The bottom of each ravine was a frightful crush of wrecked vehicles and dozens of dead soldiers sprawled across the red snow. The enemy's guns hammered these passages savagely. We kept falling over wounded and bloody men. We had to take shelter alongside the dead. Carts tipped over. Horses flailed their hooves in the air until the machine-gun bullets spilled their hot intestines into the soiled snow . . . [24]

Carts full of wounded, their horses spooked by the crush of bursting shells, were overturned in the snow, sending dozens of helpless men sprawling. Snow quickly covered the dead and dying. Despite this carnage and confusion, Degrelle wrote afterwards that he thought that the movement towards the southwest had remained "fairly orderly." Grim determination appeared to be the order of the day.

A short while later, a group of Soviet tanks approached the southern end of the *balka* and attacked his own column of wounded, but there was little that he or his men could do about it. While the tanks were untangling themselves from the wreckage, Degrelle urged his men to climb out of the *balka* and keep going, dragging a few of their wounded comrades along with them. It was now midday. Soon, the Walloons joined the general movement of thousands of troops to the southwest, though he had managed so far to keep most of his brigade together.[25]

As for the casket carrying Lippert, it was destroyed when it received a direct hit by an artillery shell. Although unhurt, both Bovy and Thyssen decided not to waste their time with the body. Besides, it had been dismembered by the shell burst and would be too difficult to carry.[26] Both men would need every bit of their resourcefulness to escape, since both were weakened from their own wounds. Later on, Degrelle and others claimed that Lippert's body was brought out by the brigade, after being ferried across the Gniloy Tikich, but this does not appear to be the case. If it had, his body was soon abandoned, for it was never seen again. Like so many other German and Walloon troops, Lucien Lippert was to be buried in an unmarked mass grave somewhere on the battlefield.

Ten kilometers to the southwest, *Maj.* Siegel had decided that he and his men had done enough for one day. By midmorning, thousands of German troops had gathered within his small bridgehead on the banks of the Gniloy Tikich. Siegel felt that his and Hummel's regiments could now disengage and make their own way to the crossing point, where he assumed everything was in order. However, when he and his men reached the creek's bank, there was no sign of a bridge anywhere. The officer he had ordered to erect an emergency bridge had apparently disappeared. All along the banks of the creek, men were seeking to cross it any way they could. Some were swimming, others were clutching boards or horses, while others were trying to crawl across patches of ice. In hopes of making some sort of bridge, Siegel and a few others shoved a *panje* wagon in the water, but was immediately swept away by the strong current. Then he and his men tried chopping down a tree, but it proved to be too short to reach the other side. There was only one option left - to swim for it.

Siegel jumped in and began to swim. The water was icy cold, but he made it across in a few strokes. Reaching the other side, he looked at his watch - it was 0914 hours. As he watched,

---

* In his account of the battle, Degrelle stated that *Wiking's* entire tank battalion had heroically sacrificed itself in this engagement east of Shanderovka, but this is not borne out by the facts. According to the tank battalion's own *Kriegstagebuch*, this was a relatively brief and successful action. It was during its return trip on the outskirts of Khilki where it was ambushed, but again, it was able to fight its way out after losing one tank. Despite this fact, Degrelle's fanciful account has been repeated in many other sources.

Obersturmführer Günther Jahnke, *a Wiking Division general staff officer in training, who witnessed many of the key events which took place during the battle.*
(Photo courtesy of Günther Jahnke)

the rest of his regiment and Hummel's swam across. Many of his men had lost their weapons, but at least they were alive. The cold, which had intensified, caused their wet clothing to freeze solid. There was only one thing left for Siegel and his men to do - follow the thousands of others who had already marched to Lysyanka. All the while, the Soviets continued to shell the opposite bank, but it was poorly directed and had little effect, due to the deep snow drifts which had accumulated along that side of the creek.

Forty-five minutes later, Siegel and his men reached the relative safety of Lysyanka. Here, he met up again with his fellow regimental commander, *Maj.* Kästner, whose regiment had arrived in Lysyanka over four hours before. Not only had Kästner's regiment remained dry (since they had entered Lysyanka over the north bridge), but he had reported Siegel as having been killed in action. Siegel also found *Hptm.* Knostmann and his men, who had attacked directed across Hill 239, awaiting their arrival. Since there was no place for his regiment to stay and no food to eat, Siegel had no choice but to order his men to continue marching towards the town of Bushanka, some eight kilometers to the

southwest, wet clothes and all, where field kitchens had been set up by *1.Pz.Div.*

At least he had managed to get most of his men and a large group of *Gren.Rgt.124* to safety. More importantly, by attacking and overrunning the Soviet positions along the woods south of Hill 239, his regiment had kept the enemy from forming a strong tank and infantry defensive barrier which could have prevented the rest of *Gruppe Stemmermann* from escaping. In contrast, Kästner's attack resulted only in his own regiment's escape. Despite the disappointing reception in Lysyanka, the "Reservist Regiment" had a great deal to be proud of, though they would have to wait several weeks for their reward. For them, the ordeal was finally over.[27]

Meanwhile, Lieb and thousands of others had arrived at the creek by noon. When they discovered that no bridges had been prepared for them, many of the men who had already endured so much became increasingly demoralized. Had they been betrayed by their leaders? Where was General Breith? Many of the men were fighting amongst themselves and cursing. Over the next several hours, in Lieb's words:

> Gradually, between 1300 and 1500, large, disorganized masses of troops piled up along the Gniloy Tikich River, east of Lysyanka. Units from all three divisions participating in the breakout were hopelessly intermingled. A few medium tanks (from Wiking) had been able to get through to the river bank, but there were no heavy weapons and artillery pieces left.[28]

As Lieb watched, the Soviet tanks on the hillside 500 meters away (Hill 222.5) that Siegel had been worried about all morning, finally swung into action. As their shells impacted among the tightly packed groups of men, panic set in. Thinking that the bridgehead was being overrun, thousands of men jumped into the creek and began to swim across. Groups of 30 or 40 men jumped blindly into the icy water to avoid what they thought was a Soviet attack. As they reached the opposite shore, they struggled up the bank and began their frozen march towards Lysyanka. Hundreds of men and horses drowned in the icy current. Lieb ordered several officers to build some sort of emergency bridge in order to ferry the casualties across, but it took several hours to carry this out. In the meantime, more men were swept away, never to be seen again. Strangely, the tanks failed to press home their attack. Although they had advanced to within several hundred meters of the bridgehead, they respectfully kept their distance.

Many men, anxious to save their own skins, selfishly abandoned wounded on the eastern bank of the creek. Not all of them, however. For example, *Uffz.* Wohler from *389.Inf.Div.* swam back and forth across the creek three times, each time carrying a wounded soldier with him using a harness made of discarded belts and leather belt support straps. Two other sergeants from his division ferried wounded across using planks to which the wren had been securely lashed. *Ofw.* Krause, from the division's antitank battalion, arrived at the bank of the creek with four other men from *389.Inf.Div.* Krause, who had distinguished himself earlier that day by knocking out several T-34s with *Panzerfäuste*, had several Soviet prisoners in tow whom he had captured when his group attacked the woodline south of Hill 239. As Krause and his men began removing their clothing in preparation for swimming the creek, their prisoners, young Russian peasants whom they had captured previously, vigorously shook their heads and, using sign language, showed the Germans how to do it right. Unbuttoning their greatcoats, the Russians slid down the banks of the creek and waded in. Using the tails of their coats as wings, all of them easily swam to the other side. Krause and his men did likewise and were soon on the opposite bank.

Krause's companion, *Gef.* Hamann, did not want to get wet, so he looked for an alternate method. A few meters away, the creek had frozen over in places, so he did what some other young Germans were doing - crawling slowly on their bellies across the ice. Hamann, a bit older and heavier, caused the ice to crack, plunging him into the water. Slowly, he hoisted himself up onto another floe of ice. Painfully, he inched across on his elbows. After half an hour of this, he reached the opposite side and collapsed with exhaustion. After a few minutes, an unknown comrade offered him a rifle butt to hold onto as he tried to stand up. Krause and his comrades were nowhere in sight. With his clothes freezing to his body, Hamann struggled painfully onwards to Lysyanka. Finally, like thousands of others, he was free.[29]

The bulk of *Wiking* reached the creek at another spot near the small village of Vsremirnyye, several hundred meters downstream from Lieb and *Maj.* Siegel's crossing site. Apparently, the Soviet troops holding Vsremirnyye were deterred from sallying forth due to the enormous numbers of Germans that had congregated along the creek - there is certainly no evidence to indicate that they made such an effort during the daylight hours. Except for shelling the Germans with mortar and artillery fire, the town's defenders did nothing. At this bridgehead, as at the one established earlier, chaos reigned. General Gille and his staff arrived around noon, to join the thousands of others from *Wiking* and *K.Abt.B*, as well as parts of the Walloon Brigade, who were milling aimlessly about the crossing site.

Gille had initially set out in his armored command vehicle with his staff earlier that morning, but was forced to continue on foot three kilometers west of Khilki when the vehicle became stuck in a gully along the escape route. Ignoring enemy fire, Gille had walked all the way to the Gniloy Tikich bolt upright, his gnarled walking stick in his hand. Urging his men forward, he refused to take cover and did not stop to rest until he and his staff had reached the creek.

At the bridgehead, Gille encountered total chaos. As at the other crossing site upstream, hundreds of men were leaping into the water. Others rode across on horseback, while others tried to paddle across on boards or wagons. Many were drowning right before his eyes. It was more than he would bear. This was not orderly! Gille had brought too many of his men along thus far and did not intend to sacrifice any more of them needlessly. Gille set to work, ordering his staff, led by his *1a, Oberstuf.* Schönfelder, his *01, Ostuf.* Westphal, and staff officer candidate Günter Jahnke to organize some sort of crossing using material at hand. Gille then sought to impose order and

discipline among the thousands of panicked troops milling about. He ordered that a half-track be driven into the water to be used as a breakwater, but this was swept away as were several *panje* wagons.

His division staff then tried to organize human chains to allow the non-swimmers to cross, but these too resulted in little success. Many were swept away to their deaths when several men lost their grip, causing the chain to break. Gille even tried to anchor one end of the human chain himself by wading into the water to his hips. He urged his officers and men to keep trying, doing his best to instill a good attitude in his division, even though by this point it was a broken wreck. A human dynamo, Gille paced back and forth, encouraging individual soldiers and SS men, or badgering them as the case required. Clad in his fur-lined greatcoat, clutching his walking stick with his mountain cap perched on his head. "Papa" Gille was in his element.[30] He even ordered that his division's sole remaining Pz. III be driven into the creek to serve as a stepping stone, but all but the top of its turret disappeared under the icy stream, as had the half-track.

Throughout the day, men from virtually every unit in the pocket continued to find their way to the various bridgeheads, cross over the creek, and stagger into Lysyanka, where they quickly overwhelmed the reception command set up by *1.Pz.Div.* to welcome them. Many men were without coats, weapons, or headgear. Others were even without boots or clothing because they had tried to bundle their uniforms up and toss them over to the other side to avoid getting them wet. Many failed in this attempt due to the width of the creek; thousands of weapons were lost this way as well. The eastern bank was also littered with coats, binoculars, cameras, machine-guns, pistols, and other personal kit that men had shed to lighten their burden before they swam across. One eyewitness said that one could have equipped an army with what the men of *Gruppe Stemmermann* had abandoned on the banks of the Gniloy Tikich that day. As bad as things had been for the first wave of escaping troops, however, it would be even worse for those who followed in their wake.

End Notes

1   Werth, p. 781.

2   *Gefechtsbericht*, K.Abt.B, 1a Nr. 200/44 geh, 24.2.1944, K.Abt. Gefechtstand, p. 4.

3   Konev in Sokolov, p. 123.

4   Schwarz, Andreas. *Chronik des Infantrie-Regiments 248,* Vol. 2. (Fürth, Germany: Josef Eckert & Sohn, 1977), p. 139.

5   *Aus feinlichen Funkverkehr*, 17.2.44. Anlage 3c zu Pz. AOK 1, 1a Nr. 158/44 gK. Vom 28.2.44.

6   Ibid, entry dated 0845 hours 17.2.44.

7   Schwarz, p. 139.

8   *Sbornik*, p. 323.

9   "Combat Operations of 5th Guards Don Red Army Cavalry Corps in the Korsun-Shevchenkovskiy Operation," *Journal of Slavic Military Studies,* pp. 351-352.

10 *Aus feindlichen Funkverkehr*, entry dated 0955 hours 17 February 1944.

11 Carell, p. 425.

12 Ibid, p. 423.

13 Lieb in DA Pam 20-234, p. 30.

14 Carell, p. 425.

15 Siegel, p. 3.

16 *Gefechtsbericht,* Generalkommando XI.A.K., Der Chef des Generalstabes, 1a Brief. B. Nr. 19/44 g. Kdos., Korps-Gefechtstand, 23.2.44, pp. 2-3.

17 Hein manuscript, p. 4.

18 Klapdor, p. 193.

19 *Kriegstagebuch Nr. 1,* I./SS Panzer Regiment 5, 9. Februar bis 30. November 1944.

20 Jahnke and Lerch, pp. 102-103 and p. 111.

21 Hahl, Fritz. *Die 6./Westland im Kessel von Tscherkassy*. (Pentling, Germany: Unpublished private manuscript, 1996), pp. 3-4.

22 Mathiew, quoted in Jahnke and Lerch, pp. 99-100.

23 Degrelle, p. 212.

24 Ibid, p. 213.

25 Ibid.

26 Mathieu in Jahnke and Lerch, p. 100.

27 Siegel, p. 4.

28 Lieb in DA Pam 20-234, p. 30.

29 Carell, p. 427.

30 Ibid, p. 427 and Jahnke and Lerch, p. 107.

Chapter Twenty Two
HELL IN THE UKRAINE

**"During the night, it looked as if . . . the encircled elements
would bring nothing else with them but their lives."**
— *Oberst. Graf von Kielmannsegg, OKH staff* [1]

By the late morning of 17 February, Konev's counter-attack had gathered full steam. Soviet tank, infantry, and artillery units from 5th Guards Tank, 4th Guards, 27th, and 52rd Armies were moving quickly to reach the corridor between Shanderovka and Lysyanka. If they arrived in time, they could cut the remaining Germans off and reap their share of glory. The Don Cossacks of Selivanov's 5th Guards Cavalry Corps were also on their way, eager to be in on the kill. By late morning, the entire German breakout route was being pounded incessantly. Even the Red Air Force managed to conduct strikes despite the mist, low-hanging clouds, and snow, which, luckily for the Germans, continued to fall throughout the day. Individual Soviet tank companies sallied forth towards the retreating German columns, biting deep before pulling back again, but on the Germans came.

One Soviet tank commander, Junior Lt. A. Krayushkin, carried out such an attack. As he observed the endless columns of Germans marching to the southeast several hundred meters away from his company's position in Komarovka, he was approached unexpectedly by his corps commander, Kirichenko. Kirichenko ordered him to charge the column instead of shooting at it from the safety of the town. Krayushkin immediately obeyed, leading his company forward. As the group of T-34s approached the Germans, who were trying to unlimber artillery to fire in their direction, the Soviets fired first. Krayushkin, in the lead tank, crashed into the column, sending bodies and pieces of equipment flying in all directions. The Germans panicked, throwing down weapons and fleeing in a disorganized mass towards the southwest with tanks in hot pursuit. Konev, who happened to be in Komarovka at that particular moment to observe the fighting, later congratulated Krayushkin and all of his tank commanders, recognizing them later for their performance by publishing their names in special orders for valor.[2]

Soviet artillery units also saw their share of action that day. In some places, guns ranging from 7.6 cm infantry howitzers to huge 15.2 cm howitzers were lined up hub to hub, keeping up a steady barrage, often at small groups of men or even individual soldiers. Many batteries rolled up to the edge of the German columns and blasted them at point-blank range and were overrun when the desperate enemy charged their positions. In the words of one Soviet eyewitness, "Frightened out of their wits and trying at any price to break out of the 'frying pan,' the enemy stopped for nothing. Frequently it came down to hand-to-hand skirmishes."

German troops heading through the "Valley of Death" between "Hell's Gate" and Hill 239. (U.S. National Archives)

One unit, the 438th Tank Destroyer Artillery Regiment under the command of Guards Colonel Novikov claimed to have knocked out two German tanks and killed up to 3,000 Germans, as well as the capture of an additional 200. One battery, the 6th, claimed to have killed 800 men alone. A Sergeant Luk'uanchikov claimed to have killed 100 with his own gun himself. While these numbers are no doubt exaggerated, it does give some idea of the intensity of the artillery fire being directed upon the struggling Germans, who inexplicably, to the Soviets at least, persisted in their desperate attempt to escape. Another German unit, estimated to consist of a regiment in size, came under fire by 2nd Battery, 139th Guards Artillery Regiment. It's commander, Senior Lieutenant Kamyshev, ordered the guns to engage the enemy with open sights. All of his guns seemed to fire at once and the German formation was shot to pieces in a hurricane of fire. The enemy took his losses and kept coming towards the Soviets. When the Germans were too close to fire effectively, the Soviet gunners abandoned their pieces and rushed at the Germans. In the fierce hand-to-hand fighting which ensued, the Soviets were overrun, the battery wiped out.

The 15th Light Artillery Brigade also distinguished itself in the fighting that day. This unit, commanded by Colonel Parovatkin, was located on the eastern outskirts of Zhurzhintsy and shelled the German columns mercilessly. One of the columns veered in the gunners' direction and began to attack. For several hours, the brigade was engaged in this fight (probably against elements of *K.Abt.B*) before it was able to drive the attackers off. This unit alone claimed to have killed 2,000

Men of Wiking Division moving single-file down the steep bank of a balka during the breakout.
(U.S. National Archives)

German officers and men, including Stemmermann, and claimed to have captured 400. Lacking infantry to actually close with and destroy the German infantry, the Soviets were forced to resort to sheer firepower to thwart their escape.

In the words of one Soviet historian, "All the artillery raised a granite wall in the path of the enemy. Together with the other branches of service it did not let the German invaders escape out of the "frying pan" and inflicted enormous losses on him."[3] While the Soviet artillery no doubt killed most of the Germans who fell that day, thousands more were escaping across the Gniloy Tikich, into the two tiny rescue corridors whose points ended at Lysyanka and Oktyabr. Here, at the outer encircling ring, Zhukov was fighting his own battle to cut off and destroy *III.Pz.Korps*. Using the bulk of three tank armies (2nd, 6th, and 5th Guards), Zhukov launched repeated attacks against the base of the narrow corridor defended by *34.* and *198.Inf. Div.*, as well as against the Lysyanka bridgehead held by *1.Pz.Div.* and *Schw.Pz.Rgt. Bäke.*

Fighting raged throughout the day, which saw waves of T-34s attacking the desperate German defenders. Breith's *III.Pz.Korps* held firm, knocking out 28 Soviet tanks and repelling waves of infantry assaults. Even the last-minute addition of the understrength 11th Guards Tank Corps from 1st Guards Tank Army, consisting of only 30 tanks, failed to dislodge the Germans. This unit, as had so many others, had been brought in late in the battle by Zhukov in an effort to achieve

enough mass to overcome the defense, but it was not enough.[4] It was now the Soviet's turn to attack into the teeth of a well laid out antitank defense, and they suffered accordingly. Even *Panthers* and *Tigers* that were no longer operational were used as static pill boxes. Although they were immobile, their 7.5 and 8.8 cm guns still cut a swath through the packs of T-34s, JS-IIs, and Shermans.

To the west of Lysyanka, both *34.* and *198.Inf.Divs.* warded off numerous Soviet assaults designed to slice of Breith's corps at the base of the salient. 74th Rifle Division hurled itself against the barbed wire entanglements at Tinovka, but *34.Inf.Div.* held firm. Von Horn's *198.Inf.Div.'s* defenses in the northern part of Vinograd were penetrated by a determined combined attack by 58th Rifle Division and 3rd Guards Airborne Division, but was able by that afternoon to restore its front line after carrying out a counterattack. Strangely, the thinly-held sectors of both *16.* and *17.Pz. Div.*, stretching from Bosovka to Chesnovka were not attacked at all. Both divisions reported that "no activity worth reporting" occurred that day.[5]

The only exception was *K.Gr. Pietsch* of *17.Pz.Div.*, consisting of *Pz.A.A.17*, located at Hill 215.7 one kilometer north of Lysyanka. This small group, consisting of one weak infantry platoon of 17 men and an assault gun, had been attached to *1.Pz.Div.* the day before. It was able protect the troops of *Gruppe Stemmermann* that had somehow gone around Zhurzhentsy to the north, while fighting off Soviet attempts to bypass its position. To the battle group's commander, *Ltn.* Pietsch, most of these groups of escaping soldiers seemed to consist of survivors of *Wiking* and the Walloon Brigade. After being given directions by Pietsch and his men, they staggered into northern Lysyanka throughout that day and into the evening.[6]

The scale of the tragedy occurring along the banks of the Gniloy Tikich, three kilometers to the east of their positions in Lysyanka seems to have eluded both *Oberstlt.* Bäke and Koll, until survivors began to reach their lines later that morning. The change of the breakout's direction had put the bulk of *XI.* and *XXXXII.A.K.* on the wrong side of the Gniloy Tikich, where no bridges had been planned or constructed. No one had foreseen this development; consequently, neither *1.Pz.Div.* nor *Schw.Pz.Rgt. Bäke* could immediately spare any forces to come to their aid. One reason for the delay in notification was the fact that Bäke's and Koll's headquarters had only one operational radio relay station left; the other sets had broken down or had been destroyed by enemy fire. Gaps in radio coverage forced both commanders to rely on couriers to pass messages back and forth.[7] Therefore, the seriousness of the situation along the banks of the river and atop Hill 239 did not become fully apparent until the breakout plan had already began to fall apart. Additionally, both men had been unable to raise either Lieb or Stemmermann by radio, thus compounding the tragedy. Attempts to route radio messages to Stemmermann through *8.Armee* also were unsuccessful.

By 1100 hours, both Koll and Bäke had realized the magnitude of the disaster. After gathering enough information from survivors who had already crossed the creek, they quickly drafted plans for their forces to relieve the pressure against the troops conducting the breakout by conducting an attack to establish a forward reception area as soon as possible. The best way to accomplish this was to order an immediate attack to regain Hill 239 and continue pushing towards Pochapintsy. If this succeeded, the escaping troops could be redirected towards north Lysyanka, where a bridge awaited. It would also encircle the considerable amount of Soviet forces still holding the line Hill 239 – Pochapintsy. In the meantime, Koll would scrape a force together in Lysyanka and send it east to cover the withdrawal across the Gniloy Tikich. Here, a platoon of *Panzergrenadiers* from *K.Gr. Heimann* and three armored vehicles from *Leibstandarte* could direct the troops breaking out to the bridges upstream or help them construct temporary bridges with the aid of *Pz.Pio.Btl.37* from *1.Pz.Div.*

The force chosen to retake Hill 239 was *Hptm.* Scherff's Tiger Battalion, now reduced in size to eight tanks. Scherff, who had been placed in acting command of *Schw.Pz.Rgt. Bäke* when Bäke was ordered to take over *K.Gr. Frank*, decided to carry out the attack with both his own battalion and the six remaining Panthers of *Pz.Rgt.23*. Scherff's force would attack from its positions north of Oktyabr, move 500 meters to the northeast and seize Hill 239, then continue the attack a kilometer and a half farther southeast until it had reached the outskirts of Pochapintsy. If his force could do this, then most of the ridgeline dominated by Hill 239 and the last obstacle to *Gruppe Stemmermann* would be in German hands. Infantry support would be provided by the few remaining half-tracks manned by the attached *Jäger* battalion. To his dismay, Scherff's attack would have to go in without artillery support - every available gun from *Oberst* Söth's artillery was being used to help repel Soviet tank assaults approaching Lysyanka from the northwest and east. The promised *Stuka* support was once again nowhere to be seen due to the low-hanging clouds and falling snow. Scherff's attack was supposed to be accompanied by a *Kampfgruppe* from *Leibstandarte*, which would follow once the hill had been taken.[8]

By 1130 hours, Scherff's force had reached the summit of Hill 239. Tanks knocked out the previous day littered the area. Surprisingly, the Germans encountered no resistance. Most of the Soviets' attention at that point was undoubtedly directed towards the northeast, where 5th Guards Tank Army was firing into masses of German troops moving east of Zhurzhintsy and at the foot of Hill 239. Fifteen minutes later, Scherff was ordered by Bäke to keep pushing towards Pochapintsy and take advantage of the Soviet's inattention. Leaving the *Panthers* atop the hill to provide rear security, while the *Jägers* cleaned out the woods south of the hill, Scherff wheeled his remaining tanks to the right and drove downhill towards the town.

After his and the other seven *Tigers* had advanced 500 meters, Scherff and his men observed three enemy tanks moving perpendicular towards them from the direction of the woodline that bounded the northern side of the road to their left. Evidently, the Soviet tanks had heard Scherff's tanks moving along the hilltop and had gone back to investigate. However, the *Panthers* atop the hillside saw them first, quickly dispatching them with five or six well-aimed shots. With that immediate

Hauptmann Walter Scherff, *Commander, Schw.Pz.Abt.503 of Schw.Pz.Rgt. Bäke, who tried to seize and hold Hill 239.*

threat taken care of, Scherff's tanks pushed on. Stopping a few hundred meters west of the town, all appeared still. At 1230 hours, there were no sign of either the enemy or their escaping comrades - Pochapintsy seemed to be a ghost town.

This surrealistic scene ended 15 minutes later when two Soviet trucks towing antitank guns exited the town and headed in their direction. Coming to a halt after driving a few meters, the crews leapt out of the trucks and prepared to place both guns into operation. Apparently, the approach of Scherff's force had been heralded by the destruction of the other Soviet tanks a few minutes before. The antitank guns were shortly followed by five T-34s which burst from the town's western edge and headed directly towards the awaiting *Tigers*. Both guns were soon put out of action, their crews chased by machine-gun fire back into the town. Three of the T-34s were soon in flames, while the other two beat a hasty retreat. Soon, Scherff and his tanks were surrounded by escaping German troops who had burst from a woodline on the town's western edge. Scherff called some of the *Jäger's* halftracks forward and told them to load wounded troops aboard, while he directed the other large group of men to keep pushing to the west. With Soviet fire intensifying and his ammunition running low, Scherff decided to pull back towards the hilltop, where the remaining *Panthers* were engaged.

Upon reaching the top of Hill 239, Scherff found the position under heavy artillery fire. His arrival was a signal for the *Panthers* to withdraw to the south; they had been tasked by Bäke to serve as *K.Gr. Frank's* reserve force. Scherff quickly inventoried his remaining ammunition and found that his tank and the others only had one-third of their basic load of 92 shells left. A few hundred meters to Scherff's left, 12 T-34s attacked south towards Oktyabr, where they ran into *K.Gr. Franks'* screen line consisting of six of his own *Panthers* plus four from *1.Pz.Div.* Seven of the Soviet tanks were quickly knocked out for the loss of one Panther. The remaining five T-34s then turned to the west, where all but one was knocked out by troops from *17.Pz.Div.*

Soviet tanks continued to launch forays from the direction of Zhurzhintsy throughout the day, rendering Scherff's position on the exposed hilltop rather tenuous. Finally, low on fuel and ammunition, he ordered his remaining Tigers at 1545 hours to withdraw down the hill towards the relative safety of German positions in Oktyabr, which itself was attacked again later that day. Throughout the battle for Hill 239, escaping German troops in groups of 40 to 60 men continuously passed through or around his position. By that point, over 6,000 men were reported to have arrived in Lysyanka.[9] Bäke himself had been extremely busy that day as he shuttled back and forth between the command post of *K.Gr. Frank* in Lysyanka and the headquarters of his own regiment in Oktyabr. In addition to the importance of easing the pressure on the withdrawing troops coming from the pocket, he also had to worry about defending Lysyanka against the ever-increasing attacks by three Soviet tank armies. The arrival of elements from a fourth tank army only increased his troubles.

Bäke was still fuming about the unauthorized withdrawal of the two battalions which had reached his lines earlier that morning. With his units stretched so thinly, he needed every available man to hold the line if *1.Pz.Div.* was to get the rest of *Gruppe Stemmermann* out of the pocket. He could not understand how the escaping troops could have lost all will to fight and described the bitterness and frustration he felt when he observed these men and others who followed callously pass by their wounded comrades without rendering assistance. How could German soldiers behave in such a manner? Bäke was especially incensed when a passing medical officer, whom he had ordered to stop and treat a wounded soldier lying by the roadside, ignored his command and kept walking towards Lysyanka.[10] Had he known, he would have realized that these men were suffering from *Kesselpsychose*, and they had lived with the constant threat of death or captivity during the past three weeks .

The contrast was instructive. To Bäke's eyes, the troops breaking out of the pocket appeared to be in good physical health and even had food to share with Scherff's tank crews. They did not seem, at least to him, that they had encountered insurmountable Soviet resistance (only later would he realize what they had actually faced between Shanderovka and Hill 239). His own troops had been fighting in the mud and snow without a break for over two weeks; they had not had any food for the past two days. The men of *Schw.Pz.Rgt. Bäke* had been

forced to ration their shells and carry fuel for their vehicles in buckets, all the while keeping their tanks in running condition. Therefore, the attitude of the men coming out of the pocket, for whom Bäke and the men of his regiment had bled themselves white, was incomprehensible.

Despite their disappointment, the officers and men of *K.Gr.Frank* and *Schw.Pz.Rgt. Bäke* continued to do their utmost for the rest of the day and into the evening to hold the towns of Lysyanka and Oktyabr and to assist the withdrawal of Stemmermann's troops. Breith's spearhead had done more than anyone could have expected under the circumstances. While they had been unable to establish a continuous corridor to the pocket, they had knocked out hundreds of Soviet tanks and had tied up the bulk of four armies. While they were surprised and shocked at the reaction of the troops streaming out of the pocket, they knew that any rescue attempt would have been impossible without their own accomplishments under difficult conditions. They still had two more days of hard fighting ahead of them.

Fortunately, more help was on the way from *Leibstandarte. K.Gr. Sandig* with less than 100 men arrived in Lysyanka at 1030 hours and were ordered by Koll to proceed to Oktyabr to augment Bäke's meager force. *K.Gr. Knittel*, from *SS-Pz.Aufkl.Abt.1* was also on the way with about 50 men. These two groups were accompanied by what was left of *SS-Pz.Rgt.1*. All it could muster were eight AFVs - one *Tiger*, two *Panthers*, four assault guns, and one self-propelled antitank gun, although this addition did substantially increase the number of tanks at Koll's disposal.[11]

Brigadeführer Wisch arrived in Lysyanka later that day and established his division headquarters in an *isba*. Although his unit was subordinated to Koll, Wisch did his best to insure that as much of his division as possible got into the fight. By late afternoon, Sandig's and Heimann's *Kampfgruppen* were in action. Sandig's force, after arriving in Oktyabr, was soon ordered to launch an attack towards Hill 222.5, three kilometers southeast of the town. This hill, which overlooked the crossing sites along the Gniloy Tikich, had been a thorn in the side of *Gruppe Stemmermann* ever since daylight. As reported by *Maj.* Siegel, a group of Soviet tanks had remained stationary at that location for most of the day and directed desultory fire against the horde of German soldiers milling about on the banks of the creek. The hill could not be left in Soviet hands as long as the exhausted survivors from the pocket kept streaming towards Lysyanka.

Sandig's men, soon joined by *K.Gr. Knittel*, were set in motion late that afternoon. After proceeding only a kilometer, this meager force of approximately 120 men was fired upon by Soviet tanks and artillery. The three accompanying *Panthers* from *K.Gr. Frank* returned the fire, but both sides quickly fought each other to a standstill. Pinned down on the icy slopes of the hill as Heimann's smaller force had been the previous day south of Hill 239, Sandig ordered his troops to retreat back the way they had come. While Sandig's men were trying the disengage, the Panther and two assault guns supporting *K.Gr. Heimann* on the southern bank of the Gniloy Tikich fired in support. All the while, troops of *Gruppe Stemmermann* marched past singly or in small groups.

According to one Soviet eyewitness:

> [The Germans] were black on the hillside, their ranks breaking and gathering, great explosions scattering them as our shells fell among them, but somehow banding together again to press on down the hill as our tanks and the SS spat at each other across the refugees.[12]

After this failed attack, Sandig could muster only four officers, nine NCOs and 54 men - the rest were either in Dr. Königshausen's aid station in Lysyanka or were lying dead on the slopes of Hill 222.5. Despite their failure, the SS troops had done all that was humanly possible and had once again lived up to their motto - *Meine Ehre heisst Treue* (My Honor is Loyalty). At the same time, the Soviets conducted another tank attack against Oktyabr which was almost lost until the combined tanks of *1.Pz.Div.* and *Schw.Pz.Rgt. Bäke* threw them out once again. By nightfall, it had become apparent to the Germans that the units holding the Lysyanka bridgehead were too weak to do anything much more than hold their own positions - and even that was in doubt. Nevertheless, the various *Kampfgruppen* held their positions in the hope that more troops would find their way out. They did, continuing all through the night and throughout the following day in a never-ending stream. By the evening of 17 February, *1.Pz.Div.* estimated that 12,000 to 15,000 men had passed through its lines. There were still thousands more en route.

Thousands of these men, many without weapons, helmets, or even boots, began to fill up the peasant shacks and outbuildings in Lysyanka. Among them were hundreds of wounded who quickly overwhelmed *1.Pz.Div.'s* aid station. There was no food, no heat, no extra clothing to provide them - nothing at all except a place to rest a bit and to recover from the shock of the ordeal that they had just endured. The men of Koll's division had not had of these things themselves for days and hardly could be expected to provide much in the way of relief. Despite the battle that raged around them, the first waves of escapees were still too overcome with emotion and fatigue to be of much use. Rather than try to organize them into some sort of usable formation, Breith and Koll thought that it would be far better to just get them out of the way. Except for a few battalions, such as Schenk's and Kästner's, nearly all the rest had lost their weapons and were incapable of serious resistance. That evening, *1.Pz.Div.* reported that "North and south Lysyanka, Bushanka, and Fronkovka are overflowing with rescued troops, most of whom are soaked through and through and wearing frozen uniforms…many of whom are wounded, all of whom are seeking some sort of shelter…"[13]

That afternoon, Koll ordered that the survivors of *Gruppe Stemmermann* be chased out of their huts and continue their march towards Bushanka. Although this order was received with disbelief, the survivors dutifully picked up their few meager belongings and began the long and painful trek towards Bushanka, where *1.Pz.Div.* had established field kitchens for them. Even here, they were still subject to death or

injury when the Soviets hammered this narrow escape corridor with intermittent artillery fire. Even T-34s made occasional forays against the escape corridor, killing and wounding many before they were knocked out or chased away by the few remaining tanks of *1.Pz.Div.* not employed in Lysyanka. It would not be over until they had reached the safety of the collection areas in the vicinity of Uman, over 30 kilometers away.

The men who were too seriously injured to be moved right away were cared for by Dr. Königshausen's medical unit in Lysyanka. Spread throughout the town in several houses, these makeshift treatment stations where men were operated on without anesthetics were a far cry from what the wounded had expected, yet it was the best that could be done for them at the time. Ironically, many men who had survived weeks of combat and had swum the icy Gniloy Tikich died here due to lack of medications, bandages, and blood plasma. To speed their evacuation, the *Luftwaffe* even landed Ju-52s and Fiesler *Storchs* on snow-covered fields along the narrow finger of land that stretched from Bushanka to Lysyanka and picked up hundreds of wounded, often under artillery fire, thus saving the lives of many men were saved who would have succumbed from their wounds had they not been quickly flown to Uman.

Most of *Gruppe Stemmermann* were unaware of what was happening atop Hill 239 and in Lysyanka that afternoon. Most of them had already turned towards the direction of Pochapintsy and were making towards Lysyanka from the south. By mid-afternoon, most of the combat units except for the rearguard had reached the relative safety of the Gniloy Tikich. Following them were the bulk of the two corps' rear service units who had degenerated into mobs or had broken up altogether. These units too began piling up along on the banks of the creek, interfering with efforts by officers like Lieb and Gille to restore some sort of order. Thousands more had congregated inside the two large *balki* along the march route - the one at the foot of the wooded hill east of Zhurzhintsy and the other, larger one at the base of Hill 239. Many gave up the fight then and there, deciding that it was better to wait the arrival of the Soviets, preferring captivity to what they perceived as the certain death that awaited them if they kept trying to break out.

Lieb remained at the bank of the creek for most of the day, ensuring that as many of his men were able to cross as possible. By 1600 hours, he noticed that the artillery fire, which had been harassing the crossing site most of the day, had ceased. Now the crossing proceeded in an almost orderly manner, in contrast to the panic that had manifested itself that morning. Satisfied that he had done all he could do, Lieb decided to head towards Lysyanka, where he could begin to organize his scattered force. He swam the Gniloy Tikich alongside his horse, but the gelding could not fight the current and was swept away. Painfully, he was able to pull himself up the opposite bank and, without pausing, crossed the snowy slope southeast of Lysyanka. Lieb finally entered the town at dusk, where he reported to the forward headquarters of *1.Pz.Div.* Along the way, he noticed that long lines of men snaked in a continuous stream towards the town. As enemy shells fell nearby, the columns veered away from them.

Above: *During the breakout, the Germans are subjected to Soviet fire from both sides as well as from the Soviets entrenched along the ridgeline from Dzurzhentsy to Pochapintsy. Here, Soviets take aim at straggling Germans. (Photo courtesy of the Battle of Korsun-Shevenkovsky Museum, Ukraine)*

Above: *Wary Soviet soldiers inspect an abandoned 15cm Infantry Howitzer stuck in a creekbed on the western outskirts of Shanderovka. (Photo courtesy of the Battle of Korsun-Shevenkovsky Museum, Ukraine)*

Lieb's arrival was greeted with joy and relief. He was the first senior officer to make it out of the pocket. At Koll's forward command post in Lysyanka, Lieb learned just how weak the relief force was. In Lysyanka, he was told that there were no more than one company of *Panzergrenadiers* and three weak companies of tanks, while Oktyabr was held by a weak infantry battalion (*Hptm.* Ebeling's) and less than a dozen tanks from *Pz.Rgt.1* and *Schw.Pz.Rgt. Bäke*. Lieb was also told about the battalions from *K.Abt.B* that had made in it (it is unknown if he was told of Schenk's and Burgfeld's decision to withdraw without orders) and was also informed that *Oberst* Fouquet was believed to have been killed in action. Shortly afterwards, *Oberst* Gädke, Stemmermann's chief of staff, appeared. Gädke had not seen his commander since early that morning, but believed that he was still inside the pocket. He had nothing further to tell Lieb except that he believed that the rearguards were still withdrawing as ordered would make their way out shortly.

Lieb's staff also made it to the relative safety of Lysyanka, arriving several hours after their commander did. His corps' chief of staff, *Oberst* Franz, had gathered most of the survivors together in the little wood south of the larger forest south of Hill 239 after taking part in the massive infantry assault west of Pochapintsy. As he and the others began moving to the edge of the forest, he heard several shots. Moments later, two Walloons approached him from the direction of the firing and reported. Apparently, an enemy machine gun blocked their escape and the little group of Walloons had already suffered casualties. Franz, an expert marksman, picked up his sniper's rifle and crawled slowly forward. At the edge of the forest 300 meters away he picked out the outlines of the Soviet machine gun crew and fired three times in rapid succession. Standing up, Franz expected the rest of his group to follow him, but they remained prone until he had started walking away from them. When the other staff members saw that Franz had indeed silenced the gun and its crew, they sheepishly stood up and followed him.

After proceeding for several hundred meters, Franz stopped and surveyed the Lysyanka valley that stretched out below them. To his surprise, he was joined by his *1a, Maj.* Hermani, who had been separated from the group earlier that day. "*Herr Oberst*," Hermani said, "now we've met in this hell unscathed we're sure to get through all the way."[14] As their group, which now numbered several hundred men, neared Hill 222.5, they were fired upon by the group of T-34s that had remained there all day. Again, men were shot down when they thought they had made it to safety. Hermani's machine pistol was shot out of his hands, but he and the rest kept running downhill towards the creek, away from the tanks. After running several hundred meters, they reached the relative safety of the bluffs bordering the eastern side of the creek.

Hermani dove in, with his damaged machine pistol hanging from his neck. As he reached the other side of the creek, he noticed that it was so cold, his winter combat uniform was beginning to harden with ice, making his uniform as "stiff as a board." After several halting steps, he fell flat on his face in the snow, but picked himself up and tried again. To remain would invite certain death, as he would certainly freeze like many others already had.[15] Behind him, *Oberst* Franz picked out a clear spot on the opposite bank and swam to it after a few short strokes. Unfortunately, his

Major i.G. Hermani, *1a of XXXXII.Armeekorps.* *(Photo courtesy of Bernd Lerch)*

coat became snagged by the branches of a low-hanging willow tree and he almost drowned as his heavy coat began to drag him down. As he felt his body going rigid from the icy water, one of his junior staff officers, *Ltn.* Güldenpfennig, reached down and hauled Franz out of the water before he was swept under.

Supported by Güldenpfennig and Hermani, Franz staggered on to Lysyanka, which they reached just as the sun began to set. There, Franz and the rest of the staff of *XXXXII.A.K.* were reunited with their corps commander, who had preceded them. Finally, they were able to rest and to warm up a bit. Later that night, Franz radioed his old friend at *8. Armee*, Speidel, telling him "We did it. Unfortunately, not in the manner that we had wished. We are collecting [our] extremely exhausted troops."[16] Conspicuously absent from the gathering was *Maj.* Ganschow. His enlisted aide swam across the creek with his dog, but Ganschow was never seen again. His riderless horse was later spotted cantering along the bank. An outstanding officer had met his fate, fulfilling the premonitions he had of his own death, yet another of the many personal tragedies that were endlessly played out along the banks of the Gniloy Tikich.

In Stemmermann's absence, Lieb assumed command of the remnants in Lysyanka. He reported that *72.Inf.Div.* and

Wiking were "completely intermingled" and had no rations, tanks, artillery, or any vehicles at all. In his opinion, neither division could in any way be able to fight. *K.Abt.B* had two regiments that had broken out intact, but they, too, lacked food and ammunition for the weapons they did bring out with them. To his dismay, Lieb learned that Koll had neither food nor ammunition to spare (hence his order to have them march to Bushanka). Later, Lieb wrote "Thus I had to order the pocket force [sic] in its miserable condition to move on westward, while I requested supply, evacuation of casualties by air, and the bringing up of vehicles and weapons from the rear."[17]

Meanwhile, near Vsremirnyye, Herbert Gille swam the creek at about the same time that Lieb did. After supervising the crossing of his division with his staff for several hours, Gille was told by his escorts that there was not much more that could be done here, and that they needed to get to Lysyanka before nightfall in order to gather the survivors of the division. Striding downhill to the near bank, Gille plunged in fully clothed. Grabbing the reins of an artillery horse, he swam by the rigid bodies of men and horses who had drowned upstream. At the opposite bank, he was helped up by members of his staff and, dripping wet in the freezing wind, began the trek towards Lysyanka. After a few hundred meters, the 46-year old Gille began to stagger under the immense mental and physical strain; he, like the others, was slowly freezing to death and had not slept for days. One of his staff officers found an abandoned horse and led it to his divisional commander, who he helped into the saddle.

An hour later, the small band of SS officers reached the forward outposts of *Leibstandarte* (probably *K.Gr. Heimann*) and were quickly led to Wisch's command post, where Gille was greeted enthusiastically by his fellow division commander. After exchanging bear hugs and downing a glass of schnapps, Gille quickly brought Wisch up to date on the situation inside the pocket and told him what his division needed. He also emphasized the urgency of sending more reinforcements to the crossing sites to protect the virtually defenseless troops while they crossed the creek.

After being fed a warm meal, they were issued fresh underwear and led to a small room, where Gille and Schönfelder were allowed to take a "good long sleep," while Wisch's division did the best it could to take care of Gille's men.[18] *Leibstandarte* had brought up its division clearing station, which soon had its hands full helping to care for the hundreds of wounded still staggering out of the pocket. The next morning, Gille and the surviving members of his staff were brought out of Lysyanka aboard Wisch's own *SPW*, while SS men sat on the front fenders looking for land mines that lay strewn about the rutted roadway.

Stemmermann's whereabouts were still unknown. He had last been seen early that morning when he decided to move his command post from Khilki against the advice of his chief of staff to a point near a natural spring southeast of Petrovskoye. Along the way, he had strayed from his staff in the confusion. Accompanied by his corps *IIa* (intelligence officer), *Maj.* Dehne and his orderly, *Ogefr.* Reichenberger, he remained totally out of contact with his staff and was unable to further influence events.

Despite the best efforts of *Oberst* Gädke and the other staff officers, Stemmermann could not be located. As it grew light, Gädke noticed that the Soviet artillery fire had increased around the spring where the headquarters was to have been situated, a bad place, he thought, to erect a command post.

Gädke galloped ahead in hopes that his commander had kept going rather than stay in the impact area. Seeking momentary concealment behind a haystack while his mount rested, Gädke met a courier from the staff of *72.Inf.Div.*, who told him that he had seen Stemmermann riding in a *Kübelwagen* towards his division's headquarters a few kilometers farther to the west. Gädke thanked the man and spurred his mount onward, perhaps feeling that he would run into Stemmermann at any moment, but it was not to be. He never saw his commander again. With nothing to show for his pains, Gädke then had no choice but to keep moving on, since by then he had no hope of finding the corps staff in the confusion. As previously related, he rode into Lysyanka later that evening after swimming the Gniloy Tikich with his horse, meeting Lieb at the headquarters of *1.Pz.Div.*[19]

Indeed, what had happened to Wilhelm Stemmermann? He never made it out of the pocket, though both *8.Armee* and *1. Pz.Armee* headquarters did not give up looking for him until several days later. According to an eyewitness, *Rttf.* Klenne, the driver for Siegfried Westphal, *Wiking's 1a*, Stemmermann commandeered his vehicle near the spring at the bottom of a *balka* southeast of Petrovskoye, and ordered Klenne to drive both him and *Maj.* Dehne towards the west. Its previous occupants, *Hstuf.* Westphal and *Obstuf.* Schönfelder, had gone to the top of the hill to observe the course of the breakout and were unaware of what was happening. At the time, Klenne was changing a flat tire, but was ordered by Stemmermann to drive over the hill anyway.

As the vehicle crested the large tree-covered hill southwest of Khilki, it got stuck and it was immediately fired upon by Soviet antitank gunners. The vehicle's windshield erupted in shattered glass as it was hit; another round tore through the passenger compartment and exploded, peppering its occupants with shrapnel. Klenne escaped with only a few cuts to the face and shattered eardrums, after diving out and seeking cover. Dehne and *Ogefr.* Reichenberger, however, caught the full force of the explosion.

When Klenne returned to his vehicle after the firing ceased, he noticed bits of flesh and hair sticking to the right shoulder of his uniform. Immediately, he knew that Stemmermann, who had been seated next to him, had been hit. Closer inspection revealed that Stemmermann sat slumped over in the car, dead from multiple shrapnel wounds in the back and head. Westphal and Schönfelder immediately ran to the car, where they saw Klenne and a *Hiwi* trying to pull Stemmermann's body out of the wreck. There was little that anyone could do now, except join the rest of the long columns of troops fleeing to the southwest. Stemmermann's fate was not reported until the following day, when Westphal, Schönfelder and Klenne finally reached their division's assembly area.

Interestingly, Moscow spread the story afterwards through the press and radio that Stemmermann had been killed by the SS because he had tried to surrender, but the facts do not support this. Numerous eyewitnesses soon verified the report that he was killed by an antitank gun shell. A Soviet propaganda film made shortly after the battle ended backs up the eyewitness statements. The film, made to highlight the victory and to raise morale in the Soviet Union, clearly shows the body lying next to a shattered *Kübelwagen* with SS license plates. He clearly had earned the *Ritterkreuz* which he was posthumously awarded. His death, however, had little impact upon the events of that day.

By mid-afternoon, the first wave of the withdrawing rearguards, primarily *Germania* and the Walloon Brigade, had reached the large mass of troops congregating in the large *balka* northwest of Pochapintsy. Some units had even skirted the northern outskirts of the town and had already reached the Gniloy Tikich. Hans Dorr's battalion from *Germania* arrived at the creek shortly before Gille decided to swim across. He had brought all of his battalion's wounded, who had been dragged along through the snow on boards or sleds. Dorr's battalion was accompanied by *Maj.* von Brese's *Pz.Gren.Rgt.108*, reduced by this point to a few hundred men. Both units had tried to protect a large column of wounded men from Soviet attack, and had been mauled in the process. Carefully, Dorr's and von Brese's men ferried the wounded men to the opposite bank and insured that all of them were brought to safety in Lysyanka.

Less fortunate was the main body of the Walloon Brigade, which had left the relative safety of the *balka* east of Zhurzhintsy a few hours before. Pressing on, Degrelle and his men saw that a group of Soviet cavalry was forming up on a hillside south of Komarovka, a kilometer to their rear. This must have been the vanguard of 63rd Cavalry Division, the first of Selivanov's Cossacks that began to arrive on the battlefield that afternoon. While the rest of his corps would not arrive until well after dark, this division had the shortest route to travel and its commander, urged on by Konev, pushed both men and horses mercilessly, lest they lose the opportunity of a lifetime. At first, Degrelle thought they were German cavalry, but a quick look through his binoculars clearly identified them as Soviet troops astride their peculiar little brown ponies.

Degrelle was aghast. After being subjected to tank fire, artillery, and machine-gun fire, would he and his men now have to endure being ridden down by saber-wielding cavalry? Where were Breith's tanks? Their only hope was to run as fast as they could and find shelter before they were overtaken by the enemy horsemen. Although wounded, Degrelle raced to the head of his formation, where he exhorted his men to hurry. Three tanks appeared from the south and his men began to cheer - finally, they had been rescued. To their dismay, the tanks began to fire into the Belgian ranks, killing and wounding many. As Degrelle came to the edge of a deep *balka*, his men hesitated. It was their only refuge, but the distance to the bottom gave him pause. Seeing no other choice, Degrelle jumped feet-first into the ravine, where his fall was broken by several feet of drifted snow. His men soon followed, piling atop one another at the bottom.

Momentarily saved, the Walloons now found that they were trapped in the ravine, along with hundreds of other German troops who had sought shelter there. While the tanks could not fire directly at them, the Walloons and Germans could not escape either. The few who had looked over the lip of the *balka*

were killed. Degrelle gathered as many of his men together as he could. As they huddled together to stay warm, many of his men began to lose heart, discarding any remaining personal effects to prevent the Soviets from taking them should they be captured.

After a few moments, what seemed to Degrelle to be a miracle occurred. From out of the mass of troops in the *balka* stepped forward two German soldiers. Each had a *Panzerfaust* that he had been carried all day long. Amazingly, while others had discarded even their weapons as being too heavy, these two soldiers had carried their seven pound anti-tank weapons as well as their rifles. Degrelle pounced on the two men, who appeared to be stupefied, and handed their burdens to two volunteers who had stepped forward, another German and a Belgian. Both men climbed to the top of the ridge, took aim at two T-34s, and fired. The loud dual reverberations of the weapons' discharge and near-simultaneous impact echoed throughout the length of the ravine. Both tanks exploded in a shower of flame and sparks. A young German officer, who had crawled to the top to witness the engagement, began to shout for joy and gesticulate wildly. At that moment, the lieutenant received the full impact of an explosive shell in his upper body. A veritable rain of blood and body tissue descended upon the horrified men in the *balka* who had seen him die. In his euphoria, the young officer had forgot about the third tank, which had fired at him the moment he stood up. In a fit of desperation, Degrelle stood up, firing his submachine gun at the tank. The others behind him took this as a sign and began to climb out of the ravine, shouting at the top of their lungs. Degrelle took off for a woodline some eight hundred meters away, with his brigade close at his heels. The mass of Germans huddling in the *balka* followed him too, as well as many of the *panje* wagons loaded with wounded that could get out of the hollow. The tank, which was only 40 meters away, hammered at them with its machine gun, but on the Belgians and Germans ran, the dense mass of troops having lost any semblance to an organized military formation.

Several hundred Cossacks who attempted to block their way were swept aside by the desperate men. The T-34 pursued the fugitives for a short while, stopping when it caught up with the column of vehicles carrying the wounded. As he had witnessed several times before, Degrelle saw over his shoulder how the T-34 drove over the carts full of wounded, whose cries of pain and fear mingled with those of the horses. But their deaths had distracted the tank's crew long enough for the rest of the mob to make it safely to the woods and some measure of concealment.

Degrelle and the hundreds of survivors pushed deeper into the woods, where they hoped to evade pursuit by their enemy altogether. Although he did not specify which patch of woods he had led his men into, it was probably the one which lay several hundred meters northwest of Hill 222.5, since it was the smaller of the two forests closest to the Gniloy Tikich. Here, in a large clearing, Degrelle attempted to rally his men, along with several thousand other Germans who had collected there throughout the day. He also encountered Fritz Kruse, commander of the ill-fated *389.Inf.Div.*, who, with his staff, had reached this point after vainly trying to locate Stemmermann's headquarters earlier that day. Kruse and his division headquarters had been employed

Soviet troops mop up the village of Shanderovka after the Germans have abandoned it, 17 February 1944.
(Photo courrtesy of the Battle of Korsun-Shevenkovsky Museum, Ukraine)

in Shanderovka to regulate the flow of traffic through the town and to round up stragglers for employment in ad hoc battle groups. When the mass of German troops evacuated Shanderovka, Kruse's task was complete and, lacking further guidance, he decided to march his men to the southwest. Kruse had experienced the same difficulties as Degrelle in arriving at this location. After being chased by tanks and shelled by artillery, he and his staff had tried to round up as many men as possible as they withdrew. Abandoned small arms were picked up; individual wounded men were helped into one of the several *panje* sleds that accompanied his headquarters. Kruse noted afterwards that, in this area at least, the movement seemed disciplined until his column reached the point between Zhurzhintsy and the forest which lay to the east, where they were halted by tank, artillery, and machine-gun fire which seemed to come at them from all sides. There, they were diverted to the southwest as had so many other groups. Atop Hill 239, the Germans saw a line of what they thought were enemy infantry, so they kept skirting south of the hill, hoping to find a place where they could slip through.* Kruse and his band pressed on and apparently crossed the road between Hill 239 and Pochapintsy, without encountering either *Hptm.* Scherff's *Tiger* tanks or the Soviets, who were fighting at the same time a mere kilometer futher to the southeast. Kruse's group then pushed on

across the open field south of Hill 239 and entered a patch of woods, wherein lay a small *balka* sited in the midst of a clearing. It was going on mid-day by this point.

Inside this relatively small *balka*, Kruse encountered over a thousand dispirited German and Walloon troops. They had sought protection from machine-gun fire, but lacked sufficient courage to leave the woods and keep going. He begged and pleaded with some of them to accompany him, but they refused, saying "We're sitting here! Tanks are everywhere! The SS tried to take the hill and were smashed!"[20] Kruse decided that it would be better to wait until darkness when he could lead his men to safety, but felt that he needed to make a personal reconnaissance first. He then crept forward to the edge of the forest, where he saw several tanks atop a hill 800 meters to the southeast (probably Hill 222.5). Through his binoculars he could see that some of the crewmembers were standing next to their vehicles, but it was impossible to tell whether they were German or Soviet. Kruse crawled forward for a better look. After a few moments, he saw two Germans approach the tanks, who then raised their hands, removed their belts and equipment, and handed them over to some of the tank crewmen. They were Soviet tanks, all right!

Kruse was then spotted by one of the tanks, which immediately began to fire at him. He ran back to the *balka*, where he was able to collect a total of about 600 officers, NCOs, and enlisted men from all branches of the *Wehrmacht* and the SS. He was thus engaged when Degrelle met up with him. Kruse was delighted when Degrelle offered to help lead the dispirited band of men in the forest to safety. At that time *Oberst* Hohn, commander of *72.Inf. Div.*, also stepped forward and offered to place the few men he had at his disposal under Kruse's command. Hohn, who

---

* The men that Kruse saw could perhaps have been from the *Jäger* unit that was providing infantry support to Scherff's tanks, although it is impossible to know for certain. At the time Kruse spotted them, it was approximately 1330 hours, at which time Scherff had temporarily occupied Hill 239. It is interesting to speculate how close Kruse and his men were to salvation, had they only known it. Lack of radio equipment or other means of communication probably contributed to the death or captivity of hundreds of men.

was wounded, had been separated from his staff several hours before and had earlier been reported killed in action, but had somehow made it to this patch of woods before the Soviets could round up him and his men. By this time, Kruse reckoned that as many as 2,500 to 3,000 troops had gathered in the woods, including sixty *panje* wagons and sleds loaded with wounded. Kruse decided that he would lead the breakout as soon as it got dark, approximately 1645 hours.

Before the breakout could begin, Kruse felt that he had to perform a personal reconnaissance of the route they would follow. Taking along his 1a, *Oberstlt.* Meier-Welcker, they proceeded south at 1430 hours for several hundred meters, until the Gniloy Tikich came into view. They sighted several Soviet tanks, though they remained undetected themselves. Luckily, they were able to locate a route that followed the contours of the terrain that would allow them to approach the creek without being seen. Their luck improved even further when several of the tanks that were closest to their position started their engines and drove off towards the north, away from the two German officers. Both men could clearly see that the route to Lysyanka was free of any other Soviet units, provided that they were able to get their large group moving quickly enough.

As they returned to the forest, artillery shells began impacting all around. Worse, it appeared as if the tanks that had moved off to the north were returning and were even heading in their direction. It seemed as if the Soviets were getting ready to attack their position. It was now about 1600 hours and the sun had begun to set when the motley collection of troops began moving out with the wounded in tow. As they left the woods, several Soviet antitank guns began firing in their direction, but with little effect. A T-34 spotted them as well, but the route of march passed along the opposite side of a narrow ridge, offering the Germans and Walloons cover. The tank shells passed harmlessly overhead. Suddenly, the point of the column encountered rifle and machine-gun fire. As it had before, Kruse's column hesitated and many men sat down in the snow. Kruse had to act quickly before defeatism set in.

With Degrelle's, Hohn's, and Meier-Welcker's help, Kruse was able to rouse the men one more time and with shouts of encouragement, got them moving again. Summoning those forward who still had weapons, Kruse and Degrelle then led them in an attack against the Soviet infantry positions which blocked their way. Shouting "Hurrah!," Kruse and his troops charged the Soviets and rapidly closed with them. It was over quickly. The Soviet troops not killed were chased away or taken prisoner. Kruse's group pressed on, crossing the abandoned railroad bed and reaching the Gniloy Tikich by 1630 hours. Turning to their right, they traced its path upstream, passing a large marsh bordering the creek that was filled with mired *panje* wagons and horses, which whinnied pitifully. These vehicles and their teams had gotten stuck when their drivers tried to negotiate the bottom land, only to be abandoned when they could proceed no further. The horses were left to die, a nightmarish scene which affected Degrelle deeply.

Kruse's group was fortunate; they had been able to approach to within 500 meters of Lysyanka before they crossed,

encountering only sporadic Soviet small arms fire along the way. They were finally able to cross the Gniloy Tikich one at a time using a narrow beam that someone had laid there that spanned the creek; whether to aid the German troops breaking out or the Soviet troops attacking is impossible to tell. At 1645 hours, the spearhead of Kruse's column began to cross. As they reached the safety of the opposite bank, Degrelle's group experienced a "heart-stopping shock" when they spotted three helmeted shadows rise up in front of them. To their relief, they were SS grenadiers from *Leibstandarte.* Degrelle and his men fell into their arms "laughing, crying and dancing with joy, as all our worry and pain fell from our shoulders," he later wrote.[21]

To insure that everyone made it to safety, Kruse returned to the rear of the formation to supervise the stragglers and wounded, while Degrelle led the first group of survivors, including most of the Walloon Brigade, into Lysyanka. Unfortunately, most of the carts and wagons carrying the wounded had become stuck in the marsh which Kruse had bypassed earlier. The wounded were offloaded and carried by their comrades, while the horses were shot because it was too difficult to pull them out. Two motor vehicles that somehow had made the trip to this point were blown up to prevent capture. His task completed, Kruse finally arrived in Lysyanka with his staff at midnight. For Kruse, Degrelle, and thousands of others whom they had led to freedom, the experience of the pocket was "nothing more than a horrible dream." In Degrelle's words, which sum up what many must have felt, "We were no longer living under a stay of execution."

The column silently trudged through the snow-covered streets of south Lysyanka as shells fell sporadically throughout the town. These survivors of *Gruppe Stemmermann* knew that they were not yet out of danger, but were safer than at any other time during the past three weeks. Officers and enlisted men alike then began to seek shelter from the snow and icy winds for the night. Although they had not had to swim the creek as had so many others before them, they were still exhausted, cold, and hungry. Dozens, even hundreds, of men tried to cram into *isbas* built to house a farm family of six to eight people. Though most of these huts were abandoned and had no fires burning in their hearths, the body warmth of men packed shoulder to shoulder was often enough to afford some respite from the cold. As they slept, many men cried out in fright or shouted incomprehensible orders directed at no one. Others would sit up bolt straight and begin to unconsciously pummel their comrades to their right and left. All had been under enormous mental strain; it would take weeks, if not months, for them to recover. Some would never recover at all. But they had survived.

End Notes

1   Glanz, "From the Dnieper to the Vistula," p. 234.
2   Rotmistrov in *Selected Readings in Military History,* pp. 332-333.
3   Telegin, A. "Under Complex Conditions," in *Selected Readings in Military History:Soviet Military History, Volume I – The Red Army, 1918 to 1945.* (Fort Leavenworth, KS: U.S. Army Combat Studies Institute, 1984), pp. 333-334.
4   Glantz, p. 160.
5   *III.Pz.Korps* KTB, entry dated 1930 hours 17 February 1944 and *1.Pz.Armee* KTB entry dated 17 February 1944, p. 1.
6   *Abschrift des Gefechtsbericht der Kampfgr. Pietsch der 17.Pz.Div., 22.2.1944.*
7   *1.Pz.Armee* KTB, entry dated 17 February 1944, p. 1.
8   Scherff in *Erinnerungen an die Tigeabteilung 503,* p. 228-229.
9   1.Pz.Div., *Gefechtsbericht über die Kämpfe der 1.Panzer-Division mit unterstellten Gruppen Frank und Pietsch vom 17.2.44 0.400 Uhr bis 18.2.44 24.00 Uhr, Div.St.Qu., den 24.February 1944,* p. 2.
10 Schw.Pz.Rgt. Bäke, Abt.1a, *Bericht über die Verbindungsaufnahme der westlich Tscherkassy eingeschlossenen Korps am 17.2.1944, Rgts.Gef.Stand, den 24.2.1944,* p. 2.
11 Lehmann and Tiemann, pp. 36-38.
12 Wykes, Alan. *Hitler's Bodyguards: SS Leibstandarte.* (New York: Ballantine Books, 1974), p. 145.
13 *1.Pz.Div. Gefechtsbericht,* p. 3.
14 Carell, p. 426.
15 Jahnke and Lerch, p. 96.
16 Radio Message, *Chef, XXXXII.A.K. an Chef A.O.K. 8,* dated 0015 hours 18 February 1944.
17 Leib in DA Pam 20-234, p. 31.
18 Lehmann and Tiemann, p. 38.
19 Anlage 1 zu Gen.Kdo. XI.A.K., 1a 19/44 g.Kdos., *Oberst i.G. Gädke meldet zu dem wahrscheinlichen Tode des der Art. Stemmermann,* 21.2.44.
20 *Kommandeur, 389.Inf. Div., 1a Nr. 200/44 geh., an das kommando XI.A.K., Ausbruch am 16.2.44, Orts Unterkunft, den 22.2.44.*
21 Degrelle, p. 221.

Chapter Twenty Three
THE REARGUARD RUNS THE GAUNTLET

"In this horrible situation, only those who still possessed great will power and physical strength had any chance of surviving . . . "
— Hans Menedetter, 88.Inf.Div.[1]

Throughout that long day, the Soviet forces relentlessly continued their efforts to block the escape route for the main body of the breakout force as well as the rearguard. Dozens of tanks made repeated forays into the corridor to cut the Germans off, but the escaping troops swerved around them or hid until the tanks had passed by. Without their own foot soldiers to provide close-in protection, Soviet tank crewmen were very reluctant to occupy vulnerable positions astride the Germans' path; thus, they initially had no way to permanently block the escape corridor. Infantry reinforcements were not forthcoming, and the units positioned in the breakout corridor (5th Guards Airborne, 41st Guards, 180th, and 202nd Rifle Divisions) had been overrun and partially encircled themselves.

While Soviet tanks and artillery killed and wounded thousands of Germans, they were no substitute for a solid line of dug-in infantry. Even the arrival of advance elements of 63rd Cavalry Division by mid-afternoon was not enough to seal the breach. By the time that their vanguard had arrived near Komarovka, nearly all of the combat elements of *Gruppe Stemmermann* had already moved several kilometers to the southwest, leaving the horsemen to content themselves with sabering German stragglers and wounded men who could not defend themselves. These unfortunate troops had been left behind or had been missed when the rearguard withdrew earlier that morning and had been trying to catch up with their comrades ever since. Many of the wounded still lay in *panje* wagons, their horses dead or taken by able-bodied men for their own escape.

Many of these stragglers were men who had been accidentally separated from their units or had deliberately absented themselves in hopes of making it through on their own. Many others were just lost. Many had given up entirely and were merely waiting to be captured. Thousands of other men – corps troops, civilian officials, Luftwaffe ground crews, civilian auxiliaries, deserters, and *Hiwis* - began to seek shelter in the many large and small *balki* that crisscrossed the breakout corridor. Leaderless, without weapons, they no longer bore any resemblance to military formations. Except for the few resolute individuals who were biding time until darkness to resume their breakout, most simply huddled in the bottom of ravines or in the small forests that dotted the area and waited - for the end, for death, for captivity.

The men who could have led them out of their predicament, leaders like Leon Degrelle and Gerhard Franz, had already

German troops crossing the Gniloy Tikich by crawling across a precarious bridge of felled trees.
(Photo by Adolf Salie, courtesy of Willy Hein)

escaped themselves at the head of their own troops. Leadership was a scarce commodity that day and most of that was possessed by the combat units. Unfortunately, the overwhelming majority of the men who sought the illusory shelter of these nameless gullies, ravines, and forests were not combat soldiers at all and were totally unprepared for the enormous mental and physical challenge that they had to face that day. By mid-afternoon, these men became the recipients of General Konev's attention, since virtually everyone else who had kept up with the breakout had made it as far as the Zhurzhintsy - Hill 239 Pochapintsy area. Intercepted Soviet radio messages attest to the ease with which these men were captured. One typical report from a Soviet battalion was intercepted at 1330 hours that stated that "One thousand [men] in the area southwest of Komarovka tried to sneak by us, but [they] did not make it. They ran in all directions [at our approach] and tried to hide in bushes and in the ravine...our troops are [currently] trying to liquidate them."[2]

By late afternoon, when the bulk of *Gruppe Stemmermann* had reached and crossed the Gniloy Tikich, the mopping up of the pocket encompassing Shanderovka, Khilki, and Komarovka had only begun. Here, Soviet troops had found thousands of wounded who had been left behind, hundreds of wrecked vehicles and guns, and an unknown number of men who simply waited to be taken prisoner. Fortunately for the Germans, many Soviet commanders failed to closely pursue the rearguards of *57.* and *88.Inf.Div.*, thus allowing them to disengage on schedule and follow the escape route that the rest of their comrades had taken. One reason perhaps why this occurred is that the pursuers stopped in the three towns mentioned above long enough to rummage through the piles of abandoned German equipment in search of luxury items unknown in the Soviet Union - pocket watches, books, writing paper, umbrellas, rubber boots, blankets, swords, underwear, champagne, and so forth.

It slowly began to dawn on the Soviets that the bulk of the Germans were getting away. Despite the fact that their troops were now killing or rounding up thousands of stragglers, Konev's subordinate commanders must have realized that most of the Germans were slipping from their grasp. Many Soviet commanders knew it, too. One intercepted Soviet radio message, this one from an unknown subordinate unit to the headquarters of 359th Rifle Division near Vsremirnyye sent during the early morning hours of 18 February, stated that:

> This morning the enemy even attacked us with about 200 men with machine pistols, but these were naturally driven off. We estimate that about 30,000 of them have made it through so far, but there aren't many fighters left among them. They were able to slip through the gate . . . "[3]

The commander of the division ordered this unit: "You will slam the gate immediately!" The fact that many thousands of Germans were escaping could not be hidden. Why Konev did not order any of his rifle divisions to attack and seize the German bridgeheads along the Gniloy Tikich remains a mystery. Perhaps he did not have any available, or if he did, they could not get there quickly enough. Perhaps he did not wish to ask his rival Zhukov for assistance, although Zhukov did have several rifle divisions that could have done so. Whatever the case, what was occurring along the banks of the Gniloy Tikich could clearly be seen from many Soviet positions, some over a kilometer away. This, of course, placed many subordinate commanders in a most uncomfortable situation.

Most did not report the fact that the Germans were getting away to their higher headquarters as the unit from 359th Rifle Division had done, on the contrary; many reported that not a single German soldier had made it through. After all, if Konev himself had promised Stalin that not a single German would escape, who were they to contradict a General of the Army? Konev's army and corps commanders then began to redouble their efforts to achieve the desired "output" that their *Front* commander required - thousands of German bodies, or at least to report that they had. Whether they were alive or not does not seem to have mattered. The airwaves were hot with orders and counter-orders instructing regiment, battalion, and company commanders to stop the remaining Germans. One example of an intercepted radio message that embodies this attitude was addressed to the commander of 5th Guards Tank Corps, which instructed him to "Ruthlessly strike the Germans [who are located] south and southwest of Zhurzhintsy and allow him no opportunity to break out towards the south!"

After three weeks of fighting, these men needed no further urging. By this point, the bloodlust must have been quite

powerful indeed; neither side asked nor received quarter. By dusk, the bulk of Selivanov's Cossack divisions finally began to arrive. While most of the German troops had broken out by that time, the horsemen still found enough left to kill. According to one account by a Maj. Kampov, who was assigned to Konev's staff, the Cossacks was particularly aggressive, slaughtering Germans in scenes reminiscent of the Middle Ages:

> Most of the time the tanks were not using their guns lest they hit their own cavalry. Hundreds and hundreds of cavalry were hacking at [the Germans] with their sabers, and massacred the Fritzes as no one had ever been massacred by cavalry before. There was no time to take prisoners. It was a kind of carnage that nothing could stop till it was over . . . I had been at Stalingrad; but never had I seen such concentrated slaughter as in the fields and ravines of that small bit of country.[4]

It is a wonder that the Soviets took any German prisoners at all, but by late afternoon they had taken so many of them it became impossible to kill them quickly, so they were increasingly rounded up and marched back to Shanderovka, where they would wait until being moved to prisoner of war camps. Besides, the sight of thousands of prisoners would prove to be a propaganda windfall, of which the Soviets would soon take full advantage.

Soviet captors also reported finding many Soviet citizens in German uniforms among the prisoners, *Hiwis* who had been unfortunate enough to be captured by their countrymen, who were not inclined to be gentle with traitors. One radio message intercepted at 1330 hours that Thursday reported that "Near Hill 193.3 (one kilometer southwest of Komarovka) more than 70 men surrendered, among them Russian women dressed as German soldiers…" The same unit reported capturing a former Soviet soldier in a German uniform who had been serving as a *Hiwi* in *112.Inf.Div.* since 1941 and who had been awarded the Iron Cross and Russian Front Medal. When they asked what they should do with the turncoat, they were told to hang him with a placard around his neck that read "Traitor to the Motherland."[5] Most of the *Hiwis* managed to break out with their German comrades, but the few who faced capture found Soviet retribution to be harsh indeed.

German troops continued to flow out of the pocket during the evening of 17/18 February in a seemingly never-ending stream. Despite the obstacles thrown in their path by both the Red Army and nature, they continued to filter past Soviet forward outposts. Strangely, the Soviet units in the Germans' path appear to have done little that night except to arrange their companies and battalions for all-round defense. Most of their activity was confined to placing artillery harassing fire throughout the length and breadth of the escape corridor. By this point, several emergency bridges had been erected at points along the Gniloy Tikich, protected by a few *Panzergrenadiers* and a tank or two. This enabled thousands of stragglers and the rearguard to cross relatively easily, in contrast to the first wave of assault troops earlier that morning.

Once arrived on the opposite bank, they were guided to Lysyanka, where they sought some degree of shelter for the night. Most of these men were soon rousted from their *isbas* and ordered to keep moving towards Bushanka and Frankovka, where warm food awaited them. Grumbling, the exhausted troops obeyed, hoping that they would get a better reception in the rear area. By midnight on 17 February, over 20,000 German soldiers had made it to the relative safety of Lysyanka - without vehicles, cannon, or tanks, but alive. Thousands more would continue to arrive throughout the evening and the next morning as well.

The breakout was not yet over, but the Soviet Propaganda Ministry felt compelled to issue an official statement trumpeting their victory at 2340 hours that evening. The Radio Moscow broadcast, intercepted by *1.Pz.Armee's* radio intelligence units, recorded an official statement issued by the Soviet Supreme Command credited to General of the Army Konev that stated:

> As a result of 14 days of uninterrupted bitter fighting, the troops of the Second Ukrainian Front ended an operation on 17 February which resulted in the liquidation of ten divisions and a brigade of the Eighth German Army that had been encircled in the area of Korsun-Shevchenkovsky. In the course of this operation, the Germans left 52,000 men dead on the battlefield. Eleven thousand soldiers and officers have surrendered. All of the enemy's equipment and weapons have been captured. In the fighting [the following units] have distinguished themselves: The troops of Lt.Gen. Trofimenko, Lt. Gen. Smirnoff, and Lt. Gen. Koroteyev; the cavalrymen of Lt. Gen. Selivanov, the tanks troops of Colonel General of Armored Troops Rotmistrov, of General Armored Troops Kirichenko and Polozkov, and the pilots of Lt. Gen. of the Air Force Goryunov.[6]

This was premature, since the battle was still in progress and would rage for two more days. Most of the Soviet units concerned were still too busy fighting to carry out a detailed body count, though they did have a good idea of how many Germans had fallen since their encirclement operation began three weeks before. At the time the Soviet statement was read, over 10,000 men of *Gruppe Stemmermann* were still en route to Lysyanka and would not reach the safety of their own lines until the following day. The broadcast also failed to mention the contribution that Zhukov, Vatutin, and First Ukrainian *Front* had made towards the success of the operation.

Worded as it was, it made it seem as if the victory was Konev's and his Front's alone, which no doubt contributed to the growing ill will that had arisen between the two men. The evidence seems to indicate that it was Konev himself who provided the information for the communiqué and who probably passed it directly to Stalin's headquarters, bypassing Zhukov, the *STAVKA* coordinator for the operation. But the impact of such a statement was undeniable. Thanks to the state of communications at that time, this message was quickly spread by the Soviet

press agency to a world-wide audience, which gave the impression that the Germans had suffered a crushing defeat. In truth, they had, though not to such a degree that the broadcast made it appear, thus igniting a debate which still continues today.

This announcement would have surprised the units comprising the rearguard of *Gruppe Stemmermann*. The regiments and battalions of *57.* and *88.Inf.Div.* had been withdrawing on schedule to phase lines Green, Black and Red. While they had been closely pressed by the pursuing Soviets, they were still able to maintain unit cohesion. Shanderovka was given up by 0800 hours on 17 February, while Khilki and the remaining part of Komarovka still in German hands would be abandoned by noon. Thereafter, the rearguard withdrew to a series of successive defensive positions that had been determined in advance.

While both divisions reported hard fighting initially, they had even more difficulty clearing a path through the immense traffic jam that stretched between Shanderovka and Khilki, which delayed their movement more than the pursuing Soviets did. Trowitz's division did not face any further difficulty until one of his regiments received heavy tank, infantry, and artillery fire from Komarovka and Khilki when it drew abreast of both towns. This fire, combined with roads that were completely stopped up with abandoned equipment and vehicles, forced Trowitz to abandon most of his remaining vehicles, except for those carrying wounded. Here, the bulk of the withdrawing *Germania* and regiments from *57.Inf.Div.* (*Gren.Rgt.199, 217,* and *676*) began to become intermingled with one another. Whenever the marching columns encountered Soviet infantry that threatened to block their path, a quick German bayonet assault nearly always forced the enemy to withdraw.

Trowitz, however, reported that soon after his division had begun its march to the southwest, many of his men began to lose their will to fight. Like the columns that had preceded them, the marching columns of *57.Inf.Div.* were attacked on both flanks by tank, artillery, and antitank gun fire. The terrain was difficult to traverse, and many men began to lose heart when they realized that they would have to fight their way out on their own. Somewhere to the north marched *88.Inf.Div.* on a parallel route, yet both divisions apparently made no attempt to operate in concert. This was probably due more to a total lack of communications than to anything else. Almost all of the rest of the division's vehicles were abandoned when they could no longer make any headway on account of the many ditches, ravines, and *balki* that crisscrossed their path.[7]

Reaching Hill 239 late in the afternoon ahead of *88.Inf.Div.*, Trowitz's troops had to overcome strong enemy resistance in order to reach the top of the ridgeline. During the fighting, his divisional column was split into two groups; the first, with Trowitz in the lead, attacked directly west across the top of the hill, where they then pushed into the patch of woods south of the hilltop. Here, they reorganized and continued their march to the Gniloy Tikich, which they reached early that evening and crossed on emergency infantry bridges erected previously. That morning, *1.Pz.Div.* even erected a small bridge that could support the weight of vehicles, thus allowing *57.Inf.Div.* to bring out two light infantry howitzers, two field kitchens, and 20 *panje* wagons loaded with wounded. Thanks to the initiative of

Exhausted SS troops pause enroute to the Gnily Tikich cross-ing. (Photo by Adolf Salie, from "Verweht sind die Spuren: Bilddokumentation 5.SS-Pz.Rgt. Wiking" [Munin Verlag] and the Wiking Division Veteran's Association)

View of the flooded Gnily Tikich looking southeast. Beyond the bend in the creek lies the Soviet occupied village Vsremirnye. (Photo from Guenther Jahnke and Bernd Lerch, "Der Kessel von Tscherkassy 1944")

Oblt. Dumberger from the transportation battalion, the division was able to get out almost all of its wounded, some six hundred men who would have otherwise perished. Trowitz himself was one of the last men of this division to cross; he waited on the opposite bank until the last of his men made it to safety during the early morning hours of 18 February. The honor of being the last belonged to *Oblt.* Kandziora of the division's *Feldgendarmerie* platoon, who did not leave his traffic direction post on the western outskirts of Shanderovka until 1400 hours.

The second group from *57.Inf.Div.* was forced to the south, where it crossed between Pochapintsy and Hill 239. It too reached the Gniloy Tikich, but unlike their more fortunate comrades two kilometers to the north, this group had to swim across. Again, this division, as had the others, lost many men to the icy current, but most made it out of the pocket. Except for Soviet tanks, which caused most of the casualties that day, nearly all of the resistance encountered was easily swept aside. Since it was one of the few units that had managed to bring out some field kitchens intact, the survivors were able to receive a warm meal once they had arrived in Lysyanka.

Uffz. Hans Gaertig, of the division's signal battalion, was one of the men who made it out with the southernmost group of *57.Inf.Div.* He described the first withdrawal from Phase Line Green vividly. "We received the whispered order to begin the breakout, passed from man to man. "No noise! No lights! Move out single file! Stay in the path stamped out [in the snow] of the man in front of you!" Detailed as an escort to a column of ambulances, he was outraged when these vehicles filled with wounded men and displaying the Red Cross were picked off one by one by Soviet tanks and artillery. After marching several hours, he was caught up in the confusion on Hill 239 and moved towards the south with many others. In his words, "[Finally], we came to a creek that was almost completely frozen over, where apparently many before us had crossed. Pieces of wood and other undefinable materials had been used to cross the not completely frozen-over creek. After crossing…we could make out our tanks, which formed the left and right flank protection for the rescue corridor."[8]

Gaertig and a few of his comrades assembled in a house in Lysyanka, where they uttered shouts of "Lads, we made it out!"

In his words, "The weeks of uncertainty fell away from us; one saw hard-bitten warriors with tears in their eyes. An old *Oberfeldwebel* said to me, 'So, now you have your front-line experience behind you' (referring to Gaertig's temporary duty with the division to gain combat seasoning as an officer candidate)." He certainly had experienced combat, far more than what he expected when he reported for duty with the division in December 1943. As a momento of what he had gone through, Gaertig carried a piece of shrapnel the size of a postage stamp. During his escape, an artillery shell had struck nearby, sending shrapnel in all directions. One piece hit him in the chest, leaving a dent in his ribcage, but failed to pierce his skin. For a long time afterwards, Gaertig could not breath without pain, but at least he had survived. Later, upon reflection, Gaertig was struck by how his unit had been able to escape relatively unscathed. He credited his own survival to a guardian angel that God himself had sent down to look over him and his comrades.

A more detailed account of *57.Inf.Div.'s* breakout was provided by staff officer *Hptm.* Hans Schiller. After disengaging from its initial position east of Shanderovka, Schiller marched with the rest of the division staff in the early morning darkness to their delaying position southeast of Khilki near the bridge where the tank from *Wiking* had fallen through the night before. At 0600, he encountered, General Trowitz, who "radiated calm confidence."After seeing that Schiller and the rest of the staff had set up the defense to his satisfaction, the general moved on to inspect his grenadiers and to reconnoiter the next phase line of the withdrawal. Schiller had not slept for days. Once he had insured that the division's escort company had set up a hasty defense of the town, he ducked under a piece of canvas stretched across the top of a foxhole. The only food left was a crust of bread, but he was so tired he fell asleep while eating it. Awoken by the sounds of impacting *Katyusha* rockets, he poked his head out of his improvised shelter and saw only smoke and drifting snow.

In a neighboring foxhole, Trowitz's aide, *Ltn.* Reiter, had remained as he awaited his commander's return. Schiller asked him what was going on, but received a sarcastic reply instead. After a brief chat, Schiller was able to determine that the withdrawal of *Gren.Rgt.199, 217*, and *646* through Shanderovka was going according to plan and that Trowitz should return momentarily. Finding that his brief catnap had refreshed him, Schiller then marched several hundred meters to the rear to take a look around, where the roofs of Khilki could be seen protruding over the rise. As he approached the village, it appeared deserted, since the unit defending the town, *Oberst* Neufellner's *Kampfgruppe* from *Div.Gr.323*, was probably arrayed on the town's northern outskirts, if it had not already withdrawn. Drawing his pistol, Schiller approached cautiously, unsure of whether the town was still in German hands. To his surprise, he heard the sound of German voices coming from one of the *isbas*. Inside sat 12 to 15 men from the *Luftwaffe*. Schiller shouted "What are you still doing here? Are you waiting for *Ivan*? Out, get out, all of you. Quickly!" The men then moved as if someone had rolled a grenade in their midst, as Schiller stood there holding the door open for them. Thinking perhaps that there might be other stragglers in the town, Schiller went from house to house. Here, he saw empty huts, smashed windows, open doors, tipped over *panje* wagons, destroyed vehicles, but not a single soul. Khilki had become a no-man's land. He turned to the south, to examine the last row of buildings, and met up with a sergeant from a combat engineer unit, who had evidently been watching Schiller from afar. He reported to the officer, stating that he was straggler from a unit that had been tasked with holding a ridgeline northeast of the town. As he spoke, his five-man squad filed out from a hut behind him. Festooned with hand grenades, all of them were armed with either machine pistols, rifles or pistols.

Schiller began to interrogate them, asking the sergeant and his men why were they hanging around and where was their unit. None of their answers satisfied him, so he ordered them to follow him, since the village appeared suspiciously peaceful. Just as he spoke, the village was rocked by a barrage that sent them all scrambling for cover. As he looked around, Schiller saw the sergeant motioning him to join him and his men in the cellar of a house, telling him that he could wait out the barrage there. After climbing down a ladder, he saw in the dim light that the cellar was occupied, but not by German troops. Instead, he saw the forms of many Ukrainian civilians, mostly women and children, and a few *Hiwis*.

Schiller and the sergeant waited until the artillery barrage lessened in intensity, then stuck their heads out to see if it was safe to exit the cellar. The artillery had shifted to the hill that lay between Schiller and the rest of the division staff, cutting him off from his comrades. The wiry sergeant, a blond 28 year-old from Berlin, told him that he was sure that they could make it out that evening, since it was known that the Soviets tended to cluster in villages or in forest during the nighttime and could be easily circumvented. He then proceeded to describe to Schiller the route they would have to take, which began to sound as if the sergeant had thought it all out. An interesting offer, Schiller thought. Just then, he saw through the falling snow the outline of a row of troops several hundred meters away from the north. They appeared to be marching in their direction, but he could not tell whether they were friend or foe.

Troops from Wiking gather on the southern bank of Gniloy Tikich after crossing. Note most men have disgarded weapons and headgear. (Photo courtesy of Guenther Jahnke and Bernd Lerch, "Der Kessel von Tscherkassy 1944")

Artillery and rocket fire now began to smash into Khilki again. The line of troops kept moving towards them. Although he could not tell whether they were Soviet troops, he decided it would be better to be safe than sorry. Turning around, Schiller screamed into the cellar, "Everybody out! The Russians are coming down the hill towards us!" The German troops quickly climbed out of the cellar and threw themselves into the snow just as another barrage impacted. Mud, snow, and shrapnel flew everywhere, but miraculously no one was hit. Schiller yelled to them to wait for the next pause in the barrage, then move out on the double towards the south, where he hoped to join the rest of the withdrawing troops and perhaps even his battalion. When the barrage momentarily ceased, he stood up and ran as fast as he could until he was out of the danger zone. Suddenly, he realized that he was alone. None of the others had followed him, perhaps trusting their own instincts more than those of an officer who they did not know.

He decided to go it alone. Clinging to ravines and larger *balki*, Schiller often slipped and rolled head-over-heels to the bottom, becoming buried in thigh-deep snow drifts. His rucksack often slipped over his head as he tumbled, but he would get up and keep walking, always to the southwest. There was no sign of the sergeant or his men. Perhaps they had been killed or taken prisoner; perhaps the men coming down the hill were German troops after all, he thought. There was no way to know for sure, so he decided to push on.

Over the next several hours, guided by his map, Schiller walked through the entire breakout corridor. On at least one occasion, he encountered a Soviet patrol, but saw hardly any of his own troops. He noticed that German weapons and equipment were strewn along the entire length and breadth of the escape route, which guided him infallibly in the right direction. Occasionally, Soviet gunners sought him out as a target; each time, he was able to evade their shells. Afraid that his legs would give out, Schiller plodded grimly onward, with the wind at his back seeming to assist his progress. Finally, reeling with fatigue, he reached the foot of the eastern slope of Hill 239 late that afternoon and pulled himself up to the top by reaching from tree trunk to tree trunk.

Survivors of the breakout, after crossing the Gniloy Tikich, march single file towards the relative safety of Lysyanka. (Photo by Adolf Salie courtesy of Willy Hein)

On the summit, he noticed how the terrain to the west leveled out into a broad valley, in the middle of which lay Lysyanka. He could hear the sounds of tank tracks and motors some distance in the west, but could see no sign of German or Soviet troops. His legs finally gave out on him, sending him reeling to the ground. As he lay trying to recover his strength, it began to snow again. Finally, he stood up and pushed on, crossing the road that ran from Hill 239 to Pochapintsy after walking a hundred meters. He pushed on along the eastern edge of the forest, fearing a Soviet ambush. After walking for what seemed like an eternity, he approached a shell crater in which he hoped to rest safely. As he approached its rim, he noticed that there were several soldiers sitting inside and eating. Schiller asked them who they were. They replied that they were breaking out from the pocket. Mystified, he told them that they seemed to be having a break, not breaking out. The group spokesman said "Naw, we're only hungry. Come on in, comrade, here is a first-class waiting room!"

Schiller soon found out that Soviet troops were blocking their escape and that they were waiting for darkness before they would resume their escape attempt. He asked them if they were part of the rearguard, but they responded that they had no idea and that they were not looking for an invitation to become one, either. Schiller decided not to wait around for darkness and told the men that they could come with him if they liked. They demurred, and one man responded with a cheery "Till we meet again tonight!" All around, Schiller could clearly hear the sound of tank and machine gun fire, but he kept moving anyway. After a quarter of an hour, he encountered a large marching column of German troops and vehicles approaching from the direction of Pochapintsy that were doing their best to avoid a Soviet artillery barrage. Since the enemy guns were firing unobserved, the shells kept impacting in the same spot repeatedly, making it easy for the escaping Germans to avoid.

Soon, he reached the southern tip of the forest that lay immediately south of Hill 239, where, to his relief, he met up with several members of the division staff who he knew, such as *Oblt.* Dehner, the *1c* of the division. Schiller's joy at seeing a friend was dampened somewhat when Dehner repeated over and

over again, "Shit, Hans, oh shit!" out of frustration. *Ltn.* Reiter, the sarcastic Sudeten who Schiller had last seen on the outskirts of Khilki lay dead in the snow. A Soviet tank had seen Reiter and some signal troops riding in a communications half-track and had fired upon them, mortally wounding the lieutenant. The only way out lay across a wide open slope upon which artillery shells could be seen impacting sporadically. Schiller, undeterred, grabbed Dehner and dragged him and some other men along with him. He would find another way out.

Pushing on, the little group found an abandoned Soviet gun position in the woods, whose barrels were pointing to the southwest. Schiller pushed the men into a log bunker camouflaged with pine branches. Here, they rested and regained their composure. He offered Dehner coffee from his field flask, but to his dismay it had frozen solid. Peeking out through an observation slit in the bunker, Schiller saw several tanks on a small hill several hundred meters downhill from their position. These were obviously Soviet, he thought. Nevertheless, he urged his comrades up one more time. Stealthily, they crept through the last bit of the forest and soon came upon a clearing where hundreds of German troops had gathered. Vehicles of all sorts were mingled together, as were the men from nearly every unit that had been in the pocket. Wounded men lay all over, begging the able-bodied to take them along.

Finally, it appeared as if one group in this mass of men had decided to attack regardless. Schiller, Dehner, and the others joined this group, which soon set off in a westerly direction down the hill in a large wedge-shaped infantry formation. Crying at the top of their lungs, the Germans began running down the hill. Strangely, there was no Soviet reaction. Looking behind, Schiller saw that several vehicles had begun to leave the safety of the woods and had begun to follow them. After less than an hour, this group reached the banks of the Gniloy Tikich. Unfortunately, the banks of the creek were being peppered with enemy tank and machine-gun fire. There was no bridge across the creek, either.

Determined not to get wet, Schiller and his small group walked along the bank a few hundred meters upstream, in hopes of finding some sort of crossing set up for them. Miraculously, just as it was beginning to grow dark they found a rather rickety-looking footbridge that led to the southern outskirts of Lysyanka, enabling the Germans to cross with dry feet.* There, they encountered the first line of outposts, who challenged them. "Freedom!" Schiller and the others yelled, the agreed-upon password for all of the troops taking part in the breakout. Ten hours and 20 kilometers after he had started, *Hptm.* Hans Schiller had made it out of the pocket.[9]

Not every soldier from *57.Inf.Div.* was as fortunate as Gaertig or Schiller. One of these men, *Gefr.* Fritz Malchow of *Füs.Btl.157*, found himself in a defensive position east of Shanderovka with the last thirty or forty men of his unit on the morning of 17 February. His group, led by *Oblt.* Brodermann, had just carried out a pre-dawn counterattack

---

* Schiller could have been in the large group in the woods that was led to safety by General Kruse and Leon Degrelle, since the details of the breakout are so similar.

along with some men from the Walloon Brigade to throw the enemy out of their position. Here, for the first time, Malchow fought Soviet infantrymen hand-to-hand, literally seeing the whites of their eyes. During the confused fighting, Malchow was separated from the rest of his comrades and found himself with *Uffz.* Meene, the battalion clerk and *Uffz.* Freese, from the battalion medical platoon. Freese had been shot through the lungs and could not walk. They were now alone in hostile territory. Malchow and Meene loaded their wounded comrade aboard a sled and began pulling him back to where they thought the battalion's position was, but could not locate it, since it had already withdrawn to the next defensive line. Brodermann reported Malchow, Freese and Meene as missing in action and afterwards wrote a letter to Malchow's parents informing them of their son's disappearance.

Soon, five other stragglers from *Gren.Rgt.217* of the division joined them. Together, they fought against both the icy wind and the terrain, taking turns towing Freese. At times, it seemed as if they were marching in the wrong direction, so disoriented had they become. Malchow noticed many other groups of German soldiers marching by, but there seemed to be no one in charge of the movement. After spending the night in the open, the small group of soldiers set out again the next morning in hopes of reaching friendly lines. They soon encountered a group of 20 to 30 Soviet horsemen, who they were able to drive off with their rifles and machine pistols. Shortly afterwards, however, a large group of Soviet infantry appeared, probably summoned by the cavalry.

Surrounded, Malchow and his comrades tried to escape in the knee-deep snow, but were unable to make good their escape. Seeing no way out, the Germans surrendered, shouting "Don't shoot! Don't fire!" To prevent a Soviet soldier from stealing his Iron Cross, First Class, Malchow took it out of his mitten where he had been hiding it and threw it into the deep snow. He and his comrades were thoroughly searched and "liberated" of any personal items such as watches, photographs, and tobacco. Those who complained or resisted were beaten for their effrontery. They were soon forced to march back to the east, accompanied by shouts of *Niemetskii Davai!* (Hurry up, Germans!). After being led back through Shanderovka, Malchow and the others were marched under guard to a larger town (probably Steblev or Korsun), where he saw thousands of other German prisoners.

When the column halted, a wounded Soviet soldier approached Malchow and struck him in the mouth with his fist, shouting *Du Kamerad kaputt!* (You're dead, comrade!). Another Soviet soldier scolded the man, telling him to stop, that the German had suffered enough. Luckily, Malchow's teeth were all intact, but his face was covered with blood. As the march through the town continued, other Soviet troops armed with machine pistols stood on street corners shouting "Are you Russian?" as they sought to find any remaining *Hiwis* in German uniform. These, Malchow noted, were shot on the spot the minute they answered yes. One guard accosted him and demanded to know whether he was Russian or not; Malchow stated emphatically that he was German.

Although they were unarmed, the German prisoners were heavily guarded. Malchow thought that, despite this fact, the

Troops and horses of Gruppe Stemmermann crossing the icy Gniloy. (Photo by Adolf Salie, first appeared in "Der Kessel von Tscherkassy-Die Flut verschlangt sich selbst, nicht uns!" by Veterans Association of Wiking and Munin Verlag, 1969)

Soviets must still have been afraid of them. Fellow prisoners who were lightly wounded were moved to the center of the formation, in order to prevent them from being sorted out by the guards and shot. The march route must have been close to the front, since he heard the familiar rattle of MG-42s somewhere in the distance. After marching for several days, Malchow and his comrades were eventually brought to a larger prisoner compound, where the SS were sorted out and separated from the Army prisoners. They were interrogated constantly. Finally, Malchow wound up in a large permanent prisoner of war camp. Here, he performed backbreaking manual labor until several years after the war, when he was eventually released.[10]

88.Inf.Div. also was able to disengage from the enemy with little difficulty. As planned, the division, with the attached *Div.Gr.323, Div.Gr.332,* and *SS-Feld Ers.Btl.5* from *Wiking,* fell back methodically throughout the day from its positions along the northern edge of the pocket, even though *Graf* Rittberg and his staff had lost radio contact with Stemmermann's headquarters earlier that morning. When the order to pull back to the last phase line failed to arrive, he made the decision to keep withdrawing on his own responsibility, since to wait for orders that might never come would invite disaster. The division's route of march would be the same one that *72.Inf.Div.* had taken the night before. At the time, no one knew what had happened along the line Zhurzhintsy - Hill 239.

However, the division's marching columns came under pressure mid-morning from the Soviets as it passed westward across the line Khilki – Komarovka. As the column marched to the southwest, it was able to maintain its tactical integrity, though many units were forced to defend themselves frequently from Soviet tank forays. Somewhere to the south, the marching groups from Trowitz's division could be seen from time to time, until they disappeared once again from view on account of the rolling terrain and falling snow.[11] When *Graf* Rittberg's troops encountered other Germans units along the route that had halted or blocked the march route, they were ordered to push their way through or bypass them altogether. Nothing was to allow their movement to fall behind schedule.

By late afternoon, the bulk of *88.Inf.Div.* arrived at the foot of Hill 239 and found a line of tanks and Soviet infantry on the top of the ridge waiting for them. *Graf* Rittberg ordered his division to attack. Most of his division was able to break through, in what he characterized as an "energetically-led assault," which consisted of elements from nearly every unit in his division. They quickly broke through the enemy security line and pushed across the hill, reaching the large forest in which so many other German soldiers had previously sought shelter. Many members of his division were forced to turn to the south, crossing Hill 222.5 (apparently free of tanks at the moment) before they reached the Gniloy Tikich.

Rittberg and the bulk of his division and attached units arrived at the banks of the creek a kilometer north of the other group. Here, he and his men found no crossings prepared for them. As he surveyed the situation, several T-34s from a position several hundred meters away began firing into the densely packed mass of men, setting off a momentary panic which *Graf* Rittberg and his other officers were only able to quell with difficulty. When he saw even officers losing their nerve and attempting to elbow their way forward to become the first in line to cross, Rittberg, a well-known competitive horseman before the war, remarked aloud sarcastically "Since when have officers had precedence in flight?"[12] With order once again restored, his division began to construct footbridges that were capable of ferrying the wounded across. By late evening, virtually all of his division was across and had reached the safety of Lysyanka. Here, they remained for only short while before they were ordered by General Lieb to continue marching towards Bushanka and Frankovka.

The last unit of the division to arrive in Lysyanka was *Hptm.* Matthias Wensauer's *II./Gren.Rgt.246*, which had been tasked to hold the northern front of the pocket along Hill 192 east of Tarashcha. It had somehow been left behind during the general confusion of the withdrawal and had to catch up with the rest of the division. Wensauer's battalion had the farthest way to go of all of the division's units, 18 kilometers in all, but was able to make its way after having to fight nearly every step. After reaching the Gniloy Tikich, these men, accompanied by hundreds of Ukrainian civilians who were trying to evade their Soviet "liberators," crossed that evening and met up with the rest of the division in Lysyanka.[13]

Not everyone from *88.Inf.Div.* made it out. One of these unlucky few was *Fw.* Jakob Raimund, a Viennese on the staff of *II./Gren.Rgt.248*. He had been tasked on the night of 16 February by the battalion adjutant, *Oblt.* Kallmann, to load 19 of the battalion's wounded on sleds for evacuation from Shanderovka during the coming breakout. Neither Kallmann nor his commander had any intention of leaving their wounded behind. After midnight, Raimund set his small convoy in motion, accompanied by a field kitchen that he had found abandoned that would serve to feed his wounded charges. As his group slowly moved west from Shanderovka, it was caught in a Soviet artillery barrage, which killed *Ofw.* Egon Steiner from the battalion's signal platoon. The route was soon completely blocked by hundreds of vehicles, forcing Raimund to order those wounded who could walk to leave the column and continue

onwards. Raimund then tried to continue with the remaining non-ambulatory wounded, halting for a rest somewhere between Khilki and Hill 239 that evening. Several of the wounded had frozen to death by that time, since they had been laying in open sleds and *panje* wagons for several days by that point.

Shortly after dark, a column of German soldiers approached, led by an *Oblt.* Lang from another unit in *88.Inf.Div.* These 47 men, still heavily armed, seemed determined to break through. Raimund decided to join them, since he was aware that his chances of making it out with just a few *Hiwis* and the wounded were about nil. The group quickly initiated an attack against a Soviet defensive position, catching its occupants, who took to their heels, by surprise. Just when the group was preparing to continue their successful night attack, they were joined by two assault guns that were incredibly still intact. These probably belonged to *StuG.Abt.239,* which had been attached to the rearguard to help provide it badly-needed fire support for its difficult mission. Somehow, they had managed to disengage from the enemy and make it through all of the obstacles that had immobilized so many other German armored vehicles.

As the reinforced group prepared to resume its attack, Raimund was overcome by exhaustion and fell sound asleep. When he awoke several hours later, he found himself alone. The lieutenant and his men had left without him! Standing up and dusting off the snow that had accumulated on top of him while he slept, Raimund set off in what he hoped was the right direction. After wandering in the darkness for what seemed like an eternity, he spotted a Soviet sentry immediately in front of him, who shouted *Ruki Verch!* at the top of his lungs. Raimund threw his weapon down and was escorted to the sentry's commanding officer, a major, who interrogated him at length. When the German refused to answer any questions, the officer ordered the guard to take him around the corner and shoot him.

Raimund, who spoke fluent Russian, turned to the officer, opened his shirt and demanded in the man's native language that he should shoot him there and then and get it over with. Impressed, the major countermanded his order and told the sentry to take Raimund over to another group of 21 German prisoners. Most of them had been prisoners since 15 February and had not had anything to eat or drink in days. Raimund said a few words in Russian to their captors and a few minutes later one of them returned with roasted potatoes and water. Shortly thereafter, he and the others were marched through Shanderovka, Steblev, Bogusslav and Kiev where they were herded together with increasing numbers of German prisoners from the pocket. Two months later, he was sent to the infamous Tombov prisoner of war camp near Moscow, where he was able to secure work as a translator. Transferred through a succession of labor camps, Raimund finally ended the war at Camp 6 at Sokolohorevska. There, he met up with his friend Wanek from his battalion, a fellow Viennese. In June 1949, he was finally released from Soviet captivity and returned home, one of the lucky few.[14]

Eberhard Heder's *SS-Feld Ers.Btl.5*, attached to *Div.Gr.323* as part of the rearguard, also made it out. Tasked to provide local security for *Stubanf.* Hans Bünning's *I./SS-Pz.Art.Rgt.5*, which had been ordered to provide fire support for the rearguard, Heder had arrayed his remaining men in an arc a kilometer west of Shanderovka. Bünning's light artillery, which was located in a deep gully on the eastern edge of Khilki, fired virtually non-stop at attacking Soviet tank and infantry units until it had nearly exhausted its remaining ammunition by 1000 hours on 17 February. Whenever a gun fired its last round, it was destroyed by its crew to prevent its capture. When Bünning walked back into Khilki with a few other men to reconnoiter their route of withdrawal, they encountered a group of Soviet sharpshooters who had infiltrated the village and were immediately fired upon.

A few moments later, the first vehicles of his battalion set off towards the southwest, with Heder's men acting as infantry escorts. As they passed by Bünning's location, they were fired upon by the Soviets, forcing many of the SS men to seek cover in a nearby ditch. A traffic jam ensued, as the driver of the lead vehicle abandoned his half-track, blocking the road. If this situation was allowed to worsen, all of the them would be quickly killed or captured. Bünning stood up and urged his men to get moving, since to lay there would only give the enemy more time to bring up reinforcements. Faced by a hail of Soviet rifle fire, the SS rose up and charged. Luckily, it was a small enemy unit, and the escape route was once again open. As Bünning stood there on a hillside awaiting his vehicle driven by his adjutant, *Ustuf.* Bülow, he was surprised when the young man drove right by without noticing him in the snowstorm. Bünning was now alone in enemy territory, so he did the only thing that he could do - he started to walk towards the illusory safety of Hill 239. A few moments later, he met up with the sergeant-major of *3.Batterie*, Hans Müller, who had also been left behind in the confusion. They hailed passing vehicles in hopes of catching a ride, but without success. Unfortunately, his white winter combat suit worked both ways - it made him hard to recognize by both friend and foe. No one wanted to stop to pick up a stranger, not when a moment's delay may have cost one's life. Finally, when another half-track drove by, Bünning and Müller raced through the mud and slush after it. With their last ounce of energy, both men leapt at the axle of the cannon it was towing and were able to climb aboard with difficulty. Thus ensconced, both men rode on for several kilometers, until this vehicle too became stuck.

His battalion moved on without him, unaware that it was missing its commander. With only a few rounds of 10.5 cm ammunition left for shooting at tanks with direct fire, the battalion had only enough left for one or two more engagements before its guns became useless. One by one, the guns and their half-tracked prime movers began to fall out of the column, as they became stuck in ditches, broke down, or were destroyed by tank or artillery fire. As they approached the icy slopes of Hill 239, the remaining vehicles kept slipping down its icy surface, forcing the crews to destroy them and their guns. One of Bünning's battery commanders, *Hstuf.* Pauck, was killed when his 15 cm *Hummel* took a direct hit. However, most of Bünning's men were able to make their way out of the pocket the same way that the others had – on foot. Bünning, at the far end of the column, rode on horseback part of the way and the rest of the way on foot after his mount was killed. He, like the others, had to swim the Gniloy Tikich as the price of obtaining safe entry to Lysyanka.[15]

Meanwhile, Heder soon found himself in the *balka* north of Pochapintsy, where a horde of leaderless men were milling about. He obtained a map from a medical officer, which allowed him to roughly determine where he was and what direction he needed to take if he and the others were to escape. To remain much longer in this position would invite certain death or capture. After a soldier shouted at the top of his lungs "Is there no officer here that can give us orders?" Heder stepped forward and told them to follow him, he was breaking out. Men began to gather around him expectantly. Since Pochapintsy was only several hundred meters to the south, Heder decided to attack it. Shouting *"Auf! Marsch – marsch!"* he set out running towards the village. The mass of men followed him.

They soon reached the edge of Pochapintsy and drove off the defending Soviet infantry. Heder stuck his head into a nearby *isba*, slipped inside and conducted a quick search of its contents. He quickly found several loaves of bread, some water, and a store of German chocolate which he and his men gobbled hungrily. Evidently, the hut's occupants had fled so precipitously that they had not had time to take their hoard with them. Thus refreshed, the Germans set out once again, passing through the northern part of the village, sweeping away any remaining Soviet troops in their path. As they reached the town's edge, Heder led the men across the open expanse of snow towards the woodline where General Lieb and *72.Inf.Div.* had broken through earlier that morning. Expecting to be overtaken by enemy tanks at any moment, he and the others reached the Gniloy Tikich, swam over to the western bank, and reached Lysyanka by mid-afternoon.[16]

Remarkably, the rearguard had lost only 20 percent of its men and was able to bring out a certain amount of its equipment, thanks to the bridges that had been thrown across the creek earlier. The men of *57.* and *88.Inf.Div.*, and their attached units from *Wiking* as well as *Div.Gr.323* and *332*, had made it out almost intact. Most made an orderly crossing of the Gniloy Tikich, and appear to have lost few men to the icy waters. The scene that had greeted them along its banks must have surely been disconcerting; everywhere lay abandoned equipment, articles of clothing, and personnel effects. Bodies of both men and horses were scattered everywhere. On the opposite bank patiently awaited the outposts of *1.Pz.Div.* and *Leibstandarte*. Once they reached the bank, all the rearguards had to do was cross over, mostly with dry feet. But many thousands of wounded and stragglers were finding their escape much more difficult.

End Notes

1   Menedetter, Hans. "Das Grauen wurde überwunden," *Alte Kameraden,* Vol. 25, No. 2, February 1974. (Stuttgart: Arbeitsgemeinschaft für Kameradenwerke und Traditionsverband e.V., 1974), pp. 29-30.

2   *Aus feindlichen Funkverkehr,* entry dated 1330 hours 17 February 1944

3   Schwarz, *Chronik des Infanterie-Regiments 248,* p. 146.

4   Werth, p. 781.

5   Anlage 3c zu Pz.AOK 1, 1a Nr. 158/44 g K. vom 28.2.44, p. 4, *Aus feinlichen Funkverkehr: Auszug aus Rundfunk Moskau* 17.2.44, 13.30 Uhr.

6   Ibid, entry dated 2340 hours 17 February 1944.

7   *Kampfbericht,* 57.Inf.Div., 1a Nr. 1/44 geh., Anlage 2 zu Gen.Kdo. XI.A.K., Div. Gef. Std., den 22.2.44, Bezug: Pz.AOK.1, v. 19.2.44 Abt.1a Nr. 370/44 geh.

8   Letter, Hans Gaertig, Homburg, Germany to author dated 14 May 1997.

9   Schiller, Hans. "Ausbruch aus dem Kessel," in Schwarz, pp. 71-81.

10 Malchow, Fritz, "Bericht über die Kämpfe im Kessel westlich Tscherkassy vom 16. Bis 19.2.1944," in Schwarz, pp. 81 to 86.

11 88.Infanterie-Division, Abt 1a Nr. 1/44 geheim. *Gefechtsmeldung für den 16.17.2.44.* Div.Gef.Stand, den 23.2.44.

12 Carell, p. 430.

13 Wensauer, Matthias. *Chronik des Infanterie-Regiments 246.* (Munich: Herausgeben anlässlich des 6. Verbandstreffens Amberg, im Mai 1962), p. 40.

14 Raimund, Jakob. "Im Kessel schliesslich doch noch gefangengenommen." In Schwarz, pp. 15 – 18.

15 Jahnke and Lerch, pp. 107-108.

16 Letter, Eberhard Heder, Dasburg, Germany to Author, 22 January 1997, p. 2.

Chapter Twenty Four
SURVIVORS' TALES

"Seeing Lysyanka in the distance, I asked a soldier to lift me out of the (ambulance), telling him I was going to crawl the rest of the way. He wouldn't do it so I had to do it by myself."
— *Feldw. Peter Reisch, 72.Inf.Div.* [1]

ith the final escape of the rearguard on the evening of 17/18 February, all organized resistance within the pocket ceased. Only the thousands of stragglers and wounded still trying to make it out were left. For the next several days, singly or in small groups, survivors kept trudging west or southwest, not stopping until they either reached safety or were killed or captured. Some groups infiltrated past Soviet positions by going north of Zhurzhintsy, approaching Oktyabr and Lysyanka from the north or northeast and thus avoiding the Gniloy Tikich altogether. Other groups went astray and found themselves deeper in Soviet territory, with surrender as their only recourse. One unfortunate group even crossed the Gniloy Tikich and completely bypassed Lysyanka before they were rounded up by Soviet outposts of 359th Rifle Division near the village of Orly. Instead of turning west after crossing the creek, they had continued marching southwest, until they were stopped a mere kilometer from the southern edge of Lysyanka.

For every soldier who voluntarily surrendered, another one kept pushing ahead. Hiding in gullies, *balki*, and forests, they kept pushing to the west or southwest, evading Soviet foot patrols, tanks and Cossacks. Thousands, including many wounded, continued to arrive at *1.Pz.Div.'s* forward outposts throughout 18 February and into the evening, when their numbers finally began to abate. By the evening of 19 February, it had ceased altogether. What these individuals endured can best be summed up in their own words, but in virtually every case is revealed the intense emotional and physical strain that their ordeal imposed upon them.

One of these men was *Uffz.* Gerhard Mayer, of *Art.Rgt.188*, who provided security for a large group of officers from *XI.A.K.* staff, including his regimental commander, *Oberst* Böhm. A habitual smoker, Mayer nervously chafed under the order that forbade the lighting of cigarettes as he waited for the assault to begin. One *Feldwebel*, who lit up a butt in a corner of a logger's hut where they were awaiting the beginning of the breakout, was struck on the face by a senior officer carrying a cane, thus providing Mayer all the incentive he needed to adhere to the order. The sergeant, however, reacted in a fury, seized his pistol and leveled it at the officer. Mayer and another comrade grabbed the man and forced the gun from his hand. The officer, now thoroughly provoked, ordered Mayer and his friend to take the sergeant out and shoot him immediately.[2]

Mayer could not believe his ears. He certainly was no executioner! Despite his feelings, he and the other soldier bundled

the sergeant up and dragged him screaming through the door. Once they were out of sight, Mayer and the other man told the sergeant to get away as fast as he could, without his pistol. The *Feldwebel*, knowing that he had just escaped death, uttered a hasty word of gratitude and disappeared into the snowstorm. Mayer chose not to go back into the hut where the staff officers were, but waited outside instead. No one would notice whether or not a shot had been fired, since the air was alive with the sound of artillery and mortar fire. He told his acting commander, *Ltn.* Pfortner, what he had done. Pfortner agreed with him and promised to cover for him if anyone asked whether or not the order had been carried out. Mayer kept the pistol and gave it to his father later for safekeeping.

Finally, after what seemed like an eternity, the group of mounted officers and their infantry escorts began moving. *Angriffsgruppe Lieb* had broken through, so the time had come for *XI.A.K.* to displace to its intermediate location. Through the snow and mist, Mayer could occasionally make out columns of German infantry with bayonets affixed marching to his left and right, scenes which, to him, seemed reminiscent of the Franco-Prussian War of 1870. For a while, it seemed as if everything was going according to plan. In the distance, he could hear the hammering sound of Soviet Maxim machine-guns and the "Hurrah!" of attacking German infantry, but all else was quiet. Occasionally, a white signal flare would soar into the sky, illuminating the colorless landscape. Suddenly, the head of the column encountered a Soviet outpost. Shots were fired and flares were set off. With a mighty shout of their own, Mayer's group, including the officers, surged towards the enemy and quickly overwhelmed them. The first men in his column fell; shots seemed to ring out from all directions. It seemed better to run than to stick around and invite further attention.

Suddenly, Soviet artillery began to impact among the formation, forcing the men to take cover. Unfortunately, Mayer's group could not keep up with the mounted officers. A liaison officer was sent to the rear to obtain assistance, and returned soon thereafter with a mounted escort. *Oberst* Böhm, who had to stay with the corps staff, shook the hands of each of his men in Mayer's group and wished them the best of luck. Then he was gone with the others, leaving the foot soldiers to make it out the best they could.

Mayer was shaken. Their group was now leaderless. No one from the group, which was composed from men of several different units, wanted to take responsibility for leading the others to safety. With several men from his unit, Mayer sought the shelter of a *balka* until he came up with a plan of his own. In the meantime, a supply unit consisting of dozens of sleds and *panje* wagon with supplies and wounded arrived and sought assistance. Its men related horror stories of how they had been attacked by Soviet tanks and artillery, forcing to leave many men behind. Mayer went back to where the column had been attacked and helped carry some of the wounded back to the *balka*, but upon his return, he discovered that most of the men from his unit had left without him. Now he was truly alone.

Mayer had no compass and no map, and only a vague idea as to which direction he should take. It was still dark. He decided to press on anyway. From time to time, he encountered other small groups who had lost contact with their units, but he continued on his own. Since the withdrawal route forced him and the others to travel cross-country through deep snow instead of along the few roads in the area, he quickly tired. He began to run into individuals or small groups of soldiers who began to give up all hope of breaking out, preferring instead to hole up in the bottom of a ravine or a *balka* until they either regained their strength or were taken prisoner. Mayer kept on, despite his aching legs. Everywhere he looked, he saw abandoned vehicles, cannon, ambulances, and carts full of wounded. Among these stalled columns Soviet shells began to rain incessantly, killing both men and horses. Mayer and a few other stragglers tried to help by pushing along a cart full of wounded, but quickly exhausted themselves. Many of the horses used to pull the carts and wagons had been unhitched by healthy men and used to further their own escape. It was a bloody end, he thought to himself.

Mayer lost all sense of time, and was possessed of a single thought: stay away from the columns! All they seemed to attract was death, and he wanted no part of it. After a period of time, he ran into a group of SS men, who were marching to the southwest. He thought to himself that he had evidently gone in the wrong direction, since he now found himself among troops from *Wiking*, which was positioned on the left flank of the breakout column. When he spoke to them, to his surprise they replied in French, identifying them as troops from the Walloon Brigade, not *Wiking*. He decided to march along with them as far as he could.

As it dawned, Mayer began to wonder where Hube's troops were. They had been marching for hours and had still not seen any sign of German tanks, only Soviet troops. As the sun slowly rose behind a heavy bank of clouds, Mayer could make out the outlines of a hill that lay nearly a kilometer to the west. He supposed it was not Hill 239, which must have been farther to his right, but a smaller one instead. Hopefully, they would find the relief force on the other side. On the crest of the hill several hundred meters to his front, Mayer could make out the outline of tanks. Surely, these must be ours, he thought. Just as he and the others began to cheer, their voices caught in their throats when they made out the silhouettes of T-34s and JS IIs.

Mayer has only a vague idea of what happened over the next several hours. Even late in his life, he has trouble finding words to describe it. It far exceeded anything he had previously encountered in the East, where he had fought in some of the war's biggest battles, such as at Voronesh and Kiev.

As he recalled, thousands of German soldiers, a horde wearing field gray, burst from several gullies, *balki*, and ravines and rushed at the tanks. A cheer rose from thousands of men as they attacked the tanks with bayonets and hand grenades. Men and horses were mowed down by tank and machine-gun fire. Still, they kept coming. To Gerhard Mayer, it was an inferno, a hell on earth.

One of the Walloons in his group was still carrying a *Panzerfaust*, which he soon put to good use. Approaching a T-34 from its blind side, he aimed and fired; moments later, it burst into flames as the white-hot explosive stream from the hollow charge set off fuel and ammunition, immolating its crew. The way temporarily cleared, the mass of men flowed "like an oily black substance" through the newly-created gap in the Soviet defense line. Somehow, he found himself and hundreds of others rushing past the tanks and into a forest, where they kept pushing on. Soviet infantry who tried to block their path were shot down mercilessly. Mayer remembers shooting some in the back with his machine pistol as they tried to run away from the onrushing Germans and their Belgian allies. Again, the ancient German battle cry sounded as the flood of troops overcame elements of 41st Guards Rifle Division, which lost nearly 2,400 of its 7,200 men during the German breakout.[3]

The Walloons' leader, a sergeant, had been shot through the arm, but he carried on as if he had not noticed, urging his countrymen and Mayer forward. Mayer soon noticed that he was the only one in the group who was not wounded. As the Gypsy fortune teller had foretold three weeks before, he began to believe that he would survive – providing that he continue to use his head! He felt that he was at the end of his strength and wondered if he had enough energy to keep going. As the small group exited the woods, they found themselves stumbling down a steep hill. Expected to be fired upon at any minute, they were surprised when they suddenly arrived at the bank of a swift-flowing creek, where a large number of German soldiers had already gathered. In the distance on the opposite bank, he could see the outlines of houses and guessed that it was probably the outskirts of Lysyanka.

He also saw a couple of tanks on the opposite bank, which he identified as *Panthers*, but they did nothing but sit there, which led him to believe that they were knocked out (actually, they were probably part of the thin security screen that *1.Pz.Div.* and *Leibstandarte* had posted there later that morning). To his profound disappointment, no bridge awaited them. Instead of reaching safety, he and the others would now have to confront one more obstacle - perhaps the most formidable one yet. Mayer could not believe that he would have to swim the creek to reach safety. Besides, the temperature was below freezing and the water did not appear to be much warmer. Every now and then, bodies of dead comrades, horses, hunks of ice, and pieces of vehicles floated by from upstream, where another group was facing the same problem. Yet swimming appeared to be the only hope for salvation.

At first, a few brave souls stripped themselves of their outer garments and dove in. Many were swept away by the powerful current and drowned. Others, like *Uffz.* Werner Hilss of *389.Inf.Div.*, crossed by holding onto horses' bridles. When his horse could not climb the opposite bank, Hilss watched sadly as it was swept away and drowned. Many other men were involuntarily pushed in when several Soviet tanks began firing on their position from a distance, creating panic among the densely packed mass of soldiers. Many soldiers who thought they had reached safety at the creek found their deaths instead. Mayer and his Walloon comrades sought safety in the lee of the hill that abutted the banks of the creek. Suddenly, a T-34 charged the bridgehead, firing its cannon and machine-guns at the large group of men standing along the edge of the creek. Mayer spotted a *Panzerfaust* lying at his feet and picked it up, even though he did not know how to use it. One of the Walloons did and grabbed it from his hands. White with terror, Mayer watched as the shot missed, exploding harmlessly next to the passing tank.

Fortunately, the tank crewmen did not see where the shot had come from, otherwise they would have killed Mayer and the others. After a few moments, it departed in the direction from whence it had come, granting the Germans a small breathing space. Mayer decided that it was high time to leave. Approaching the bank of the creek, he attempted to throw his machine pistol to the opposite side, but failed to throw it hard enough and watched helplessly as it sank. He then threw his pistol belt, map case, and bread bag in the water but saved his newly-acquired pistol by stuffing it in the pocket of his camouflaged jacket. As he was standing on the bank debating whether or not to jump in, a tank shell exploded several meters behind him. Something hit him hard in the back, knocking the breath out of him. Needing no further urging, Mayer leapt into water. After a couple of strong strokes, he reached the opposite bank, where a comrade helped him out of the water.

Dripping with freezing water, Mayer joined a long column of men trudging towards Lysyanka. As they approached the town, shells began to fall about them. Instead of seeking cover like the others, Mayer ran on as fast as he could, since he felt that if he lay down in the snow, he would not have the strength to rise up again. Although he was sweating heavily, he noticed that the outer layer of clothing had frozen solid. His trousers had ripped along the seams near his knees where the frozen fabric had yielded to the constant motion, but he no longer cared. He knew that with every step, he was getting farther and farther away. As he walked, it occurred to him that he had made it out without a scratch. Apparently, he had only been struck by a piece of dirt when the shell had burst nearby. He soon forgot his troubles, the biting cold, and the hunger when the realization that he was free had finally sank home. For the third time, he had escaped from a pocket. What mattered the wet clothes, the wind, the cold?, he thought. He was safe.

A few steps later, Mayer reached the edge of Lysyanka, where he quickly found an *isba* where he could warm up a bit and dry out his clothes. Like the others, he was soon disappointed when he was urged to keep moving towards the west. There was no warm food, no warm clothing, no welcoming committee. After snatching only two or three hours of sleep in the hut, he was ordered to put his clothes back on. As he turned to put his clothing back on, he was angered to discover that someone had taken his insulated winter combat suit while he slept. This distressed him deeply, since he would need every article of

clothing he had to prevent from freezing to death. As he stuck his head outside, he realized that it was still snowing and the wind had not abated at all. At that very moment, a Ukrainian civilian happened by, clad in a fur-lined jacket. Without scruple, Mayer demanded that the hapless man hand over his jacket, which he did under protest. When Mayer put it on, he noted that it had as many holes in it as it had lice, but at least it sufficed to keep him warm. Dressed, in his words, like a "waiting room whore," rather than as a German soldier, Mayer and his comrades were chased out of town by *1.Pz.Div.*, which needed room in the town for the ever-increasing number of arriving wounded. Onwards to Bushanka trekked Mayer and the Walloons, passing by dozens of wrecked tanks and vehicles, testimony to the ferocity of the fighting that had taken place during the relief effort. In a double column that followed the frozen ruts made by tanks, the survivors of *Gruppe Stemmermann* continued their march towards the collecting areas set up for them farther to the rear. Like thousands of others, Mayer had made it out, thanks to his determination not to be taken prisoner and the help provided by his comrades.

Willy Hein was another who refused to quit. After parting ways with Gerd Schumacher's tanks two kilometers west of Komarovka at 0700 hours on the morning of 17 February, he fell in with a group of SS men who were marching to the west. Two hours later, the group reached the large forest in the center of the escape corridor, where many men from virtually every unit in the pocket had sought shelter. When Hein asked them why they had not kept marching, one soldier told him that the enemy were blocking their escape path. Inside the forest, Hein discovered a Pz. III from the tank training company of his battalion, with the crew dead inside. With the help of other men from his division, he was able to remove the bodies and get the vehicle started. Although it only had a short 5 cm gun, he felt it was better than nothing, so the tank with its improvised crew drove to the edge of the woods and began firing at Soviet targets, forcing the enemy to pull back several hundred meters. With that, Hein directed the driver to move out of the woods and drive towards the southwest. Hein had unwittingly unleashed a veritable human tidal wave with several hundred men following in the tank's wake.[4]

After advancing one hundred meters or so, the tank's engine gave out. Apparently, the radiator had been damaged in a previous fight, causing the engine to overheat. Hein ordered the crew to bail out and join the others on foot. Before leaving the tank, he removed the breech block and stuffed a hand grenade in the barrel, thus rendering the vehicle useless when it fell into enemy hands. By 1000 hours, Hein and the rest of his group had reached the large *balka* at the foot of Hill 239, but it soon became obvious to him that no advance along this route was possible, judging by the heavy fire coming from that direction. A few minutes later, a towed artillery battery from *Wiking* arrived at the edge of the *balka*, led by *Hstuf.* Zäh. When Zäh's vehicles failed to negotiate the steep slope of the hill, he ordered all of the guns to be unlimbered and unceremoniously dumped into the ravine. He and his men soon joined Hein's group.

Shortly thereafter, a Soviet officer appeared at the edge of the *balka* and demanded that the Germans surrender, but was

The rearguard of 1st Panzer Division, their tanks blown up to keep them from falling into the hands of the Soviets, arrive in a reception area. (Photo courtesy of von Dörnberg)

Survivors of Wiking assemble in Lysyanka.
(Photo by Adolf Salie courtesy of Willy Hein)

chased away by several warning shots from a carbine. Before Hein could assemble his group and continue pushing on, the southern exit of the *balka* was blocked by several T-34s which had been positioned some 400 meters away. Forty soldiers decided to give up then and there; shucking their weapons, shoulder straps and equipment, they approached the tanks with their arms raised over their heads. As Hein and the others watched in horror, the tanks mowed them down with machine-gun fire after they had approached to within 100 meters. That was all the incentive Hein and the others needed to make up their minds.

Gathering 500 to 600 men about him, Hein led an attack towards the tanks. As the men stormed forward, a mighty "Hurrah!" erupted among their ranks. To the German's relief, the tanks backed off, after shooting many of the onrushing foot soldiers. Apparently, the tanks did not want to be overrun by infantry when they had none of their own to provide close-in protection. The large group kept running and soon reached the safety of a small forest, where they were able to catch their breath and rest a bit. Hein was exhausted, since he had been suffering from infection and a high fever as a result of his previous injuries sustained during the battle for Olshana. Periodically, other groups of German soldiers passed by their sanctuary and the sounds of fighting could be heard a kilometer to the north in the vicinity of Hill 239. Hein saw a long column of *panje* wagons carrying wounded come down the road from Hill 239 to Pochapintsy. How they had made it this far was a mystery, but that road marked the farthest extent of their progress. As he and his comrades watched in horror, several T-34s chased the column of wounded down the hill and quickly rolled over them.

By 1400 hours, Hein and the others had reached the edge of the smaller forest northwest of Hill 222.5, where he decided to wait until darkness. Here, they encountered a large group of men who had previously sought shelter there. Hein saw Leon Degrelle and *Oberst* Hohn from *72.Inf.Div.* trying to instill order and get the men moving again. When Hohn saw Hein, he ordered him to assemble all of the men from *Wiking* that were scattered throughout the woods and to take charge of them. While he gathered the men from his division, it had begun to grow dark, making his task immensely more difficult.

Periodically, Soviet artillery fire fell randomly throughout the forest. Somewhere to the west, the column of Germans and Walloons had already begun their escape. Hein ordered the large group to shed any remaining unnecessary equipment and follow him. It was now 2100 hours, by Hein's estimation.

After proceeding down a long, open slope, Hein and his group passed through a marshy area, where dozens of *panje* wagons and other vehicles had gotten stuck and had been abandoned. Then, they were at the creek. Silently, his column walked forward single file, lest the Soviet outpost hear them. The only sounds that could be heard was that of Soviet troops shouting commands and the firing of *Katyushas* somewhere in the distance. At the the Gniloy Tikich crossing, his men filed one by one across a large log that had been thrown over the creek. He himself was the last to cross from his group. As Hein staggered over the log, a man came up and offered him his hand to hold on to steady him. Safe on the opposite side, he thanked the man who had helped him. In the misty twilight, Hein recognized the good Samaritan - it was none other than Leon Degrelle himself, who had stayed behind to insure that as many of the stragglers and wounded got out as possible.[5]

Shortly thereafter, the group entered Lysyanka. Hein looked about for his division command post. Since his head and face were still swathed in bandages, he was directed to an aid station to receive some sort of treatment before being sent onward. As he staggered through the shattered town, he saw an empty school house with a metal standard bearing a "G" emblazoned upon it near the entrance. Figuring that the G stood for Gille, he went inside. Along the wall sat a row of apathetic men, whose joy at escaping from the pocket had soon worn off. After a while, as more and more men sought shelter in the school, he began to spot familiar faces, which raised Hein's own spirits considerably.

As he watched, a soldier burst into the room wearing a black panzer uniform. He carried a tank's MG-34 and was draped with machine-gun belts. It was none other than *Uscha.* Edgar Schweichler, the gunner from Hein's old tank. When Schweichler had heard that Hein had made it to safety, he had set out in search of his commander. When he saw Hein, he set his machine-gun down and reported to him matter-of-factly in his

East Prussian dialect "*Obersturmführer, Unterscharführer* Schweichler reports back from the pocket." Hein then exclaimed "Schweichler, man, how did you make it out?" To which he replied, "*Obersturmführer*, the only bad part about it was that I haven't been able to shit for the past 24 hours. Beg permission to be dismissed so I can attend to it." An Army *Oberleutnant* then said to Hein "I envy your men such as this!"[6]

Walter Notz from *Eisenbahn-Pioniereinheit Schäfer* made it out as well. His small group of combat engineers had fought with the rearguard and made it to the banks of the Gniloy Tikich on the morning of 18 February with little difficulty. However, they were surprised when they found thousands of men milling about it banks. He witnessed hundreds of men diving in and swimming across, some even mounted on horseback. While the water was chest deep at this particular crossing point, the current was stronger than anyone realized. Notz watched helplessly as many men were swept away when they had nearly reached the opposite bank. He soon joined a group of other engineers who were trying to construct an emergency bridge.

Some soldiers drove two assault guns that had been abandoned nearby into the creek to use as a foundation for a bridge, but the tops of both vehicles disappeared in the icy swirling water. Doggedly, the engineers kept trying, but due to incessant Soviet shelling, they soon gave up their efforts. Finally, some one came up with the idea of forming a human chain as a means of helping their comrades cross to safety, especially the wounded. Those who lost their grip while negotiating the creek were swept downstream to their deaths. Finally, standing on top of the hulls of the two sunken assault guns, they were able to steady themselves. Many man were then able to cross until Notz and his comrades were forced to abandon their efforts due to the cold. On the opposite bank, Notz and the others urged men who had collapsed in the snow from exhaustion to get up and continue marching; to wait too long would only invite death by hypothermia. Many of these survivors begged Notz and his comrades to shoot them and put them out of their misery, but they refused. Instead, they hoisted these men to their feet and got them on their way.

Notz's group arrived in Lysyanka that afternoon. By that point, most of the town had been cleared of the survivors and wounded of *Gruppe Stemmermann*. Only outposts and patrols remained. Soaking wet, with their clothing frozen to their bodies, they entered an undamaged *isba* and quickly lit a fire to warm themselves. They soon found a stash of uncooked frozen potatoes and proceeded to cook them in the oven. One enterprising *Pionier* found a large bucket and started heating water in it so they could wash themselves. After eating their hastily prepared meal, the first they had eaten in several days, they laid down to catch a quick nap. Before they had fallen asleep, they were abruptly awoken by a sentry from *1.Pz.Div.* and told to clear out. Soon, Notz and his comrades were on the march again, this time towards Bushanka, following the footprints of tens of thousands of men who had gone before them.[7]

Ustf. Fritz Hahl made it out too. After a harrowing march from the edge of Komarovka, he was able to get his company from *Westland* as far as the outskirts of Pochapintsy, where they sought refuge in a small wood mid-morning on 17 February.

Aching from a shrapnel wound in his back, Hahl saw that a Soviet infantry unit roughly the same size as his was approaching their position. As they closed to within 50 meters of the Germans, Hahl ordered his men to stand up and prepare to rush their opponent. Strangely, the Soviets did not fire at them but instead demanded their surrender.

Hahl, a young SS officer who knew full well what would occur were he and his men to be made prisoner, ordered his men to attack without hesitation. Seconds later, both formations crashed into each other and the fighting quickly became hand-to-hand. Hahl's experience in many such previous encounters had proven that Soviet troops usually panicked when surprised, thus offering a slight advantage. He was proven right in this instance when the stunned enemy broke contact and fled, leaving the way clear for his company to continue. After marching for several more hours, they found themselves standing on the northern bank of the Gniloy Tikich. Some 500 meters away, several T-34s were shooting at them and thousands of other German troops attempting to cross.

With his company now scattered, Hahl decided to swim across. Hanging his machine-pistol around his neck, he dove into the icy water. Keeping his head up, he swam to the opposite shore. He quickly began to tire as his heavy parka became waterlogged, making it harder to fight the powerful current. Finally, he reached the safety of the creek's edge, where he grabbed the roots of a low-hanging tree and pulled himself laboriously up the steep bank. Next to him an *Obersturmführer* from *Germania* was doing the same. Their clothing, like the others, soon froze, making walking difficult. Together, both men made their way safely through sporadic Soviet artillery fire to Lysyanka. Next to a shed they spotted a Tiger, whose commander was standing in the hatch looking at them through binoculars. As they approached, they asked him whether or not they had made it out of the pocket.

Rather than replying by way of an answer the tank commander grinned wolfishly at them. Hahl and the other officer were overcome with joy and hugged each other unashamedly. Hahl felt the tension of the past three weeks drain from his body. He had made it! And good thing, too. All he had left to fight with was an empty machine pistol, a Luger with but three rounds in its magazine, and an egg grenade in his pocket. On his feet, Hahl wore only a pair of rubber boots - his good leather ones had been burnt up when his vehicle had been destroyed in earlier fighting. It did not matter though. He was free.[8] After meeting up with some members of his company, he too was soon on the march again.

Franz Figur, the chaplain of *72.Inf.Div.*, also made it out after he became separated from the rest of the divisional staff during the morning of 17 February. Nicknamed the division's *Evangelische-Spirituoose abwehr-Kanone* (*ESaK*, or Lutheran Spiritual Defense Cannon),* Figur had been hearing confessions and administering last rites for thousands of dying soldiers for weeks. Accompanied by two enlisted medics, he sought to detour around a Soviet infantry position on the southern slope of Hill 239. When the enlisted men begged the chaplain to get up

---

* A play on the acronym for anti-tank gun, or PaK.

and follow them, he demurred, stating that he was too tired to continue. They left without him and immediately fell into the hands of a Soviet patrol. Figur and another soldier crawled on their hands and knees until they had put as much distance between them and the enemy as possible.

A few hours later, he caught a ride on a passing *panje* carrying wounded. Shortly thereafter, the wagon reached the banks of the Gniloy Tikich, which appeared to be covered with thousands of men. Artillery shells impacted sporadically and no one seemed to be in charge. As he turned around to fetch his rucksack from the wagon, he was surprised to see that his rucksack with food, as well as the wagon, has disappeared, leaving him only his cane and a spoon as his sole possessions. Like the others, the chaplain was forced to swim across and reached the safety of Lysyanka with difficulty. As he reached the town's outskirts, he recalled General Hube's promise to the troops of Gruppe Stemmermann, "Hold on, I'll get you out!" Now these words, spoken over the radio several weeks before, seemed more than a little ironic.

As proof of what he had gone through, Figur later received an entry in his *Soldbuch* (Paybook) granting him credit for one day of close combat, a rarity indeed for a divisional chaplain! To come to an understanding of how he and the others had made it out, Figur recalled a line from Psalm 139, Verse 5, that states "Behind me and before me, you protect me and rest your hand upon me." How else could the survival of so many men be explained?, he thought. After, they had been surrounded on all sides by the Soviets, yet they had come through. Only the protecting hand of God, as he saw it, could be the cause of their deliverance. Figur was not the only survivor who thought this.[9]

One of these men who credited the Almighty for his deliverance was *Uscha.* Fernand Kaisergruber of the Walloon Brigade. Kaisergruber, a native of Brussels, had been one of the first to join the Walloon Legion in August 1941, when it was known at the time as the *Corps Franc Wallonie* (Free Corps Wallonia) and registered in the Army as *Inf.Btl.373.* Engaged in the East from November 1941 to June 1943, he had fought in the Ukraine, the Don Front, and in the Caucasus. He was transferred to the *Waffen-SS* with the rest of his formation, which had in the meantime been renamed *5.SS-Freiwilligen Brigade "Wallonien."* A small, wiry soldier, he was known throughout the brigade for his wit and toughness. By February 1944, Kaisergruber was one of the few remaining original members of the old Free Corps Wallonia; most of his comrades had fallen at various locations in the East during the past two year's of fighting.

Before the breakout, Kaisergruber's company had been defending a position on the Walloon Brigade's flank north of Novo Buda, where it tied in with the right flank of a battalion from *Germania*. The position itself consisted merely of a series of foxholes laid out in an open field that stretched across several hundred meters of farmland from the town's northern outskirts to the forest held by the troops from *Wiking*. By the evening of 16 February, it was no longer much of a position. Kaisergruber's company had shrunk to seventeen men. In each foxhole lay one or two men, surrounded by the dead bodies of both comrades and Soviet soldiers. From this position, they had

SS-Unterscharführer Fernand Kaisergruber, *Walloon Brigade, shown here convalescing from wounds after escaping from the pocket, April 1944. (Photo courtesy of Fernand Kaisergruber)*

repelled numerous enemy infantry assaults for several days and were eagerly awaiting the word to fall back so they could join in the breakout.[10]

The command to pull out, however, never got to Kaisergruber and his comrades. In the confusion that accompanied the withdrawal from Novo Buda on the night of 16/17 February, Leon Degrelle and his staff either forgot about them or the messenger who would have delivered the order got lost. It can no longer be determined what happened, but the effect upon Kaisergruber and the others was the same. As it began to become light on the morning of 17 February, the commander of the small unit became concerned and sent patrols out to the left and right to see whether their neighbors were still in their positions. To his surprise and dismay, he discovered that they were alone. Both the Walloon Brigade and the battalion from *Germania* had withdrawn several hours before. Fortunately, the Soviet attacks against their position had ceased; otherwise they would have already been outflanked.

The leader of the little band ordered Kaisergruber and the others to fall in on the company command post, then set them in motion towards Shanderovka. Here confusion reigned supreme; of their brigade, there was nothing to be seen. Therefore, the commander dissolved the company and ordered his men to make it out as best they could. Kaisergruber fell in with nine of his friends and began marching through the snow towards the southwest. To their left and right marched other groups of men, evidently headed in the same direction. He remembered feeling confident that day, that he and his comrades would have little trouble breaking out. The only food he had left was a roast chicken leg that he carried in the pocket of his uniform. Although it was cold, the temperature was of little concern, because he and the others were stimulated by the thought of the upcoming escape as well as by the body heat brought about by their physical exertions. It was still snowing heavily, carpeting the ground with a thick white blanket.

To orient themselves, Kaisergruber and the others picked out a hill to their front and marched until they reached its summit. Once this goal had been reached, they would pick out another in the same direction and continue. In this manner, they made it nearly halfway through the escape corridor without incident. Although artillery shells burst in the distance, everything else seemed calm and peaceful. As it grew lighter, however, enemy shells seemed to strike closer to their position. Still, Kaisergruber felt little need to worry. It was, after all, a rather wide-open plain they were traversing and they made very small targets. To be safe, they would occasionally throw themselves into the snow when shells burst nearby. Somehow, he and two others had become separated from the rest of the group, but decided to continue anyway.

As they pressed on, they were overtaken by a German half-track carrying five or six men, who ducked whenever a shell burst nearby. Kaisergruber and his two comrades decided to walk behind the vehicle, since it compacted the snow as it moved along, thus making it easier for the Walloons to walk. It was a mistake. Soon, it seemed as if every Soviet gunner was trying to hit the half-track. Shells fell everywhere, as the vehicle turned to the left and the right to make a more difficult target. The Walloons watched as one man, who was riding on the left front fender, fell off and was run over by the vehicle's tracks. Amazingly, he sprung up as soon as the vehicle passed over him and jumped on the rear bumper. Apparently, the soft soil and snow cushioned the weight of the vehicle, instead of allowing the tracks to crush him.

Slowly, the vehicle pulled away from them and the artillery fire died down. They soon overtook another marching group, with many women dressed in German uniforms, marching southwest. When Kaisergruber asked one of the Germans who the women were, he was surprised to hear that they were entertainers from a German theatrical group that had arrived in the Kanev salient days before being trapped inside the pocket. He had spotted them only because the shoulders of their greatcoats were too broad and the tails too long for them; otherwise, they marched as resolutely and as silently as the men. What became of them later is unknown, though most of them undoubtedly were killed or captured.

After several hours, the three Walloons began to relax when it seemed as if they would make it out of this mess after all. One of Kaisergruber's friends, André Bourdouxhe, even began to tell jokes. A few rifle shots rang out from the right, so

the three men veered a few meters to the left. It all seemed like a lark after the tense moments they had experienced earlier that morning. By mid-morning, the snowfall had temporarily ceased. They had reached a point south of Petrovskoye where the breakthrough route had narrowed to a width of eight hundred meters. To their dismay, they saw to the right and left Soviet cannons and anti-tank guns lined up almost hub to hub only four hundred meters away. Each gun appeared to have a pile of ammunition crates stacked next to it. Suddenly, they began to fire directly at them. Kaisergruber and the others had never experienced anything like this before and began to run away as fast as they could. Behind them, shells began to impact where they had been standing moments before.

Reaching the safety of a small ravine, the three Walloons followed a path that led from the bottom to the top of a neighboring hill, several hundred meters away. When they arrived, the saw that an elderly German major wearing a white camouflaged suit and a mountain cap was sitting on its summit with his rucksack between his legs. As they approached, they noticed that he was playing with a pistol in his hands. Kaisergruber motioned to him with a wave of his head that they were moving towards the southwest, but he refused to acknowledge their presence. Evidently, he was a reserve officer who had lost the will to go on. Unable to elicit a response from the man, the three younger Walloons kept marching.

After they had gone less than 20 steps, they heard a pistol shot. As they turned around, they saw the major slowly topple over. The three ran back to him to see if they could offer assistance, but he was dead. To Kaisergruber, this officer's action was a rather poor example of leadership. He and the others could not comprehend how the man could have taken his own life with safety so near. To have survived weeks of encirclement, combat, and deprivation, only to have ended one's life seemed a waste. The three men pressed on in silence, Kaisergruber making up his mind that he would make it out, no matter what.

It was now about 0800 hours. Shells fell everywhere it seemed, but they began to think that they were living a charmed life. When a Soviet tank blocked their path and seemed about to run them down, the flame of a *Panzerfaust* erupted from a concealed position and destroyed it and its crew. Somewhere up ahead, the near-simultaneous detonation of another sent a second T-34 up in flames. Thick smoke was seen pouring out of both of them. From one tank, a crewman bailed out, himself enveloped in flames. Screaming, he ran across the path of a group of German soldiers before he was cut down with machine-gun fire. Kaisergruber was shocked. A man was a man, and it did not matter what side he was on when he died. Somehow, the scene offended him, even though he knew that the death of the tank and its crew meant that he and more of his comrades would escape.

With renewed hope, the three Walloons pressed on. During a brief pause, Kaisergruber remarked to one of his friends that if they made it out, he would be satisfied even if he was not filmed for the *Deutsche Wochenschau*, but would accept orchestra seats for a viewing. With a hearty laugh, the three pressed on. In the distance, artillery fire intensified. Feeling hungry, Kaisergruber reached into his pocket for a chicken leg he had placed their earlier. When we pulled it out, he noticed that it was covered with lint, tobacco, dirt and sugar, but he did not care. He began gnawing on the leg bone with gusto and passed it around. Just then, Soviet shells began to burst quite nearby.

All of a sudden, the world seemed to turn upside down in a kaleidoscope of mud, snow, and fire. Kaisergruber awoke with a sharp pain in his head. As he opened his eyes, his two friends were nowhere to be seen. Instead, two other men he knew from his company, Lux and Dominé, were standing a few meters away shouting at him, but he could not hear a word they were saying. To his amazement, they walked away from him and disappeared from view. He found to his dismay that he was paralyzed and could neither speak nor hear. A shell must have fallen rather close by.

Stunned, he lay in the snow. After several minutes, he began to recover his senses as well as the ability to move his limbs. Feeling something wet on the side of his face, he ran his hand over his cheek to see whether he was bleeding. He was surprised to see his hand covered with brain matter and concluded that he had suffered a serious head wound. He was also covered in blood from head to toe. Looking about him, he spotted the shattered bodies of his two comrades Bourdouxhe and Delreux, laying nearby. Their blood stained the snow bright red. Suddenly, he realized that it was their brains and blood on him. He tried to stand, but fell when his left leg gave out. To his shock, he saw that his shin had been broken by a shell fragment. Rolling up his trouser leg to apply a first aid dressing, he was even more stunned to see the jagged edge of the bone protruding through the skin. In addition, he had been hit on the right foot as well and had lost the tip of a finger.

The enormity of his situation began to sink in. Without assistance, he knew he would die. As he sat there, he felt the bits of tissue and blood freezing in his hair. Resolved to survive, he bandaged the wound on his left leg the best he could. Since he could not walk, he crawled across the snow, leaving a trail of blood. After continuing for over an hour, he rolled over on his back and stared at the sky. Too tired to continue, he was slowly beginning to succumb to both shock and hypothermia. His hands were so stiff from cold he could not even inspect his wounds. Fortunately, the cold worked in his favor, since it restricted the circulation of blood in the affected area, minimizing blood loss. However, at the time he saw the cold as his enemy and began to grow discouraged.

A passing horseman spotted him lying in the snow and left his column to ride over to the wounded man. The man, whose name Kaisergruber no longer remembers, was a medic from *Art.Rgt.86*. He dismounted and approached, intent on helping him. When he saw the seriousness of the wounds, he helped Kaisergruber up onto the horse's back. In this manner, they traveled several kilometers. Shortly thereafter, shrapnel from an artillery burst hit the horse in the head, killing it and sending Kaisergruber crashing into the snow. In agony, he lay in the snow and begged the man to leave him and to save himself. Ignoring his pleas, the medic picked him up and helped him to walk on his good leg. Everywhere, other German soldiers seemed to be walking past them.

After several detours, the two men came upon another riderless horse that was standing in the middle of an open field. Again, the medic helped Kaisergruber into the saddle and they proceeded in this manner until they reached the Gniloy Tikich north of Lysyanka. Somehow, the two men had crossed over the ridgeline between Hill 239 and Zhurzhintsy without attracting the Soviet's attention and now found themselves on the town's northern outskirts. They soon found themselves in a small clearing at the bank of the creek. Artillery burst throughout the area. Suddenly, a *panje* loaded with wounded came barreling down the hill from the east. The driver, with a crazed look on his face, wrongly thought that speed would suffice to effect a crossing. The wagon with its horses and wounded crashed into the water; as it was rapidly swept away by the current, the cries of the wounded and the screams of the horses reverberated throughout the area.

Kaisergruber's helper then told him to hold onto the horse's reins and led the horse into the water. Fortunately, it did not panic and was a good swimmer. After a few moments, both men and the horse were safe on the opposite bank. The medic helped him off of the horse, and turned to go. The Walloon asked him where he was going; he replied that he was going back to pick up more wounded. Kaisergruber never saw his livesaver again. As he sat safely on the opposite bank, his clothes began to freeze solid. The water-logged leather in his boots had also hardened. To his surprise, the combination of ice, frozen clothing and leather sufficed to make a crude splint for his broken leg; in this manner, he was able to walk after a fashion. He soon spotted the outlines of two Panthers and a Tiger hidden between several peasant huts. A few minutes later, he limped into Lysyanka, where he fell into the arms of pickets from *1.Pz.Div.* Kaisergruber was brought to an *isba* in the center of the town, where he was provided rudimentary first aid before being evacuated further, after almost being overlooked. To this day, he believes that the man who saved him was a guardian angel sent down from heaven to deliver him to safety.[11]

For every Kaisergruber who was helped by a kindly soul, there were many others who were ignored by their comrades. One of these unfortunate men was *Oscha*. Fiebelkorn, who had been wounded several days before in Novo Buda when his tank was knocked out. As he bailed out from his burning vehicle, he broke an ankle. He had since been evacuated to the battalion dressing station in Shanderovka, where he remained instead of being sent to the field hospital, which was to be turned over to the Soviets. When the breakout began, Fiebelkorn had taken a seat in his battalion commander's large 18-ton half-track that was towing several wheeled ambulances. When that vehicle was hit, killing Köller and wounding several others, Fiebelkorn received additional wounds. A passing *panje* wagon from another unit picked up him and some of the other wounded.

Soon, the rest of the battalion's tanks became involved in a battle with 14 T-34s that had attacked from the direction of Zhurzhintsy, while the wagons loaded with wounded sought shelter in a nearby wood. When the fighting had subsided, the driver of the wagon unhitched the horses and rode off with them, stranding Fiebelkorn and several others. An unnamed *Sturmbannführer* who happened to be passing by helped him down from the wagon and assisted him as he tried to walk. Just then, an explosive shell destroyed the wagon and killed the officer. Miraculously, Fiebelkorn was untouched. He quickly sought the shelter of a nearby shellhole where he lay for two or three hours. Several times fellow German soldiers passed by him, and each time he implored them to help. None stopped; a few muttered apologies for not helping and continued on.

At sunrise the next day, Fiebelkorn decided to climb out and keep heading west. He had a wife and child to look after and did not want to die a nameless death or become a captive. Painfully, he limped onwards. He soon encountered two other wounded men attempting to escape and fell in with them. Later that morning, they realized that they had been going in the wrong direction and had somehow strayed into the Soviet positions. Rather than continue, they dug a shelter in a deep snowdrift on the edge of a ditch and waited for darkness to resume their journey. As the sun began to set, Fiebelkorn attempted to rouse his newfound comrades, but both were suffering from advanced hypothermia and shock, dying shortly thereafter. Alone, he trudged back to the northwest, in the direction where he hoped salvation lay.

Late in the evening of 18 February, he finally reached the German outpost line. When he was brought to the field dressing station in Lysyanka, the doctors discovered that both of his feet, his hands, and his right knee were frozen, in addition to his earlier wounds. He then lost consciousness, and did not regain his senses until he was being unloaded from a Ju-52 at the airfield in Uman. After treatment for his wounds and injuries, he was evacuated to a proper field hospital in Poland. When he wrote to his wife, who had not heard from him in months, he told her simply that he had made it out safely from the pocket and that his only injuries were to his right hand. She was pregnant with their second child and he did not want to upset her.[12]

Many of the wounded and those who had been separated from their units were ultimately captured. *Hstuf.* Kurt Schröder, commander of *I./Germania,* was one of these. He and thirteen other men had decided to await darkness in a small wood near a Soviet-held town. After consulting his map, Schröder determined that they had strayed too far south, so he intended to lead them back to the northwest where he hoped the rescue force lay. As the small group began to carefully slip through the forest, they were spotted by an alert Soviet sentry who ordered them to halt. One of Schröder's men, a native of Upper Silesia, yelled something back in Russian, which evidently satisfied the enemy soldier enough to let them pass through the middle of a Soviet artillery battery without being noticed. The Germans guessed that they were following the proper heading. According to the map, Schröder thought that they had approached to within two or three kilometers from the Gniloy Tikich. They were almost free.

By midnight, the group was completely exhausted. After marching for several hours through knee-deep snow, they felt that they could not take another step, and they still had not reached the creek. Gustav Schreiber, a veteran *Hauptscharführer* travelling with Schröder's group, advised him that it would be better if they sought shelter in a hollow for the night and try again in the morning. Schröder had

his doubts, but decided to heed the man's advice. He would soon regret it and would have kept moving if he knew what awaited them the next morning.

After spending a cold night in the open, Schröder was awakened by the sound of an MG-42 firing nearby, so he sent a sergeant and another man forward to investigate. After an hour, the two men returned and panted that they were being pursued by a group of Soviet infantry. Moments later, they found their position surrounded by the enemy, who were yelling to them in German to surrender immediately. One of his sergeants, a paymaster, jumped out of the hole and tried to make a run for it, but was shot in the head and collapsed at the bottom of the hole in front of his comrades. Schröder and the rest raised their hands and were quickly searched by their captors. *Hschaf.* Schreiber, who wore the Knight's Cross he had earned the previous November for valor on Foxtail Island, snatched the medal from around his neck and hurled it into the snow to prevent it being made a trophy. For these thirteen SS men, the shooting war was over and another one had begun.

Schröder and the others were led back on foot to a collecting area, where he found twelve other men from his battalion who had been captured. As an officer, he was soon separated from his troops and was interrogated frequently by successively higher levels of Soviet commanders. He was led out twice to be shot, but each time his life was spared at the last minute by Soviet officers who intervened in his behalf. Stripped of his SS uniform, he was provided a *Hauptmann's* uniform from captured stocks. After a week, he was flown with ten other officers in an American-made C-47 transport to Moscow and was imprisoned in the infamous Lubyanka, which also served as the headquarters of the NKVD. Three weeks of intensive interrogation followed. Many of these sessions were recorded, and played back to him whenever his story changed from one session to another.

Finally, he was sent to a large POW camp on the outskirts of Moscow, where he was greeted by German, Italian, and Hungarian officers. Here, members of the National Free Germany Committee and the League of German Officers tried to recruit him to their cause, but each time he refused. For two weeks, men such as Wilhelm Pieck, Walter Ulbricht, and General Dr. Otto Körfes met with him. Should he be converted to their way of thinking, it would have been a major propaganda victory for the Soviets; it was not every day that an SS officer became a communist.

Each time, Schröder refused. Finally, in frustration, he was hauled out of the camp by his captors and placed in solitary confinement at another prison in Moscow. After languishing in a tiny unheated cell for three weeks and enduring endless interrogations, which usually involved matters that were far above what he would be privy to, he was taken out and shipped to the POW camp near Krasnogorsk. Here, he was tried for war crimes and sentenced to a 25 year sentence at hard labor because he had served in the *Waffen-SS.* After being shipped around to various prison camps in the vast Soviet *Gulag* system during the next several years, he was finally released on 22 September 1953 and shipped back to Germany in a freight train with 1,000 other former German soldiers. Ten days later, he arrived at the processing camp in Friedland, where members of his family greeted him. Nine years and eight months later, he was back at his home in Herleshausen, thousands of miles and a lifetime removed from the battlefields of Cherkassy.[13]

Another one of the thousands of prisoners the Soviets rounded up between 17 and 19 February was *Unterarzt* Dr. Peter Dohrn from *San.Kp.172* of *72.Inf.Div*. Dohrn was one of the four medical officers who volunteered to remain behind with 12 other enlisted medical personnel to care for the thousands of non-ambulatory German casualties that had been left in Shanderovka. In fact, it was Dohrn who had been ordered to carry the personal note from General Stemmermann and hand it to the first Soviet commander who entered Shanderovka in order to secure proper treatment for the wounded. At the time, Dohrn had not thought of Stemmermann's humane act as a virtual death sentence for the wounded, but immediately began to have second thoughts about the wisdom of surrendering to the Soviets.

Once the first assault wave had departed Shanderovka on the evening of 16/17 February, Dohrn decided to try to evacuate as many of the wounded as he could, rather than turn them over, thus violating a direct order. It did not matter to him – as a doctor, he was dedicated to saving as many lives as possible. With the help of other medical personnel, he was able to secure a column of empty *panje* wagons and even a truck. Several hundred of the wounded men were quickly helped into the vehicles and the convoy set off into the darkness. Dohrn and the others were brought to a halt when the lead vehicle in the column encountered the massive traffic jam on the western outskirts of Shanderovka brought about earlier when the tank from *Wiking* crashed through the bridge over the creek.

To make matters worse, Dohrn's truck was stolen at gun point by a German infantry *Leutnant* who evidently needed it more than he did. Salvoes from *Katyushas* impacted throughout the length of the small valley, but luckily none of Dohrn's men were hit. Finally, his convoy was able to cross the bridge at dawn, though by that point he and his men were about to get caught up in the battle being waged by the rearguard against the pursuing Soviets. After the column had proceeded several kilometers, Dohrn saw a line of infantry occupying a low hill to the northwest. These turned out to be enemy troops, who attacked the column, cutting it in half. Dorhn, at the head of the column, urged the drivers to spur on their mounts. With luck, he hoped to reach the safety of a nearby wood. To his dismay, artillery soon began to strike the woods, inflicting further casualties.

Subsequent attempts to break out miscarried when the Soviets shelled the first person or wagon to leave the woodline. Dohrn decided to try again in the morning. When it grew light, he made out a long line of Soviet troops that had virtually surrounded the forest. Dohrn had no choice but to give himself and the others up to their captors. For once, the Soviets were relatively good-natured. Dohrn grew concerned, however, when he saw the enemy sorting out the walking wounded from the stretcher cases. Thinking quickly, Dohrn handed over the envelope with the message from General Stemmermann to the nearest Soviet officer, a major, who led him away from the others. Although the man apparently could not read German, the envelope apparently conveyed something of importance and he

led Dohrn to see his regimental commander. Dohrn credited this with saving his life.

Dohrn then marched with the ambulatory wounded back to Shanderovka. After being interrogated in Smela, he was eventually flown to Moscow, where he was told that he was going to the Lubyanka prison. Apparently, that facility was filled up with recent arrivals, so he was luckily diverted to Camp 27 near Moscow instead. After serving as a doctor is Camp 188 near Tambov until the war ended, he was suddenly released in August 1946 and allowed to go home. To this day, he still has no idea why he was released early, but is glad that he had presented Stemmermann's letter to the Soviet officer. What became of the wounded who were unable to walk, or of the rest of the wounded who remained behind in Shanderovka, he never found out.

One wounded man taken prisoner later witnessed the death of *Oberst* Fouquet, commander of *K.Abt.B*. This officer, *Ltn.* Joachim Ohlendorf of *Gren.Rgt.266*, had been wounded in the early morning hours of 17 February during *Hptm.* Knostmann's spontaneous assault of Hill 239. Ohlendorf sustained shrapnel injuries to his head when a grenade exploded next to him during the confused fighting that followed in the forest south of the hill. As he lay in the snow stunned, his comrades assumed that he was dead and carried on their assault, leaving him behind. Ohlendorf, alone, attempted to bandage his wounds, expected a subsequent attacking wave from his division to appear out of the night at any minute. Unbeknownst to him, the rest of his regiment had been driven to the south by heavy Soviet fire. When no one appeared, he stood up and walked back towards the eastern side of the hill, where he hoped to see where the rest of his division had gone.

On the edge of the road that ran from Hill 239 to Pochapintsy he heard someone moan. There, in a snow bank on the roadside lay a seriously wounded German officer wearing a heavy fur coat. Feeling exposed on the edge of the road, Ohlendorf helped him walk to a small copse of trees, where he hoped that they would not be seen by the enemy. They had only gone a short distance when the man slipped from Ohlendorf's grasp and collapsed. The officer told him his name: *Oberst* Fouquet. Ohlendorf tried to console him and told him that more of their troops would arrive any minute and take them along with them. Ohlendorf wanted to stay with the *Oberst* as long as he could, but he knew that there was very little he could do for him. The two lay in the snow for an indeterminate amount of time. Suddenly, as it began to dawn, a patrol could be heard approaching.

To his surprise, it was a Soviet patrol of eight men led by a lieutenant, who had seen the German's trail in the snow and had decided to investigate. The Soviet officer ordered some of his men to stand Fouquet up, but were unable to since he was barely conscious. Ohlendorf was unable to witness what happened next, since he was led away by two of his captors. After he had gone a few meters, he heard a pistol shot. When he tried to turn his head and see what had happened, he was beaten by one of his guards. It was obvious to him that the Soviets had shot Fouquet, since they were unable to carry him and could not be bothered with a seriously wounded man, even if he was a senior officer. It was a tragic end for such a brave and dedicated soldier. Though only an acting commander, Fouquet had more than justified the faith that General Lieb had placed in him when Lieb was ordered to assume temporary command of *XXXXII.A.K.* and hand his division over to someone else.

Ohlendorf was then led to a nearby village (probably Zhurzhintsy), where he was interrogated by a Soviet major. While he was reading Ohlendorf's *Soldbuch*, he ordered a guard to remove the German's wristwatch and other papers from his pockets. The Soviet officer then laid a map upon the table, and asked Ohlendorf to indicate his unit's position on the map, which was covered with various tactical markings. The *Leutnant* demurred, stating that this was not his map, but must have belonged to the German officer who the Soviet major's men had shot. The leader of the patrol was called in and interrogated by his commander. When the patrol leader informed him that he had ordered Fouquet shot, the Soviet major began to strike him about the head and shoulders while shouting various unintelligible invectives at the man. Evidently, the major was angered by the fact that a very valuable prisoner had been murdered without his permission, a prisoner who could have provided a great deal of useful information.

Ohlendorf was then led away, where his wounds were treated by a doctor. After a few moments, he was brought something to eat. Another officer appeared and gave him a glass of vodka to drink, evidently either as a painkiller or a sign of comradeship. Although the officer spoke German, he did not ask Ohlendorf any military questions, engaging instead in small talk which lasted late into the morning. Several days later, he was brought with hundreds of other prisoners to a nearby rail station, where he and the other wounded troops were loaded aboard a Soviet hospital train. A few hours later, they arrived in Kiev. To his disappointment, none of the other 40 or so men in the railcar belonged to his division. When their Soviet escorts discovered that the hospitals in Kiev were full of wounded, their railcar was uncoupled and hitched to a freight train which was supposed to take them to Moscow, but bypassed the city instead.

The train continued traveling to the northeast. Several of the wounded had died during the journey, since there was only one Soviet doctor for several hundred men. The doors were rarely opened during their journey and their railcar stank like a midden. It had gotten much colder and Ohlendorf and the others had torn apart the wooden lining of the railcar and stuffed it into the small oven that sufficed to heat the interior. As for food, they were sometimes given raw grain, while other times they were issued canned rations. On 3 April 1944, the train finally arrived at a remote POW camp somewhere in the vicinity of Kirov. There, they were at first billeted in an abandoned schoolhouse, which served as the camp hospital, where 60 men to a room were quartered in bunks. Ohlendorf and the others underwent delousing and were allowed to bathe.

The medical treatment they received was rudimentary. Soon, many men had contacted typhus, though Ohlendorf had thankfully been inoculated several months before. Many other men contacted measles and died. Ohlendorf's head wound soon became infected. After seven days in this camp, he was separated from the others because of his rank, and was quartered in a room in the hospital with six other officers. Here he roomed

with the well-known Berlin orchestra conductor Hans Carste, a dentist from Hannover, and a Jewish doctor from Bratislava who had been assigned to the camp from a local *Gulag* labor battalion as its chief doctor. He was allowed to serve as the camp's medical officer providing that he was observed by Soviet female doctors.

Ohlendorf befriended all three of these men, who went out of their way to insure that the *Leutnant* received adequate medical care. Through the doctor, he learned that he was the only one of the 40 men from the railcar that had brought them to the camp who had survived. In October 1944, he was transferred to a forest camp near Krasnogorsk, then to another camp a few weeks later 40 kilometers east of Moscow for "prominent prisoners." Here, he met Field Marshal Paulus, Walter Ulbricht, Comrades Pieck and Grotewohl, and several others, including the future head of East Germany's *Nationale Volksarmee*, General Heinz Hoffmann.

From Pastor Gollwitzer, Ohlendorf learned of the cruel fate of many of his comrades, who had disappeared in the Lubyanka prison. In May 1945, Ohlendorf was transferred to an officer's camp near Susdal, located in a former cloister. Here, he learned the end of World War Two when the camp commander greeted him cheerfully and informed him that the war was over. He was then sent to the town of Vladimir to recover from a bout of sickness, followed by a stint in the town's tractor factory and work in a road construction detail. Finally, he was allowed to return to Germany in August 1948, three and a half years after the harrowing breakout from Cherkassy.[14]

Incredibly, some men evaded their captors and kept making their way out of the pocket for days afterward. One of the men who claimed to be the last out of the pocket was Theodor Vogelsang, a driver from *Gren.Rgt.124* of *72.Inf.Div.* Vogelsang had been with a horse-drawn column, which had been shot up by Soviet tanks and artillery fire south of Petrovskoye on the morning of February 17. He and another man decided to leave the column, when their leader, a *Leutnant*, indicated his intention of surrendering to the Soviets at the first possible opportunity. After marching for several hours, both men sought the protection of a gully, where they covered themselves with their shelter quarters and waited until dawn.

The next morning, they continued their journey. By midmorning on 18 February, they came across a long, deep *balka* at the base of a large hill (probably Hill 239). They and several others had been marching all day and needed another place to stay, where they could wait until the approach of darkness. In the meantime, the battlefield had become remarkably still. Later that afternoon, they spotted a small group of German soldiers led by an elderly *Oberstleutnant* marching by their position in a single file. Vogelsang and the others jumped up and begged the officer to take them along. The sounds of Soviet tanks could now be heard everywhere, but visibility was reduced by the heavy snowfall to scarcely a hundred meters, which assisted their exit from the *balka*.

Vogelsang knew none of the men with whom he was travelling. All that mattered was that they seemed to be marching in the right direction. By this time, the sun was about to set. The officer stopped and studied his map, then indicated that they should turn and go to the left. Evidently they had strayed off course. After marching an additional five kilometers, they came to a small footbridge over a wide creek. Not a single soul was to be seen anywhere - they were completely alone. By this time, night had fallen and It was eerily quiet. Silently, Vogelsang and the others crossed the bridge, where they encountered a German outpost, which directed them to the rear. He later recalled his feelings of joy and relief upon encountering the sentry; it seemed to him, as to so many others, that a huge weight had fallen from his heart.

After marching for two kilometers, the small group arrived in Lysyanka, where they sought shelter in an outbuilding that was still occupied by Ukrainian civilians. They told Vogelsang that Soviet troops had occupied the same house four days before. It was now early morning of 19 February. That morning, a German soldier who belonged to the rearguard awoke them. Lysyanka was being evacuated, he told them, and if they remained another hour, they would certainly become prisoners. That was all Vogelsang and his comrades needed to hear; they hastily grabbed up their belongings and started marching. As they passed through the town, they saw no sign of other survivors; certainly, they were among the last to make it out of the pocket.

Two kilometers southwest of Lysyanka, they encountered a collection point, where they were given something to eat. Transport aircraft could be seen landing in the distance, where they were picking up wounded men to be evacuated to Uman. They passed the improvised airfield as quickly as possible, for they knew that if the weather cleared, Soviet fighter-bombers would soon appear. Three days later, in the division's assembly area north of Uman, Vogelsang was back with his comrades of *8.Kompanie* who had since given him up for dead.[15] No additional survivors were reported after that date. *Gruppe Stemmermann* had passed into history.

End Notes

[1] Reisch, Peter. *"Ausbruch aus dem Kessel westlich von Tscherkassy."* (Undated manuscript, courtesy of the 72nd Infantry Division Veteran's Association), p. 4.

[2] Mayer, pp. 139-146.

[3] Glantz, "From the Dnieper to the Vistula," p. 171

[4] Hein manuscript, pp. 4-5.

[5] Interview with Willy Hein, Lauenburg, Germany, 25 June 1996.

[6] Klapdor, p. 196.

[7] Letter, Walter Notz, Reichenbach, Germany to author, 10 July 1997, pp. 7-8.

[8] Hahl manuscript, pp. 4-5.

[9] Figur, Franz. "Der ESAK im Kessel." (Trier, Germany: Unpublished Manuscript, courtesy of the 72nd Infantry Division Veteran's Association, 1976), p. 3.

[10] Interview with Fernand Kaisergruber of Brussels, Belgium at Novo Buda,Ukraine, 29 June 1996.

[11] Kaisergruber, Fernand. *Nous N'Irons pas a Touapse: du Donetz au Caucase de Tscherkassy L'Oder.* (Brussels: Privately Published, 1993), pp. 231-236

[12] Abschrift, Bericht über den SS-Oberscharführer Fiebelkorn, *Kriegstagebuch*, 5.SS-Panzer Regiment *Wiking*, 9. Februar bis 30. November 1944.

[13] Jahnke and Lerch, pp. 111-112.

[14] Ohlendorf, Joachim. "Bericht über die Gefangennahme und Gefangenschaft in der USSR." (Lübeck, Germany: Unpubished manuscript, courtesy of the 72nd Infantry Division Association, April 1976), pp. 2-3.

[15] Vogelsang, Theodor, "Die Letzten aus Tscherkassy," in Schwarz, pp. 49-52.

CONGRATULATIONS AND RECRIMINATIONS

Chapter Twenty Five

VICTORY CELEBRATIONS ON BOTH SIDES

"West of Cherkassy contact was made with further elements of the freed battle group, in spite of numerous enemy counterattacks, which were repulsed, and extremely difficult terrain conditions . . . "
— *Wehrmacht communiqué, 19 February 1944*[1]

T he staff of *Heeresgruppe Süd* had sat by the telephones all night in a state of great suspense, awaiting the news of whether the troops had begun to make their way out of the Pocket. In the early morning hours of 17 February, Manstein and his staff were gratified to hear that *III.Pz.Korps* had established contact with the leading spearheads of *Gruppe Stemmermann*. As soon as confirmation from *1.Pz.Armee* was received, the officer on duty, *Hptm.* Stahlberg, passed the message on to the *1a* of the *OKH* Operations Branch, *Oberst Graf* Kielmansegg.

In his diary for that day, Kielmansegg wrote "0410 hours in the morning. Breith and Stemmermann meet. Thank God. During the night, it looked as if, in an act of despair, the encircled elements would bring out nothing else with them but their lives."[2] Back in Uman, after relaying the word of the breakout to East Prussia, Stahlberg then awoke Manstein to tell him that both corps were in the process of breaking out, as well as to congratulate him.[3]

The Field Marshal later took satisfaction from the fact that the bulk of both corps had gotten out. He was distressed by the report that General Stemmermann had apparently been killed during the breakout, as well as by the fact that most of the wounded could not be evacuated. Despite this, in his words, "It had thus been possible to spare both corps the fate suffered by *6. Armee* at Stalingrad."[4] Events had proven that Manstein's decision to have been the correct one.

Had Hitler known what Manstein intended, he very likely would have countermanded his army group commander. When he was informed of the breakout after it had actually begun, he had no choice but to retroactively consent. Manstein's staff wondered throughout the day of 17 February when Hitler would make his call, but it never came. Stahlberg and others credited Manstein's independent decision to counter Hitler's orders as a morally courageous act that resulted in saving the lives of thousands of men.[5]

Manstein also realized that the divisions that had broken out would not be available for use immediately, since they would all have to be rebuilt. The loss, however temporary, of two corps of six and a half divisions would adversely impact his ability to resist additional Soviet offensives, but this fact was largely counterbalanced by the "joy of having saved at least the fighting men of the two corps."[6] The fact that both *XI.* and *XXXXII.A.K.* had lost nearly all of their equipment was another blow, since the guns, tanks, and other equipment could only be partially replaced by a Germany's overburdened

The Ross River hydro-electric dam at Korsun, used by the Germans as a bridge and destroyed during the retreat, as it appeared after the war. (Photo courtesy of the Battle of Korsun-Shevchenkovsky Museum, Ukraine)

industrial base in the sixth year of the war. More importantly, Manstein had demonstrated to his army group that he would move heaven and earth to free them if they were encircled. In his own mind, he had finally removed the stain of Stalingrad from his reputation. He need not have been concerned; by the late winter of 1944 he had proven to both his colleagues and his Soviet enemies that he still possessed the finest operational and tactical mind in the *Wehrmacht*.

While most of the men from *Gruppe Stemmermann* had been indeed able to make their way out, the battlefield, from the air at least, indicated otherwise. A trail of destroyed or abandoned German vehicles stretched to the west in a virtually unbroken column from Gorodishche to Korsun, then made a bend to the south, where the trail continued through Steblev and Shanderovka, ending in an vast graveyard of vehicles that filled the entire valley. Subsequent aerial reconnaissance photos confirmed these initially unbelievable reports. Both corps had lost nearly everything. Thousands of bodies could clearly be seen from the air as well.

One German pilot to view the devastation was *Oblt.* Erich Hartmann of *7./JG 52*. As he flew over the area with his wingman, *Oblt.* Walter Krupinski, several days after the breakout had succeeded, he spotted the mass of destroyed vehicles and the bodies of his countrymen scattered throughout the battlefield between Shanderovka and Hill 239. Hartmann shuddered at the morbid spectacle and gained a new appreciation for the lot of the average soldier. While he and the other

Destroyed German equipment line the road from Steblev to Shanderovka. (Photo courtesy of the Battle of Korsun-Shevchenkovsky Museum, Ukraine)

pilots flew high above in their fast fighter aircraft, down below the infantrymen fought, as he called it, in a "frozen purgatory." His sortie over, he flew his Messerschmidt back to his base at Uman with a "profound feeling of relief."[7]

Breith's spearhead stayed in Oktyabr and Lysyanka awaiting the arrival of more stragglers. Few were expected after 19 February, so General Hube issued the order to prepare to abandon the forward reception area that evening. Breith's corps was then to withdraw in stages until its divisions had pulled back to their original starting points between Risino and Tinovka. Once the survivors of *Gruppe Stemmermann* had arrived at their reception areas near Uman, German efforts for the remainder of February would be devoted towards reestablishing contact between the *1.Pz.* and *8.Armee*. This was accomplished with relatively little fighting, for a temporary calm had settled over this part of the Eastern Front.

It must not have seemed very calm to the troops of *1., 16.,* and *17.Pz.Div., Schw.Pz.Rgt. Bäke,* or *Leibstandarte,* who had to withdraw under heavy pressure by Marshall Zhukov. Nor was the escape route for the survivors of *Gruppe Stemmermann* safe, either. On several occasions, Soviet tanks and infantry attempted to slice through the narrow salient connecting Bushanka and Lysyanka and cut off both the remnant of *Gruppe Stemmermann* as well as the relief forces. Men who had thought themselves safe were killed by artillery, air attack, or roaming T-34s. They would not truly be out of harm's way until they reached their planned assembly areas near Uman, a distance of over 50 kilometers.

Most of the wounded were evacuated to Uman aboard ambulances or *panje* wagons and would have to endure several days of exposure to the cold winter air before they could receive proper medical treatment. Many of the casualties who had made it out of the pocket were airlifted directly from Lysyanka to Uman. While this speeded up the evacuation, it also exposed the wounded once again to death or injury, should they be attacked by Soviet fighters. On several occasions, these vulnerable aircraft were pounced upon by Soviet fighters, and more than one was lost.

Fernand Kaisergruber, who was evacuated from Lysyanka after a harrowing journey aboard a *panje* wagon to a forward airfield, was deathly afraid of being shot down. He fully expected

to die, watching in horror as the helpless aircraft he was in was shot full of holes. He reflected anxiously on the other seriously wounded men who would be killed or wounded again only minutes away from the field hospital in Uman, but fortunately he had a bumpy, if uneventful, flight. It was not enough that he had almost been overlooked by search parties when Lysyanka's medical treatment stations were abandoned - to be shot down in a medical evacuation aircraft would be the final indignity. It seemed to Kaisergruber that he would not be safe until he was back home in a hospital in his native Belgium![8]

Breith's divisions were forced to defend themselves against numerous attacks by elements of the Soviet 1st, 2nd, 5th Guards, and 6th Tanks Armies from 17 to 20 February. The Germans holding the outskirts of Oktyabr and Lysyanka were subjected to relentless enemy forays into their lines. They experienced considerable difficulty not only in evacuating wounded men coming out of the pocket, but in obtaining fuel and ammunition. The snow continued to fall, creating deep drifts which blocked the roads and kept the supply trucks from getting up to the forward units. Defensive positions, which were seized by the enemy, were retaken in desperate counterattacks, which found men from the Thuringian *1.Pz.Div.* fighting shoulder to shoulder with *Leibstandarte.* Both *16.* and *17.Pz.Div.* repelled numerous attempts by large numbers of Soviet tanks and troops to penetrate the German salient from the north. Throughout that day and the next, the ground troops were supported in their defensive efforts by *VIII.Flieger-Korps,* which conducted numerous strikes against Soviet troop concentrations whenever the weather permitted.[9] Somehow, the thin German perimeter held throughout 18 February and into the night.

By that evening, over 30,000 men from *Gruppe Stemmermann* had reached the safety of Lysyanka and had begun their trek to Uman, but the flow of men coming out of the pocket had now turned to a trickle. General Koll did not expect many more to make their way out. Since the continued presence of the relief forces in the Lysyanka bridgehead would only serve to draw in more Soviet forces determined to cut them off, Hube decided that night to order Breith to begin withdrawing his units the following day. Now that the Cherkassy Pocket was no more, the Soviets would be free to move their forces elsewhere, and the commander of *1.Pz.Armee* intended to be ready to parry the

Abandoned or destroyed German vehicles, outskirts of Shanderovka. (Photo courtesy of the Battle of Korsun-Shevchenkovsky Museum, Ukraine)

Abandoned 105mm Light Field Howitzer Model 18 with corpse of gunner, as well as many destroyed or abandoned vehicles, western outskirts of Shanderovka. (Photo courtesy of the Battle of Korsun-Shevchenkovsky Museum, Ukraine)

blow when it came. It would do neither him nor his army any good should his units holding the escape corridor be cut off. There were other intelligence indications that the enemy was beginning to concentrate forces on his left and right flanks, plus there was the matter of attending to the gap between his army and General Wöhler's *8.Armee*.

For its part, *8.Armee* began to do the same. *XXXXVII. Pz.Korps*, stalled on the hills overlooking Zvenigorodka since 15 February, would pull back both *11.* and *13.Pz.Div.* and replace them with an infantry division. All of Vormann's remaining armor would be desperately needed in the weeks to come and the necessity to provide them time to reconstitute their shattered ranks had become pressing indeed. Fortunately, the timely arrival of *2.Fallsch.Jg.Div.* helped Vormann shore up his front while the battered panzer divisions withdrew. However, he was not to remain long in his position as corps commander, where he had proven himself, at least to his army commander, as a difficult subordinate. At Wöhler's request, Vormann was relieved of his duties on 5 March 1944 and placed on the general officer's active reserve list awaiting future special employment. His next assignment would not occur until he replaced *Gen. der Inf.* Hans Jordan as commander of *9.Armee* on 27 June 1944, while that army was in the process of being destroyed during Operation Bagration, the great Soviet summer offensive of 1944 which resulted in the near annihilation of Army Group Center.[10]

In Oktyabr, *Hptm.* Scherff and *Oblt.* Dörnberg prepared to evacuate the village and destroy their non-recoverable damaged Tigers and Panthers. As he prepared his own tank for the trip back to Lysyanka, Scherff was dismayed to discover that his vehicle had sustained battle damage to its right track, thus immobilizing it. Sadly, he and his crew had no choice but to prepare it for demolition, after he had moved to take command of another Tiger. Slowly, *Kgr. Frank* and *Schw.Pz.Rgt. Bäke* brought in their forward outposts on the evening of 19 February and began surreptitiously withdrawing downhill towards the crossing sites in north Lysyanka. While this was occurring, General Koll ordered his division to conduct a thorough search of every building and dwelling in Lysyanka, because no one, not even Dr. Königshausen, the division's surgeon, truly knew how

many survivors of *Gruppe Stemmermann* had sought shelter without their knowledge. Despite their best efforts, it is likely that a small number of survivors were still in the village when the Soviets retook it on 20 February.

Somehow, a local Soviet commander had gotten wind of the evacuation of Oktyabr and initiated a counterattack on the evening of 19 February to seize it before the Germans were ready to give it up. After several hours of fighting, Dörnberg and his remaining tanks were forced to abandon the town, though in the fighting his tanks and several Panthers from *Pz.Rgt.23* were able to knock out 23 T-34s. All that the Soviets gained when they occupied the town that evening was the smoldering hulks of German and Soviet tanks. The town itself had been nearly destroyed and consisted of little more than dozens of bare chimneys. Dead bodies still lay everywhere. Dörnberg made it back to Lysyanka on foot when he was forced to blow up his own crippled tank.

Troops of *16.Pz.Div.* holding Chesnovka a few kilometers to the northwest of Dörnberg's position were also forced to withdraw from that town before they were ready to as well. The Germans had too few men and tanks to hold much longer; the Soviet superiority in numbers had now become truly overwhelming. By nightfall, the divisions and battle groups of *III. Pz.Korps* had only 15 *Pz.IVs*, ten *Panthers*, six *Tigers*, and 12 Sturmgeschütze operational - a total of 43 in all, less than a quarter of what they had when Operation "Wanda" began two weeks before.[11] While many other tanks were being repaired, these would not be available for days, if not weeks. Other tanks that could not be repaired or recovered would be blown up, which brought about the complete loss of over a dozen Tigers and Panthers that had been used as pill boxes in the Lysyanka area. The Soviet tank armies facing them had easily three or four times as many by this point.

Despite the fact that the breakout by *Gruppe Stemmermann* had been less successful than anticipated, General Hube was quite pleased with his own army's performance. On 19 February, he issued an official order of the day directed at the survivors from the pocket and his own troops, in recognition of their achievement. It read in part:

SS survivors of the breakout gather after crossing the Gniloy Tikich. (IWM photo shown in Andrew Mollo's "A Pictorial History of the SS," Stein and Day, 1977)

37 survivors of Wiking's tank battalion enrout to assembly areas in Poland where the battalion will be rebuilt. (Photo courtesy of Bernd Lerch and the Wiking Division's Veteran's Association)

The Russians have failed to reach their goal! He has already announced to the world that he has destroyed ten of our divisions and killed over 50,000 [of you]. Today, however, the majority of you have been freed by the brave [troops of] III.Pz.Korps. You saved yourselves by your tough and unbreakable defensive spirit as well as the skillful blows of III.Pz.Korps which came to your relief in your hour of need. We are also sincerely thankful for the sacrifices of our comrades from VIII.Flieger-Korps, who supplied you from the air and evacuated many of the wounded.

The majority of you are free . . . I give you my thanks and highest recognition to all of you, who, weapon in hand, fought your way through and denied the Russians their long sought-after victory. Each of you have fought as the Führer demanded and trusted in the might of your weapons and the superiority of your leadership once again. We will never forget our fallen. With bitter hearts, we think of our severely wounded comrades whom we were forced to leave behind to the Russians, and those who could not find their way to freedom. We will extract our revenge on the Russians. As always, in good or in difficult days, long live the Führer![12]

As elements of *1.Pz.Div.* began to pull out on 18 February, *Hptm.* Ernst Schenk's *Rgt.Gr.110* was still holding its position in the exposed field on the northwestern outskirts of Lysyanka. His misgivings had been justified the previous day when his battalion was attacked by Soviet tanks and infantry. Since they had no anti-tank weapons, his men were experienced enough to let the tanks pass over their foxholes and slit trenches; once they had gone by, Schenk and his men rose from the ground and eliminated the accompanying infantry. The tanks were dealt with later by some of *1.Pz.Div.'s* Panthers. The following day, Schenk received the order to withdraw and follow the route that the rest of the survivors had taken. "Easier said than done," he thought. He had heard rumors that Soviet tanks

were roaming up and down the *Rollbahn* attempting to cut off the forces in Lysyanka yet again.

Taking no chances, Schenk ordered his men to march in a westerly direction across the fields where they could find cover, thus avoiding the road altogether. When a group of T-34s was spotted athwart the road several hundred meters to their right, he ordered his men to follow the contours of a small creek that paralleled the road, a sound decision since they would be out of the tanks' line of sight. After following the terrain for several hours, they finally arrived in Bushanka, where they were provided some food before being ordered to keep marching. It did not matter to Schenk or his men - they had somehow made it through, although they brought out with them only what they could carry on their backs. Looking back, Schenk recalled at the time that nearly everyone looked towards the heavens and thanked God for allowing them to make it out. Nothing ever came of Schenk's supposed refusal to obey *Oberstlt.* Bäke's order to place his battalion at his disposal. Evidently, *Oberst* Viebig had indeed given the order for him and *Hptm.* Burgfeld not to stop until they reached Lysyanka. The matter was dropped, as attested by the fact that Schenk was promoted to major shortly thereafter.[13]

A more immediate concern for General Hube was what to do with the thousands of men streaming out of the pocket. While both he and Manstein believed that *Gruppe Stemmermann* would suffer heavy casualties during the breakout, no one had thought that they would lose all of their equipment in the process. Without rations or sufficient field kitchens of their own, there was little that the surviving units could do to provide sustenance for their men. Nor was there much in the way of shelter for them along the corridor that stretched from Lysyanka to Bushanka, since the few available *isbas* and other buildings were already in use by the relief forces or had been packed with men from the first units which had broken out. The overtaxed supply staffs of *III.Pz.Korps* could do little for them either, since they were completely occupied with providing their own units with fuel and ammunition. Even that was a larger task than they could handle, as evidenced by *1.Pz.Div.* and *Schw.Pz.Rgt. Bäke's* difficulty in keeping their forward units supplied with sufficient quantities of gasoline and tank ammunition.

1.Pz.Armee had at least foreseen the need to set up receiving areas for the divisions of *XI.* and *XXXXII.A.K.*, where the scattered battalions and regiments could be reassembled and given back to their commanders. It was hoped that they would quickly be restored to a combat-ready status, but these plans were dashed when the condition of the units coming out of the pocket was reported. An order issued by *1.Pz.Armee* on 18 February stated that "the effects of the fighting of the last few weeks on the troops is to be overcome as quickly as possible," but this was quickly recognized as being unrealistic.[14]

The order specified which localities each division or regiment was to occupy upon arrival on the northern outskirts of Uman. Once Hube had learned of Stemmermann's death, he recalled the actual commander of *XXXXII.A.K.*, Gen.d.Inf. Franz Mattenklott, who had been on furlough, and ordered him to proceed immediately to Mankovka where he was tasked with reforming the shattered units assembling there. The survivors would now be grouped under the heading of *Gruppe Mattenklott* and would remain under his command until they were evacuated to Poland to be rebuilt or sent back to their original units. He was allocated an area bounded by the towns of Ivanki, Rogi, Zendsovka, Verchnyashka, Leshchinovka, Dobra, Nesterovka, and Kishchintsy to be used as assembly points for his new command.

Within this area lay many other smaller villages, where units would sort themselves out by battalion and company. For example, *88.Inf.Div.* was allocated the villages of Selenyi Gai, Kratchkovka, Polkovnishche, Ivanki, and Monastyrek. All of these localities offered little more than the barest necessities needed to provide shelter for the men while they awaited transport, since for the most part these villages consisted of little more than a few *isbas* with a barn or two. Where possible, *1. Pz.Armee's Oberquartiermeister* (Chief Logistics Officer, or *O.Qu.*) provided them with a field kitchen to serve welcome hot meals and beverages.

The army's *O.Qu.* also had to comb through his stocks of supplies to round up as much clothing as possible, especially greatcoats and boots, to replace those lost during the breakout. Many troops who had stripped to their underwear in order to swim the Gniloy Tikich had lost even their uniforms. Thousands of caps, belts, gloves, scarves, underwear, and socks had to be found in the various depots maintained by the army's service and supply units. Even with this effort, there was not enough to go around and many men had to endure the cold and dampness in the same summer uniforms they were wearing on the day of the breakout.

As items such as toilet articles, shoe polish, and writing material were in short supply and were considered luxury items, the troops would have to make do until a source of supply could be found. The SS survivors fared the same. According to Fritz Hahl of *Wiking*, "For every 20 men, there was one razor. Despite this, our morale was good," especially when it was rumored that everyone would be granted generous leaves.[15] To assist Mattenklott in providing a modicum of logistical planning and support, the supply staff of *Art.Div.z.b.V.311* was attached to his headquarters, as well as a company of military police from Army Group South.

Some of the thousands of German prisoners taken during 17-18 February marching into captivity on the outskirts of Shenderovka. In addition to German soldiers can be seen many Ukrainian auxilliaries and German civilian employees of the Reichsbahn. Few of them would ever be seen alive again. (Photo courtesy of the Battle of Korsun-Shevchenkovsky Museum, Ukraine)

The units began to trickle into their new collection areas as early as the evening of 18 February. Here, they were met by reception commandos from *Heerestreifen-Gruppe 11* (Army Traffic Direction Control Group 11) who set up a line of roadblocks to control and guide the men into their new local billeting areas as they arrived from Frankovka or Bushanka. They would also pass along a series of instructions to the commanders of units coming out of the pocket, which were to be implemented without delay. First, commanders were to report the strength of their units as soon as possible to *Gruppe Mattenklott's* headquarters in Mankovka and update this information as frequently as possible. Second, they were to make up detailed lists of all men missing in action or believed to have been left behind in Shanderovka. Thirdly, each division coming out of the pocket was to appoint a local defense commander for each of its billeting areas. Units would have to construct local defensive positions before they could allow themselves to rest.

Another order was issued that day which spelled out Army Group South's long-term intentions regarding how it planned to restore the combat strength of the units comprising *Gruppe Mattenklott*. As soon as possible, the units would be assembled and moved by rail to training areas in the vicinity of Lemberg (Lviv) and Tarnopol, where they would be rebuilt as much as possible within the rear area of the army group on Poland's eastern border. The order did not apply to those troops on leave status who would continue to serve in whatever ad-hoc unit, such as *Urlauber Regiment Baacke*, until they had been released to rejoin their units, though any of these men who were in *8. Armee's* sector were ordered to be transferred to *1.Pz.Armee*, so their eventual reintegration with their units could more readily take place.* The order also stated that *Gruppe Mattenklott* was now under the command and control of *1.Pz.Armee*, and was released from attachment to *8.Armee*.[16]

---

* *Oberstlt.* Karl Baacke never rejoined his division. During there treat of *8.Armee* from the Ukraine that April, he was killed in action.

Some who got away. Survivors of the breakout recuperate in eastern Poland, Spring 1944. (Bundesarchiv 241/2200/35)

Any units whose division headquarters were not encircled were to be returned as expeditiously as possible, since it was felt that these units, whose own divisions still had the means to support them, would be reintegrated into the army group's order of battle much more quickly and efficiently. This order affected Brese's battlegroup from *14.Pz.Div.*, the two regiments from *213.Sich.Div.* as well as the battalions from *167.* and *168.Inf.Div.* They would get no rest at all, but would instead be sent almost immediately back into combat. At least these soldiers would be reunited with their comrades. The return of *Maj.* Brese's regiment to *14.Pz.Div.* was a cause for celebration, since it was assumed that he and his men had perished in the breakout. The division commander, *Gen.Maj.* Unrein, personally greeted him upon his returned and insured that his regiment would quickly be re-outfitted with the necessary weapons and equipment. He also redirected all available replacements to Brese.[17]

The shattered units of *Gruppe Mattenklott* slowly arrived on foot in their temporary billeting area. The joy that they had originally felt when they arrived in Lysyanka had been replaced by a numbing fatigue brought about by the need to march over 50 kilometers. Along the way, they sought shelter for the night in peasant huts or outbuildings, warmed only by the body heat of their comrades. While they had been able to obtain cups of *Ersatz* (artificial) coffee and soup along the way, none of them received a decent meal until three or four days after they had broken out. Many men had no weapons or headgear and looked more like an army of beggars than members of what was considered at the time to still be the world's finest military force.

Most felt just lucky to be alive. Others felt guilty that they had made survived when close friends had perished. Many others were shaken by what they had seen and experienced, especially the sight of the wounded they had been forced to abandon along the way.

Slowly, units began to collect at their reception areas. Survivors would scan the ranks of their shattered units for familiar faces and would jump for joy when they were reunited with a comrade whom they had given up for dead. Order began to reassert itself, as the surviving officers and senior NCOs began to shout orders instructing men to clean their weapons, write letters home to loved ones, or to square away their uniforms. Platoons and companies began to reform, then battalions. Acting commanders were found to replace those who had fallen in battle. Requests were submitted for replacement clothing, boots and weapons. Men with minor illnesses were treated if possible. But, most of all, the men rested. Of all the things that had been lacking during the three-week battle, an uninterrupted night's sleep was what they missed the most.

As he marched with his remaining Walloons towards the assembly area they were to share with *Wiking* at Michailovka, Leon Degrelle took the time to enjoy the winter scenery. Away from immediate danger, he could now afford to relax a bit, noting the colorful Ukrainian windmills, painted blue, lilac, and pale green, which dotted the landscape. Upon arrival at the reception area, he remarked upon the contrast between what he and his men had just experienced and the almost comic seriousness of the rear area.

We reached a large village. There the [breakout] corridor came to an end. German order immediately reasserted itself. Dozens of big fellows from the rear, well-fed, their cheeks as appetizing as beefsteaks, held big placards on which were inscribed the names of each of the units. It was necessary to reform the platoons and companies. The lifers (career soldiers) were already bellowing out orders. If the Stabsfeldwebeln were blustering, it meant that the adventure was truly over.[18]

Although he was not aware of it at the time, the *Führer* himself had been inquiring as to his whereabouts for the past two days.

For their part, both *1.Pz.Armee's* and Army Group South's leadership were shocked at the condition of the units coming out of the pocket. Not only had they lost practically all of their equipment and heavy weapons, but three weeks of encirclement had turned the troops themselves into physical and mental wrecks. Officer and NCO casualties had been extremely high, thus making it even more difficult for units to be whipped back into shape. General Wenck reported that:

> These troops have weeks of enormous burdens and, on account of the breakout, an overwhelming physical exhaustion behind them. The inner substance is still there, despite these stresses they have endured. One must not fail to recognize that only the few soldiers who possess inborn toughness would be able to withstand such strain more than once. Only through quickly applied assistance and care, combined with the possibility of rest in the days immediately following the breakout, can this condition of exhaustion be quickly overcome.[19]

Had Manstein saved his men from one hell only to deliver them into another, darker one, one characterized by the symptoms of *Kesselpsychose*? The first reports, though shocking, soon gave way to faith in the legendary resiliency of the average German, as attested to by Wenck, with some reservations:

> The Army is of the opinion, based on the weight of available evidence, that all parts [of the surviving forces], both leadership and troops, have performed their duty to the utmost limits of the capabilities of men and material and have accomplished the most that anyone could have hoped to expect from this operation: Saving nearly 35,000 German soldiers from captivity.[20]

1.Pz.Armee also, by way of explanation for the troops psychological condition, stated that "It must be recognized that these troops were encircled since 28 January and, consciously or unconsciously, had the fate of Stalingrad before their eyes." Wenck was not alone in his clear-headed estimation, but there were many others who could not believe that German soldiers had been so deeply affected or how they could have simply abandoned millions of *Reichmarks* worth of equipment to the Soviets.

Indeed, the aftermath of the breakout from the Cherkassy Pocket immediately provoked controversy within both Army Group South and in Germany itself. Some way had to be found to explain the magnitude of the loss and to squelch a host of rumors that were being spread by the Soviets, such as one that alleged that the SS murdered Stemmermann. On 18 February, *1.Pz.Armee* also requested information about several sensitive topics, perhaps in the hope that it would head off criticism of how the army itself had handled the battle.[21]

Not only did it request that each unit of *Gruppe Mattenklott* submit a detailed after-action report that dealt only with that particular unit's activities during the breakout, but also demanded to know whether Hill 239 had been occupied by *1.Pz.Div.*, why did the units not bring out their heavy equipment and vehicles, and why did *1.Pz.Div.* not help them recover their equipment. At this particular point in the battle's immediate aftermath, many suspected that *1.Pz.Div.* did not do enough to help *Gruppe Stemmermann* fight its way out of the pocket. Another message was sent at nearly the same time demanding an explanation of the circumstances surrounding General Stemmermann's death. All of these needed to be answered, not only to protect *1.Pz.Armee's* reputation, but to help forestall any Soviet propaganda designed to sow further dissent among the German ranks.

In the meantime, Generals Lieb and Gille, as well as Leon Degrelle, had been summoned to the *Wolfschanze* in East Prussia in order to be personally decorated by Adolf Hitler. In order to take advantage of their observations and experiences before they departed, General Hube called a meeting at his headquarters in Uman on 20 February. Not only did Hube and Wenck attend, but Wöhler and Speidel also flew in to participate in the meeting. Lieb's chief of staff, *Oberst* Franz, and Gille's *1a*, *Ostubaf.* Schönfelder also attended, since they were intimately involved in operations encompassing the initial encirclement and the breakout, as well as the many battles fought in between. The main topics and the candor of its attendees makes this event stand out as a singular instance where the failures and successes of the recent battle were frankly and openly discussed, especially since it took place at a time when members of the *Wehrmacht* were increasingly reluctant to air their personal views.

Hube led off the discussion by stating that in his opinion, the goals of the relief operation, that is, the encirclement of the Soviet forces as well as the rescue of *Gruppe Stemmermann* followed by a counteroffensive designed to retake Kiev, were too ambitious to be accomplished by the forces available, and that the objectives should have been strictly limited to the relief operation itself and the closing of the gap between his and Wöhler's army. This, he thought, would still have enabled both armies to trap and destroy a large portion of the enemy's forces and would have created the prerequisites for further operations. Enough forces were at hand, Hube thought, to meet these limited goals.

The men of 1st Panzer Regiment's 1.Kompanie bury their Battailion commander, Hauptmann Cramer, after the battle. (Photo courtesy of von Dörnberg)

The first relief attempt, he thought, began well enough, but was forced to be called off on account of the mud and poor terrain. He made no mention of the Soviet response to his thrust, though Vatutin's forces no doubt contributed immensely to Hube's inability to attain his objectives. The second attempt, he related, caught the enemy by surprise and enabled Breith's spearheads to seize three bridgeheads and reach the Gniloy Tikich at Lysyanka before his attack culminated upon the western slopes of Hill 239. Once again, the German forces were brought to a halt by the poor road conditions, which, in Hube's opinion, made the operation one that "murdered our motor vehicles." Here, in front of Lysyanka, *1.Pz.Div.* met a concentrated enemy defense which it simply could not overcome by its dwindling battalions and their ever-shrinking number of tanks.

Instead of conducting a phased and orderly operation, Hube concluded that *III.Pz.Korps* was forced to find a way to break into the pocket by the quickest and shortest route; even that desperate attempt was not enough. In the end, of course, *1.Pz.Div.* failed, but Stemmermann's troops were able to make it out on their own by simply overrunning the enemy positions along Hill 239, though at horrific cost. It was, in Hube's words, a "primitive way to break out," attended by the loss of all of both encircled corps' equipment and the lives of many of their soldiers, not to mention the thousands of wounded that Stemmermann and Lieb were forced to leave behind.

Wöhler spoke next, relating the course of *XXXXVII. Pz.Korps'* attempt to break through to *Gruppe Stemmermann* along his army's left flank. Not only did this corps face the same problems of weather and terrain that Breith's did, but it had far fewer available forces to work with and consequently was not able to achieve the desired mass to punch through the Soviet defensive belt south of Zvenigorodka. While he believed that the Iskrenoye bridgehead showed some initial promise, the fact that Vormann could not capitalize on it due to enemy resistance and the loss of the bridge over the Shpolka River forced him to look further west, where he eventually employed just two divisions (*11.* and *13.Pz.Div.*) and *Gruppe Haack* to achieve a decision south of Zvenigorodka.

In retrospect, Wöhler stated that he had expected too much of Vormann's corps and that the best he could have hoped for was for him to have tied up as much of the enemy's forces as possible that could have been used against Breith's relief attempt. While this belatedly exonerated Vormann, *XXXXVII. Pz.Korps* did indeed manage to pin down the bulk of Rotmistrov's 5th Guards Tank Army until the last two days of the operation, no small achievement. Despite its limited strength, Vormann's corps still managed to destroy 120 Soviet tanks during the last week of the battle.

Wöhler concluded that there was very little that his army could have done to prevent the encirclement. The initiative lay solely with the enemy, who used his overwhelming numerical superiority to dictate the course of the battle, leaving *8.Armee* few options with which to counter Konev's thrusts. Wöhler simply did not have enough men and tanks on his left wing available to stop the enemy, though he felt that his men contributed significantly to *1.Pz.Armee's* relief attempt.

General Lieb spoke after Wöhler, concentrating on the combat operations of *Gruppe Stemmermann*. Lieb stated frankly that the wisest course of action would have been the evacuation of the Kanev salient in December, which would have prevented both corps from being encircled in the first place. Hube responded by saying that this was not possible in view of the significant role the position along the Dnieper would play in future operations, an allusion to Hitler's desire to conduct a counteroffensive in order to regain Kiev. After Lieb had spoken, the discussion shifted to the topic of the *Luftwaffe* airlift. Nearly all of the participants were unanimous in their opinion that despite the extreme limitations imposed upon the *Luftwaffe* by the weather, mud, and the Red Air Force, the airlift was far more successful than anyone had hoped. For its exemplary performance, Wöhler felt that Seidemann's *VIII. Flieger-Korps* deserved the highest recognition.

Then it was General Gille's turn to speak. He asked the others why had the pocket been allowed to shrink so much, a factor that he thought had considerably limited *Gruppe Stemmermann's* freedom of maneuver. He felt that it would have been better had the encircled forces tried to keep the pocket as large as possible. Wöhler replied, stating that on account of the dwindling strength of the two corps in the pocket, combined with the very real threat that the Soviets might cut it in two as well as the need to create a reserve to effect the link-up with *III. Pz.Korps*, he was forced to order Stemmermann to continually shrink the size of the pocket. Hube, who had been at Stalingrad himself, reminded everyone that the decision not to yield an inch of ground had cost *6.Armee* dearly.

The topic of discussion then switched to the actual breakout. Lieb was the first to speak. He outlined the general course of the initial attack and the many difficulties that his units faced after crossing the line of departure. The loss of so many vehicles was due, in large part, to the unsuitable terrain, shortage of fuel, mud and snow, as well as enemy action. There was simply no way that he and his men could have broken out without leaving their equipment behind. Lieb believed that his men had enough to eat until the last days of the encirclement, and compared the breakout itself, in terms of physical exertion, as being little more than an "alpine tour." The most difficult part, in his opinion, was when the mass of the escaping troops encountered the icy Gniloy Tikich and realized that they had no choice but to swim across to escape capture. Many men, in Lieb's opinion, could not physically rise to the challenge and drowned while they tried to swim to the creek's opposite bank.

Gille then asked why had they broken out towards the direction of Lysyanka, when it seemed that the encircled forces could have broken out by way of Olshana much earlier. Wöhler told him that this was considered, but it readily became apparent that the Soviets were concentrating the bulk of their forces along the southern front of the pocket in their attempt to slice it in half, so a breakout in that direction would have encountered great difficulties. In addition, *XXXXVII.Pz.Korps* was too weak to break through, having already expended most of its strength during the early phase of the encirclement when Vormann tried to close the gap between his corps and Stemmermann's near Kapitanovka.

Gille then asked whether they could have waited two or three more days to begin the breakout. In his opinion, all of the offensive preparations were too hurriedly made, which resulted in a poorly organized attack that quickly fell apart when it encountered significant enemy forces. Hube then asked Leon Degrelle, as the only commander of a troop unit, what was his opinion of the matter. Degrelle replied, in "lively French," that he thought that his men could not have possibly held on any longer than they did. To him, it was not merely a matter of personal courage, but a question of sheer physical strength and endurance. Before he could continue, he was cut off by Gille, who stated that although the Walloons were very good while attacking, they were somewhat soft in regards to conducing a defense or holding out for a long period of time. Hube then countered Gille's remark by stating that he was entirely satisfied that the field commanders and troops had done everything that was humanly possible to hold their positions and had accomplished everything expected of them. Gille's condescending remark in front of the others showed that the Waffen-SS still had a few things to learn about German-Belgian cooperation.

The next subject discussed involved psychological issues. Hube asked his fellow conferees how effective they thought the Soviet propaganda was, especially the actions of the National Free Germany Committee and the League of German Officers. Oberst Franz stated that he was of the opinion that it had no effect whatsoever; in any case, he did not think that anyone took it very seriously. Lieb disagreed, saying that he thought the dan-

Destroyed Panzer Mark IV of Wiking on the edge of Khilki, Spring 1944. (Photo courtesy of the Battle of Korsun-Shevchenkovsky Museum, Ukraine)

ger posed by General Seydlitz and the others was very great indeed, especially in the manner in which Seydlitz's personally-targeted propaganda was designed to separate the officers from the men. Hube agreed, stating that this was something that the *Wehrmacht* had never faced before in the East, and that new measures needed to be designed in order to counter this sort of thing in the future. He thought that Hitler's idea for Lieb, Gille, and Degrelle to fly to the *Führerhauptquartier* so soon after the battle was a good idea, because it would allow them to publicly deny the increasingly fantastic claims being made by the Soviet Ministry of Propaganda.

Hube felt that, if done properly, the death of General Stemmermann could be used to good advantage for Germany's own propaganda counteroffensive. When the next *Wehrmachtsbericht* was issued, he felt that much should be made of the fact that Stemmermann died while leading his troops out of the pocket on foot. Already, Soviet claims of the numbers of German troops killed and captured was continuing to rise, a claim which needed to be countered immediately with their own accounts of the battle's outcome. Not only did they have to reassure the German people that this battle was no second Stalingrad, but Hube was aware that Germany had to demonstrate to its allies that it was in control of the situation. In no way could this battle be talked of in terms of failures by the troops, but rather an outcome resulting from the weather and terrain. As for the lost equipment, it should be glossed over.

In closing, Hube thought that it would be best if the propaganda theme concentrated on the fact that the encircled troops were successfully freed from their encircling ring and the fact that the enemy was unable to destroy the encircled divisions due to the decisive success of the German defenders. The meeting then broke up and Lieb, Gille, and Degrelle, still wearing their torn and dirty field uniforms, boarded their He-111 for their flight to Rastenburg.[22]

Afterwards, Hube directed Wenck to publish the minutes of the conference, and draw up a list of conclusions to be placed in the army's *Kriegstagebuch* as a *Kommandosache* (commander's addendum). Most noteworthy were a number of factors which Hube and Wenck both felt were above their ability to influence; i.e., decisions that had been exclusively reserved for

Hitler. Among the factors that heavily influenced or could have influenced the outcome of the battle were the following: an early withdrawal from the Dnieper Bend region; the recall of *24.Pz.Div.* at a decisive phase of the fighting; Direction of *1. Pz.Armee's* relief attack after the recall of *24.Pz.Div.*; the questions concerning the aerial resupply effort (especially in regards to the condition of the airfields and liaison with the Luftwaffe with ground units); the possibility that both armies and Army Group South could have followed another course other than the dictated relief axis of advance; as well as other ancillary issues.

In retrospect, most of these were matters over which neither Hube nor Wöhler had much control; still, they felt duty bound to mention these as possibly contributing to the less than successful outcome of the battle. It is unknown whether the results of their conversations ever reached the highest levels of the *OKH*; Manstein himself makes no mention of them in his memoirs. They were immediately classified as secret documents and perhaps never saw the light of day throughout the remaining months of the Third Reich. It is instructive to note that most of the commanders at the conference knew why the pocket had come about and why the relief operation had ultimately failed; yet, they refrained from criticizing Hitler's role in the entire affair, choosing instead to put the blame on the "High Command" rather than directly at Hitler himself. Fear of Hitler's

wrath and an unwillingness to pin the blame where it belonged had now become nearly universal among the German officer corps after the third year of war in the East.

Only a few hardy souls, Manstein and Model included, were bold enough to criticize Hitler to his face. Most of their peers had either been previously relieved of command or had chosen the easier path of unquestioning obedience. When Germany most badly needed its most talented leadership, such men became increasingly harder to find. While German leadership as well as operational and tactical proficiency had begun to display signs of decay, that of the Red Army clearly began to show signs of improvement. Although the Soviet generalship also feared contradicting their dictator to his face, Stalin at least was giving them less reason to do so, especially when they continued to present him with victories seemingly as impressive as the Korsun-Shevchenkovsky Operation. Soon, however, the Soviets' grand claims of victory would be challenged by their adversary's, which would attempt to score its own propaganda triumph.

End Notes

[1] Buchner, p. 69.

[2] Glanz, "From the Dnieper to the Vistula," p. 234.

[3] Stahlberg, p. 328.

[4] Manstein, p. 517.

[5] Stahlberg, p. 328.

[6] Ibid.

[7] Toliver, Raymond and Constable, Trevor. *The Blond Knight of Germany: The True Story of Erich Hartmann, the Greatest Fighter Ace of All Time.* (New York: Ballantine Books, 1973 edition), p. 93.

[8] Kaisergruber, p. 44.

[9] *1.Pz.Armee* KTB, entry dated 18 February 1944, p. 4.

[10] Adair, Paul. *Hitler's Greatest Defeat: The Collapse of Army Group Center, June 1944.* (London: Arms and Armor Press, 1994), p. 118.

[11] *Panzerlage III.Pz.Korps,* 1330 hours, 19 February 1944.

[12] Oberbefehlshaber, 1.Panzerarmee, *Tagesbefehl,* 19 February 1944.

[13] Letter, Ernst Schenk, Dinkelsbühl, Germany to author, 20 August 1996, p. 3.

[14] Pz.AOK 1 an III.Pz.Korps. *Ordnen der aus dem Einschliessungsraum durchgebrochenen Verbände des XI. und XXXXII.A.K.,* 2100 hours 18 February 1944.

[15] Hahl, *Panzergrenadiere der Panzerdivision Wiking im Bild,* p. 198.

[16] Radio Message, *Heeresgruppe Süd an Pz.AOK 1, Bezug H.Gr.Süd* 1A *Nr. 842/44,* dated 1445 hours 18 February 1944.

[17] Grams, pp. 180-181.

[18] Degrelle, p. 224.

[19] *PzAOK 1, Abt.1a, Stellungnahme zu den Gefechtsberichten der Gruppe Stemmermann und des III.Pz.Korps über die Kämpfe vom 16. Bis 18.2.44. Armee H.Qu., den 28.2.44, Anlage 4 zu Pz.AOK. 1, Abt.1a, Nr. 158/44 g.Kdos.v.28.2.44,* p. 3.

[20] Ibid.

[21] *Stellungnahme zu den Gefechtsberichten der Gruppe Stemmermann.*

[22] *Besprechung bei Pz.AOK.1 anlässlich der Berufung Generalleutnant Lieb, Gruppenführer Gille und Obersturmführer Degrelle in des Führerhauptquartier, 20 February 1944,* pp. 1-10.

Chapter Twenty Six

AN AUDIENCE WITH THE FÜHRER

**"I felt myself broken, devoured by those terrible weeks, but . . .
there was glory for our heroic legion . . . "**

— *Leon Degrelle*[1]

hile the Germans began to rebuild the two shattered corps, the victorious Soviets combed through the wreckage in the Shanderovka valley and counted the dead, guided by thousands of crows that had gathered nearby. General Zhukov remarked later that "I have never seen, and never again saw, such a vast number of corpses in such a small area. The Germans had made a hopeless attempt to extricate themselves...we had not planned a bloodbath."[2] Thousands of bodies, both German and Soviets, were buried in mass graves, though separately. The mass graves of the Soviet Union's fallen heroes were soon marked even before the war ended with impressive memorials that still stand today.

The German mass graves went unmarked. The only exception was that of the body of General Stemmermann. According to Major Kampov of Konev's staff, his body was found in a *balka* next to the ruins of a German staff car in the vicinity of Zhurzhintsy. In his account:

> Stemmermann was dead, right enough. I saw his body as it lay there. Our people had laid him out on a rough wooden table in a barn. There he lay, complete with his orders and medals. He was a little old man, with gray hair; he must have been a Korps student in his younger days, judging from the big [dueling] scar on one cheek. For a moment we wondered whether it wasn't a fake; perhaps an ordinary soldier had been dressed up in a general's uniform. But all of Stemmermann's papers were found on the body . . . We buried him decently . . . The rest were dumped in holes in the ground; if we started making individual graves - we don't do that for our own people - we would have needed an army of gravediggers at Korsun . . . and there was no time to waste . . . But dead generals aren't all that frequent, so we could give him a proper burial.[3]

 ❖ ❖ ❖

Stemmermann's remains were placed in a rough pine board casket and interred in a small cemetery in the village of Brane Polye, a few kilometers away from where he fell. To this day, a Ukrainian family still tends his burial plot, the only known individual German grave from the battle. Stemmermann's walking cane was found by a Soviet enlisted man and now resides in the collection at the Battle of Korsun-Shevchenkovsky Museum.

Body of **General Wilhelm Stemmermann**, *found on the battlefield south of Zhurzhentsy (from a Soviet periodical). (Photo courtesy of the Battle of Korsun-Shevchenkovsky Museum, Ukraine)*

The vast amount of abandoned equipment, destroyed vehicles, prisoners, and thousands of dead provided a rich bounty for the Soviet Union's propaganda ministry. Every day, it seemed that the German death toll rose higher, a dubious claim which was proclaimed throughout the world by the Soviet media and accepted at face value by their Western Allies. These statements were proving to be a great source of concern to Hitler, hence his decision to recall Lieb, Gille, and Degrelle to his headquarters in order to personally decorate them.

One broadcast that originated in England was intercepted three days after the first Soviet broadcast was conducted 17 February. The announcer claimed that Konev's forces had completely wiped out the pocket and had killed 55,000 German soldiers and had captured an additional 18,200. The Soviets also claimed to have shot down 471 German aircraft, destroyed 271 tanks, and destroyed or captured 994 guns and artillery pieces. At least 10,000 vehicles and 6,418 horses were also claimed to

Gille *and* **Degrelle** *being greeted by* **Hitler** *at Wolfschanze immediately after the battle.* **Hermann Fegelein**, *Waffen-SS liason officer for Reichsführer-SS Heinrich Himmler, stands in the background.*

have been captured or destroyed on the battlefield. Similar claims in other languages were intercepted. The Soviets were succeeding in painting the outcome of the Battle of Cherkassy as a decisive German defeat.

All of the initial broadcasts claimed that no one had escaped from the pocket. Furthermore, some were buttressed by German POW accounts, which seemed to add authenticity to the Soviet's claims. It was, in the words of one Soviet chronicler, a "second Stalingrad."[4] Certainly, the total number of dead and wounded Germans claimed - which ranged from 70,000 initially to 73,200 - was a number that approached the scale of the German loss at the city along the Volga. At first, the Soviets claimed to have killed or captured more Germans than were physically present in the pocket by a least 10,000, but becomes more understandable when one considers that they believed at the time that they had encircled the bulk of *8. Armee*, some 100,000 men. Of course, this had not been the case at all, but the propaganda ministry had to find some way to make the body count agree with its claims to have wiped out most of Wöhler's forces.

Nor were the numbers of tanks, guns, and aircraft claimed to have been destroyed accurate either. The total was greater than what the entire Army Group South had available at the time. Losses in tanks had indeed been high, with between 100 and 150 totally destroyed. The number of German aircraft the Soviets claimed to have destroyed was more than the total number that were operational at that time for the entire Eastern Front. In fact, only 32 Ju-52s had been shot down. An additional 113 aircraft had been damaged, but these were subsequently repaired. Losses in fighter aircraft and *Stukas* had been negligible. While all of *Gruppe Stemmermann's* artillery, howitzers, and mortars were lost, this number only approximated a quarter of the Soviets claims. The numbers of destroyed vehicles and guns had to match what the Soviets claimed were actually in the pocket when the encirclement was completed, which made it appear, to Stalin at least, that the Red Army had indeed achieved the

"output" promised at the beginning of their offensive.

To counter the Soviet's claim, the *OKW* issued no less than three *Wehrmachtsberichte*, each of them successively more impressive than the other. The first one, issued 18 February, was rather short and matter of fact. It stated that "After fighting off heavy enemy counterattacks, contact was reestablished with powerful German battle groups cut off for a week in the area west of Cherkassy, which had fought their way through to the Panzer units coming to their relief . . ."[5] This claim was factually misleading. The troops had been cut off for three weeks, not one, and could hardly be described as "powerful" by the time they established contact with their rescuers. However, a subsequent communiqué put an even more favorable spin on the outcome, a reflection of the fact that the German's own propaganda machine had begun to be brought into play to counter the Soviet's claims.

The communiqué issued 20 February was the most detailed of the three issued concerning the battle. According to the extract:

> The OKW announces that, in regards to the 18 February report of the freeing of the German battle group surrounded west of Cherkassy, that the recovery of the freed divisions is complete. The troops of the Army and Waffen-SS under the command of General der Artillerie Stemmermann and Generalleutnant Lieb, surrounded since 28 January, held fast against an assault by far superior forces in a heroic defensive battle, and then in bitter fighting broke through the enemy's encircling ring.[6]

This was true enough, but continued in the following vein: "Leaders and troops have acted in ways that will go down in German military history as shining examples of heroic steadfastness, audacious offensive spirit, and a willingness to sacrifice oneself for one's comrades." It also claimed that during the battle the combined forces of *1.Pz.* and *8.Armee* destroyed 728 Soviet tanks and 800 guns and artillery pieces, as well as the capture of thousands of prisoners. Taken in this light, it would seem that the whole battle was practically fought to a draw, if not to a decisive German victory.

It was, in fact, a decisive defeat for the Third Reich and a great victory for the Soviet Union, though not without cost. The Red Army did not release casualty figures during the war, though one reliable source has indicated that the Soviets suffered at least 80,188 killed and wounded during this particular operation.[7] Losses in tanks and self-propelled guns had also been particularly high, though the Soviet archives do not mention specific numbers. *1.Pz.Armee* and *8.Armee* claimed to have destroyed over 700 tanks during the course of the battle from 24 January to 18 February. This incredibly high figure is borne out by tallying daily totals listed in both armies' *Kriegstagebücher* for their two attacking corps as well as reports by *Gruppe Stemmermann*.

The damage to the eight Panzer divisions which took part in the relief effort would not be made good for a long time afterwards and they would be unprepared to face the next round of Soviet offensives which would take place in early March, when they would all be badly needed. The German relief forces had also probably lost from 20,000 to 25,000 men killed, wounded, and captured as well. Whatever the losses suffered by either side, the Red Army could replace theirs much faster, and, more importantly, it had achieved its operational goals - the elimination of the threat to the flank of First Ukrainian *Front* and destruction of the encircled forces. Though the Germans in the pocket had not been annihilated, they had been destroyed as effective fighting organizations.

How many German soldiers had survived the encirclement and the subsequent break out? The exact answer was not available for several days because survivors kept trickling into the assembly areas where *Gruppe Mattenklott* was reforming its units. *General Koll of 1.Pz.Div.* gave his best estimate on 18 February that some 30,000 men had broken out, and this figure was used by many others afterwards as the correct figure, but this was only an educated guess. As the days passed, the number continued to rise. Men who had been assumed dead or captured continued to show up at their units. Others who had temporarily taken up with other units outside of the pocket made their way back too in the days that followed.

By 29 February, enough information was available for General Mattenklott to tabulate the final human cost of the battle. Of approximately 60,000 men who had been encircled in January (including *Hiwis*), some 4,161 wounded had been flown out and 36,262 had broken out from 17-19 February, for a grand total of 40,423. Thus, a soldier's chances of surviving the pocket were roughly two out of three. Unfortunately, his chances of being killed or wounded were the same, since only 28,767 men came through without injury. Most of the wounded were evacuated further to the rear. After convalescence, most would rejoin their original regiments, which in the meantime had moved into Poland.

Shortly after the bulk of the survivors were assembled, it soon became evident that all of the shattered divisions would have to be moved further into the zone of the interior for rehabilitation and reconstitution. Additionally, none of them could be rebuilt with the stocks from Army Group South's depots - there simply was not enough to go around, not to mention the ever-increasing demands being placed upon the *O.Qu.* Therefore, on 20 February, Manstein decided to ship both *XI.* and *XXXXII. A.K.*, with *57., 72., 88., 389.Inf.Div.* and *K.Abt.B* to the Demba training area, located in the *General Gouvernement* (Poland).[8] *Wiking* was ordered to proceed to the Bergen training area, while the Walloon Brigade would proceed to the Wildflecken training area after a victory parade in Belgium. While these units would have a better chance of being rebuilt further to the west, they would no longer be under von Manstein's army group.

Gruppe Mattenklott would start loading for their rail journey to Poland on 23 February, at the earliest. In the meantime, Manstein decided to visit their assembly areas on 24 February. Accompanied by General Busse and his chief aide, *Oberst* von Merkel, the Field Marshal flew from his old headquarters at Proskurov to the airfield at Uman that morning, where he was met by Mattenklott and his staff. The group then proceeded by Volkswagen to Pomoinik, where 25 officers representing every unit that had been inside the pocket were assembled, as well as a group of enlisted men from *72.Inf.Div.* After speaking to the officers, Manstein presented awards for valor to both officers and men, then sat down to share a lunch prepared by one of the field kitchens that had made it out of the pocket. By 1300 hours, he was back on the road, returning to Proskurov at 1520 hours, where the situation on the army group's left wing had begun to deteriorate.[9] *4.Pz.Armee's XIII.A.K.* had been attacked near Rovno by an overwhelming Soviet force, requiring von Manstein's full attention.

While their units were being formed into *Gruppe Mattenklott*, Lieb, Gille, and Degrelle flew to Rastenburg after their conference at Uman aboard a Ju-52, arriving on the evening of 20 February. Here, the two SS officers were whisked away in a limousine to their accommodations by an escort provided by *Reichsführer-SS* Heinrich Himmler. Degrelle later recalled how out of place he felt, when he stated that "In the automobile which drove me from the airport I could feel hundreds of lice devouring my body. My uniform was filthy."[10] He was also still wearing the heavy felt winter boots he had worn during the breakout and his uniform was torn in several places. While he was led to a waiting hot bath, his first in months, a squad of SS men took his uniform from him and cleaned and mended it as best they could. Prior to dressing, Degrelle discovered that Himmler had presented him a gift of a new undershirt, since his old one was full of holes and lice-ridden. Thus refreshed, Degrelle and Gille joined Himmler for the 40 kilometer drive to Hitler's *Wolfschanze*.

Here, the group was led into the perimeter of the compound, illuminated by floodlights and heavily guarded. Once led inside the wooden meeting hall, the group was greeted by Hitler himself, who seized Degrelle's hand and said "I've been very worried about you." Degrelle's admiration for the *Führer* was not lessened by Hitler's frail appearance, in fact, it increased, since he credited it to the fact that Hitler's back was bent from "studying maps interminably and from bearing the weight of the world . . ."[11] It did not occur to the Walloon leader at the time that it was Hitler himself who was directly responsible for the destruction of his beloved brigade, since it was he who had decreed that the salient along the Dnieper be held at all costs.

Degrelle and Gille, now reunited with Lieb, were led to a large hall in the building, where Hitler presented the two generals with the Oak Leaves to their Knight's Crosses and Degrelle with his first award of the Knight's Cross. The award ceremony was immediately followed by a press conference which was broadcast live throughout Germany and the occupied areas as proof indeed that *Gruppe Stemmermann* had fought its way out of the Cherkassy Pocket and had not been destroyed, as the Soviets had claimed. Hitler's press chief, Dr. Otto Dietrich, allowed each of the three men to make a few prepared statements. In the glare of flashbulbs, they briefly related their experiences and how well their troops had fought, stressing repeatedly that the mass of the encircled troops had fought their way free.

Their appearance embarrassed the Soviet propaganda ministry, which had to adjust its official story in light of the fact that

Shortly afterwards, **Gille** *would be flown into the encircled town of Kovel in eastern Galicia, where he was tasked by the Führer to organize the defense of that town until a hurriedly assembled relief force could be rushed to rescue it. In this battle, units of Wiking would make up both the encircled force and relief force!*
(Photo by Adolf Salie courtesy of Willy Hein)

General Gille *and his entourage arrive in Lublin to confer awards to survivors of the breakout from the Wiking Division. To his right is the Division's First General Staff Officer (or 1a),* **Obersturmbannführer Mannfred Schoenfelder**.
(Photo by Adolf Salie courtesy of Willy Hein)

some Germans had indeed been able to make it out of the pocket. To explain this discrepancy, ministry officials then announced that a few thousand fanatical SS troops had broken out when General Gille led a tank attack that linked up with the relief force. Another Soviet explanation for their appearance in Rastenburg was that all three men had been flown out of the pocket, abandoning their men to die. General Konev also had to modify his original report, although it is unknown whether Stalin ever held his initial incorrect report against him. He probably did not, since he was promoted shortly thereafter. In the amended statement, Konev wrote:

> In carrying out your order, the troops of the Front on 17 February completely routed, destroyed and partially (emphasis added) captured the surrounded enemy grouping consisting of nine infantry divisions, one tank division, and one motorized brigade.[12]

Back in Rastenburg, a very much alive Theo Lieb found himself in the limelight. Perhaps carried away by the excitement and the media attention, Lieb, when asked who had made the decision to break out of the pocket, declared that he himself had done so on his own responsibility. This provoked an angry inquiry two days later by Manstein, who learned about the incident after hearing the interview on the *Deutsche Soldatensender* (German Armed Forces radio). The field marshal fired off a personal message on 22 February to Hube at *1.Pz.Armee* demanding that he set the record straight, since it was Manstein, through *8.Armee's* commander, who had made the decision to order a breakout.[13]

It was here perhaps where Lieb earned the sobriquet that would follow him wherever he went for the rest of his career - forever after, he would be known as the "Lion of Cherkassy." While it had probably been coined sarcastically, Lieb wore the

title as a badge of honor.[14] Who could deny that he had earned it, for had he not led the assault force that broke out of the encirclement? Despite the honors heaped upon him by Hitler and his superb handling of *XXXXII.A.K.*, Lieb was not selected to command a corps again, though he did command *34.Inf.Div.* along the Franco-Italian border from June to October 1944. The war's end found him holding a nominal assignment in northern Italy. Perhaps Manstein's wrath had shortened his career, perhaps Lieb had done so himself with his outspokenness; at any rate, fate was a great deal kinder to him than to Wilhelm Stemmermann.

While the ceremonies were ending at Rastenburg, *Gruppe Mattenklott* began entraining as scheduled on 23 February, starting with *Wiking's* remnants, soon followed by *K.Abt.B.* Over the next two weeks, nearly all of the units to be rebuilt shipped out with all of their remaining equipment - 547 horses, 116 wagons, 22 sleds, and 35 motor vehicles.[15] The remaining field pieces brought out by Kästner's regiment and a regiment from *Div.Grp.332* were given to other units of *1.Pz.Armee.* Additionally, there was a large number of horses and wagons, as well as a few trucks, belonging to service units left outside the pocket when it was formed, and which had since been serving temporarily with other units, such as *Gr. Haack*. These units with their equipment, most of which came from *88.* and *389.Inf. Div.*, would follow their divisions at a later date.

It took as many trains to move all of the shattered divisions to Poland as it took to move one full-strength infantry division, so great was the loss of vehicles and equipment. As to the divisions themselves, however, some had obviously suffered more than others, such as *389.Inf.Div.*, which had borne the brunt of Konev's initial offensive. Rather than disbanding such units, which may have been the more efficient course to follow, Hitler, as he had done after Stalingrad the year before, chose to rebuild all of those that had been encircled, except *K.Abt.B.* By doing so, he could show the world that while his units had been encircled, they had not been annihilated. While bloodied, they

Field Marshal von Manstein *talking to his troops of 72.Inf.Div. who have just escaped from the Cherkassy Pocket. To his left is his aide-de-camp,* **Oberst Merkel**. *(Brian L. Davis, "German Army Uniforms and Insignia 1933-45")*

Oberst Franz, *Chief of Staff of Lieb's XXXXII.Armeekorps, being interviewed on radio immediately after the breakout. (Paul Carell, "Der Russlandkrieg: Fotografiert von Soldaten, Ullstein Verlag, 1968")*

would soon be back in the German Army's order of battle, after they had incorporated thousands of replacement and returning wounded back into their ranks. There, all five of the remaining divisions would continue to give a good account of themselves for the remainder of their active field service.

General Kruse's division, which had been reduced to 1,932 men present for duty (including *Hiwis*) by 18 February 1944, was sent to the Milowitz training area in Czechoslovakia, where it absorbed the two grenadier regiments of *Schatten-Division Milowitz* (a so-called "shadow division") as well as an artillery battalion.* Considered completely rebuilt for front-line service, it was back in action again that summer with Army Group North. Surrounded in Courland with the rest of that Army Group in September 1944, it was later evacuated to Germany by sea. After several months of combat, the *Rheingold* Division was finally cut off on the Hela Peninsula and forced to surrender to the Soviets in April 1945. Kruse himself relinquished command of his division on 15 March and did not serve again in a command capacity until chosen to lead *Höhere Artilleriekommando 314*, an army-level artillery headquarters, on 10 March 1945.[16]

The Bavarian *57.Inf.Div.* suffered likewise. Reduced to an active strength of 2,950 men, its remnants were shipped to the Debica training area in Poland. Here, the attached *Gren.Rgt.676* was renamed *Gren.Rgt.164* and became an integral part of the division. Additionally, two artillery battalions from *Art.Rgt.86* from *Div.Gr.112* were incorporated into *Art.Rgt.157*, becoming its *I./* and *II./Abteilungen*, respectively. Certified as ready for combat, it was shipped once more to the East, and was assigned to Army Group Center. Here, during the great Soviet summer offensive of 1944, Operation Bagration, *57.Inf.Div.*, along with its commander, *Gen.Maj.* Adolf Trowitz, was encircled in the pocket near Mogilev along with most of *4.Armee* and forced to

capitulate. Only one battalion from *Gren.Rgt.217* was able to escape. It was temporarily incorporated into *K.Abt.C* before it was finally assigned to *299.Inf.Div.* in September 1944. Trowitz himself returned from Soviet captivity in 1955.

The Trier-Mosel *72.Inf.Div.* came out of the pocket with an effective strength of 3,815 men. Instead of being reconstituted at the Demba camp, it was sent instead to the Hrubieszov training area in Poland. Here, it was merged on 24 March with the *Division-Generalgouvernement*, a so-called *Walküre* (Valkyrie) division then forming in Poland.* Restored to its former authorized strength and led by officers such as *Oberst* Hohn (soon promoted to *Gen.Lt.*), Robert Kästner and Rudolf Siegel (both of whom were quickly promoted to *Oberstleutnant*), it performed creditably that summer in the Vistula bend battles. Smashed during the Soviet January 1945 breakout from the Vistula bridgehead, the division was back in action in March, finally falling into Soviet captivity in May 1945.

The Bavarian-Austrian *88.Inf.Div.* was rebuilt in Demba, incorporating various *Divisions-Gruppen* that had been in the pocket into its ranks. *Div.Gr.323* was dissolved and its personnel used to fill out the division's other battalions. A new *Gren.Rgt.246* was supposed to have raised, but instead the decision was made to incorporate *Oberst* Viebig's *Div.Gr.112* into a new regiment instead. This regiment was created by the merging of *Hptm.* Burgfeld's *Rgt.Gr 258* and Ernst Schenk's *Rgt.Gr.110*, and re-titled *Gren.Rgt.110*, commanded by Viebig. The division was assigned to Army North Ukraine's reconstituted *XXXXII.A.K.* along with *72.Inf.Div.*, fighting side-by-side with Hohn's troops during the Vistula bend battles. *Gen.Lt. Graf* Rittberg led the division until it was smashed in January 1945 during the Soviet breakout from the Baranov bridgehead, a blow from which it never recovered. The remnants

---

* *Schatten-Divisionen* were an experiment in creating replacement divisions without rear services. They were intended to be absorbed by burnt-out divisions since experience showed that rear services often remained intact relative to the combat unit. (Source: Tessin)

* *Walküre* was a code word used in the Replacement Army for the emergency mobilization of new divisions. Typically, each *Wehrkreis* was tasked to provide a battalion or even a regiment from its manpower in training. Units formed from this program were intended to be used against unrest at home or in occupied territories. (Source: Tessin)

were then incorporated into several *Kampfgruppen*, which were eventually forced to surrender to the Soviets.

K.Abt.B was completely disbanded on 10 March and its 5,213 survivors scattered. *Div.Gr.112*, as previously mentioned, was assigned to *88.Inf.Div. Div.Gr.255* and *332*, with *Rgt.Gr. 465, 475, 677* and *678* were amalgamated with other units and their numbers stricken from the rolls. Only *Rgt.Gr.676* lived on, incorporated in *57.Inf.Div.* as *Gren.Rgt.164*. Several other remaining battalions or companies were renumbered and assigned to the Balkans. Today, however, no veteran's organization from any of these three *Divisionsgruppen* remain - it is as if 10,000 men had disappeared from the pages of history without a trace, with Cherkassy as their only epitaph.

Of all of the divisions trapped in the Cherkassy Pocket, none did more than any other to ensure the continued survival of *Gruppe Stemmermann* than *5.SS-Pz.Div. Wiking*. Whether at Steblev or Olshana, Ossitnyashka or Shanderovka, the men, tanks, and half-tracks of *Wiking* seemed to have been everywhere. As the pocket's only truly mobile force, its regiments and battalions, particularly its tank battalion, counterattacked and shored up one crumbling sector of the pocket, only to have to march dozens of kilometers to do the same at another location on the opposite side.

While some of its battalions performed marginally, on balance the division performed feats of arms which constantly threw back Soviet attacks while inflicting great loss to the enemy. It also suffered the highest casualty rate of any unit inside the pocket as well, escaping on 17/18 February with only 8,278 men out of the 14,000 men who had filled out its ranks at the end of January. Only *389.Inf.Div.* lost more men, though most of these losses were suffered during the initial stages of the Soviet offensive. *Wiking* also lost all of its tanks, artillery, and other armored vehicles. In terms of *Reichmarks*, its losses were the most expensive and difficult to replace, in contrast to the infantry divisions, which were chiefly equipped with horse-drawn vehicles and guns.

Initially ordered to the Bergen training area in Germany to be rebuilt, its men were dismayed to learn on 4 March that they would be proceeding to Lublin instead of Bergen. Men who had been promised leave in Germany, some of whom had not been home in over three years, had their hopes dashed when they learned that they would proceed no farther, except for Germanic volunteers and the wounded. Those who had already departed on leave before the order reached them were stopped at rail stations in Silesia and brought back to Lublin. Here, the division struggled to rebuild, but was unable to make much headway due to the almost complete lack of replacement equipment. Thus occupied, the division staff was surprised to receive a call from *OKW* ordering them to prepare a *Kampfgruppe* to be ready to depart for Kovel immediately. Gille immediately flew to Kovel aboard a Fiesler Storch to carry out an estimate of the situation.

The garrison of Kovel, an important railway junction on the edge of the Pripet marshes between Army Groups South and Center, had been threatened with encirclement by the rapid approach of a Soviet offensive timed to take advantage of operations occurring farther south involving *1.Pz.Armee*. Should it fall, the lines of communication between the two army groups

would be severed, necessitating a detour of several hundred kilometers. Consequently, Gille was ordered to proceed to Kovel immediately with the bulk of *Germania* and *Westland*, while the rest of *Wiking* would be given time to rebuild. For the weary SS men who had only just escaped from the Cherkassy Pocket, it would only be more of the same.

Gille and his men defended the six-kilometer-square fortress of Kovel from 15 March to 6 April 1944 before they were relieved by elements of their division who had not been in the pocket at all - *I./SS-Pz.Rgt.5*, equipped with brand-new Panthers, and *III./SS-Pz.Gren.Rgt. Germania*, equipped with half-tracks. These units had been forming in the west during the battle; their first action involved freeing members of their own division in Kovel. Finally, the survivors of the Kovel garrison were allowed to rejoin their division, receiving their long over-due leaves, though many survivors of Cherkassy perished in the bitter fighting for the desolate railway town.

Wiking fought for the remainder of the war in the East, most prominently in Galicia and Poland during the summer and autumn of 1944, where it helped stop the great Soviet summer offensive at the gates of Warsaw. It took part in the abortive relief of Budapest in December 1944, as well as another attempt in January 1945. Nearly surrounded in the desperate battle of Stuhlweissenburg during Germany's final offensive in the East, it surrendered to the Americans in Austria in May 1945. Regarded by the Soviets as a tough and dangerous opponent, *Wiking* earned an enviable reputation among its peers in the *Waffen-SS*.

It is a singular fact that, unlike several other better-known SS divisions, it was one of the few SS divisions that fought on the Eastern Front that was not charged by the Soviets with a variety of war crimes. Its commander, Herbert Gille, went on to command the *IV.SS-Pz.Korps*, comprising *Wiking* as well as the *Totenkopf* divisions, proving that he could command a corps as ably as he had a division. Certainly, nothing could be more difficult than that day along the Gniloy Tikich on 17 February 1944, when he tried to organize a crossing for thousands of desperate, frightened men.

Of the various corps troops, only 1,474 from both *XI.* and *XXXXII.A.K.* were reported as being fit for duty. Indeed, most of the casualties incurred during the breakout came from the various service and support units who were incapable of resisting Soviet tank and cavalry attacks. While *XI.A.K.* was sent to the Demba training area to be reconstituted and to receive a new corps commander, *XXXXII.A.K.*, after a brief rest near Przemsyl in Galicia, was thrown into battle once again on 18 March, where it led several understrength divisions involved in the relief of Kovel, including the newly-raised armored *Kampfgruppe* from *Wiking*.

As for the Walloon Brigade, its remaining 632 members, all that remained of the 2,000-strong organization that had arrived along the Dnieper in November of the previous year, were shipped by rail to Belgium via Wildflecken, where the Belgian collaborationist government had arranged a series of homecoming parades for them. Degrelle led the procession through the city of Charleroi on 1 April at the helm of an armored half-track on loan from the *12.SS-Pz.Div. Hitlerjugend*, which was stationed nearby. Following this appearance, the brigade made a triumphal procession through the streets of Brussels, where high-ranking German and Belgian officials, including Sepp Dietrich, the *Leibstandarte's* former commander, reviewed them from the steps of the Bourse, the Belgian stock exchange. Degrelle then began a round of speaking engagements in Belgium and France designed to drum up support for the collaborationist governments in both countries and to draw more recruits into the ranks of his formation. After being granted generous furloughs, the men of the brigade were ordered to report to the Wildflecken training area in Germany at the end of April to begin the brigade's reformation.

After several months, it was then sent to Estonia during the summer of 1944, where it took part in the epic battle of Narva, where the multinational *III.SS-Pz.Korps*, consisting of Walloons, Dutch, Danes, and Norwegians, fought a series of pitched engagements against the Red Army. In October 1944, the brigade was upgraded to a division (at least on paper), and renamed *28.SS-Freiwilligen-Gren.Div. Wallonien*. Many convalescing veterans, such as Fernand Kaisergruber, requested to be returned to duty with their comrades. The Walloon Division was finally destroyed by the Soviets in Pomerania during the latter half of April 1945. Degrelle, who rose to the rank of *SS-Standartenführer*, escaped captivity and trial for treason by fleeing to Spain aboard a He-111, where he learned that his native country had condemned him to death in absentia. Here, he continued to write and support his former troops who were forced to endure years of incarceration and privation by the post-war Belgian government.

While *Wiking* was soon back in action in Kovel, one unit had even harder luck. Not only were the four battalions from *213.Sich.Div.* - two from *Sich.Rgt.318* and two from *Sich.Rgt.177* - not designated to go to a training area to be rebuilt, but their 442 survivors were ordered to march to rejoin the rest of their division, then involved in heavy fighting in *4.Pz.Armee's* sector near Luboml. After assembling in Uman, the survivors were linked up with elements of both regiments that had been caught outside of the pockets, bringing their total number to 1,150 men. *Oberst* Erich Mielke, the actual commander of *Sich.Rgt.318* who had also been with the rest of the division at Luboml, was ordered on 18 February to proceed immediately to the Uman area in order to supervise the movement of both regiments.

After a brief period of reorganization, Mielke and his men started for Luboml on 7 March in two columns. The northern one, under the command of *Oberstlt*. Dr. Bloch, consisting of the infantry, marched westward along a route which led parallel to the front, while the wheeled vehicle column under Mielke took a more southerly route. The following day, the remaining 24 motor vehicles were forced to a halt near Teplik on account of an enormous traffic jam. Mielke dismounted from his staff car and proceeded in a halftrack to the front of the column. Finding no one in charge, he directed traffic for several hours. Hundreds of trucks and *panje* wagons were jammed nose to tail for miles and his efforts had little effect.

With the traffic finally moving again, Mielke and his remaining vehicles were stopped two days later by the sound of heavy fighting near the village of Pogoreloye. A few hundred meters ahead, the convoy had been stopped by Soviet tanks, infantry, and antitank guns. Mielke assembled a small force of perhaps 100 drivers armed only with rifles and pistols. This small force was soon put to flight by the enemy, which was present in at least battalion size. In frustration, Mielke watched as the drivers in the convoy abandoned their vehicles and began running away to the west across the open field. Most of the hundreds of vehicles in their column were soon in flames, as T-34s rode up and down the *Rollbahn* machine-gunning and crushing cars and trucks. Mielke himself was forced to flee, catching a ride to Bershad, where he hoped to link up with his other marching column.

At about the same time, the great Soviet offensive designed to trap *1.Pz.Armee* involving First and Third Ukrainian *Fronts* had begun, cutting Mielke off from the rest of his men for good. While Mielke and several hundred thousand men were soon part of another wandering pocket, the so-called *Hube-Kessel*, the rest of his regiment and *Sich.Rgt.177* were redirected through *4.Pz.Armee's* sector after enduring several weeks of heaving fighting in the Trans-Dniester and Bukovina regions. Their whereabouts remained unknown to Army Group South for several weeks, though they were finally located in April 1944 near the town of Sokal 120 kilometers miles north of Lemberg in Poland. In the interim, Mielke was severely wounded, and evacuated to Germany. After their ordeal, the home guardsmen were finally allowed their well-earned rest, though their division was back in action that summer with Army Group Center, where it was eventually destroyed in August.[17]

The men of First and Second Ukrainian *Fronts* also drew a brief reprieve, though it was to be much shorter than that enjoyed by the German survivors of the encirclement. Both *Fronts* were brought back up to strength not only in troops, but in tanks, artillery, and other equipment. Without the German salient between them, they could now work in close cooperation. After a three week lull, the Soviet forces began a subsequent operation in mid-march whose goal was to drive the Germans out of the Ukraine forever.

The Red Army's Korsun-Shevchenkovsky Operation was a success in more ways than one. Not only had it forced Manstein to use up the rest of his armor, it had caused Army Group South's front to become dangerously overextended. The gap caused by the loss of two experienced infantry corps could not be made good. Hitler continued to insist that von Manstein and Army Group A to his south hold on to every square inch of Ukrainian soil. This would bring about the collapse of the German front in the Ukraine, the temporary encirclement of *1.Pz.Armee*, the destruction of *17.Armee* in the Crimea, and the advance of the Red Army to the Rumanian border in April 1944.

The Battle of Cherkassy had also validated Red Army encirclement doctrine. Not only had the forces of Konev, Zhukov, and Vatutin successfully encircled a large grouping of German forces, they had fought to a standstill a powerful relief force consisting of eight of Hitler's best panzer divisions. Generals and historians could argue about the number of Germans who had escaped. The important thing was that the Red Army had fought the best the Germans had on nearly even terms and had won. The battle had also taught Soviet commanders the importance of not underestimating their opponent. The *Wehrmacht* would still be able to deal powerful blows against its opponents as late as April 1945, but it would never again be triumphant.

Zhukov and Konev benefited as well. Following the operation, Konev was promoted to the rank of Marshal of the Soviet Union, the highest rank in the Red Army and went on to become one of Stalin's most capable and ambitious commanders. Zhukov temporarily assumed command of Vatutin's *Front* when the latter was killed by Ukrainian nationalist partisans in late March 1944. Both Zhukov and Konev went on to greater successes during the summer of 1944, when their *Fronts* helped crush Army Group Center and in the race towards Berlin, when their rivalry reached its wartime climax.

A fitting epitaph to the Battle of Cherkassy was provided by *Uffz.* Gerhard Mayer from *Art.Rgt.188*. After surviving the breakout and the subsequent march to the assembly areas near Uman, Mayer and his comrades were elated to receive the rations that had been undeliverable during the encirclement. In the Ukrainian village where they were quartered, the gaunt survivors of his regiment were able to gorge on food they had not eaten for weeks - sausage, bread, cheese, and marmalade. They were able to draw four times their normal coffee and tobacco ration, and stuffed themselves for several days.They also received gifts from the Reich's administrator of the Ukraine in the form of candy, beer, schnapps, wine, and a variety of other luxury items. Best of all, Mayer was elated to hear that he had been awarded a 21 day furlough. His luck improved even more, when he was told that he would go home on the first train. Less than three months after his previous furlough, he was going home again.

Laden like a pack animal with food - eggs, sardines, tinned meat, cigarettes and *Schoko-Kola* - he made his way to the railway station in Uman and was soon on his way. His sole burden was a suitcase carrying personal items for *Ltn.* Pfortner that he had promised to deliver to his home in Germany. As compensation, he was allowed to board a first-class compartment in Cracow, where he was also ordered to undergo the mandatory delousing before entering Germany proper. He considered this a waste of delousing spray, since he was not infested - evidently, he wrote later, his lice had all either frozen to death or had drowned in the Gniloy Tikich!

Upon arrival at his home near Heilbronn, Mayer's family was overjoyed, since they had given him up for dead. They had been listening to Radio London and believed the report that everyone who had been in the Cherkassy Pocket had either been killed or captured. After celebrating his return with his family and some old friends, he then checked into *Wannentalkaserne*, the barracks in Heilbronn where field artillerymen of his regiment were required to report while on home leave. As a "Cherkassy Hero," he quickly found that he had become an object of interest and sympathy to his military superiors and peers, who constantly badgered him to tell his version of the battle. Since his uniform was worn out, he used his hoard of cigarettes to acquire a new one, complete with mountain cap, ski trousers and a field blouse with newly attached NCO braid on the collar.

Thus attired, he began to enjoy his hard-earned leave. But he was not allowed to enjoy it the way he had planned; instead of spending time by himself or with his family, he found himself besieged everywhere he went by those curious to know what had the Battle of Cherkassy been like. After a visit to his old civilian firm, he stopped by his old haunt, *Kaffee Schmieg*, for a cup of coffee and was immediately surrounded by former associates who begged him to "tell it like it was."

He felt that he had no choice but to adhere to the official version of events as broadcast by the *Wehrmachtsbericht*, since it at least was more factual that the accounts being reported by civilian newspapers and radio stations, which were blatant misrepresentations of what had occurred. Nor could he tell them the unvarnished truth, since this could be misinterpreted as "defeatism," a crime in Nazi Germany. Judging by what he had heard on the radio, which was broadcasting *Schönfäberei* (fairly tales) about the battle, Mayer thought that one could gain the impression that Army Group South had inflicted a tremendous blow to the Soviets and was now on the march towards Moscow. What had really happened to him and the others in Shanderovka, in Lysyanka, and in the valley of the Gniloy Tikich was something, he thought, that he could never tell his old friends around the *Stammtisch*. They would never understand or believe him. The only one he felt that he could tell the truth to was his father, and then only in bits and pieces. Although he was one of the lucky ones, the Battle of the Cherkassy Pocket was the most terrible thing that he had ever experienced. Like thousands of other survivors, the trauma of those three weeks along the Dnieper remained with him for the rest of his life.[18]

End Notes

[1] Degrelle, p. 227.

[2] Sokolov, p. 91.

[3] Werth, pp. 781-782.

[4] Erickson, p. 179.

[5] Buchner, p. 69.

[6] Ibid.

[7] Glantz, David and House, Jonathan. *When Titans Clashed: How the Red Army Stopped Hitler.* (Lawrence, Kansas: University Press of Kansas, 1995), p. 298.

[8] Oberkommando, Heeresgruppe Süd, an Pz.AOK. 1, *Neugliederung und Auffrischung der Gen.Kdos. Roem. 11. Und Roem. 42. A.K. mit unterstellten Verbände,* 1950 hours 20 February 1944.

[9] Heeresgruppe Süd an Pz.AOK.1, *Zeitplan für Besuch des Oberbefehlhabers bei 1.Pz.Armee,* 1245 hours 23 February 1944.

[10] Degrelle, p. 225.

[11] Ibid, p. 226.

[12] *Voyenno-Istoricheskiy Zhurnal,* No. 2 "Documents on Korsun-Shevchenkovsky Given," (Moscow: Voyenno-Istoricheskiy Zhurnal, Feb. 1984), p. 40.

[13] Radio message, Heeresgruppe Süd Nr. 936/44 G.Kdos., Generalfeldmarschall von Manstein an Oberbefehlshaber der 1.Panzer Armee, dated 1850 hours 22 February 1944.

[14] Letter from Dr. Georg Meyer, *Militärgeschichtliches Forschungsamt,* Freiburg, Germany to author, 13 May 1996.

[15] *Abschlussmeldung,* Gruppe Mattenklott an Pz.AOK. 1, 2000 hours 3 March 1944.

[16] Numbers of survivors for each division is found in Gruppe Mattenklott's closing report, Meldung Gruppe Mattenklott, *Stärken der Truppenteile,* dated 1740 hours 29 February 1944. Information on division's subsequent histories is found in Samuel Mitcham Jr.'s *Hitler's Legions: The German Army Order of Battle, World War II.* (New York: Stein and Day, 1985).

[17] Kommandeur, Sich.Rgt. 318 an Pz.AOK.1, *Versammlung und Inmarschsetzung der Sich.Rgter 177 und 318 zur Sich.Div.213,* Orts-Unterkünft, 21 March 1944, pp. 1-2.

[18] Mayer manuscript, pp. 153-154.

EPILOGUE

"Cherkassy was no military victory—but was not our salvation from certain destruction a kind of victory?"
—Wiking veterans association, 1963 [1]

Both sides claimed victory in the aftermath of the Battle of the Cherkassy Pocket. The Germans claimed a victory (though a Pyrrhic one, at best) because they had extricated the bulk of the encircled corps' manpower. The Soviet Union, for its part, claimed that not a man had escaped. In fact, it was a significant Soviet operational and tactical victory. Two German corps had been shattered. All their equipment lay abandoned on the battlefield. The Red Army claimed to have killed over 55,000 Germans and to have captured another 18,000, although it later admitted that a few had managed to escape. The Red Army inflicted heavy casualties upon the German relief force as well, claiming later to have knocked out over 500 German tanks of the encircled units and the relief columns.[2] Although this number, too, was exaggerated, *XXXXVII.Pz.Korps* was reduced to an empty shell and *III.Pz.Korps* was crippled as an effective offensive force. Both sides had suffered nearly equally in terms of men killed, wounded, and missing - approximately 60,000 to 80,000 men each.

But what was more significant than these casualty figures, as impressive as they are, was the fact that the flanks of First and Second Ukrainian *Fronts* were now secure and that the remaining German armored forces in Army Group South had been crippled. This weakening of Manstein's panzer divisions, combined with Hitler's continued insistence on holding ground at all cost (despite the demonstrated failure of this doctrine during the Battle of Cherkassy), made the subsequent Soviet clearing of the Ukraine relatively easy. Launched on 4 March 1944, the Proskurov-Chernovtsy Operation had forced the *1.Pz.* and *8.Armee* out of the Ukraine by 30 March.[3] Although an ambitious encirclement scheme was attempted, both German armies managed to escape to the west, due in part to the serious depletion of Soviet armor strength in the Cherkassy battle. By 17 April 1944, all German forces had been cleared from the Ukraine and Black Sea coast, and the Red Army stood on the Rumanian border.

The Battle of Cherkassy made this and other subsequent operations possible. The Soviet victory flowed from a number of factors. First, as mentioned in the second chapter, force ratio trends had begun to favor the Soviet Union. The overall quality of their equipment had also improved substantially. The mobility of the Red Army was superior, due in part to its fleet of Lend-Lease trucks. Increasing reliance on massive artillery preparations along narrow frontages was beginning to make up for the shortage of infantry. Evolving operational and tactical

Reverse slope of Hill 239 today, looking downhill towards Lysyanka. Schw.Pz.Rgt. Bäke tried several times to get its Tigers up this slope, but each time was driven back down by dozens of attacking Soviet tanks. (Photo by author)

doctrine, coupled with more experienced commanders and staff, had begun to equal the German's level of effectiveness, which had declined. Hitler's stand-fast decree also helped the Red Army achieve success, because it forced the Germans to fight the kind of battles they could not win with the meager resources available during the third year of war with the Soviet Union. In nearly every category, the Red Army was becoming increasingly powerful. Against this, even German operational mastery, as practiced by Manstein, could only delay the inevitable.

The Soviet plan, though not brilliant, was thoroughly prepared and adequately executed. Although the situation offered the opportunity to fight a set-piece battle of encirclement á la Stalingrad, Zhukov and the *Front* commanders amassed the force ratios required to quickly encircle and eliminate the German grouping within three weeks. This departure contrasted with Stalingrad, where nearly three months were required to wipe out the encircled *6.Armee*. A combination of dense grouping of attacking forces, massive artillery preparations, and two tank armies launching deep attacks practically guaranteed success, at least on paper. An ambitious deception operation, coupled with diversionary attacks, was designed to mislead the Germans as to the actual date, location, and size of the attack. Although this aspect of the plan was not as successful as hoped, the number of Soviet forces employed did succeed in surprising the Germans.

*View of Gniloy Tikich today, looking north from bridge at Lysyanka. Many men crossed the creek using felled trees like this one.
(Photo by author)*

The offensive phase of the operation, launched with great vigor, quickly succeeding in encircling the Germans in the Kanev salient. Efforts to split up the pocket failed, as the encircled forces rapidly formed an all-round defense and warded off Red Army attempts to break in. Hitler's stand-fast order helped the Soviets, since it prevented the encircled forces from withdrawing from the Dnieper River line and attacking to link up with the German relief force. The Germans, for their part, reacted quickly and organized a powerful force designed to restore contact with the forces in the salient as well as to encircle and destroy the besieging Soviet forces.

Each side continued to feed more troops into the battle, especially armored formations. As force ratios inside and outside the pocket gradually became equal, weather intervened to slow the tempo of operations on both sides, forcing the combat to degenerate into a slugging match. Finally, when it became apparent that the relief force could not penetrate into the pocket, the encircled forces broke out through a ring of Soviet armor. Despite panic and confusion, as well as frightful loss of life, the bulk of the entrapped Germans, some 36,000 men, fought their way to freedom. The individual soldiers of both sides proved without a doubt that they were capable of awesome feats of dedication and bravery. But other than this, what had the operation proven?

Examination of the planning and execution of the battle plan reveals many elements of Soviet operational design that were to become standard for the remainder of the war and echo opera-

tional concepts which are practiced by many other armed forces of the world even today. Most notable were the Red Army's use of deep attacks by armored forces, deception operations, diversionary attacks, echelonment in depth, and the use of artillery to create the conditions for a tactical breakthrough. The battle also witnessed application of Soviet tactical aviation in support of ground operations. Not all of these operational elements were executed effectively, though they were tried with varying degrees of success. The deep attack by the two tank armies that carried out the initial encirclement was extremely well executed.

Without regard to their flanks, Rotmistrov's and Kravchenko's spearheads were used to punch a hole in the German defenses and penetrate into the German operational depths, cutting the lines of communication to the two corps in the salient. Previously, Soviet armor had been reluctant to attack deep without close cooperation with advancing infantry formations. Using armor to punch a hole was also a departure from previous experience, since the infantry armies, with tank support, usually did this. At Cherkassy, infantry armies lacked their own organic armor support, proving that they no longer possessed the power to create the initial penetration by themselves. This use of armor to create its own penetrations violated the stereotype, thereby confusing and surprising the German defenders, who were accustomed to Soviet armor keeping pace with the infantry.

During the battle, the Soviets constantly sought to force the Germans to conform to the Red Army's operational plan, often with great success. The Red Army's commanders and units dis-

Author and Fernand Kaisergruber, veteran of the Walloon Brigade and survivor of the breakout, pose in front of a Joseph Stalin II. In the background is the palace which houses the collection of battlefield artifacts. Used as a field hospital during the war, it was badly damaged but has been restored since. (Photo by author)

played considerable agility throughout this operation, as demonstrated by their ability to rapidly shift operational reserves, the tank armies and corps, from one axis to another. Rapid concentration of these forces astride the path of the German relief effort caused it to culminate, or reach its peak, just several kilometers short of the encircled forces, leaving them no choice but to break out on their own at great cost.

The deception plan practiced by General Konev was very ambitious and would have worked had his troops been sufficiently trained and disciplined to carry it out. Its failure led the Germans to anticipate the time and place of the attack. This failure also gave the Germans time to move mobile reserves to the area, which significantly slowed the creation of the Soviet's outer encirclement ring. For subsequent operations, the Red Army perfected its use of operational *maskirovka*, as demonstrated by its overwhelming success during Operation Bagration during June to July 1944, when strategic and operational surprise were achieved, contributing directly to the annihilation of Army Group Center.

During the Battle of Cherkassy, the diversionary attacks, poorly synchronized, allowed the Germans to divine the true Soviet intention, which was the encirclement and destruction of the German corps in the Kanev salient. The diversionary attacks launched by the First and Second Ukrainian *Fronts* were either easily warded off by the Germans or dealt with by yielding ground in the face of encirclement, as *6.Armee* had done in the Nikopol area. Thus, Manstein was able to move his armor freely

without having to worry about another serious attack. Subsequent diversionary operations launched by the Soviets during the summer of 1944 were planned and executed so thoroughly that the Germans believed they were main efforts or initial phases of a main effort. These diversions caused Hitler and the *OKH* to focus their attention on where they believed the next attack would take place rather than the actual location.

Examples of the use of diversionary attacks were the attacks against Finland and the clearing operation in the Crimea, both of which occurred in May 1944. These attacks caused the Germans to believe that the main effort for the summer of 1944 would occur either in the south Ukraine, or further to the north, where Army Group North was threatened by an attack to pin it against the Baltic. The unforeseen offensive against Army Group Center resulted in complete strategic and operational surprise, leading to the total destruction of German forces in Byelorussia.

The Battle of Cherkassy also saw a further refinement in the Red Army's use of echelonment in depth. Here, vast stretches of the Soviet front line were nearly denuded of troops, enabling the First and Second Ukrainian *Fronts* to build up staggering force ratios with divisions closely echeloned behind one another. This echelonment applied especially to the tank armies, whose positioning of tank and mechanized corps allowed Soviet commanders to continually feed fresh units into battle, thus maintaining the attack's tempo. Faulty or delayed commitment of these echelons often led to gaps or loss of momentum, which the Germans exploited whenever possible.

Fernand Kaisergruber holding the cane purported to be that of General Wilhelm Stemmermann, on display at the Battle of Korsun-Shevchenkovsky Museum. (Photo by author)

In Operation Bagration, the echelonment of forces, especially tank and mechanized corps, was handled extremely well, permitting Field Marshal Wilhelm Busch's Army Group Center no breathing space whatsoever, an indicator that Soviet staffs had become very competent in this complex type of operation. Subsequent developments also indicated that the Red Army had perfected the command and control techniques required to mount such operations. During their Cherkassy offensive, the commitment of the First and Second Tank Armies into the flanks and path of the German relief attack during the latter part of the operation surprised the Germans and indicated that the Red Army was attaining an ability already possessed by the Germans.

The use of artillery to blast a narrow hole through the German defenses, followed by the commitment of tank formations to exploit the gap, was also used with great success during the battle. The inability of the Soviet artillery, however, to keep up with the advancing tank and mechanized formations, mainly due to the poor conditions of the road network, led to accusations that a scarcity of artillery prevented the quick dispatch of the encircled German forces. This shortcoming would be dealt with in the future by devoting more attention and resources to the preparation of the fire support aspect of operations. More engineer and transportation assets, as well as more time to carry out preparations, would also occur in subsequent operations.

The support provided by Soviet tactical aviation during the battle was not very effective. Lack of coordination meant that most air support was planned independently of ground operations and was wasted on shooting up German supply routes in the pocket rather than concentrating on German defensive positions or attacking armored spearheads of the relief force. Soviet tactical aviation could have been used to augment deep attacks against relief forces with attacks of its own, but the air effort was poorly integrated into the operational plan.

These tactical air assets, had they attacked in depth to shatter the German relief operation or the command and control nexus at Uman, might have brought the Battle of the Cherkassy Pocket to a rapid conclusion. In future operations, Soviet tactical aviation would be more closely integrated into the ground operation. During Operation Bagration, for example, German survivors recounted numerous instances of front line positions being obliterated by well-executed air attacks and of their tank columns being ravaged by air attack as they tried to stop the Soviet advance through Byelorussia.[4]

Finally, one last lesson was relearned during the course of the battle. Because the Soviets had underestimated German capabilities, the Red Army failed to roll back the German main defensive line during the course of the encirclement. This lack of foresight eased the Germans' task considerably, in that the distance from the new front line near Uman, the direction from which *III.Pz.Korps* would launch its relief attack, was only 40 kilometers from the pocket. Although it was a hard 40 kilometers, the Germans got close enough to Stemmerman's beleaguered force so that his troops were able to fight their way through. This development contrasted with Stalingrad, where the relief column had to fight its way through over 150 kilometers of Soviet defenses and never got closer than 50 kilometers to Paulus' army.

Zhukov's failure to repeat his performance at Stalingrad, where he had also been Stalin's *STAVKA* representative, is inexplicable, leading the historian to conclude that Zhukov thought the offensive would attain its goals quickly. As a result, far more effort was devoted to annihilating the Germans in the Kanev salient *do kontsa* than was desirable. The spearheads of Rotmistrov and Kravchenko should have kept pushing the German front line further back. The fact that they did not do so gave the Germans the breathing space they needed to hurriedly assemble a relief effort.

Although the Soviets did not strike as deeply as they could and should have, the attack by the two tank armies towards their link-up point at Zvenigorodka, even while disregarding their flanks, proved that the Soviets had judged the most vulnerable part of the German defenses correctly. The seizure of this town not only caused the collapse of the German front line in the Dnieper Bend, but nearly brought about the rapid dissolution of the encircled German forces. Only skillful leadership by Generals Lieb and Stemmerman, as well as the slowness of the Soviet infantry armies, allowed the Germans to create an all-around defense in the pocket.

All of these shortcomings slowed the execution of the operation and permitted the Germans time to recover their balance. However, once the German relief attack had commenced, Zhukov, Konev, and Vatutin were able to quickly organize a defense that integrated all of the available Red Army combat elements and coordinated their actions. This effort worked to a great degree. Although the opposing armor force ratios became nearly equal, the two German panzer corps could not break through, despite the fact that they destroyed two to three times the number of tanks that they lost. Even Soviet tactical aviation was used effectively to illuminate the battlefield with incendiary bombs during the course of the German breakout on the night of 16/17 February.

In subsequent operations, the Red Army would push far deeper with its tank and mechanized formations into the German's operational depths, leaving the reduction of any remaining enemy pockets to the following infantry armies. This was amply demonstrated during Operation Bagration, when tank, mechanized, and cavalry corps focused strictly on carrying out their assigned deep attacks. Not only would this disrupt the German defenses, it would continually unbalance any relief effort that the Germans could assemble because they would be frittered away trying to shore up a crumbling front line rather than be used for a concentrated attack to rescue any encircled units.

The growing versatility of the Red Army was proven during this battle beyond a doubt. Though this attribute had been a hallmark of previous German operations, the Soviets also demonstrated their ability to shift forces rapidly, tailor them to circumstances, and switch from one role or mission to another rapidly and efficiently. The transition of the 5th Guards Tank Army from the deep attack to a deliberate defense near Zvenigorodka in the path of the attacking *XXXXVII.Pz.Korps* is a case in point.

Thus, it can be said that the result of the Battle of Cherkassy, from the Soviet perspective, was significant because it validated their emerging operational concepts, taught new ones, and allowed the Red Army to perfect techniques during subsequent operations in the summer of 1944 which would witness the Red Army's complete strategic and operational mastery over the *Wehrmacht*. Many of these operational concepts still apply today and deserve closer study by Western military professionals, since encirclement operations and the search for a modern battle of Cannae remain prominent features in contemporary military history and thought.

While the Red Army gained a great deal of experience in the conduct of large-scale mechanized operations during this battle, the Germans were unable to profit from many of the lessons they had learned themselves. Zhukov, Konev and Vatutin clearly believed that the Germans would not be able to react quickly enough to the encirclement to be able to respond decisively. By the time the Germans had gathered sufficient forces to relieve their encircled corps, so the Soviets thought, it would be too late for them to do anything about it. Here, they were clearly wrong. During the Battle of the Cherkassy Pocket, the Red Army again underestimated German capabilities, still formidable even during the third year of the Russo-German War.

Manstein correctly read the true nature of the diversionary attacks and threw everything he had into the relief attempt. Furthermore, he flatly disregarded Hitler's order to attack towards Kiev, concentrating instead on the bulk of the Soviet forces attacking the pocket. It would be an interesting exercise

to see how the German relief attack would have fared had the weather been more cooperative. Stalin and his marshals were right to be greatly concerned by Manstein's Operation Wanda, which forced Stalin at least on one occasion to personally intervene in the conduct of operations.

Fortunately for the Soviets, Manstein would be relieved of command by Hitler on 30 March 1944 and replaced by Field Marshal Walter Model, who assumed command of a now-renamed Army Group North Ukraine. However, despite Model's considerable talent as a tactical improviser, his formidable willpower, and his good relations with the *Führer*, he could accomplish very little against an enemy who had the initiative everywhere. By the summer of 1944 German tactical and operational expertise had become irrelevant in the face of growing Soviet superiority in numbers, equipment, and operational expertise. Even Manstein would have been hard pressed to redress the balance.

The *Ostheer* also lost once of its last truly effective army commanders when *Gen.O.* Hans Hube was killed when his Ju-52 crashed 21 April 1944 on its return flight from Hitler's residence at Obersalzberg. He had only just received the Diamonds to his Knight's Cross the previous day from Hitler for *1.Pz.Armee's* performance at Cherkassy and the recently concluded breakout from the *Hubekessel*. This offensive sought to entrap and destroy Hube's Army and to drive the Germans from the remainder of Ukrainian soil they still occupied. After several tense weeks, Hube was able to break out of the pocket near the town of Buchach, bringing out all of his men and most of his equipment. With the death of one of Germany's last practitioners of operational-level mechanized warfare, the Soviets would find their task during the summer of 1944 much easier.

Besides Hitler's sacking of one of his most talented subordinates, the Soviets benefited from other actions of Hitler's. His stand-fast decree had been further augmented by the *Festung* or fortified locality concept, which carried the stand-fast doctrine to its ultimate mindless culmination. Under this concept, any town of even minor importance could be designated a "fortress" and its garrison ordered to hold out at all costs until relieved. This drained away large numbers of troops and the local commander's initiative at a time when both would be badly needed elsewhere. This stubborn doctrine contributed greatly to the string of Soviet successes during the Spring and Summer of 1944, such as at Brody, Tarnopol, Minsk, Bobruisk, and Mogilev. Even more damaging was the continual erosion of the strategic effectiveness of German general staffs at the corps level and higher.

This was primarily brought about by Hitler's continuing arrogation of all operational and even many tactical decisions to himself. In many cases, commanders and staffs could only withdraw or move to subsequent positions with Hitler's permission. By the time that a request to conduct such a movement had been relayed to and approved by Hitler at his headquarters in Rastenburg over 1,000 kilometers away, the situation had usually become dire. When his permission, if given, had been received, it was usually too late. A case in point in the inability of Stemmermann to receive permission to withdraw *72.Inf.Div.* to the *Hamsterstellung* southwest of Smela. Approval for such a move could only be granted once the various staffs had forwarded

1996: The author with several participants of the battle. From L to R: author, Hans Fischer, SS-Pz.Rgt.5, Irmtraut Hein, Willy Hein, SS-Pz.Rgt.5, and Fernand Kaisergruber, Walloon Brigade. (Photo by author)

the request through proper channels to the *OKH*. Once permission had been granted for *Oberst* Hohn's division to pull back, it was almost too late, since the Soviets had nearly outflanked the position from both the north and the south.

Under the old Prussian general staff system, the local commander would have been permitted to make such a decision on his own, since no one better than he would have a correct grasp of the situation. But this was not often the case during the Battle of the Cherkassy Pocket. Obedience to Hitler's dictates made talented men such as Generals Busse and Speidel little more than uniformed clerks passing and relaying messages. Even army commanders, men such as Hube and Wöhler, often found their hands tied. An exception to this tendency was General Lieb, who purposely denuded his portion of the Dnieper defensive line, leaving only a thin infantry screen to observe the Soviets, while at the same time loudly proclaiming that he was "holding the Dnieper Front."

When pressed, his troops quickly withdrew on schedule to alternate positions that had been laid out in advance, such as that which occurred when *K.Abt.B* withdrew during Operation *Winterreise*. The records seem to indicate that Lieb notified his headquarters of these actions only after they had been completed. Thus, in Lieb's mind, seeking forgiveness after the fact was better than seeking permission that would be denied. How widespread were such cases of deliberate deception cannot be ascertained, though it would make for a fascinating study. In contrast, General Stemmermann seems to have adhered much more

closely to the directives from *8.Armee*. Certainly, if Hitler had followed the advice of Manstein, Hube, Wöhler, Lieb and Stemmermann and had authorized a withdrawal from the Kanev Salient, the Battle of Cherkassy would never have happened. Had *XI.* and *XXXXII.A.K.* both been allowed to pull back to a new line in good order, the course of the fighting in the Ukraine during the spring and summer of 1944 would have been much different.

Manstein's willingness to disobey Hitler has already been discussed, and was a key factor in Hitler's decision to relieve him. Had he not ordered the breakout to commence on his own responsibility, it is doubtful whether any of the men of *Gruppe Stemmermann* would have made it out. Examples such as the sacking of Manstein showed the rest of the general staff what penalty awaited them should they follow the dictates of their own consciences and the instincts ingrained by a traditional general staff education. Most, though not all, recognized this new reality and began to act accordingly, much to the detriment of the men whom they were responsible for. This increasingly blind obedience to Hitler or *Kadavergehorsam* contributed to the string of disasters that befell Nazi Germany in both the East and the West during the Summer of 1944. No amount of tactical expertise at the division level and below or quality of individual soldiers and weapons could redress the balance.

While debate during the war about the outcome of the battle was muted, probably to conceal the scale of the disaster from the German people and its armed forces, the outcome of

Cherkassy proved to be quite controversial after the war. The debate was aided by the fact that nearly all of the records of the battle, including *Kriegstagebücher* of the units concerned, reports, orders, and after-actions reports were found cataloged and archived by the Americans, who promptly removed them to the United States for study. They lay undisturbed in the U.S. National Archives until the early 1950s, when conflict with the Soviet Union appeared imminent. Allowed to gain access to these records for the first time, many former German high-ranking officers and American military historians pored over them in order to derive lessons learned which could be applied in the field by both NATO forces and the newly-created army of West Germany, the *Bundeswehr*. One of the first products of this endeavor, appearing in 1953, was U.S. Department of the Army Pamphlet 20-234, *Operations of Encircled Forces: German Experiences in Russia*, extensively quoted from in the body of this manuscript. Edited by former Generals Erhard Raus and Oldwig von Natzmer, it provides detailed accounts of several battles of encirclement, with two chapters devoted to the Battle of the Cherkassy Pocket alone

While the U.S. Army was more interested in how to profit from the German's experiences, German military scholars began a heated debate about the battle and sought to apportion blame. The first account to appear was Nikolaus von Vormann's *Tscherkassy*, published in 1954. In this excellent work, Vormann not only described the operations of his *XXXXVII.Pz.Korps*, he also provided an insider's account on the course of the battle. While thought by some to be an attempt by the author to salvage his military reputation, it is still considered to be one of the most detailed and thoughtful analyses of the battle from the point of view of a general staff-trained military historian. Noteworthy was Vormann's indirect criticism of *8.Armee's* General Wöhler and his chief of staff Speidel, who he felt made unreasonable demands of his divisions while at the same time failing to do their utmost to support him. His account was and still is used extensively by those who sought to determine what went wrong during the relief operation and the breakout.

More critical was former *Gen.d.Inf.* Edgar Röhricht's *Probleme der Kesselschlacht*, which appeared in 1958. A thorough study of all of the major battles of encirclement that took place on the Eastern Front from 1941 to 1945, it is another excellent example of a German general staff historical study. Röhricht devotes an entire chapter to the Battle of Cherkassy as a *Kessel-Probleme* (historical analysis or case study of a battle of encirclement), although he himself was not actually at the scene of the events described. In this chapter, the author repeats what had been known during the war about the disaster's causes, such as the pointlessness of holding on to the Kanev Salient, the failure to order an early breakout, and Manstein's over-ambitious plan to encircle and destroy the Soviets while simultaneously liberating the entrapped forces. But Röhricht reserves most of his criticism for the conduct of *III.Pz.Korps'* relief effort, especially that of *1.Pz.Div.*, for allegedly failing to secure sufficient crossings along the Gniloy Tikich and for failing to hold Hill 239.

That such criticisms are unfair have already been amply demonstrated in view of that division's effort to seize the hill while holding off dozens of determined Soviet tank-led counter-attacks. With the forces available, there was little else that General Koll and his men could have done. What is remarkable is that *1.Pz.Div.* was able to accomplish so much with so few men and tanks. Röhricht's criticism may perhaps be understood in light of the fact that, as an infantry officer, he was still somewhat skeptical of the role of armor and had even been criticized for his distaste of tank troops. As late as 1947, he was lambasted by none other than former Chief of Staff of the *OKH, Gen.O.* Heinz Guderian, father of the German armored force. In a criticism of a paper that Röhricht wrote for Colonel S.L.A. Marshall about tank-infantry cooperation, Guderian wrote "This study shows that the author had just as little peacetime training experience as wartime combat experience."[5] While perhaps an unfair characterization, it does illustrate the source of some of Röhricht's own criticism of Breith's relief effort.

Röhricht's study does make some observations that others have ignored or failed to detect. For example, he points out that the repeated radio messages sent in the clear from both *1.Pz.* and *8.Armee* to the encircled troops informing them that the rescue forces were on their way and exhorting them to hold on engendered a false sense of optimism that collapsed when *III.* and *XXXXVII.Pz.Korps* failed to arrive as promised. Such *Befehls-Optimismus* (i.e., keeping morale up with official statements) should be avoided in future conflicts, Röhricht stated.[6] He also criticized *III.Pz.Korps* for not making it absolutely clear on 15 February when the breakout order was being written that it did not yet have possession of Hill 239.

Röhricht believes that had Stemmermann known this to be the case, he would have adjusted his breakout plan accordingly. Perhaps; there is now no way of knowing if this would have mattered. There was only one way out of the pocket by that point, and it was via the line Hill 239 - Zhurzhintsy. Statements such as the one made by General Speidel that the true situation was withheld from Stemmermann to prevent demoralization, while convenient, does not square with the facts. The more likely case was that everyone assumed that *1.Pz.Div.* would have occupied the hill by 16 February. As events were to prove, it did not, with tragic results.

Another point that Röhricht made was that *Gruppe Stemmermann* should have been attached to *1.Pz.Armee* for the breakout operation. It made no sense to have the relief force and encircled force operate under separate army headquarters. Unity of command would have been greatly enhanced had Stemmermann and Lieb been reporting directly to Hube; it would have certainly speeded up vital communications between the two forces. As it was, anything going from the pocket to Hube's headquarters had to be passed through *8.Armee* first.

Röhricht also decried the fact that no single *führende Persönlichkeit* (dynamic leading personality) was at Lysyanka personally directing the fighting, yet another criticism directed at Generals Koll and Breith. Whether this would have made any difference is questionable. Given the limited means of radio communication at hand, it is doubtful whether any one man could have exercised the degree of leadership that Röhricht felt was necessary. The closest to this archetype was General Gille's attempt to rally his troops at the Gniloy Tikich,

Monument to the Battle of the Cherkassy Pocket in municipal cemetary, Bad Windsheim, Germany, site of annual veteran's commermoration ceremony since 1974.

but even his span of control was limited to those who could see him and hear his voice.

Regardless of their merits, Röhricht's and Vormann's accounts were the first detailed analyses of the battle to appear in Germany. Soon, they were followed by a plethora of divisional histories that filled in many of the gaps in the action. In 1966, Paul Carell published the second part of his monumental account of the war in the East, *Verbrannte Erde* (Scorched Earth), devoting an entire chapter to the Battle of Cherkassy. In his treatment of the battle, he integrates official histories, postwar accounts, and veterans' interviews to present the first truly balanced account of the fighting from an operational perspective. Though he did not dwell on the tactical details, his account remains as probably the best quick read of the battle.

Since these early works, other accounts of the battle have appeared in Germany and Austria, as well as in the Soviet Union, where the Soviet Army studied the battle as late as 1986. German and Austrian veterans' organizations have also devoted a great deal of print to it, seeking to gain closure for those terrible events of January and February 1944. They also seek to show succeeding generations how much of their youth they sacrificed for their country, even though their cause was not a just one. How deeply the battle affected these men is attested by the fact that surviving veterans still gather annually on the third weekend of February to commemorate the battle and to honor their fallen comrades.

This event, known as the *Tscherkassy-Treffen* (Cherkassy Meeting) takes place at the city cemetery of the Franconian town

of Bad Windsheim, where the veterans erected a monument to mark the battle. Each year since 1974, hundreds of veterans and their family members have traveled from all over Europe to hear speeches and to lay wreaths. In February 1998, a delegation from Estonia composed of veterans of the *SS-Sturmbataillon Narva* participated in the event. For the first time since the collapse of the Soviet Union, these former German allies were allowed to visit and to meet old German comrades they had not seen for over 50 years. After the ceremonies, the veterans and their families retreat to local pubs where they recount exploits and remember friends of days past.

Other veterans have been even more adventuresome. In 1996, for example, *Wiking's* veteran's association chartered a cruise ship to navigate the mighty Dnieper River from Kiev to the Black Sea, stopping at several points along the way where their division had been heavily engaged. When it stopped at Kanev, the former SS men and their families boarded buses for the one-hour trip to the town of Korsun-Shevchenkovsky, where they toured the former Soviet museum commemorating the battle and to walk the ground they had once trod 52 years before. At one point, they even watched a Soviet propaganda film recounting the battle, which was composed primarily of combat footage. The silence that accompanied the screening was mute testimony that the events had scarred them all, even though they had all built new lives after the war and had fathered several generations of young Germans whose knowledge of the war and its human costs grow increasingly dimmer. A chance meeting with a group of Soviet veterans of the same battle revealed that neither group bore a grudge against the other and that each had respected the other's combat prowess. They had far more in common than they could imagine.

There is no monument to this day to the German soldiers who fought and died during the Battle of the Cherkassy Pocket. While Soviet monuments dot the landscape between Kanev and Lysyanka, an attempt by Korsun-Shevchenkovsky and its German sister city to construct a joint memorial commemorating the battle miscarried when the German city council insisted that the monument bear inscriptions that the German soldiers were fighting in a criminal cause and had committed numerous criminal acts on Ukrainian soil. This proved to be too much even for the mayor of Korsun-Shevchenkovsky, who ended all discussions on the monument in 1996. Evidently, and rightly so, he believed that such a monument would prove to be too divisive at a time when he wanted to promote better relations between the two countries. Perhaps truth is the war's final victim, but today the Ukrainians bear no grudges.

The events that took place along the banks of the Dnieper and the Gniloy Tikich have long since passed into obscurity. There was no Stalingrad on the Dnieper, as the Soviets claimed, but the Germans had experienced a major defeat. Even if the salvation of most of the fighting troops of *Gruppe Stemmermann* had been accomplished, it mattered little how many had escaped the Soviet noose. In the grand scheme of things, the calculus of the war was turning increasingly against the Germans.

Today, the thousands of dead, both German and Soviet, sleep for eternity under several feet of rich black Ukrainian *chernozem*. There is little save deteriorating Soviets monuments and T-34s to mark where heavy fighting took place. The landscape of Cherkassy is again at peace. Soon, the remaining veterans of both sides will pass away, leaving only their bravery and dedication to duty as their final monument. May the heroism and sacrifice of the ordinary German and Soviet soldier during these terrible days never be forgotten.

End Notes

[1] Truppenkameradschaft *Wiking, Der Kessel von Tscherkassy: die Flut verschlangt sich selbst, nicht uns!* (Hannover, Germany: H. Bothe Druck, 1963), Schlusswort.

[2] Werth, p. 774.

[3] Matsulenko, pp. 143-144.

[4] Buchner, pp. 172-173.

[5] Macksey, Kenneth. *Guderian: Creator of the Blitzkrieg.* (Novato, CA: Presidio Press, 1992), p. 240.

[6] Röhricht, Edgar. *Probleme der Kesselschlacht: dargestellt an Einkreisungs-Operationen im zweiten Weltkrieg.* (Karlsruhe, Germany: Condor-Verlag GmbH, 1958), p. 158. Note: from the series *Deutsche Truppenführung im 2.Weltkrieg*).

ACKNOWLEDGEMENTS

This book represents the culmination of several years of research and is my first effort at publishing. I did not do it entirely alone, of course. This would not have been possible but for the contribution of many individuals who donated their time, talent, and patience to help me bring this project to fruition. First and foremost, I would like to thank three veterans of the battle who stuck with me while I was writing this: the late Willy Hein, of Lauenburg, Germany who passed away in October 2000; Fernand Kaisergruber, of Brussels; and Hans Menedetter of Weidling, Austria. They provided me with dozens of photographs, articles, and pages of personal manuscripts that provided the bedrock of this book. Their enthusiasm and willingness to help provided the first boost I needed to begin serious work on this manuscript. Monsieur Kaisergruber of the Walloon Brigade also accompanied me to Ukraine, where we toured the battlefield together. His keen memory helped me on many occasions to visualize the flow of events as as they occurred at that time, a service for which I am deeply indebted to him.

Through their good offices, these three put me in contact with many other veterans of the battle who were also very willing to assist: Eberhard Heder of Dasburg, Germany; Hans Fischer of Lüneburg, Germany, and Günther Ploen. Dr. Roland Foerster of the Bundesarchiv-Militärarchiv in Freiburg and the staff of the Bundesarchiv Photograph Archive in Koblenz also provided much needed assistance. In addition, I would also like to thank the staff of Alte Kameraden Magazine of Stuttgart, who so graciously ran my story describing our trip to Ukraine. This article attracted the attention of over a dozen German survivors of the battle who had not previously revealed their experiences - including Hans Eppo Freiherr von Doernberg, Günther Feisthauer, Hans Merkel, Ernst Schenck, the late Walter Notz, Justiz von Oechselhäuser, Hans Queitzsch, Walter Schäfer-Kehnert, Karl Schierholz, Alfred-Enno Porst, and Hans Gaertig. The recounting of their experiences helped round out the story from the perspective of the soldiers who did the bulk of the fighting and dying in the battle.

I would like to acknowledge the help provided by Klaus Schulz of Meerbusch, Germany, whose contacts with Alte Kameraden as well as other veteran's organizations and his translation capabilities helped paved the way; Rolf Stoves, whose contacts and document archive proved invaluable, and Studiendirektor Fredrich Pohl, who helped check my work's accuracy with many veterans of the battle. Thanks also are in order for the contribution made by the late Helmuth Spaeter of the *Grossdeutschland* division, who was able to shed light on the actions of that division's tank regiment in the battle.

I thank the veterans organizations of 72nd, 88th, 255th, and 323rd Infantry Divisions, and 5th SS Panzer Division "*Wiking*," who loaned or gave me vast amounts of material, of which I was only able to use a fraction, including Dr. Wolfgang Brandstetter, Jupp Stefan, Fritz Beer, Dr. Juergen Stech, Wolfgang Dreesen, Gerhard Meyer, Harald Baumann, Guenther Lange, Franz Hahl, Erhard Schmidt, and Willi Spindler. The authors of *Der Kessel von Tscherkassy*, Bernd Lerch and Günther Jahnke, also provided me a great deal of useful material.

In Ukraine, I am indebted to the services of our tour guide Yuri Vertiporoch, who endured not only many questions but put his Volkswagen Golf at our service, as well as the staff of the Korsun-Shevchenkovsky Battle Museum in Korsun-Shevchenkovsky, Ukraine. Their generous decision to grant me access to their archives as well as arranging interviews with several Soviet veterans of the battle, including Mikhail Hadai and Alexei Fedorovich, provided much-needed Soviet primary source material to balance that of the Germans.

In the United States, I am indebted to Frederick C. Clemens, Donald Houston, French MacLean, Dr. Bruce Menning, Edward G. Miller, George Petersen, and Emilie Stewart. I would also like to make special mention of the contributions of David Glantz and Juergen Buehring - Dave for providing me with a wealth of translated Soviet material and Juergen, whose patient tutoring and translation of German made this entire project a great deal of fun. To each and every one of you, I offer my most sincere thanks.

AUTHOR'S NOTES ON SOURCES

This manuscript relies to a large extent upon materials found in veteran's personal archives, records archives, and major research libraries that are not readily accessible to the public. For example, microfilmed copies of the German daily operational logbooks exist in several U.S. governmental or military archives. Known as *Kriegstagebücher*, these reports, ranging from army group to regimental level, provide an account of the action as it unfolded. These microfilms, available now from the U.S. National Archives, provide a catalog of unit status reports, reports from higher headquarters, analysis of military intelligence reports, and occasionally the private thoughts of unit commanders. They are excellent tools for tracking the operation from a German perspective as the action unfolds. Of particular interest were those files contained in microfilm groups T-311, T-312, and T-313. The Battle of Cherkassy was exceptional in that most of the actual records survived the war and had been apparently grouped together and stored in a different location than the rest of the German Army's operational records, which were largely destroyed during the latter part of the war by Allied bombing. Since a series of investigations and studies were carried out during the war to determine what went wrong during the battle, virtually every report, every radio message and *Kommandosache* were preserved together, much to the author's good fortune.

In addition, many unit after-action reports are available in these microfilm groupings. Remarkable for their frank and graphic nature, the reports filed by the units that broke out of the pocket provide the researcher with a rare view into the human element of this battle and highlight the importance of moral factors in the Germans' escape from the Soviet trap. These records, though available for study since the early 1950s, have rarely been used in subsequent accounts and shed new light on the events of over fifty years ago. They constitute perhaps the best available primary source on German actions and are relatively free of the post-war rationalization of many of the available German secondary sources.

Similarly, the detailed wartime Soviet after-action report of the operation, printed in the September-October 1944 edition of *Sbornik materialov po izucheniiu optya voiny* or *Sborniki* (Collection of Materials on the Study of War Experience) is a critical, relatively unvarnished account which is often at odds with the official story presented by the former Soviet Union. Interestingly, the tactical action depicted in this report parallels the German records quite closely. As one compares the *Sborniki* side by side with the German accounts, dates, places, and unit movements correspond almost exactly. Of course, the perceived outcomes of particular engagements may vary, but this phenomenon is common in tactical reports. This report, only recently retrieved and declassified by a dedicated group of Sovietologists is but a fraction of the amount of material stored within Russian archives and gives a tantalizing glimpse of how *glasnost* may yet illuminate the "Great Patriotic War."

Another particularly useful source is a series of art of war symposia held at the U.S. Army War College at Carlisle Barracks, Pennsylvania from 1984 -1986. These symposia were conducted for the express purpose of teaching future brigade and division commanders the complexities of the operational art as practiced by the Soviet Union during World War II. The symposium proceedings volume most useful for this thesis is "From the Don to the Dnieper: Soviet Offensive Operations November 1943 to August 1944." Chaired by Colonel David M. Glantz, this particular symposium analyzed the relevant phases of the war in the East in great detail. Most notable was the symposium's use of actual participants in the operations to conduct presentations. Their testimony, coupled with the use of actual German and Soviet records, offered an extraordinary opportunity to analyze the various operations as they unfolded from the perspective of the belligerents. This effort still stands as a milestone in the study of the Russo-German War.

There are numerous postwar accounts of the operation by German participants. In addition to Manstein's account, the most noteworthy are *Tscherkassy* by the commander of the ill-fated *XXXXVII.Pz.Korps*, Nikolaus von Vormann, and Leon Degrelle's epic *Campaign in Russia*, which relates the experiences of the Belgian *Waffen-SS* legion in the operation. Numerous other German unit histories chronicle events from the foxhole perspective, including materials from 1st Panzer Division, 1st SS Panzer Division "*Leibstandarte Adolf Hitler*," 5th SS Panzer Division "*Wiking*", and 72nd Infantry Division. Although these sources suffer from weaknesses common to this genre (i.e., one-sidedness and the glossing over of ideology), they graphically depict the nature of the fighting from the soldier's perspective.

Reference has also been made to the accounts of the operation given by several of the key Soviet participants, such as those by Marshals Georgi K. Zhukov, Ivan S. Konev, and Pavel M. Rotmistrov. These are noteworthy in that they often contradict each other's version of events, an illustration of the role played by competing personalities. Another useful source is recently declassified documents concerning the operation, which provide translated versions of the actual *Front* operations orders for the Korsun-Shevchenkovsky Operation as well as the order issued by the *STAVKA*. These sources, coupled with a different perspective that seeks to objectively investigate all aspects of the Battle of Cherkassy, allow the researcher to conduct an analysis of the operation to determine its overall significance.

Numerous secondary sources were used to provide additional background and context for the operation. Most important in this regard are the official U.S. Army history of the war in Russia already mentioned and Paul Carell's sweeping and dramatic work, *Scorched Earth*. Once touted as Germany's Cornelius Ryan, Carell blended veterans' interviews with official accounts, with emphasis on the human aspect of conflict. Another recent addition to this body of material is Alex Buchner's *Ostfront 1944*, which deals with the destruction of the *Ostheer*. Buchner devotes an entire chapter to the Battle of Cherkassy, providing a wealth of narrative accounts by German survivors of the encirclement.

Former Soviet secondary sources, while numerous, do not give detailed information on the actual day-to-day conduct of what Russian and Ukrainian military historians still refer to as the Korsun-Shevchenkovsky Operation. Nearly every official account provides identical descriptions and analysis of the operation, even down to the number of supposed German casualties, but do not report on movements of corps and divisions. Examples of this type of coverage are provided in the *Official History of the Great Patriotic War*, as already mentioned. In a sense, to read one is to read them all. Far more detailed and less biased are the various Soviet military publications, including the *Soviet Military Review and Voyenno-Istoricheskiy Zhurnal*.

Lastly, monographs and letters contributed by the veterans themselves round out the account. In fact, the contributions by over two dozen German survivors of the battle provide a rare glimpse into what the average *Landser* was forced to endure during three weeks of hellish combat. Their personal papers, photographs, maps and other articles from their private archives allowed the author to piece together much of the tactical action that took place at the small unit level that brings much of the action to life. Most of the material provided was written shortly after the war, when memories of events were still fresh in their minds. Just as useful were nearly a dozen interviews the author personally conducted with veterans, both German and Soviet.

APPENDIX 1 — GERMAN ORDER OF BATTLE

(Organization of units engaged as of 28 January 1944)

Heeresgruppe Süd (Army Group South) G.F.M. Erich von Manstein

   1.Panzerarmee (PzAOK 1) Gen.O. Hans-Valentin Hube

III.Panzerkorps (Pz.Korps)	Gen.d.Pz.Tr. Hermann Breith
1.Pz.Div.	Gen.Maj. Richard Koll
16.Pz.Div.	Gen.Maj. Hans-Ulrich Back
17.Pz.Div.	Gen.Lt. Karl-Friedrich von der Meden
1.SS-Pz.Div. "Leibstandarte Adolf Hitler"	SS-Brig.Fhr. Theodor Wisch
Schw.Pz.Rgt. Bäke	Oberstlt. Dr. Franz Bäke

VII.Armeekorps (A.K.)	Gen.d.Inf. Ernst-Eberhard Hell
34.Inf.Div.	Gen.Lt. Friedrich Höchbaum
75.Inf.Div.	Gen.Lt. Helmuth Beukemann
198.Inf.Div.	Gen.Maj. Hans-Joachim von Horn

Gruppe Stemmermann   Gen.d.Art. Wilhelm Stemmermann
   Army Troops:
   Armee Nachr.Rgt.570
   Eisenbahn Pionier Einheit Schäfer
   Eisenbahn-Betriebs Kompanie 108
   Landesschutz-Btl.867
   Armenisches Inf.-Btl.810

   XI. Armeekorps   Gen.d.Art. Wilhelm Stemmermann
   Corps Troops:
   StuG.Abt.239
   Artillerie-Kommandeure (ArKo) 6
       Beob.Abt.67
   II./Heeres-Art.Abt.800 (17 cm)
   H.Art.Abt.842 (10 cm Kan.)
   I./H.Art.Abt.108 (10.5 cm le.F.H.)
   Pi.Rgt. Stab 601
   Pi.Btl.666
   Bau-Pi.Btl.410
   Bau.Btl.155

   57.Inf.Div. *Gen.Maj. Adolf Trowitz*
           Gren.Rgt.199
           Gren.Rgt.217
           Gren.Rgt.676 (attached)
   72.Inf.Div. *Oberst* Dr. Hermann Hohn
           Gren.Rgt.105
           Gren.Rgt.124
           Gren.Rgt.266
   389.Inf.Div. *Gen.Lt.* Kurt Kruse
           Gren.Rgt.544
           Gren.Rgt.545
           Gren.Rgt.546
           1 battalion, *Gren.Rgt.331* (detached from *167.Inf.Div.*)
           1 battalion, *Gren.Rgt.339* (detached from *167.Inf.Div.*)

XXXXII.Armeekorps Gen.Lt. Theobald Lieb (*mdFb**)
    Corps Troops:
    ArKo 107
    Beob.Bttr.75 (Pz.)
    lei.Beob.Abt.14
    I. /Art.Rgt.248 (from 168.Inf.Div.)
    Pi.Rgt.Stab 4
    Pi.Rgt.Stab 26
    Bau Pi.Btl.213

  88.Inf.Div. Gen.Lt. Georg *Graf* von Rittberg
    Gren.Rgt.245
    Gren.Rgt.248
    II./Gren.Rgt.246
  Attached:
    Div.Gr.323
    Sich.Rgt.318 (from *213.Sich.Div.*)
    II., III., Sich.Rgt.177 (from *213.Sich.Div.*)
    Gren.Rgt.417 (from *168.Inf.Div.*)

  Korpsabteilung B Oberst Hans-Joachim Fouquet
    Div.Gr.112
      Regiments-Gruppe (Rgt.Gr.) 110
      Rgt.Gr.258
    Div.Gr.255
      Rgt.Gr.465
      Rgt.Gr.475
    Div.Gr.332
      Rgt.Gr.677
      Rgt.Gr.678

  5.SS-Panzer Division "Wiking" SS-Brig.Fhr. Herbert Otto Gille
    SS-Pz.Gren.Rgt.9 "Germania"
    SS-Pz.Gren.Rgt.10 "Westland"
    I. Abt.,SS-Pz.Rgt.5
  Attached:
    SS-Freiwilligen-Sturmbrigade "Wallonie"
    SS-Freiwilligen-Pz.Gren.Btl. "Narwa"

8.Armee (AOK 8) Gen.d.Inf. Otto Wöhler

  XXXXVII.Pz.Korps   Gen.Lt. Nikolaus von Vormann
    3.Pz.Div.   Gen.Maj. Fritz Bayerlein, Oberst Lang
    11.Pz.Div.   Gen.Lt. Wend von Wietersheim
    13.Pz.Div.   Gen.Maj. Hans Mikosch
    14.Pz.Div.   Gen.Lt. Martin Unrein
    10.Pz.Gren.Div.   Gen.Maj. Walter Herold
    106.Inf.Div.   Gen.Lt. Werner Forst
    282.Inf.Div.   Gen.Maj. Hermann Frenking
    320.Inf.Div.   Gen.Lt. Georg Postel
    376.Inf.Div.   Gen.Lt. Alexander Edler von Daniels

VIII.Flieger-Korps General der Flieger Hans Seidemann

---

* MdFB-*mit der Führung beauftragt* (acting commander)

APPENDIX 2 — SOVIET ORDER OF BATTLE

KORSUN SCHEVCHENKOVSKY OPERATION

STAVKA Coordinator for operation (later acting commander, First Ukrainian Front): Marshal of the Soviet Union Georgi Konstantinovich Zhukov

First Ukrainian Front General of the Army Nikolai Fedorovich Vatutin

27th Army Lt.Gen. Sergei Georgievich Trofimenko
    Army Troops:
        881st Heavy Artillery Regiment
        480th and 492nd Mortar Regiments
        329th Guards Mortar Regiment
        298th Guards Self-propelled Artillery Regiment
        713th, 1892nd Self-propelled Artillery Regiments
        25th, 38th Engineer Battalions
    Rifle Divisions:
        180th, 206th and 337th Rifle Divisions
        54th, 159th Fortified Regions

40th Army Lt.Gen. Filipp. Fedoseevich Zhmachenko
    Army Troops:
        33rd Light Artillery Brigade
        111th Guards Howitzer Artillery Regiment
        1528 Howitzer Artillery Regiment
        28th Heavy Howitzer Artillery Brigade
        4th, 317th Guards Heavy Antitank Regiments
        680th Heavy Artillery Regiment
        9th, 10th Heavy Mortar Regiments
        493rd Mortar Regiment
        9th Anti-aircraft Artillery Regiment
        1898th Self-propelled Artillery Regiment
        14th Engineer Battalion
        4th, 21st Security Battalions
    50th Rifle Corps
        38th, 240th, and 340th Rifle Divisions
        4th Guards Airborne Division
    51st Rifle Corps
        42nd Guards Rifle Division
        163rd, 232nd Rifle Divisions
    104th Rifle Corps
        58th, 74th, and 133rd Rifle Divisions

6th Tank Army Lt.Gen. Andrei G. Kravchenko
    5th Mechanized Corps
        2nd, 9th, and 45th Mechanized Brigades
        233rd Tank Brigade
        745th, 1228th Self-propelled Artillery Regiments
        1827th Heavy Self-propelled Artillery Regiment
        64th Engineer Battalion
    5th Guards Tank Corps
        20th, 21st, and 22nd Guards Tank Brigades
        6th Guards Motorized Rifle Brigade
        1416th, 1458th, and 1462nd Self-propelled Artillery Regiments

1667th Heavy Antitank Regiment
181st Engineer Battalion
47th Rifle Corps (attached)
136th, 167th, and 359th Rifle Divisions

1st Tank Army (Arriving 15/16 February) Lt.Gen. Mikhail E. Katukov
(one Brigade)

2nd Tank Army (Arriving 4 February) Lt.Gen. Semen I. Bogdanov
3rd Tank Corps
16th Tank Corps

Second Ukrainian Front General of the Army Ivan Stepanovich Konev

4th Guards Army Maj.Gen. Aleksandr Ivanovich Ryshov
Army Troops:
42nd Light Artillery Brigade
97th, 98th Heavy Howitzer Artillery Brigade
568th, 1328th Gun Artillery Regiment
466th Mortar Regiment
27th Anti-Aircraft Artillery Division
20th Guards Rifle Corps
5th, 7th Guards Airborne Divisions
62nd Guards Rifle Division
31st Rifle Division
21st Guards Rifle Corps
69th, 94th Guards Rifle Divisions
252nd, 375th Rifle Divisions

52nd Army Lt.Gen. Konstantin Apollonovich Koroteyev
Army Troops:
1322nd Heavy Artillery Regiment
38th Anti-Aircraft Artillery Regiment
490th Mortar Regiment
568th Artillery Regiment
17th Guards Mortar Regiment
438th Antitank Regiment
133rd, 135th, and 366th Engineer Regiments
73rd Rifle Corps
254th, 294th Rifle Divisions
78th Rifle Corps
373rd Rifle Division

53rd Army Lt.Gen. Ivan Vasil'evich Galanin
Army Troops:
78th Guards Rifle Division
214th Rifle Division
63rd, 122nd Antitank Rifle Battalions
16th Artillery Division (with five brigades)
31st Light Artillery Brigade
1327th Gun Artillery Regiment
33rd Heavy Mortar Brigade
1316th Howitzer Artillery Regiment
30th Anti-Aircraft Artillery Division
189th Separate Tank Brigade
26th Guards Rifle Corps
1st Guards Airborne Division
25th Guards Rifle Division

6th Rifle Division
48th Guards Rifle Corps
 14th, 66th, and 89th Guards Rifle Divisions
75th Rifle Corps
 138th, 213th, and 233rd Rifle Divisions

5th Guards Tank Army General of Tank Troops Pavel Rotmistrov
 Army Troops:
  678th Howitzer Artillery Regiment
  689th Self-propelled Artillery Regiment
  6th Anti-Aircraft Artillery Division
  994th Separate Artillery Regiment
  377th Separate Engineer Brigade
 18th Tank Corps
  110th, 170th, 181st Tank Brigades
  32nd Mechanized Brigade
 20th Tank Corps
  8th Guards Tanks Brigade
  80th and 155th Tanks Brigades
  7th Mechanized Brigade
 29th Tank Corps
  25th, 31st, and 32nd Tank Brigades
  53rd Mechanized Brigade

5th Guards Cavalry Cossack Corps Maj.Gen. A. G. Selivanov
 11th, 12th Guards Cavalry Divisions
 63rd Cavalry Division

2nd Air Army Lt.Gen. of Aviation Stepan Akimovich Krasovsky
 10th Fighter Air Corps
 254th, 291st, 264th Ground Attack Air Divisions
 326th Night Bomber Air Division

5th Air Army Lt.Gen. of Aviation Sergei Kondrat'evich Goryunov
 1st Guards Bomber Division
 1st Ground Attack Air Corps
 4th Fighter Air Corps

APPENDIX 3 — TABLE OF GERMAN RANK EQUIVALENTS

Wehrmacht	Waffen-SS	Abbreviation	U.S. Equivalent
Generalfeldmarschall	N/A	G.F.M.	General of the Army
Generaloberst	SS-Oberstgruppenführer und Generaloberst der Waffen-SS	Gen.O./Obstgruf.	General
General der Infantrie, Kavalerie, etc.	SS-Obergruppenführer und General der Waffen-SS	Gen.d.Inf./Ogruf.	Lieutenant General
Generalleutnant	SS-Gruppenführer und Generalleutnant der Waffen-SS	Gen.Lt./Gruf.	Major General
Generalmajor	SS-Brigadeführer und Generalmajor der Waffen-SS	Gen.Maj./Brig.Fhr.	Brigadier General
Oberst	SS-Standartenführer	O./Staf.	Colonel
Oberstleutnant	SS-Obersturmbannführer	Oberstlt./Ostubaf.	Lieutenant Colonel
Major	SS-Sturmbannführer	Maj./Stubaf.	Major
Hauptmann or Rittmeister	SS-Hauptsturmführer	Hptm./Hstuf.	Captain
Oberleutnant	SS-Obersturmführer	Oberlt./Ostuf.	First Lieutenant
Leutnant	SS-Untersturmführer	Lt./Ustuf.	Second Lieutenant
Stabsfeldwebel	SS-Sturmscharführer	Stabs Fw./none	Sergeant Major
Oberfeldwebel	SS-Hauptscharführer	Ofw./Hscha.	Master Sergeant
Feldwebel	SS-Oberscharführer	Fw./Oscha.	Sergeant First Class
Unteroffizier	SS-Unterscharführer	Uffz./Uscha.	Staff Sergeant
Obergefreiter	SS-Rottenführer	Ogefr./Rttf.	Coporal/Specialist
Gefreiter	SS-Sturmmann	Gef./Strm.	Private First Class
Obergrenadier, Oberkannonier, etc.	SS-Obergrenadier, etc.	none	Private Second Class
Grenadier, Kanonier, Funker, etc.	SS-Grenadier, etc.	none	Private

APPENDIX 4 — SURRENDER LEAFLET FROM THE FREE GERMAN COMMITTEE

NATIONAL FREE GERMANY COMMITTEE
LEAGUE OF GERMAN OFFICERS

Officers and Soldiers
of 72.I.D., 57.I.D., 389.I.D., SS-Division WIKING
and attached units!

You are surrounded and are facing destruction. You can no longer expect help. The tragedy of Stalingrad repeats itself. Then, 200,000 of your comrades were killed on Hitler's orders. You are threatened with the same fate. Hitler will also forbid you to accept every offer to surrender by the Red Army.

Take your fate into your own hands!

There exists in Russia a powerful German freedom movement, which has taken as its task, the freeing of Germany from the tyranny of Hitler and the opening of peace negotiations. Also marching in this Free Germany movement is the League of German Officers under the command of General der Artillerie Walther von Seydlitz. The undersigned are empowered as members of the League of German Officers opposite your sector to make contact with you. We have gone through the hell of Stalingrad and therefore know of your misery.

Come to us and take protection under the League of German Officers. Make contact with us. Send emissaries to us to whom we can give exact instructions. Each emissary should make himself recognizable at the front with a white cloth and demand to speak with one of the undersigned officers. We guarantee every emissary an unhindered return to his unit. The Red Army staff have appropriate instruction.

Comrades! Act before it is too late! Do not sacrifice yourself for Hitler. Germany needs you to rebuild. Come and fight with us for peace and for a free and independent Germany!

In the field, 4 February 1944   (signed)

Steidle
Oberst and Rgt.C.O. of Gren.Rgt.767, 376.I.D.
Vice-President of the League of German Officers

Röckl
Oblt. and Batterie Chef, II./Art.Rgt.46 (mot.)
Member of the Managing Board

Büchler
Maj. and C.O. of I/Flak Rgt.241
Member of the Managing Board

APPENDIX 5 — GLOSSARY OF GERMAN AND SOVIET TERMS AND ABBREVIATIONS

Term	Definition
Abteilung (Abt.)	A German unit of company size or greater, normally of battalion size.
Armeekorps (A.K.)	Infantry Corps
Armee-Oberkommando (AOK)	Army Headquarters
Aufklärungsabteilung (Aufkl.Abt.)	Reconnaissance Battalion
Balka, Balki	Russian for deep gully or ravine common to Ukraine.
Beobachtungs-Abteilung (Beo.Abt.)	Artillery Observation Battalion
Chernozem	Rich, black Ukrainian soil
Davai!	"Hurry up!"
Division (Div., or D.)	Division
Divisionsgruppe (Div.Gr.)	Unit formed from remnants of infantry division, normally consisted of two infantry battalions, an artillery battery, and headquarters. Equivalent to an infantry regiment in strength.
Do kontsa (Ru.)	Soviet doctrinal term meaning, "to the utmost," or "to the last man."
Front	A Soviet army group
Frontovnik	Red Army slang for infantryman
Führer	Hitler's title as German chief of state
Gruppe (Gr.)	Section or group, can denote larger ad-hoc formations such as an Armeegruppe or Gruppe Stemmermann.
Guards	An honorific designation given to Soviet units which had distinguished themselves in combat.
Guards Cavalry Cossack Corps	Soviet Guards horse-mounted unit augmented with self-propelled guns and medium tanks.
Guards Tank Army (GTA)	Soviet Guards Tank Army which had larger number of tank and artillery units assigned, as well as higher priority for replacements.
Hiwi, Hilfswillige	Russian auxiliaries serving with German units on the Eastern Front in various noncombatant capacities.
Infanterie-Division (Inf.Div., or I.D.)	German Army infantry division
Isba	Typical thatched Russian or Ukrainian farmer's hut, usually consisted of one room with large stove in the center.
Ju-52	The German Junkers 52 trimotor transport airplane
Kampfgruppe (Kgr.)	A temporary ad hoc organization, which may be anything from a platoon to an army group in size plus attached troops, normally identified by its commander's name.
Katyusha	"Little Kate," Soviet nickname for the 12.2 cm multiple rocket launcher. Known as the "Stalin Orgel" (Stalin's organ) by the Germans.
Kommissar	Soviet political officer; often served as a shadow commander. Insured that Soviet officers and troops remained faithful to the dictates of the Communist Party.
Kraftfahrzeug (Kfz.)	Any German motor vehicle, except armor
Korpsabteilung (K.Abt.)	A means of designating German divisions which had been seriously reduced in strength through combat losses. Normally consisted of from two to three Divisionsgruppen and was depicted on the map using a corps standard.
Knight's Cross of the Iron Cross	The *Ritterkreuz*, the highest class of the Iron Cross and the most prized of the German World War II military decorations.
Landeschützen-Bataillon (Ldsch.Btl.)	German local defense battalion, formed from older reservist. Often used for local security duties in the occupied regions.
Lastkraftwagen (Lkw.)	German cargo truck of various makes
Leichtes Infanteriegeschütz (le.IG)	Light infantry gun, usually 7.5 cm le.IG 18.
Leichte Feldhaubitze (le.FH)	Light field howitzer, usuall 10.5 cm 18.

Maskirovka	Soviet doctrinal term for operational and tactical deception using a variety of means - such as imaginary communications networks, dummy field positions, and concealment.
Nachrichtenabteilung (Nachr.Abt.)	Signal Battalion
NKVD	*Narodnyi Komissariat Venutrennikh Del* (People's Commissariat for Internal Affairs, the Soviet internal security organization, which even fielded combat units for use behind the front lines.
OKH	*Oberkommando des Heeres.* The German Army High Command, responsible for operations on the Eastern Front. After December 1941, its command position was held by Hitler himself.
OKW	Oberkommando der Wehrmacht. The German Armed Forces High Command.
Ostheer	German Army's unofficial name for its group of forces fighting on the Eastern Front.
Panje	Russian or Ukrainian peasant cart or sled pulled by a one or a pair of sturdy ponies native to the region.
Panzerfaust	A recoilless antitank grenade launcher designed to be used against armor at ranges from 25 to 100 meters. It consisted of a steel launching tube, which contained a percussion-fired propellant charge, and a hollow-charge antitank grenade mounted at the end. Could penetrate up to six inches of rolled steel plate.
Panzergrenadier (Pz.Gren.)	Armored Infantryman
Panzerjäger (Pz.Jäg.)	Antitank soldier or antitank system
Panzerarmeeoberkommando (Pz.AOK)	German Tank Army Headquarters
Pionier (Pi.)	Combat Engineer
Regimentsgruppe (Rgt.Gr.)	German unit formed from remnants of infantry regiment, normally consisted of three infantry companies, a heavy company, and headquarters. Equivalent to an infantry battalion in strength
Ruki Verch!	Russian for "Hands Up!" (i.e., Surrender!)
Schutzenpanzerwagen (SPW)	Armored Personnel Carrier
Sicherungs-Regiment (Sich.Rgt.)	Line of communications security regiment, often consisted of older *Landes-Schüzten* personnel. Often committed to front line combat when situations dictated.
SS	*Schutzstaffel*, or Elite Guard of the Nazi Party.
STAVKA	Stavka Verkhovnovo, Glavnokommandovaniya, or the Soviet Supreme Command
Stuka	Nickname for Junkers Ju-87 *Sturzkampfflugzeug*, or dive bomber.
Sturmovik	Ilyushin Il2 ground attack aircraft
Tankodesantniki	Soviet slang for tank-mounted mechanized infantrymen who rode into battle holding on to special rails welded to the turrets of the tanks they rode on. Usually suffered heavy casualties in battle.
Unichtozhenie	Soviet doctrinal term for the total liquidation or annihilation of an enemy. Usually applied to encirclement doctrine.
Waffen-SS	Combat units of the SS
Wehrmacht	The German Armed Forces

APPENDIX 6 — BREAKOUT ORDERS FROM GRUPPE STEMMERMANN

Appendix 1 to
Gen.Kdo.XI.A.K.
Ia 19/44 geh.Kdos.
Headquarters, 15.2.44

Group Stemmermann
Ia Nr. 236/44 Secret

Command for the Breakout

1.) The enemy will continue his efforts through concentrated attacks to further constrict the size of the pocket.

2.) Group Stemmermann will break out at 2300 hours, 16 February towards the southwest through the enemy's lines of encirclement, with concentrated forces, in order to link up with *III.Pz.Korps.* As a prerequisite for success, both corps must reinforce the western front of the pocket, so that the current main defense line there can be held under all circumstances.

3.) Accordingly, I command that:

a) As the situation permits, both corps headquarters will begin moving the strongest forces available by this evening to begin reinforcing our western front. As the line of departure, the heights around Khilki, Khilki itself, and Komarovka must remain in our hands. Limited attacks may be conducted only if the seizure or retaking of key terrain is necessary for use as forward assault positions.

b) The assault force, under the command of *Generalleutnant* Lieb, will break through at 2300 hours on 16 February along the general line Khilki-Komarovka after forming up in open areas immediately behind the main defense line. It will use a tightly massed assault formation and punch its way through in a column by way of Zhurzhintsy all the way to Hill 239. The speed of the advance is the key to our success. For locations of forward assembly areas and the route of advance of the attack force, see map overlays.

c) For the conduct of the attack, *XI. A.K.* will place the following at the disposal of the assault force: *72.I.D.* and *SS-Wiking* with approximately 2/3 of the combat forces of each division. Both will reinforce them selves with detailed drivers and other support personnel of the destroyed supply convoys and disbanded staffs there of.

4.) Tasks for *Generealleutnant* Lieb:

He is responsible for ensuring that the forward assembly areas of the troops are occupied noiselessly and according to plan by 2300 hours. *The SS-Wiking* has the responsibility for the relief in place by 1900 hours 16 February of elements from *72.I.D.* holding Komarovka. He will direct the course of the assault from his position with the center assaulting column so that he can remain in contact with the other columns on his left and right. He must report his progress by radio using code names for each of the assigned phase lines.

5.) Tasks for the Divisions:

Forward assembly areas are shown on the enclosed map overlays. The movement must take place with deeply echeloned columns and must follow the designated routes. You must advance silently and fall upon the enemy with bayonets affixed. Emphasize offensive spirit.

6.) Tasks for the Rearguard:

The Rearguard will cover the backs of the assault units at Line Green, which you must occupy by 2230 hours 16 February 1944. At the radioed command "Displace," *57.I.D.* will disengage from the enemy and follow the route taken by the *SS-Wiking*, while *88.I.D.* will follow the route taken by *72.I.D.*

7.) Artillery:

You are to take as many guns with you as possible through the use of multiple teams of horses. The number of guns to take along will be based on the amount of available ammunition. Guns will be used primarily for direct fire. Guns that become stuck or cannot be brought along will be blown up on the spot.

8.) Destruction of equipment:

Divisional commanders are responsible for ensuring that all equipment that cannot be taken along be destroyed in accordance with previous instructions.

9.) Units are to form *Hiwi* wagon columns to bring along those who are wounded during the breakout.

10.) Units are released from the requirement to evacuate male civilians.

11.) Units will refrain under all circumstances from committing any violations of international law, since any such acts will only endanger our wounded [in Shanderovka], who will soon fall into the hands of the enemy.

Signed: STEMMERMANN

Appendix:
1 Map with overlay 1:100,000 with reporting grids
Distribution:
XXXXII.A.K.
72.I.D.
57.I.D.
389.I.D.
SS-Wiking
Arko

APPENDIX 7 — GERMAN PRESENT FOR BATTLE UNIT STRENGTHS AFTER THE BREAKOUT*

Unit	Officers	Troops	Hiwis	Total
Corps Troops XXXXII.A.K.	41	565	13	619
Corps Troops XI. A.K.	34	814	7	855
88.Inf.Div.	108	3,055	117	3,280
389.Inf.Div.	70	1,829	33	1,932
72.Inf.Div.	91	3,524	200	3,815
57.Inf.Div.	99	2,598	253	2,950
Korps-Abt.B	172	4,659	382	5,213
SS-Wiking (Including Wallonie)[1]	196	8,057	25	8,278
Elements of 213.Sich.Div.	22	418	2	442
Elements of 14.Pz.Div. (von Brese)	14	453	2	467
Elements of 168.Inf.Div.	12	601	29	642
Sturmgeschütz Abteilung 239	unk.	150	0	150
Leichte Beob.Btl. 14	8	116	1	124
Totals:	867	26,836	1,064	28,767
Wounded Flown out of the Pocket:				4,161
Wounded evacuated from Lysyanka 17-20 February:				7,496
Total Survivors:				40,423

---

* Source: *Abschlussmeldung Gruppe Mattenklott*, 2.3.44.
[1] Not present: SS-Pz.Rgt.5 with II./Pz.Rgt.5, III./Germania and III./Westland

APPENDIX 8 — THE LUFTWAFFE'S AERIAL SUPPLY EFFORT

During the period from 29 January to 20 February 1944, *VIII.Flieger-Korps*, operating in support of both *Gruppe Stemmermann* and units from *1.Pz. and 8.Armee* accomplished the following:

Amount of supplies flown in or dropped into the Cherkassy Pocket
From 29 January-16 February 1944:

Ammunition:	867.7 tons
Fuel:	82,948.8 gallons
Medical Supplies:	4 tons
Wounded flown out:	4,161

Amount of supplies airdropped to spearheads of *III.Pz.Korps* from 12-20 February 1944:

Ammunition:	316 tons
Fuel:	57,024 gallons
Food:	24.1 tons
Containers of medical supplies (VAB):	4

Amount of supplies airdropped to spearheads of *XXXXVII.Pz.Korps* from 12-16 February 1944:

Ammunition:	9 tons
Fuel:	17,265 gallons

Wounded flown out of Lysyanka area to Uman from 19-20 February 1944: 2,483

Totals:

Ammunition:	1,192.7 tons
Fuel:	157, 237.8 gallons
Food:	24.1 tons
Medical supplies:	4 tons plus 4 VAB containers

APPENDIX 9 — COMPARATIVE SIZES OF GERMAN AND SOVIET COMMANDS

German	Soviet
1. *Army Groups* On the Eastern Front 4 to 5 plus the Twentieth Mountain Army and the Finnish Army to Sept. 1944	1. *Fronts* 10 to 12
2. Armies Two to four in an army group	2. Armies three to nine in a *front*
3. Corps (including Panzer Corps) two to seven in an army	3. Rifle Corps An average of three in an army
4. Divisions two to seven in a corps	4. Divisions two to three in a corps

Authorized Strengths Divisions		Authorized Strengths Armored Corps and Divisions	
Panzer Divisions (103 to 125 tanks)	14,000 to 17,000	Tank Corps (189 tanks)	10,500
Motorized Divisions (48 tanks)	14,000	Mechanized Corps (186 tanks)	16,000
Infantry Division, 9 battalions Infantry Division, 6 battalions	15,000 12,700	Rifle Divisions	9,375
Artillery Divisions (113 guns)	3,380	Guards Rifle Divisions Artillery Divisions (210 guns)	10,585 6,550

Source: Earl F. Ziemke, *Stalingrad to Berlin: The German Defeat in the East*, App. B.

APPENDIX 10 — KNIGHT'S CROSS RECIPIENTS*

Knight's Cross with Oakleaves and Swords

Rank, Name, Unit and Award Date

Oberstlt. Dr. Franz Bäke, *Schw.Pz.Rgt. Bäke,* 21.2.44
SS-Ogruf. Herbert Gille, *5.SS-Pz.Div. Wiking,*
20.2.44
Maj. Josef Bregenzer, *Gren.Rgt.245, 88.Inf.Div.,*
17.3.44

Knight's Cross with Oakleaves

Gen.Lt. Hermann Breith, *III.Pz.Korps, 21.2.44*
Maj. Heinz Wittchow von Brese-Winiary,
Pz.Gren.Rgt.108, 14.Pz.Div., 6.4.44
Oberst Dr. Hermann Hohn, *72.Inf.Div.,* 1.3.44
Maj. Robert Kästner, *Gren.Rgt.105, 72.Inf.Div.,*
21.2.44
Gen.Maj. Theobald Lieb, *XXXXII.A.K.,* 18.2.44
Gen.Lt. Wilhelm Stemmermann, *XI. A.K.,* 18.2.44
Brigfhr. Theodor Wisch, *1.SS-Pz.Div. LSSAH,*
12.2.44
Obergef. Hermann Bebel, *Füs.Btl.88, 88.Inf.Div.,*
18.2.44
Oblt. Rudolf Becker, *Pz.Gren.Rgt.66, 13.Pz.Div.,*
23.2.44
Ofw. Christian Braun, *Gren.Rgt.308, 198.Inf.Div.,*
15.7.44

Knight's Cross

Hptm. Georg Burgfeld, *Div.Gr.112, K.Abt.B,*
21.2.44
Ostuf. Heinrich Debus, *SS-Pz.A.A. 5,* 15.5.44
Hstuf. Leon Degrelle, *5.SS-Sturm-Brig. Wallonien,*
20.2.44
Uffz. Joseph Dimmig, *Div.Gr.112, K.Abt.B,* 21.2.44
Ostubaf. Fritz Ehrath, *SS-Pz.Gren.Rgt.9 Germania,*
23.2.44
Uscha. Gerhard Fischer, *SS-Pz.Jg.Abt.5,* 15.5.44
Oberst Heinrich Gaedke, *XI.A.K.,* 7.4.44
Ofw. Franz Gössmann, *Gren.Rgt.199 "List,"*
57.Inf.Div., 14.5.44
Lt. Friedrich Grammel, *Gren.Rgt.544, 389.Inf.Div.,*
4.5.44
Ostuf. Eberhard Heder, *SS-Feld Ausb.Btl. 5,*
18.11.44
Lt. Wilhelm Haehnel, *Art.Rgt.157, 57.Inf.Div.,*
21.2.44
Ostuf. Willy Hein, *I./SS-Pz.Rgt.5,* 15.5.44

Stubaf. Heinrich Heimann, *SS-Stug.Abt.1 LSSAH,*
23.2.44
Oscha. Fritz Henke, *SS-Stug.Abt.1 "LSSAH,"*
12.2.44
Oberst Kurt Hummel, *Gren.Rgt.124, 72.Inf.Div.,*
15.5.44
Oblt. Wilhelm Isselhorst, *Gren.Rgt.258, Div.Gr.112,*
21.2.44
Hstuf. Heinrich Kling, *SS-Pz.Rgt.1 "LSSAH,"*
23.2.44
Uffz. Walter Knorr, *Pz.Gren.Rgt.108, 14.Pz.Div.,*
6.3.44
Hptm. Georg Knostmann, *Gren.Rgt.266, 72.Inf.Div.,*
15.5.44
Stubaf. Herbert Kuhlmann, *I./SS-Pz.Rgt.1, LSSAH,*
13.2.44
Ostubaf. Rudolf Lehmann, *1.SS-Pz.Div.LSSAH,*
23.2.44
Gen.Lt. Theobald Lieb, *XXXXII.A.K.,* 7.2.44
Ostuf. Werner Meyer, *SS-Pz.Gren.Rgt.9 Germania,*
15.5.44
Maj. Heinrich Murken, *Gren.Rgt.124, 72.Inf.Div.,*
21.2.44
Oberst Karl Neufellner, *Art.Rgt.86, K.Abt.B,* 6.4.44
Fw. August Niemann, *Pi.Btl.112, K.Abt.B,* 15.5.44
Fw. Oskar Penkert, *Pz.Gren.Rgt.108, 14.Pz.Div.,*
23.2.44
Maj. Paul Penth, *Gren.Rgt.677, Div.Gr.332,* 14.5.44
Ostubaf. Joachim Richter, *SS-Pz.Art.Rgt.5,* 23.2.44
Gen.Maj. Georg *Graf* von Rittberg, *88.Inf.Div.,*
21.2.44
Oblt. Matthias Roth, *Gren.Rgt.105, 72.Inf.Div.,*
21.2.44
Oblt. Walter Scherf, *Schw.Pz.Abt.503, Schw.Pz.Rgt.*
"Bäke," 23.2.44
Hptm. Harry Schlingmann, *Pi.Btl.112, K.Abt.B,*
14.2.44
Hstuf. Walter Schmidt, *SS-Pz.Gren.Rgt.9 Germania,*
5.4.44
Ostubaf. Manfred Schönfelder, *5.SS-Pz.Div. Wiking,*
23.2.44
Ostuf. Kurt Schumacher, *I./SS-Pz.Rgt.5,* 15.5.44
Maj. Rudolf Siegel, *Gren.Rgt.266, 72.Inf.Div.,*
23.2.44
Maj. Karl von Sivers, *Pz.Rgt.15, 11.Pz.Div.,* 6.3.44
Maj. Christian Sonntag, *Div.Gr.255, K.Abt.B,*
12.2.44
Oblt. Karl-Heinz Sorge, *Pz.Rgt.6, 3.Pz.Div.,* 7.2.44
Hptm. Fritz Steinbacher, *Art.Rgt.172, 72.Inf.Div.,*
21.2.44
Uffz. Hermann Tanczos, *Art.Rgt.157, 57.Inf.Div.,*
21.2.44
Gen.Maj. Adolf Trowitz, *57.Inf.Div.,* 21.2.44

Oberst Hans Viebig, *Gren.Rgt.258, K.Abt.B*, 21.2.44
Ustuf. Helmut Wendorff, *SS-Pz.Rgt.1 "LSSAH,"*
12.2.44
Oberstlt. Alfred Wittmann, *Gren.Rgt.546,*
389.Inf.Div., 15.5.44
Lt. Friedrich Zempel, *Füs.Btl.112, K.Abt.B,* 4.5.44
Hptm. Manfred Zimmermann, *Gren.Rgt.199 "List,"*
57.Inf.Div., 14.5.44

* List does not include Luftwaffe recipients

Source: Walther-Peer Fellgiebel, *Die Träger des Ritterkreuzes des Eisernen Kreuzes 1939-1945*

APPENDIX 11 — CORRELATION OF FORCES

MAJOR COMBAT ELEMENTS LOCATED VICINITY KANEV SALIENT, 24 JANUARY 1944

Soviet		German	
First Ukrainian *Front* (Vatutin)		*1.Pz.Armee* (Hube)	
27th Army	(28,350)	*VII.Armeekorps*	(25,000)
40th Army	(33,720)	*LXII.Armeekorps**	(30,000)
6th Tank Army	(24,420) 190 Tanks/SP guns		
Second Ukrainian *Front* (Konev)		*8.Armee* (Wöhler)	
52nd Army	(15,900)	*XI.Armeekorps**	(35,000) 40 Tanks/SP guns
4th Gds Army	(46,000) 126 Tanks/SP guns	*XLVII.Pz.Korps*	(50,000) 60 Tanks/SP guns (35,000 engaged)
53rd Army	(54,000)		
5th Gds Tank Army	(22,300) 197 Tanks/SP guns	**TOTAL:**	130,000 men, 100 Tanks/SPs
Other:	(20,300)		
TOTAL:	245,000 men, 513 Tanks/SP guns		

Force ratios Soviet/German: troops 2:1, armor 5:1, artillery 7:1, tactical aviation 4:1

* Encircled Corps

Source: Glantz, David. 1985 *Art of War Symposium*, "From the Dnieper to the Vistula: Soviet Offensive Operations from November 1943 to August 1944." (Carlisle Barracks, PA: U.S. Army War College, 1985), p. 128.

BIBLIOGRAPHY

Books

Buchner, Alex. *Ostfront 1944: The German Defensive Battle on the Russian Front, 1944.* (Atglen, PA: Schiffer Publishing, 1991).
Carell, Paul. *Scorched Earth: The Russian-German War 1943-1944.* (New York: Ballantine Books, 1971).
Clark, Alan. *Barbarossa - The Russian-German Conflict 1941-45.* (New York: Quill Books, 1985).
Degrelle, Leon. *Campaign in Russia: The Waffen-SS on the Eastern Front.* (Torrance, CA: Institute for Historical Review, 1985).
Donnhauser, Anton J. *Der Weg der 11.Panzer-Division.* (Bad Wörishofen, Germany: Holzmann Druck Service, 1979).
Erickson, John. *The Road to Berlin.* (London: McMillan and Company, Ltd. 1983).
Fellgiebel, Walther-Peer. *Die Träger des Ritterkreuzes des Eisernen Kreuzes 1939-1945.* (Wölfersheim-Berstadt, Germany: Podzun-Pallas Verlag, 1996).
Garthoff, Raymond L. *Soviet Military Doctrine.* (Glencoe, IL: The RAND Corporation, 1953).
Glantz, David M. *Soviet Military Deception in the Second World War.* (London: Frank Cass and Company, LTD, 1989).
Glantz, David M. and House, Jonathan M., *When Titans Clashed: How the Red Army Stopped Hitler.* (Lawrence, KS: University of Kansas Press, 1995).
Grams, Rolf. *Die 14.Panzer-Division 1940-1945.* (Friedberg, Germany: Podzun-Pallas Verlag, 1986).
Graser, Gerhard. *Zwischen Kattegat und Kaukasus: Weg und Kämpfe der 198.Infanterie-Division.* (Tübingen, Germany: Kameradhilfswerk der ehemaligen 198.Infanterie-Division, 1961).
Hahl, Fritz. *Panzergrenadiere der Panzerdivision "Wiking" im Bild.* (Osnabrück, Germany: Munin Verlag, 1984).
Haupt, Werner. *Krim- Stalingrad - Kaukasus: Die Heeresgruppe Süd 1941-45.* (Friedberg, Germany: Podzun-Pallas Verlag, 1977).
Hausser, Paul. *Waffen-SS im Einsatz.* (Oldendorf, Germany: Schütz Verlag GmbH, 1953).
Hinze, *Dr.* Rolf. *Rückzugskämpfe in der Ukraine 1943-1944.* (Meerbusch, Germany: Verlag Dr. Rolf Hinze, 1991).
Höhne, Heinz. *The Order of the Death's Head.* (New York: Ballantine Books, 1983).
Kaisergruber, Fernand. *Nous N'Irons Pas A Touapse: Du Donetz au Caucase dez Tscherkassy a L'Oder.* (Brussels: Privately published, 1990).
Kern, Erich. *Dance of Death.* (New York: Charles Scribner's Sons, 1951).
Klapdor, Ewald. *Mit dem Panzerregiment 5 Wiking im Osten.* (Siek, Germany: Privately published by Ewald Klapdor, 1981).
Konev, Ivan Stepanovich. *Der Kessel von Korsun-Schewtschenkowski, in Aufzeichnungen eines Frontoberbefehlshabers 1943/44.* (East Berlin: Militärverlag der Deutschen Demokratischen Republik).
Krainjukow, Konstantin. *Vom Dnepr zur Weichsel.* (East Berlin: Militärverlag der Deutschen Demokratischen Republic, 1982).
Landwehr, Richard and Roba, Jean-Louis. *The Wallonen: The History of the 5th SS-Sturmbrigade and the 28th SS Volunteer Panzergrenadier Division.* (Glendale, Oregon: Weapons and Warfare Publications, 1984).
Lehman, Rudolf and Tieman, Ralf. *The Leibstandarte, Vol. IV.* (Winnipeg, Canada: J.J. Fedorowicz Publishing, Inc. 1993).
Lerch, Bernd, Dr. and Jahnke, Günter. *Der Kessel von Tscherkassy 1944.* (Donauwörth, Germany: Merkle Druck Service, 1996).
Lewerenz, Hermann. *Die Tätigkeit der Bevollmächtigen des Nationalkomitees Freies Deutschland am Kessel von Korsun-Schewtschenkowski,* from *Sie kämpften für Deutschland: zur Geschichte des Kampfes der Bewegung, Freies Deutschland bei der 1. Ukrainischen Front der Sowjetarmee.* (Berlin: Verlag des Ministeriums für Nationale Verteidigung, 1959).
Lewin, Ronald. *Hitler's Mistakes.* (New York: William and Morrow, Inc., 1984).
Lucas, James. *War on the Eastern Front.* (New York: Stein and Day, 1979).
von Manstein, Erich. *Lost Victories.* (Novato, CA: Presidio Press, 1982).
Matsulenko, Viktor A. *Operatsii I boi na Okruzheniye* (Encirclement Operations and Combat). (Moscow: Voyenizdat, 1983).
Menedetter, Hans-Kurt. *Chronik des Artillerie-Regiment 188 der 88.Infanterie-Division.* (Fürth, Germany: Josef Eckert und Sohn, 1960).
Mehner, Kurt. *Die Deutsche Wehrmacht 1939-1945: Führung und Truppe.* (Norderstedt, Germany: Militair-Verlag Klaus D. Patzwall, 1993).
Meiser, Anton. *Die Hölle von Tscherkassy: Ein Kreigstagebuch 1943-1944.* (Schnellbach, Germany: Verlag Siegfried Bublies, 1998).
Mitcham, Samuel W. *Hitler's Legions.* (New York: Stein and Day, 1985).
Neuman, Peter. *The Black March.* (New York: Bantam Books, 1971).
Newton, Steven H. *German Battle Tactics on the Russian Front.* (Atglen, PA: Schiffer Publishing, Ltd., 1994).
Orgill, Douglas. *T-34-Russian Armor.* (New York: Ballantine Books Inc., 1971).
Perrett, Bryan. *Knights of the Black Cross: Hitler's Panzerwaffe and its Leaders.* (New York: St. Martin's Press, 1986).
Pierek, Perry. *Hungary 1944-1945: The Forgotten Tragedy.* (Nieuegein, The Netherlands: Aspekt b.v., Second Edition, 1998).
Röhricht, Edgar. *Probleme der Kesselschlacht.* (Karlsruhe, Germany: Condor-Verlag GmbH, 1958).

Rubbel, Alfred. *Erinnerungen an die Tigerabteilung 503 1942-1945*. (Berlin: Privately published, 1990).

Rudel, Hans-Ullrich. *Stuka Pilot*. (New York: Bantam Books, 1973).

Sajer, Guy. *The Forgotten Soldier*. (New York: Ballantine Books, Inc. 1971).

Schenk, Ernst. and Ullmer, Hans. *Das Badische Infanterie-Regiment 110*. (Heidelberg, Germany: privately published manuscript, 1957).

Schneider, Jost. *Their Honor Was Loyalty*. (San Jose, CA: R. James Bender Publishing, 1977).

Schwarz, Dr. Andreas. *Datentafel 323.Infanterie-Division*. (Fürth, Germany: Josef Eckert und Sohn, 1966).

Schwarz, Dr. Andreas, *Die 88.Infanterie-Division*. (Amberg, Germany: privately published unit history, February 1956).

Schwarz, Dr. Andreas. *Chronik des Infanterie-Regiments 248* (drei Teile). (Fürth, Germany: Josef Eckert und Sohn, 1977.

Seaton, Albert. *The Russo-German War, 1941-1945*. (Novato, CA: Presidio Press, 1993).

Shukman, Harold, ed. *Stalin's Generals*. (New York: Grove Press, 1993).

Shtemenko, Sergei. *The Soviet General Staff at War 1941-45*. (Moscow:Progress Publishers, 1986).

Sokolov, Sergei. *Battles Hitler Lost*. (New York: The Berkley Publishing Group, 1986).

Spaeter, Helmuth. *The History of the Panzerkorps Grossdeutschland, Vol. 2*. (Winnipeg, Canada: J.J. Fedorowicz Publishing, Inc., 1995).

Stahlberg, Alexander. Bounden Duty: *The Memoirs of a German Officer 1939-45*. (London: Brassey's, 1990).

Stein, George H. *The Waffen-SS: Hitler's Elite Guard at War*. (Ithaca, NY: Cornell University Press, 1966).

Stoves, Rolf. *Die 1.Panzerdivision*. (Bad Nauheim, Germany: Hans-Henning Podzun Verlag, 1961).

Strassner, Peter. *European Volunteers*. (Winnipeg, Manitoba: J.J. Fedorowicz Publishing, 1988).

Traditionsgemeinschaft 72.Infanterie-Division. Die 72.Infanterie-Division 1939-1945. (Friedberg, Germany: Podzun-Pallas Verlag GmbH, 1982).

Traditionsverband 3.Panzer Division. Geschichte der 3.Panzer-Division. (Berlin: Verlag Günter Richter, 1967).

Truppenkameradshaftsverband 5. SS-Panzer-Regiment "Wiking." Verweht sind die Spuren. (Osnabrück, Germany: Munin Verlag, 1979).

Truppenkameradschaftsverband "Wiking." Der Kessel von Tscherkassy: Die Flut verschlangt sich selbst, nicht uns! (Osnabrück, Germany: Munin Verlag, 1969).

Verlag des Ministeriums für Nationale Verteidigung. Sie kämpften für Deutschland: zur Geschichte des Kampfes der Bewegung "Freies Deutschland" bei der 1. Ukrainischen Front der Sowjetarmee. (Berlin: Verlag des Ministeriums für Nationale Vertidigung, 1959).

von Vormann, Nikolaus. *Tscherkassy*. (Heidelberg, Germany: Kurt Vowinckel Verlag, 1954).

Wagener, Carl. *Heeresgruppe Süd*. (Bad Nauheim, Germany: Podzun Verlag, 1969).

Wensauer, Matthias. *Chronik des Infanterie-Regiments 246*. (Munich: Traditionsverband 88.I.D. e.V., 1962).

Werth, Alexander. *Russia at War 1941-1945*. (New York: E.P. Dutton & Co., Inc. 1964).

Werthen, Wolfgang. *Geschichte der 16.Panzer-Division 1939-1945*. (Friedberg, Germany: Podzun-Pallas Verlag, 1958).

Williamson, Gordon. *Loyalty Is My Honor: Personal accounts from the Waffen-SS*. (Osceola, WI: Motorbooks International Publishers, 1995).

Zentner, Christian. *Soldaten im Einsatz - Tapferkeit und Pflichterfüllung in Angriff und Verteidigung*. (Hamburg, Germany: Jahr Verlag KG, 1982).

Zhukov, Georgi. *Reminiscences and Reflections*. (Moscow: Progress Publishers, 1985).

Ziemke, Earl F. *Stalingrad to Berlin - the German Defeat in the East*. (Washington, D.C.: U.S. Government Printing Office, 1968).

Aue, A. "Die Handlungen der sowjetischen Panzertruppen in der Kesselschlacht von Korsun Schewtschenkowski." *Militärwesen*, Volume 4, April 1964. (East Berlin: Zeitschrift für Militärpolitik und Militärtheorie, 1964).

Periodicals and Articles

Der Freiwillige. "Das Schicksal der Verwundeten im Kessel von Tscherkassy." (Osnabrück, Germany: Munin-Verlag, November 1982 to April 1983).

Heder, Eberhard. "Tscherkassy-Gedenken 45 Jahre." (Osnabrück, Germany: *Der Freiwillige*, Nr. 6, June 1989).

Hilss, Werner. "Ein Reitpferd zog mich durch den Fluss: Durch eiskaltes Wasser aus dem Kessel von Tscherkassy." *Alte Kameraden*, 2/1990. (Stuttgart, Germany: Arbeitsgemeinschaft für Kameradenwerk und Traditionsverbände e.V. 1990).

Isserson, G., "Razvitiye teorii sovetakogo operativnogo iskusstva v 30-ye gody" (The Development of the Theory of Soviet Operational Art in the 1930s), *Voyenno-istoricheskiy Zhurnal*, No. 1 (January 1965). (Moscow: Voyenno-istoricheskiy Zhurnal).

Jahnke, Günter. "Eine Richtigstellung." *Der Freiwilliger*, February 1993. (Osnabrück, Germany: Munin-Verlag GmbH, 1993), pp. 27-28.

The Journal of Slavic Military Studies. "The Korsun-Shevchenkovskii Operation, January-February 1944." (London: Frank Cass and Company, June 1994).

Loza, Dmitriy. "How Soviets Fought in U.S. Shermans." *Armor*, July-August 1996, pp. (Fort Knox, Kentucky: Armor Magazine, 1996), pp. 21-31.

Menedetter, Hans-Kurt. "Das Grauen wurde überwunden: Das Artillerie-Regiment 188, 88.Infanterie-Division im Kessel westlich Tscherkassy," in *Alte Kameraden*, Volume 22, February 1974. (Stuttgart, Germany: Arbeitsgemeinschaft für Kameradenwerke und Traditionsverband e.V., 1974.)

Menedetter, Hans-Kurt. "Vor 35 Jahren - Tscherkassy, Winterdrama am Gniloj Tikitsch" in *Der Kamerad*, Nr. 2, February 1979. (Vienna: Der Österreichischen Kameradschaftbundes, 1979.)

Menedetter, Hans. "Tscherkassy - ein Ring um zwei Korps." *Deutsche Soldatenjahrbuch* 1987. (Munich: Schild Verlag, 1987.)

Soviet Military Review. "The Korsun-Shevchenkovsky Operation." (Moscow: Soviet Military Review Magazine, February 1969.)

Voyenno-Istoricheskiy Zhurnal. "Documents on Korsun-Shevchenskovskiy Operation Given." (Moscow: Voyenno-Istoricheskiy Zhurnal, February 1984.)

Letters and Unpublished Manuscripts

Dohrn, Dr. Peter. "Bericht von Unterartzt Dr. med. Peter Dohrn, 2.Sanitäts-Kompanie 172, 72.Infanterie-Division." (undated private manuscript, courtesy of the 72nd Infantry Division Veteran's Association.)

von Dörnberg, Freiherr Hans Eppo (1st Panzer Division), Oberaula, Germany. Letters to author, 14 February, 4 May, and 2 June 1997. Letters in authors possession.

Feisthauer, Günther (213th Security Division), Hamburg, Germany. Letters to author, 8 May, 2 June, and 2 November 1997. Letters in author's possession.

Figur, Fritz. "Der ESAK in Kessel." (unpublished private manuscript courtesy of the 72nd Infantry Division Veterans' Association.)

Fischer, Hans (5th SS-Panzer Regiment "Wiking".) "Der weite weg einer Kamera." (Versmold, Germany: unpublished private manuscript, copy in author's possession, 1994.)

Fischer, Hans. "Erlebnisbericht Einsatz Januar 1944." (Versmold, Germany: Unpublished private manuscript in author's possession, January 1998.)

Gaertig, Hans (57th Infantry Division), Homburg, Germany. Letter to author 14 May 1997. Letter in author's possession.

Hahl, Fritz. "Die 6.Kompanie des Regiments Westland im Kessel von Tscherkassy." (Pentling, Germany: unpublished private manuscript, May 1995.)

Heder, Eberhard, Warburg, Germany to author. Correspondence from May 1995 to December 1997. Letters in author's possession.

Hein, Willy. "Meine Erblebnisse im Kessel von Tscherkassy, 26 Januar bis 18 February 1944." (Lauenburg, Germany: undated private manuscript in author's possession.)

Hein, Willy. "Kurzer kriegsgeschichtlicher Vortrag über die Aufstellung und den Einsatz des Panzer-Regiments 5 Wiking." (Lauenburg, Germany: unpublished private manuscript, April 1992.)

Hein, Willy, Lauenburg, Germany to author, correspondence from December 1994 to January 1997. Letters in author's possession.

Kathagen, Fritz. "Chronik der 2./SS Panzer Nachrichten Abteilung 5." (Osnabrück, Germany: undated privately published manuscript.)

Kaisergruber, Fernand (5th SS Volunteer Brigade 'Wallonia"), Brussels to author. Correspondence from August 1995 to January 1997. Letters in author's possession.

Letter, Georg Tartler to Willy Hein, Lauenburg, Germany, 13 November 1994. Copy in author's possession.

Mayer, Gerhard. "Im Kessel von Tscherkassy bei Regimentsstab Artillery-Regiment 188, 88.Infanterie-Division." (Heilbronn, Germany: Unpublished private manuscript, 1986.)

Mennedetter, Hans (88th Infantry Division), Weidling, Austria to author, correspondence from May 1995 to January 1997. Letters in author's possession.

Notz, Walther (Eisenbahnpionier Gruppe "Schäfer"), Reichenbach, Germany to author, correspondence from June to December 1997. Letters in author's possession.

von Öchselhäuser, Justus (Heavy Panzer Regiment "Bäke"), Himmelpfort, Germany to author, 29 March 1997. Letter in author's possession.

Ogrowsky, Adolf. "Die Versorgung der kämpfenden Truppe mit Verpflegung im Stadtkessel von Tscherkassy und im grossen Kessel von Kanew-Korsun." (Speyer, Germany: unpublished manuscript, courtesy of the 72nd Infantry Division Veteran's Association, August 1975.)

Ohlendorf, Joachim. "Bericht über die Gefangnahme und Gefangenschaft in der UdSSR." (Lübeck, Germany: unpublished private manuscript, courtesy of the 72nd Infantry Division Veteran's Association, April 1976.)

Ploen, Günther. "Morgen wird n' Ding gedreht." (Kaltenkirchen, Germany: unpublished private manuscript, September 1995.)

"Programm zum Appell der Angehörigen der ehemalige deutsche 8.Armee anlässlich des Gedenktages der Kessel von Tscherkassy." (Amberg, Germany: privately published ceremonial program book, 16 February 1974.)

Quietzsch, Hans (Korpsabteilung B), Halle, Germany to Klaus Schulz, 1 December 1997. Letter in author's possession.

Reisch, Peter. "Ausbruch aus dem Kessel westlich von Tscherkassy." (unpublished private manuscript courtesy of the 72nd Infantry Division Veteran's Association.)

Roth, Matthias. "Tscherkassy." (undated private manuscript, courtesy of the 72nd Infantry Division Veteran's Association.)

Schäfer-Kehnert, Walter (11th Panzer Division.) Kriegstagebuch in Feldpostbriefen 1940-1945. (Remagen, Germany: private ly published manuscript, 1988.)

Schenk, Ernst (Korpsabteilung B), Dinkelsbühl, Germany to author, 26 July, 20 August and 18 November 1996, and 14 January 1997. Letters in author's possession.

Schierholz, Karl (Korpsabteilung B), Butjadingen, Germany to author, 6 April, 19 August and 25 September 1997. Letters in author's possession.

Schiller, Hans (57th Infantry Division), "Ausbruch aus dem Kessel." (Nuremberg, Germany: unpublished private manuscript, 1975.) Copy of article courtesy of Hans Menedetter, Weidling, Austria.

Spaeter, Helmuth, Eching/Ammersee, Germany (Pz.Gren.Div. "Grossdeutschland") to author, 16 January 1996. Letter in author's possession.

Stoves, Rolf, Norderstedt, Germany (1st Panzer Division), Letter to author 10 January 1997. Letter in author's possession.Strathoff, Karl-Heinz. "Erinnerungen an die Kämpfe um und bei Tscherkassy." (Unna, Germany: unpublished private manuscript, courtesy of the 72nd Infantry Division Veteran's Association, April 1975.)

Official Documents

Adjutant, 318th Security Regiment. Den Einsatz des Sicherungs-Regiment 318, 213 Sicherungs-Division, von Sommer 1943 bis Sommer 1944.

Department of the Army Pamphlet 20-234, Operations of Encircled Forces: German Experiences in Russia. (U. S. Government Printing Office, 1952.)

Glantz, David M. "From the Dnepr to the Visula - Soviet Offensive Operations November 1943- August 1944," 1985 Art of War Symposium. (Carlisle Barracks, PA: U. S. Army War College, 1985.)

Kästner, Oberstleutnant Robert. "3. Mitteilungsblatt für das Offizier-Korps des Grenadier-Regiments 105, 72.Infanterie Division," 20 March 1944.

Kriegstagebuch Nr. 1 mit Gefechtsberichte, 1.Abteilung, SS-Panzer Regiment 5 "Wiking," 9 February to 30 November 1944.

Morzik, Fritz. German Air Force Airlift Operations in WWII. (U.S. Air University: U.S. Air Force Historical Division, 1961.) Red Army 1944 Field Service Regulations.

Sasso, Claude R., "Soviet Night Operations in World War II," Leavenworth Papers, No.6. (Fort Leavenworth, KS: U.S. Government Printing Office, 1982.)

Sbornik materialov po izucheniiu optya voiny (Collection of materials on the study of war experience), No.14. (Moscow: Voennoe Izdatel'stvo Narodnogo Komissariata Oborony, 1945.) Translated version presented in Journal of Slavic Military Studies. (London: Frank Cass and Company, June 1994.)

Selected Readings in Military History: Soviet Military History,Volume I - The Red Army 1918-45. (Fort Leavenworth: Combat Studies Institute, 1984.)

Siegel, Oberstleutnant Rudolf. "Bericht über die Kämpfe des Grenadier-Regiments 266 der 72.Infanterie-Division im Kessel von Tscherkassy und des grossen Kessels von Korssun in der Zeit vom 22.11.1943 bis 17.2.1944."

World War Two German Military Studies. (Vol. 1, p-143d.) "Breakout From Encirclement in the Cherkassy Pocket by the 105th Infantry Regiment, 72nd Infantry Division, February 1944." (United States Government: U.S. Army Europe Historical Division, 1954.)

Material on Microfilm

National Archives, Washington DC
    Oberkommando Heeresgruppe Süd, Ia Kriegstagebüch Nr. 0765/44, Group T-311, Roll 40.

National Archives, Washington DC
    Armeeoberkommando 8, Ia, Kriegstagebuch Nr. 3, 20 January - 18 February 1944, Group T-312, Roll 64.

National Archives, Washington DC
    Armeeoberkommando 8, Kriegstagebuch Meldungen u. Befehle, 20 January-18 February 1944, Group T-312, Roll 66.

National Archives, Washington DC
    Armeeoberkommando 8, Chefsachen January-June 1944, Group T-312, Roll 65.

National Archives, Washington DC

Panzerarmeeoberkommando 1, Ia, Kriegstagebuch Nr. 13, 5-18 February 1944, Group T-313, Roll 69. National Archives, Washington DC

Panzerarmeeoberkommando 1, An der Gruppe Mattenklott, February - March 1944, Group T-313, Roll 69. National Archives, Washington DC

Generalkommando XI Armeekorps, Ia Meldungen und Befehle, 28 January - 11 March 1944, Group T-313, Roll 72. National Archives, Washington DC

Generalkommando XXXXII Armeekorps, Chef des Generalstabes, Ia Meldungen und Befehle Nr. 158/44, Group T-313, Roll 72.

Author's Interviews

Dreesen, Wolfgang, Korsun-Shevchenkovsky, Ukraine 29 June 1996.

Fedorovich, Alexei, Korsun-Shevchenkovsky, Ukraine 29 June 1996.

Fischer, Hans, Lauenburg, 25 June 1996 and Niedernhall, Germany 19 September 1998.

Hadai, Mikhail Yakelovich, Korsun-Shevchenkovsky, Ukraine 1 July 1996.

Hahl, Franz, Niedernhall, Germany, 19 September 1998.

Heder, Eberhard, Niedernhall, Germany, 19 September 1998.

Hein, Willy, Lauenburg, Germany, 25-26 June 1996.

Jahnke, Günther, Niedernhall, Germany, 19 September 1998.

Kaisergruber, Fernand. Brussels, Belgium, 21 June - 3 July 1996.

Lange, Günther, Korsun-Shevchenkovsky, Ukraine 29 June 1996.

Menedetter, Hans-Kurt, Weidling, Austria, 2-3 July 1996.

Ploen, Günther, Lauenburg, Germany, 25-26 June 1996.

Stoves, Rolf, Heidelberg, 6 August 1998

INDEX